A Smithsonian Book of

COMIC-BOOK COMICS

Edited by
Michael Barrier
and
Martin Williams

Copublished by
Smithsonian Institution Press and
Harry N. Abrams, Inc., New York

Printed in the United States

Library of Congress Cataloging in Publication Data
Main entry under title:

A Smithsonian book of comic-book comics.

Bibliography: p.
1. Comic books, strips, etc.—United States. I. Barrier, J. Michael. II. Williams, Martin T. III. Smithsonian Institution. PN6726.S58 741.5'973
81-607842   AACR2
ISBN 0-87474-228-5 (SIP)
ISBN 0-8109-0696-1 (HNA)

All of the stories in this volume have been reproduced from their first comic-book printings.

Printed in the United States of America by American Book-Stratford Press, Inc.

Contents

Acknowledgments

The names of the copyright holders who have generously contributed to this volume appear on the comics pages that follow. And we owe special thanks to the following individuals, for help of many kinds.

C. C. Beck, Glenn Bray, Steve Brewster, Steve Brumbaugh, Pete Costanza, Ann Durell, Will Eisner, Harlan Ellison, William M. Gaines, Steve Geppi, Don Glut, Wallace I. Green, Mary C. Janaky, Barbara Johnson, Jenette Kahn, Bob Kane, Selby Kelly, Jim Lawson, Paul Levitz, Chuck McCleary, Mercy Macabeo, Sheldon Mayer, Wendall Mohler, Eileen Opatut, Ethan Roberts, Joe Shuster, Jerry Siegel, Bill Spicer, Terry Stroud, J. R. Taylor, Bill Tighe, Larry R. Vasquez, Kim Weston, John C. Worrell, Craig Yoe.

And the following have an especially strong claim on our gratitude.

John Benson, Rick Durell, Don and Maggie Thompson.

Introduction

The comic book as we know it today—with its slick covers, newsprint-paper insides, and crude colors, all in a package measuring about seven by ten inches—was a long time in being born.

The comic book was the child of the newspaper comic strip, and the comic strip was born in the United States late in the nineteenth century. Several elements that had been separately present in European culture for centuries—drawings in sequence that told a story, "balloons" filled with dialogue, caricature—were combined by American cartoonists, as what quickly came to be called comic strips, in American newspapers beginning in the 1890s. Within a few years, daily comic strips and Sunday comics sections in color were widely featured in American newspapers.

Some newspaper comics offered extended narratives—stories that were told over many days, and in many drawings—almost from the start. And although the full-color Sunday comics were often presented in a grid pattern—rows of boxed drawings, or panels, of the same size—cartoonists sometimes dealt with the comics page as a whole, giving their panels different shapes and arranging them in unusual ways.

Many ingredients of the comic book—the comic-strip form, the extended narrative, the page as a basic unit along with the panel—were thus present in newspaper strips from around the turn of the century. (The Sunday comics section—very thick and colorful in those early days—was itself a comic book of a sort.) But just as the comic strip took a curiously long time to assume its definitive shape, so too did the comic book.

For about three decades, publishers experimented with formats of many kinds. They first reprinted newspaper strips in books (both hard and soft covers), making what one might call early comic books. In 1929, one publisher tried something different—a weekly publication made up of completely new comics. Called *The Funnies,* it died after a few issues, perhaps because it was tabloid size (twice as large as a modern comic book) and so looked too much like a Sunday comics section.

In 1933, comic books of approximately the modern size and shape were published by Eastern Color Printing Company—but as premiums, to be given away by retailers and manufacturers to their customers. No one thought about selling these comic books directly to readers until M. C. Gaines, a salesman at Eastern Color, tested the market by putting ten-cent price stickers on a few copies and leaving them at two newsstands. The comic books quickly sold out, and this led—after a few false starts—to the publication of

Famous Funnies No. 1 in May 1934. *Famous Funnies* was sold on newsstands for a dime, and it was soon being published on a monthly schedule. It was the first true comic book in the modern sense.

But, like the premium comic books that preceded it, *Famous Funnies* was composed of reprinted newspaper strips. The first comic book made up entirely of new material did not appear until early in 1935; this was *New Fun* No. 1. In later years, comic books with new material came to dominate the field, eclipsing the comic books made up of reprints.

So, depending on the definition one uses, the first comic book was published anywhere from early in the century to as late as 1935. But the real turning point in the comic book's history probably came in the summer of 1932.

Jerry Siegel, a student at Glenville High School in Cleveland, and his classmate, Joe Shuster, had become friends because of a shared interest in comic strips, particularly heroic fantasies like *Tarzan* and *Buck Rogers.* They began to make comic strips of their own; Siegel wrote and Shuster illustrated. As Siegel later told the story to a writer for the *Saturday Evening Post,* the idea for the new strip came to him one hot night in 1932, as he was trying to fall asleep:

"I am lying in bed counting sheep when all of a sudden it hits me. I conceive a character like Samson, Hercules, and all the strong men I ever heard tell of rolled into one. Only more so. I hop right out of bed and write this down, and then I go back and think some more for about two hours and get up again and write that down. This goes on all night at two-hour intervals, until in the morning I have a complete script."

That morning, Siegel rushed to Shuster's house, and they whipped up the script and the drawings for twelve installments of a daily newspaper strip—two weeks' worth—to submit to newspaper syndicates. The strip was called *Superman.* The established syndicates were uniformly unflattering in their assessments of Siegel and Shuster's samples and *Superman* gathered a large pile of rejection slips. When *Superman* finally found a home, in 1938, it was in the first issue of a monthly comic book, *Action Comics,* wherein the strips had been cut up and the panels rearranged to make a thirteen-page feature.

Within a short time, *Action Comics*—with *Superman* in each issue—was selling almost a million copies every month, the bimonthly *Superman* comic book was selling well over a million copies per issue, and the character had spread from comic books to radio and the movies. And to the newspapers—by 1941, *Superman* as a daily strip signed by Siegel and Shuster, was running in 230 papers.

If, in the mid-1930s, just one syndicate editor had come to a different decision and given *Superman* a test run, the history of comic books would surely have been different. Had *Superman* squeezed onto the newspaper comics pages before 1938, the strip probably would have wound up in a reprint comic book, and a second-hand *Superman* of that kind could not have changed comic books the way that *Action Comics* and the *Superman* bimonthly did.

Superman alerted publishers to the riches to be gained from offering readers the larger-than-life costumed super-hero, and within a couple of years the newsstands were filled with comic books starring such characters, and comic books themselves had become big business. Some of the new heroes were super-human, like Superman, although they usually had fewer powers than Superman did, and some of them had powers that Superman did not (the ability to burst into flame, for example, or to stretch one's body into all sorts of improbable shapes). Other heroes were not super-human, but had well-developed muscles and specialized skills; they were not the heirs of Superman so much as of the masked, law-into-their-own-hands vigilantes (the Phantom, the Lone Ranger, the Green Hornet, and others) who had become popular through comic strips, radio, and pulp fiction. However, the new comic-book vigilantes were clad in costumes far more garish than simple masks. The exemplar was Batman, whose adventures became the lead feature in *Detective Comics* (published by National, the company that brought out the *Superman* titles) a year after Superman's debut. Batman quickly became the second most popular of the super-heroes; his bimonthly comic book was selling 800,000 copies per issue by 1941.

Not all comic-book heroes had the sustained success of Superman and Batman, but starting in the early 1940s other kinds of comic books, from many different publishers, found favor with millions of readers. The Walt Disney characters Mickey Mouse and Donald Duck began appearing monthly in *Walt Disney's Comics and Stories* in the fall of 1940, and other comic books with animated-cartoon characters soon followed. Another genre was the comic book with teenage characters; the *Archie* feature, which first appeared in 1941 as a filler in a super-hero comic book, spawned a multitude of imitators. The western—that staple of Americana—made the transition to comic books with ease, and cowboy movie stars like Roy Rogers and Gene Autry became comic-book stars as well. Romance comic books flourished in the postwar years, sharing the appeal of radio soap operas and confession magazines.

Of the many new genres, the one that ultimately had the greatest effect on the industry was the crime comic book. Crime was always present in the super-hero comic books—the heroes usually proved themsleves to be heroes by defeating criminals—but in the new crime comics, the emphasis was on the crimes themselves. A wave of such comic books started with *Crime Does Not Pay* in 1942 and crested in the postwar years. The success of the frequently lurid and violent crime comic books encouraged one publisher, E. C., to go a step further, and in 1950 it introduced three horror titles—*The Crypt of Terror, The Vault of Horror,* and *The Haunt of Fear.* Other publishers quickly scented a bonanza, and the comic racks filled up with bloody axes, severed heads, and rotting corpses.

Comic books had been criticized in print since 1940 or so; because most of the readers were children, some people worried that comic books—crude and violent as many of them were—might be damaging young minds. The crime and horror comic books were found especially alarming, and a storm of indignation finally struck the industry with full force in 1954. Comic books were dumped on bonfires; comic books were denounced in Congress; comic books were solemnly condemned by psychiatrists as the root of a host of social evils. (And, more important for business, distributors started refusing to accept some comic books from the publishers.) As the movie producers had done twenty years earlier, the comic-book publishers responded to charges of immorality by drawing up an extremely strict code and entrusting its enforcement to a panel recruited from outside the industry. Only one major publisher—Dell, whose comic books starred such licensed characters as Donald Duck and the Lone Ranger and had attracted little criticism—could afford to shun the new Comics Code.

The adoption of the Comics Code in October 1954 marked the end of sixteen years of flamboyant success for the comic-book industry. Many publishers left the business in the 1950s, and total circulation fell sharply. Despite occasional bursts of prosperity (like the one that accompanied the public's interest in the *Batman* television show of the 1960s), comic books have never come close to equaling their popularity in the 1940s and early 1950s. Once ubiquitous on newsstands and in drug stores, variety stores, and supermarkets, comic books in recent years have been slipping slowly out of sight.

Even when comic books were at the peak of their success,

very little of that success trickled down—in the form of money or artistic freedom—to the writers and cartoonists who were producing the magazines.

For the most part, comic books did not attract established, main-line magazine publishers. They attracted publishers that were already on the fringes—companies that specialized in pulp fiction or movie-fan magazines or, at best, mass-market children's books. Such publications were produced mostly according to formulas, with the formulas determined by whatever sold well. The publishers were accustomed to dealing with formula writers, and everything that passed through their hands was therefore treated like hackwork. In such an atmosphere, there was not much incentive to try to make comic-book stories into artistic statements.

And if a feature turned out to have great commercial value, it was the publisher, not the artist or writer, who profited. (Siegel and Shuster were paid only ten dollars a page for the *Superman* story that was published in *Action Comics* No. 1—and they were required by the publisher to sign away all rights to the character. Although they continued to work on the *Superman* comic books and strips, it was as employees only.) The artists and writers who worked on comic books were often not allowed to sign their work, and many saw comic books only as a rung on the ladder leading up to a contract for a syndicated newspaper strip, or to writing for radio or slick magazines, or to a career in commercial art.

In short, there was no reason to believe that the comic book, when it was flourishing in the 1940s and 1950s, would give birth to stories of enduring value. But it did.

The comic books' readers can take part of the credit. Readers often responded with delight to those few comics that broke free of the formulas or turned them to new purposes. *Captain Marvel, Uncle Scrooge, Little Lulu,* and the early *Mad* won the allegiance of hundreds of thousands of readers. But of course the readers could not bring such comic books into being by themselves.

On at least one occasion, a group of comics creators— supported by an enlightened publisher—set out to do work well above the industry norm. That happened in the early 1950s at E.C., the company that spawned the horror-comic boom. Cushioned by the profits from E.C.'s crime and horror titles, the company's editors and artists put their best efforts into science-fiction and war comic books that were aimed at more mature readers (and did not sell as well as crime and horror). E.C.'s patience with slow-selling titles paid off spectacularly when the satirical *Mad,* edited and written by Harvey Kurtzman, became a best seller after a rocky start.

Another cartoonist did not have to seek out a mature audience; it came built in. Will Eisner's *Spirit*—the adventures of a masked crime-fighter—was distributed as a small comic-book section with Sunday newspapers, and as such was read by adults as well as by children—perhaps more by adults than by children. Although Eisner worked under severe deadline pressures—turning out a seven-page story every week—he worked under few pressures of any other kind, and many episodes of *The Spirit* were so formula-free that the title character played only a limited role in them.

But outstanding stories usually emerged in another way. A single cartoonist was hired to perform a specific, limited task; often—but not always—he was hired to both write and draw his stories. The cartoonist set out to do the work in the spirit of a craftsman; and slowly, he became something more than a craftsman.

For example, a few cartoonists started with conventional super-heroes—C. C. Beck with Captain Marvel, Jack Cole with Plastic Man—and put them at the center of stories that were far more witty and charming than comic-book conventions had seemed to permit. Other cartoonists, like Walt Kelly and George Carlson, found havens in comic books intended for very young children. Many such comic books were published in the 1940s, especially by Dell, which brought out *Animal Comics, Fairy Tale Parade, Raggedy Ann and Andy,* and *Santa Claus Funnies.* It was in these low-key Dell comic books that Kelly perfected the skills that he put to use in his famous *Pogo.* Unlike Kelly, who worked in comic books in the early stages of his career, Carlson came to comic books—to *Jingle Jangle Comics*—after many years as a cartoonist and illustrator. He saw—and seized—an opportunity to cap his career with very free and inventive stories about such zanies as the Pie-Face Prince.

Other cartoonists wrote and drew humorous features to be used as "comic relief" in titles that were dominated by characters meant to be taken more seriously. Both Sheldon Mayer and Basil Wolverton filled this role in the 1940s—Mayer with this *Scribbly* feature, Wolverton with *Power house Pepper* and other features. Since they worked on the edges of the spotlight, Mayer and Wolverton could indulge comic fancies even to the point of mocking the super-heroes that were the mainstay of the industry.

In the 1940s, it was common for a cartoonist to be paired with an existing character and to draw the stories with that character in issue after issue, perhaps for years. Such pairings did not lead inevitably to distinguished work; but sometimes, a gifted cartoonist could find unsuspected possibilities in an established character. That happened when Carl Barks was assigned to the *Donald Duck* feature in *Walt Disney's Comics and Stories,* and when John Stanley was asked to write and draw the new *Little Lulu* comic book. Both cartoonists turned out brilliant stories in which the familiar characters were transformed and enriched.

Other cartoonists, too—far more than could be represented in this book—did comic-book work that reflects high levels of both craft and caring.

Comic books did not seek out truly original talents. But in its heyday, the field was so large and so fluid that talented people could find ways to do exceptional work—and, sometimes, extraordinary work.

Our volume is intended to be not so much a survey or a sampler as a statement about the comic book at its best. Therefore, most of our choices are here because of our own convictions about their quality. We considered several thousand stories in making our selections. One or the other or both of us read all, or almost all, of the comic-book work of some of the creators represented here (Barks, Stanley, Kelly, Carlson) and large selections from the others. We also sought and received valuable advice from several people whose names you will find in our acknowledgments. But the choices here are our own.

To reduce the criteria for our selections to a few words would be difficult, but perhaps we can say that we have looked for compelling stories whose creators have made use of the medium itself—who have made their words and pictures work together to achieve results not possible in any other medium.

It will not come as a surprise, to anyone who has glanced at this volume's table of contents, that we think most highly of the humor features, even those that treated the conventions of the comic book itself and the concept of the super-heroes themselves with humor. And it will soon be evident also that our own list of the major talents of the comic book would begin with Carl Barks, Walt Kelly, John Stanley, C. C. Beck, Will Eisner . . .

Our cut-off date for this collection has been the adoption of the Comics Code in October 1954 (the first comic books that had been subjected to the Code's requirements were published in the spring of 1955). Nothing published after the Code took effect will be found here. The adoption of the Code marked a distinct change in the industry, although some comic books with real vitality—like Stan Lee's collaborations with Jack Kirby and Steve Ditko in the Marvel super-hero comics (*Fantastic Four, Amazing Spider-Man*) of the mid-1960s—have been published under the Code.

Inevitably there are dozens of popular features that are not included in this volume; *Blackhawk* and *The Heap* are two much-admired examples. We have been forced to exclude the work of many highly regarded artists; Alex Toth, for one. Many artists were not well served by the writers whose scripts they illustrated, and we have felt that the features included in this book should be distinguished in writing as well as drawing. There are also genres and types of comics that we have not represented. We have no romance comics and no westerns. There are no teenage comics here, and hence no examples from the very durable *Archie* magazines. We include no examples of the comics based on classic novels, plays, and poems, and none of the comics based on movies or—except for the Disney ducks—on the supposed adventures of movie stars, such as Bob Hope, Jerry Lewis, or others. We have also avoided those comics that were based on newspaper strips—those that offer not reprints but new material about their characters.*

All of the features in this book are, of course, comic-book originals. And it is our conviction that although some may show the work of assistants, none were in any sense ghosted, and all are ultimately the work of the men we have identified as the authors.

But enough. It is high time for the reader to begin to enjoy that work.

Michael Barrier
Martin Williams

---

* Those latter magazines, incidentally, were often turned out by the syndicate that distributed the strip and were probably never seen by the newspaper strip's author or authors. A few conscientious strip artists did directly supervise their comic-book ghosts. And a small few even worked, with assistants, on the comic-book adventures of their characters.

About "Superman"

As we have seen, comic-book originals began to appear in 1935; the first was a magazine called *New Fun.* In its first issue, *New Fun* (its name was soon changed to *More Fun*) was anything but impressive. Some of its features had a professional look; more of them looked like the work of promising amateurs; and some seemed to be the work of amateurs of little promise. Many of them were indeed the work of eager teenagers in their conception, their scripting, and their drawing. But from *More Fun* came the magazines *New Adventure, Detective Comics,* and *Action Comics,* and from these came the whole line of National Periodical Publications, now called DC Comics and now part of a huge conglomerate.

Two things intervened to make all that possible: the arrival of the feature called *Superman* in 1938 and the one called *Batman* in 1939, both in comic books published by National Comics. Indeed, at second hand, the sustained success of these features probably made a whole industry possible and, thus, at third hand made the contents of this book possible.

Superman, as we have said, came from Jerry Siegel, who wrote it, and Joe Shuster, who drew it. They had been contributing to *More Fun* and *Detective Comics* since 1936, but they originally intended *Superman* to be a newspaper strip and had submitted it unsuccessfully to almost every syndicate there was. Harry Donenfeld purchased it for *Action Comics* and had its daily-format panels pasted into a thirteen-page feature. Three years later *Superman* was appearing in three comic books simultaneously and still other *Superman* adventures had newspaper distribution as well.

The idea of a secret identity for Superman (he is otherwise, of course, Clark Kent, "mild-mannered reporter") could have come from such heroes of pulp fiction as the Shadow and the Spider or their radio counterparts like the Green Hornet or from the several films based on the Zorro character—but, in the Scarlet Pimpernel of the British novelist Baroness Orczy, the idea dates back earlier than they.

Philip Wylie's 1930 science-fiction novel, *Gladiator,* has often been suggested as Superman's inspiration. An equally handy suggestion could have come from John Carter, the hero of Edgar Rice Burroughs's Martian adventures. Carter was an American mysteriously teleported to Mars in the 1860s. There he discovered that the lesser pull of Martian gravity made his earthling's muscles exceedingly powerful: he could leap to great heights, run in great strides, and fight with superior strength. Substitute Krypton for Mars, reverse the idea, and one has Kryptonian Clark Kent-Superman on earth, "able to leap tall buildings at a single bound." Indeed, in his initial conception, superior strength and leaping power on earth, plus a skin impenetrable to bullets, were Superman's super powers. The ability to fly unlimited distances and X-ray vision—such powers came later.

On the other hand, one does not have to look for conscious sources for *Superman* or look too far to account for his appeal. The promotional material for the 1978 *Superman* movie made the matter virtually specific in the blurb, "with Marlon Brando as Jor-El, who gave his only son to save the world." Intended or not (and the allusion would not *have* to be conscious), only the word "begotten" seems to be missing from the sentence.

Superman: conceived in a magic land in the sky (the planet Krypton), from a superior group of beings and fathered by a wise and powerful member of that group (Jor-El), threatened in his infancy with death (the destruction of Krypton), sent to earth, raised in humble surroundings (the farming Kent family), the possessor of great powers that he uses to save mankind.

Superman is one version of the hero with a thousand faces—to employ the title of Joseph Campbell's excellent book on the subject—and his appeal should therefore not surprise us. But Superman is a crude version of the hero; if you will, an elementary one. Unlike his more developed analogues in all the world's great religions, Superman does not offer love or goodwill, self-knowledge or contemplation as keys to man's salvation. He offers his own physical powers. Ultimately Superman's message for man rests only in his own superior strength and lies in his power to be an enforcer of his own judgement of what is good and what is evil.

For our Superman choice here, rather than jump forward to his later appearances in his own *Superman* comics, we have chosen the less frequently reprinted first appearance in *Action Comics* No. 1, with Siegel's episodic scripting (designed for daily newspapers, remember) and Shuster's cartoon-oriented drawing style. Superman's origin is barely sketched; Krypton is unnamed; Kent's newspaper is called the *Daily Star;* and although there is a "Lois," there is no Perry White and no Jimmy Olsen.

M.W.

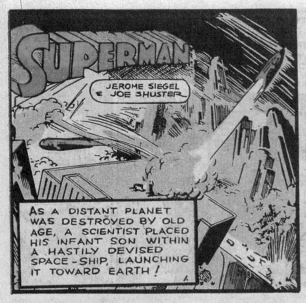

SUPERMAN
JEROME SIEGEL & JOE SHUSTER
AS A DISTANT PLANET WAS DESTROYED BY OLD AGE, A SCIENTIST PLACED HIS INFANT SON WITHIN A HASTILY DEVISED SPACE-SHIP, LAUNCHING IT TOWARD EARTH!
WHEN THE VEHICLE LANDED ON EARTH, A PASSING MOTORIST, DISCOVERING THE SLEEPING BABE WITHIN, TURNED THE CHILD OVER TO AN ORPHANAGE
ATTENDANTS, UNAWARE THE CHILD'S PHYSICAL STRUCTURE WAS MILLIONS OF YEARS ADVANCED OF THEIR OWN, WERE ASTOUNDED AT HIS FEATS OF STRENGTH
WHEN MATURITY WAS REACHED, HE DISCOVERED HE COULD EASILY:
LEAP 1/8TH OF A MILE; HURDLE A TWENTY-STORY BUILDING . . .
RAISE TREMENDOUS WEIGHTS . . .
. . . RUN FASTER THAN AN EXPRESS TRAIN . . .
. . AND THAT NOTHING LESS THAN A BURSTING SHELL COULD PENETRATE HIS SKIN!
EARLY, CLARK DECIDED HE MUST TURN HIS TITANIC STRENGTH INTO CHANNELS THAT WOULD BENEFIT MANKIND
AND SO WAS CREATED . . .
SUPERMAN! CHAMPION OF THE OPPRESSED, THE PHYSICAL MARVEL WHO HAD SWORN TO DEVOTE HIS EXISTENCE TO HELPING THOSE IN NEED!
A SCIENTIFIC EXPLANATION OF CLARK KENT'S AMAZING STRENGTH
KENT HAD COME FROM A PLANET WHOSE INHABITANTS' PHYSICAL STRUCTURE WAS MILLIONS OF YEARS ADVANCED OF OUR OWN.
UPON REACHING MATURITY, THE PEOPLE OF HIS RACE BECAME GIFTED WITH TITANIC STRENGTH!
--INCREDIBLE? NO! FOR EVEN TODAY ON OUR WORLD EXIST CREATURES WITH SUPER-STRENGTH!
THE LOWLY ANT CAN SUPPORT WEIGHTS HUNDREDS OF TIMES ITS OWN
THE GRASSHOPPER LEAPS WHAT TO MAN WOULD BE THE SPACE OF SEVERAL CITY BLOCKS

From *Action Comics* No. 1, June 1938.

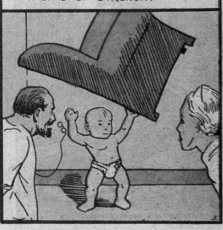

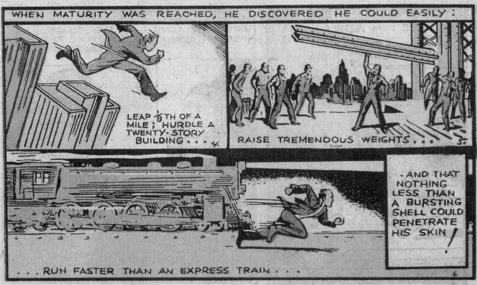

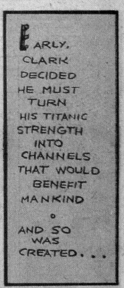

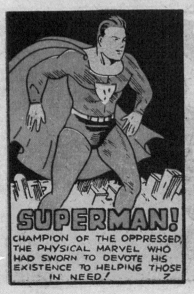

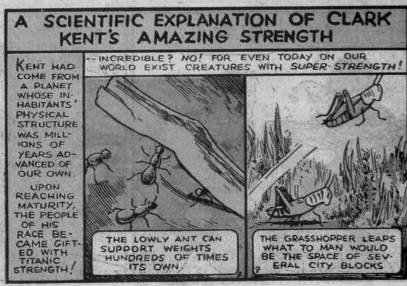

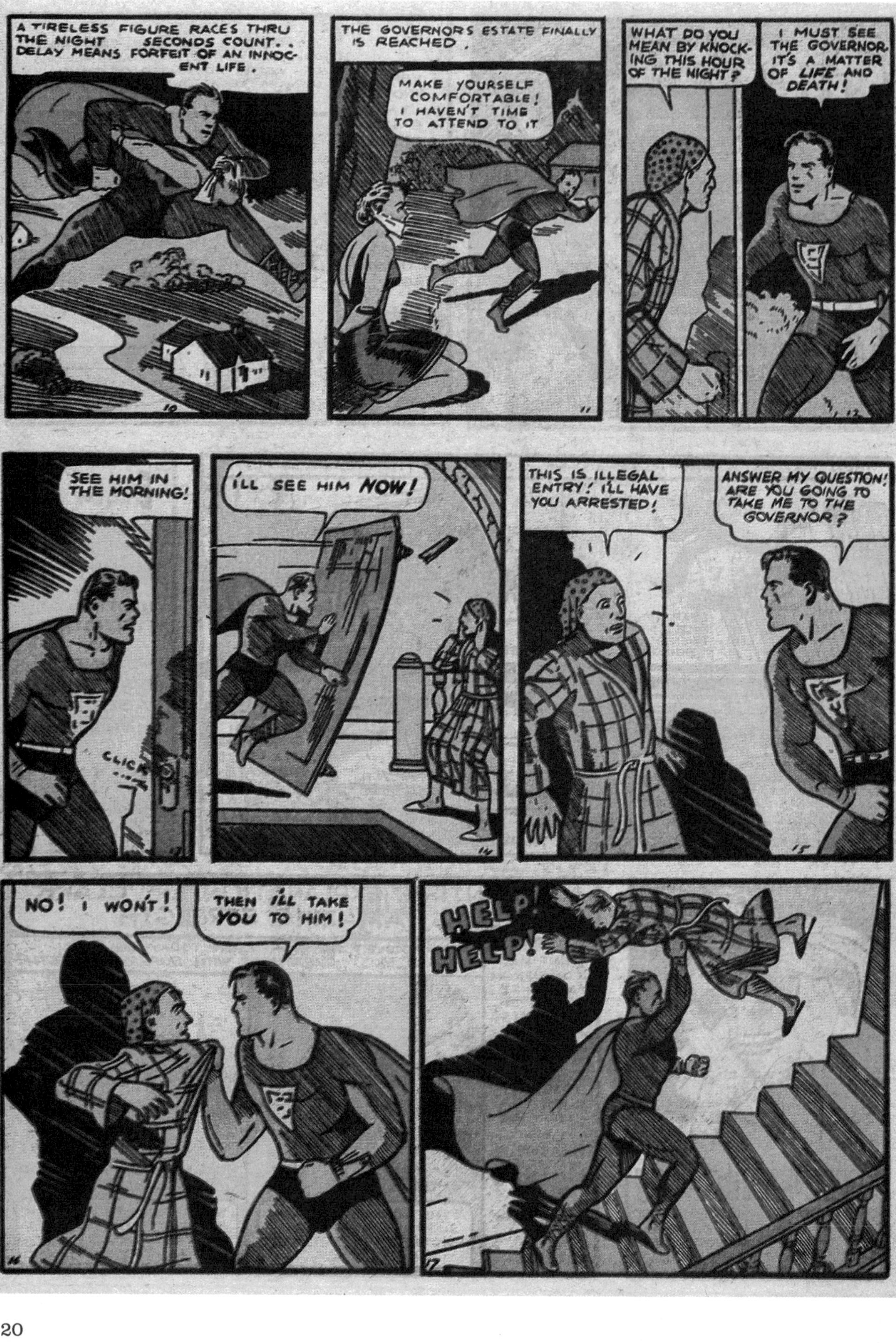
A TIRELESS FIGURE RACES THRU THE NIGHT SECONDS COUNT. . DELAY MEANS FORFEIT OF AN INNOCENT LIFE.
THE GOVERNORS ESTATE FINALLY IS REACHED.
MAKE YOURSELF COMFORTABLE! I HAVEN'T TIME TO ATTEND TO IT
WHAT DO YOU MEAN BY KNOCKING THIS HOUR OF THE NIGHT?
I MUST SEE THE GOVERNOR. IT'S A MATTER OF LIFE AND DEATH!
SEE HIM IN THE MORNING!
CLICK
I'LL SEE HIM NOW!
THIS IS ILLEGAL ENTRY! I'LL HAVE YOU ARRESTED!
ANSWER MY QUESTION! ARE YOU GOING TO TAKE ME TO THE GOVERNOR?
NO! I WON'T!
THEN I'LL TAKE YOU TO HIM!
HELP! HELP!

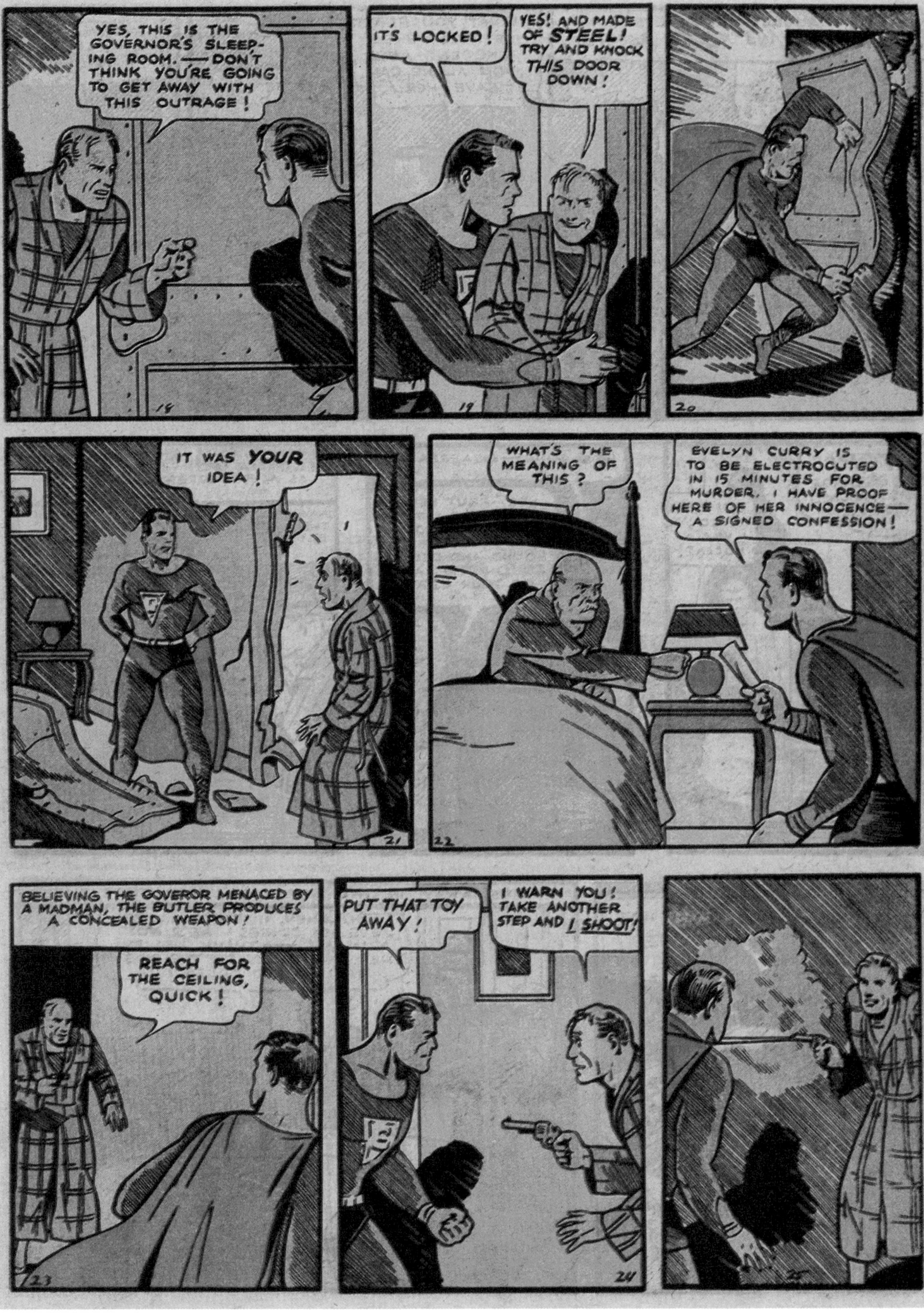
YES, THIS IS THE GOVERNOR'S SLEEPING ROOM. —— DON'T THINK YOU'RE GOING TO GET AWAY WITH THIS OUTRAGE!
IT'S LOCKED!
YES! AND MADE OF STEEL! TRY AND KNOCK THIS DOOR DOWN!
IT WAS YOUR IDEA!
WHAT'S THE MEANING OF THIS?
EVELYN CURRY IS TO BE ELECTROCUTED IN 15 MINUTES FOR MURDER. I HAVE PROOF HERE OF HER INNOCENCE — A SIGNED CONFESSION!
BELIEVING THE GOVEROR MENACED BY A MADMAN, THE BUTLER PRODUCES A CONCEALED WEAPON!
REACH FOR THE CEILING, QUICK!
PUT THAT TOY AWAY!
I WARN YOU! TAKE ANOTHER STEP AND I SHOOT!

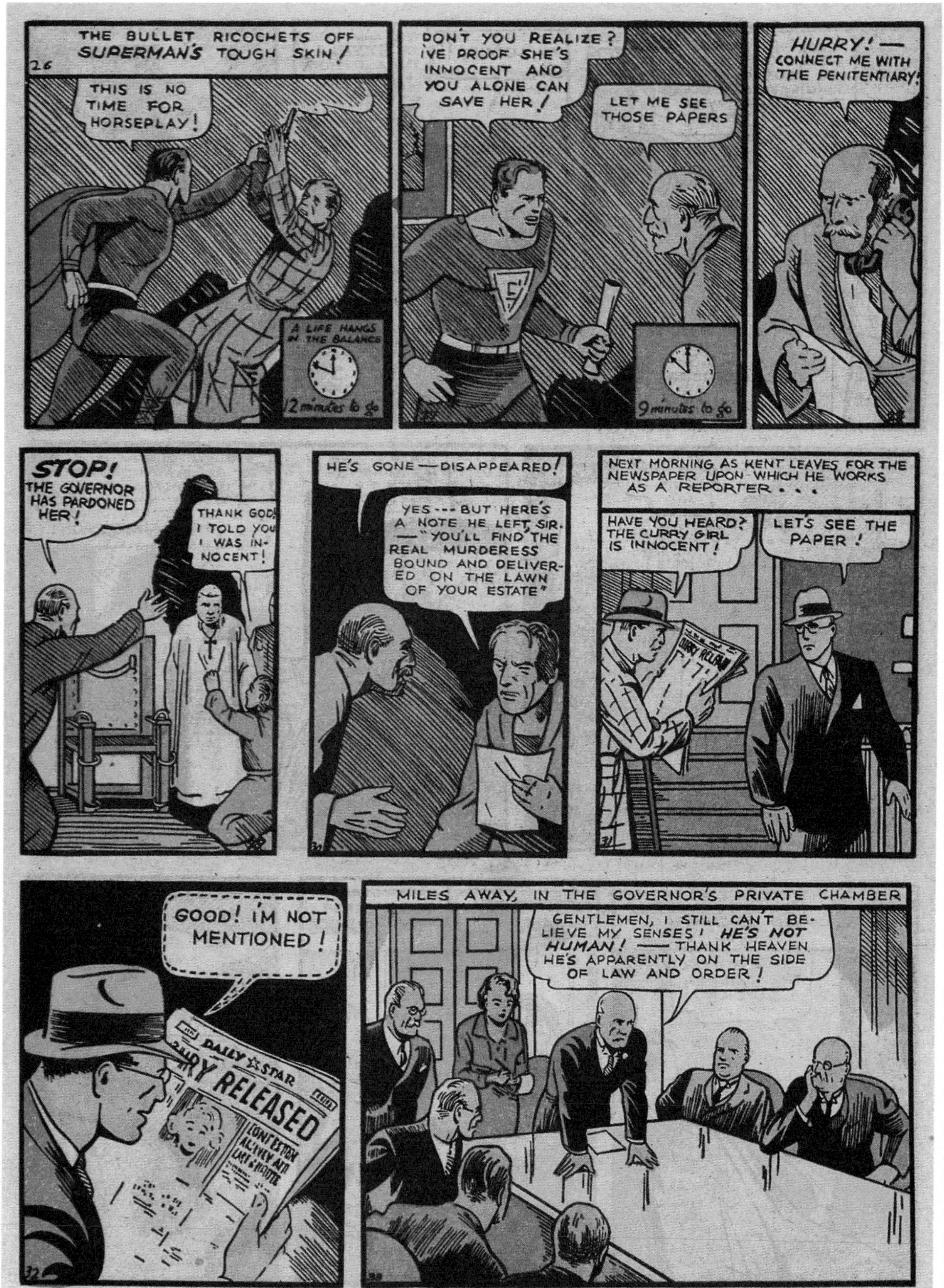

THE BULLET RICOCHETS OFF SUPERMAN'S TOUGH SKIN!
THIS IS NO TIME FOR HORSEPLAY!
A LIFE HANGS IN THE BALANCE
12 minutes to go
DON'T YOU REALIZE? I'VE PROOF SHE'S INNOCENT AND YOU ALONE CAN SAVE HER!
LET ME SEE THOSE PAPERS
9 minutes to go
HURRY! — CONNECT ME WITH THE PENITENTIARY!
STOP! THE GOVERNOR HAS PARDONED HER!
THANK GOD! I TOLD YOU I WAS INNOCENT!
HE'S GONE — DISAPPEARED!
YES --- BUT HERE'S A NOTE HE LEFT, SIR. — "YOU'LL FIND THE REAL MURDERESS BOUND AND DELIVERED ON THE LAWN OF YOUR ESTATE"
NEXT MORNING AS KENT LEAVES FOR THE NEWSPAPER UPON WHICH HE WORKS AS A REPORTER . . .
HAVE YOU HEARD? THE CURRY GIRL IS INNOCENT!
LET'S SEE THE PAPER!
GOOD! I'M NOT MENTIONED!
DAILY STAR
RELEASED
MILES AWAY, IN THE GOVERNOR'S PRIVATE CHAMBER
GENTLEMEN, I STILL CAN'T BELIEVE MY SENSES! HE'S NOT HUMAN! — THANK HEAVEN HE'S APPARENTLY ON THE SIDE OF LAW AND ORDER!

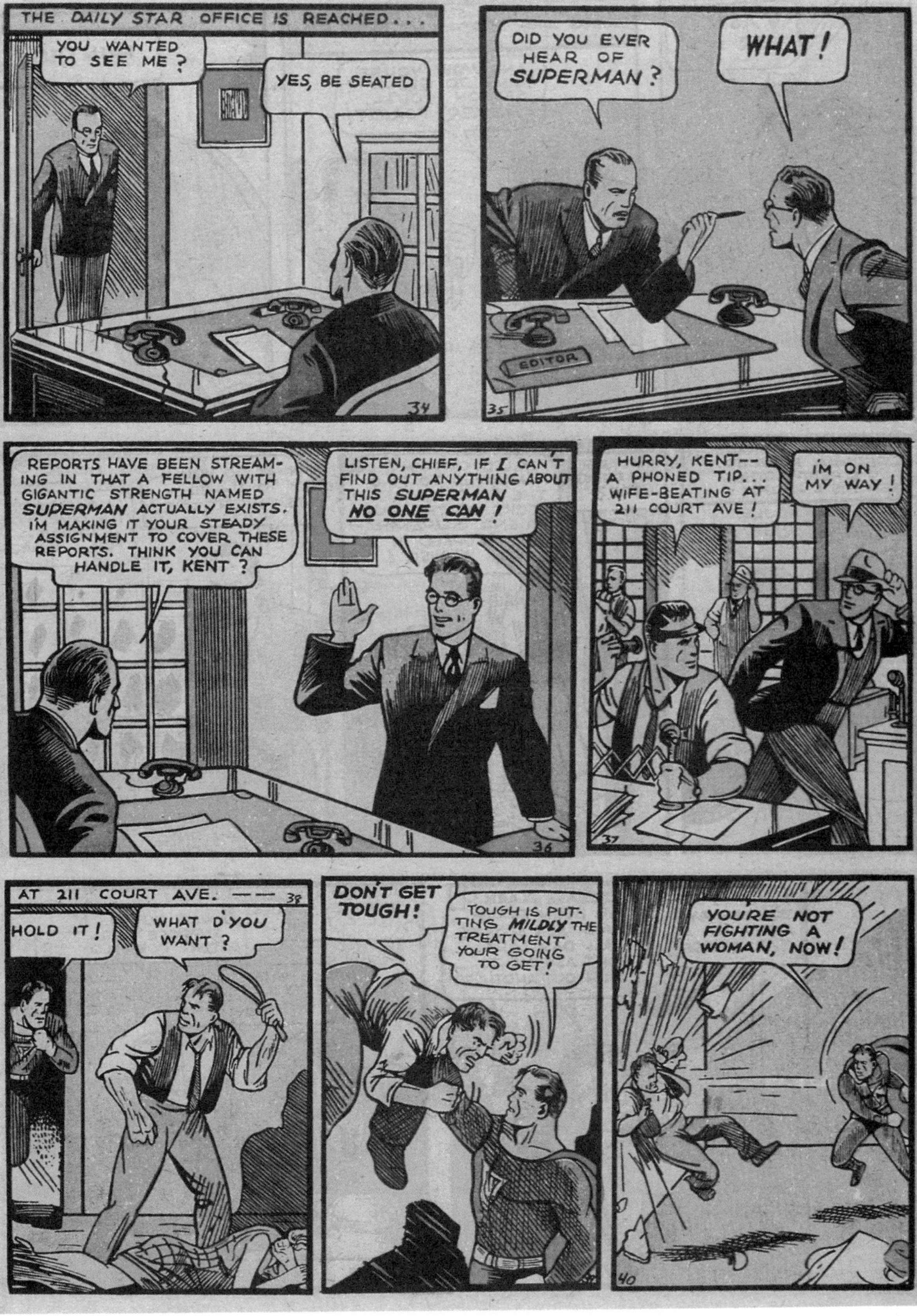
THE DAILY STAR OFFICE IS REACHED...
YOU WANTED TO SEE ME?
YES, BE SEATED
DID YOU EVER HEAR OF SUPERMAN?
WHAT!
EDITOR
REPORTS HAVE BEEN STREAMING IN THAT A FELLOW WITH GIGANTIC STRENGTH NAMED SUPERMAN ACTUALLY EXISTS. I'M MAKING IT YOUR STEADY ASSIGNMENT TO COVER THESE REPORTS. THINK YOU CAN HANDLE IT, KENT?
LISTEN, CHIEF, IF I CAN'T FIND OUT ANYTHING ABOUT THIS SUPERMAN NO ONE CAN!
HURRY, KENT-- A PHONED TIP... WIFE-BEATING AT 211 COURT AVE!
I'M ON MY WAY!
AT 211 COURT AVE. ---
HOLD IT!
WHAT D'YOU WANT?
DON'T GET TOUGH!
TOUGH IS PUTTING MILDLY THE TREATMENT YOUR GOING TO GET!
YOU'RE NOT FIGHTING A WOMAN, NOW!

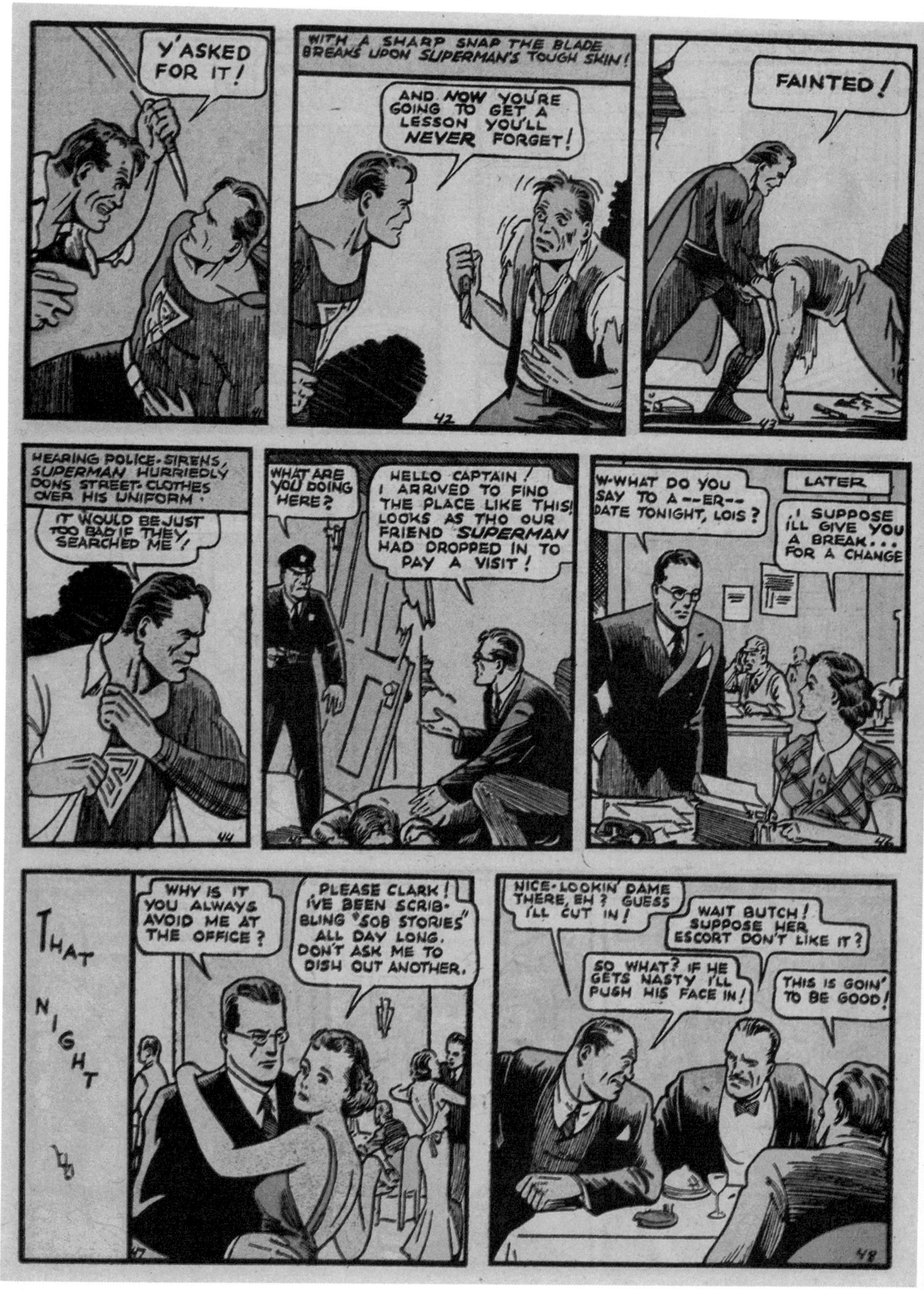
Y'ASKED FOR IT!
WITH A SHARP SNAP THE BLADE BREAKS UPON SUPERMAN'S TOUGH SKIN!
AND NOW YOU'RE GOING TO GET A LESSON YOU'LL NEVER FORGET!
FAINTED!
HEARING POLICE-SIRENS, SUPERMAN HURRIEDLY DONS STREET-CLOTHES OVER HIS UNIFORM.
IT WOULD BE JUST TOO BAD IF THEY SEARCHED ME!
WHAT ARE YOU DOING HERE?
HELLO CAPTAIN! I ARRIVED TO FIND THE PLACE LIKE THIS! LOOKS AS THO OUR FRIEND SUPERMAN HAD DROPPED IN TO PAY A VISIT!
W-WHAT DO YOU SAY TO A --ER-- DATE TONIGHT, LOIS?
LATER
I SUPPOSE I'LL GIVE YOU A BREAK... FOR A CHANGE
THAT NIGHT
WHY IS IT YOU ALWAYS AVOID ME AT THE OFFICE?
PLEASE CLARK! I'VE BEEN SCRIBBLING "SOB STORIES" ALL DAY LONG. DON'T ASK ME TO DISH OUT ANOTHER.
NICE-LOOKIN' DAME THERE, EH? GUESS I'LL CUT IN!
WAIT BUTCH! SUPPOSE HER ESCORT DON'T LIKE IT?
SO WHAT? IF HE GETS NASTY I'LL PUSH HIS FACE IN!
THIS IS GOIN' TO BE GOOD!

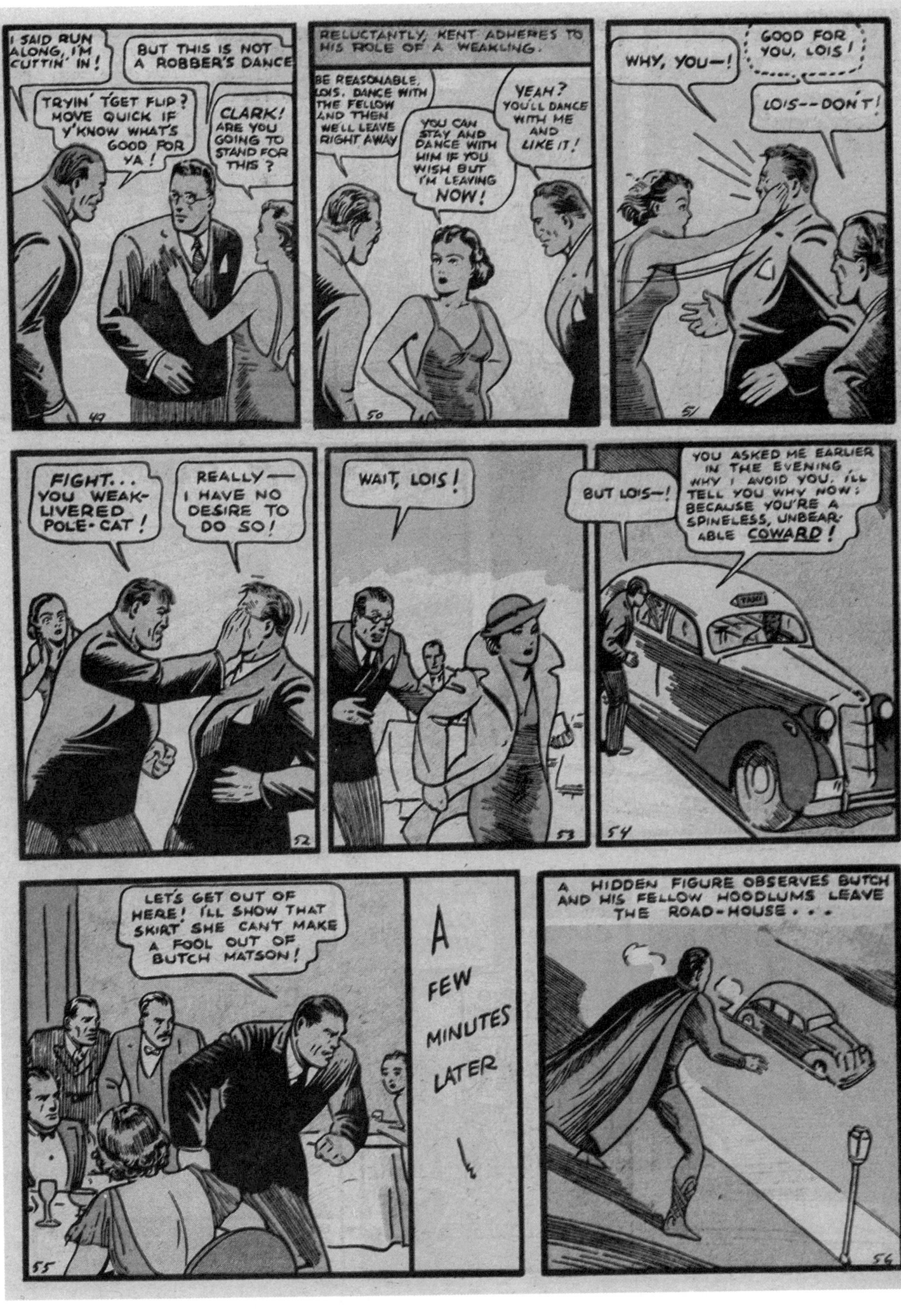
I SAID RUN ALONG, I'M CUTTIN' IN!
BUT THIS IS NOT A ROBBER'S DANCE
TRYIN' T'GET FLIP? MOVE QUICK IF Y'KNOW WHAT'S GOOD FOR YA!
CLARK! ARE YOU GOING TO STAND FOR THIS?
49
RELUCTANTLY, KENT ADHERES TO HIS ROLE OF A WEAKLING.
BE REASONABLE, LOIS. DANCE WITH THE FELLOW AND THEN WE'LL LEAVE RIGHT AWAY
YOU CAN STAY AND DANCE WITH HIM IF YOU WISH BUT I'M LEAVING NOW!
YEAH? YOU'LL DANCE WITH ME AND LIKE IT!
50
WHY, YOU—!
GOOD FOR YOU, LOIS!
LOIS--DON'T!
51
FIGHT... YOU WEAK-LIVERED POLE-CAT!
REALLY— I HAVE NO DESIRE TO DO SO!
52
WAIT, LOIS!
53
BUT LOIS—!
YOU ASKED ME EARLIER IN THE EVENING WHY I AVOID YOU. I'LL TELL YOU WHY NOW: BECAUSE YOU'RE A SPINELESS, UNBEARABLE COWARD!
TAXI
54
LET'S GET OUT OF HERE! I'LL SHOW THAT SKIRT SHE CAN'T MAKE A FOOL OUT OF BUTCH MATSON!
55
A FEW MINUTES LATER
A HIDDEN FIGURE OBSERVES BUTCH AND HIS FELLOW HOODLUMS LEAVE THE ROAD-HOUSE...
56

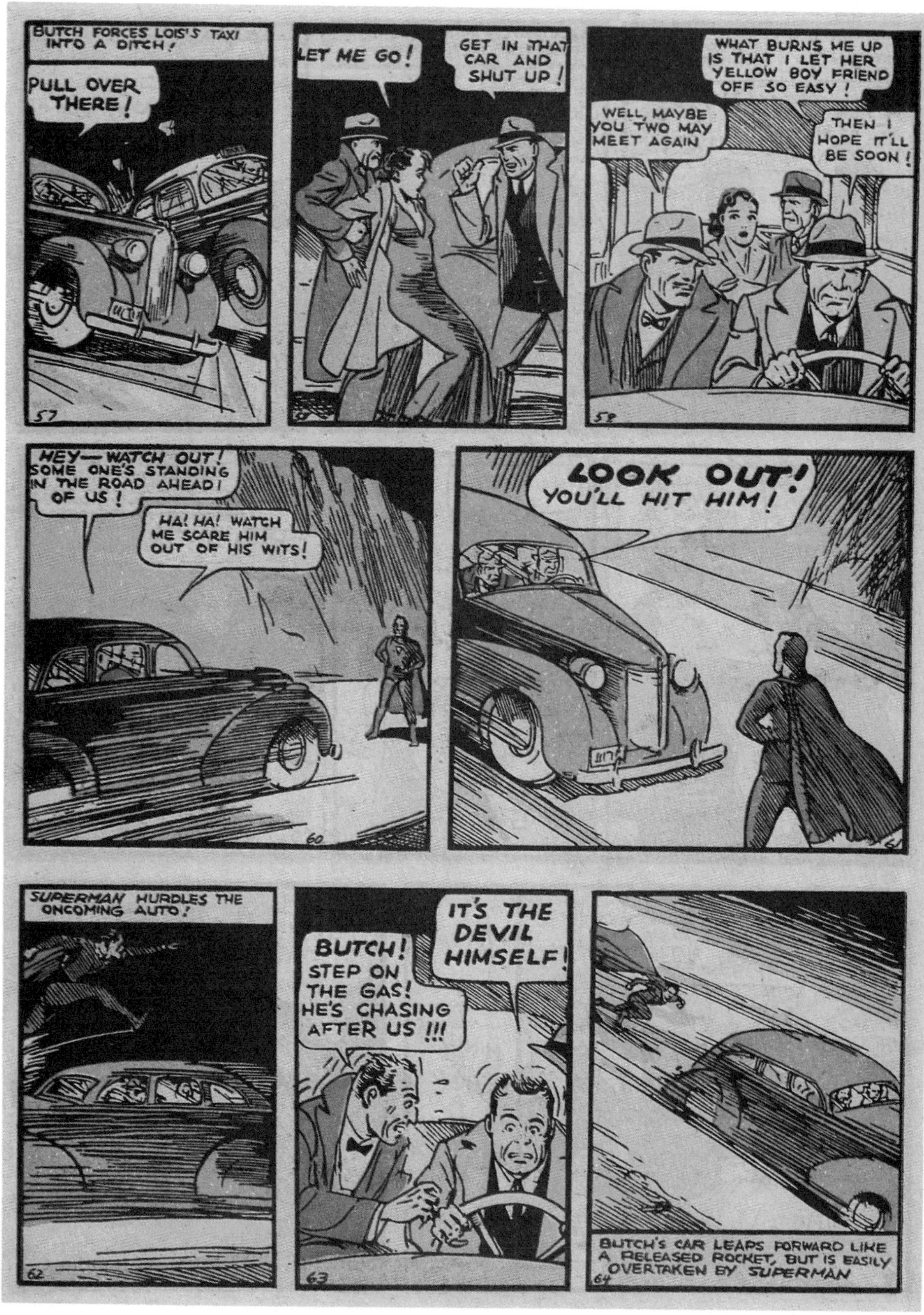
BUTCH FORCES LOIS'S TAXI INTO A DITCH!
PULL OVER THERE!
57
LET ME GO!
GET IN THAT CAR AND SHUT UP!
WHAT BURNS ME UP IS THAT I LET HER YELLOW BOY FRIEND OFF SO EASY!
WELL, MAYBE YOU TWO MAY MEET AGAIN
THEN I HOPE IT'LL BE SOON!
59
HEY—WATCH OUT! SOME ONE'S STANDING IN THE ROAD AHEAD OF US!
HA! HA! WATCH ME SCARE HIM OUT OF HIS WITS!
60
LOOK OUT! YOU'LL HIT HIM!
61
SUPERMAN HURDLES THE ONCOMING AUTO!
62
BUTCH! STEP ON THE GAS! HE'S CHASING AFTER US !!!
IT'S THE DEVIL HIMSELF!
63
BUTCH'S CAR LEAPS FORWARD LIKE A RELEASED ROCKET, BUT IS EASILY OVERTAKEN BY SUPERMAN
64

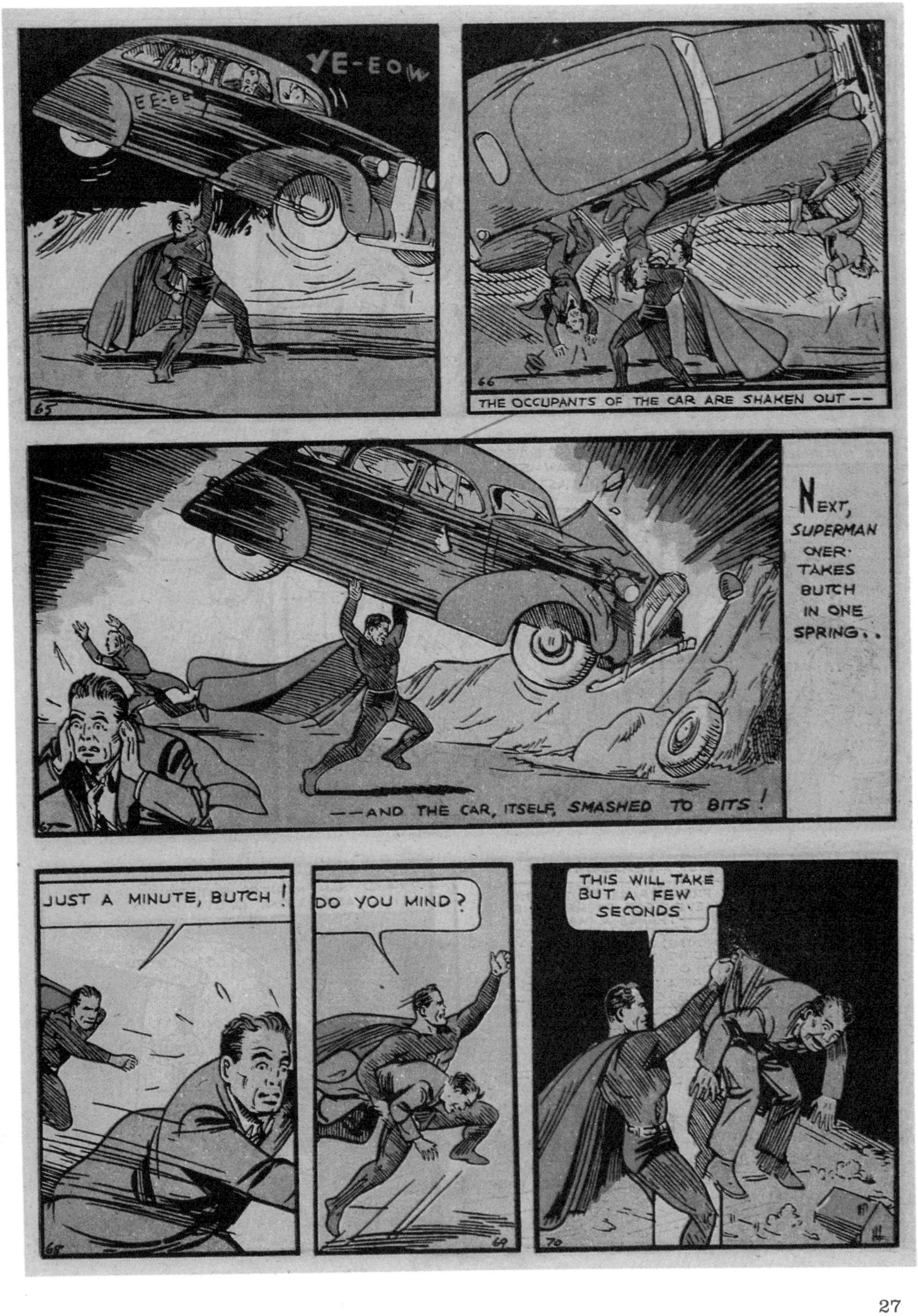
YE-EOW
EE-EE
THE OCCUPANTS OF THE CAR ARE SHAKEN OUT --
--AND THE CAR, ITSELF, SMASHED TO BITS!
NEXT, SUPERMAN OVER-TAKES BUTCH IN ONE SPRING..
JUST A MINUTE, BUTCH!
DO YOU MIND?
THIS WILL TAKE BUT A FEW SECONDS

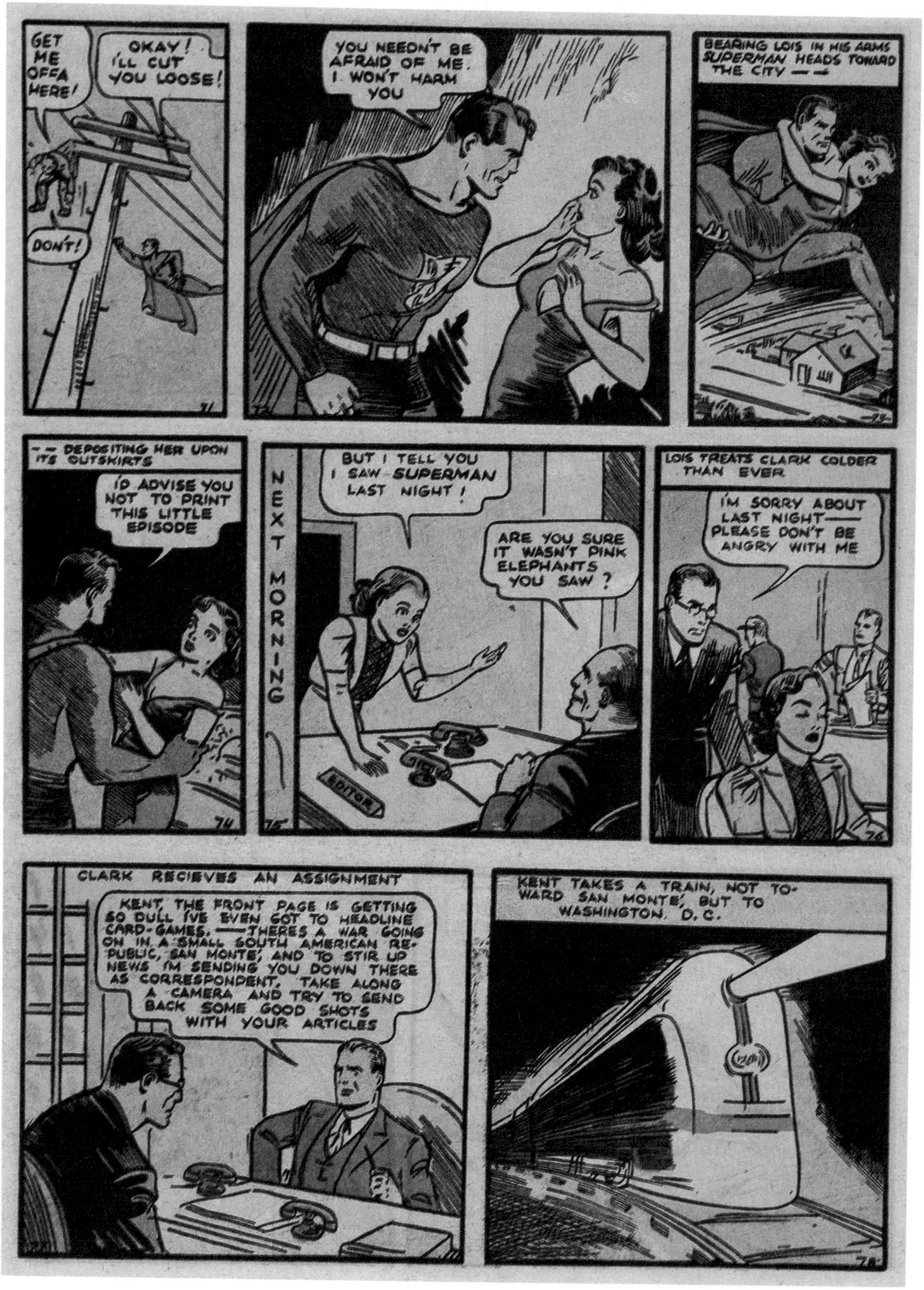
GET ME OFFA HERE!
OKAY! I'LL CUT YOU LOOSE!
DON'T!
YOU NEEDN'T BE AFRAID OF ME. I WON'T HARM YOU
BEARING LOIS IN HIS ARMS SUPERMAN HEADS TOWARD THE CITY --
-- DEPOSITING HER UPON ITS OUTSKIRTS
I'D ADVISE YOU NOT TO PRINT THIS LITTLE EPISODE
NEXT MORNING
BUT I TELL YOU I SAW SUPERMAN LAST NIGHT!
ARE YOU SURE IT WASN'T PINK ELEPHANTS YOU SAW?
EDITOR
LOIS TREATS CLARK COLDER THAN EVER
I'M SORRY ABOUT LAST NIGHT—— PLEASE DON'T BE ANGRY WITH ME
CLARK RECIEVES AN ASSIGNMENT
KENT, THE FRONT PAGE IS GETTING SO DULL I'VE EVEN GOT TO HEADLINE CARD-GAMES. ——THERES A WAR GOING ON IN A SMALL SOUTH AMERICAN REPUBLIC, SAN MONTE, AND TO STIR UP NEWS I'M SENDING YOU DOWN THERE AS CORRESPONDENT. TAKE ALONG A CAMERA AND TRY TO SEND BACK SOME GOOD SHOTS WITH YOUR ARTICLES
KENT TAKES A TRAIN, NOT TOWARD SAN MONTE, BUT TO WASHINGTON, D.C.

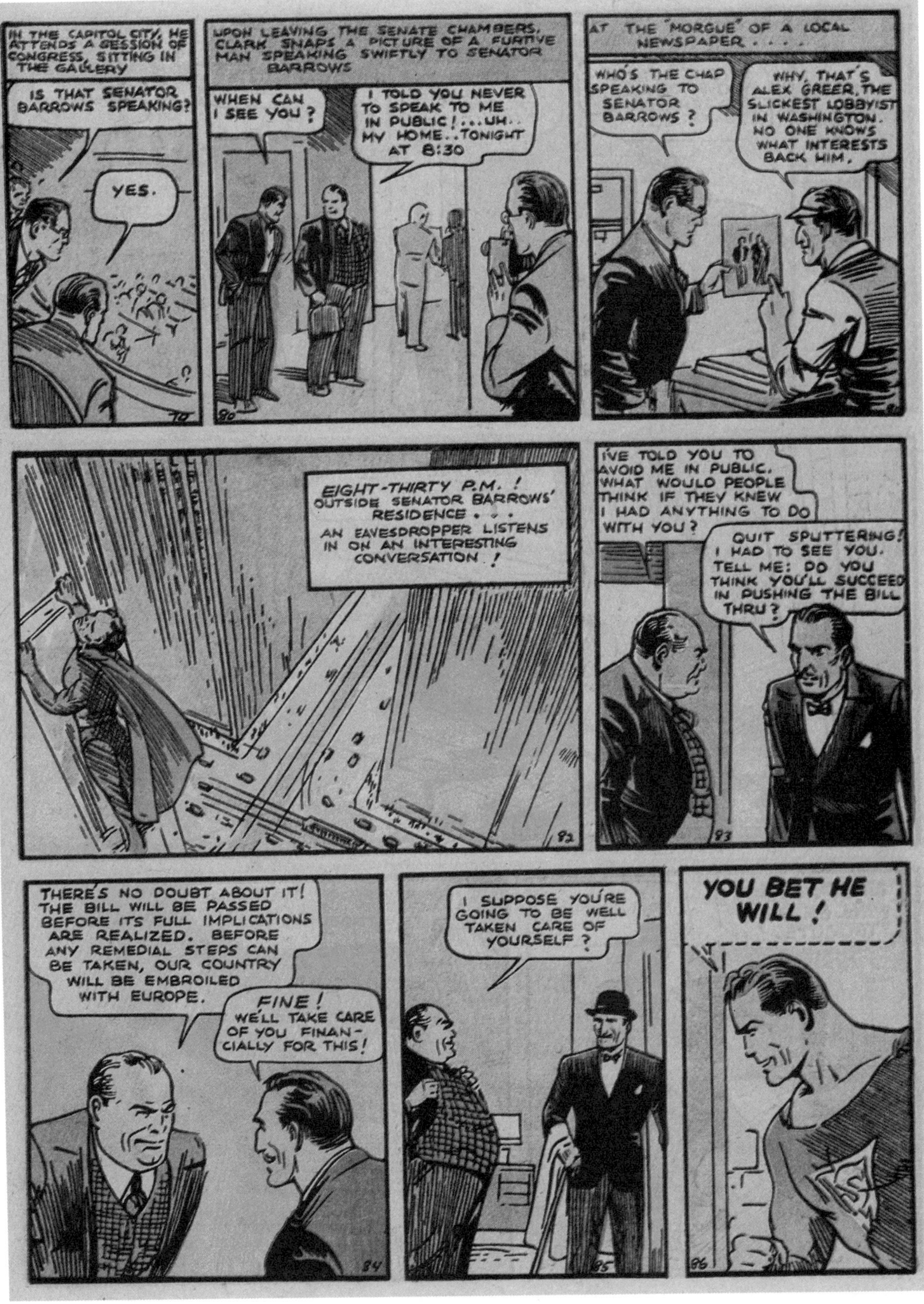

IN THE CAPITOL CITY, HE ATTENDS A SESSION OF CONGRESS, SITTING IN THE GALLERY
IS THAT SENATOR BARROWS SPEAKING?
YES.
UPON LEAVING THE SENATE CHAMBERS, CLARK SNAPS A PICTURE OF A FURTIVE MAN SPEAKING SWIFTLY TO SENATOR BARROWS
WHEN CAN I SEE YOU?
I TOLD YOU NEVER TO SPEAK TO ME IN PUBLIC!...UH.. MY HOME..TONIGHT AT 8:30
AT THE "MORGUE" OF A LOCAL NEWSPAPER....
WHO'S THE CHAP SPEAKING TO SENATOR BARROWS?
WHY, THAT'S ALEX GREER, THE SLICKEST LOBBYIST IN WASHINGTON. NO ONE KNOWS WHAT INTERESTS BACK HIM.
EIGHT-THIRTY P.M.! OUTSIDE SENATOR BARROWS' RESIDENCE... AN EAVESDROPPER LISTENS IN ON AN INTERESTING CONVERSATION!
I'VE TOLD YOU TO AVOID ME IN PUBLIC. WHAT WOULD PEOPLE THINK IF THEY KNEW I HAD ANYTHING TO DO WITH YOU?
QUIT SPUTTERING! I HAD TO SEE YOU. TELL ME: DO YOU THINK YOU'LL SUCCEED IN PUSHING THE BILL THRU?
THERE'S NO DOUBT ABOUT IT! THE BILL WILL BE PASSED BEFORE ITS FULL IMPLICATIONS ARE REALIZED. BEFORE ANY REMEDIAL STEPS CAN BE TAKEN, OUR COUNTRY WILL BE EMBROILED WITH EUROPE.
FINE! WE'LL TAKE CARE OF YOU FINANCIALLY FOR THIS!
I SUPPOSE YOU'RE GOING TO BE WELL TAKEN CARE OF YOURSELF?
YOU BET HE WILL!

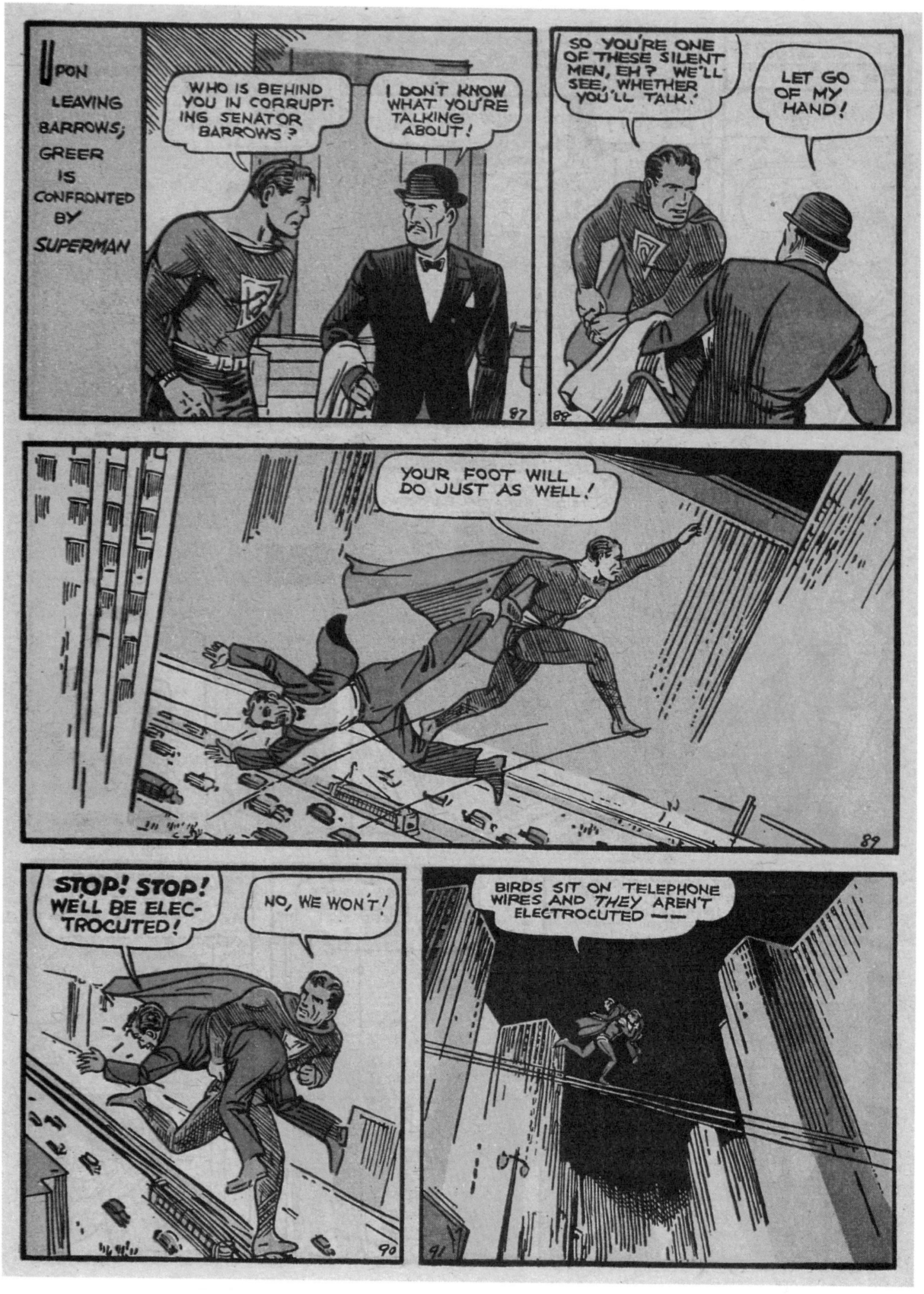
UPON LEAVING BARROWS; GREER IS CONFRONTED BY SUPERMAN
WHO IS BEHIND YOU IN CORRUPTING SENATOR BARROWS?
I DON'T KNOW WHAT YOU'RE TALKING ABOUT!
87
SO YOU'RE ONE OF THESE SILENT MEN, EH? WE'LL SEE, WHETHER YOU'LL TALK.
LET GO OF MY HAND!
88
YOUR FOOT WILL DO JUST AS WELL!
89
STOP! STOP! WE'LL BE ELECTROCUTED!
NO, WE WON'T!
90
BIRDS SIT ON TELEPHONE WIRES AND THEY AREN'T ELECTROCUTED ——
91

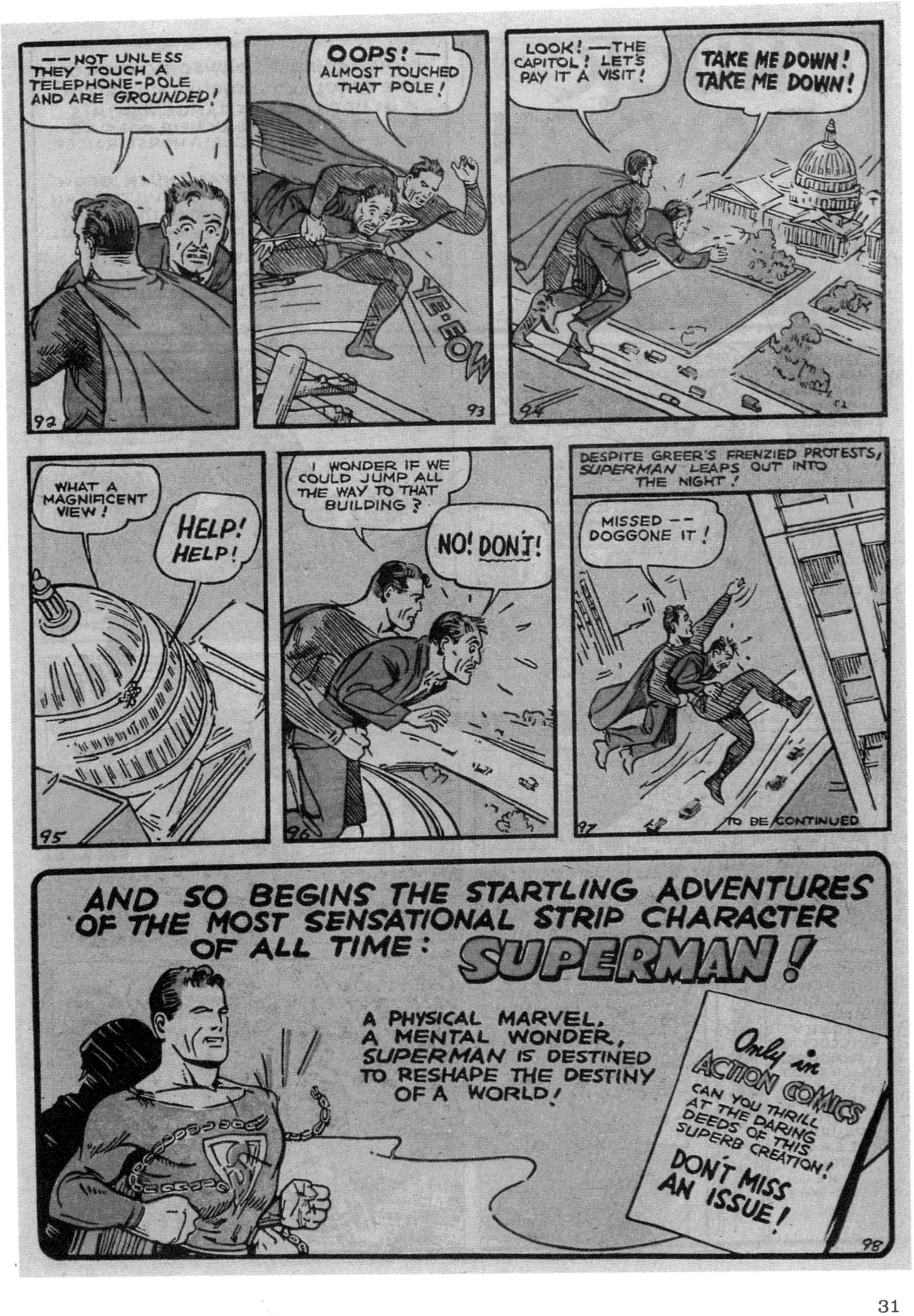

-- NOT UNLESS THEY TOUCH A TELEPHONE-POLE AND ARE GROUNDED!
92
OOPS! — ALMOST TOUCHED THAT POLE!
YE-EOW
93
LOOK! — THE CAPITOL! LET'S PAY IT A VISIT!
TAKE ME DOWN! TAKE ME DOWN!
94
WHAT A MAGNIFICENT VIEW!
HELP! HELP!
95
I WONDER IF WE COULD JUMP ALL THE WAY TO THAT BUILDING?
NO! DON'T!
96
DESPITE GREER'S FRENZIED PROTESTS, SUPERMAN LEAPS OUT INTO THE NIGHT!
MISSED -- DOGGONE IT!
97
TO BE CONTINUED
AND SO BEGINS THE STARTLING ADVENTURES OF THE MOST SENSATIONAL STRIP CHARACTER OF ALL TIME: SUPERMAN!
A PHYSICAL MARVEL, A MENTAL WONDER, SUPERMAN IS DESTINED TO RESHAPE THE DESTINY OF A WORLD!
Only in ACTION COMICS CAN YOU THRILL AT THE DARING DEEDS OF THIS SUPERB CREATION!
DON'T MISS AN ISSUE!
98

About "Batman"

Just as we have included Superman's first appearance, we have also selected Bob Kane's first six-page account of *The Bat-Man* (as it was called) from *Detective Comics* No. 27. And even less than the first Superman appearance is it concerned with its hero's fictional origin.

The details of the Batman's creation are somewhat obscure and even controversial. National Comics editor Whitney Ellsworth frankly wanted a bizarre character who would be as popular as the company's Superman. He went to Kane, who had been working regularly with writer Bill Finger, and between them they worked out the Batman.

A bat-costumed night-stalker had appeared more than once in pulp magazines—on either side of the law. And Kane, incidentally, points to a striking analogy in his early Batman depiction and Leonardo's notebook designs for his flying devices.

Batman was, by day, Bruce Wayne, a man with inherited millions, a rather bored character who was friend to the city's Police Commissioner Gordon. Acting on information he casually gathered from Gordon, Wayne became the Batman by night, a self-trained strongman, gymnast, and acrobat, with high intelligence—a costumed vigilante who preyed on the fears, superstitions, and insecurities of criminals to stalk them and turn them over to the police (or occasionally, in the early days, to shoot them himself).

Wayne, it was later revealed, had been orphaned when his well-to-do parents were killed in a street holdup, and he decided to devote his life to fighting crime, or rather, of course, to one-man vigilante justice. The feature's other regular characters, Alfred, Kane's butler, and Robin, the Boy Wonder (a young orphaned circus acrobat whom Wayne adopted), came later.

So did the colorful recurring criminals: The Joker, the Penguin, the horrifying Two-Face, and the rest. And there the inspiration, like the inspiration for the feature's flat, angular, poster-like drawing style, was in part Chester Gould's *Dick Tracy* newspaper strip. As *Batman* evolved, a brooding, threatening quality was sustained in its predominantly black, night-time panels.

Kane had begun his comic-book career at age twenty; at first it was mostly devoted to humor strips, plus a couple of thrillers he worked on with Bill Finger. He remained with *Batman* well into the 1960s. Meanwhile, the feature's quick success had led to several comic books, to the employment of artist Jerry Robinson to share the work, to a newspaper strip version, to two movie serials—long before the campy TV version of the 1960s.

M.W.

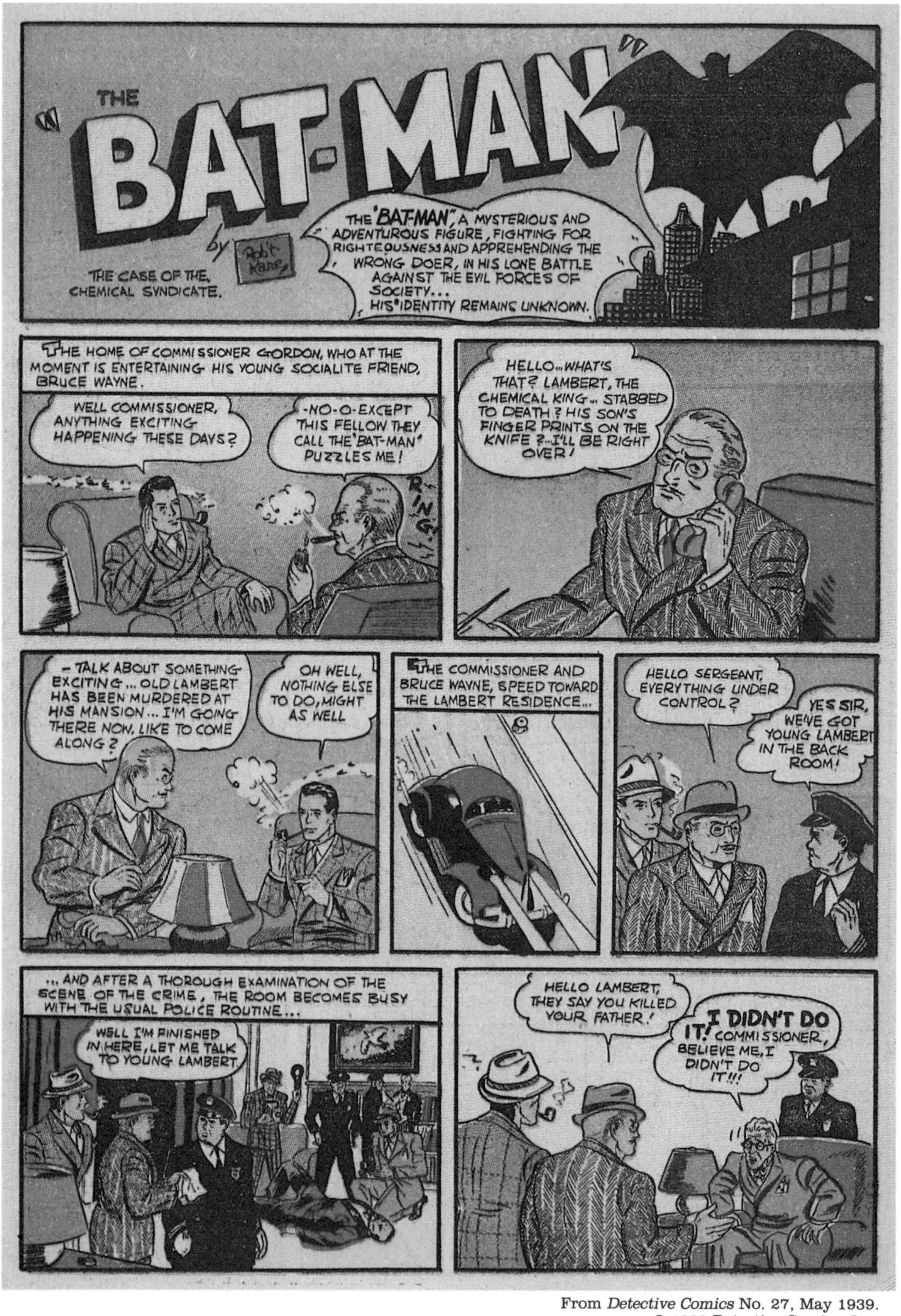

"THE BAT-MAN"
by Rob't Kane
THE CASE OF THE CHEMICAL SYNDICATE.
THE 'BAT-MAN', A MYSTERIOUS AND ADVENTUROUS FIGURE, FIGHTING FOR RIGHTEOUSNESS AND APPREHENDING THE WRONG DOER, IN HIS LONE BATTLE AGAINST THE EVIL FORCES OF SOCIETY... HIS IDENTITY REMAINS UNKNOWN.
THE HOME OF COMMISSIONER GORDON, WHO AT THE MOMENT IS ENTERTAINING HIS YOUNG SOCIALITE FRIEND, BRUCE WAYNE.
WELL COMMISSIONER, ANYTHING EXCITING HAPPENING THESE DAYS?
-NO-O-EXCEPT THIS FELLOW THEY CALL THE 'BAT-MAN' PUZZLES ME!
R-ING-G
HELLO...WHAT'S THAT? LAMBERT, THE CHEMICAL KING... STABBED TO DEATH? HIS SON'S FINGER PRINTS ON THE KNIFE?...I'LL BE RIGHT OVER!
-TALK ABOUT SOMETHING EXCITING... OLD LAMBERT HAS BEEN MURDERED AT HIS MANSION... I'M GOING THERE NOW. LIKE TO COME ALONG?
OH WELL, NOTHING ELSE TO DO, MIGHT AS WELL
THE COMMISSIONER AND BRUCE WAYNE, SPEED TOWARD THE LAMBERT RESIDENCE...
HELLO SERGEANT, EVERYTHING UNDER CONTROL?
YES SIR, WE'VE GOT YOUNG LAMBERT IN THE BACK ROOM!
... AND AFTER A THOROUGH EXAMINATION OF THE SCENE OF THE CRIME, THE ROOM BECOMES BUSY WITH THE USUAL POLICE ROUTINE...
WELL I'M FINISHED IN HERE, LET ME TALK TO YOUNG LAMBERT.
HELLO LAMBERT, THEY SAY YOU KILLED YOUR FATHER!
I DIDN'T DO IT! COMMISSIONER, BELIEVE ME, I DIDN'T DO IT!!!

From *Detective Comics* No. 27, May 1939.

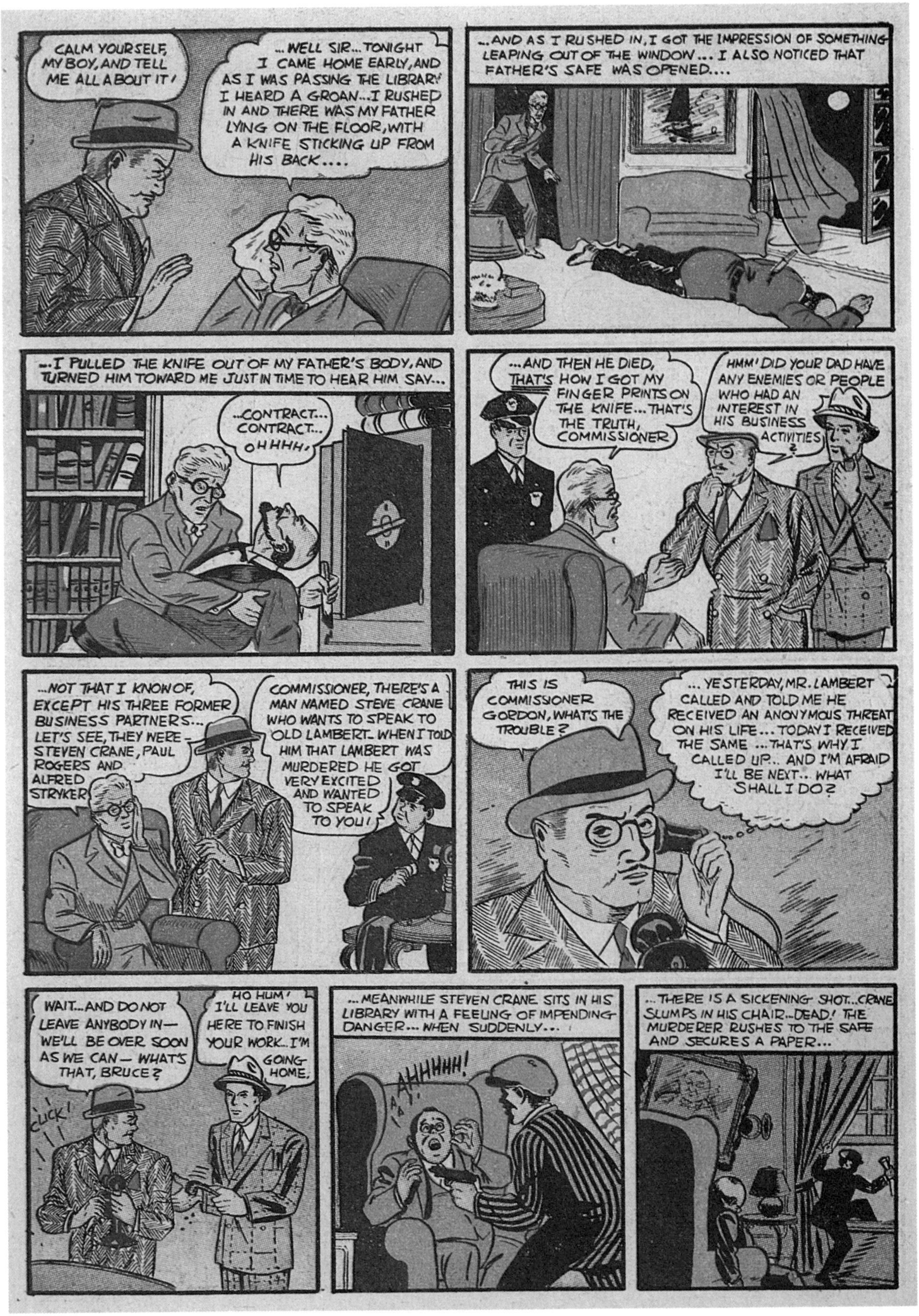
CALM YOURSELF, MY BOY, AND TELL ME ALL ABOUT IT!
...WELL SIR... TONIGHT I CAME HOME EARLY, AND AS I WAS PASSING THE LIBRARY I HEARD A GROAN... I RUSHED IN AND THERE WAS MY FATHER LYING ON THE FLOOR, WITH A KNIFE STICKING UP FROM HIS BACK....
...AND AS I RUSHED IN, I GOT THE IMPRESSION OF SOMETHING LEAPING OUT OF THE WINDOW... I ALSO NOTICED THAT FATHER'S SAFE WAS OPENED....
...I PULLED THE KNIFE OUT OF MY FATHER'S BODY, AND TURNED HIM TOWARD ME JUST IN TIME TO HEAR HIM SAY...
...CONTRACT... CONTRACT... OHHHH!
...AND THEN HE DIED, THAT'S HOW I GOT MY FINGER PRINTS ON THE KNIFE... THAT'S THE TRUTH, COMMISSIONER
HMM! DID YOUR DAD HAVE ANY ENEMIES OR PEOPLE WHO HAD AN INTEREST IN HIS BUSINESS ACTIVITIES?
...NOT THAT I KNOW OF, EXCEPT HIS THREE FORMER BUSINESS PARTNERS... LET'S SEE, THEY WERE - STEVEN CRANE, PAUL ROGERS AND ALFRED STRYKER
COMMISSIONER, THERE'S A MAN NAMED STEVE CRANE WHO WANTS TO SPEAK TO OLD LAMBERT- WHEN I TOLD HIM THAT LAMBERT WAS MURDERED HE GOT VERY EXCITED AND WANTED TO SPEAK TO YOU!
THIS IS COMMISSIONER GORDON, WHAT'S THE TROUBLE?
... YESTERDAY, MR. LAMBERT CALLED AND TOLD ME HE RECEIVED AN ANONYMOUS THREAT ON HIS LIFE... TODAY I RECEIVED THE SAME ...THAT'S WHY I CALLED UP... AND I'M AFRAID I'LL BE NEXT... WHAT SHALL I DO?
WAIT...AND DO NOT LEAVE ANYBODY IN— WE'LL BE OVER SOON AS WE CAN— WHAT'S THAT, BRUCE?
HO HUM! I'LL LEAVE YOU HERE TO FINISH YOUR WORK...I'M GOING HOME.
CLICK!
...MEANWHILE STEVEN CRANE SITS IN HIS LIBRARY WITH A FEELING OF IMPENDING DANGER... WHEN SUDDENLY...
AHHHHH!
...THERE IS A SICKENING SHOT...CRANE SLUMPS IN HIS CHAIR...DEAD! THE MURDERER RUSHES TO THE SAFE AND SECURES A PAPER...

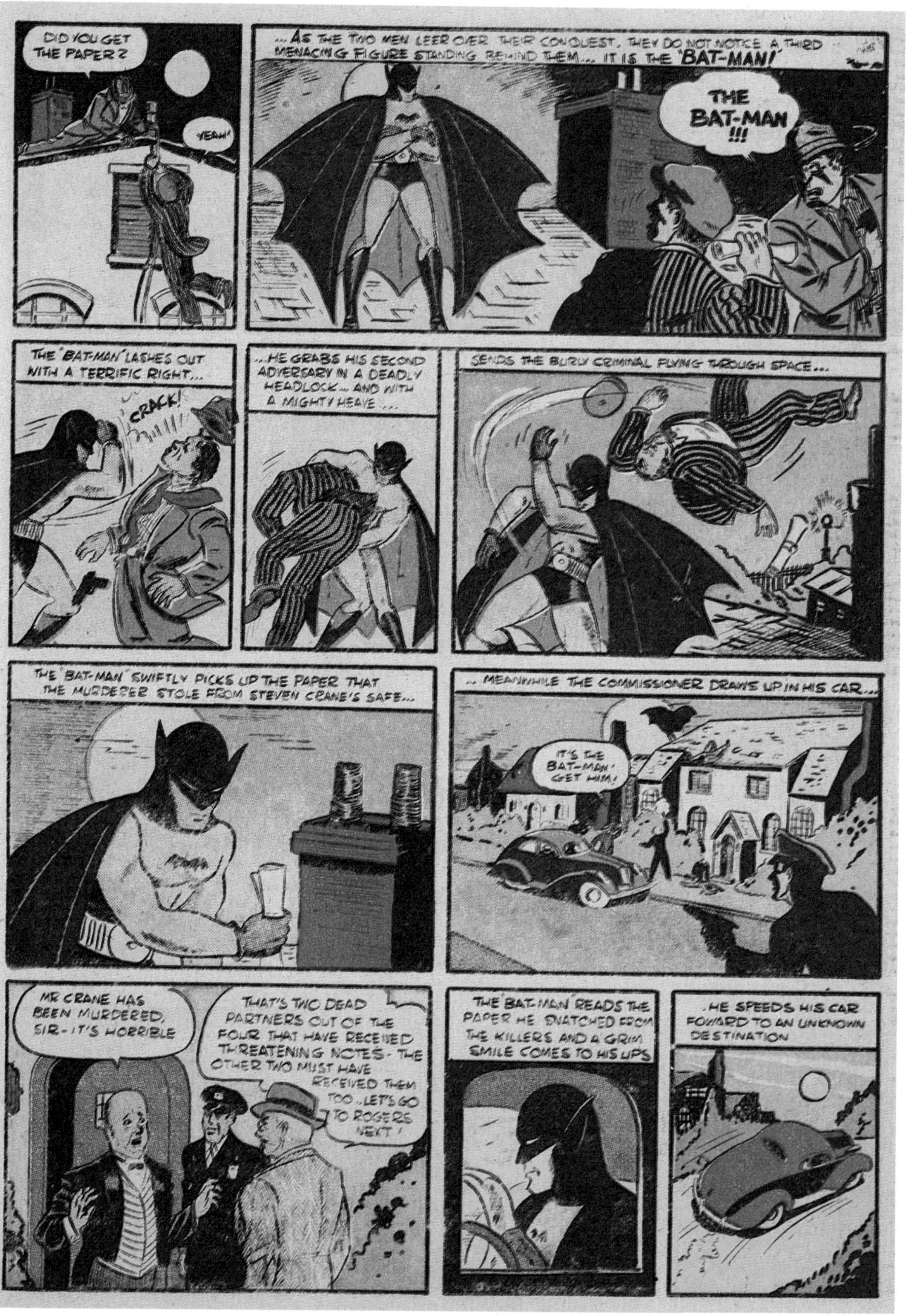
DID YOU GET THE PAPER?
YEAH!
...AS THE TWO MEN LEER OVER THEIR CONQUEST, THEY DO NOT NOTICE A THIRD MENACING FIGURE STANDING BEHIND THEM... IT IS THE "BAT-MAN!"
THE BAT-MAN !!!
THE "BAT-MAN" LASHES OUT WITH A TERRIFIC RIGHT...
CRACK!
...HE GRABS HIS SECOND ADVERSARY IN A DEADLY HEADLOCK... AND WITH A MIGHTY HEAVE....
SENDS THE BURLY CRIMINAL FLYING THROUGH SPACE...
THE "BAT-MAN" SWIFTLY PICKS UP THE PAPER THAT THE MURDERER STOLE FROM STEVEN CRANE'S SAFE...
...MEANWHILE THE COMMISSIONER DRAWS UP IN HIS CAR...
IT'S THE BAT-MAN GET HIM!
MR CRANE HAS BEEN MURDERED, SIR - IT'S HORRIBLE
THAT'S TWO DEAD PARTNERS OUT OF THE FOUR THAT HAVE RECEIVED THREATENING NOTES - THE OTHER TWO MUST HAVE RECEIVED THEM TOO.. LET'S GO TO ROGERS NEXT!
THE BAT-MAN READS THE PAPER HE SNATCHED FROM THE KILLERS AND A GRIM SMILE COMES TO HIS LIPS
.HE SPEEDS HIS CAR FOWARD TO AN UNKNOWN DESTINATION

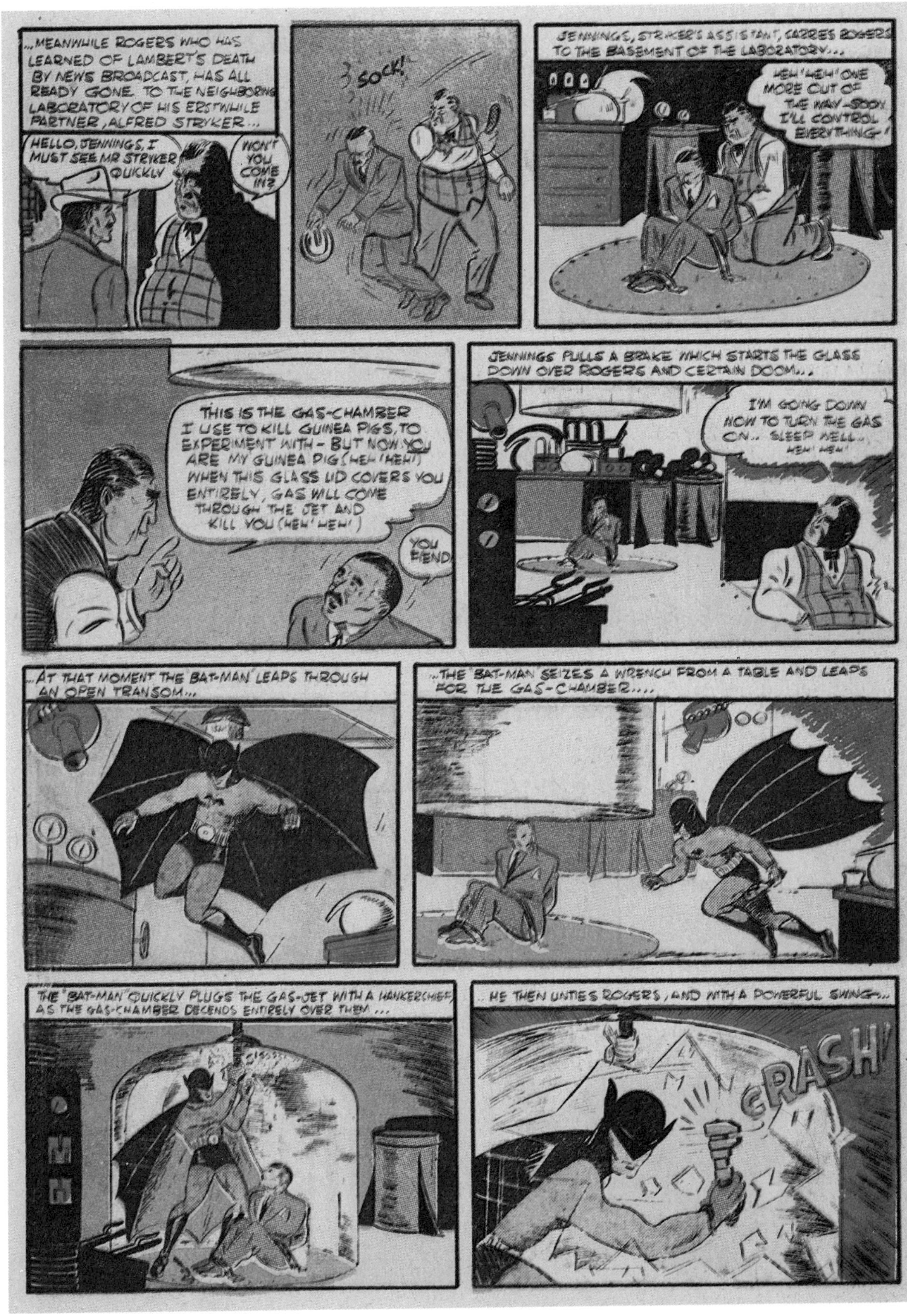

...MEANWHILE ROGERS WHO HAS LEARNED OF LAMBERT'S DEATH BY NEWS BROADCAST, HAS ALL READY GONE TO THE NEIGHBORING LABORATORY OF HIS ERSTWHILE PARTNER, ALFRED STRYKER...
HELLO, JENNINGS, I MUST SEE MR STRYKER QUICKLY
WON'T YOU COME IN?
SOCK!
JENNINGS, STRYKER'S ASSISTANT, CARRES ROGERS TO THE BASEMENT OF THE LABORATORY...
HEH' HEH' ONE MORE OUT OF THE WAY-SOON I'LL CONTROL EVERYTHING!
THIS IS THE GAS-CHAMBER I USE TO KILL GUINEA PIGS, TO EXPERIMENT WITH - BUT NOW YOU ARE MY GUINEA PIG (HEH' HEH') WHEN THIS GLASS LID COVERS YOU ENTIRELY, GAS WILL COME THROUGH THE JET AND KILL YOU (HEH' HEH')
YOU FIEND
JENNINGS PULLS A BRAKE WHICH STARTS THE GLASS DOWN OVER ROGERS AND CERTAIN DOOM...
I'M GOING DOWN NOW TO TURN THE GAS ON.. SLEEP WELL.. HEH' HEH'
...AT THAT MOMENT THE BAT-MAN LEAPS THROUGH AN OPEN TRANSOM...
...THE BAT-MAN SEIZES A WRENCH FROM A TABLE AND LEAPS FOR THE GAS-CHAMBER....
THE 'BAT-MAN' QUICKLY PLUGS THE GAS-JET WITH A HANKERCHIEF, AS THE GAS-CHAMBER DECENDS ENTIRELY OVER THEM...
...HE THEN UNTIES ROGERS, AND WITH A POWERFUL SWING...
CRASH!

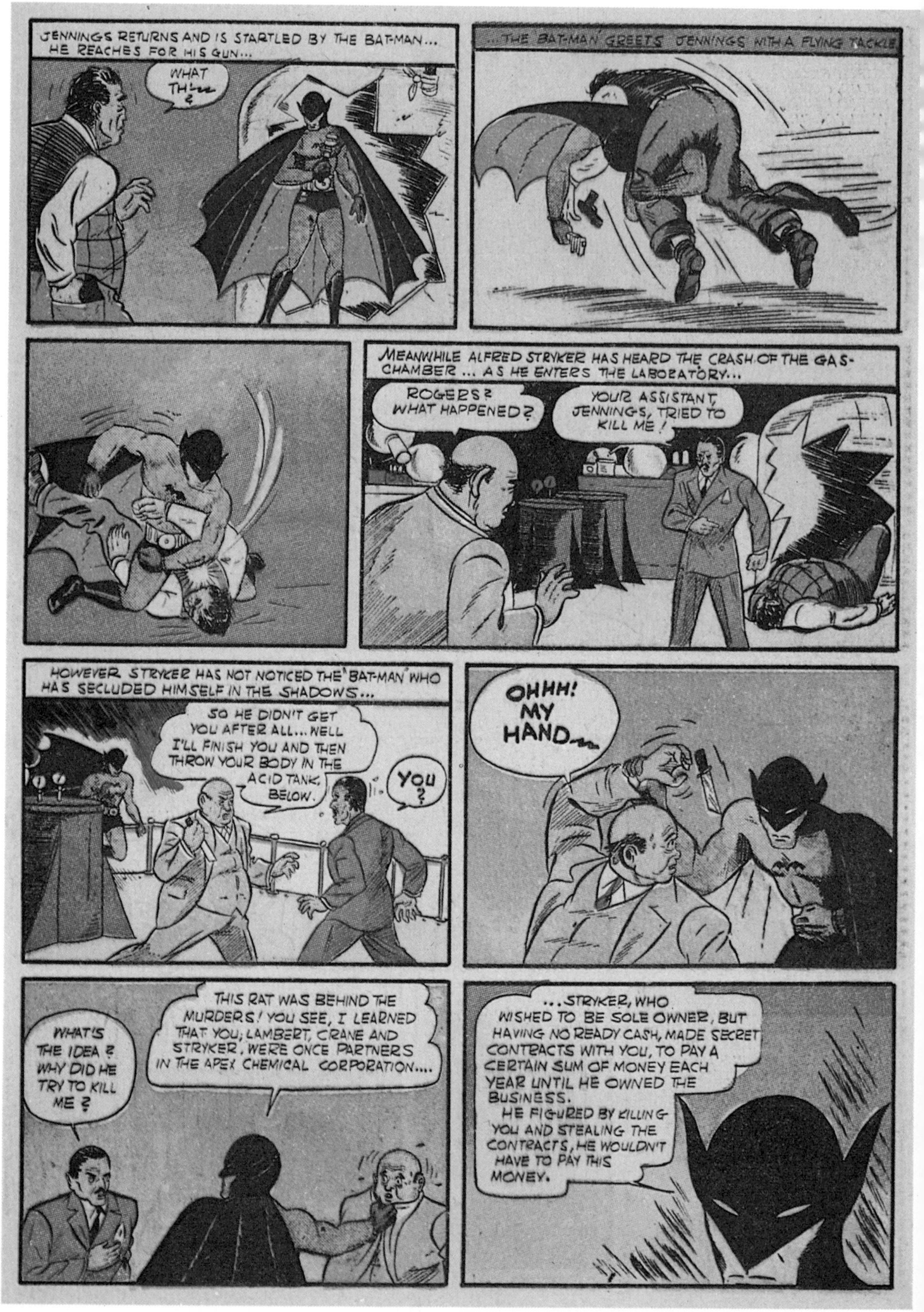

JENNINGS RETURNS AND IS STARTLED BY THE BAT-MAN... HE REACHES FOR HIS GUN...
WHAT TH-- ?
...THE BAT-MAN GREETS JENNINGS WITH A FLYING TACKLE
MEANWHILE ALFRED STRYKER HAS HEARD THE CRASH OF THE GAS-CHAMBER ... AS HE ENTERS THE LABORATORY...
ROGERS? WHAT HAPPENED?
YOUR ASSISTANT, JENNINGS, TRIED TO KILL ME!
HOWEVER STRYKER HAS NOT NOTICED THE "BAT-MAN" WHO HAS SECLUDED HIMSELF IN THE SHADOWS...
SO HE DIDN'T GET YOU AFTER ALL...WELL I'LL FINISH YOU AND THEN THROW YOUR BODY IN THE ACID TANK, BELOW.
YOU ?
OHHH! MY HAND--
WHAT'S THE IDEA? WHY DID HE TRY TO KILL ME?
THIS RAT WAS BEHIND THE MURDERS! YOU SEE, I LEARNED THAT YOU, LAMBERT, CRANE AND STRYKER, WERE ONCE PARTNERS IN THE APEX CHEMICAL CORPORATION....
...STRYKER, WHO WISHED TO BE SOLE OWNER, BUT HAVING NO READY CASH, MADE SECRET CONTRACTS WITH YOU, TO PAY A CERTAIN SUM OF MONEY EACH YEAR UNTIL HE OWNED THE BUSINESS.
HE FIGURED BY KILLING YOU AND STEALING THE CONTRACTS, HE WOULDN'T HAVE TO PAY THIS MONEY.

HMM, A VERY CLEVER SCHEME, AND BEING THE CONTRACTS WERE A STRICT SECRET BETWEEN THE FOUR OF US, OUR HEIRS OR THE OUTSIDE WORLD WOULDN'T KNOW A THING ABOUT THEM... BUT HOW DID YOU KNOW ALL THIS?

I SECURED THIS CONTRACT FROM ONE OF HIS HIRED KILLERS

... SUDDENLY, STRYKER, WITH THE STRENGTH OF A MAD MAN, TEARS HIMSELF FREE FROM THE GRASP OF THE BAT-MAN...

— SURE... I DID IT! BUT YOU WON'T SEND ME TO THE 'CHAIR' FOR IT!!! I'LL —

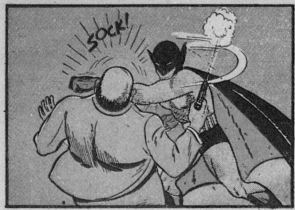

SOCK!

HE'S FALLING RIGHT INTO THE ACID TANK!

YA-AA-AA-AA...

A FITTING ENDING FOR HIS KIND.

... HOW CAN I EVER THANK YO... WHY— GONE!

THE NEXT DAY, YOUNG BRUCE WAYNE IS AGAIN A VISITOR AT THE COMMISSIONER'S HOUSE... WHO HAS JUST FINISHED TELLING BRUCE, THE LATEST EXPLOITS OF THE 'BAT-MAN'.

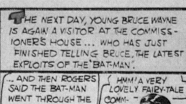

.. AND THEN ROGERS SAID THE BAT-MAN WENT THROUGH THE SKYLIGHT!

HMM! A VERY LOVELY FAIRY-TALE COMMISSIONER, INDEED

AFTER BRUCE WAYNE HAS GONE...

...BRUCE WAYNE IS A NICE YOUNG CHAP- BUT HE CERTAINLY MUST LEAD A BORING LIFE... SEEMS DISINTERESTED IN EVERYTHING—

..BRUCE WAYNE RETURNS HOME TO HIS ROOM... A LITTLE LATER HIS DOOR SLOWLY OPENS...

...AND REVEALS ITS OCCUPANT...IF THE COMMISSIONER COULD SEE HIS YOUNG FRIEND NOW... HE'D BE AMAZED TO LEARN THAT HE IS THE *BAT-MAN!*

Rob't Kane

FINIS

WATCH FOR A NEW THRILLING 'BAT-MAN' STORY...

NEXT MONTH

39

About "Scribbly" and Sheldon Mayer

The following early sequence from Sheldon Mayer's *Scribbly* is heartening evidence that the implicit pomposity of the costumed super-heroes received romping, low-comic comment almost from the moment of their arrival (and in a comic book from National, the home of the most popular super-heroes).

The *Scribbly* feature did not quite begin with this uninhibited super-hero buffoonery. In the first issue of *All-American Comics,* it introduced the adventures of a would-be boy cartoonist, and it developed and explored that premise for ten subsequent years, not only in *All-American* but in the young protagonist's own magazine. Mayer was also editor of *All-American,* and *Scribbly* was a comic interlude among the more earnest doings of *The Green Lantern, The Atom,* and a *Rescue on Mars.* Predictably, perhaps, Scribbly sometimes confused his own life with the events in his cartoonist's fantasies.

Mayer was born in 1917 in New York City, where he worked as an assistant (and occasional ghost) to several established cartoonists, beginning in 1932. By 1936, in addition to his other work, Mayer had begun to help with the editing of a new comic-book line for Dell, and thus he was a founding professional of the comic book. He held the editorship of *All-American* and its related titles for ten years, and he continued to write features of all kinds for National Comics after that. After *Scribbly,* however, Mayer's most respected feature was another humor strip, *Sugar and Spike,* begun in 1956 and continued through 1971. It was his own reaction to the many derivative comic-book imitations of Hank Ketcham's newspaper feature, *Dennis the Menace,* and his own determination not to do another one. In *Sugar and Spike,* Mayer came up with two spunky infants, merrily observing and involving themselves in the adult world, but communicating in a gibberish baby talk that only they (and the reader) understood.

As we join the *Scribbly* saga, the formidable Ma Hunkel has bought a grocery store, and some racketeers have made the mistake of trying to collect "protection money" from her. She has mussed them up and they have fled in their car—not knowing that Ma's daughter Sisty and Scribbly's brother Dinky have locked themselves in the rumble seat.

M.W.

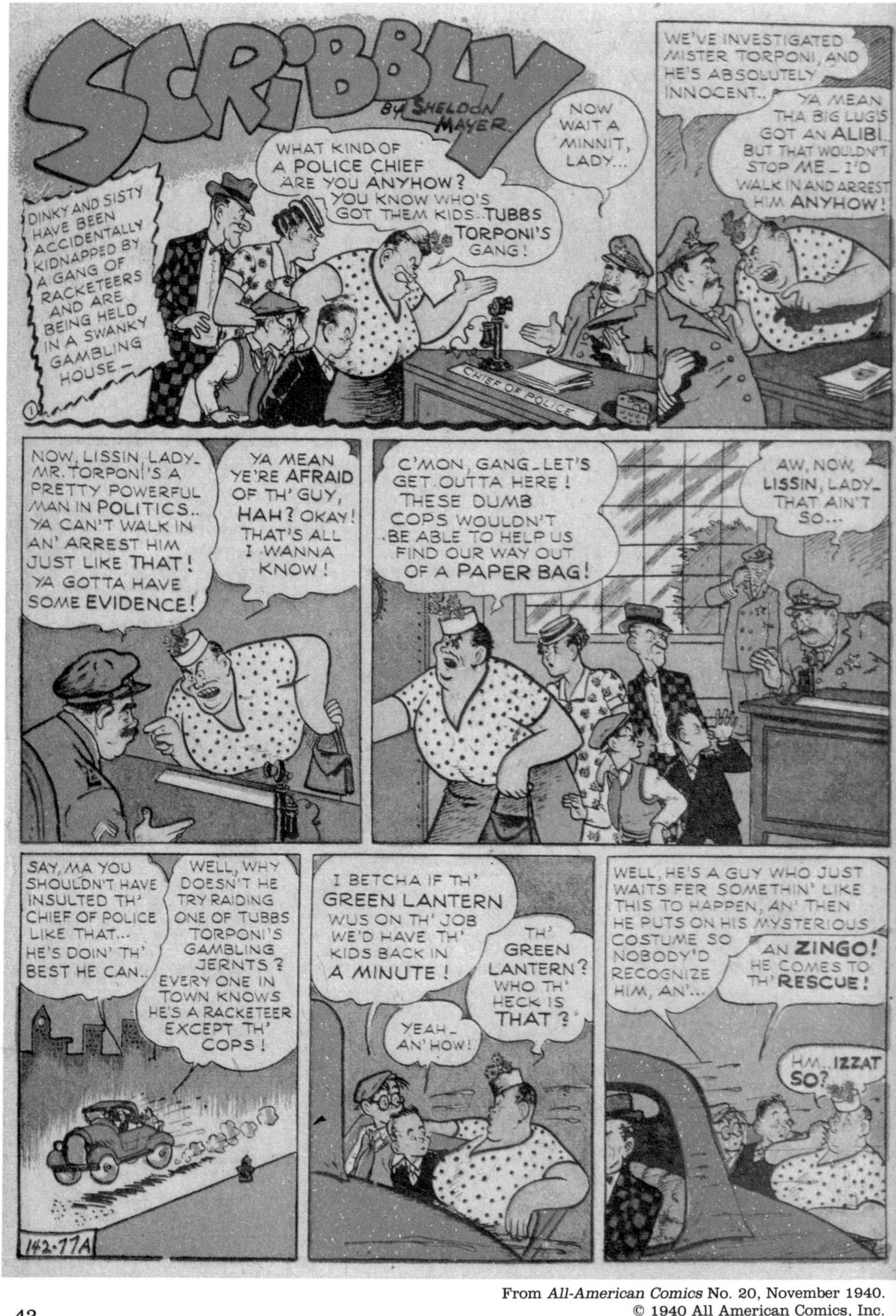
SCRIBBLY
BY SHELDON MAYER
DINKY AND SISTY HAVE BEEN ACCIDENTALLY KIDNAPPED BY A GANG OF RACKETEERS AND ARE BEING HELD IN A SWANKY GAMBLING HOUSE—
WHAT KIND OF A POLICE CHIEF ARE YOU ANYHOW? YOU KNOW WHO'S GOT THEM KIDS..TUBBS TORPONI'S GANG!
NOW WAIT A MINNIT, LADY...
CHIEF OF POLICE
WE'VE INVESTIGATED MISTER TORPONI, AND HE'S ABSOLUTELY INNOCENT..
YA MEAN THA BIG LUG'S GOT AN ALIBI.. BUT THAT WOULDN'T STOP ME — I'D WALK IN AND ARREST HIM ANYHOW!
NOW, LISSIN, LADY— MR. TORPONI'S A PRETTY POWERFUL MAN IN POLITICS.. YA CAN'T WALK IN AN' ARREST HIM JUST LIKE THAT! YA GOTTA HAVE SOME EVIDENCE!
YA MEAN YE'RE AFRAID OF TH' GUY, HAH? OKAY! THAT'S ALL I WANNA KNOW!
C'MON, GANG—LET'S GET OUTTA HERE! THESE DUMB COPS WOULDN'T BE ABLE TO HELP US FIND OUR WAY OUT OF A PAPER BAG!
AW, NOW, LISSIN, LADY— THAT AIN'T SO...
SAY, MA YOU SHOULDN'T HAVE INSULTED TH' CHIEF OF POLICE LIKE THAT... HE'S DOIN' TH' BEST HE CAN..
WELL, WHY DOESN'T HE TRY RAIDING ONE OF TUBBS TORPONI'S GAMBLING JERNTS? EVERY ONE IN TOWN KNOWS HE'S A RACKETEER EXCEPT TH' COPS!
I BETCHA IF TH' GREEN LANTERN WUS ON TH' JOB WE'D HAVE TH' KIDS BACK IN A MINUTE!
TH' GREEN LANTERN? WHO TH' HECK IS THAT?
YEAH— AN' HOW!
WELL, HE'S A GUY WHO JUST WAITS FER SOMETHIN' LIKE THIS TO HAPPEN, AN' THEN HE PUTS ON HIS MYSTERIOUS COSTUME SO NOBODY'D RECOGNIZE HIM, AN'...
AN ZINGO! HE COMES TO TH' RESCUE!
HM..IZZAT SO?
142-77A

From *All-American Comics* No. 20, November 1940.

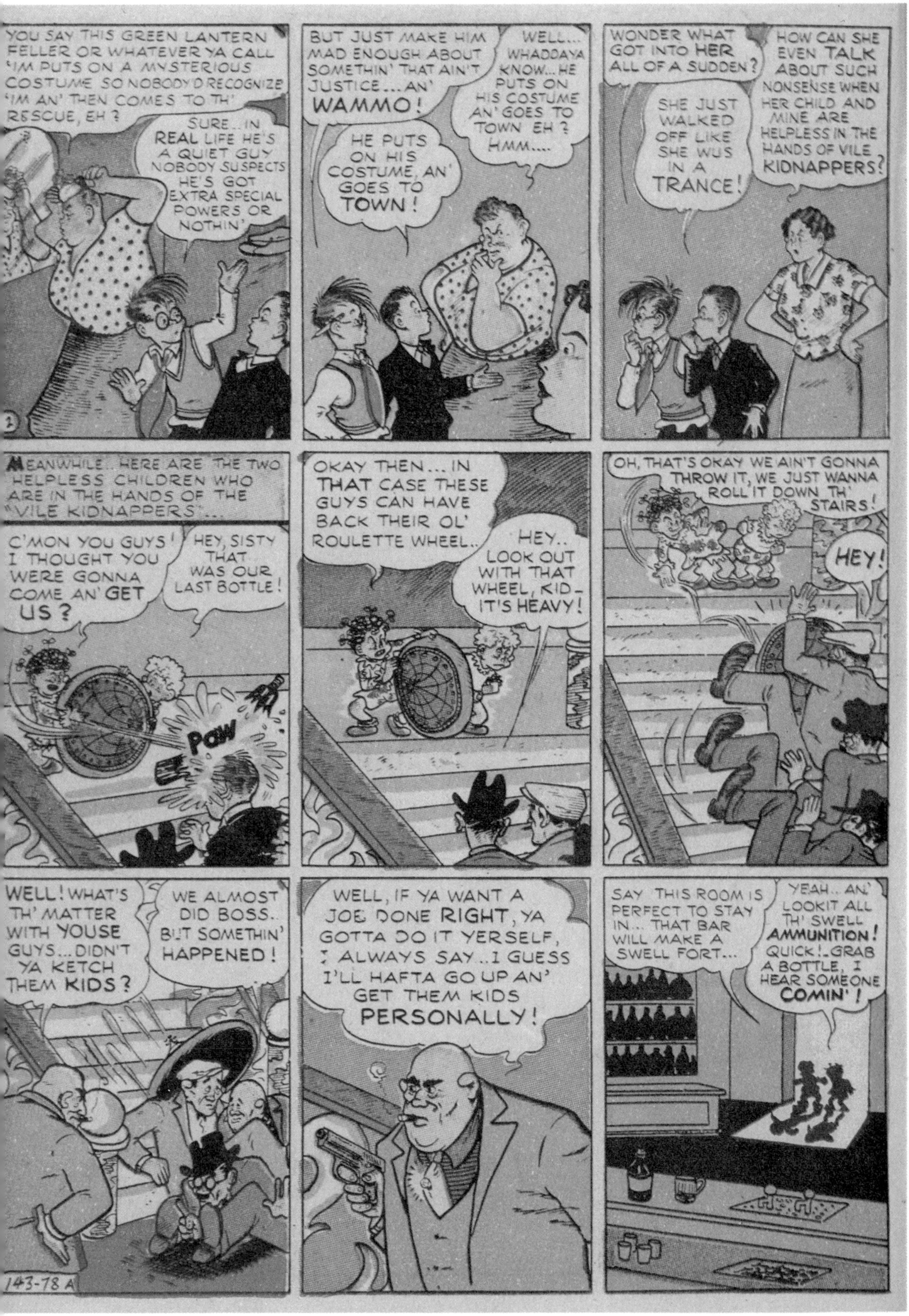

YOU SAY THIS GREEN LANTERN FELLER OR WHATEVER YA CALL 'IM PUTS ON A MYSTERIOUS COSTUME SO NOBODY'D RECOGNIZE 'IM AN' THEN COMES TO TH' RESCUE, EH ?
SURE...IN REAL LIFE HE'S A QUIET GUY NOBODY SUSPECTS HE'S GOT EXTRA SPECIAL POWERS OR NOTHIN'
BUT JUST MAKE HIM MAD ENOUGH ABOUT SOMETHIN' THAT AIN'T JUSTICE... AN' WAMMO!
HE PUTS ON HIS COSTUME, AN' GOES TO TOWN !
WELL... WHADDAYA KNOW...HE PUTS ON HIS COSTUME AN' GOES TO TOWN EH ? HMM....
WONDER WHAT GOT INTO HER ALL OF A SUDDEN ?
SHE JUST WALKED OFF LIKE SHE WUS IN A TRANCE!
HOW CAN SHE EVEN TALK ABOUT SUCH NONSENSE WHEN HER CHILD AND MINE ARE HELPLESS IN THE HANDS OF VILE KIDNAPPERS?
MEANWHILE...HERE ARE THE TWO HELPLESS CHILDREN WHO ARE IN THE HANDS OF THE "VILE KIDNAPPERS"...
C'MON YOU GUYS ! I THOUGHT YOU WERE GONNA COME AN' GET US ?
HEY, SISTY THAT WAS OUR LAST BOTTLE !
PAW
OKAY THEN... IN THAT CASE THESE GUYS CAN HAVE BACK THEIR OL' ROULETTE WHEEL..
HEY.. LOOK OUT WITH THAT WHEEL, KID - IT'S HEAVY!
OH, THAT'S OKAY WE AIN'T GONNA THROW IT, WE JUST WANNA ROLL IT DOWN TH' STAIRS!
HEY!
WELL! WHAT'S TH' MATTER WITH YOUSE GUYS...DIDN'T YA KETCH THEM KIDS?
WE ALMOST DID BOSS.. BUT SOMETHIN' HAPPENED !
WELL, IF YA WANT A JOB DONE RIGHT, YA GOTTA DO IT YERSELF, I ALWAYS SAY..I GUESS I'LL HAFTA GO UP AN' GET THEM KIDS PERSONALLY!
SAY THIS ROOM IS PERFECT TO STAY IN... THAT BAR WILL MAKE A SWELL FORT...
YEAH.. AN' LOOKIT ALL TH' SWELL AMMUNITION! QUICK!..GRAB A BOTTLE, I HEAR SOMEONE COMIN'!
143-78 A

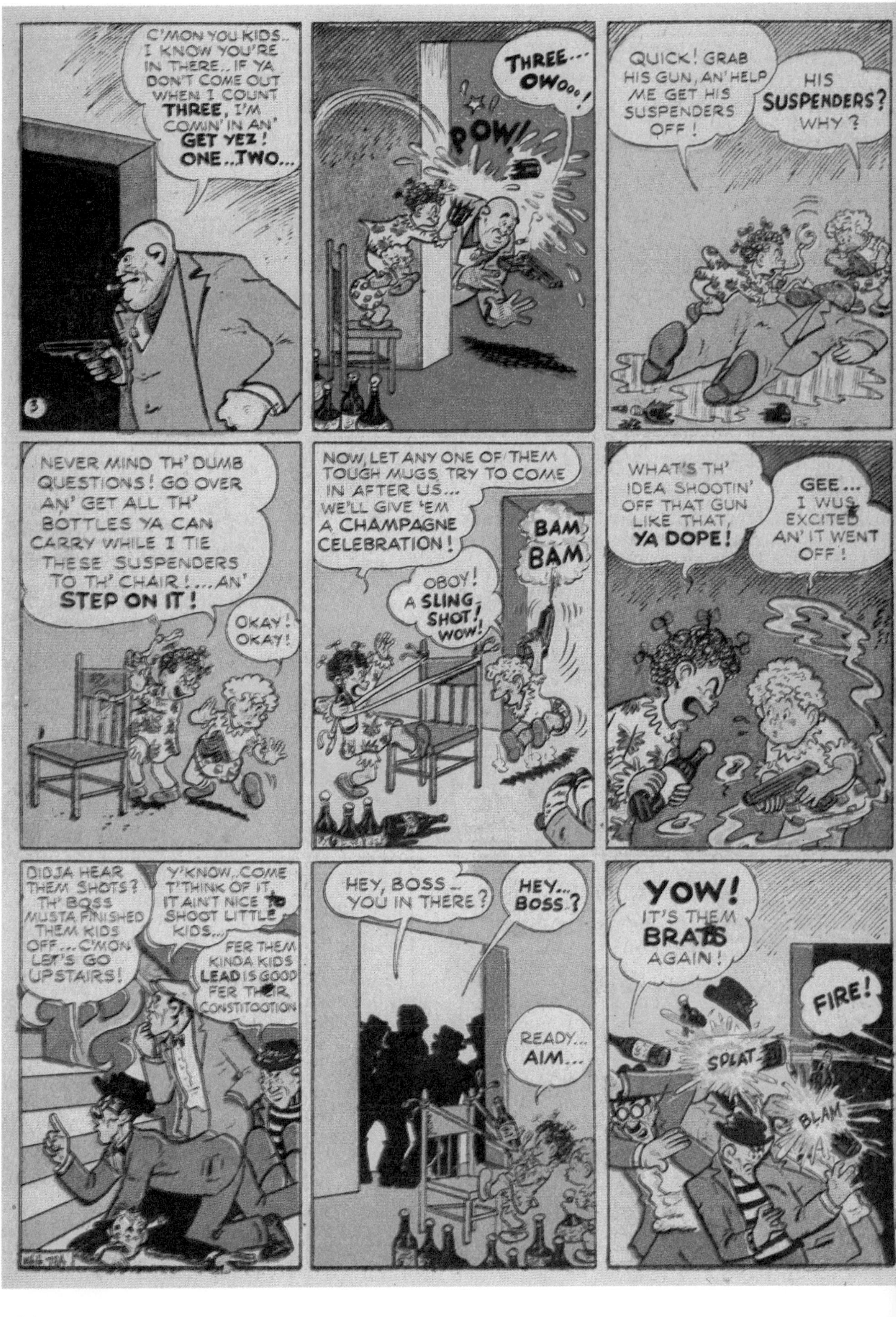
C'MON YOU KIDS.. I KNOW YOU'RE IN THERE.. IF YA DON'T COME OUT WHEN I COUNT THREE, I'M COMIN' IN AN' GET YEZ! ONE..TWO...
THREE... OWooo!
POW!
QUICK! GRAB HIS GUN, AN' HELP ME GET HIS SUSPENDERS OFF!
HIS SUSPENDERS? WHY?
NEVER MIND TH' DUMB QUESTIONS! GO OVER AN' GET ALL TH' BOTTLES YA CAN CARRY WHILE I TIE THESE SUSPENDERS TO TH' CHAIR!...AN' STEP ON IT!
OKAY! OKAY!
NOW, LET ANY ONE OF THEM TOUGH MUGS TRY TO COME IN AFTER US... WE'LL GIVE 'EM A CHAMPAGNE CELEBRATION!
OBOY! A SLING SHOT! WOW!
BAM BAM
WHAT'S TH' IDEA SHOOTIN' OFF THAT GUN LIKE THAT, YA DOPE!
GEE... I WUS EXCITED AN' IT WENT OFF!
DIDJA HEAR THEM SHOTS? TH' BOSS MUSTA FINISHED THEM KIDS OFF... C'MON LET'S GO UPSTAIRS!
Y'KNOW..COME T'THINK OF IT, IT AIN'T NICE TO SHOOT LITTLE KIDS...
FER THEM KINDA KIDS LEAD IS GOOD FER THEIR CONSTITOOTION
HEY, BOSS.. YOU IN THERE?
HEY... BOSS.?
READY... AIM...
YOW! IT'S THEM BRATS AGAIN!
FIRE!
SPLAT
BLAM

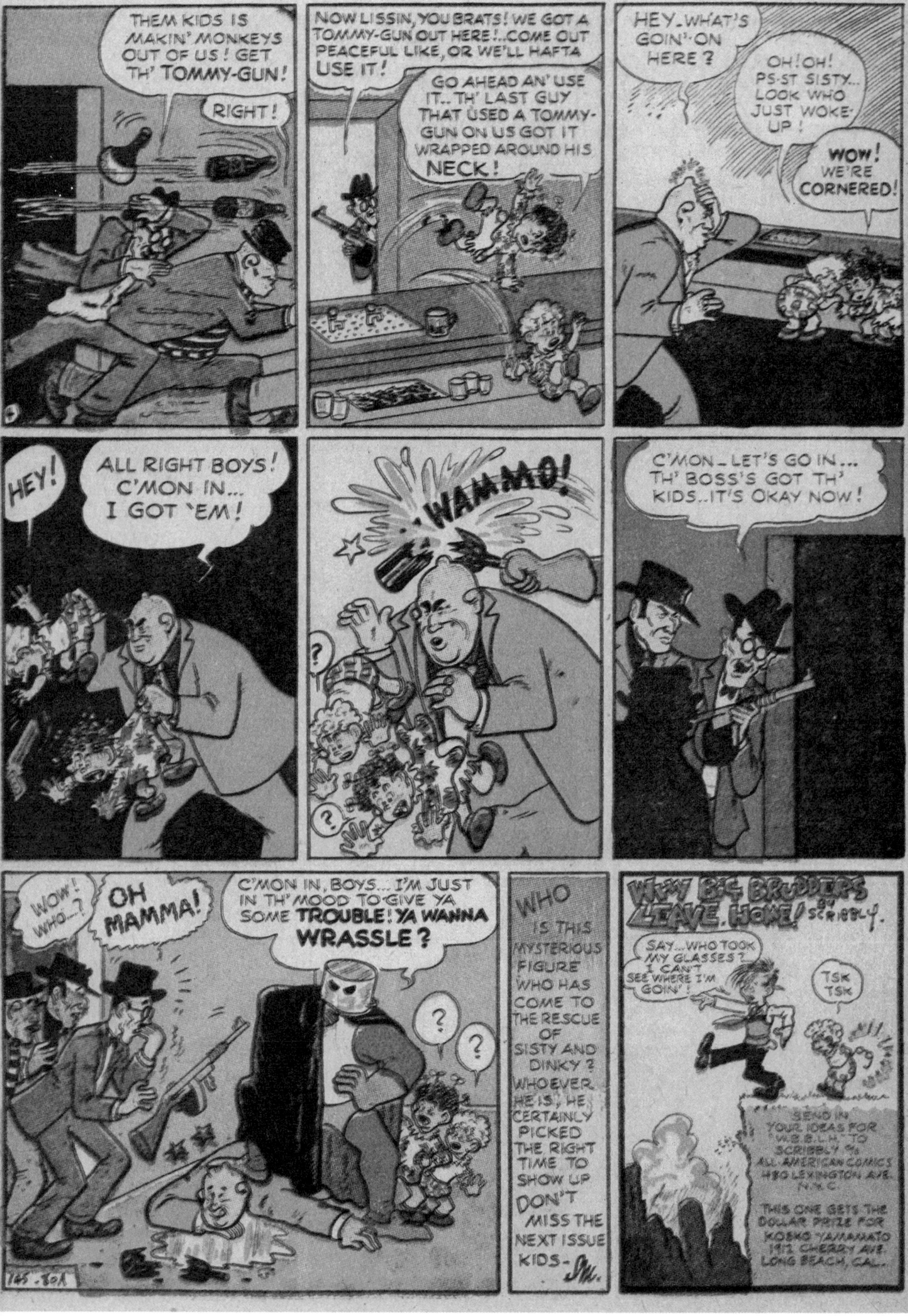
THEM KIDS IS MAKIN' MONKEYS OUT OF US! GET TH' TOMMY-GUN!
RIGHT!
NOW LISSIN, YOU BRATS! WE GOT A TOMMY-GUN OUT HERE!..COME OUT PEACEFUL LIKE, OR WE'LL HAFTA USE IT!
GO AHEAD AN' USE IT.. TH' LAST GUY THAT USED A TOMMY-GUN ON US GOT IT WRAPPED AROUND HIS NECK!
HEY_WHAT'S GOIN'-ON HERE?
OH! OH! PS-ST SISTY... LOOK WHO JUST WOKE-UP!
WOW! WE'RE CORNERED!
HEY!
ALL RIGHT BOYS! C'MON IN... I GOT 'EM!
WAMMO!
C'MON_LET'S GO IN... TH' BOSS'S GOT TH' KIDS..IT'S OKAY NOW!
WOW! WHO..?
OH MAMMA!
C'MON IN, BOYS... I'M JUST IN TH' MOOD TO GIVE YA SOME TROUBLE! YA WANNA WRASSLE?
WHO IS THIS MYSTERIOUS FIGURE WHO HAS COME TO THE RESCUE OF SISTY AND DINKY? WHOEVER HE IS, HE CERTAINLY PICKED THE RIGHT TIME TO SHOW UP DON'T MISS THE NEXT ISSUE KIDS-
WHY BIG BRUDDERS LEAVE HOME! BY SCRIBBLY.
SAY...WHO TOOK MY GLASSES? I CAN'T SEE WHERE I'M GOIN'!
TSK TSK
SEND IN YOUR IDEAS FOR "W.B.B.L.H." TO SCRIBBLY % ALL-AMERICAN COMICS 480 LEXINGTON AVE. N.Y.C.
THIS ONE GETS THE DOLLAR PRIZE FOR KOSKO YAMAMATO 1912 CHERRY AVE. LONG BEACH, CAL.

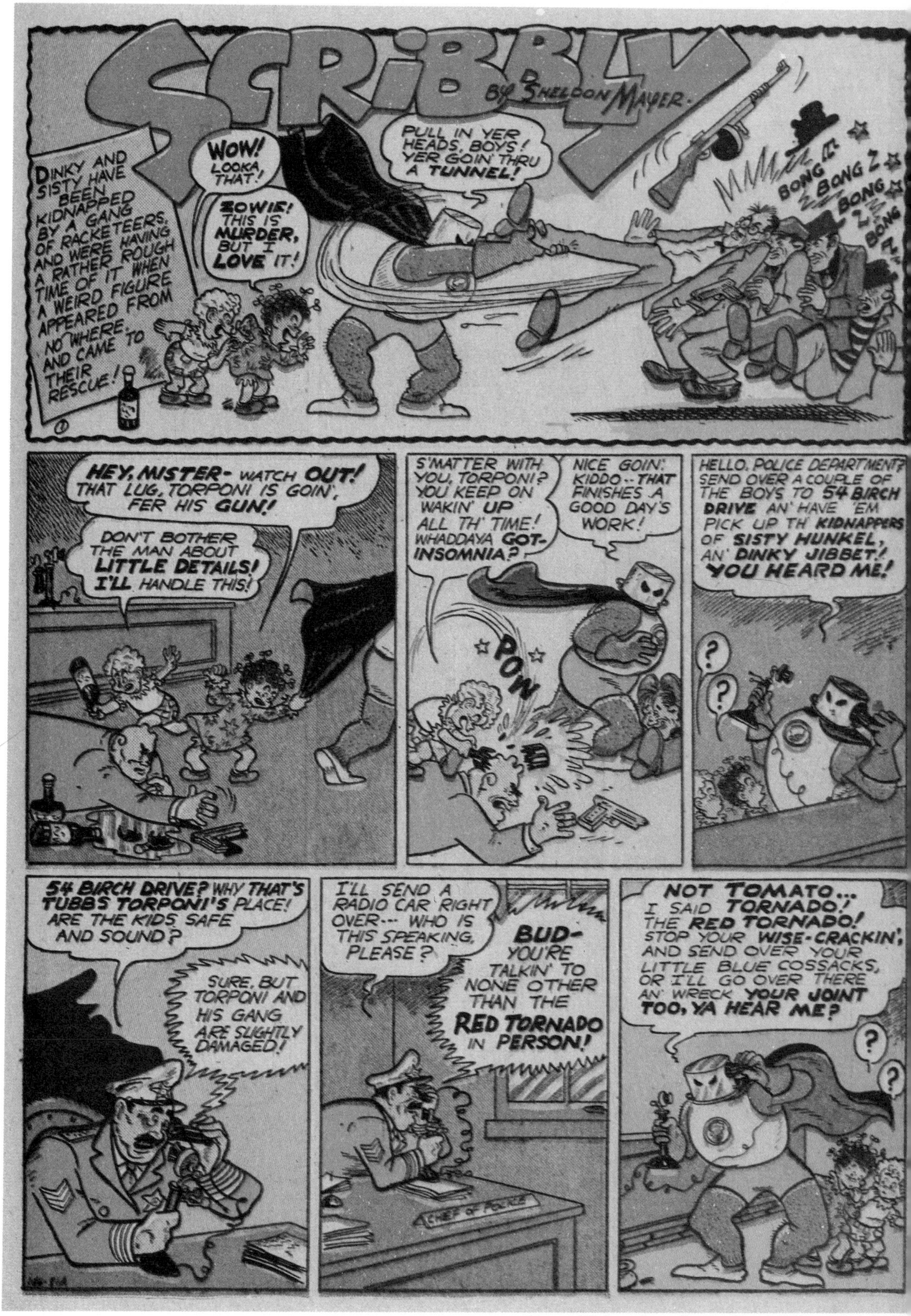
SCRIBBLY
BY SHELDON MAYER.
DINKY AND SISTY HAVE BEEN KIDNAPPED BY A GANG OF RACKETEERS, AND WERE HAVING A RATHER ROUGH TIME OF IT WHEN A WEIRD FIGURE APPEARED FROM NO WHERE, AND CAME TO THEIR RESCUE!
WOW! LOOKA THAT!
ZOWIE! THIS IS MURDER, BUT I LOVE IT!
PULL IN YER HEADS, BOYS! YER GOIN' THRU A TUNNEL!
BONG BONG BONG BONG
HEY, MISTER- WATCH OUT! THAT LUG, TORPONI IS GOIN', FER HIS GUN!
DON'T BOTHER THE MAN ABOUT LITTLE DETAILS! I'LL HANDLE THIS!
S'MATTER WITH YOU, TORPONI? YOU KEEP ON WAKIN' UP ALL TH' TIME! WHADDAYA GOT- INSOMNIA?
NICE GOIN' KIDDO -- THAT FINISHES A GOOD DAY'S WORK!
POW
HELLO, POLICE DEPARTMENT? SEND OVER A COUPLE OF THE BOYS TO 54 BIRCH DRIVE AN' HAVE 'EM PICK UP TH' KIDNAPPERS OF SISTY HUNKEL, AN' DINKY JIBBET! YOU HEARD ME!
54 BIRCH DRIVE? WHY THAT'S TUBBS TORPONI'S PLACE! ARE THE KIDS SAFE AND SOUND?
SURE, BUT TORPONI AND HIS GANG ARE SLIGHTLY DAMAGED!
I'LL SEND A RADIO CAR RIGHT OVER--- WHO IS THIS SPEAKING, PLEASE?
BUD- YOU'RE TALKIN' TO NONE OTHER THAN THE RED TORNADO IN PERSON!
CHIEF OF POLICE
NOT TOMATO... I SAID TORNADO! THE RED TORNADO! STOP YOUR WISE-CRACKIN', AND SEND OVER YOUR LITTLE BLUE COSSACKS, OR I'LL GO OVER THERE AN' WRECK YOUR JOINT TOO, YA HEAR ME?

From *All-American Comics* No. 21, December 1940.

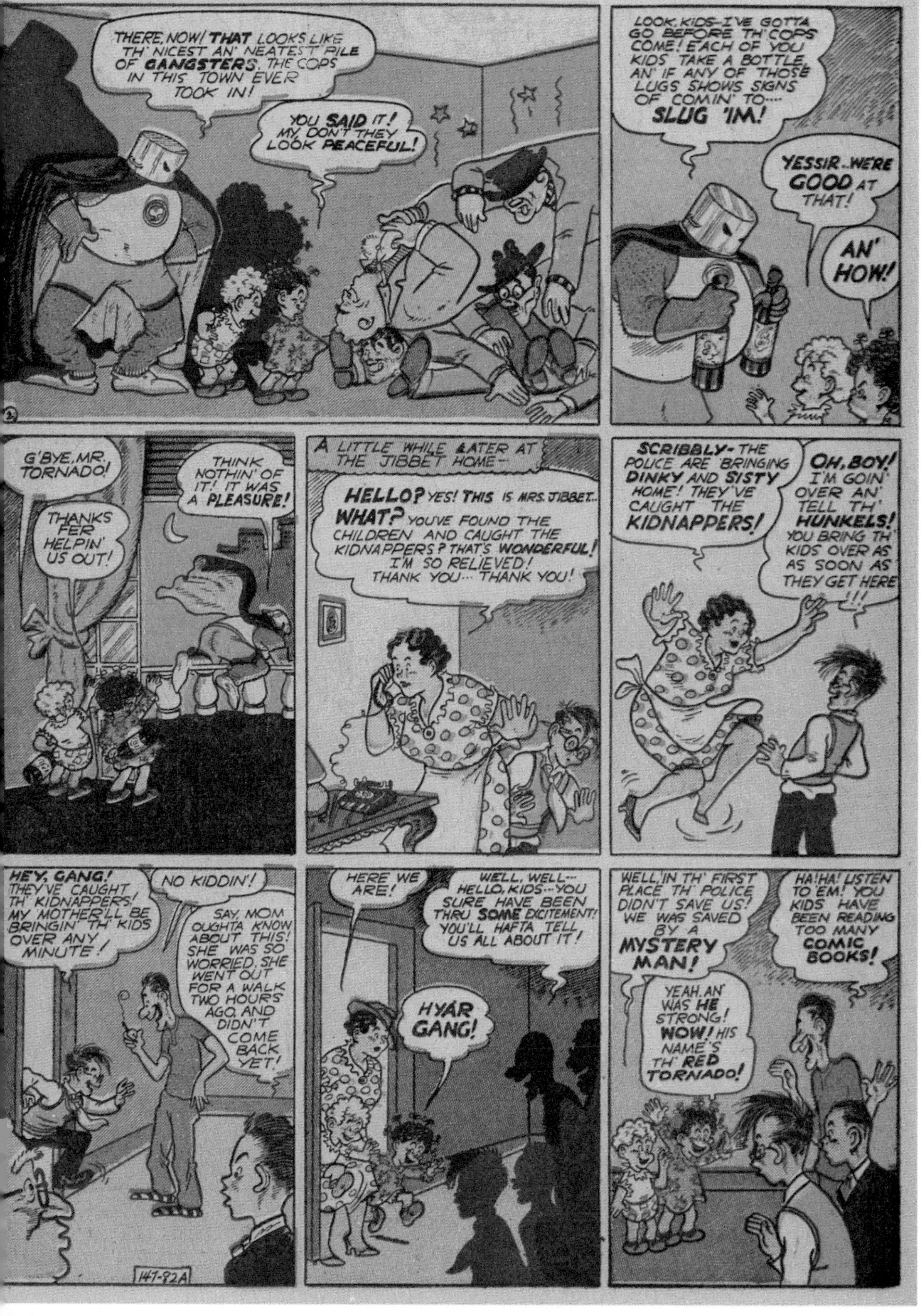
THERE, NOW! THAT LOOKS LIKE TH' NICEST AN' NEATEST PILE OF GANGSTERS THE COPS IN THIS TOWN EVER TOOK IN!
YOU SAID IT! MY, DON'T THEY LOOK PEACEFUL!
LOOK, KIDS—I'VE GOTTA GO BEFORE TH' COPS COME! EACH OF YOU KIDS TAKE A BOTTLE, AN' IF ANY OF THOSE LUGS SHOWS SIGNS OF COMIN' TO.... SLUG 'IM!
YESSIR..WE'RE GOOD AT THAT!
AN' HOW!
G'BYE, MR. TORNADO!
THINK NOTHIN' OF IT! IT WAS A PLEASURE!
THANKS FER HELPIN' US OUT!
A LITTLE WHILE LATER AT THE JIBBET HOME—
HELLO? YES! THIS IS MRS. JIBBET... WHAT? YOU'VE FOUND THE CHILDREN AND CAUGHT THE KIDNAPPERS? THAT'S WONDERFUL! I'M SO RELIEVED! THANK YOU... THANK YOU!
SCRIBBLY- THE POLICE ARE BRINGING DINKY AND SISTY HOME! THEY'VE CAUGHT THE KIDNAPPERS!
OH, BOY! I'M GOIN' OVER AN' TELL TH' HUNKELS! YOU BRING TH' KIDS OVER AS AS SOON AS THEY GET HERE!!!
HEY, GANG! THEY'VE CAUGHT TH' KIDNAPPERS! MY MOTHER'LL BE BRINGIN' TH' KIDS OVER ANY MINUTE!
NO KIDDIN'!
SAY, MOM OUGHTA KNOW ABOUT THIS! SHE WAS SO WORRIED, SHE WENT OUT FOR A WALK TWO HOURS AGO, AND DIDN'T COME BACK YET!
147-82A
HERE WE ARE!
WELL, WELL... HELLO, KIDS...YOU SURE HAVE BEEN THRU SOME EXCITEMENT! YOU'LL HAFTA TELL US ALL ABOUT IT!
HYAR GANG!
WELL, IN TH' FIRST PLACE TH' POLICE DIDN'T SAVE US! WE WAS SAVED BY A MYSTERY MAN!
HA! HA! LISTEN TO 'EM! YOU KIDS HAVE BEEN READING TOO MANY COMIC BOOKS!
YEAH, AN' WAS HE STRONG! WOW! HIS NAME'S TH' RED TORNADO!

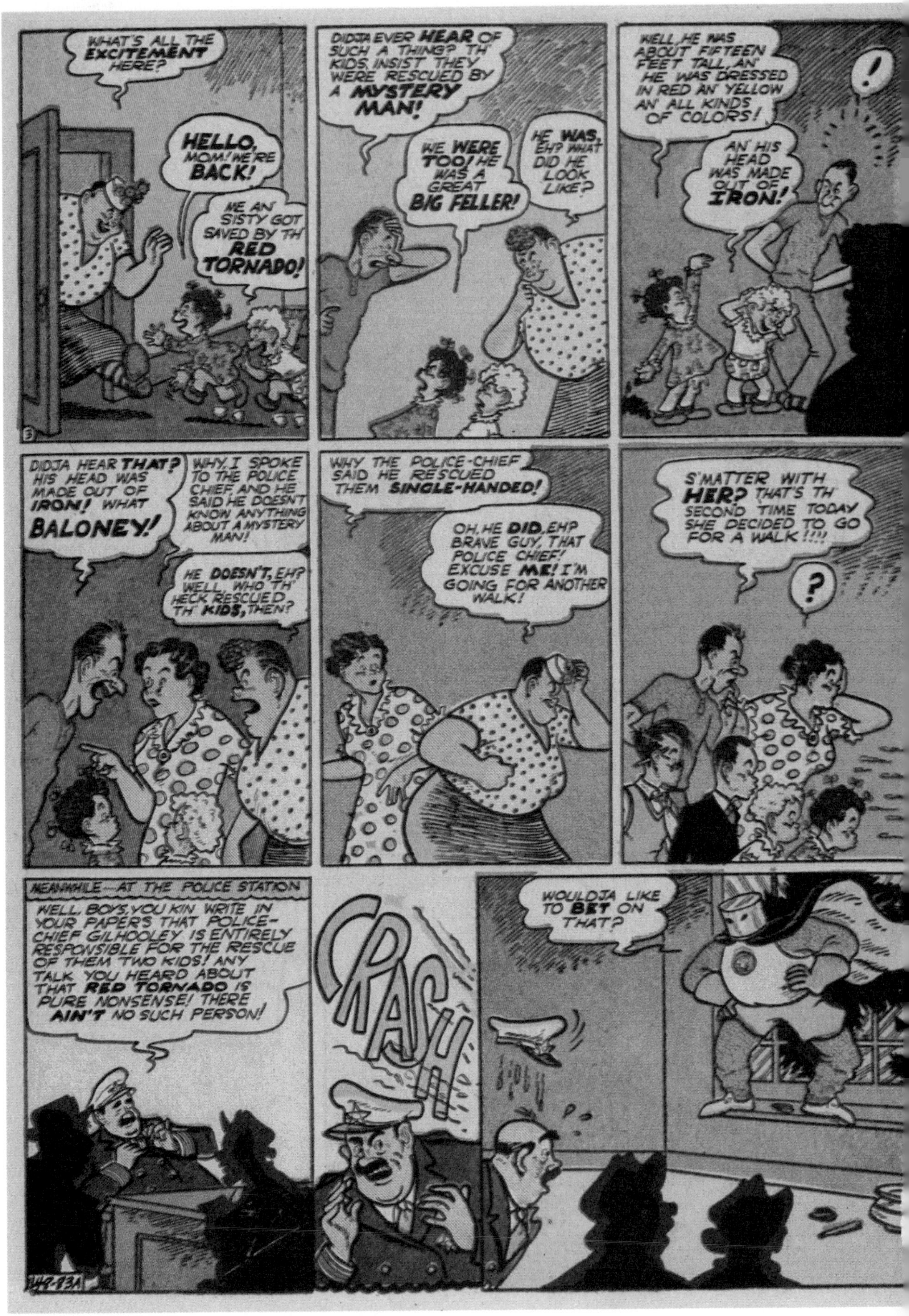

WHAT'S ALL THE EXCITEMENT HERE?
HELLO, MOM! WE'RE BACK!
ME AN' SISTY GOT SAVED BY TH' RED TORNADO!
DIDJA EVER HEAR OF SUCH A THING? TH' KIDS INSIST THEY WERE RESCUED BY A MYSTERY MAN!
WE WERE TOO! HE WAS A GREAT BIG FELLER!
HE WAS, EH? WHAT DID HE LOOK LIKE?
WELL, HE WAS ABOUT FIFTEEN FEET TALL, AN' HE WAS DRESSED IN RED AN' YELLOW AN' ALL KINDS OF COLORS!
AN' HIS HEAD WAS MADE OUT OF IRON!
!
DIDJA HEAR THAT? HIS HEAD WAS MADE OUT OF IRON! WHAT BALONEY!
WHY, I SPOKE TO THE POLICE CHIEF, AND HE SAID HE DOESN'T KNOW ANYTHING ABOUT A MYSTERY MAN!
HE DOESN'T, EH? WELL, WHO TH' HECK RESCUED TH' KIDS, THEN?
WHY THE POLICE-CHIEF SAID HE RESCUED THEM SINGLE-HANDED!
OH, HE DID, EH? BRAVE GUY, THAT POLICE CHIEF! EXCUSE ME! I'M GOING FOR ANOTHER WALK!
S'MATTER WITH HER? THAT'S TH' SECOND TIME TODAY SHE DECIDED TO GO FOR A WALK!!!!
?
MEANWHILE—AT THE POLICE STATION
WELL, BOYS, YOU KIN WRITE IN YOUR PAPERS THAT POLICE-CHIEF GILHOOLEY IS ENTIRELY RESPONSIBLE FOR THE RESCUE OF THEM TWO KIDS! ANY TALK YOU HEARD ABOUT THAT RED TORNADO IS PURE NONSENSE! THERE AIN'T NO SUCH PERSON!
CRASH
WOULDJA LIKE TO BET ON THAT?

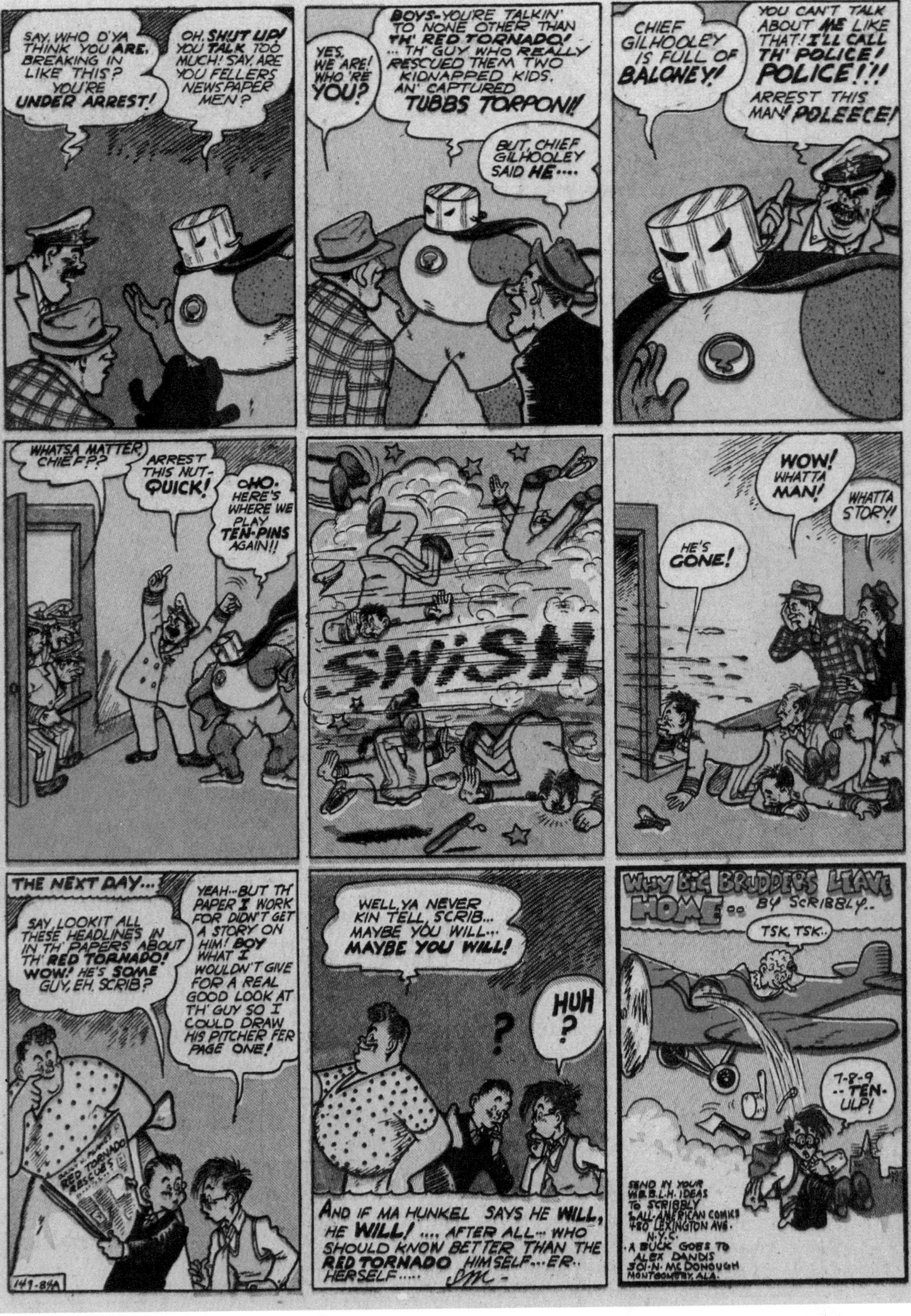
SAY, WHO D'YA THINK YOU ARE, BREAKING IN LIKE THIS? YOU'RE UNDER ARREST!
OH, SHUT UP! YOU TALK TOO MUCH! SAY, ARE YOU FELLERS NEWSPAPER MEN?
YES, WE ARE! WHO 'RE YOU?
BOYS-YOU'RE TALKIN' TO NONE OTHER THAN TH' RED TORNADO! ... TH' GUY WHO REALLY RESCUED THEM TWO KIDNAPPED KIDS, AN' CAPTURED TUBBS TORPONI!
BUT, CHIEF GILHOOLEY SAID HE....
CHIEF GILHOOLEY IS FULL OF BALONEY!
YOU CAN'T TALK ABOUT ME LIKE THAT! I'LL CALL TH' POLICE! POLICE!!! ARREST THIS MAN! POLEECE!
WHATSA MATTER, CHIEF??
ARREST THIS NUT-QUICK!
OHO. HERE'S WHERE WE PLAY TEN-PINS AGAIN!!
SWISH
WOW! WHATTA MAN!
WHATTA STORY!
HE'S GONE!
THE NEXT DAY...
SAY, LOOKIT ALL THESE HEADLINES IN TH' PAPERS ABOUT TH' RED TORNADO! WOW! HE'S SOME GUY, EH, SCRIB?
YEAH...BUT TH' PAPER I WORK FOR DIDN'T GET A STORY ON HIM! BOY WHAT I WOULDN'T GIVE FOR A REAL GOOD LOOK AT TH' GUY SO I COULD DRAW HIS PITCHER FER PAGE ONE!
RED TORNADO RESCUES
147-84A
WELL, YA NEVER KIN TELL, SCRIB... MAYBE YOU WILL... MAYBE YOU WILL!
?
HUH ?
AND IF MA HUNKEL SAYS HE WILL, HE WILL! .... AFTER ALL... WHO SHOULD KNOW BETTER THAN THE RED TORNADO HIMSELF...ER.. HERSELF.....
WHY BIG BRUDDERS LEAVE HOME.. BY SCRIBBLY..
TSK. TSK..
7-8-9 --TEN-ULP!
SEND IN YOUR W.B.B.L.H. IDEAS TO SCRIBBLY ALL-AMERICAN COMICS 480 LEXINGTON AVE. N.Y.C.
A BUCK GOES TO ALEX DANDIS 301-N. MC DONOUGH MONTGOMERY, ALA.

SCRIBBLY BY SHELDON MAYER

WELL, WHAT *ABOUT* IT? ARE YA GONNA QUIT OVER-CHARGIN' YER *CUSTOMERS?*

YES! YES! I WON'T DO IT ANY MORE—I PROMISE! PLEASE LET ME ALONE!

LATELY, SOME STRANGE THINGS HAVE HAPPENED IN SCRIBBLY'S NEIGHBORHOOD. EVERY TIME ANY STORE-KEEPER WAS CAUGHT SHORT-CHANGING, OR OVER-CHARGING A CUSTOMER, A STRANGE, WEIRD FIGURE VISITED HIM, AND....

OKAY! NOW, YOU'RE GONNA SEND TWO POUNDS OF PORK-CHOPS *FREE* TO EACH AN' EVERY ONE OF YER CUSTOMERS! *THAT'LL* HELP MAKE UP FER ALL OF TH' GYPPIN' YA'VE BEEN DOIN SINCE YA'VE BEEN IN BUSINESS! *YA HEAR ME?*

YESSIR! YESSIR! I'LL DO IT, *GLADLY!*

NEXT DAY—

EXTRY! EXTRY! GET TH' LATEST NEWS ABOUT TH' **RED TORNADO!**

SAY, SCRIB, IT SEEMS AS THO' TH' **RED TORNADO** CONFINES ALL HIS ACTIVITIES TO YOUR NEIGHBORHOOD!

YEAH—IT SURE LOOKS THAT WAY, DON'T IT?

YEAH. SO HERE'S YOUR ASSIGNMENT! I WANT YOU TO STICK AROUND YOUR HOME UNTIL YOU GET A GLIMPSE OF THAT MYSTERY-MAN, AND I WANT YOU TO DRAW A SKETCH OF HIM! WE'LL BE THE ONLY PAPER IN TOWN TO PUBLISH HIS PICTURE!

HUH?

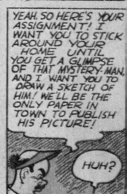

HIM AN' HIS *IDEAS!*

DIDJA EVER *HEAR* OF SUCH A THING, MRS. HUNKEL? I GOTTA HANG AROUND TH' NEIGHBORHOOD UNTIL I GET A LOOK AT THE **RED TORNADO!** I GOTTA DRAW HIS PITCHER!

HM— IZZAT SO?

HA! THIS IS GONNA BE EASIER FOR HIM THAN HE THINKS! HERE'S WHERE TH' **RED TORNADO** DOES ANOTHER GOOD DEED!

150-85A

From *All-American Comics* No. 22, January 1941.
© 1940 All American Comics, Inc.
Renewal © 1968 DC Comics, Inc.

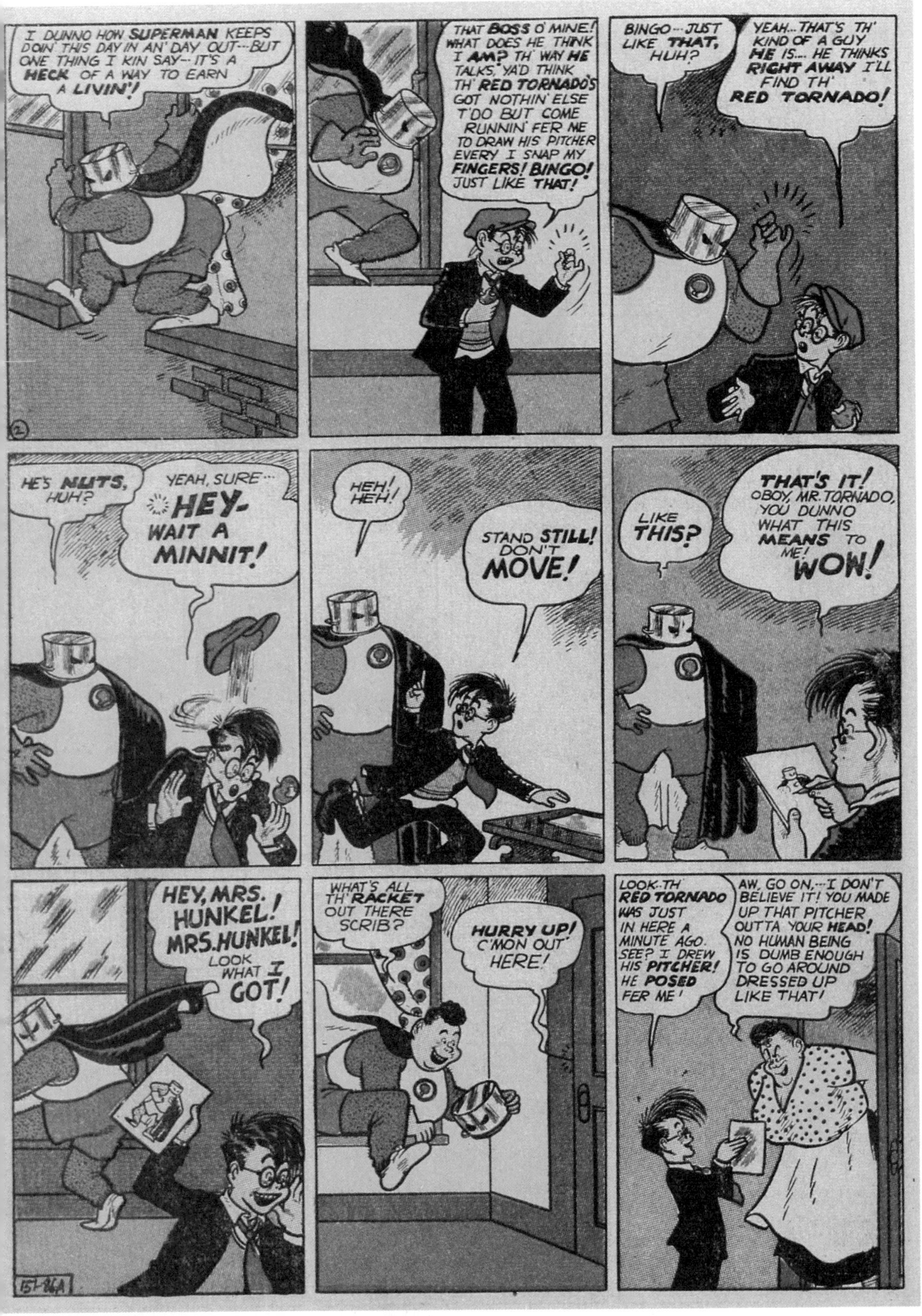
I DUNNO HOW SUPERMAN KEEPS DOIN' THIS DAY IN AN' DAY OUT--BUT ONE THING I KIN SAY--IT'S A HECK OF A WAY TO EARN A LIVIN'!
THAT BOSS O' MINE! WHAT DOES HE THINK I AM? TH' WAY HE TALKS, YA'D THINK TH' RED TORNADO'S GOT NOTHIN' ELSE T'DO BUT COME RUNNIN' FER ME TO DRAW HIS PITCHER EVERY I SNAP MY FINGERS! BINGO! JUST LIKE THAT!
BINGO--JUST LIKE THAT, HUH?
YEAH...THAT'S TH' KIND OF A GUY HE IS... HE THINKS RIGHT AWAY I'LL FIND TH' RED TORNADO!
HE'S NUTS, HUH?
YEAH, SURE... HEY- WAIT A MINNIT!
HEH! HEH!
STAND STILL! DON'T MOVE!
LIKE THIS?
THAT'S IT! OBOY, MR. TORNADO, YOU DUNNO WHAT THIS MEANS TO ME! WOW!
HEY, MRS. HUNKEL! MRS. HUNKEL! LOOK WHAT I GOT!
WHAT'S ALL TH' RACKET OUT THERE SCRIB?
HURRY UP! C'MON OUT HERE!
LOOK-TH' RED TORNADO WAS JUST IN HERE A MINUTE AGO. SEE? I DREW HIS PITCHER! HE POSED FER ME!
AW, GO ON,--I DON'T BELIEVE IT! YOU MADE UP THAT PITCHER OUTTA YOUR HEAD! NO HUMAN BEING IS DUMB ENOUGH TO GO AROUND DRESSED UP LIKE THAT!

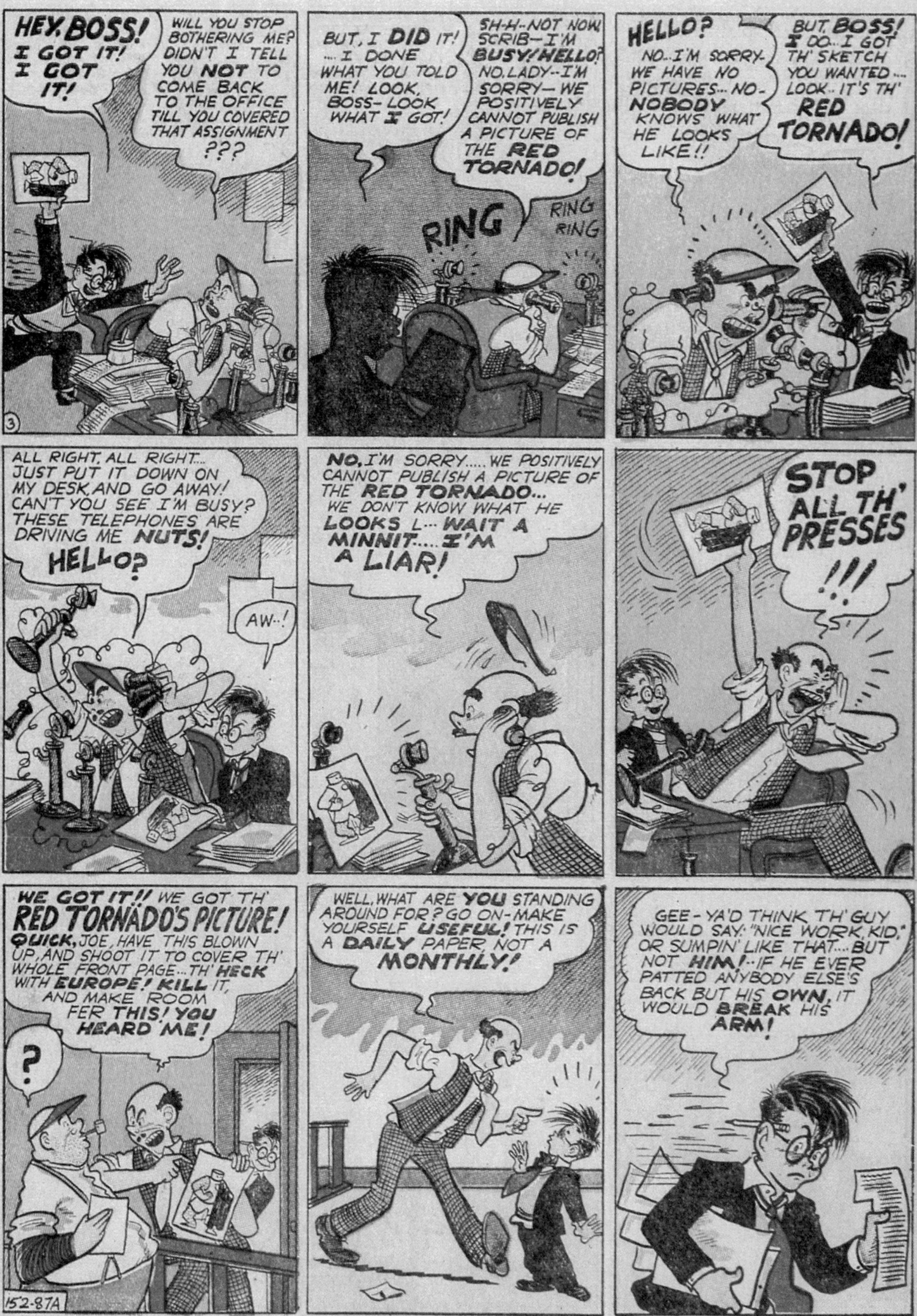
HEY, BOSS! I GOT IT! I GOT IT!
WILL YOU STOP BOTHERING ME? DIDN'T I TELL YOU NOT TO COME BACK TO THE OFFICE TILL YOU COVERED THAT ASSIGNMENT ???
3
BUT, I DID IT! ... I DONE WHAT YOU TOLD ME! LOOK, BOSS- LOOK WHAT I GOT!
SH-H--NOT NOW, SCRIB-- I'M BUSY! HELLO? NO, LADY--I'M SORRY-- WE POSITIVELY CANNOT PUBLISH A PICTURE OF THE RED TORNADO!
RING
RING RING
HELLO?
NO...I'M SORRY-- WE HAVE NO PICTURES...NO-NOBODY KNOWS WHAT HE LOOKS LIKE!!
BUT, BOSS! I DO...I GOT TH' SKETCH YOU WANTED... LOOK...IT'S TH' RED TORNADO!
ALL RIGHT, ALL RIGHT... JUST PUT IT DOWN ON MY DESK, AND GO AWAY! CAN'T YOU SEE I'M BUSY? THESE TELEPHONES ARE DRIVING ME NUTS!
HELLO?
AW--!
NO, I'M SORRY..... WE POSITIVELY CANNOT PUBLISH A PICTURE OF THE RED TORNADO... WE DON'T KNOW WHAT HE LOOKS L... WAIT A MINNIT..... I'M A LIAR!
STOP ALL TH' PRESSES !!!
WE GOT IT!! WE GOT TH' RED TORNADO'S PICTURE! QUICK, JOE, HAVE THIS BLOWN UP, AND SHOOT IT TO COVER TH' WHOLE FRONT PAGE...TH' HECK WITH EUROPE! KILL IT, AND MAKE ROOM FER THIS! YOU HEARD ME!
?
152-87A
WELL, WHAT ARE YOU STANDING AROUND FOR? GO ON--MAKE YOURSELF USEFUL! THIS IS A DAILY PAPER, NOT A MONTHLY!
GEE - YA'D THINK TH' GUY WOULD SAY: "NICE WORK, KID," OR SUMPIN' LIKE THAT... BUT NOT HIM!--IF HE EVER PATTED ANYBODY ELSE'S BACK BUT HIS OWN, IT WOULD BREAK HIS ARM!

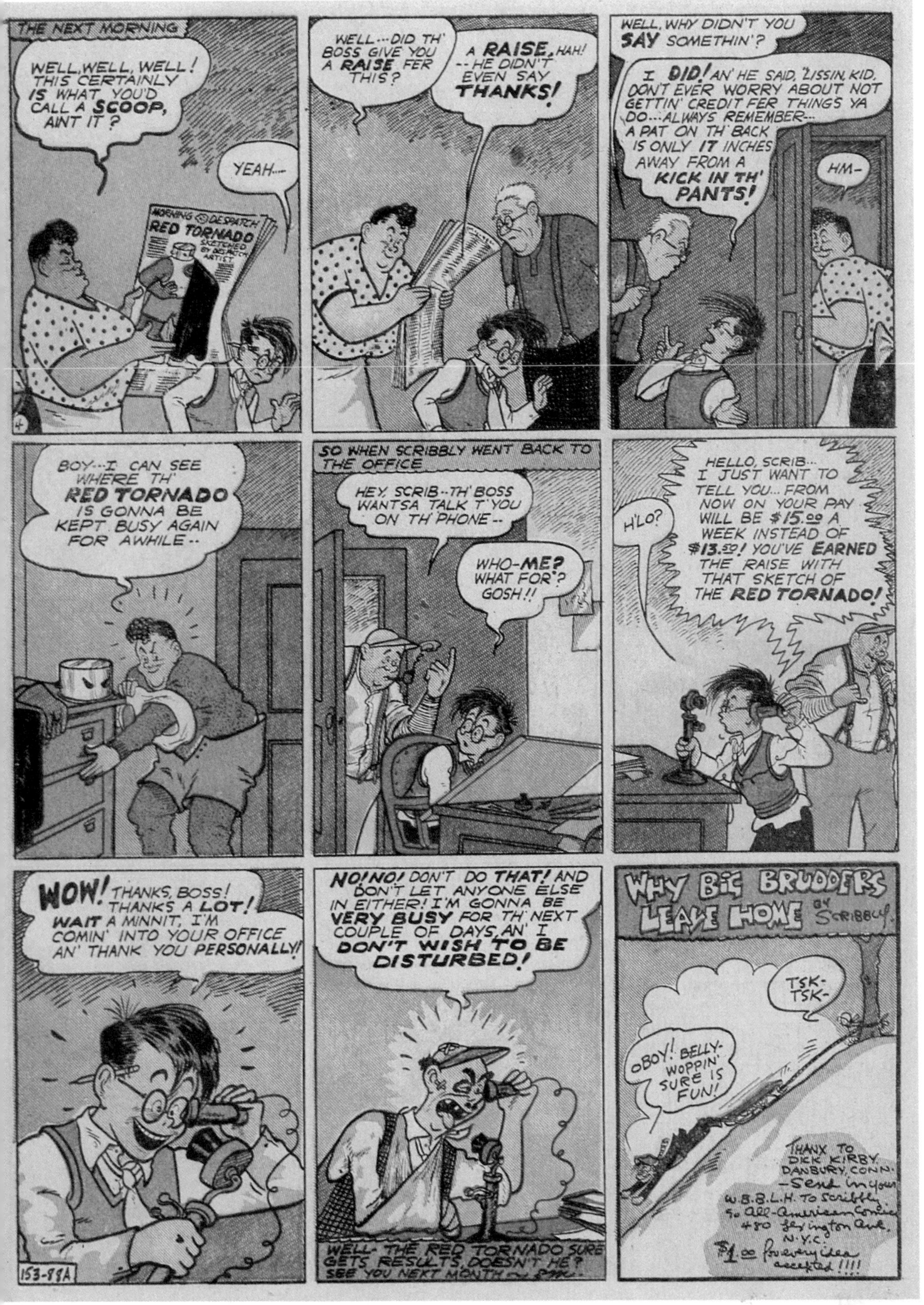
THE NEXT MORNING
WELL, WELL, WELL! THIS CERTAINLY IS WHAT YOU'D CALL A SCOOP, AINT IT?
YEAH....
MORNING DESPATCH
RED TORNADO
SKETCHED BY DESPATCH ARTIST
WELL...DID TH' BOSS GIVE YOU A RAISE FER THIS?
A RAISE, HAH! --HE DIDN'T EVEN SAY THANKS!
WELL, WHY DIDN'T YOU SAY SOMETHIN'?
I DID! AN' HE SAID, "LISSIN, KID, DON'T EVER WORRY ABOUT NOT GETTIN' CREDIT FER THINGS YA DO...ALWAYS REMEMBER... A PAT ON TH' BACK IS ONLY 17 INCHES AWAY FROM A KICK IN TH' PANTS!
HM-
BOY...I CAN SEE WHERE TH' RED TORNADO IS GONNA BE KEPT BUSY AGAIN FOR AWHILE--
SO WHEN SCRIBBLY WENT BACK TO THE OFFICE
HEY, SCRIB--TH' BOSS WANTSA TALK T' YOU ON TH' PHONE--
WHO-ME? WHAT FOR'? GOSH!!
H'LO?
HELLO, SCRIB... I JUST WANT TO TELL YOU... FROM NOW ON YOUR PAY WILL BE $15.00 A WEEK INSTEAD OF $13.50! YOU'VE EARNED THE RAISE WITH THAT SKETCH OF THE RED TORNADO!
WOW! THANKS, BOSS! THANKS A LOT! WAIT A MINNIT, I'M COMIN' INTO YOUR OFFICE AN' THANK YOU PERSONALLY!
NO! NO! DON'T DO THAT! AND DON'T LET ANYONE ELSE IN EITHER! I'M GONNA BE VERY BUSY FOR TH' NEXT COUPLE OF DAYS, AN' I DON'T WISH TO BE DISTURBED!
WELL- THE RED TORNADO SURE GETS RESULTS, DOESN'T HE? SEE YOU NEXT MONTH
153-88A
WHY BIG BRUDDERS LEAVE HOME BY SCRIBBLY
TSK-TSK-
OBOY! BELLY-WOPPIN' SURE IS FUN!
THANX TO DICK KIRBY DANBURY, CONN.
-Send in your W.B.B.L.H. To Scribbly % All-American Comics 480 Lexington Ave. N.Y.C.
$1.00 for every idea accepted!!!!

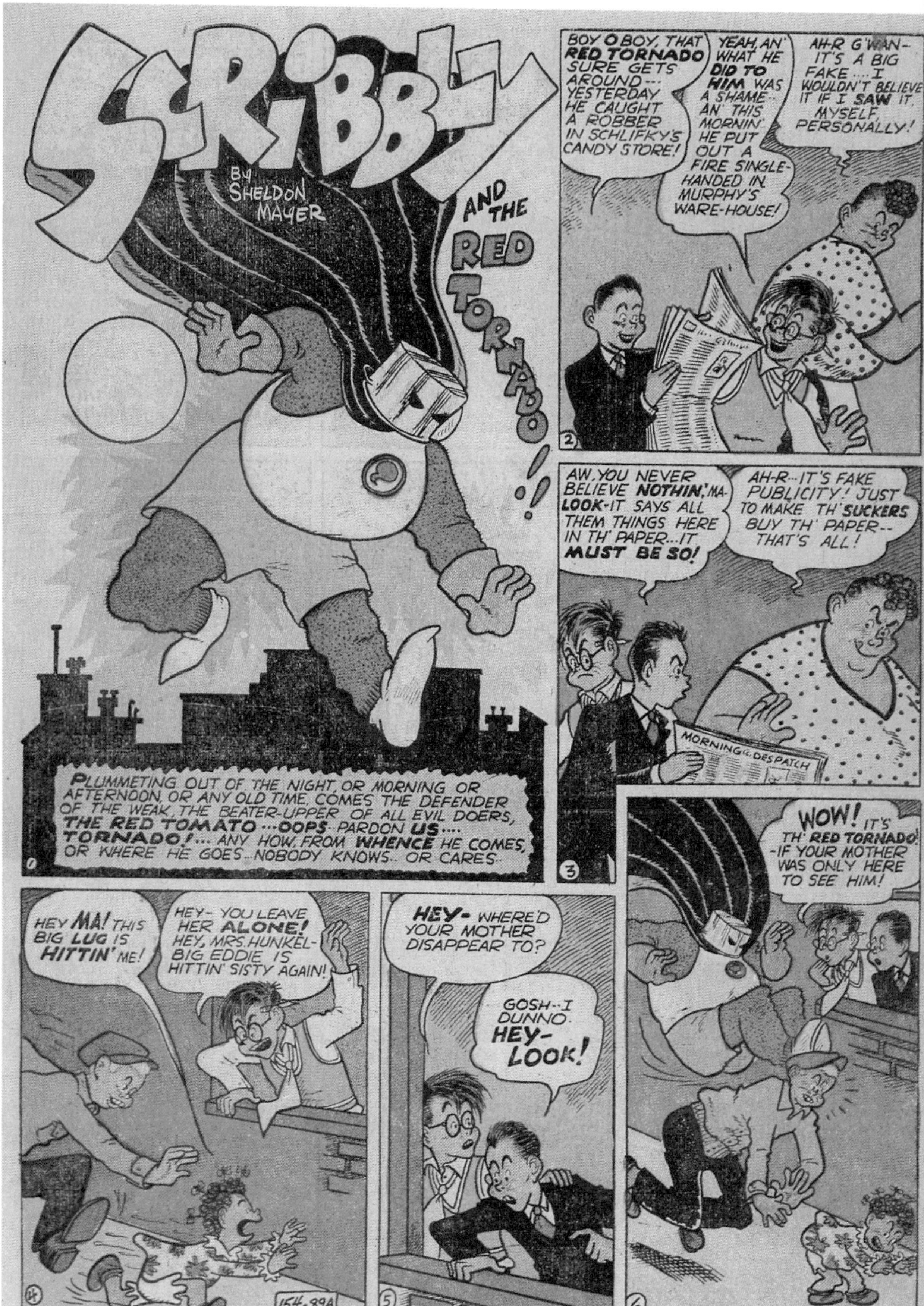

SCRIBBLY
BY SHELDON MAYER
AND THE RED TORNADO!!
PLUMMETING OUT OF THE NIGHT, OR MORNING OR AFTERNOON, OR ANY OLD TIME, COMES THE DEFENDER OF THE WEAK, THE BEATER-UPPER OF ALL EVIL DOERS, THE RED TOMATO ...OOPS-PARDON US.... TORNADO!... ANY HOW, FROM WHENCE HE COMES, OR WHERE HE GOES...NOBODY KNOWS.. OR CARES.
BOY O BOY, THAT RED TORNADO SURE GETS AROUND--- YESTERDAY HE CAUGHT A ROBBER IN SCHLIFKY'S CANDY STORE!
YEAH, AN' WHAT HE DID TO HIM WAS A SHAME-- AN' THIS MORNIN' HE PUT OUT A FIRE SINGLE-HANDED IN MURPHY'S WARE-HOUSE!
AH-R G'WAN-- IT'S A BIG FAKE ....I WOULDN'T BELIEVE IT IF I SAW IT MYSELF, PERSONALLY!
AW, YOU NEVER BELIEVE NOTHIN', MA. LOOK-IT SAYS ALL THEM THINGS HERE IN TH' PAPER...IT MUST BE SO!
AH-R...IT'S FAKE PUBLICITY! JUST TO MAKE TH' SUCKERS BUY TH' PAPER-- THAT'S ALL!
MORNING DESPATCH
HEY MA! THIS BIG LUG IS HITTIN' ME!
HEY- YOU LEAVE HER ALONE! HEY, MRS. HUNKEL- BIG EDDIE IS HITTIN' SISTY AGAIN!
154-89A
HEY- WHERE'D YOUR MOTHER DISAPPEAR TO?
GOSH--I DUNNO. HEY- LOOK!
WOW! IT'S TH' RED TORNADO! -IF YOUR MOTHER WAS ONLY HERE TO SEE HIM!

From *All-American Comics* No. 23, February 1941.

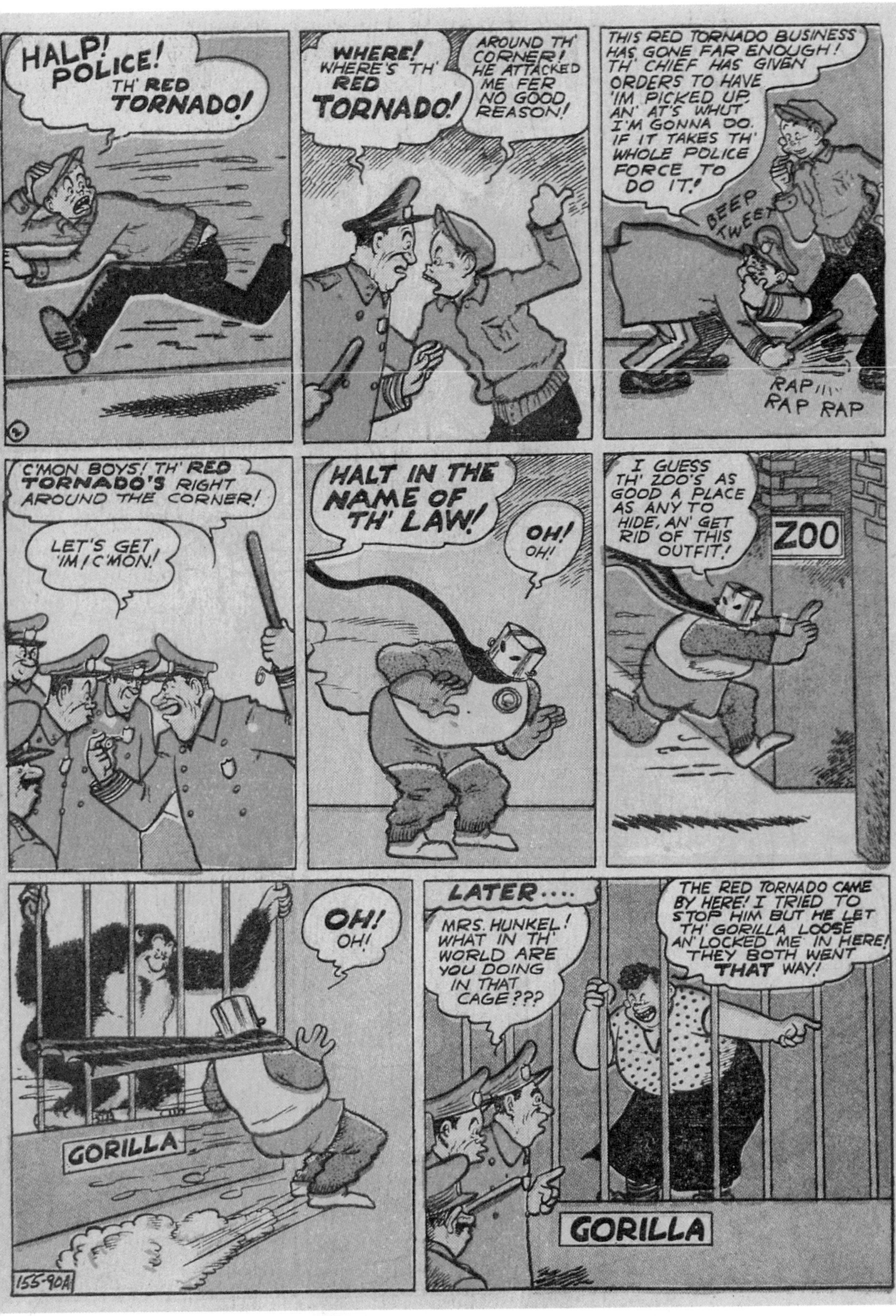
HALP! POLICE! TH' RED TORNADO!
WHERE! WHERE'S TH' RED TORNADO!
AROUND TH' CORNER! HE ATTACKED ME FER NO GOOD REASON!
THIS RED TORNADO BUSINESS HAS GONE FAR ENOUGH! TH' CHIEF HAS GIVEN ORDERS TO HAVE 'IM PICKED UP, AN' AT'S WHUT I'M GONNA DO. IF IT TAKES TH' WHOLE POLICE FORCE TO DO IT!
BEEP
TWEET
RAP
RAP RAP
C'MON BOYS! TH' RED TORNADO'S RIGHT AROUND THE CORNER!
LET'S GET 'IM! C'MON!
HALT IN THE NAME OF TH' LAW!
OH! OH!
I GUESS TH' ZOO'S AS GOOD A PLACE AS ANY TO HIDE, AN' GET RID OF THIS OUTFIT!
ZOO
OH! OH!
GORILLA
155-90A
LATER....
MRS. HUNKEL! WHAT IN TH' WORLD ARE YOU DOING IN THAT CAGE???
THE RED TORNADO CAME BY HERE! I TRIED TO STOP HIM BUT HE LET TH' GORILLA LOOSE AN' LOCKED ME IN HERE! THEY BOTH WENT THAT WAY!
GORILLA

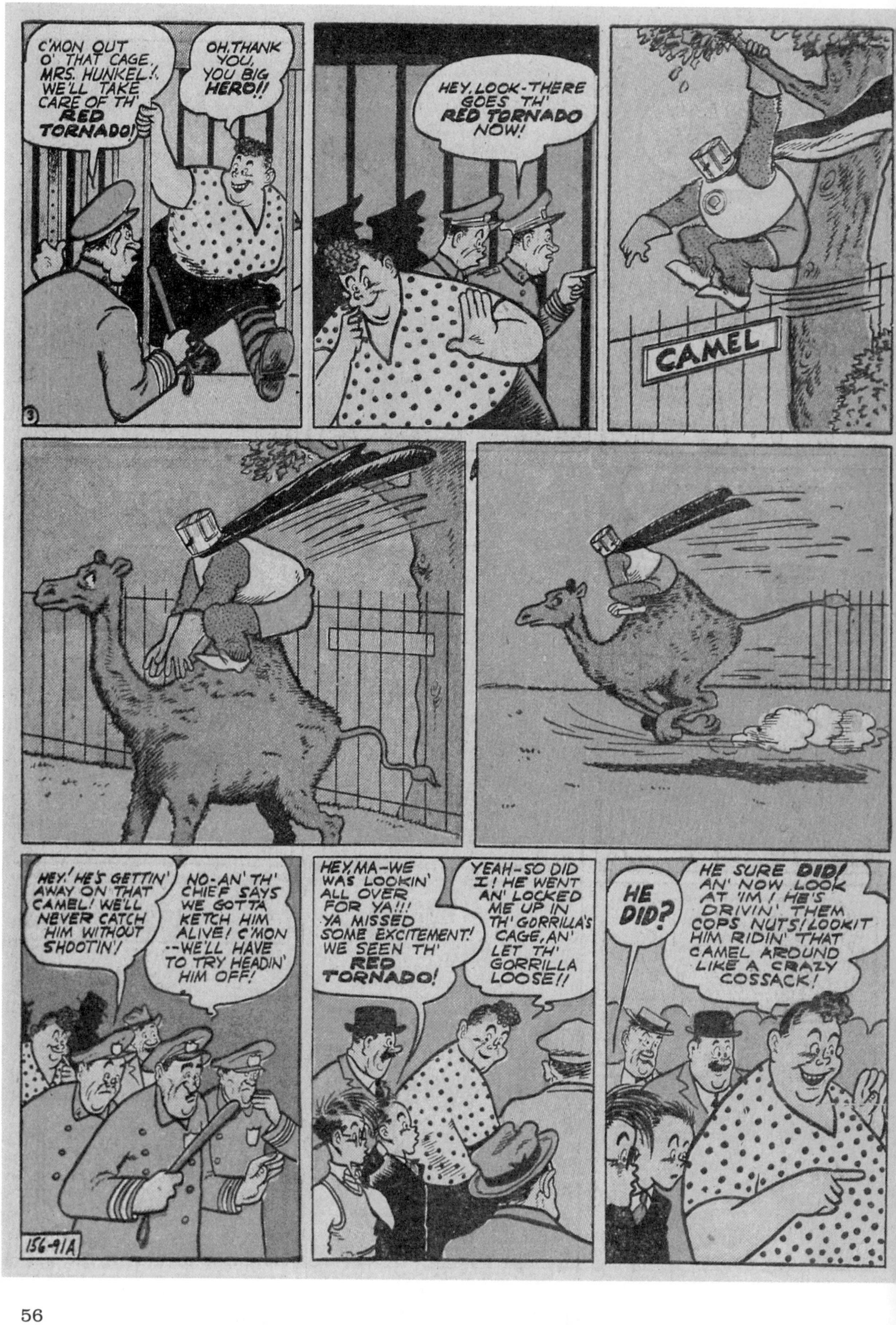
C'MON OUT O' THAT CAGE, MRS. HUNKEL!. WE'LL TAKE CARE OF TH' RED TORNADO!
OH, THANK YOU, YOU BIG HERO!!
3
HEY, LOOK-THERE GOES TH' RED TORNADO NOW!
CAMEL
HEY! HE'S GETTIN' AWAY ON THAT CAMEL! WE'LL NEVER CATCH HIM WITHOUT SHOOTIN'!
NO-AN' TH' CHIEF SAYS WE GOTTA KETCH HIM ALIVE! C'MON --WE'LL HAVE TO TRY HEADIN' HIM OFF!
156-91A
HEY, MA-WE WAS LOOKIN' ALL OVER FOR YA!!! YA MISSED SOME EXCITEMENT! WE SEEN TH' RED TORNADO!
YEAH-SO DID I! HE WENT AN' LOCKED ME UP IN TH' GORRILLA'S CAGE, AN' LET TH' GORRILLA LOOSE!!
HE DID?
HE SURE DID! AN' NOW LOOK AT 'IM! HE'S DRIVIN' THEM COPS NUTS! LOOKIT HIM RIDIN' THAT CAMEL AROUND LIKE A CRAZY COSSACK!

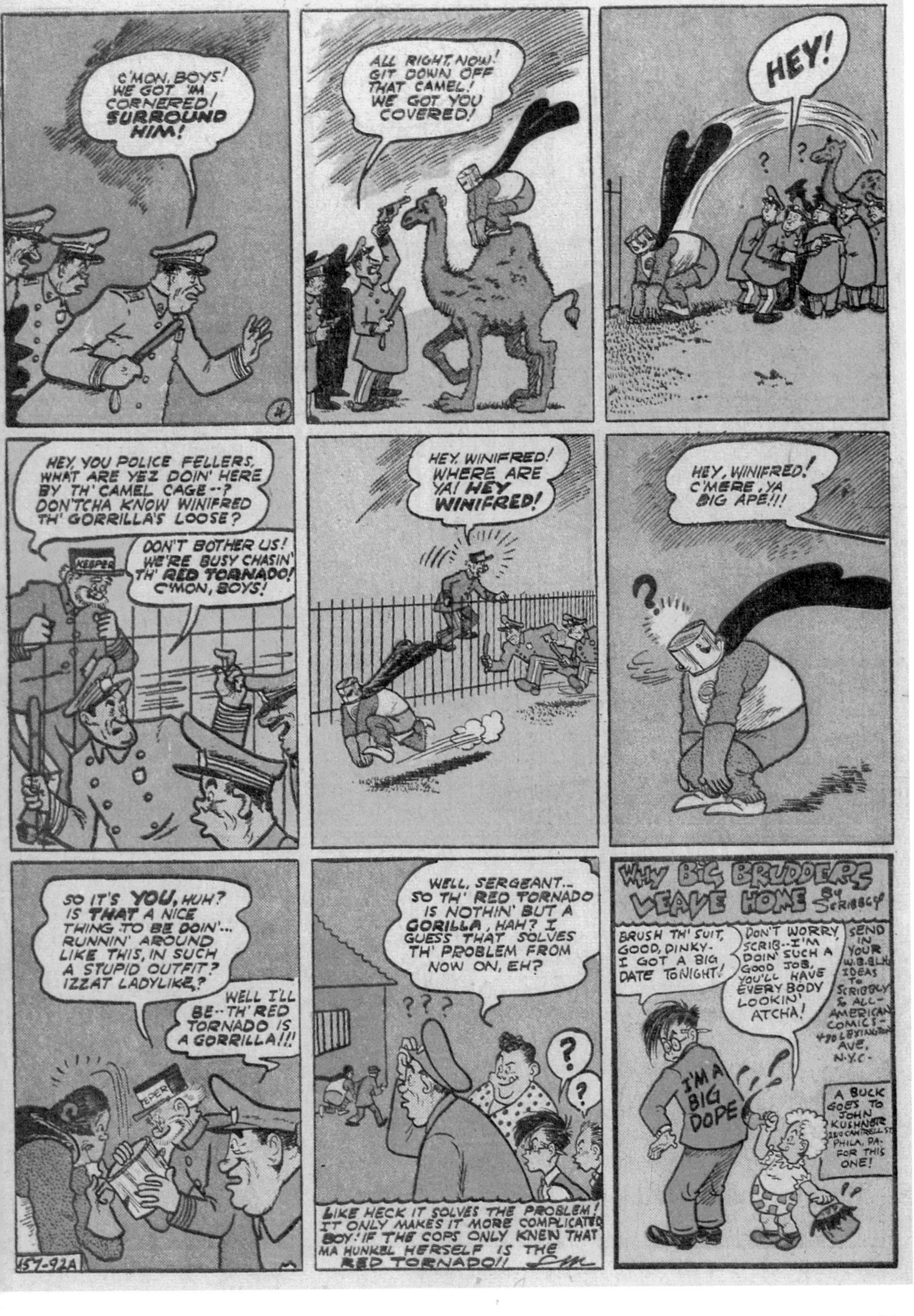
C'MON, BOYS! WE GOT 'IM CORNERED! SURROUND HIM!
ALL RIGHT, NOW! GIT DOWN OFF THAT CAMEL! WE GOT YOU COVERED!
HEY!
?
?
HEY, YOU POLICE FELLERS, WHAT ARE YEZ DOIN' HERE BY TH' CAMEL CAGE--? DON'TCHA KNOW WINIFRED TH' GORRILLA'S LOOSE?
KEEPER
DON'T BOTHER US! WE'RE BUSY CHASIN' TH' RED TORNADO! C'MON, BOYS!
HEY, WINIFRED! WHERE ARE YA! HEY WINIFRED!
HEY, WINIFRED! C'MERE, YA BIG APE!!!
?
SO IT'S YOU, HUH? IS THAT A NICE THING TO BE DOIN'... RUNNIN' AROUND LIKE THIS, IN SUCH A STUPID OUTFIT? IZZAT LADYLIKE?
WELL I'LL BE--TH' RED TORNADO IS A GORRILLA!!!
WELL, SERGEANT... SO TH' RED TORNADO IS NOTHIN' BUT A GORILLA, HAH? I GUESS THAT SOLVES TH' PROBLEM FROM NOW ON, EH?
???
?
?
LIKE HECK IT SOLVES THE PROBLEM! IT ONLY MAKES IT MORE COMPLICATED BOY! IF THE COPS ONLY KNEW THAT MA HUNKEL HERSELF IS THE RED TORNADO!!
WHY BIG BRUDDERS LEAVE HOME BY SCRIBBLY
BRUSH TH' SUIT, GOOD, DINKY- I GOT A BIG DATE TONIGHT!
DON'T WORRY, SCRIB--I'M DOIN' SUCH A GOOD JOB, YOU'LL HAVE EVERY BODY LOOKIN' ATCHA!
SEND IN YOUR W.B.B.L.H. IDEAS TO SCRIBBLY & ALL-AMERICAN COMICS- 480 LEXINGTON AVE, N.Y.C-
I'M A BIG DOPE
A BUCK GOES TO JOHN KUSHNER PHILA, PA- FOR THIS ONE!
157-92A

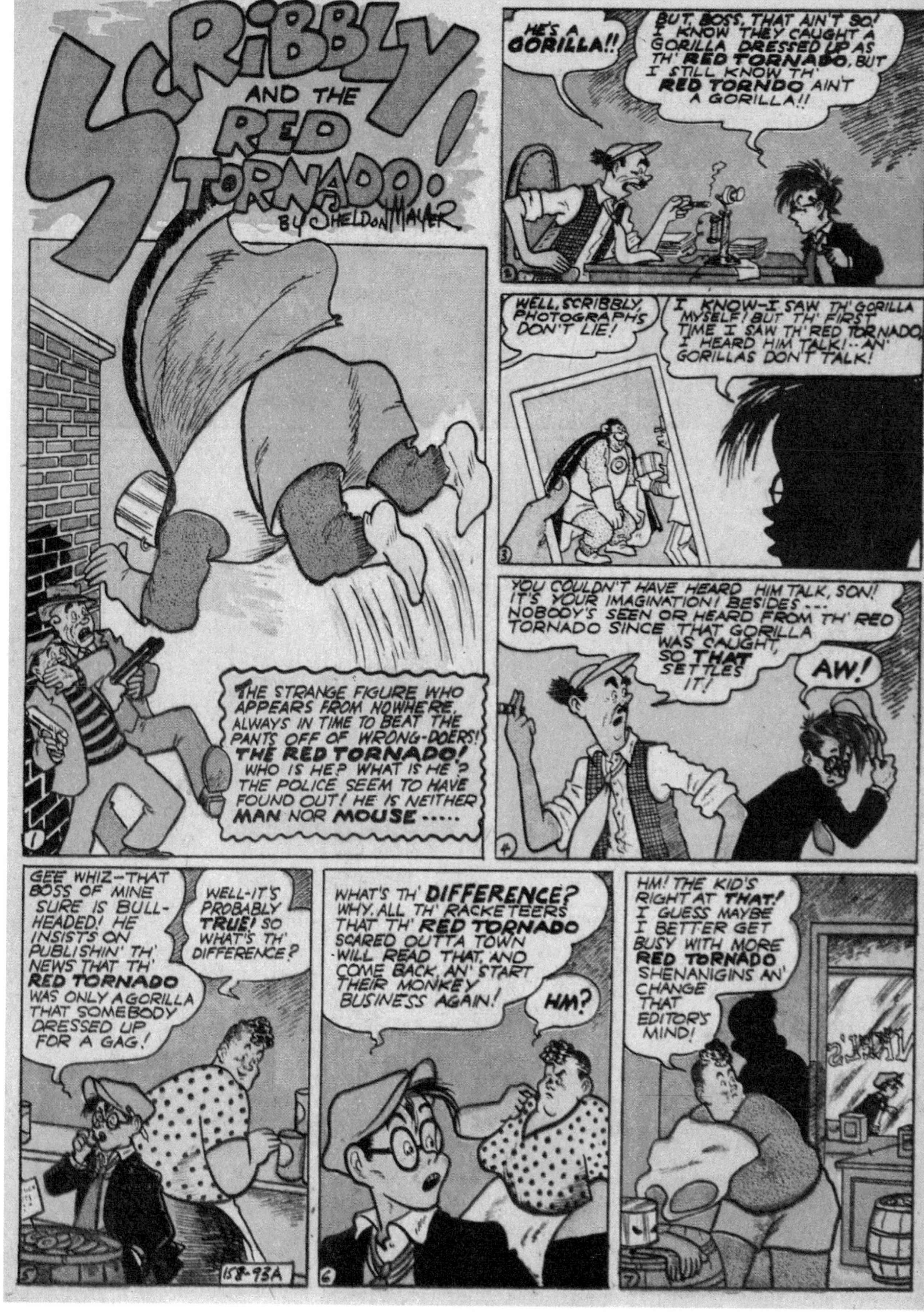
SCRIBBLY AND THE RED TORNADO!
BY SHELDON MAYER
HE'S A GORILLA!!
BUT, BOSS, THAT AIN'T SO! I KNOW THEY CAUGHT A GORILLA DRESSED UP AS TH' RED TORNADO, BUT I STILL KNOW TH' RED TORNDO AINT A GORILLA!!
THE STRANGE FIGURE WHO APPEARS FROM NOWHERE, ALWAYS IN TIME TO BEAT THE PANTS OFF OF WRONG-DOERS! THE RED TORNADO! WHO IS HE? WHAT IS HE? THE POLICE SEEM TO HAVE FOUND OUT! HE IS NEITHER MAN NOR MOUSE.....
WELL, SCRIBBLY, PHOTOGRAPHS DON'T LIE!
I KNOW—I SAW TH' GORILLA MYSELF! BUT TH' FIRST TIME I SAW TH' RED TORNADO, I HEARD HIM TALK!.. AN' GORILLAS DON'T TALK!
YOU COULDN'T HAVE HEARD HIM TALK, SON! IT'S YOUR IMAGINATION! BESIDES--- NOBODY'S SEEN OR HEARD FROM TH' RED TORNADO SINCE THAT GORILLA WAS CAUGHT, SO THAT SETTLES IT!
AW!
GEE WHIZ—THAT BOSS OF MINE SURE IS BULL-HEADED! HE INSISTS ON PUBLISHIN' TH' NEWS THAT TH' RED TORNADO WAS ONLY A GORILLA THAT SOMEBODY DRESSED UP FOR A GAG!
WELL-IT'S PROBABLY TRUE! SO WHAT'S TH' DIFFERENCE?
WHAT'S TH' DIFFERENCE? WHY, ALL TH' RACKETEERS THAT TH' RED TORNADO SCARED OUTTA TOWN WILL READ THAT, AN' COME BACK, AN' START THEIR MONKEY BUSINESS AGAIN!
HM?
HM! THE KID'S RIGHT AT THAT! I GUESS MAYBE I BETTER GET BUSY WITH MORE RED TORNADO SHENANIGINS AN' CHANGE THAT EDITOR'S MIND!
158-93A

From *All-American Comics* No. 24, March 1941.

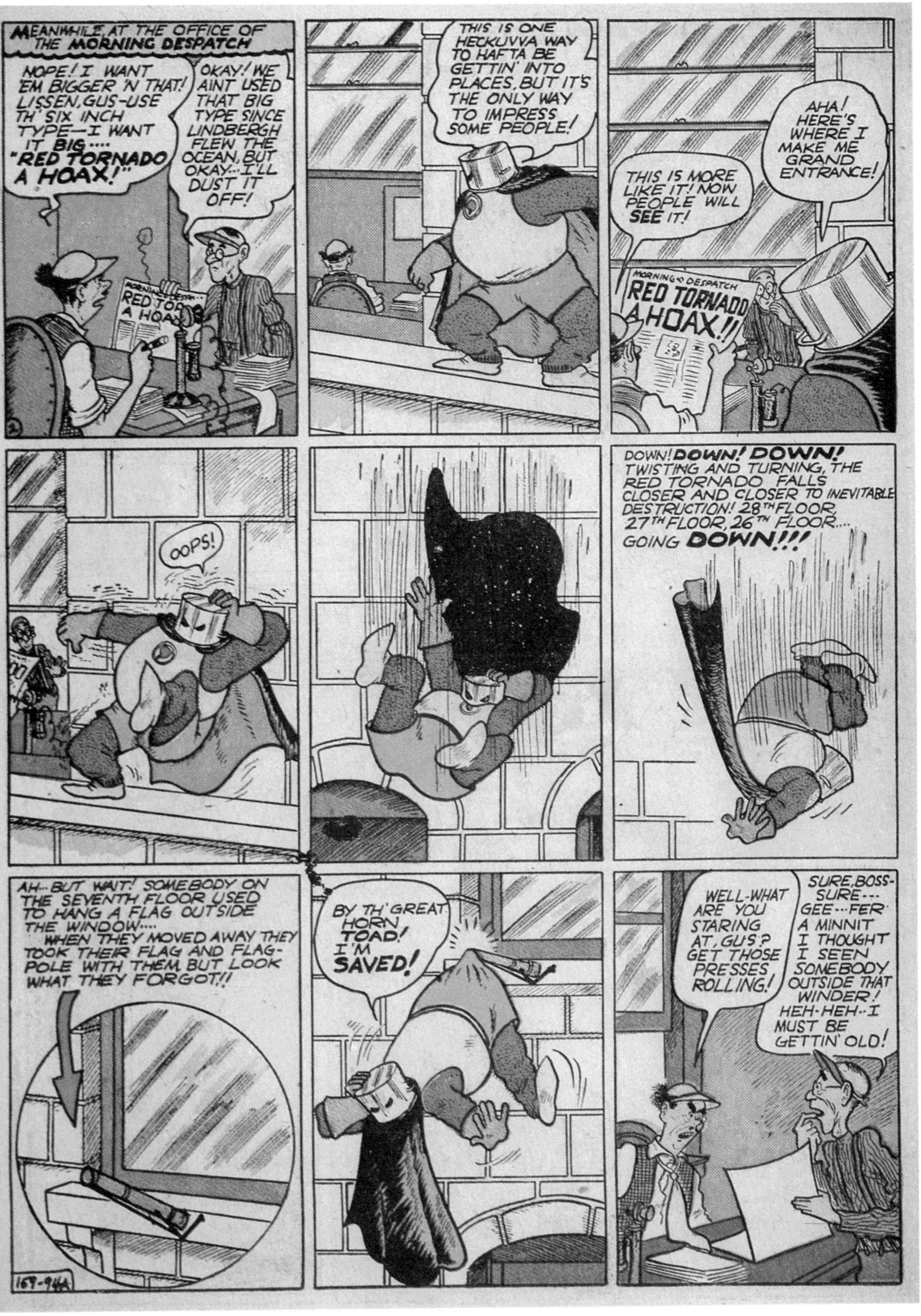
MEANWHILE, AT THE OFFICE OF THE MORNING DESPATCH
NOPE! I WANT 'EM BIGGER 'N THAT! LISSEN, GUS-USE TH' SIX INCH TYPE—I WANT IT BIG.... "RED TORNADO A HOAX!"
OKAY! WE AINT USED THAT BIG TYPE SINCE LINDBERGH FLEW THE OCEAN, BUT OKAY...I'LL DUST IT OFF!
RED TORNADO A HOAX
THIS IS ONE HECKUVVA WAY TO HAFTA BE GETTIN' INTO PLACES, BUT IT'S THE ONLY WAY TO IMPRESS SOME PEOPLE!
AHA! HERE'S WHERE I MAKE ME GRAND ENTRANCE!
THIS IS MORE LIKE IT! NOW PEOPLE WILL SEE IT!
MORNING DESPATCH
RED TORNADO A HOAX!!
OOPS!
DOWN! DOWN! DOWN! TWISTING AND TURNING, THE RED TORNADO FALLS CLOSER AND CLOSER TO INEVITABLE DESTRUCTION! 28TH FLOOR, 27TH FLOOR, 26TH FLOOR.... GOING DOWN!!!
AH...BUT WAIT! SOMEBODY ON THE SEVENTH FLOOR USED TO HANG A FLAG OUTSIDE THE WINDOW.... WHEN THEY MOVED AWAY THEY TOOK THEIR FLAG AND FLAG-POLE WITH THEM, BUT LOOK WHAT THEY FORGOT!!
BY TH' GREAT HORN TOAD! I'M SAVED!
WELL-WHAT ARE YOU STARING AT, GUS? GET THOSE PRESSES ROLLING!
SURE, BOSS-SURE---GEE---FER A MINNIT I THOUGHT I SEEN SOMEBODY OUTSIDE THAT WINDER! HEH-HEH--I MUST BE GETTIN' OLD!
159-94A

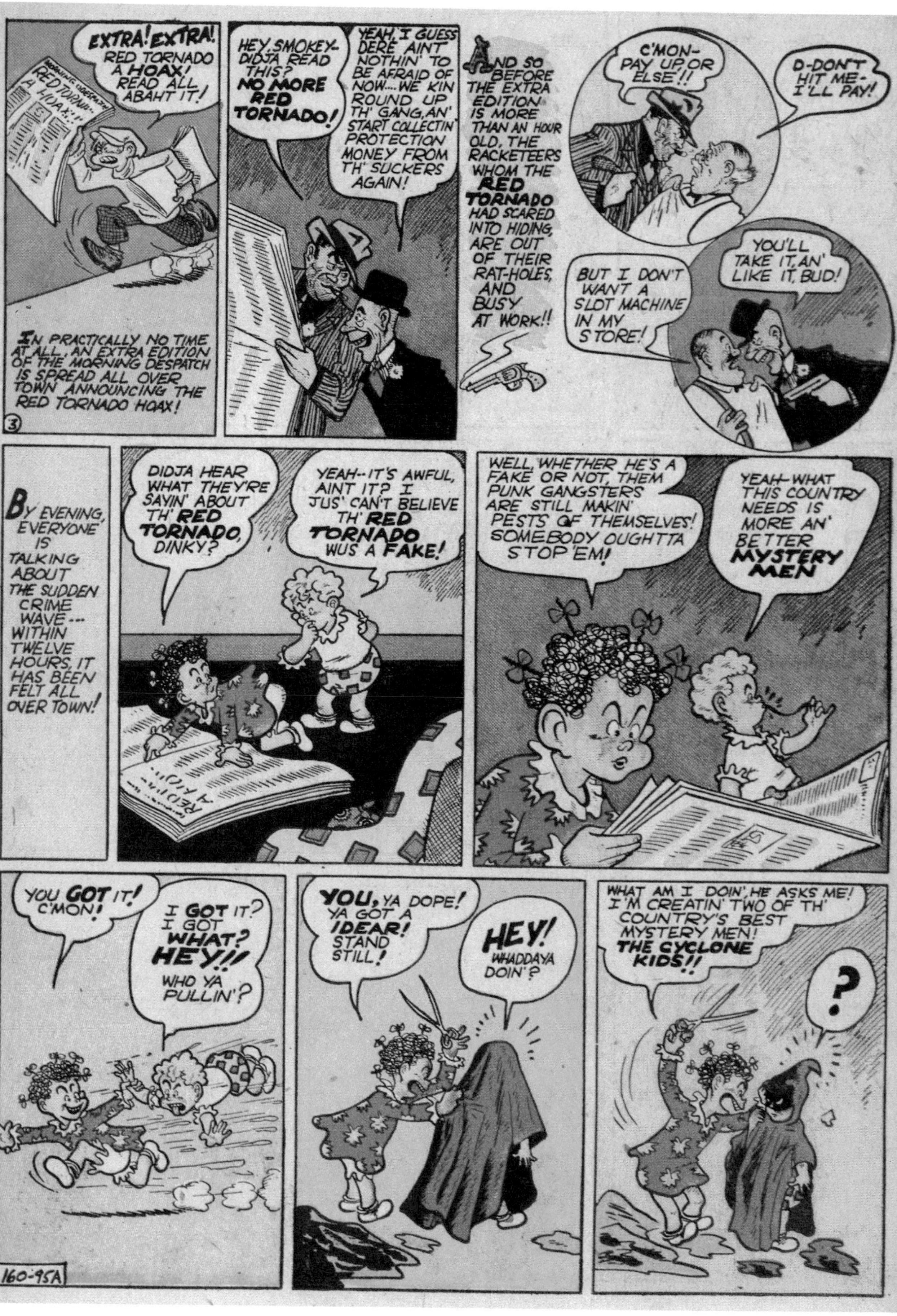
EXTRA! EXTRA! RED TORNADO A HOAX! READ ALL ABAHT IT!
MORNING DESPATCH RED TORNADO A HOAX!!
IN PRACTICALLY NO TIME AT ALL, AN EXTRA EDITION OF THE MORNING DESPATCH IS SPREAD ALL OVER TOWN ANNOUNCING THE RED TORNADO HOAX!
3
HEY, SMOKEY- DIDJA READ THIS? NO MORE RED TORNADO!
YEAH, I GUESS DERE AINT NOTHIN' TO BE AFRAID OF NOW.... WE KIN ROUND UP TH' GANG, AN' START COLLECTIN' PROTECTION MONEY FROM TH' SUCKERS AGAIN!
AND SO BEFORE THE EXTRA EDITION IS MORE THAN AN HOUR OLD, THE RACKETEERS WHOM THE RED TORNADO HAD SCARED INTO HIDING, ARE OUT OF THEIR RAT-HOLES, AND BUSY AT WORK!!
C'MON- PAY UP, OR ELSE!!
D-DON'T HIT ME- I'LL PAY!
YOU'LL TAKE IT, AN' LIKE IT, BUD!
BUT I DON'T WANT A SLOT MACHINE IN MY STORE!
BY EVENING, EVERYONE IS TALKING ABOUT THE SUDDEN CRIME WAVE--- WITHIN TWELVE HOURS, IT HAS BEEN FELT ALL OVER TOWN!
DIDJA HEAR WHAT THEY'RE SAYIN' ABOUT TH' RED TORNADO, DINKY?
YEAH-- IT'S AWFUL, AINT IT? I JUS' CAN'T BELIEVE TH' RED TORNADO WUS A FAKE!
WELL, WHETHER HE'S A FAKE OR NOT, THEM PUNK GANGSTERS ARE STILL MAKIN' PESTS OF THEMSELVES! SOMEBODY OUGHTTA STOP 'EM!
YEAH- WHAT THIS COUNTRY NEEDS IS MORE AN' BETTER MYSTERY MEN
YOU GOT IT! C'MON!
I GOT IT? I GOT WHAT? HEY!! WHO YA PULLIN'?
YOU, YA DOPE! YA GOT A IDEAR! STAND STILL!
HEY! WHADDAYA DOIN'?
WHAT AM I DOIN', HE ASKS ME! I'M CREATIN' TWO OF TH' COUNTRY'S BEST MYSTERY MEN! THE CYCLONE KIDS!!
?
160-95A

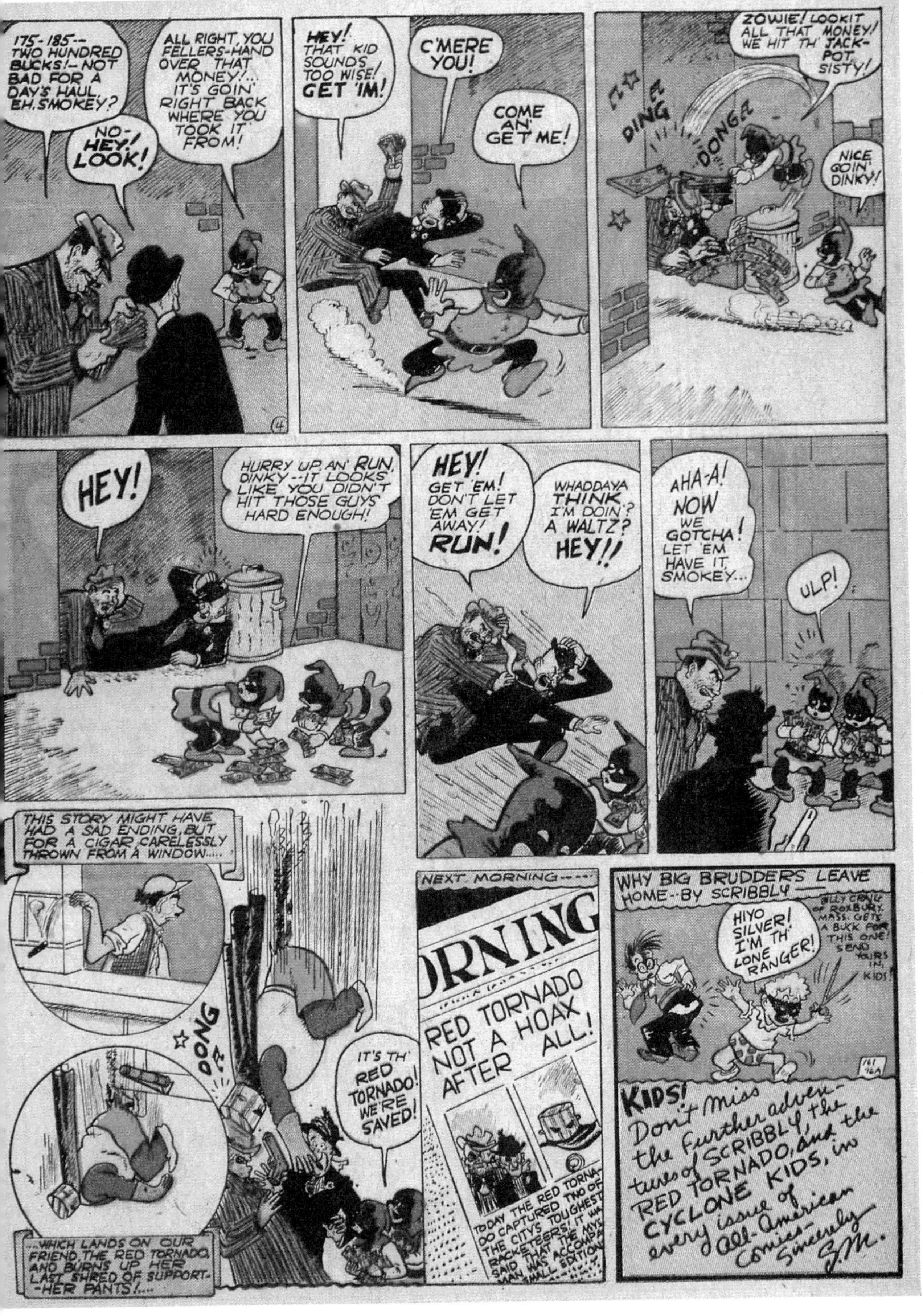

175-185-- TWO HUNDRED BUCKS!-- NOT BAD FOR A DAY'S HAUL, EH, SMOKEY?
ALL RIGHT, YOU FELLERS-HAND OVER THAT MONEY!... IT'S GOIN' RIGHT BACK WHERE YOU TOOK IT FROM!
NO- HEY! LOOK!
HEY! THAT KID SOUNDS TOO WISE! GET 'IM!
C'MERE YOU!
COME AN' GET ME!
ZOWIE! LOOKIT ALL THAT MONEY! WE HIT TH' JACK-POT, SISTY!
DING
DONG
NICE GOIN', DINKY!
HEY!
HURRY UP AN' RUN, DINKY--IT LOOKS LIKE YOU DIDN'T HIT THOSE GUYS HARD ENOUGH!
HEY! GET 'EM! DON'T LET 'EM GET AWAY! RUN!
WHADDAYA THINK I'M DOIN'? A WALTZ? HEY!!
AHA-A! NOW WE GOTCHA! LET 'EM HAVE IT, SMOKEY...
ULP!
THIS STORY MIGHT HAVE HAD A SAD ENDING, BUT FOR A CIGAR CARELESSLY THROWN FROM A WINDOW.....
DONG
IT'S TH' RED TORNADO! WE'RE SAVED!
...WHICH LANDS ON OUR FRIEND, THE RED TORNADO, AND BURNS UP HER LAST SHRED OF SUPPORT--HER PANTS!....
NEXT MORNING----
ORNING
RED TORNADO NOT A HOAX AFTER ALL!
TODAY THE RED TORNADO CAPTURED TWO OF THE CITY'S TOUGHEST RACKETEERS! IT WAS SAID THAT THE MYS
WHY BIG BRUDDERS LEAVE HOME--BY SCRIBBLY
BILLY CRAIG OF ROXBURY, MASS. GETS A BUCK FOR THIS ONE! SEND YOURS IN, KIDS!
HIYO SILVER! I'M TH' LONE RANGER!
KIDS! Don't miss the further adventures of SCRIBBLY, the RED TORNADO, and the CYCLONE KIDS, in every issue of All-American Comics-- Sincerely S.M.

About "Plastic Man" and Jack Cole

Plastic Man was the creation of Jack Cole, a man whose life came close to true tragedy.

Cole was born in 1918 in New Castle, Pennsylvania. He once took a correspondence course in cartooning, but he was a man with the natural talents of a cartoonist. By 1937, he was already at work in comic books, turning out gag features built around more or less traditional "big foot" characters. Within two years, however, he was meeting the demand for super-heroes and adventure by editing, drawing, and writing several features, including the durable *Daredevil*. Cole also worked as an assistant to Will Eisner, particularly on the daily newspaper version of *The Spirit* that ran in the early 1940s.

Meanwhile, the magazine *Police Comics* had appeared in 1941, and in it Cole's inventive *Plastic Man,* a light-hearted feature with a crime-fighting hero who did have a super-power, but a super-power with decidedly comic implications. Clearly, *Plastic Man,* featuring what Joe Brancatelli has called "breathless story telling and a refined, semi-slapstick," combined elements of Cole's "realistic" present and his "big foot" past in a single feature. The balance was not perfectly achieved, however, until the appearance of *Police Comics* No. 13 and the arrival of a maladroit sidekick in Woozy Winks, an out-and-out traditional clown, right down to his costume.

By 1943, Plastic Man ("Plas" to his admirers) had his own comic book, and the feature thrived under Cole's guidance through 1950. Others took over the comic book, and it lasted until 1956. (And there have been revivals since, including an animated TV version in 1979.)

Cole meanwhile had begun a career as a panel cartoonist in such publications as *Collier's* and the *Saturday Evening Post*. By 1955, he had begun a regular collection of *Females by Cole* in *Playboy*. In 1958, a humorous Cole "family strip" called *Betsy and Me* began daily newspaper syndication by the Chicago *Sun-Times*. But on August 15th of that year, Jack Cole took his own life. He left no note and gave no explanation.

We have chosen Plastic Man's first appearance for inclusion here, and the adventure of the arrival of Woozy Winks.

M.W.

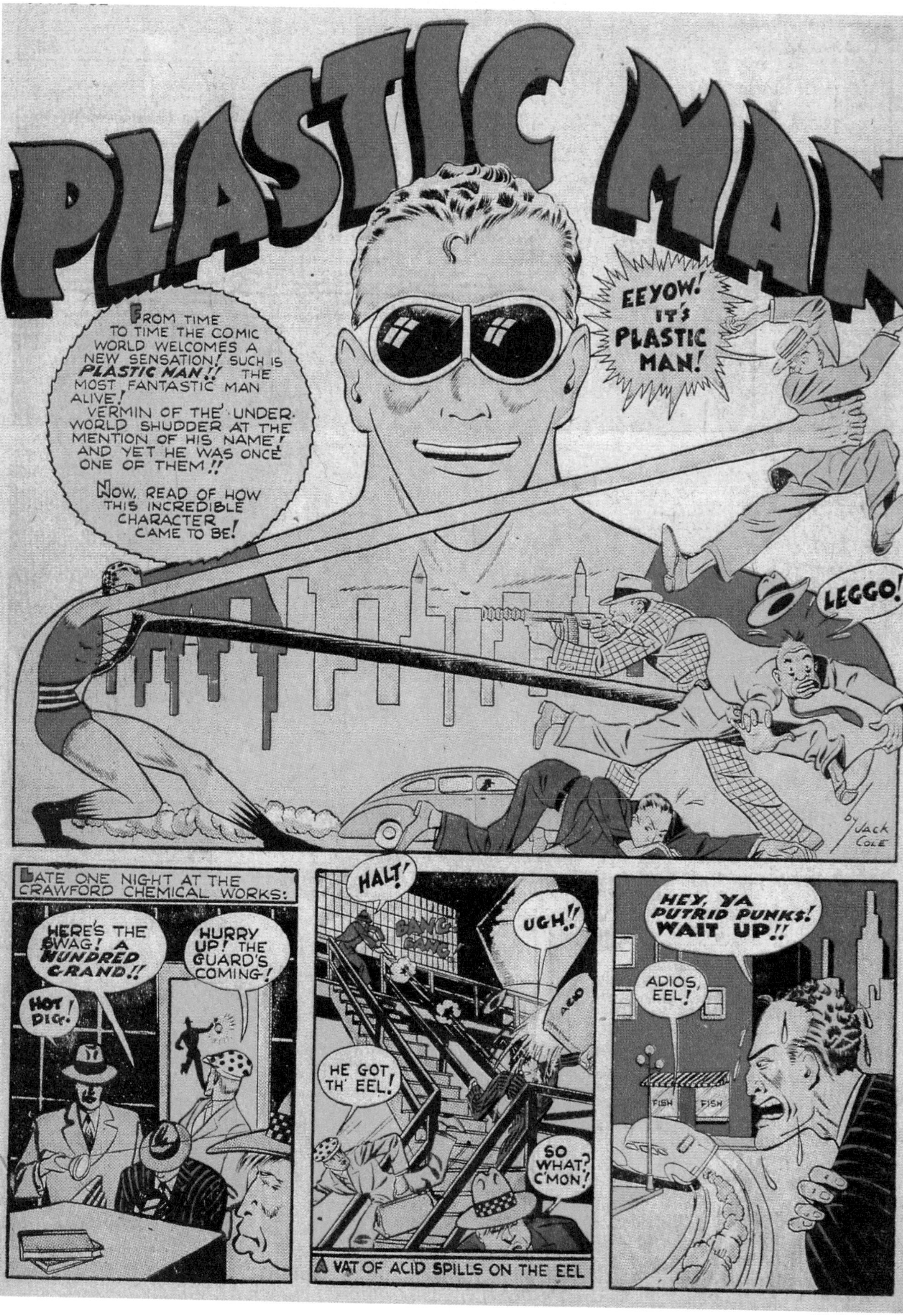
PLASTIC MAN
FROM TIME TO TIME THE COMIC WORLD WELCOMES A NEW SENSATION! SUCH IS PLASTIC MAN!! THE MOST FANTASTIC MAN ALIVE! VERMIN OF THE UNDER-WORLD SHUDDER AT THE MENTION OF HIS NAME! AND YET HE WAS ONCE ONE OF THEM!!
NOW, READ OF HOW THIS INCREDIBLE CHARACTER CAME TO BE!
EEYOW! IT'S PLASTIC MAN!
LEGGO!
by JACK COLE
LATE ONE NIGHT AT THE CRAWFORD CHEMICAL WORKS:
HERE'S THE SWAG! A HUNDRED GRAND!!
HOT DIG!
HURRY UP! THE GUARD'S COMING!
HALT!
UGH!!
HE GOT TH' EEL!
SO WHAT? C'MON!
ACID
A VAT OF ACID SPILLS ON THE EEL
HEY, YA PUTRID PUNKS! WAIT UP!!
ADIOS, EEL!
FISH
FISH

From *Police Comics* No. 1, August 1941.

TH' YELLOW +6*6!! GOTTA GET AWAY.... SOMEHOW.... SOMEPLACE! **CURSE THIS ACID!** IT'S IN THE WOUND AND STINGIN' LIKE BLAZES!!!

LATER IN A DAZE THE EEL WANDERS THROUGH SWAMPS:

MUST...KEEP GOING!! COPS COMING!!

THEN UP A MOUNTAIN SIDE:

LEGS WON'T WORK.... HEAD REELING!! CAN'T GO ON!

THEN, UNCONSCIOUSNESS:

SOME TIME LATER HE AWAKENS:

OH, MY HEAD! WHERE AM I? WHO ARE—??

YOU ARE IN **REST-HAVEN**, SON!

IN HEAVEN?? ME? QUIT TH' KIDDIN'! WHERE I'M GOIN' THE COLDEST DAY IS °300 ABOVE!

REST-HAVEN, MY BOY... A MOUNTAIN RETREAT FAR FROM THE TROUBLED WORLD!

I FOUND YOU ON THE TRAIL THIS MORNING, **EEL O'BRIAN!**

HOW DO YOU KNOW MY NAME?

THE POLICE TRAILED YOU HERE BUT I TURNED THEM AWAY!!

YOU... YOU DID THIS... TOOK A CHANCE LIKE **THAT** FOR ME? WHY??

BECAUSE SOMETHING TOLD ME THAT HERE IS A MAN WHO COULD BECOME A VALUABLE CITIZEN IF HE ONLY HAD THE CHANCE!

COME, WON'T YOU TELL ME YOUR STORY?

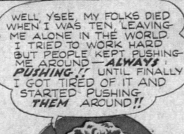

WELL, Y'SEE, MY FOLKS DIED WHEN I WAS TEN, LEAVING ME ALONE IN THE WORLD. I TRIED TO WORK HARD BUT PEOPLE KEPT PUSHING ME AROUND—**ALWAYS PUSHING!!** UNTIL FINALLY I GOT TIRED OF IT AND STARTED PUSHING **THEM** AROUND!!

EEL TELLS HIS STORY

I'D **COMPLETELY** LOST FAITH IN MANKIND UNTIL.... WELL, YOU'VE GIVEN ME A NEW SLANT ON THINGS!

BUT THE IMPORTANT THING RIGHT NOW IS TO REST AND GET WELL!

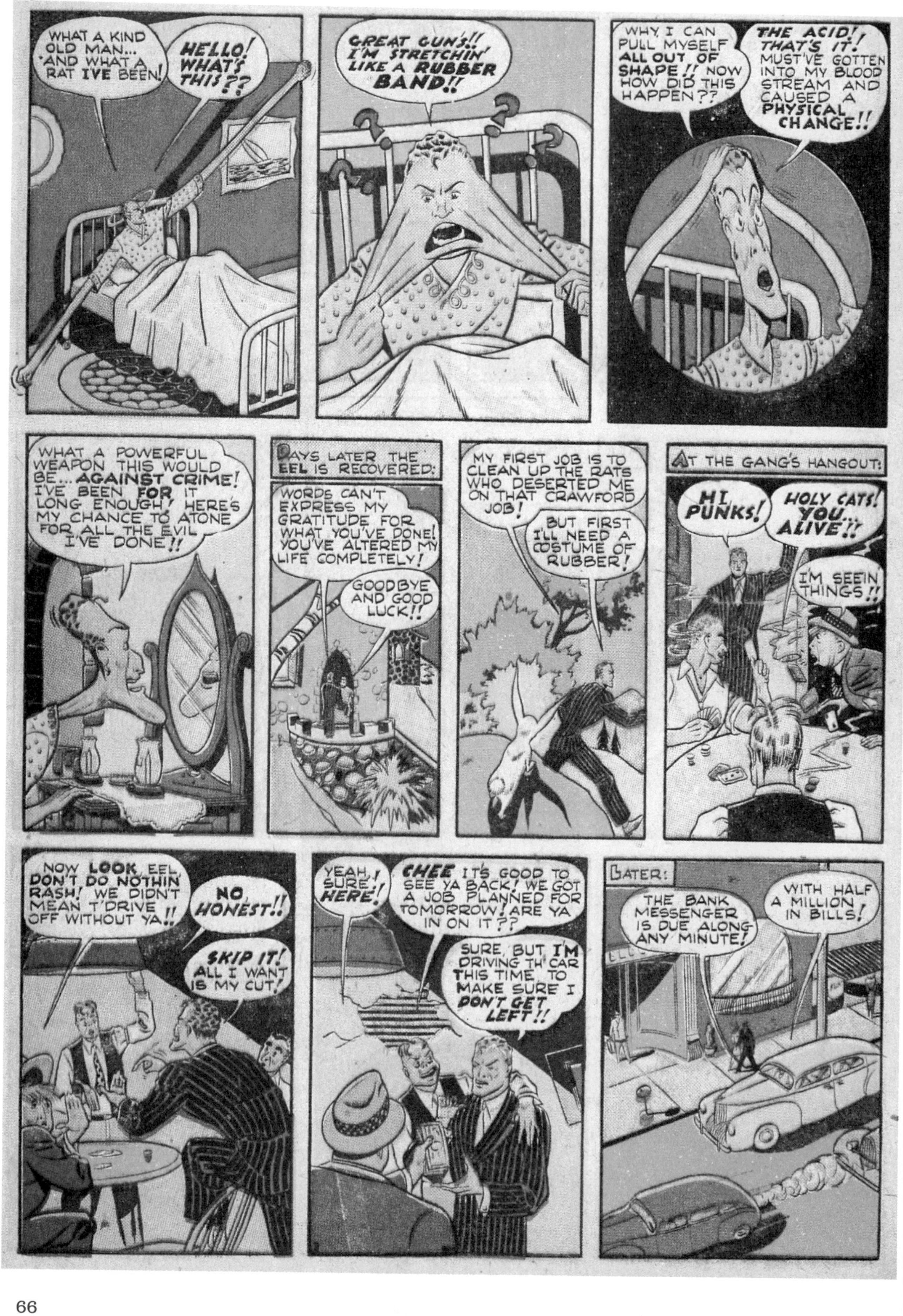

WHAT A KIND OLD MAN... AND WHAT A RAT I'VE BEEN!
HELLO! WHAT'S THIS??
GREAT GUNS!! I'M STRETCHIN' LIKE A RUBBER BAND!!
WHY, I CAN PULL MYSELF ALL OUT OF SHAPE!! NOW HOW DID THIS HAPPEN??
THE ACID! THAT'S IT! MUST'VE GOTTEN INTO MY BLOOD STREAM AND CAUSED A PHYSICAL CHANGE!!
WHAT A POWERFUL WEAPON THIS WOULD BE... AGAINST CRIME! I'VE BEEN FOR IT LONG ENOUGH! HERE'S MY CHANCE TO ATONE FOR ALL THE EVIL I'VE DONE!!
DAYS LATER THE EEL IS RECOVERED:
WORDS CAN'T EXPRESS MY GRATITUDE FOR WHAT YOU'VE DONE! YOU'VE ALTERED MY LIFE COMPLETELY!
GOODBYE AND GOOD LUCK!!
MY FIRST JOB IS TO CLEAN UP THE RATS WHO DESERTED ME ON THAT CRAWFORD JOB!
BUT FIRST I'LL NEED A COSTUME OF RUBBER!
AT THE GANG'S HANGOUT:
HI PUNKS!
HOLY CATS! YOU... ALIVE!!
I'M SEEIN' THINGS!!
NOW LOOK EEL, DON'T DO NOTHIN' RASH! WE DIDN'T MEAN T'DRIVE OFF WITHOUT YA!!
NO, HONEST!!
SKIP IT! ALL I WANT IS MY CUT!
YEAH, SURE! HERE!
CHEE IT'S GOOD TO SEE YA BACK! WE GOT A JOB PLANNED FOR TOMORROW! ARE YA IN ON IT??
SURE, BUT I'M DRIVING TH' CAR THIS TIME TO MAKE SURE I DON'T GET LEFT!!
LATER:
THE BANK MESSENGER IS DUE ALONG ANY MINUTE!
WITH HALF A MILLION IN BILLS!

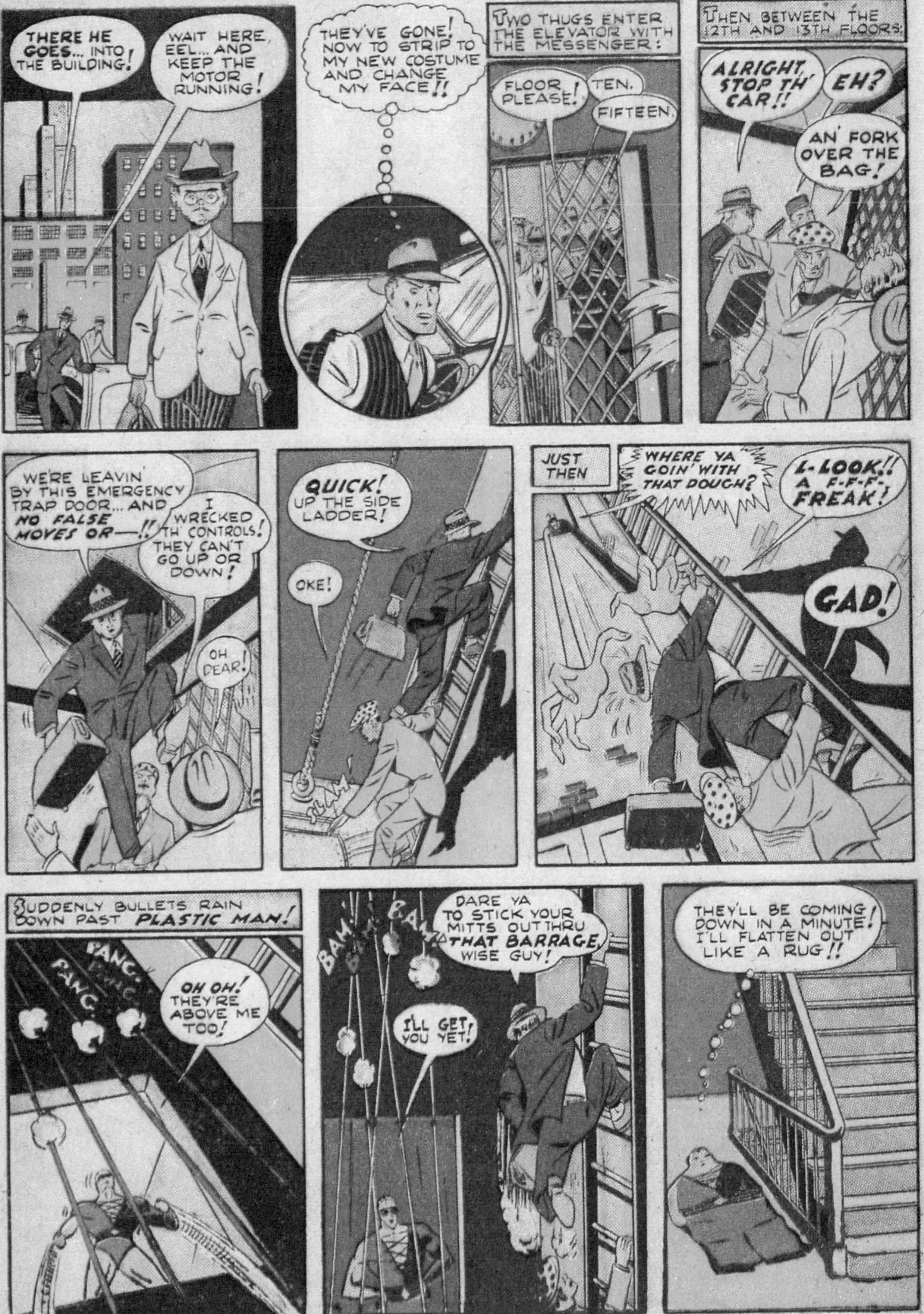
THERE HE GOES... INTO THE BUILDING!
WAIT HERE, EEL... AND KEEP THE MOTOR RUNNING!
THEY'VE GONE! NOW TO STRIP TO MY NEW COSTUME AND CHANGE MY FACE!!
TWO THUGS ENTER THE ELEVATOR WITH THE MESSENGER:
FLOOR PLEASE!
TEN.
FIFTEEN.
THEN BETWEEN THE 12TH AND 13TH FLOORS:
ALRIGHT, STOP TH' CAR!!
EH?
AN' FORK OVER THE BAG!
WE'RE LEAVIN' BY THIS EMERGENCY TRAP DOOR... AND NO FALSE MOVES OR—!!
I WRECKED TH' CONTROLS! THEY CAN'T GO UP OR DOWN!
OH DEAR!
QUICK! UP THE SIDE LADDER!
OKE!
JUST THEN
WHERE YA GOIN' WITH THAT DOUGH?
L-LOOK!! A F-F-F-FREAK!
GAD!
SUDDENLY BULLETS RAIN DOWN PAST PLASTIC MAN!
PANG
PANG
OH OH! THEY'RE ABOVE ME TOO!
BAM
DARE YA TO STICK YOUR MITTS OUT THRU THAT BARRAGE, WISE GUY!
I'LL GET YOU YET!
THEY'LL BE COMING DOWN IN A MINUTE! I'LL FLATTEN OUT LIKE A RUG!!

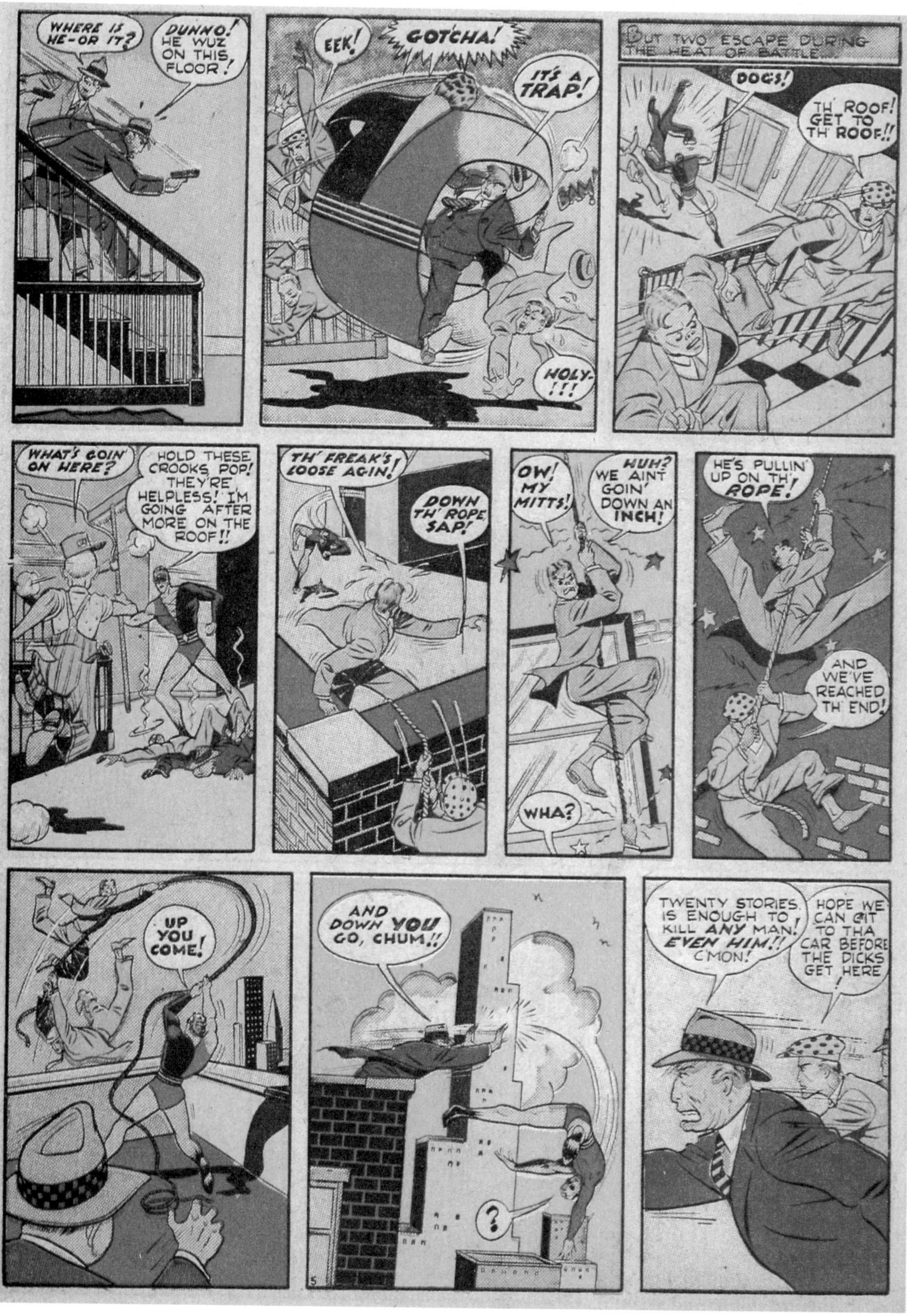
WHERE IS HE-OR IT?
DUNNO! HE WUZ ON THIS FLOOR!
EEK!
GOTCHA!
IT'S A TRAP!
HOLY-!!!
BUT TWO ESCAPE DURING THE HEAT OF BATTLE...
DOGS!
TH' ROOF! GET TO TH' ROOF!!
WHAT'S GOIN' ON HERE?
HOLD THESE CROOKS, POP! THEY'RE HELPLESS! I'M GOING AFTER MORE ON THE ROOF!!
TH' FREAK'S LOOSE AGIN!
DOWN TH' ROPE, SAP!
OW! MY MITTS!
HUH? WE AINT GOIN' DOWN AN INCH!
WHA?
HE'S PULLIN' UP ON TH' ROPE!
AND WE'VE REACHED TH' END!
UP YOU COME!
AND DOWN YOU GO, CHUM!!
?
TWENTY STORIES IS ENOUGH TO KILL ANY MAN! EVEN HIM!! C'MON!
HOPE WE CAN GIT TO THA CAR BEFORE THE DICKS GET HERE!

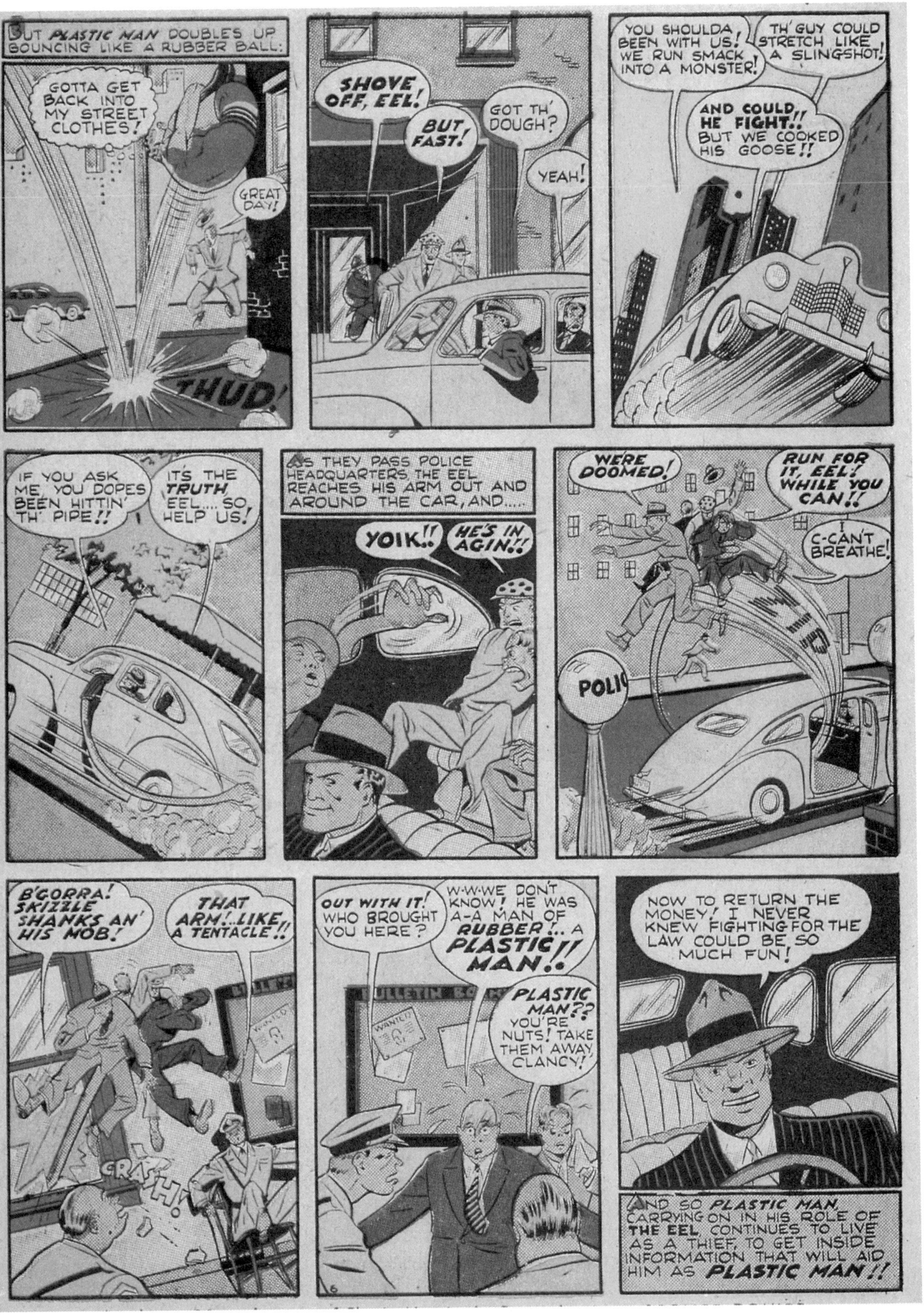
BUT PLASTIC MAN DOUBLES UP BOUNCING LIKE A RUBBER BALL:
GOTTA GET BACK INTO MY STREET CLOTHES!
GREAT DAY!
THUD!
SHOVE OFF, EEL!
BUT FAST!
GOT TH' DOUGH?
YEAH!
YOU SHOULDA BEEN WITH US! WE RUN SMACK INTO A MONSTER!
TH' GUY COULD STRETCH LIKE A SLINGSHOT!
AND COULD HE FIGHT!! BUT WE COOKED HIS GOOSE!!
IF YOU ASK ME, YOU DOPES BEEN HITTIN' TH' PIPE!!
IT'S THE TRUTH, EEL.... SO, HELP US!
AS THEY PASS POLICE HEADQUARTERS, THE EEL REACHES HIS ARM OUT AND AROUND THE CAR, AND....
YOIK!!
HE'S IN AGIN!!
WE'RE DOOMED!
RUN FOR IT, EEL! WHILE YOU CAN!!
I C-CAN'T BREATHE!
POLIC
B'GORRA! SKIZZLE SHANKS AN' HIS MOB!
THAT ARM!..LIKE A TENTACLE!!
CRASH!
OUT WITH IT! WHO BROUGHT YOU HERE?
W-W-WE DON'T KNOW! HE WAS A-A MAN OF RUBBER!.. A PLASTIC MAN!!
BULLETIN BO
WANTED
PLASTIC MAN?? YOU'RE NUTS! TAKE THEM AWAY, CLANCY!
NOW TO RETURN THE MONEY! I NEVER KNEW FIGHTING FOR THE LAW COULD BE SO MUCH FUN!
AND SO PLASTIC MAN, CARRYING ON IN HIS ROLE OF THE EEL, CONTINUES TO LIVE AS A THIEF, TO GET INSIDE INFORMATION THAT WILL AID HIM AS PLASTIC MAN!!

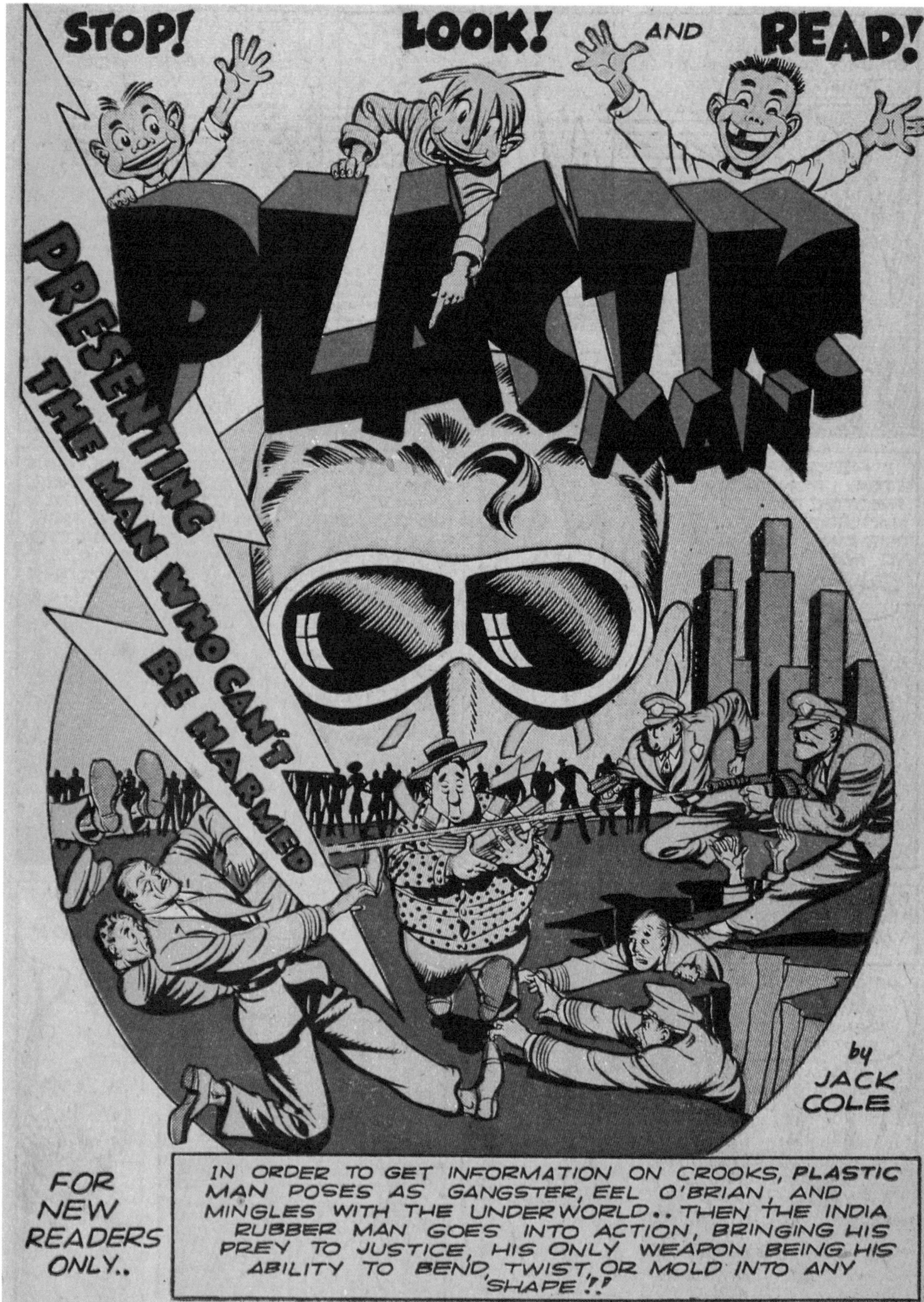
STOP! LOOK! AND READ!
PLASTIC MAN
PRESENTING THE MAN WHO CAN'T BE HARMED
by JACK COLE
FOR NEW READERS ONLY..
IN ORDER TO GET INFORMATION ON CROOKS, PLASTIC MAN POSES AS GANGSTER, EEL O'BRIAN, AND MINGLES WITH THE UNDERWORLD.. THEN THE INDIA RUBBER MAN GOES INTO ACTION, BRINGING HIS PREY TO JUSTICE, HIS ONLY WEAPON BEING HIS ABILITY TO BEND, TWIST, OR MOLD INTO ANY SHAPE!!

From *Police Comics* No. 13, November 1942.

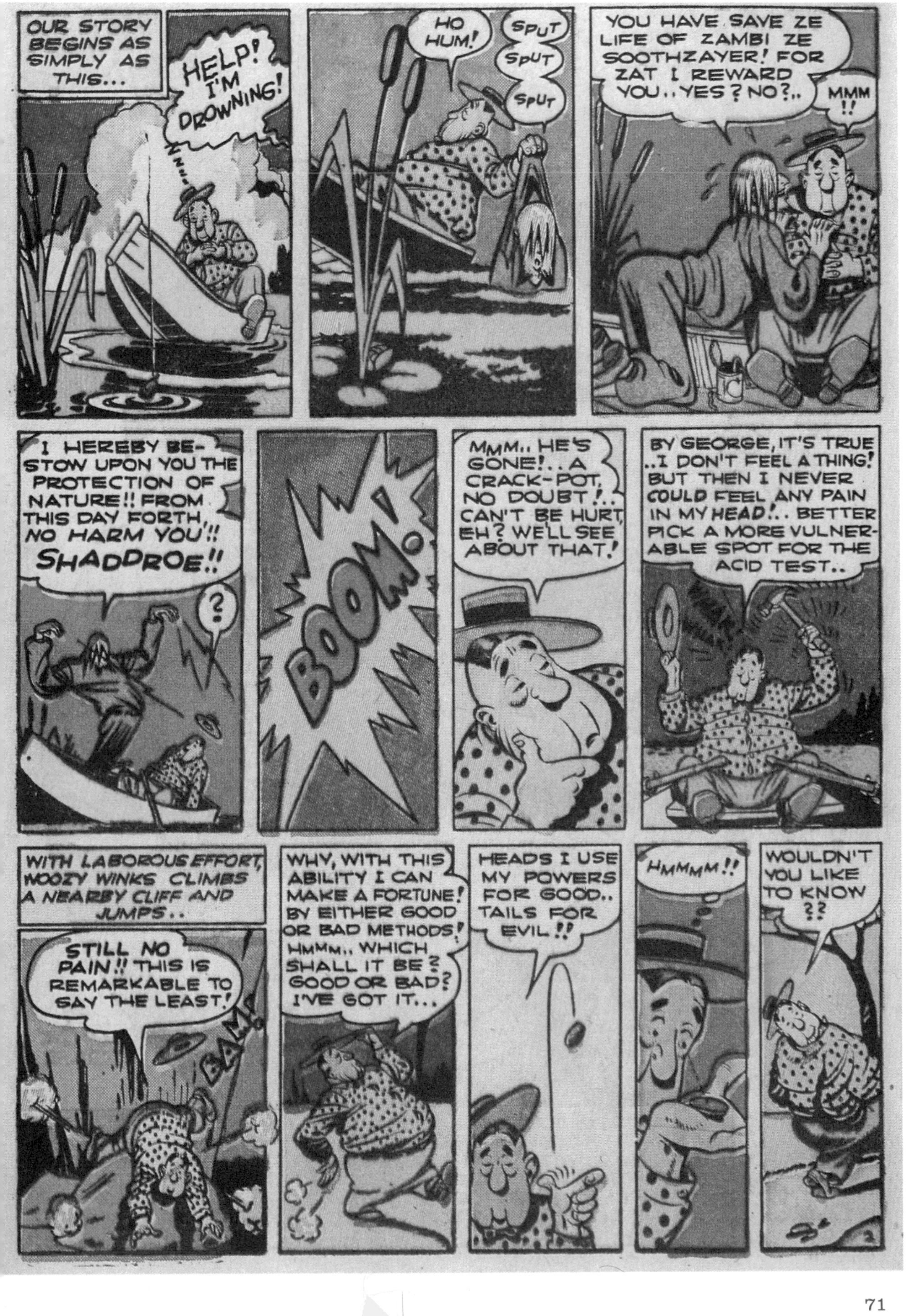

OUR STORY BEGINS AS SIMPLY AS THIS...
HELP! I'M DROWNING!
HO HUM!
SPUT SPUT SPUT
YOU HAVE SAVE ZE LIFE OF ZAMBI ZE SOOTHZAYER! FOR ZAT I REWARD YOU.. YES? NO?..
MMM !!
I HEREBY BE-STOW UPON YOU THE PROTECTION OF NATURE!! FROM THIS DAY FORTH, NO HARM YOU!! SHADDROE!!
?
BOOM!
MMM.. HE'S GONE!.. A CRACK-POT, NO DOUBT!.. CAN'T BE HURT, EH? WE'LL SEE ABOUT THAT!
BY GEORGE, IT'S TRUE ..I DON'T FEEL A THING! BUT THEN I NEVER COULD FEEL ANY PAIN IN MY HEAD!.. BETTER PICK A MORE VULNER-ABLE SPOT FOR THE ACID TEST..
WITH LABOROUS EFFORT, WOOZY WINKS CLIMBS A NEARBY CLIFF AND JUMPS..
STILL NO PAIN!! THIS IS REMARKABLE TO SAY THE LEAST!
BAM!
WHY, WITH THIS ABILITY I CAN MAKE A FORTUNE! BY EITHER GOOD OR BAD METHODS! HMMM.. WHICH SHALL IT BE? GOOD OR BAD? I'VE GOT IT...
HEADS I USE MY POWERS FOR GOOD.. TAILS FOR EVIL!!
HMMMM!!
WOULDN'T YOU LIKE TO KNOW ??

SOME TIME LATER, THE POLICE RECEIVE A CALL..

THIS IS HOMER TWITCHEL, THE GREAT SCULPTER.. HOMER COME QUICKLY.. MY PRICELESS STATUES HAVE BEEN STOLEN!

OKAY, HOMER ..DON'T GET SO UPSET ABOUT IT !!

DON'T GET UPSET, HE SAYS!

HEY PLASTIC! THINK YOU CAN STOP RUBBERING OUT THE WINDOW LONG ENOUGH TO ANSWER A CALL?

OH, OH.. GOTTA GO MIKE!

C* !!# JUS' WHEN I HAD Y'LICKED!

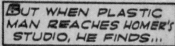

BUT WHEN PLASTIC MAN REACHES HOMER'S STUDIO, HE FINDS...

?? THE PLACE IS EMPTY!! IF THIS IS A JOKE..!

THAT'S QUEER.. THE WORD "HELP" SPELLED OUT IN CLAY ON THIS BOOK..

HANS & GRETHEL

HELP

BUT WHY ON A BOOK ?? AND WHY, "HANS AND GRETHEL"?? ..UNLESS..

HANS AND GRETHEL DROPPED BREAD CRUMBS TO MARK A TRAIL.. PERHAPS HOMER TWITCHEL DROPPED CLAY!

AH, HERE'S A PIECE!

OUT INTO THE STREET HE FOLLOWS THE TRAIL..

HERE'S ANOTHER!

PLASTIC MAN, GUTTER SNIPING! TCH! TCH! TCH!!

WHY, DADDY ?

MEANWHILE NOT FAR AWAY...

OHHHHHH.... MY LIFE'S WORK.. RUINED! WHY DID YOU DO IT? WHY KIDNAP ME?

BOSS' ORDERS!.. NOW WHERE DID I PUT THAT SAW?

3

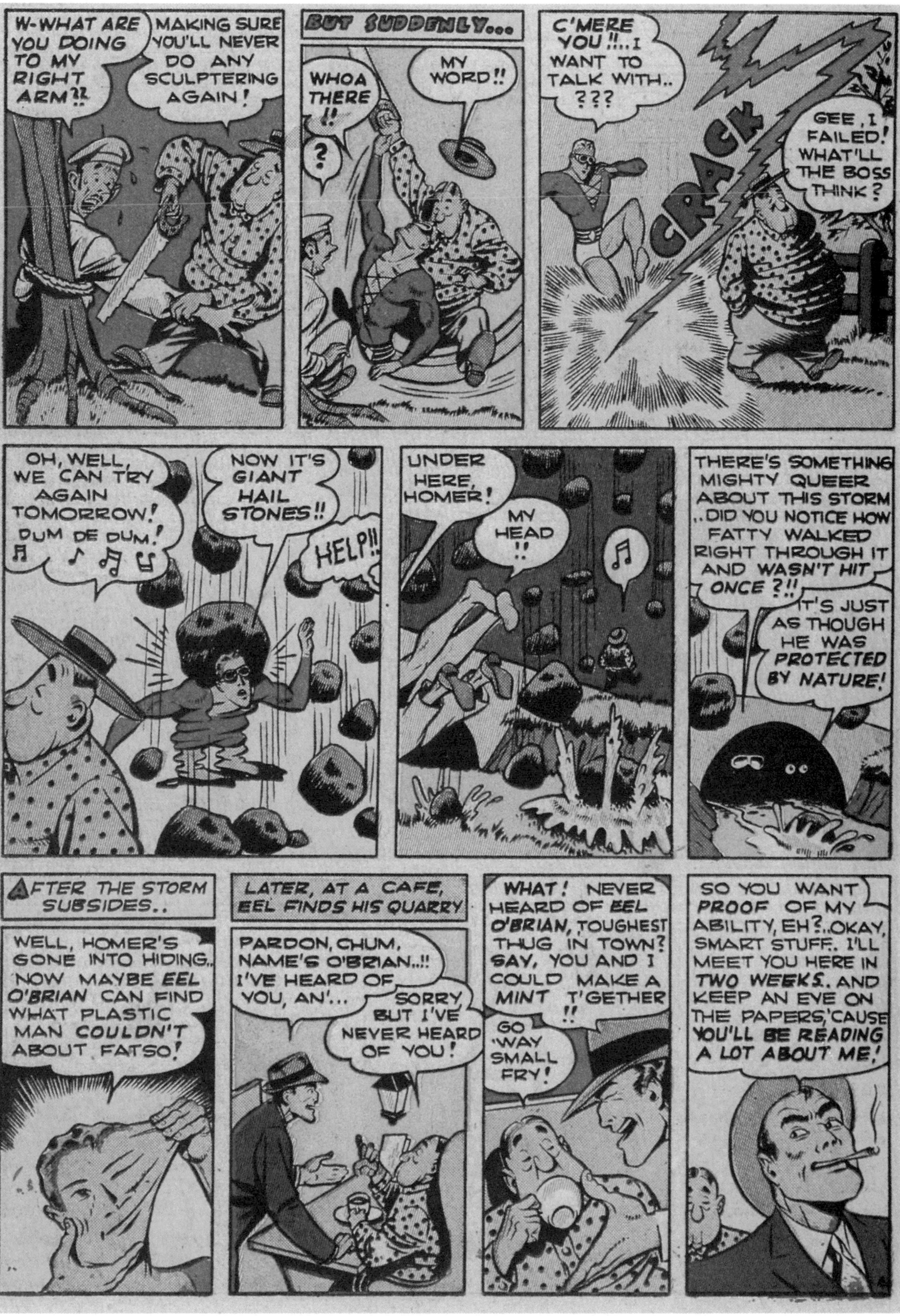
W-WHAT ARE YOU DOING TO MY RIGHT ARM??
MAKING SURE YOU'LL NEVER DO ANY SCULPTERING AGAIN!
BUT SUDDENLY...
WHOA THERE !!
?
MY WORD!!
C'MERE YOU!!...I WANT TO TALK WITH.. ???
CRACK
GEE, I FAILED! WHAT'LL THE BOSS THINK?
OH, WELL, WE CAN TRY AGAIN TOMORROW! DUM DE DUM!
NOW IT'S GIANT HAIL STONES!!
HELP!!
UNDER HERE, HOMER!
MY HEAD !!
THERE'S SOMETHING MIGHTY QUEER ABOUT THIS STORM ..DID YOU NOTICE HOW FATTY WALKED RIGHT THROUGH IT AND WASN'T HIT ONCE?!!
IT'S JUST AS THOUGH HE WAS PROTECTED BY NATURE!
AFTER THE STORM SUBSIDES..
WELL, HOMER'S GONE INTO HIDING.. NOW MAYBE EEL O'BRIAN CAN FIND WHAT PLASTIC MAN COULDN'T ABOUT FATSO!
LATER, AT A CAFE, EEL FINDS HIS QUARRY
PARDON, CHUM. NAME'S O'BRIAN..!! I'VE HEARD OF YOU, AN'...
SORRY BUT I'VE NEVER HEARD OF YOU!
WHAT! NEVER HEARD OF EEL O'BRIAN, TOUGHEST THUG IN TOWN? SAY, YOU AND I COULD MAKE A MINT T'GETHER !!
GO 'WAY SMALL FRY!
SO YOU WANT PROOF OF MY ABILITY, EH?..OKAY, SMART STUFF.. I'LL MEET YOU HERE IN TWO WEEKS.. AND KEEP AN EYE ON THE PAPERS, 'CAUSE YOU'LL BE READING A LOT ABOUT ME!

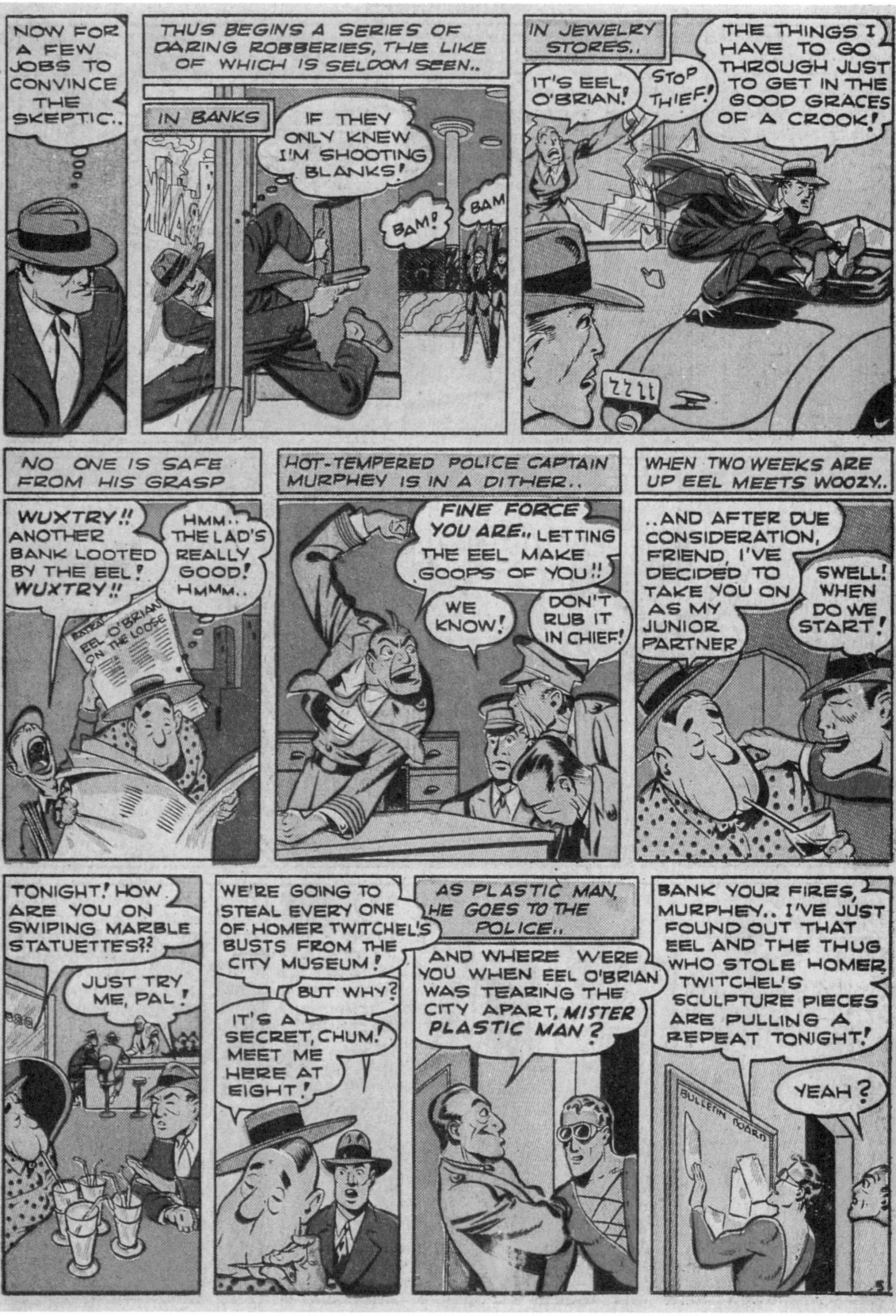

NOW FOR A FEW JOBS TO CONVINCE THE SKEPTIC..
THUS BEGINS A SERIES OF DARING ROBBERIES, THE LIKE OF WHICH IS SELDOM SEEN..
IN BANKS
IF THEY ONLY KNEW I'M SHOOTING BLANKS!
BAM!
BAM
IN JEWELRY STORES..
IT'S EEL O'BRIAN!
STOP THIEF!
THE THINGS I HAVE TO GO THROUGH JUST TO GET IN THE GOOD GRACES OF A CROOK!
NO ONE IS SAFE FROM HIS GRASP
WUXTRY!! ANOTHER BANK LOOTED BY THE EEL! WUXTRY!!
HMM.. THE LAD'S REALLY GOOD! HMMM..
EEL O'BRIAN ON THE LOOSE
HOT-TEMPERED POLICE CAPTAIN MURPHEY IS IN A DITHER..
FINE FORCE YOU ARE.. LETTING THE EEL MAKE GOOPS OF YOU!!
WE KNOW!
DON'T RUB IT IN CHIEF!
WHEN TWO WEEKS ARE UP EEL MEETS WOOZY..
..AND AFTER DUE CONSIDERATION, FRIEND, I'VE DECIDED TO TAKE YOU ON AS MY JUNIOR PARTNER
SWELL! WHEN DO WE START!
TONIGHT! HOW ARE YOU ON SWIPING MARBLE STATUETTES??
JUST TRY ME, PAL!
WE'RE GOING TO STEAL EVERY ONE OF HOMER TWITCHEL'S BUSTS FROM THE CITY MUSEUM!
BUT WHY?
IT'S A SECRET, CHUM! MEET ME HERE AT EIGHT!
AS PLASTIC MAN, HE GOES TO THE POLICE..
AND WHERE WERE YOU WHEN EEL O'BRIAN WAS TEARING THE CITY APART, MISTER PLASTIC MAN?
BANK YOUR FIRES, MURPHEY.. I'VE JUST FOUND OUT THAT EEL AND THE THUG WHO STOLE HOMER TWITCHEL'S SCULPTURE PIECES ARE PULLING A REPEAT TONIGHT!
BULLETIN BOARD
YEAH?

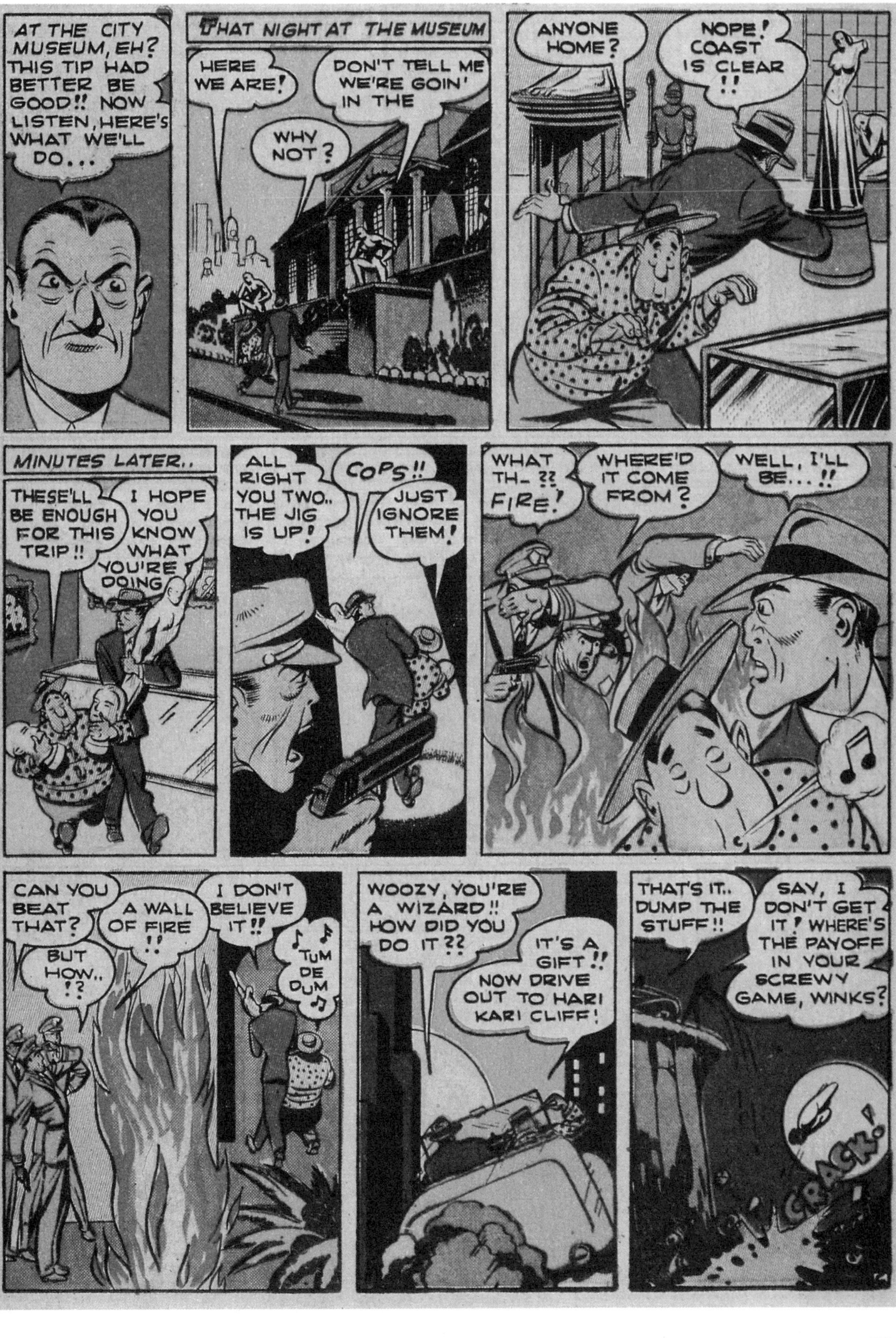
AT THE CITY MUSEUM, EH? THIS TIP HAD BETTER BE GOOD!! NOW LISTEN, HERE'S WHAT WE'LL DO...
THAT NIGHT AT THE MUSEUM
HERE WE ARE!
DON'T TELL ME WE'RE GOIN' IN THE
WHY NOT?
ANYONE HOME?
NOPE! COAST IS CLEAR !!
MINUTES LATER..
THESE'LL BE ENOUGH FOR THIS TRIP!!
I HOPE YOU KNOW WHAT YOU'RE DOING
ALL RIGHT YOU TWO.. THE JIG IS UP!
COPS!!
JUST IGNORE THEM!
WHAT TH- ?? FIRE!
WHERE'D IT COME FROM?
WELL, I'LL BE...!!
CAN YOU BEAT THAT?
A WALL OF FIRE !!
I DON'T BELIEVE IT!!
BUT HOW.. !?
TUM DE DUM
WOOZY, YOU'RE A WIZARD!! HOW DID YOU DO IT??
IT'S A GIFT!! NOW DRIVE OUT TO HARI KARI CLIFF!
THAT'S IT.. DUMP THE STUFF!!
SAY, I DON'T GET IT! WHERE'S THE PAYOFF IN YOUR SCREWY GAME, WINKS?
CRACK!

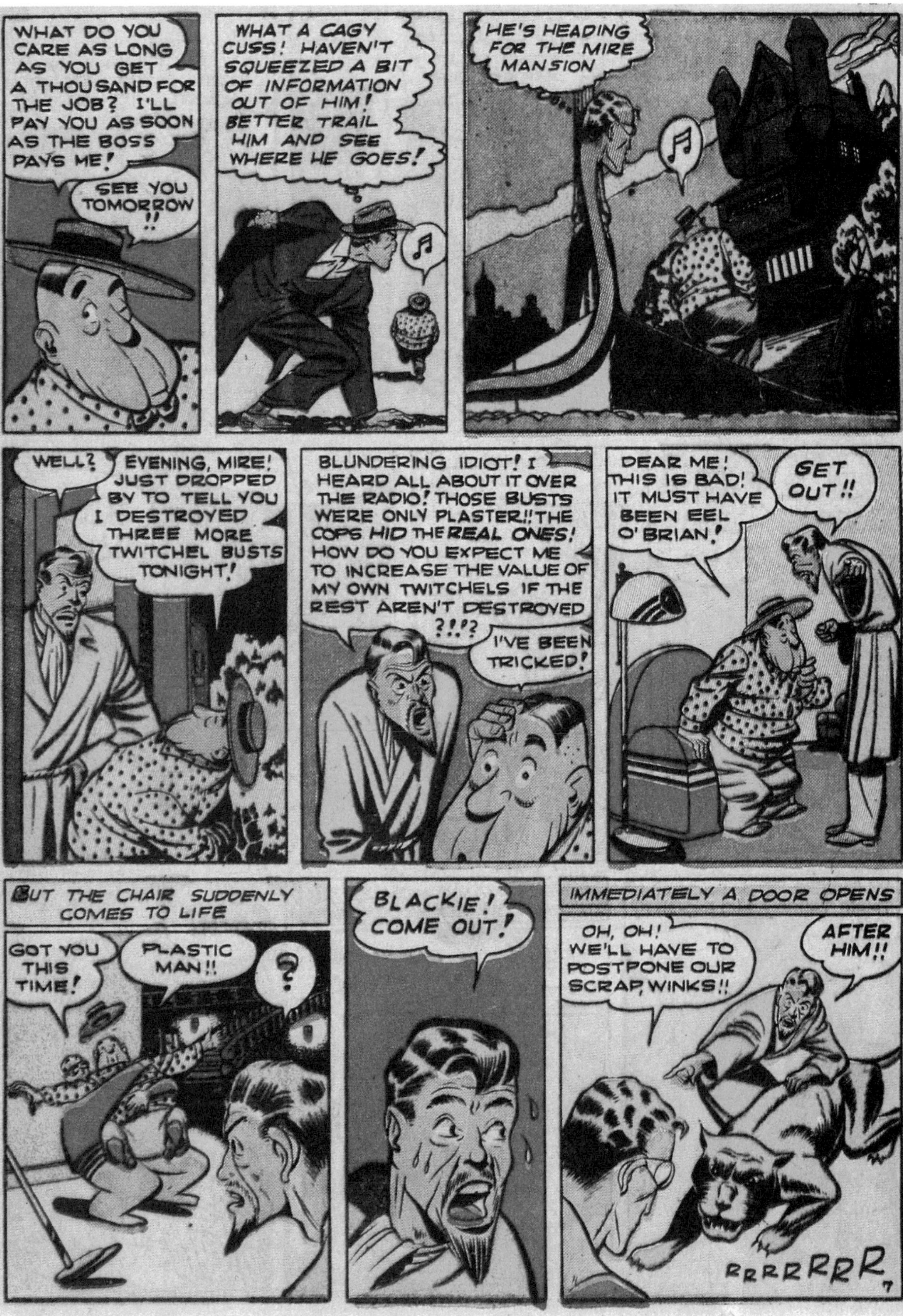
WHAT DO YOU CARE AS LONG AS YOU GET A THOUSAND FOR THE JOB? I'LL PAY YOU AS SOON AS THE BOSS PAYS ME!
SEE YOU TOMORROW !!
WHAT A CAGY CUSS! HAVEN'T SQUEEZED A BIT OF INFORMATION OUT OF HIM! BETTER TRAIL HIM AND SEE WHERE HE GOES!
HE'S HEADING FOR THE MIRE MANSION
WELL?
EVENING, MIRE! JUST DROPPED BY TO TELL YOU I DESTROYED THREE MORE TWITCHEL BUSTS TONIGHT!
BLUNDERING IDIOT! I HEARD ALL ABOUT IT OVER THE RADIO! THOSE BUSTS WERE ONLY PLASTER!! THE COPS HID THE REAL ONES! HOW DO YOU EXPECT ME TO INCREASE THE VALUE OF MY OWN TWITCHELS IF THE REST AREN'T DESTROYED ?!!?
I'VE BEEN TRICKED!
DEAR ME! THIS IS BAD! IT MUST HAVE BEEN EEL O'BRIAN!
GET OUT!!
BUT THE CHAIR SUDDENLY COMES TO LIFE
GOT YOU THIS TIME!
PLASTIC MAN!!
?
BLACKIE! COME OUT!
IMMEDIATELY A DOOR OPENS
OH, OH! WE'LL HAVE TO POSTPONE OUR SCRAP, WINKS!!
AFTER HIM!!
RRRRRRR
7

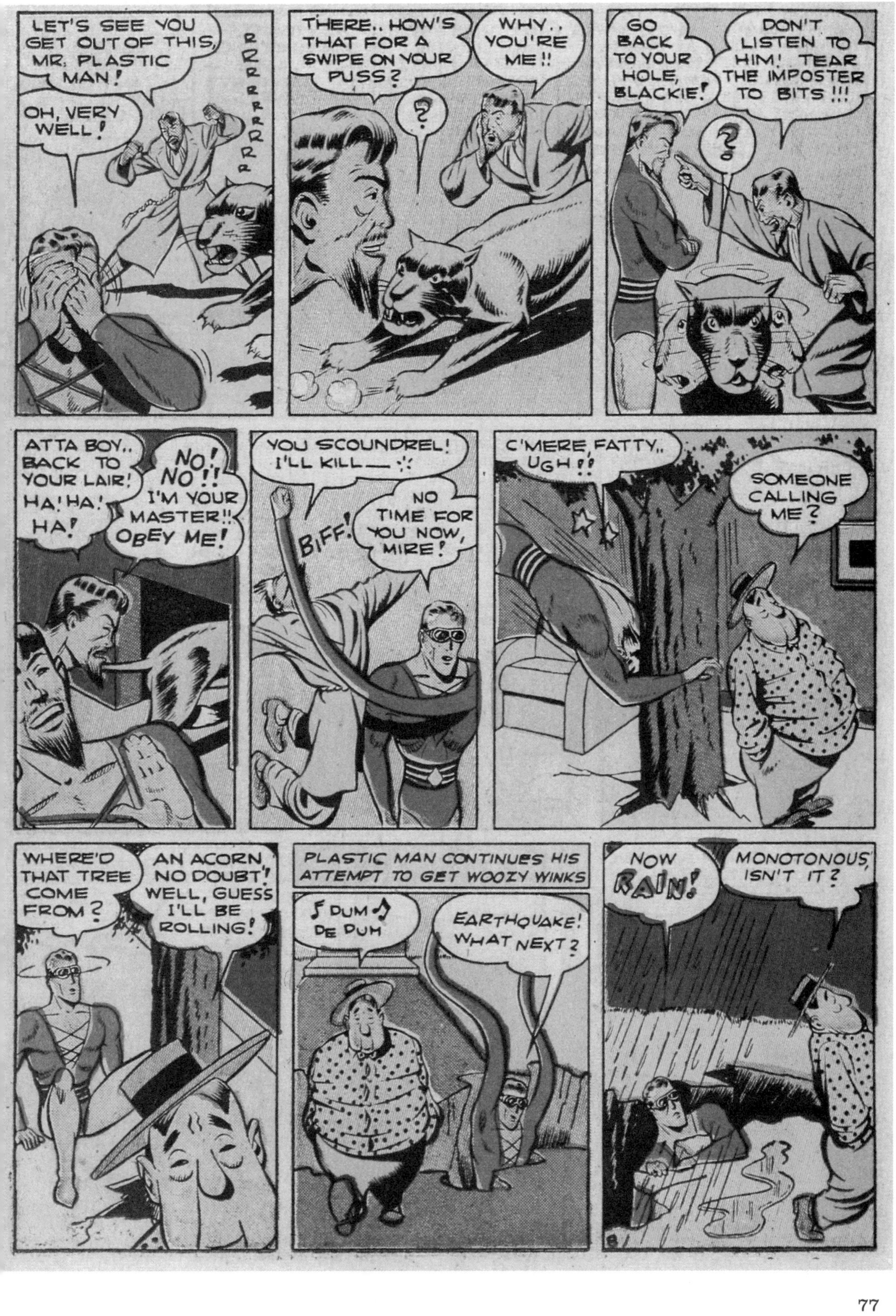
LET'S SEE YOU GET OUT OF THIS, MR. PLASTIC MAN!
RRRRRRRRRR
OH, VERY WELL!
THERE.. HOW'S THAT FOR A SWIPE ON YOUR PUSS?
WHY.. YOU'RE ME!!
?
GO BACK TO YOUR HOLE, BLACKIE!
DON'T LISTEN TO HIM! TEAR THE IMPOSTER TO BITS!!!
?
ATTA BOY.. BACK TO YOUR LAIR! HA! HA! HA!
NO! NO!! I'M YOUR MASTER!! OBEY ME!
YOU SCOUNDREL! I'LL KILL—
BIFF!
NO TIME FOR YOU NOW, MIRE!
C'MERE, FATTY.. UGH!!
SOMEONE CALLING ME?
WHERE'D THAT TREE COME FROM?
AN ACORN NO DOUBT! WELL, GUESS I'LL BE ROLLING!
PLASTIC MAN CONTINUES HIS ATTEMPT TO GET WOOZY WINKS
DUM DE DUM
EARTHQUAKE! WHAT NEXT?
NOW RAIN!
MONOTONOUS, ISN'T IT?

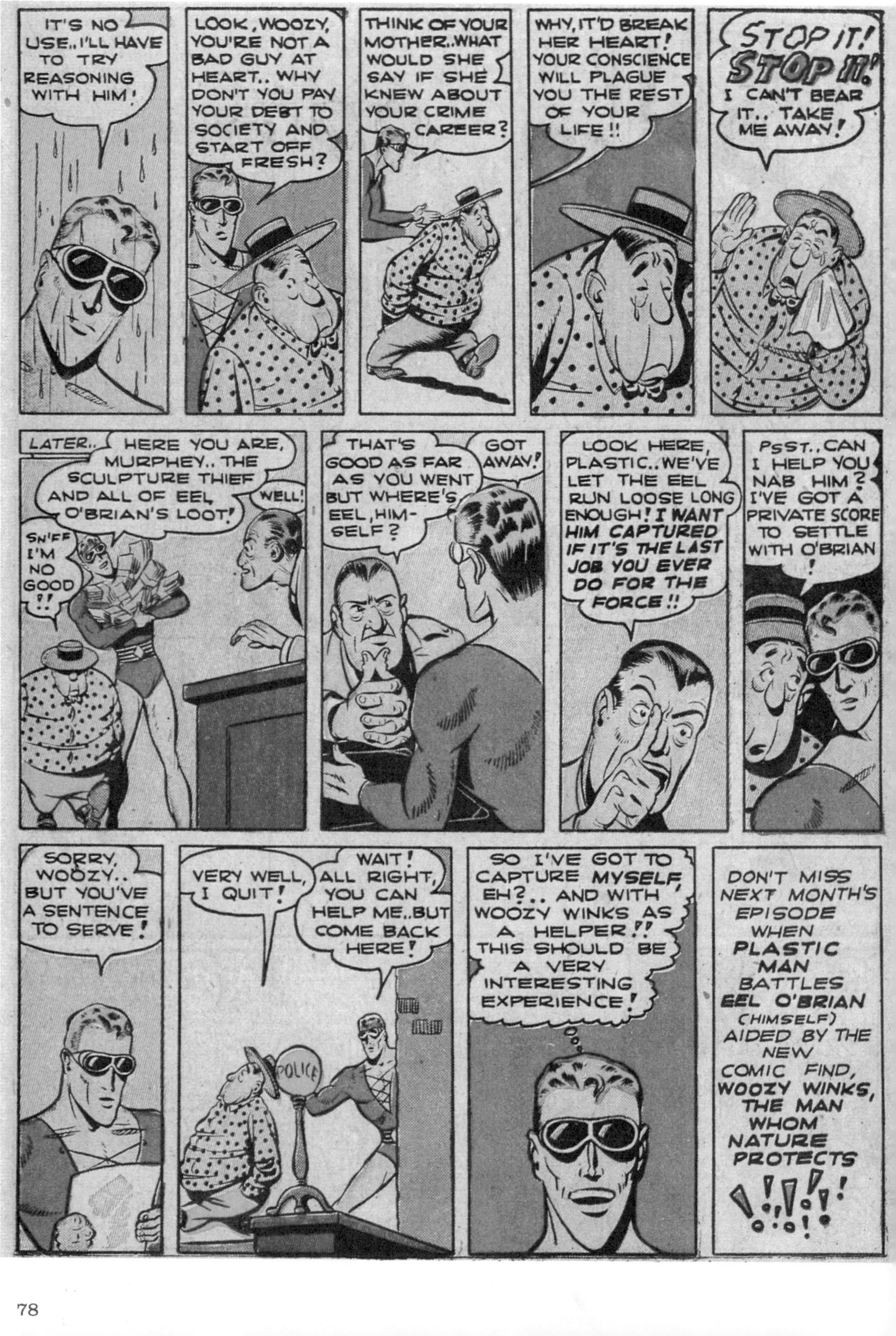
IT'S NO USE.. I'LL HAVE TO TRY REASONING WITH HIM!
LOOK, WOOZY, YOU'RE NOT A BAD GUY AT HEART.. WHY DON'T YOU PAY YOUR DEBT TO SOCIETY AND START OFF FRESH?
THINK OF YOUR MOTHER..WHAT WOULD SHE SAY IF SHE KNEW ABOUT YOUR CRIME CAREER?
WHY, IT'D BREAK HER HEART! YOUR CONSCIENCE WILL PLAGUE YOU THE REST OF YOUR LIFE!!
STOP IT! STOP IT! I CAN'T BEAR IT.. TAKE ME AWAY!
LATER..
HERE YOU ARE, MURPHEY.. THE SCULPTURE THIEF AND ALL OF EEL O'BRIAN'S LOOT!
WELL!
SNIFF I'M NO GOOD!!
THAT'S GOOD AS FAR AS YOU WENT BUT WHERE'S EEL, HIMSELF?
GOT AWAY!
LOOK HERE, PLASTIC..WE'VE LET THE EEL RUN LOOSE LONG ENOUGH! I WANT HIM CAPTURED IF IT'S THE LAST JOB YOU EVER DO FOR THE FORCE!!
PSST.. CAN I HELP YOU NAB HIM? I'VE GOT A PRIVATE SCORE TO SETTLE WITH O'BRIAN!
SORRY, WOOZY.. BUT YOU'VE A SENTENCE TO SERVE!
VERY WELL, I QUIT!
WAIT! ALL RIGHT, YOU CAN HELP ME..BUT COME BACK HERE!
POLICE
SO I'VE GOT TO CAPTURE MYSELF, EH?.. AND WITH WOOZY WINKS AS A HELPER!! THIS SHOULD BE A VERY INTERESTING EXPERIENCE!
DON'T MISS NEXT MONTH'S EPISODE WHEN PLASTIC MAN BATTLES EEL O'BRIAN (HIMSELF) AIDED BY THE NEW COMIC FIND, WOOZY WINKS, THE MAN WHOM NATURE PROTECTS
!!!!!

About "Captain Marvel" and C. C. Beck

Captain Marvel was the result, first, of an executive decision, and, following on that, of the fortuitous coming together of exceptional talents.

The decision came when Fawcett Publications declared itself a relatively late entrant into the highly profitable comic-book field. C. C. Beck, a cartoonist who had contributed gag panels to Fawcett's humor magazines, was brought together with writer Bill Parker. They came up with an orphaned big-city newsboy who could transform himself into a super-being. Billy Batson was lured into an abandoned subway station by a mysterious figure, led past grotesque depictions of the Seven Deadly Enemies of Man (actually the Seven Deadly Sins of medieval Catholic theology), and taken to an ancient, enthroned magician who was somehow Egyptian. This sage gave Billy a magic word, "Shazam," based on the initials of a polyglot of Biblical characters, Greek and Roman deities, and mythic heroes. Uttering this word, Billy would invoke a lightning bolt and convert himself into Captain Marvel. (And, incidentally, as if to domesticate the whole picture, the Captain was physically modeled on the actor Fred MacMurray, and the Captain's archenemy, Dr. Sivana, on C. C. Beck's neighborhood pharmacist.)

Beck's graphic renderings were simple, uncluttered, cartoon-oriented, and appropriately humorous. And Captain Marvel was a huge success. He was soon appearing in a whole group of magazines and had spun off a Captain Marvel, Jr., a Mary Marvel—even a Marvel Bunny.

Beck needed a whole roomful of assistants to help out. The foremost of these was Pete Costanza, who worked directly with Beck and also supervised the other helpers. Meanwhile, in 1941, the feature had found its perfect author in the fanciful Otto Binder. Binder understood that the *Captain Marvel* stories were best treated as light-hearted children's fare, and knew that strong rationalizations and pseudo-scientific explanations of its magic events and magic powers were not only unnecessary, they might simply get in the way of the psychological truths the magic imparted. Binder's introduction of Tawky Tawny, a "civilized," talking jungle tiger, was indicative: Billy befriends him and he becomes a sports-jacketed American suburbanite, confirming for the feature's readers that the savage impulse can be domesticated—with a sense of humor.

Both Charles Calvin Beck and Otto Binder came from the American Midwest. Beck was born in Zumbrote, Minnesota, in 1910. He studied at the Chicago Academy of Fine Arts and the University of Minnesota, and was a humor illustrator for Fawcett by 1933. Binder was born a year after Beck in

Bessemer, Michigan, and had been writing for pulp and short-story magazines and, beginning in 1939, for comic books.

The various Marvel-family comic books continued with high success until 1953. National Comics had brought legal action against Fawcett, claiming that the Captain infringed upon its Superman copyrights, and Fawcett finally decided that fighting the suit wasn't worth the money and the effort. (Insiders insist, incidentally, that there were other, less successful super-heroes that were closer to Superman in conception than was Captain Marvel.)

Our selection, *Captain Marvel Battles the Plot Against the Universe,* comes from 1949 and the one-hundredth issue of *Captain Marvel Adventures.* Its title is perhaps the only awkward moment in this little masterpiece of breakneck whimsy, as Binder's plotting is rendered and embellished in Beck's and Costanza's drawings. The elements are, as usual, wonderfully preposterous: pseudo-science, traditional myth, space travel, time travel—all are invoked with no inhibition, and the feature's pseudo-heaven (the Rock of Eternity) is prominently featured. If a new magic metal is needed to get the story started, let's have one: shazamium. If another is needed to keep it going, let's have another: sivanium. If a third is required to resolve things, so be it: marvelium. Most indicative of the tone of it all, the artists give us Captain Marvel's torture at the hands of Sivana in the "splash panel" to Part 3—he gets some ink on his red suit from a squirt gun, some itching powder, and (torture of tortures!) a swift kick in the behind.

The story is sustained by an innocent, unapologetic fascination with its own willful fancy, and by our delight in following that fancy—those things, plus an absolute refusal to take itself seriously. And to bring it all off involves a balance of attitudes, of story elements, of pictures—and balances within balances—that are not nearly so easy to achieve and to sustain as they seem.

Otto Binder died in 1974, but C. C. Beck has remained active, and he illustrated the first few issues of a revived *Captain Marvel* comic book (titled *Shazam!*) in the 1970s. Ironically, the comic book was published by National, the company that had put the Captain out of business twenty years earlier.

M.W.

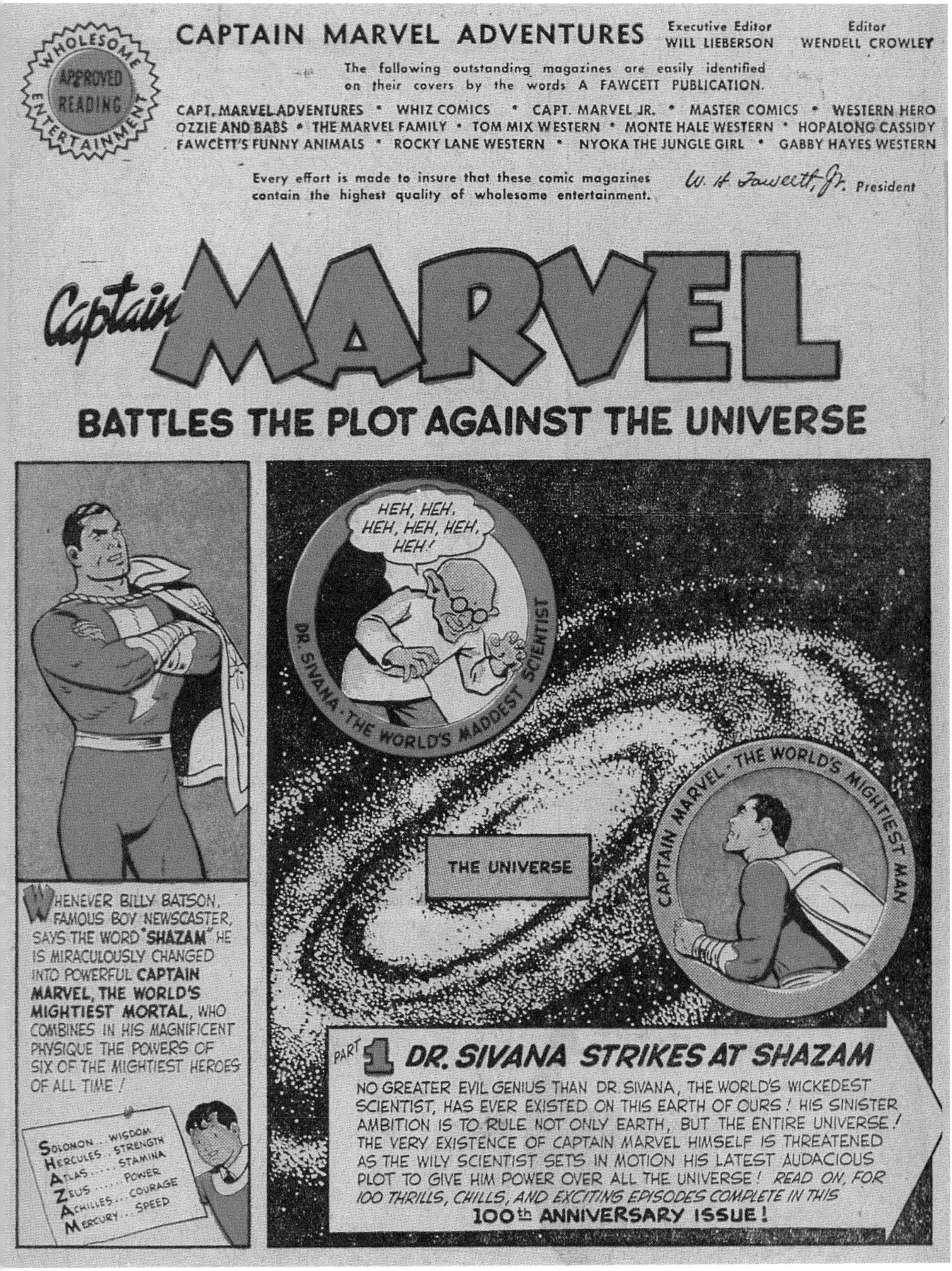
WHOLESOME APPROVED READING ENTERTAINMENT
CAPTAIN MARVEL ADVENTURES
Executive Editor WILL LIEBERSON
Editor WENDELL CROWLEY
The following outstanding magazines are easily identified on their covers by the words A FAWCETT PUBLICATION.
CAPT. MARVEL ADVENTURES • WHIZ COMICS • CAPT. MARVEL JR. • MASTER COMICS • WESTERN HERO
OZZIE AND BABS • THE MARVEL FAMILY • TOM MIX WESTERN • MONTE HALE WESTERN • HOPALONG CASSIDY
FAWCETT'S FUNNY ANIMALS • ROCKY LANE WESTERN • NYOKA THE JUNGLE GIRL • GABBY HAYES WESTERN
Every effort is made to insure that these comic magazines contain the highest quality of wholesome entertainment.
W. H. Fawcett, Jr. President
Captain MARVEL
BATTLES THE PLOT AGAINST THE UNIVERSE
HEH, HEH, HEH, HEH, HEH, HEH!
DR. SIVANA · THE WORLD'S MADDEST SCIENTIST
THE UNIVERSE
CAPTAIN MARVEL · THE WORLD'S MIGHTIEST MAN
WHENEVER BILLY BATSON, FAMOUS BOY NEWSCASTER, SAYS THE WORD "SHAZAM" HE IS MIRACULOUSLY CHANGED INTO POWERFUL CAPTAIN MARVEL, THE WORLD'S MIGHTIEST MORTAL, WHO COMBINES IN HIS MAGNIFICENT PHYSIQUE THE POWERS OF SIX OF THE MIGHTIEST HEROES OF ALL TIME!
SOLOMON... WISDOM
HERCULES.. STRENGTH
ATLAS...... STAMINA
ZEUS...... POWER
ACHILLES... COURAGE
MERCURY... SPEED
PART 1 DR. SIVANA STRIKES AT SHAZAM
NO GREATER EVIL GENIUS THAN DR. SIVANA, THE WORLD'S WICKEDEST SCIENTIST, HAS EVER EXISTED ON THIS EARTH OF OURS! HIS SINISTER AMBITION IS TO RULE NOT ONLY EARTH, BUT THE ENTIRE UNIVERSE! THE VERY EXISTENCE OF CAPTAIN MARVEL HIMSELF IS THREATENED AS THE WILY SCIENTIST SETS IN MOTION HIS LATEST AUDACIOUS PLOT TO GIVE HIM POWER OVER ALL THE UNIVERSE! READ ON, FOR 100 THRILLS, CHILLS, AND EXCITING EPISODES COMPLETE IN THIS 100th ANNIVERSARY ISSUE!

From *Captain Marvel Adventures* No. 100, September 1949.

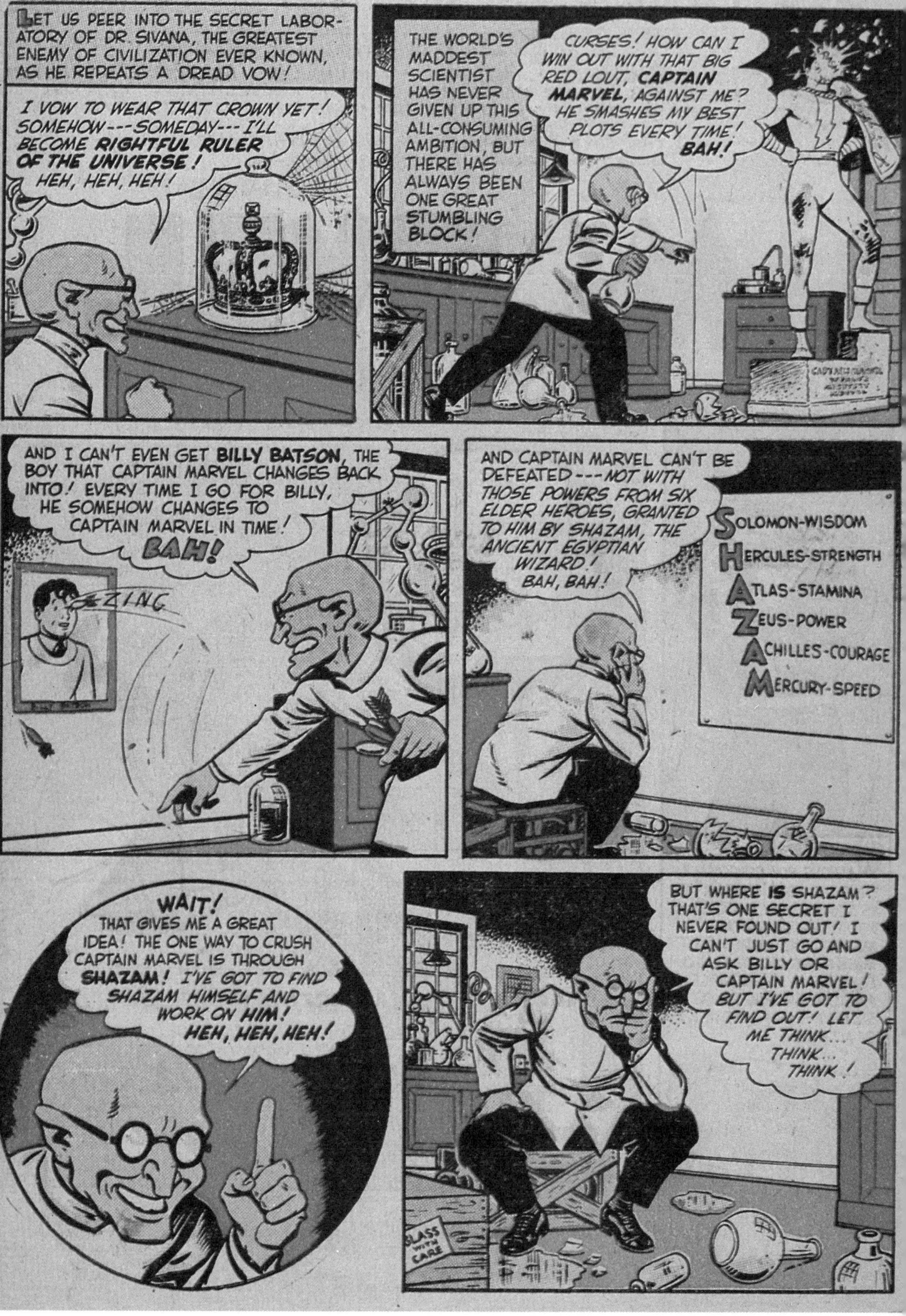
LET US PEER INTO THE SECRET LABORATORY OF DR. SIVANA, THE GREATEST ENEMY OF CIVILIZATION EVER KNOWN, AS HE REPEATS A DREAD VOW!
I VOW TO WEAR THAT CROWN YET! SOMEHOW---SOMEDAY--- I'LL BECOME **RIGHTFUL RULER OF THE UNIVERSE!** HEH, HEH, HEH!
THE WORLD'S MADDEST SCIENTIST HAS NEVER GIVEN UP THIS ALL-CONSUMING AMBITION, BUT THERE HAS ALWAYS BEEN ONE GREAT STUMBLING BLOCK!
CURSES! HOW CAN I WIN OUT WITH THAT BIG RED LOUT, **CAPTAIN MARVEL**, AGAINST ME? HE SMASHES MY BEST PLOTS EVERY TIME! **BAH!**
AND I CAN'T EVEN GET **BILLY BATSON**, THE BOY THAT CAPTAIN MARVEL CHANGES BACK INTO! EVERY TIME I GO FOR BILLY, HE SOMEHOW CHANGES TO CAPTAIN MARVEL IN TIME! **BAH!**
ZING
AND CAPTAIN MARVEL CAN'T BE DEFEATED---NOT WITH THOSE POWERS FROM SIX ELDER HEROES, GRANTED TO HIM BY SHAZAM, THE ANCIENT EGYPTIAN WIZARD! BAH, BAH!
SOLOMON-WISDOM
HERCULES-STRENGTH
ATLAS-STAMINA
ZEUS-POWER
ACHILLES-COURAGE
MERCURY-SPEED
WAIT! THAT GIVES ME A GREAT IDEA! THE ONE WAY TO CRUSH CAPTAIN MARVEL IS THROUGH **SHAZAM**! I'VE GOT TO FIND SHAZAM HIMSELF AND WORK ON **HIM**! **HEH, HEH, HEH!**
BUT WHERE **IS** SHAZAM? THAT'S ONE SECRET I NEVER FOUND OUT! I CAN'T JUST GO AND ASK BILLY OR CAPTAIN MARVEL! BUT I'VE GOT TO FIND OUT! LET ME THINK... THINK... THINK!
GLASS WITH CARE

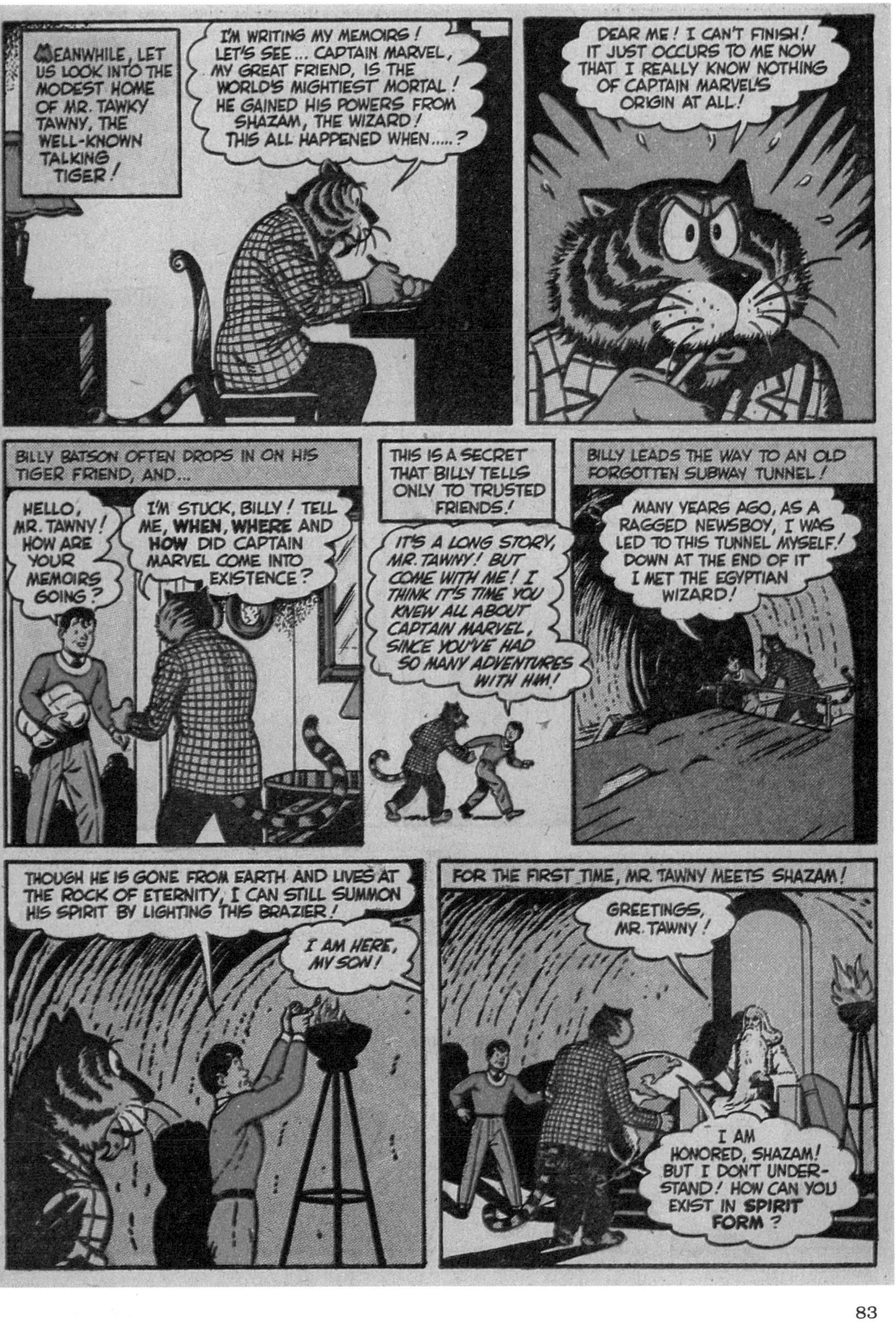
MEANWHILE, LET US LOOK INTO THE MODEST HOME OF MR. TAWKY TAWNY, THE WELL-KNOWN TALKING TIGER!
I'M WRITING MY MEMOIRS! LET'S SEE... CAPTAIN MARVEL, MY GREAT FRIEND, IS THE WORLD'S MIGHTIEST MORTAL! HE GAINED HIS POWERS FROM SHAZAM, THE WIZARD! THIS ALL HAPPENED WHEN.....?
DEAR ME! I CAN'T FINISH! IT JUST OCCURS TO ME NOW THAT I REALLY KNOW NOTHING OF CAPTAIN MARVEL'S ORIGIN AT ALL!
BILLY BATSON OFTEN DROPS IN ON HIS TIGER FRIEND, AND...
HELLO, MR. TAWNY! HOW ARE YOUR MEMOIRS GOING?
I'M STUCK, BILLY! TELL ME, WHEN, WHERE AND HOW DID CAPTAIN MARVEL COME INTO EXISTENCE?
THIS IS A SECRET THAT BILLY TELLS ONLY TO TRUSTED FRIENDS!
IT'S A LONG STORY, MR. TAWNY! BUT COME WITH ME! I THINK IT'S TIME YOU KNEW ALL ABOUT CAPTAIN MARVEL, SINCE YOU'VE HAD SO MANY ADVENTURES WITH HIM!
BILLY LEADS THE WAY TO AN OLD FORGOTTEN SUBWAY TUNNEL!
MANY YEARS AGO, AS A RAGGED NEWSBOY, I WAS LED TO THIS TUNNEL MYSELF! DOWN AT THE END OF IT I MET THE EGYPTIAN WIZARD!
THOUGH HE IS GONE FROM EARTH AND LIVES AT THE ROCK OF ETERNITY, I CAN STILL SUMMON HIS SPIRIT BY LIGHTING THIS BRAZIER!
I AM HERE, MY SON!
FOR THE FIRST TIME, MR. TAWNY MEETS SHAZAM!
GREETINGS, MR. TAWNY!
I AM HONORED, SHAZAM! BUT I DON'T UNDERSTAND! HOW CAN YOU EXIST IN SPIRIT FORM?

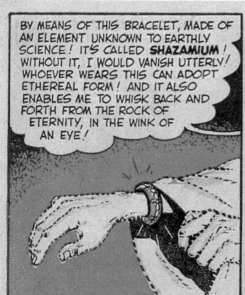

BY MEANS OF THIS BRACELET, MADE OF AN ELEMENT UNKNOWN TO EARTHLY SCIENCE! IT'S CALLED **SHAZAMIUM**! WITHOUT IT, I WOULD VANISH UTTERLY! WHOEVER WEARS THIS CAN ADOPT ETHEREAL FORM! AND IT ALSO ENABLES ME TO WHISK BACK AND FORTH FROM THE ROCK OF ETERNITY, IN THE WINK OF AN EYE!

NOW I MUST GO! YOU HAVE DONE WELL, MR. TAWNY, AIDING CAPTAIN MARVEL IN THE GREAT FIGHT AGAINST EVIL!

THANK YOU, GREAT SIR!

LATER, BACK AT MR. TAWNY'S HOME...

NOW I CAN FINISH MY MEMOIRS! THANKS, BILLY!

JUST ONE THING, MR. TAWNY--- DON'T WRITE DOWN **WHERE** THAT FORGOTTEN TUNNEL IS! NOBODY ELSE MUST EVER FIND THAT OUT! GOOD NIGHT!

BUT MEANWHILE, SIVANA HAS COME TO THE HOME OF MR. TAWNY!

I'VE FINALLY FIGURED IT OUT! MR. TAWNY IS A CLOSE FRIEND OF BILLY AND CAPTAIN MARVEL! HE OUGHT TO KNOW **WHERE SHAZAM IS**! AFTER BILLY IS OUT OF SIGHT, I'LL STRIKE!

FOR THE FIRST TIME, SIVANA AND MR. TAWNY MEET!

SIVANA! I RECOGNIZE YOU FROM YOUR PICTURES! YOU'RE THE MOST EVIL GENIUS ON EARTH!

GREETINGS, MR. TAWNY! I SEE MY REPUTATION PRECEDES ME! HEHHHH!

YOU MADE A MISTAKE COMING HERE!

DID I?

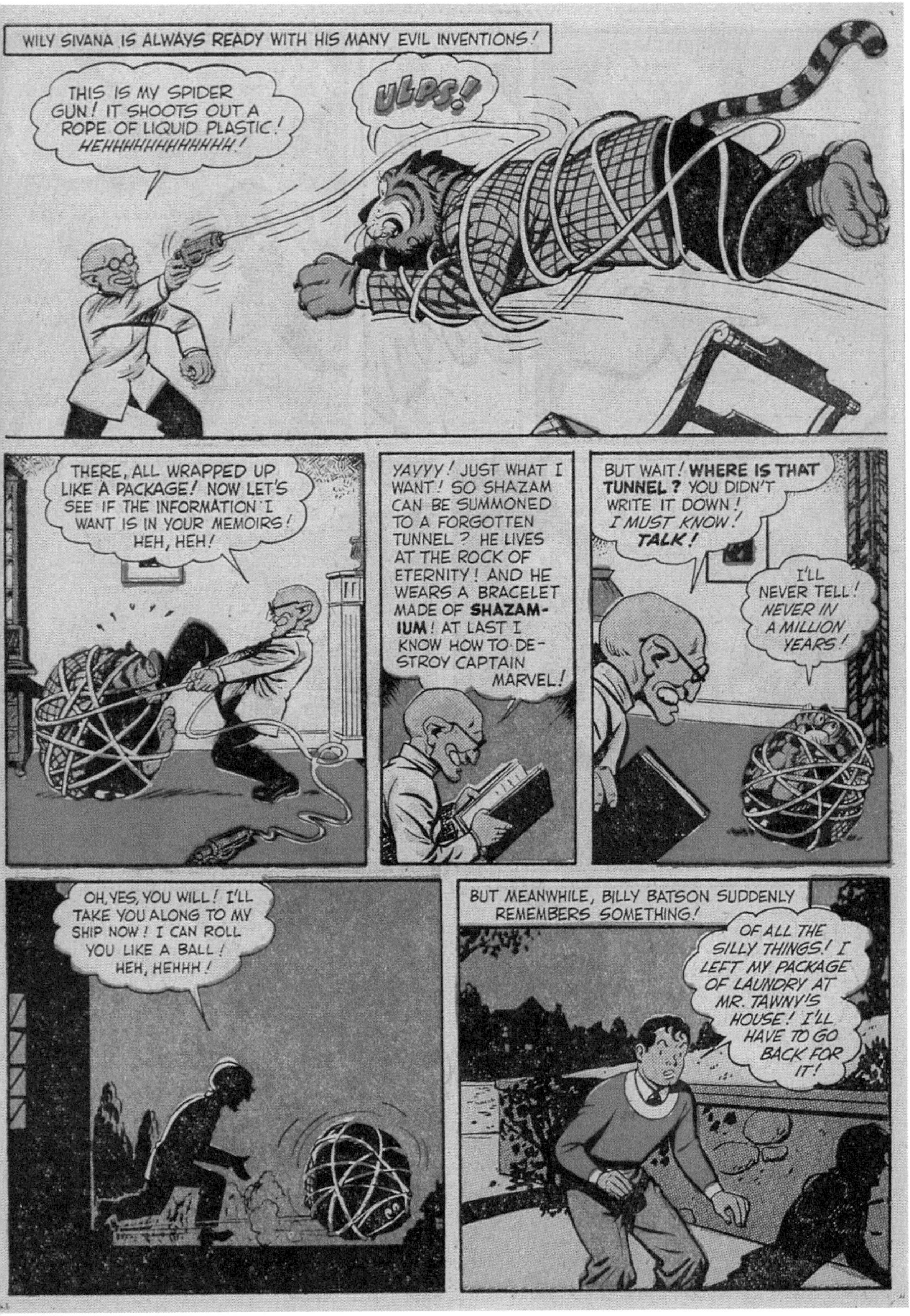
WILY SIVANA IS ALWAYS READY WITH HIS MANY EVIL INVENTIONS!
THIS IS MY SPIDER GUN! IT SHOOTS OUT A ROPE OF LIQUID PLASTIC! HEHHHHHHHHHHHH!
ULPS!
THERE, ALL WRAPPED UP LIKE A PACKAGE! NOW LET'S SEE IF THE INFORMATION I WANT IS IN YOUR MEMOIRS! HEH, HEH!
YAYYY! JUST WHAT I WANT! SO SHAZAM CAN BE SUMMONED TO A FORGOTTEN TUNNEL? HE LIVES AT THE ROCK OF ETERNITY! AND HE WEARS A BRACELET MADE OF SHAZAMIUM! AT LAST I KNOW HOW TO DESTROY CAPTAIN MARVEL!
BUT WAIT! WHERE IS THAT TUNNEL? YOU DIDN'T WRITE IT DOWN! I MUST KNOW! TALK!
I'LL NEVER TELL! NEVER IN A MILLION YEARS!
OH, YES, YOU WILL! I'LL TAKE YOU ALONG TO MY SHIP NOW! I CAN ROLL YOU LIKE A BALL! HEH, HEHHH!
BUT MEANWHILE, BILLY BATSON SUDDENLY REMEMBERS SOMETHING!
OF ALL THE SILLY THINGS! I LEFT MY PACKAGE OF LAUNDRY AT MR. TAWNY'S HOUSE! I'LL HAVE TO GO BACK FOR IT!

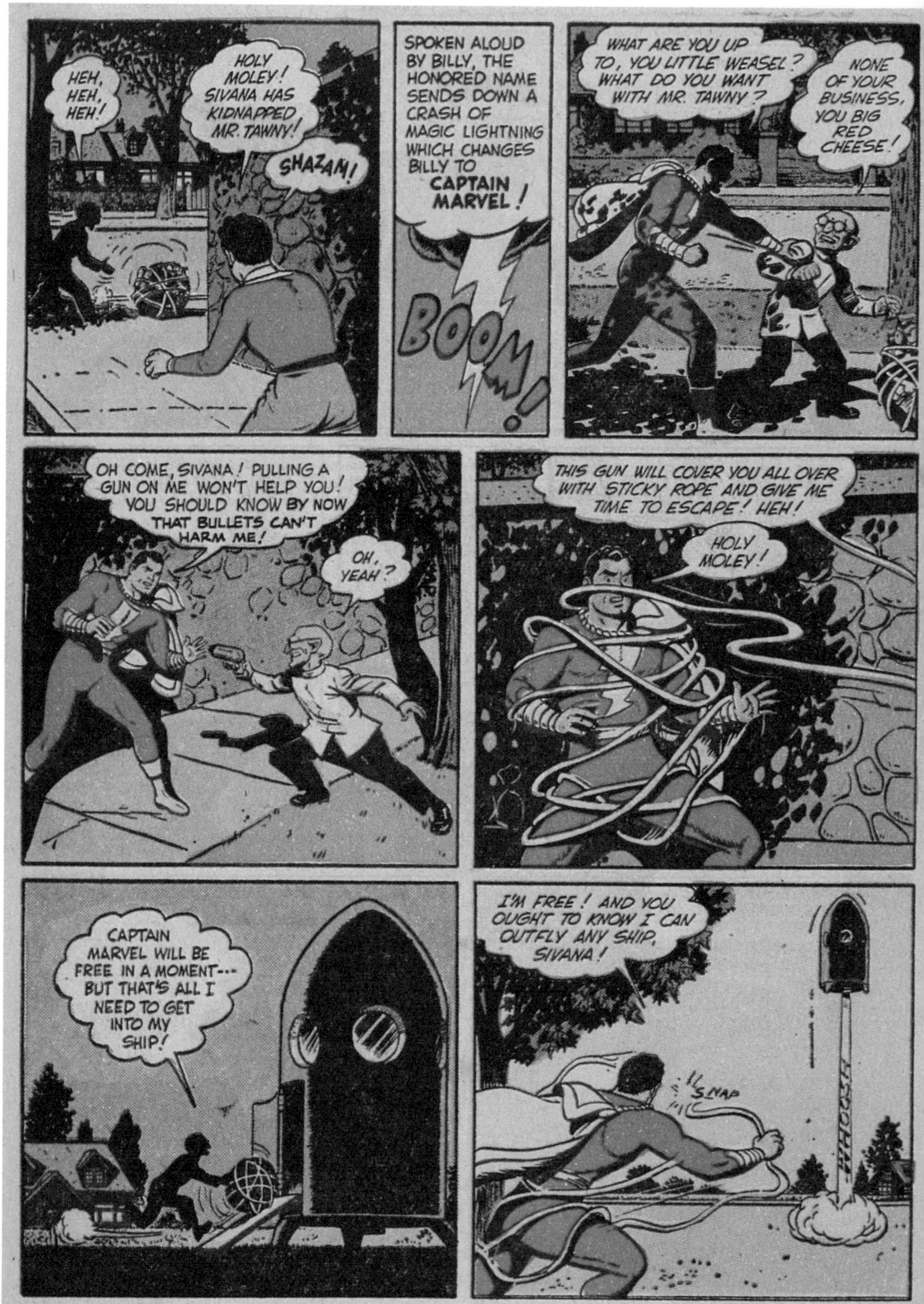
HEH, HEH, HEH!
HOLY MOLEY! SIVANA HAS KIDNAPPED MR. TAWNY!
SHAZAM!
SPOKEN ALOUD BY BILLY, THE HONORED NAME SENDS DOWN A CRASH OF MAGIC LIGHTNING WHICH CHANGES BILLY TO CAPTAIN MARVEL!
BOOM!
WHAT ARE YOU UP TO, YOU LITTLE WEASEL? WHAT DO YOU WANT WITH MR. TAWNY?
NONE OF YOUR BUSINESS, YOU BIG RED CHEESE!
OH COME, SIVANA! PULLING A GUN ON ME WON'T HELP YOU! YOU SHOULD KNOW BY NOW THAT BULLETS CAN'T HARM ME!
OH, YEAH?
THIS GUN WILL COVER YOU ALL OVER WITH STICKY ROPE AND GIVE ME TIME TO ESCAPE! HEH!
HOLY MOLEY!
CAPTAIN MARVEL WILL BE FREE IN A MOMENT--- BUT THAT'S ALL I NEED TO GET INTO MY SHIP!
I'M FREE! AND YOU OUGHT TO KNOW I CAN OUTFLY ANY SHIP, SIVANA!
SNAP

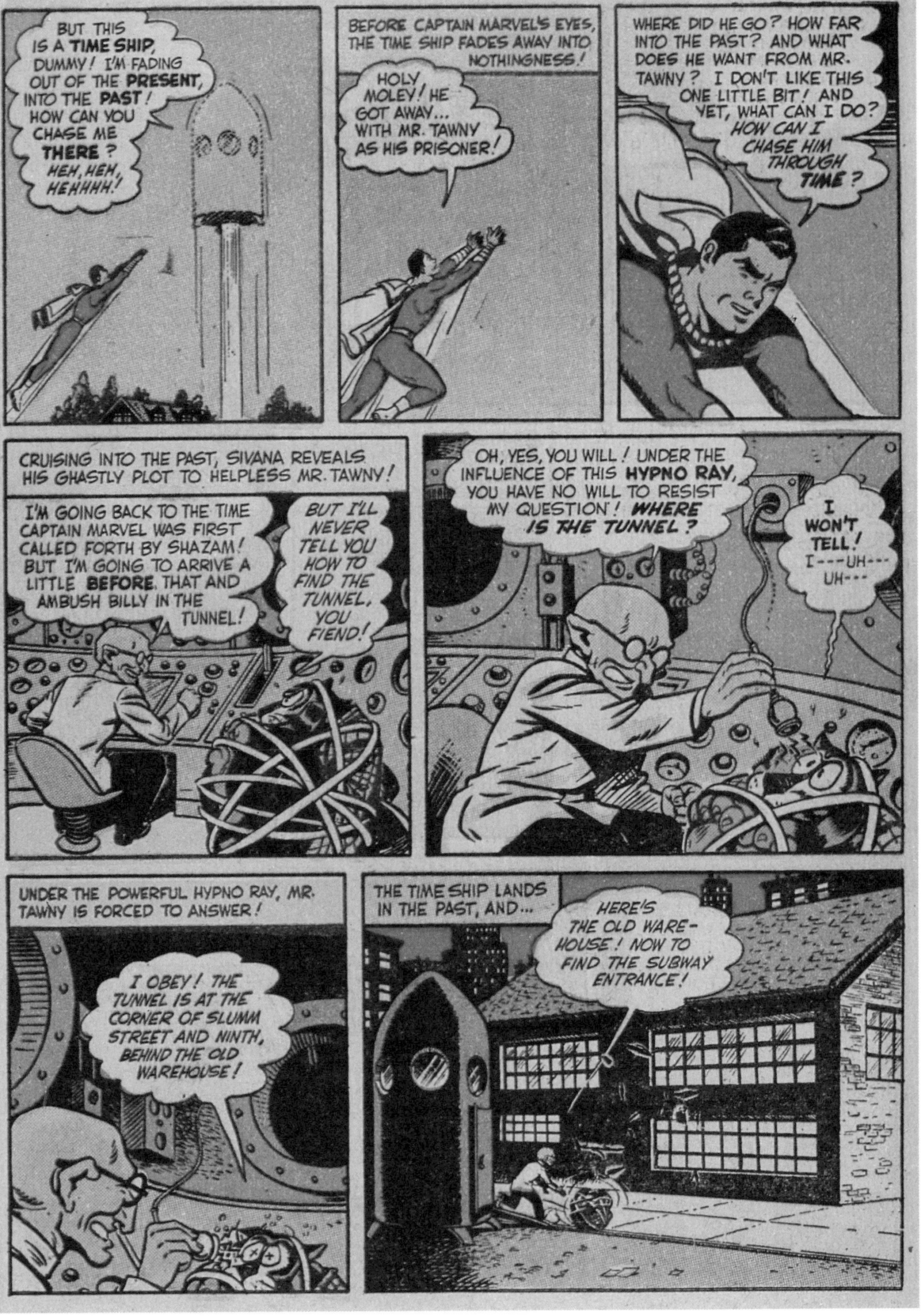

BUT THIS IS A TIME SHIP, DUMMY! I'M FADING OUT OF THE PRESENT, INTO THE PAST! HOW CAN YOU CHASE ME THERE? HEH, HEH, HEHHHH!
BEFORE CAPTAIN MARVEL'S EYES, THE TIME SHIP FADES AWAY INTO NOTHINGNESS!
HOLY MOLEY! HE GOT AWAY... WITH MR. TAWNY AS HIS PRISONER!
WHERE DID HE GO? HOW FAR INTO THE PAST? AND WHAT DOES HE WANT FROM MR. TAWNY? I DON'T LIKE THIS ONE LITTLE BIT! AND YET, WHAT CAN I DO? HOW CAN I CHASE HIM THROUGH TIME?
CRUISING INTO THE PAST, SIVANA REVEALS HIS GHASTLY PLOT TO HELPLESS MR. TAWNY!
I'M GOING BACK TO THE TIME CAPTAIN MARVEL WAS FIRST CALLED FORTH BY SHAZAM! BUT I'M GOING TO ARRIVE A LITTLE BEFORE THAT AND AMBUSH BILLY IN THE TUNNEL!
BUT I'LL NEVER TELL YOU HOW TO FIND THE TUNNEL, YOU FIEND!
OH, YES, YOU WILL! UNDER THE INFLUENCE OF THIS HYPNO RAY, YOU HAVE NO WILL TO RESIST MY QUESTION! WHERE IS THE TUNNEL?
I WON'T TELL! I---UH--- UH---
UNDER THE POWERFUL HYPNO RAY, MR. TAWNY IS FORCED TO ANSWER!
I OBEY! THE TUNNEL IS AT THE CORNER OF SLUMM STREET AND NINTH, BEHIND THE OLD WAREHOUSE!
THE TIME SHIP LANDS IN THE PAST, AND...
HERE'S THE OLD WARE-HOUSE! NOW TO FIND THE SUBWAY ENTRANCE!

HERE IT IS! WE'RE BACK IN TIME **BEFORE** BILLY BATSON FIRST ENTERED! I'VE. TIMED ALL THIS PERFECTLY!

SUBWAY

THE SEVEN DEADLY ENEMIES OF MAN, EH? WE'LL HIDE BEHIND ONE OF THOSE STATUES!

THE SEVEN DEADLY ENEMIES OF MAN

PRIDE ENVY GREED HATRED SELFISHNESS LAZINESS

I WANT YOU TO SEE THIS, MR. TAWNY! SOON BILLY WILL COME! I'LL NAB HIM HERE, **BEFORE** HE REACHES THE THRONE OF SHAZAM --- AND **BEFORE** CAPTAIN MARVEL IS CREATED! AND YOU WON'T BE ABLE TO YELL TO WARN HIM! HEHHH!

MEANWHILE, OUTSIDE, THE BILLY BATSON OF THE PAST IS MET BY A MYSTERIOUS, DARK FIGURE!

HE'S BECKONING ME TO FOLLOW??

WHY ARE YOU TAKING ME INTO THIS OLD ABANDONED SUBWAY TUNNEL?

THIS IS THE BILLY BATSON OF YEARS BACK --- A YOUNG NEWSBOY WHO DOES NOT KNOW THAT HE HAS BEEN SELECTED BY SHAZAM TO BECOME THE FUTURE CAPTAIN MARVEL! HE DOES NOT YET KNOW OF THE GREAT AND BLAZING CAREER FOR WHICH HE IS DESTINED AS THE WORLD'S MIGHTIEST MORTAL! THIS IS BILLY BATSON **BEFORE** CAPTAIN MARVEL EVER EXISTED!

AS IT ALL ONCE HAPPENED IN THE PAST, BILLY IS LED THROUGH THE CAVERN OF THE SEVEN DEADLY ENEMIES OF MAN!

THE SEVEN DEADLY ENEMIES OF MAN

PRIDE ENVY GREED HATRED SELFISHNESS LAZINESS

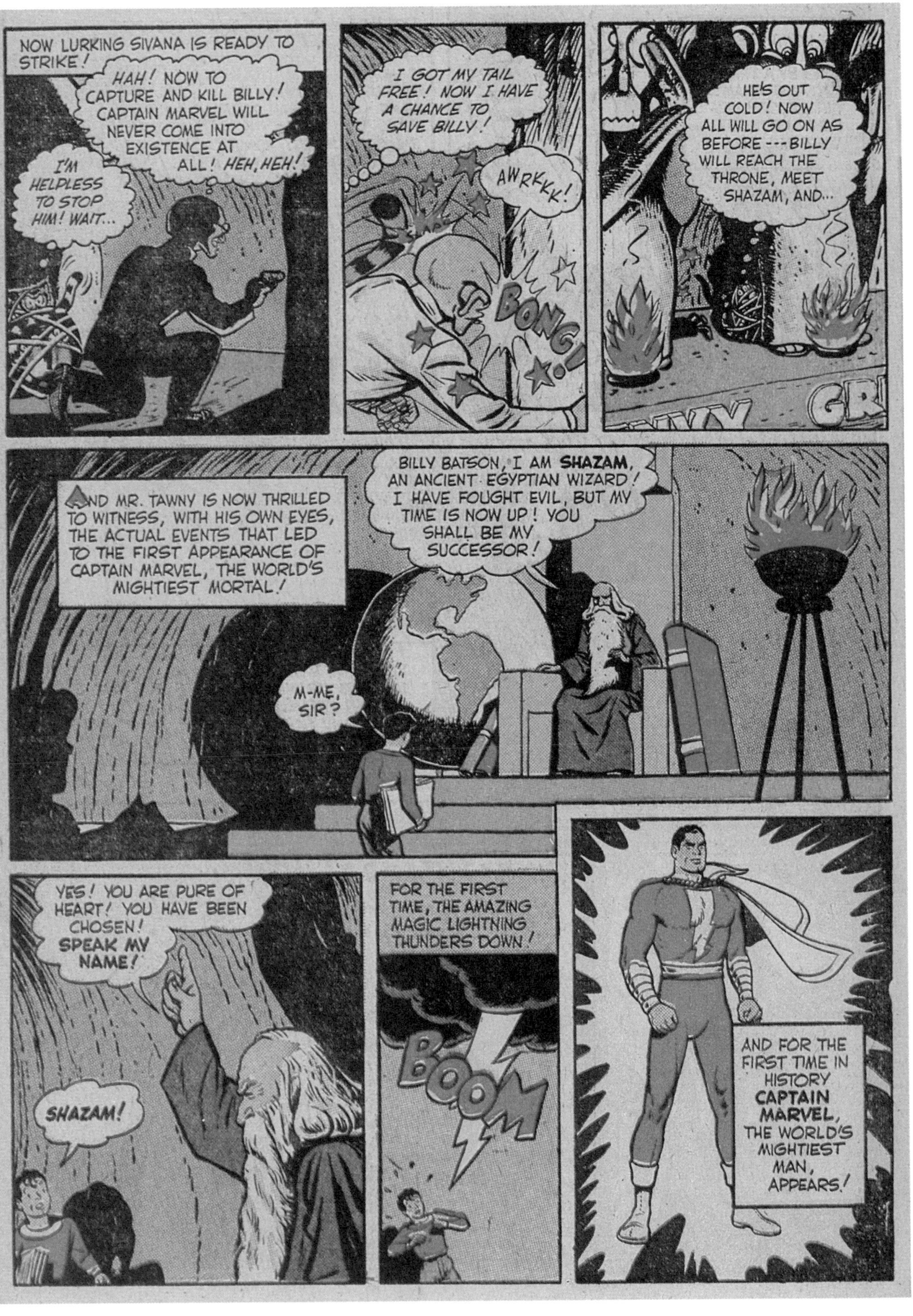
NOW LURKING SIVANA IS READY TO STRIKE!
HAH! NOW TO CAPTURE AND KILL BILLY! CAPTAIN MARVEL WILL NEVER COME INTO EXISTENCE AT ALL! HEH, HEH!
I'M HELPLESS TO STOP HIM! WAIT...
I GOT MY TAIL FREE! NOW I HAVE A CHANCE TO SAVE BILLY!
AWRKKK!
BONG!
HE'S OUT COLD! NOW ALL WILL GO ON AS BEFORE --- BILLY WILL REACH THE THRONE, MEET SHAZAM, AND...
AND MR. TAWNY IS NOW THRILLED TO WITNESS, WITH HIS OWN EYES, THE ACTUAL EVENTS THAT LED TO THE FIRST APPEARANCE OF CAPTAIN MARVEL, THE WORLD'S MIGHTIEST MORTAL!
BILLY BATSON, I AM SHAZAM, AN ANCIENT EGYPTIAN WIZARD! I HAVE FOUGHT EVIL, BUT MY TIME IS NOW UP! YOU SHALL BE MY SUCCESSOR!
M-ME, SIR?
YES! YOU ARE PURE OF HEART! YOU HAVE BEEN CHOSEN! SPEAK MY NAME!
SHAZAM!
FOR THE FIRST TIME, THE AMAZING MAGIC LIGHTNING THUNDERS DOWN!
BOOM
AND FOR THE FIRST TIME IN HISTORY CAPTAIN MARVEL, THE WORLD'S MIGHTIEST MAN, APPEARS!

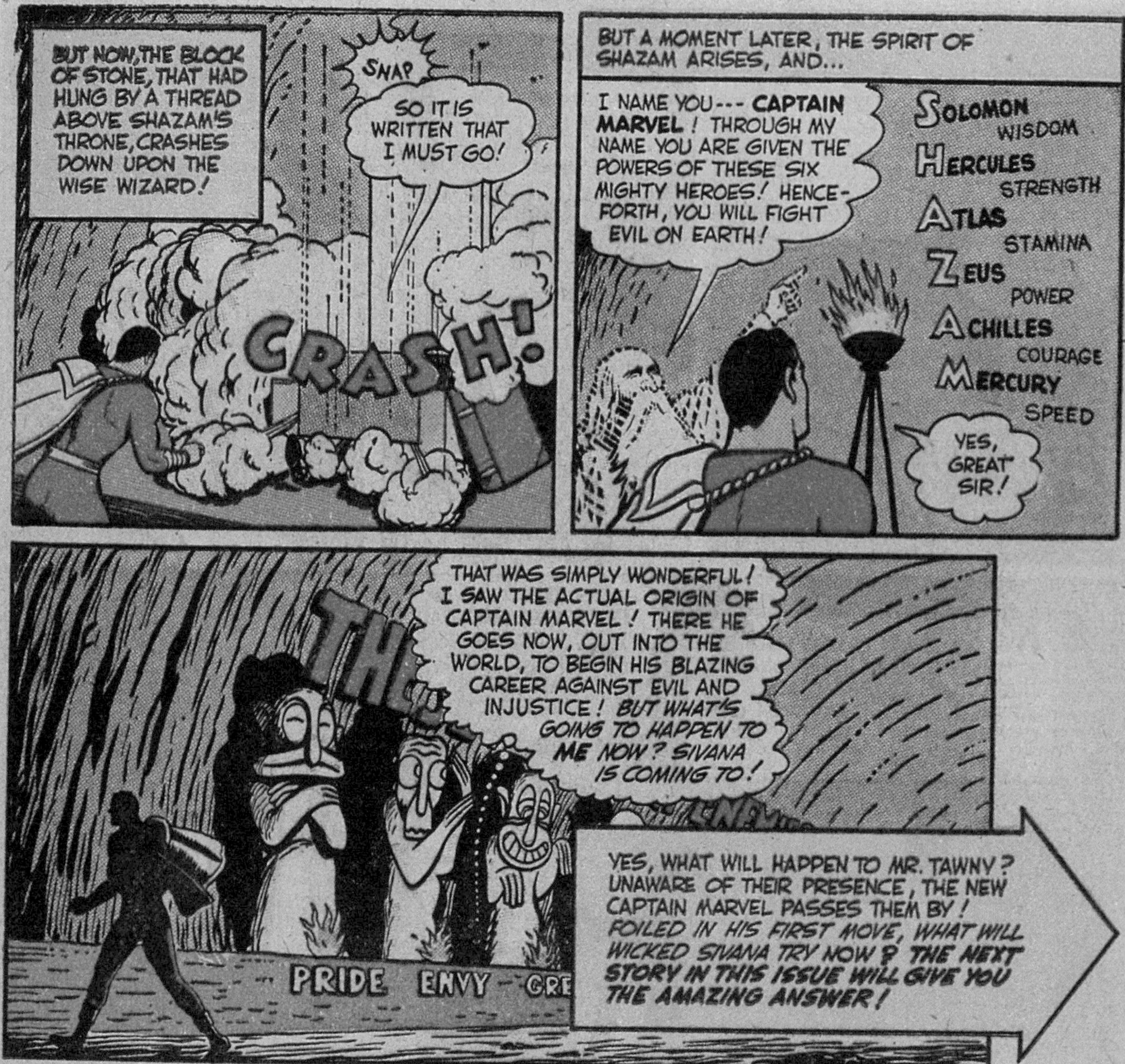
BUT NOW, THE BLOCK OF STONE, THAT HAD HUNG BY A THREAD ABOVE SHAZAM'S THRONE, CRASHES DOWN UPON THE WISE WIZARD!
SNAP
SO IT IS WRITTEN THAT I MUST GO!
CRASH!
BUT A MOMENT LATER, THE SPIRIT OF SHAZAM ARISES, AND...
I NAME YOU--- CAPTAIN MARVEL! THROUGH MY NAME YOU ARE GIVEN THE POWERS OF THESE SIX MIGHTY HEROES! HENCE-FORTH, YOU WILL FIGHT EVIL ON EARTH!
SOLOMON WISDOM
HERCULES STRENGTH
ATLAS STAMINA
ZEUS POWER
ACHILLES COURAGE
MERCURY SPEED
YES, GREAT SIR!
THAT WAS SIMPLY WONDERFUL! I SAW THE ACTUAL ORIGIN OF CAPTAIN MARVEL! THERE HE GOES NOW, OUT INTO THE WORLD, TO BEGIN HIS BLAZING CAREER AGAINST EVIL AND INJUSTICE! BUT WHAT'S GOING TO HAPPEN TO ME NOW? SIVANA IS COMING TO!
PRIDE ENVY
YES, WHAT WILL HAPPEN TO MR. TAWNY? UNAWARE OF THEIR PRESENCE, THE NEW CAPTAIN MARVEL PASSES THEM BY! FOILED IN HIS FIRST MOVE, WHAT WILL WICKED SIVANA TRY NOW? THE NEXT STORY IN THIS ISSUE WILL GIVE YOU THE AMAZING ANSWER!

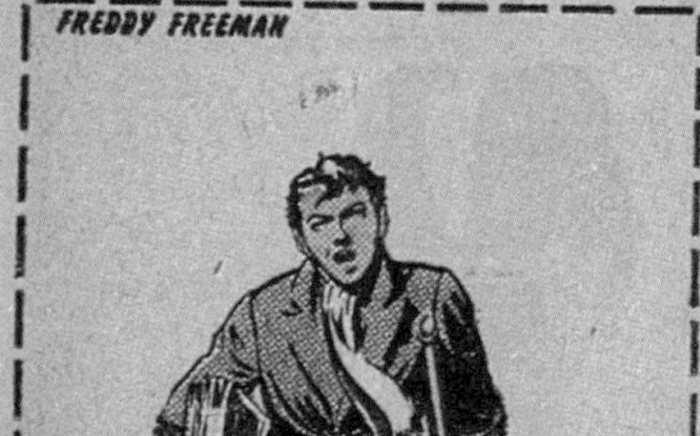
FREDDY FREEMAN
Copyright 1949 FAWCETT PUBLICATIONS, INC.

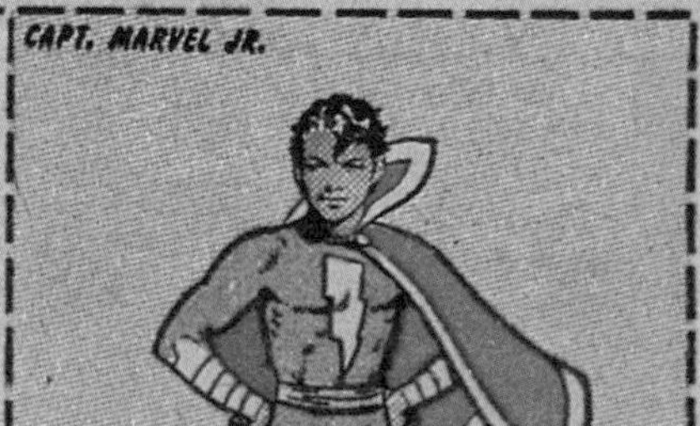
CAPT. MARVEL JR.
Copyright 1949 FAWCETT PUBLICATIONS, INC.

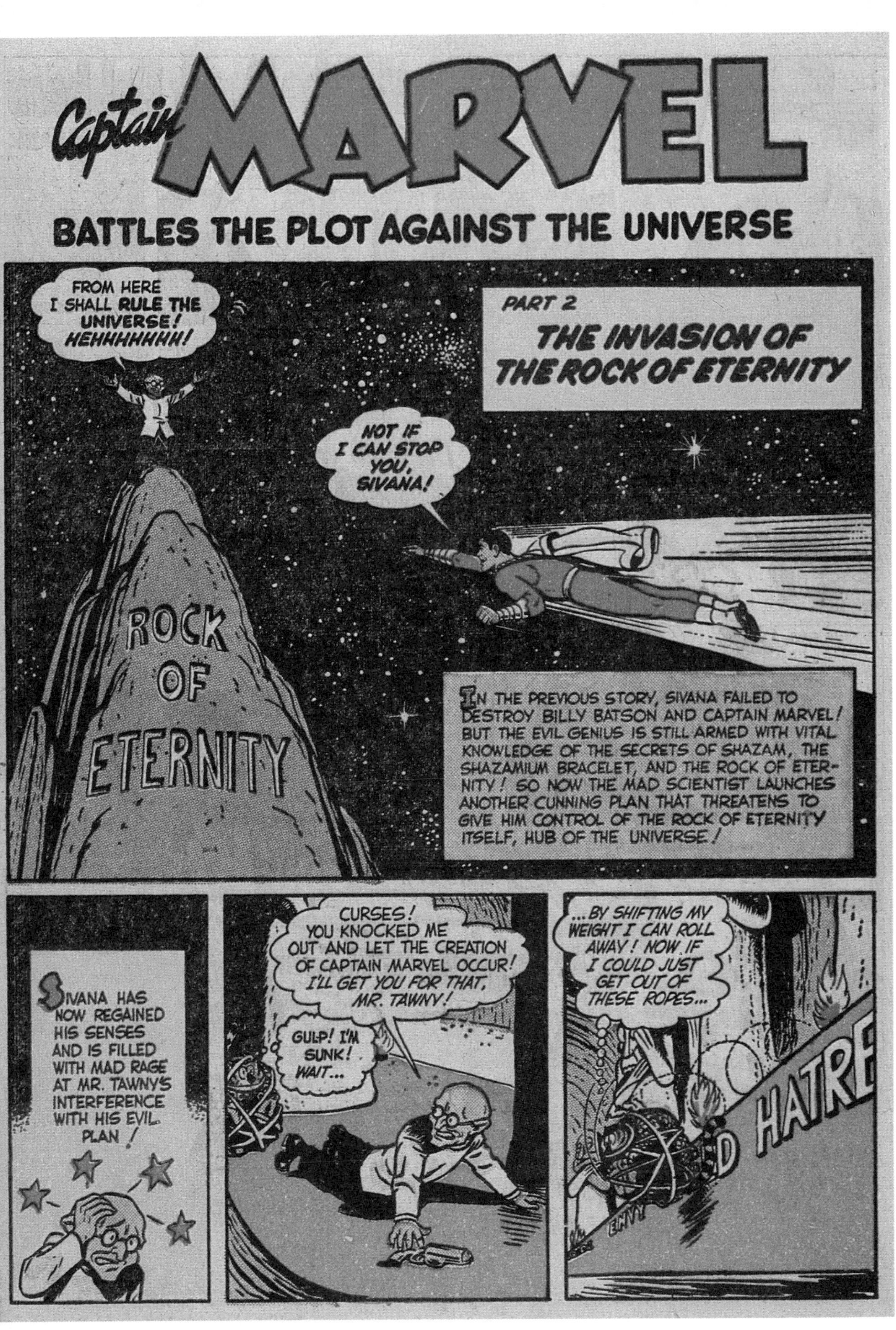
Captain MARVEL
BATTLES THE PLOT AGAINST THE UNIVERSE
FROM HERE I SHALL RULE THE UNIVERSE! HEHHHHHHH!
PART 2
THE INVASION OF THE ROCK OF ETERNITY
NOT IF I CAN STOP YOU, SIVANA!
ROCK OF ETERNITY
IN THE PREVIOUS STORY, SIVANA FAILED TO DESTROY BILLY BATSON AND CAPTAIN MARVEL! BUT THE EVIL GENIUS IS STILL ARMED WITH VITAL KNOWLEDGE OF THE SECRETS OF SHAZAM, THE SHAZAMIUM BRACELET, AND THE ROCK OF ETERNITY! SO NOW THE MAD SCIENTIST LAUNCHES ANOTHER CUNNING PLAN THAT THREATENS TO GIVE HIM CONTROL OF THE ROCK OF ETERNITY ITSELF, HUB OF THE UNIVERSE!
SIVANA HAS NOW REGAINED HIS SENSES AND IS FILLED WITH MAD RAGE AT MR. TAWNY'S INTERFERENCE WITH HIS EVIL PLAN!
CURSES! YOU KNOCKED ME OUT AND LET THE CREATION OF CAPTAIN MARVEL OCCUR! I'LL GET YOU FOR THAT, MR. TAWNY!
GULP! I'M SUNK! WAIT...
...BY SHIFTING MY WEIGHT I CAN ROLL AWAY! NOW IF I COULD JUST GET OUT OF THESE ROPES...
D HATRE

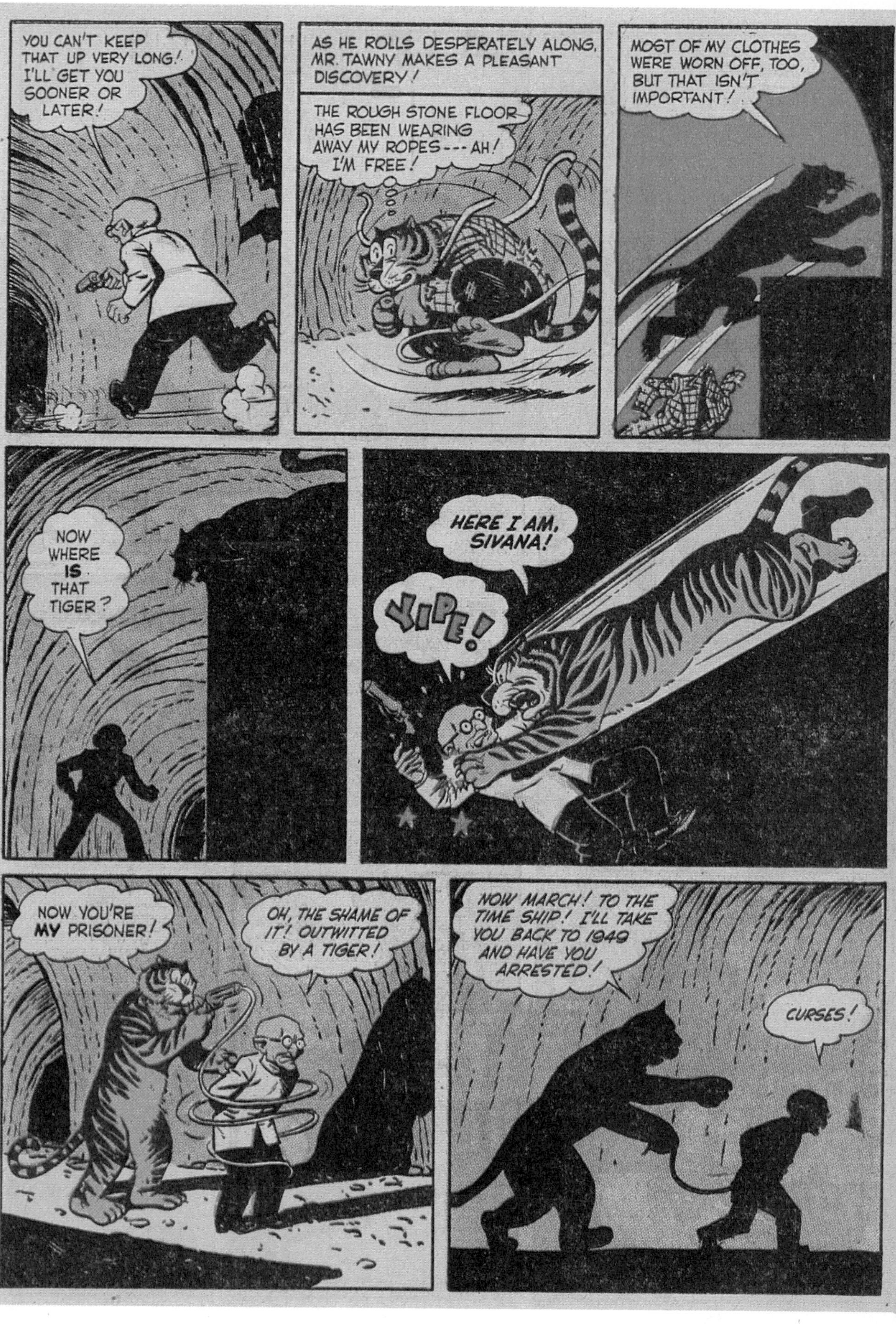
YOU CAN'T KEEP THAT UP VERY LONG! I'LL GET YOU SOONER OR LATER!
AS HE ROLLS DESPERATELY ALONG, MR. TAWNY MAKES A PLEASANT DISCOVERY!
THE ROUGH STONE FLOOR HAS BEEN WEARING AWAY MY ROPES---AH! I'M FREE!
MOST OF MY CLOTHES WERE WORN OFF, TOO, BUT THAT ISN'T IMPORTANT!
NOW WHERE IS THAT TIGER?
HERE I AM, SIVANA!
YIPE!
NOW YOU'RE MY PRISONER!
OH, THE SHAME OF IT! OUTWITTED BY A TIGER!
NOW MARCH! TO THE TIME SHIP! I'LL TAKE YOU BACK TO 1949 AND HAVE YOU ARRESTED!
CURSES!

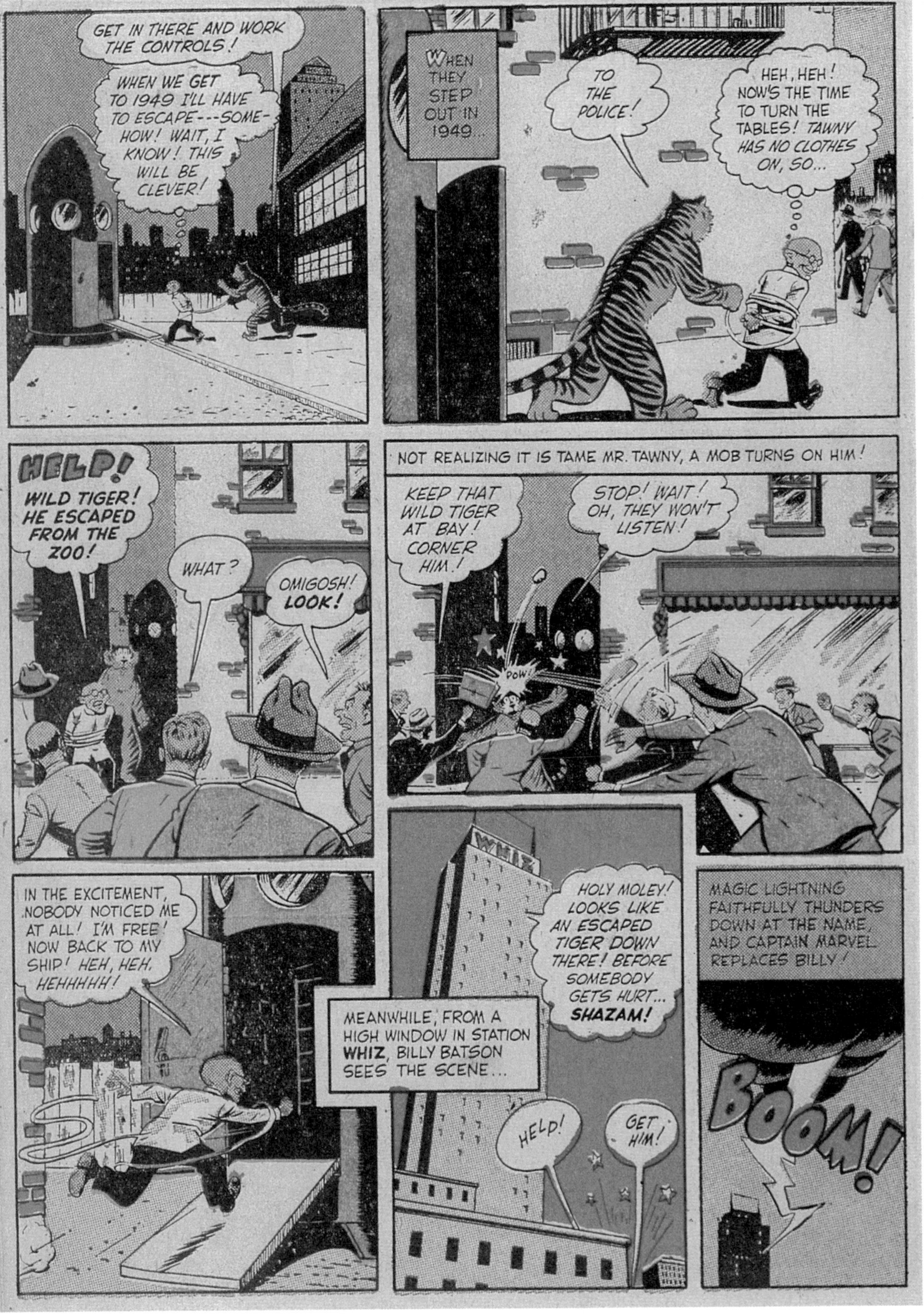

GET IN THERE AND WORK THE CONTROLS!
WHEN WE GET TO 1949 I'LL HAVE TO ESCAPE---SOMEHOW! WAIT, I KNOW! THIS WILL BE CLEVER!
WHEN THEY STEP OUT IN 1949...
TO THE POLICE!
HEH, HEH! NOW'S THE TIME TO TURN THE TABLES! TAWNY HAS NO CLOTHES ON, SO...
HELP!
WILD TIGER! HE ESCAPED FROM THE ZOO!
WHAT?
OMIGOSH! LOOK!
NOT REALIZING IT IS TAME MR. TAWNY, A MOB TURNS ON HIM!
KEEP THAT WILD TIGER AT BAY! CORNER HIM!
STOP! WAIT! OH, THEY WON'T LISTEN!
POW!
IN THE EXCITEMENT, NOBODY NOTICED ME AT ALL! I'M FREE! NOW BACK TO MY SHIP! HEH, HEH, HEHHHHH!
WHIZ
MEANWHILE, FROM A HIGH WINDOW IN STATION WHIZ, BILLY BATSON SEES THE SCENE...
HOLY MOLEY! LOOKS LIKE AN ESCAPED TIGER DOWN THERE! BEFORE SOMEBODY GETS HURT... SHAZAM!
HELP!
GET HIM!
MAGIC LIGHTNING FAITHFULLY THUNDERS DOWN AT THE NAME, AND CAPTAIN MARVEL REPLACES BILLY!
BOOM!

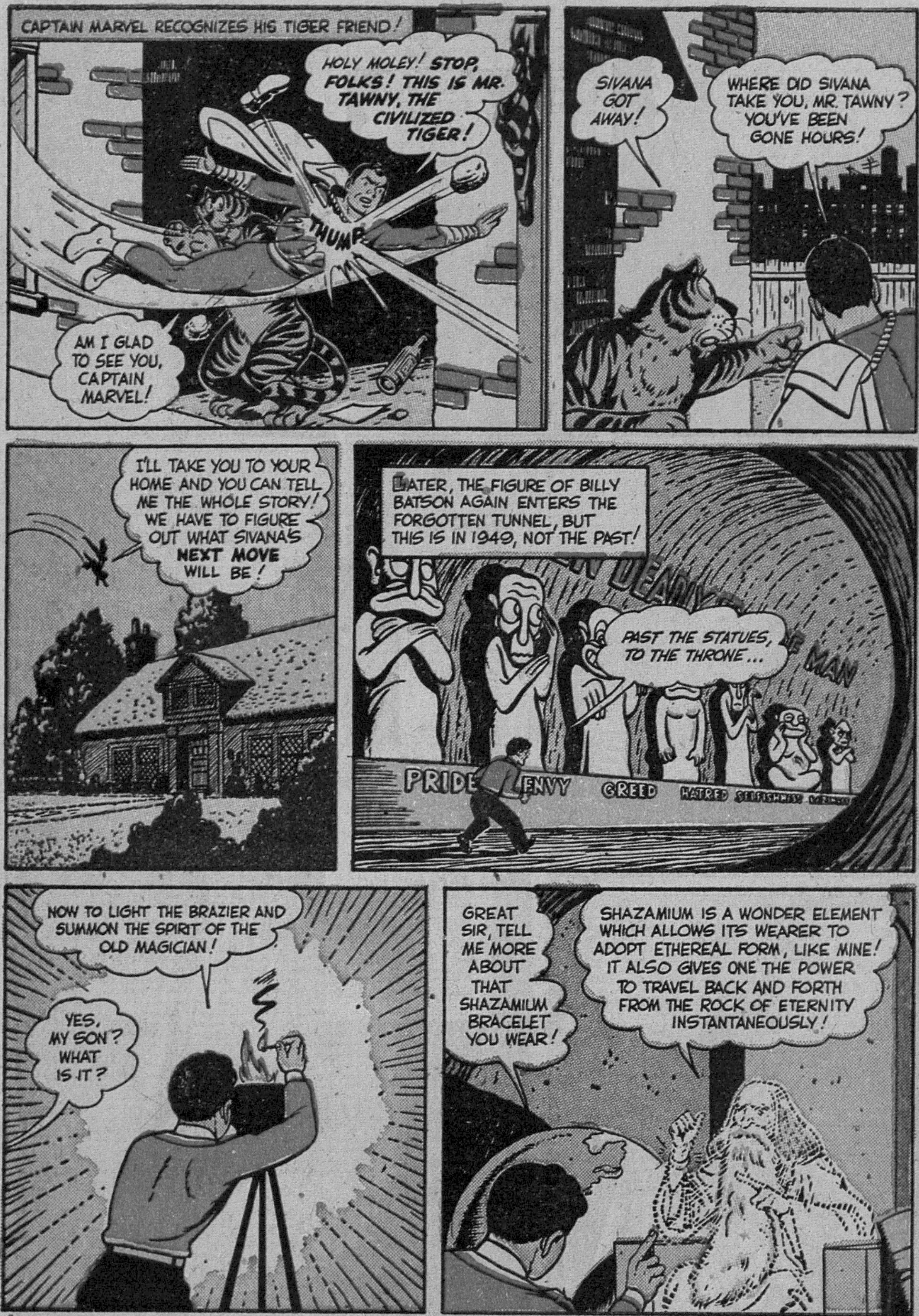
CAPTAIN MARVEL RECOGNIZES HIS TIGER FRIEND!
HOLY MOLEY! STOP, FOLKS! THIS IS MR. TAWNY, THE CIVILIZED TIGER!
THUMP
AM I GLAD TO SEE YOU, CAPTAIN MARVEL!
SIVANA GOT AWAY!
WHERE DID SIVANA TAKE YOU, MR. TAWNY? YOU'VE BEEN GONE HOURS!
I'LL TAKE YOU TO YOUR HOME AND YOU CAN TELL ME THE WHOLE STORY! WE HAVE TO FIGURE OUT WHAT SIVANA'S NEXT MOVE WILL BE!
LATER, THE FIGURE OF BILLY BATSON AGAIN ENTERS THE FORGOTTEN TUNNEL, BUT THIS IS IN 1949, NOT THE PAST!
PAST THE STATUES, TO THE THRONE...
PRIDE
ENVY
GREED
HATRED
NOW TO LIGHT THE BRAZIER AND SUMMON THE SPIRIT OF THE OLD MAGICIAN!
YES, MY SON? WHAT IS IT?
GREAT SIR, TELL ME MORE ABOUT THAT SHAZAMIUM BRACELET YOU WEAR!
SHAZAMIUM IS A WONDER ELEMENT WHICH ALLOWS ITS WEARER TO ADOPT ETHEREAL FORM, LIKE MINE! IT ALSO GIVES ONE THE POWER TO TRAVEL BACK AND FORTH FROM THE ROCK OF ETERNITY INSTANTANEOUSLY!

DO YOU WISH TO SEE IT CLOSELY, BILLY? HERE, TAKE IT--- BUT RETURN IT QUICKLY! WITHOUT IT ON MY ARM, I WOULD FADE AWAY INTO NOTHINGNESS IN 24 HOURS! IT MEANS LIFE TO ME!

BUT NOW, THERE ARISES AN OMINOUS, MOCKING CHUCKLE!

HEH, HEH, HEH, HEH, HEH, HEH, HEHH!

BILLY! THAT EVIL CHUCKLE! YOU SOUND LIKE SIVANA!

STARTLING REVELATION!

I AM SIVANA, SHAZAM! HEH, HEH! OF ALL MY CLEVER DISGUISES, THIS HAS BEEN THE MOST CUNNING OF ALL! IT WAS THE ONE WAY I COULD GET THE GREAT SHAZAMIUM BRACELET IN MY HANDS! HEHHHHH!

OH, WHAT HAVE I DONE? WITHOUT THAT BRACELET, I AM POWERLESS!

EXACTLY WHAT I FIGURED! HEH! I FAILED TO STOP THE CREATION OF CAPTAIN MARVEL, BUT NOW I HAVE YOU IN MY POWER, SHAZAM! I'LL PUT ON THE BRACELET!

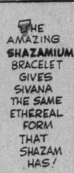

THE AMAZING **SHAZAMIUM** BRACELET GIVES SIVANA THE SAME ETHEREAL FORM THAT SHAZAM HAS!

MY HAND PASSES RIGHT THROUGH SOLID MATTER! HEH, HEH! THIS IS BETTER THAN BEING A GHOST!

AND YOU'RE MY PRISONER, SHAZAM! NOW OFF TO THE ROCK OF ETERNITY!

I AM HELPLESS TO RESIST!

IN THE WINK OF AN EYE, THROUGH THE POWER OF THE SHAZAMIUM BRACELET, THEY ARE HURLED BEYOND SPACE AND TIME TO THE ROCK OF ETERNITY, WHERE SHAZAM HAS DWELLED!

FROM HERE, I WILL SOON **RULE THE UNIVERSE!** HEH, HEH, HEHHHHH!

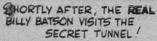
SHORTLY AFTER, THE REAL BILLY BATSON VISITS THE SECRET TUNNEL!

MR. TAWNY TOLD ME THE WHOLE STORY OF SIVANA'S VISIT TO THE PAST, AND HIS ATTEMPT TO DESTROY ME! I THINK SHAZAM HIMSELF MAY BE IN DANGER NOW! I'D BETTER WARN HIM!

NOW, AS USUAL, I LIGHT THE BRAZIER TO SUMMON HIS SPIRIT!

HEH, HEH!

BILLY BATSON RECEIVES THE SHOCK OF HIS LIFE!

HOLY MOLEY! THAT'S NOT THE EGYPTIAN WIZARD! IT'S SIVANA!

YES, MY SON! WHAT CAN I DO FOR YOU? OH HEH, HEH, HEH, HEH, HEH, HEH!

CAPTAIN MARVEL WILL TAKE CARE OF YOU! SHAZAM!

GO AHEAD! CHANGE TO THAT RED OX! I'M NOT WORRIED! ♫ HUM DE DUM ♫

THE MAGIC LIGHTNING COMES AS USUAL, FOR AS LONG AS SHAZAM EXISTS, THE WORD WILL NOT FAIL BILLY!

BOOM!

I'LL GRAB YOU AND --- HOLY MOLEY! IT'S LIKE GRABBING SMOKE!

SURE! I'M IN ETHEREAL FORM NOW, JUST LIKE OLD SHAZAM! ALL YOUR MIGHTY STRENGTH CAN'T HARM ONE HAIR OF MY HEAD --- IF I HAD ANY! HEH, HEHHHHHH!

AND LOOK! WITHOUT THIS SHAZAMIUM BRACELET, OLD SHAZAM WILL FADE AWAY INTO LIMBO, IN 24 HOURS! AND WITH HIS PASSING, YOU, TOO, WILL VANISH! IN 24 HOURS THERE WON'T BE ANY MORE CAPTAIN MARVEL! HEHHH!

HOLY MOLEY!

SIVANA PRONOUNCES A DREAD DOOM FOR THE WORLD'S MIGHTIEST MORTAL!

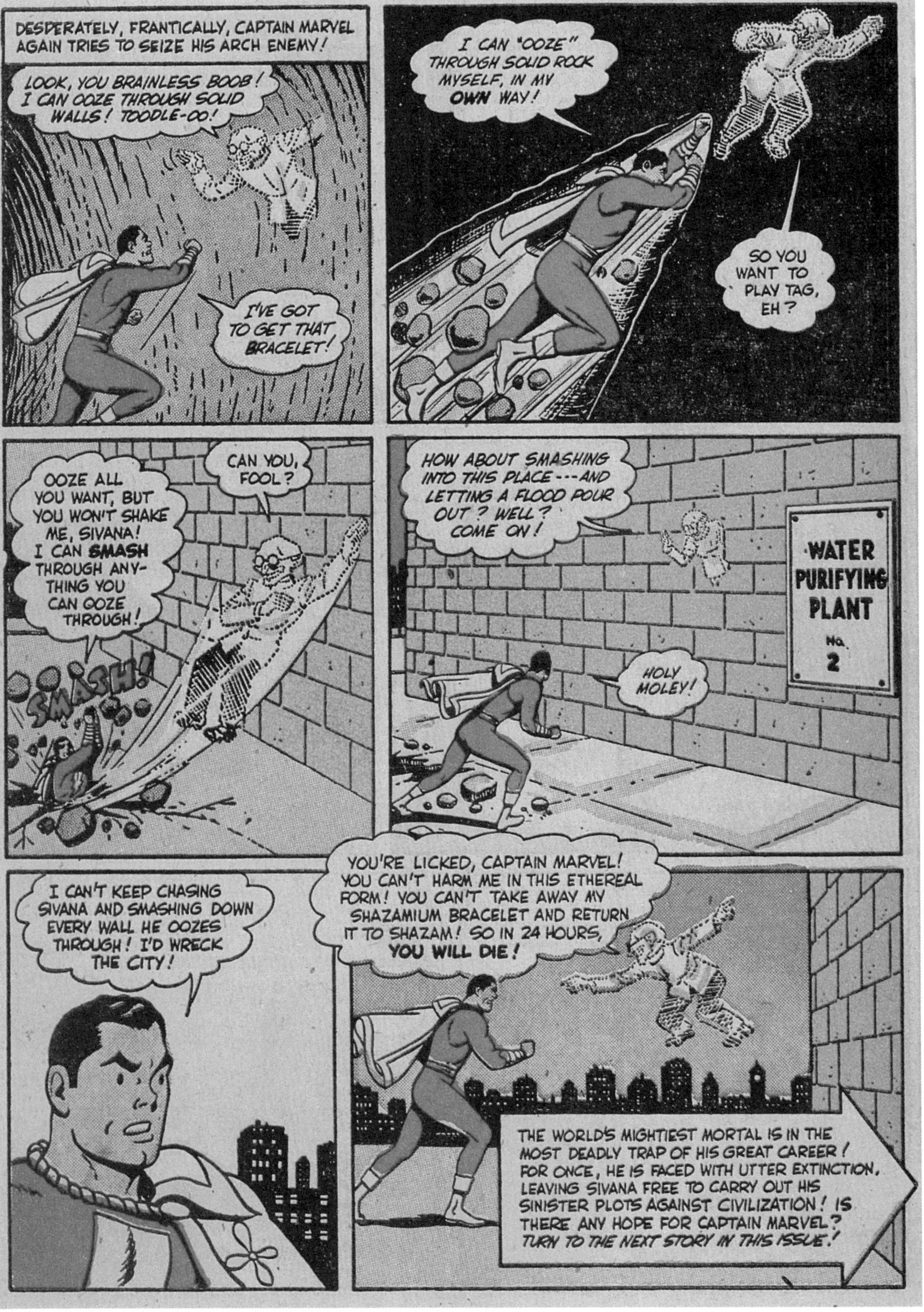

DESPERATELY, FRANTICALLY, CAPTAIN MARVEL AGAIN TRIES TO SEIZE HIS ARCH ENEMY!
LOOK, YOU BRAINLESS BOOB! I CAN OOZE THROUGH SOLID WALLS! TOODLE-OO!
I'VE GOT TO GET THAT BRACELET!
I CAN "OOZE" THROUGH SOLID ROCK MYSELF, IN MY OWN WAY!
SO YOU WANT TO PLAY TAG, EH?
OOZE ALL YOU WANT, BUT YOU WON'T SHAKE ME, SIVANA! I CAN SMASH THROUGH ANYTHING YOU CAN OOZE THROUGH!
CAN YOU, FOOL?
SMASH!
HOW ABOUT SMASHING INTO THIS PLACE---AND LETTING A FLOOD POUR OUT? WELL? COME ON!
WATER PURIFYING PLANT No. 2
HOLY MOLEY!
I CAN'T KEEP CHASING SIVANA AND SMASHING DOWN EVERY WALL HE OOZES THROUGH! I'D WRECK THE CITY!
YOU'RE LICKED, CAPTAIN MARVEL! YOU CAN'T HARM ME IN THIS ETHEREAL FORM! YOU CAN'T TAKE AWAY MY SHAZAMIUM BRACELET AND RETURN IT TO SHAZAM! SO IN 24 HOURS, YOU WILL DIE!
THE WORLD'S MIGHTIEST MORTAL IS IN THE MOST DEADLY TRAP OF HIS GREAT CAREER! FOR ONCE, HE IS FACED WITH UTTER EXTINCTION, LEAVING SIVANA FREE TO CARRY OUT HIS SINISTER PLOTS AGAINST CIVILIZATION! IS THERE ANY HOPE FOR CAPTAIN MARVEL? TURN TO THE NEXT STORY IN THIS ISSUE!

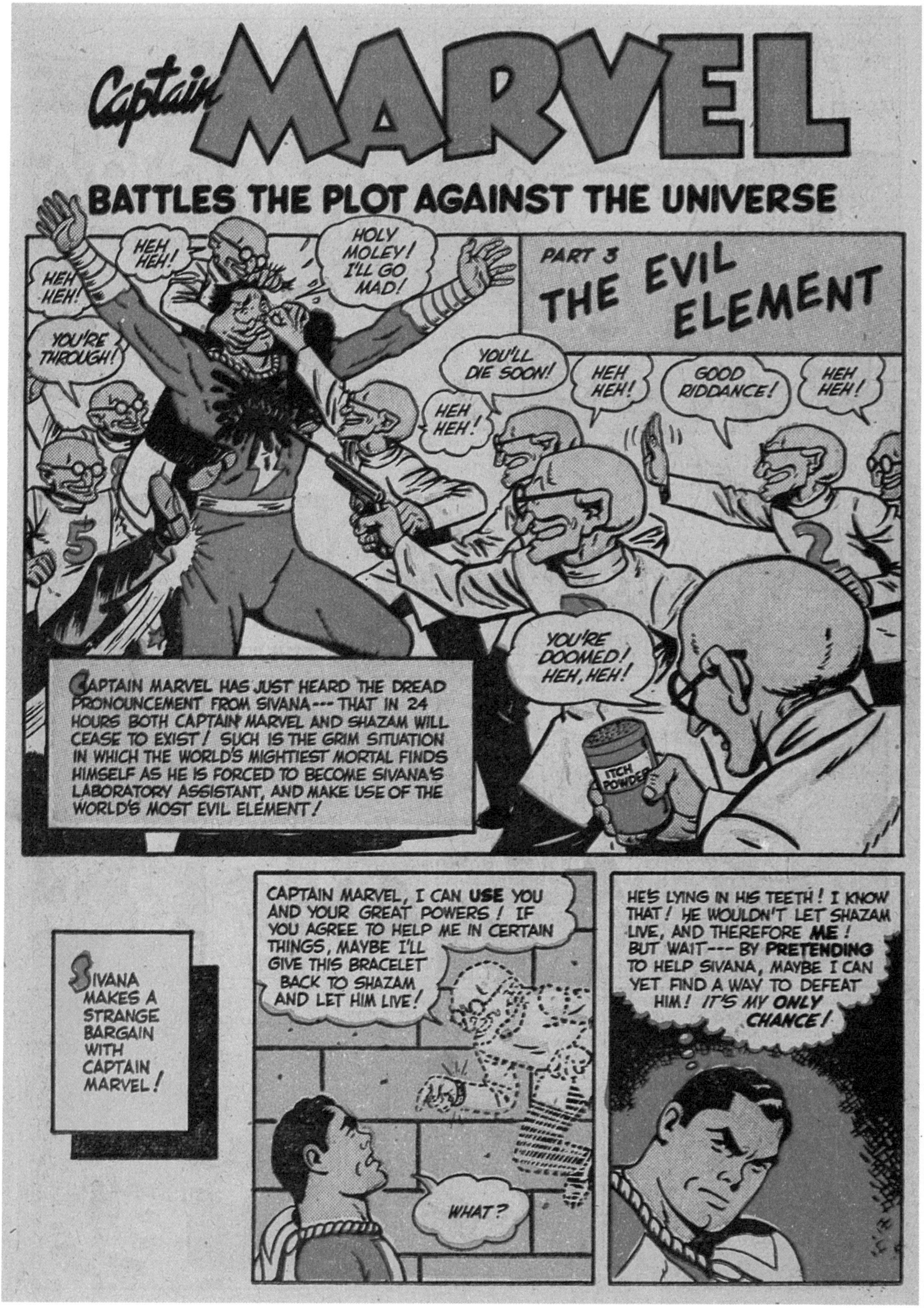
Captain MARVEL
BATTLES THE PLOT AGAINST THE UNIVERSE
PART 3 THE EVIL ELEMENT
HEH HEH!
HEH HEH!
HOLY MOLEY! I'LL GO MAD!
YOU'RE THROUGH!
YOU'LL DIE SOON!
HEH HEH!
HEH HEH!
GOOD RIDDANCE!
HEH HEH!
YOU'RE DOOMED! HEH, HEH!
ITCH POWDER
CAPTAIN MARVEL HAS JUST HEARD THE DREAD PRONOUNCEMENT FROM SIVANA--- THAT IN 24 HOURS BOTH CAPTAIN MARVEL AND SHAZAM WILL CEASE TO EXIST! SUCH IS THE GRIM SITUATION IN WHICH THE WORLD'S MIGHTIEST MORTAL FINDS HIMSELF AS HE IS FORCED TO BECOME SIVANA'S LABORATORY ASSISTANT, AND MAKE USE OF THE WORLD'S MOST EVIL ELEMENT!
SIVANA MAKES A STRANGE BARGAIN WITH CAPTAIN MARVEL!
CAPTAIN MARVEL, I CAN USE YOU AND YOUR GREAT POWERS! IF YOU AGREE TO HELP ME IN CERTAIN THINGS, MAYBE I'LL GIVE THIS BRACELET BACK TO SHAZAM AND LET HIM LIVE!
WHAT?
HE'S LYING IN HIS TEETH! I KNOW THAT! HE WOULDN'T LET SHAZAM LIVE, AND THEREFORE ME! BUT WAIT--- BY PRETENDING TO HELP SIVANA, MAYBE I CAN YET FIND A WAY TO DEFEAT HIM! IT'S MY ONLY CHANCE!

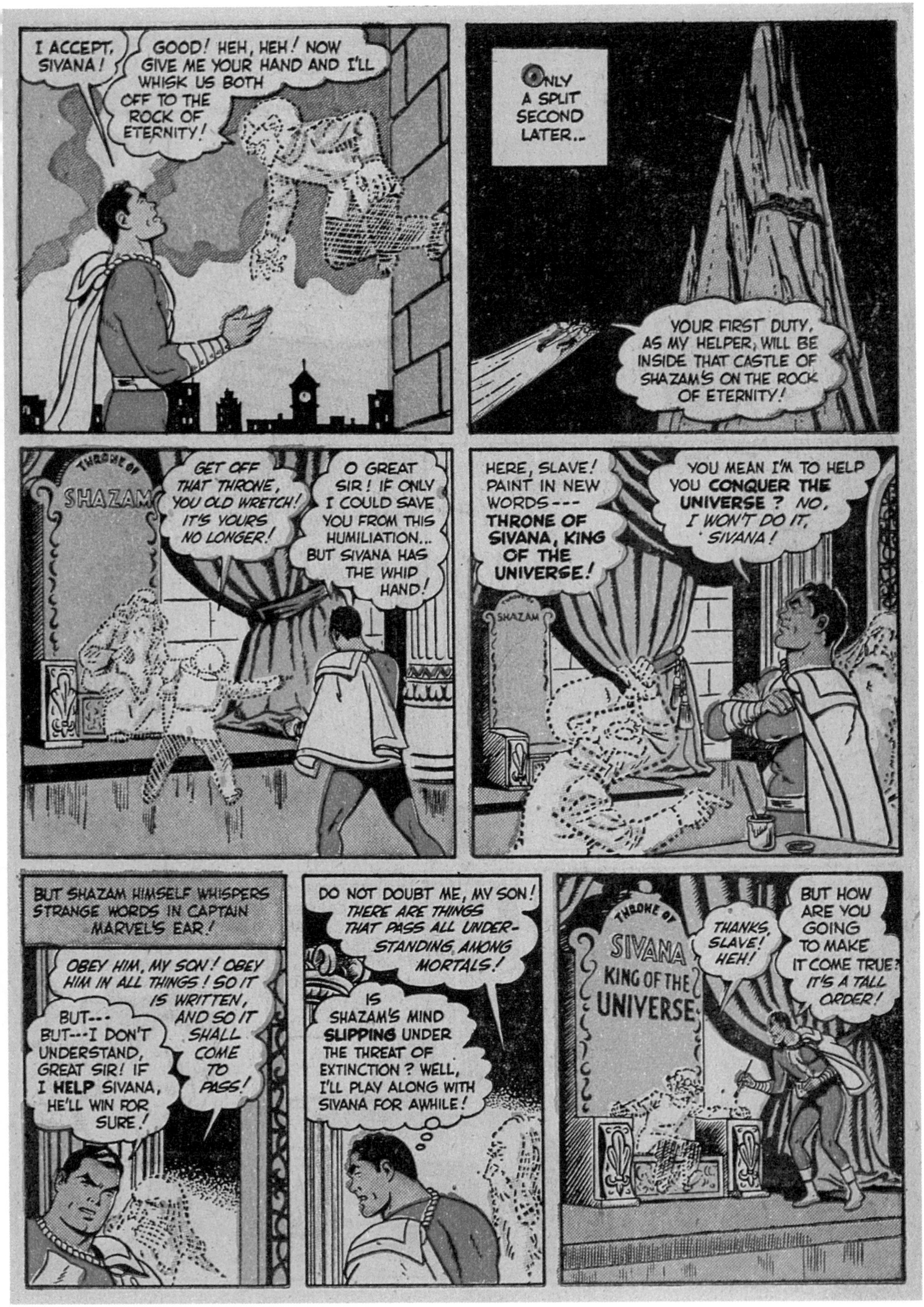
I ACCEPT, SIVANA!
GOOD! HEH, HEH! NOW GIVE ME YOUR HAND AND I'LL WHISK US BOTH OFF TO THE ROCK OF ETERNITY!
ONLY A SPLIT SECOND LATER...
YOUR FIRST DUTY, AS MY HELPER, WILL BE INSIDE THAT CASTLE OF SHAZAM'S ON THE ROCK OF ETERNITY!
THRONE OF SHAZAM
GET OFF THAT THRONE, YOU OLD WRETCH! IT'S YOURS NO LONGER!
O GREAT SIR! IF ONLY I COULD SAVE YOU FROM THIS HUMILIATION... BUT SIVANA HAS THE WHIP HAND!
HERE, SLAVE! PAINT IN NEW WORDS--- **THRONE OF SIVANA, KING OF THE UNIVERSE!**
YOU MEAN I'M TO HELP YOU **CONQUER THE UNIVERSE**? NO, I WON'T DO IT, SIVANA!
SHAZAM
BUT SHAZAM HIMSELF WHISPERS STRANGE WORDS IN CAPTAIN MARVEL'S EAR!
OBEY HIM, MY SON! OBEY HIM IN ALL THINGS! SO IT IS WRITTEN, AND SO IT SHALL COME TO PASS!
BUT--- BUT---I DON'T UNDERSTAND, GREAT SIR! IF I **HELP** SIVANA, HE'LL WIN FOR SURE!
DO NOT DOUBT ME, MY SON! THERE ARE THINGS THAT PASS ALL UNDERSTANDING AMONG MORTALS!
IS SHAZAM'S MIND **SLIPPING** UNDER THE THREAT OF EXTINCTION? WELL, I'LL PLAY ALONG WITH SIVANA FOR AWHILE!
THRONE OF SIVANA KING OF THE UNIVERSE
THANKS, SLAVE! HEH!
BUT HOW ARE YOU GOING TO MAKE IT COME TRUE? IT'S A TALL ORDER!

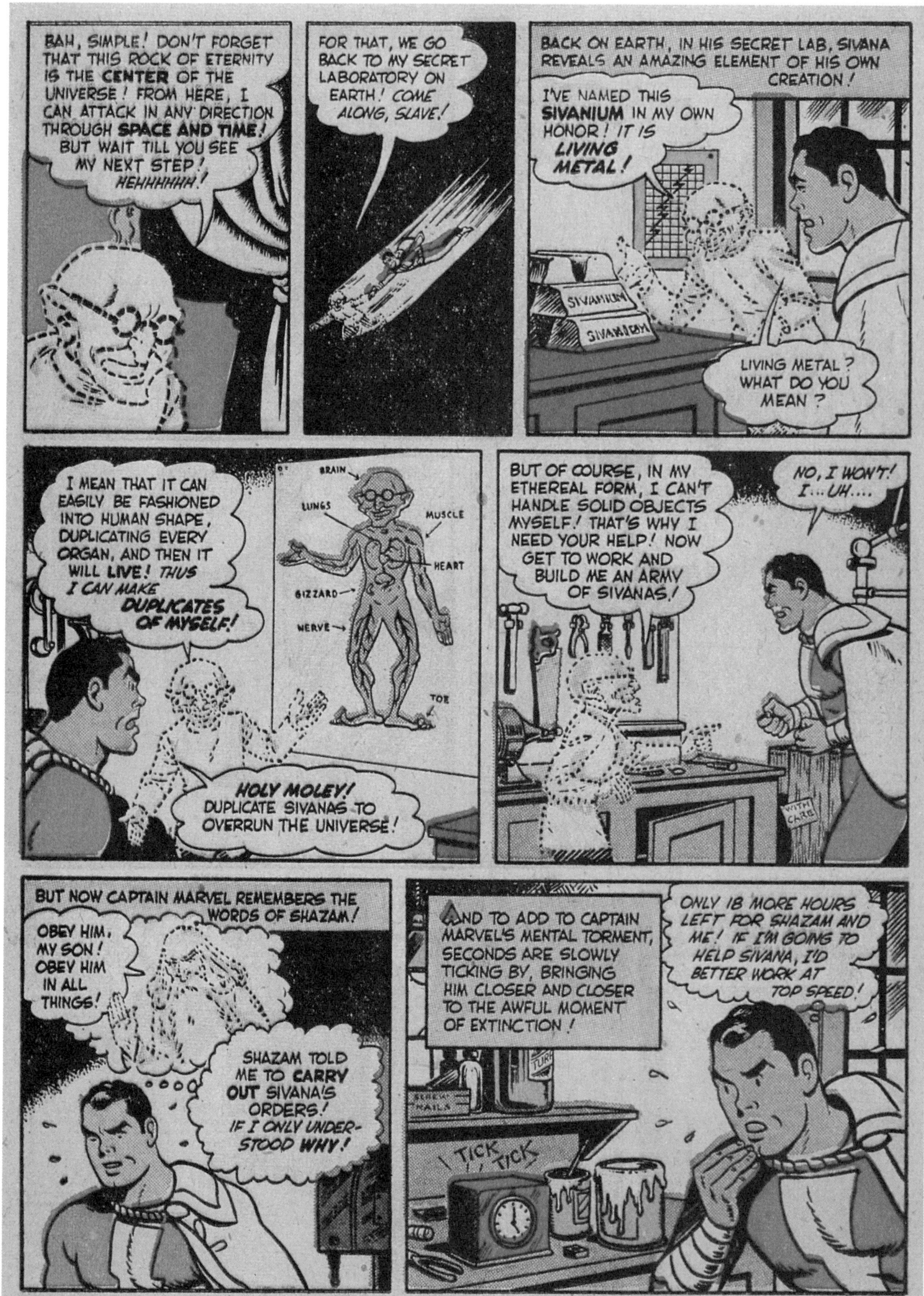

BAH, SIMPLE! DON'T FORGET THAT THIS ROCK OF ETERNITY IS THE CENTER OF THE UNIVERSE! FROM HERE, I CAN ATTACK IN ANY DIRECTION THROUGH SPACE AND TIME! BUT WAIT TILL YOU SEE MY NEXT STEP! HEHHHHHH!
FOR THAT, WE GO BACK TO MY SECRET LABORATORY ON EARTH! COME ALONG, SLAVE!
BACK ON EARTH, IN HIS SECRET LAB, SIVANA REVEALS AN AMAZING ELEMENT OF HIS OWN CREATION!
I'VE NAMED THIS SIVANIUM IN MY OWN HONOR! IT IS LIVING METAL!
SIVANIUM
LIVING METAL? WHAT DO YOU MEAN?
I MEAN THAT IT CAN EASILY BE FASHIONED INTO HUMAN SHAPE, DUPLICATING EVERY ORGAN, AND THEN IT WILL LIVE! THUS I CAN MAKE DUPLICATES OF MYSELF!
BRAIN
LUNGS
MUSCLE
HEART
GIZZARD
NERVE
TOE
HOLY MOLEY! DUPLICATE SIVANAS TO OVERRUN THE UNIVERSE!
BUT OF COURSE, IN MY ETHEREAL FORM, I CAN'T HANDLE SOLID OBJECTS MYSELF! THAT'S WHY I NEED YOUR HELP! NOW GET TO WORK AND BUILD ME AN ARMY OF SIVANAS!
NO, I WON'T! I...UH....
WITH CARE
BUT NOW CAPTAIN MARVEL REMEMBERS THE WORDS OF SHAZAM!
OBEY HIM, MY SON! OBEY HIM IN ALL THINGS!
SHAZAM TOLD ME TO CARRY OUT SIVANA'S ORDERS! IF I ONLY UNDERSTOOD WHY!
AND TO ADD TO CAPTAIN MARVEL'S MENTAL TORMENT, SECONDS ARE SLOWLY TICKING BY, BRINGING HIM CLOSER AND CLOSER TO THE AWFUL MOMENT OF EXTINCTION!
ONLY 18 MORE HOURS LEFT FOR SHAZAM AND ME! IF I'M GOING TO HELP SIVANA, I'D BETTER WORK AT TOP SPEED!
SCREWS NAILS
TICK, TICK

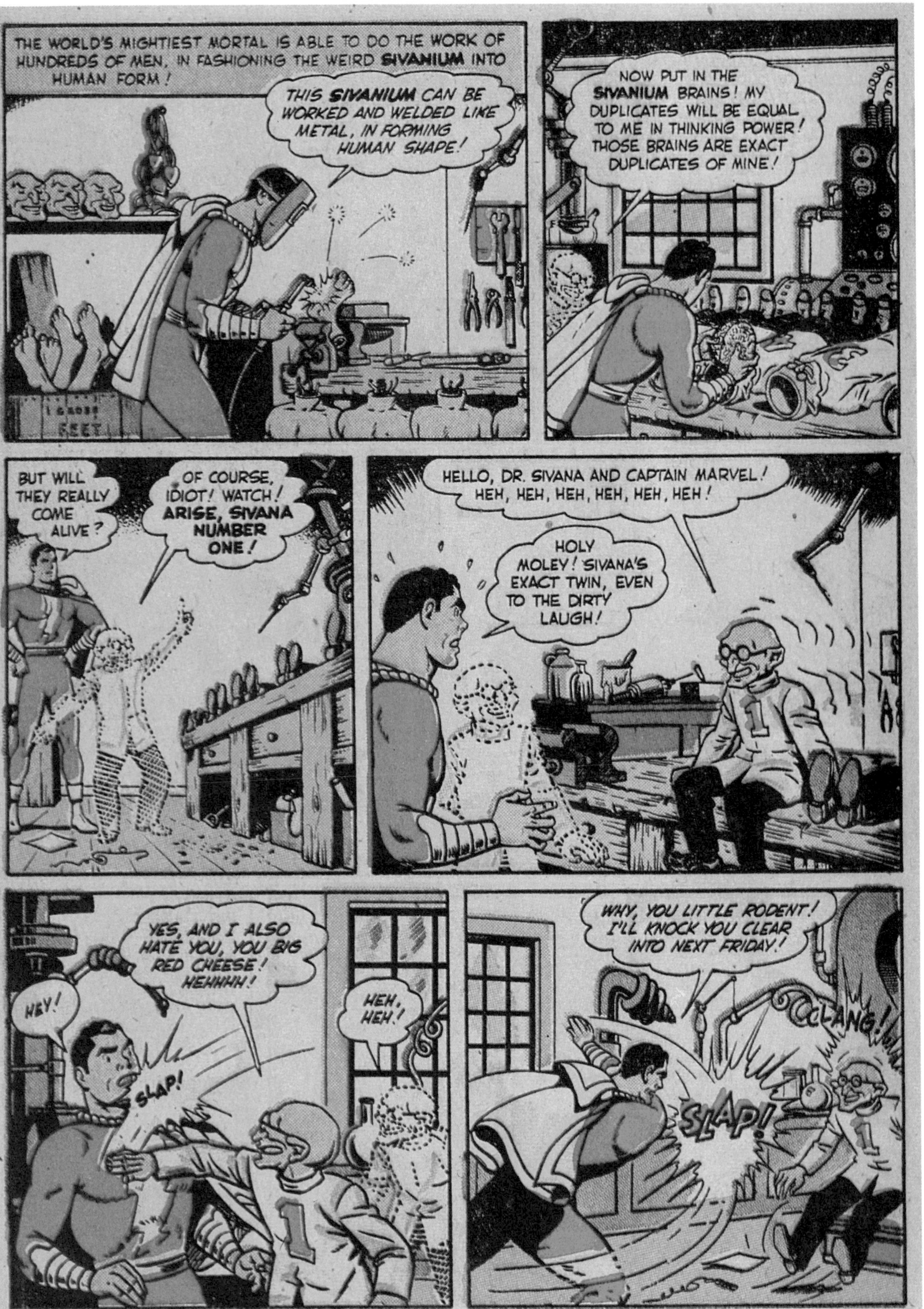

THE WORLD'S MIGHTIEST MORTAL IS ABLE TO DO THE WORK OF HUNDREDS OF MEN, IN FASHIONING THE WEIRD SIVANIUM INTO HUMAN FORM!
THIS SIVANIUM CAN BE WORKED AND WELDED LIKE METAL, IN FORMING HUMAN SHAPE!
1 GROSS FEET
NOW PUT IN THE SIVANIUM BRAINS! MY DUPLICATES WILL BE EQUAL TO ME IN THINKING POWER! THOSE BRAINS ARE EXACT DUPLICATES OF MINE!
BUT WILL THEY REALLY COME ALIVE?
OF COURSE, IDIOT! WATCH! ARISE, SIVANA NUMBER ONE!
HELLO, DR. SIVANA AND CAPTAIN MARVEL! HEH, HEH, HEH, HEH, HEH, HEH!
HOLY MOLEY! SIVANA'S EXACT TWIN, EVEN TO THE DIRTY LAUGH!
HEY!
YES, AND I ALSO HATE YOU, YOU BIG RED CHEESE! HEHHHH!
HEH, HEH!
SLAP!
WHY, YOU LITTLE RODENT! I'LL KNOCK YOU CLEAR INTO NEXT FRIDAY!
CLANG!
SLAP!

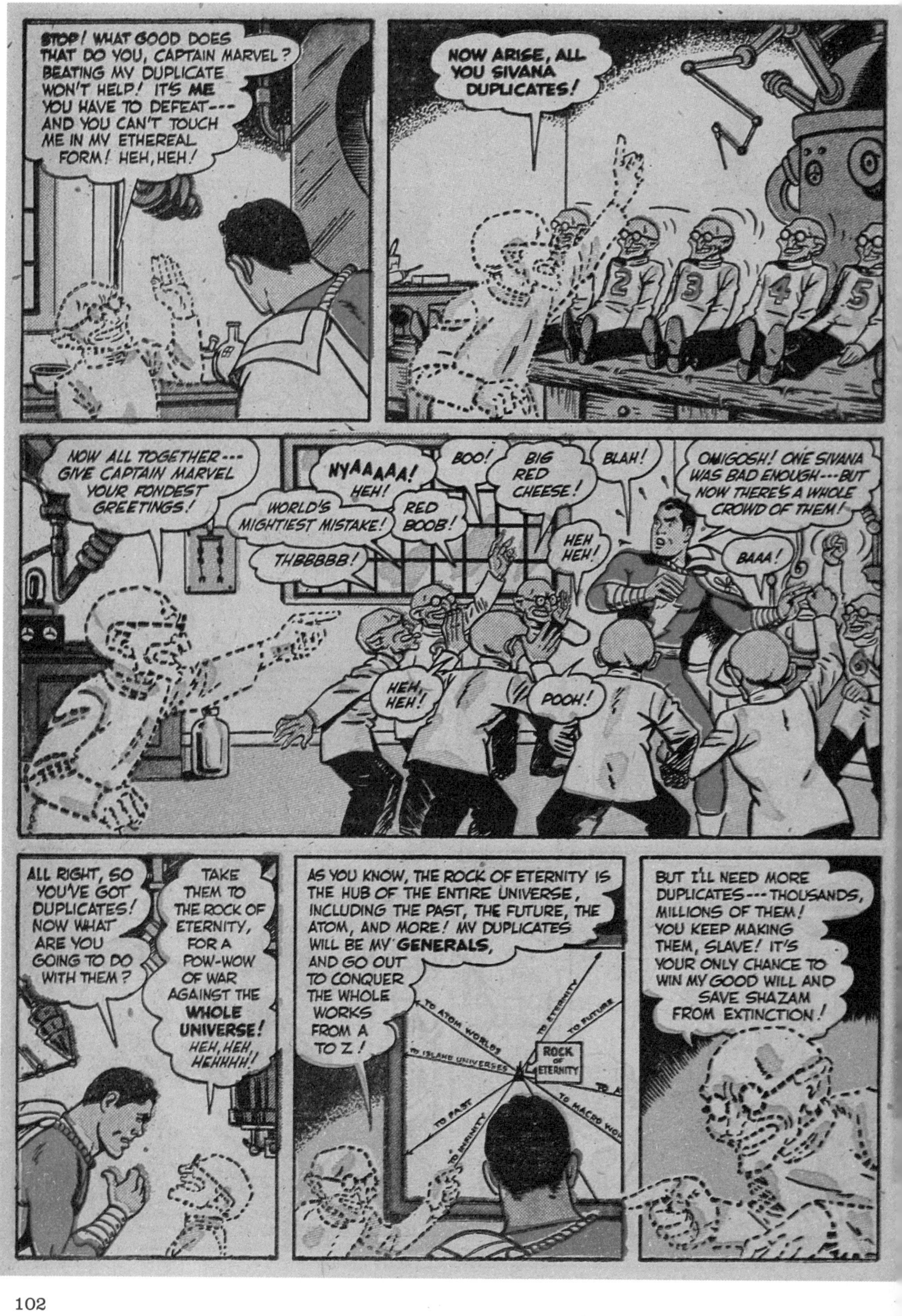

STOP! WHAT GOOD DOES THAT DO YOU, CAPTAIN MARVEL? BEATING MY DUPLICATE WON'T HELP! IT'S ME YOU HAVE TO DEFEAT--- AND YOU CAN'T TOUCH ME IN MY ETHEREAL FORM! HEH, HEH!
NOW ARISE, ALL YOU SIVANA DUPLICATES!
2
3
4
5
NOW ALL TOGETHER--- GIVE CAPTAIN MARVEL YOUR FONDEST GREETINGS!
NYAAAAA! HEH!
WORLD'S MIGHTIEST MISTAKE!
RED BOOB!
THBBBBB!
BOO!
BIG RED CHEESE!
BLAH!
HEH HEH!
OMIGOSH! ONE SIVANA WAS BAD ENOUGH---BUT NOW THERE'S A WHOLE CROWD OF THEM!
BAAA!
HEH, HEH!
POOH!
ALL RIGHT, SO YOU'VE GOT DUPLICATES! NOW WHAT ARE YOU GOING TO DO WITH THEM?
TAKE THEM TO THE ROCK OF ETERNITY, FOR A POW-WOW OF WAR AGAINST THE WHOLE UNIVERSE! HEH, HEH, HEHHHH!
AS YOU KNOW, THE ROCK OF ETERNITY IS THE HUB OF THE ENTIRE UNIVERSE, INCLUDING THE PAST, THE FUTURE, THE ATOM, AND MORE! MY DUPLICATES WILL BE MY GENERALS, AND GO OUT TO CONQUER THE WHOLE WORKS FROM A TO Z!
TO ATOM WORLDS
TO ETERNITY
TO FUTURE
TO ISLAND UNIVERSES
ROCK OF ETERNITY
TO PAST
TO INFINITY
BUT I'LL NEED MORE DUPLICATES--- THOUSANDS, MILLIONS OF THEM! YOU KEEP MAKING THEM, SLAVE! IT'S YOUR ONLY CHANCE TO WIN MY GOOD WILL AND SAVE SHAZAM FROM EXTINCTION!

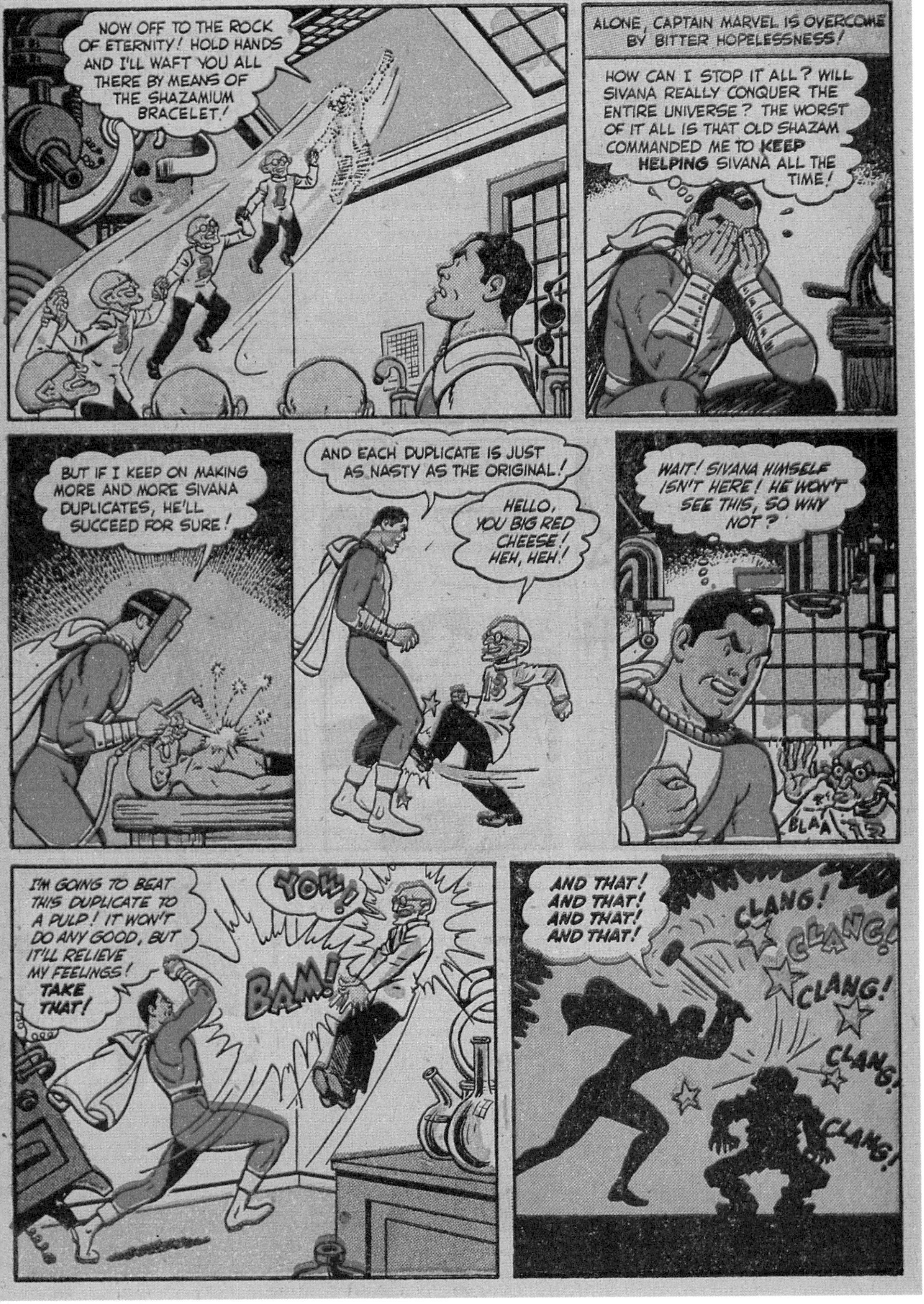
NOW OFF TO THE ROCK OF ETERNITY! HOLD HANDS AND I'LL WAFT YOU ALL THERE BY MEANS OF THE SHAZAMIUM BRACELET!
ALONE, CAPTAIN MARVEL IS OVERCOME BY BITTER HOPELESSNESS!
HOW CAN I STOP IT ALL? WILL SIVANA REALLY CONQUER THE ENTIRE UNIVERSE? THE WORST OF IT ALL IS THAT OLD SHAZAM COMMANDED ME TO KEEP HELPING SIVANA ALL THE TIME!
BUT IF I KEEP ON MAKING MORE AND MORE SIVANA DUPLICATES, HE'LL SUCCEED FOR SURE!
AND EACH DUPLICATE IS JUST AS NASTY AS THE ORIGINAL!
HELLO, YOU BIG RED CHEESE! HEH, HEH!
WAIT! SIVANA HIMSELF ISN'T HERE! HE WON'T SEE THIS, SO WHY NOT?
BLAA
I'M GOING TO BEAT THIS DUPLICATE TO A PULP! IT WON'T DO ANY GOOD, BUT IT'LL RELIEVE MY FEELINGS! TAKE THAT!
YOW!
BAM!
AND THAT! AND THAT! AND THAT! AND THAT!
CLANG!
CLANG!
CLANG!
CLANG!
CLANG!

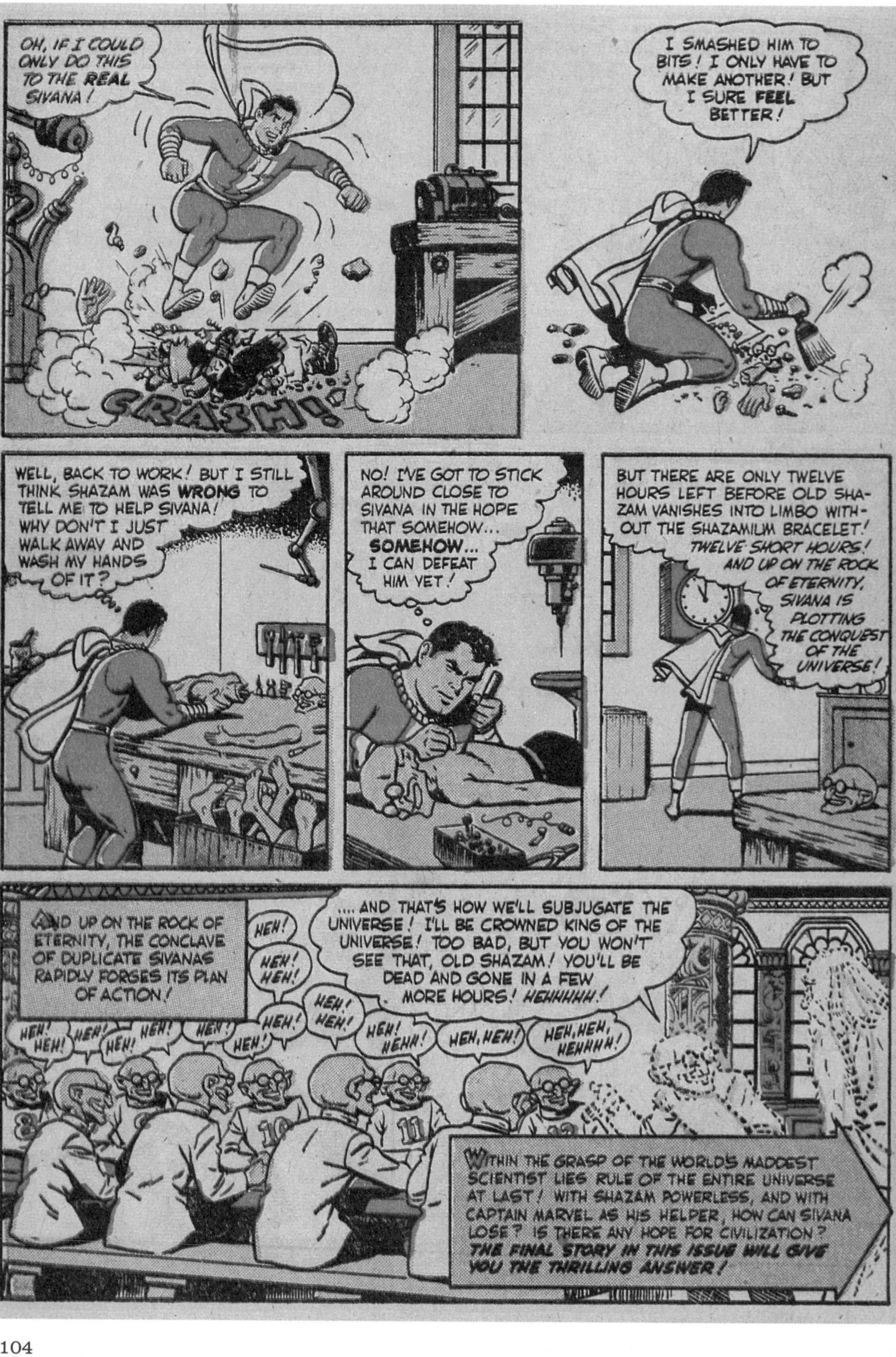
OH, IF I COULD ONLY DO THIS TO THE REAL SIVANA!
CRASH!
I SMASHED HIM TO BITS! I ONLY HAVE TO MAKE ANOTHER! BUT I SURE FEEL BETTER!
WELL, BACK TO WORK! BUT I STILL THINK SHAZAM WAS WRONG TO TELL ME TO HELP SIVANA! WHY DON'T I JUST WALK AWAY AND WASH MY HANDS OF IT?
NO! I'VE GOT TO STICK AROUND CLOSE TO SIVANA IN THE HOPE THAT SOMEHOW... SOMEHOW... I CAN DEFEAT HIM YET!
BUT THERE ARE ONLY TWELVE HOURS LEFT BEFORE OLD SHAZAM VANISHES INTO LIMBO WITHOUT THE SHAZAMIUM BRACELET!
TWELVE SHORT HOURS! AND UP ON THE ROCK OF ETERNITY, SIVANA IS PLOTTING THE CONQUEST OF THE UNIVERSE!
AND UP ON THE ROCK OF ETERNITY, THE CONCLAVE OF DUPLICATE SIVANAS RAPIDLY FORGES ITS PLAN OF ACTION!
HEH!
HEH! HEH!
....AND THAT'S HOW WE'LL SUBJUGATE THE UNIVERSE! I'LL BE CROWNED KING OF THE UNIVERSE! TOO BAD, BUT YOU WON'T SEE THAT, OLD SHAZAM! YOU'LL BE DEAD AND GONE IN A FEW MORE HOURS! HEHHHHH!
HEH! HEH!
HEH!
HEH!
HEH!
HEH!
HEH!
HEH! HEH!
HEH! HEHH!
HEH, HEH!
HEH, HEH, HEHHHH!
WITHIN THE GRASP OF THE WORLD'S MADDEST SCIENTIST LIES RULE OF THE ENTIRE UNIVERSE AT LAST! WITH SHAZAM POWERLESS, AND WITH CAPTAIN MARVEL AS HIS HELPER, HOW CAN SIVANA LOSE? IS THERE ANY HOPE FOR CIVILIZATION?
THE FINAL STORY IN THIS ISSUE WILL GIVE YOU THE THRILLING ANSWER!

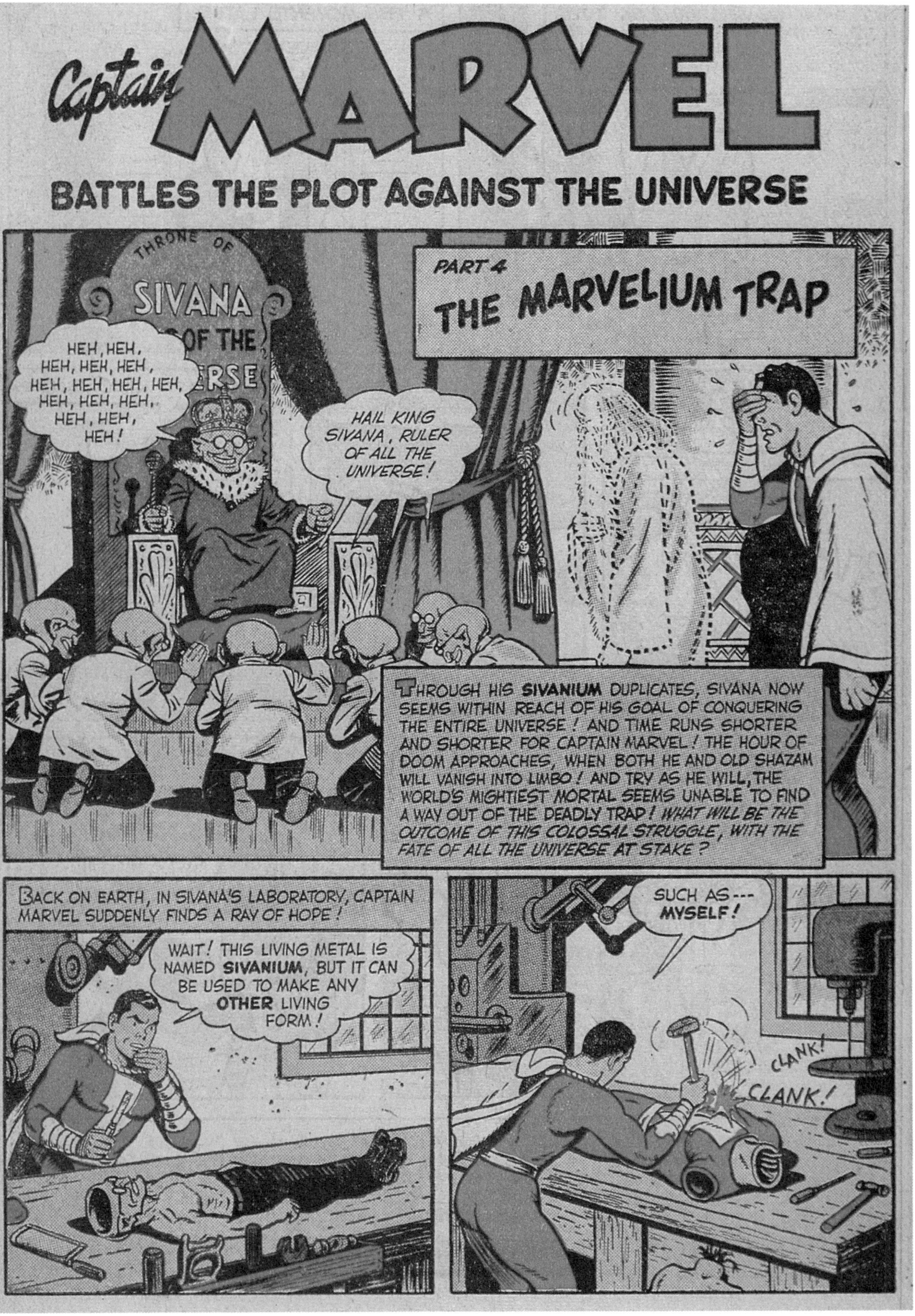
Captain MARVEL
BATTLES THE PLOT AGAINST THE UNIVERSE
PART 4
THE MARVELIUM TRAP
THRONE OF SIVANA ... OF THE ...ERSE
HEH, HEH, HEH, HEH, HEH, HEH, HEH, HEH, HEH, HEH, HEH, HEH, HEH, HEH, HEH!
HAIL KING SIVANA, RULER OF ALL THE UNIVERSE!
THROUGH HIS SIVANIUM DUPLICATES, SIVANA NOW SEEMS WITHIN REACH OF HIS GOAL OF CONQUERING THE ENTIRE UNIVERSE! AND TIME RUNS SHORTER AND SHORTER FOR CAPTAIN MARVEL! THE HOUR OF DOOM APPROACHES, WHEN BOTH HE AND OLD SHAZAM WILL VANISH INTO LIMBO! AND TRY AS HE WILL, THE WORLD'S MIGHTIEST MORTAL SEEMS UNABLE TO FIND A WAY OUT OF THE DEADLY TRAP! WHAT WILL BE THE OUTCOME OF THIS COLOSSAL STRUGGLE, WITH THE FATE OF ALL THE UNIVERSE AT STAKE?
BACK ON EARTH, IN SIVANA'S LABORATORY, CAPTAIN MARVEL SUDDENLY FINDS A RAY OF HOPE!
WAIT! THIS LIVING METAL IS NAMED SIVANIUM, BUT IT CAN BE USED TO MAKE ANY OTHER LIVING FORM!
SUCH AS --- MYSELF!
CLANK!
CLANK!

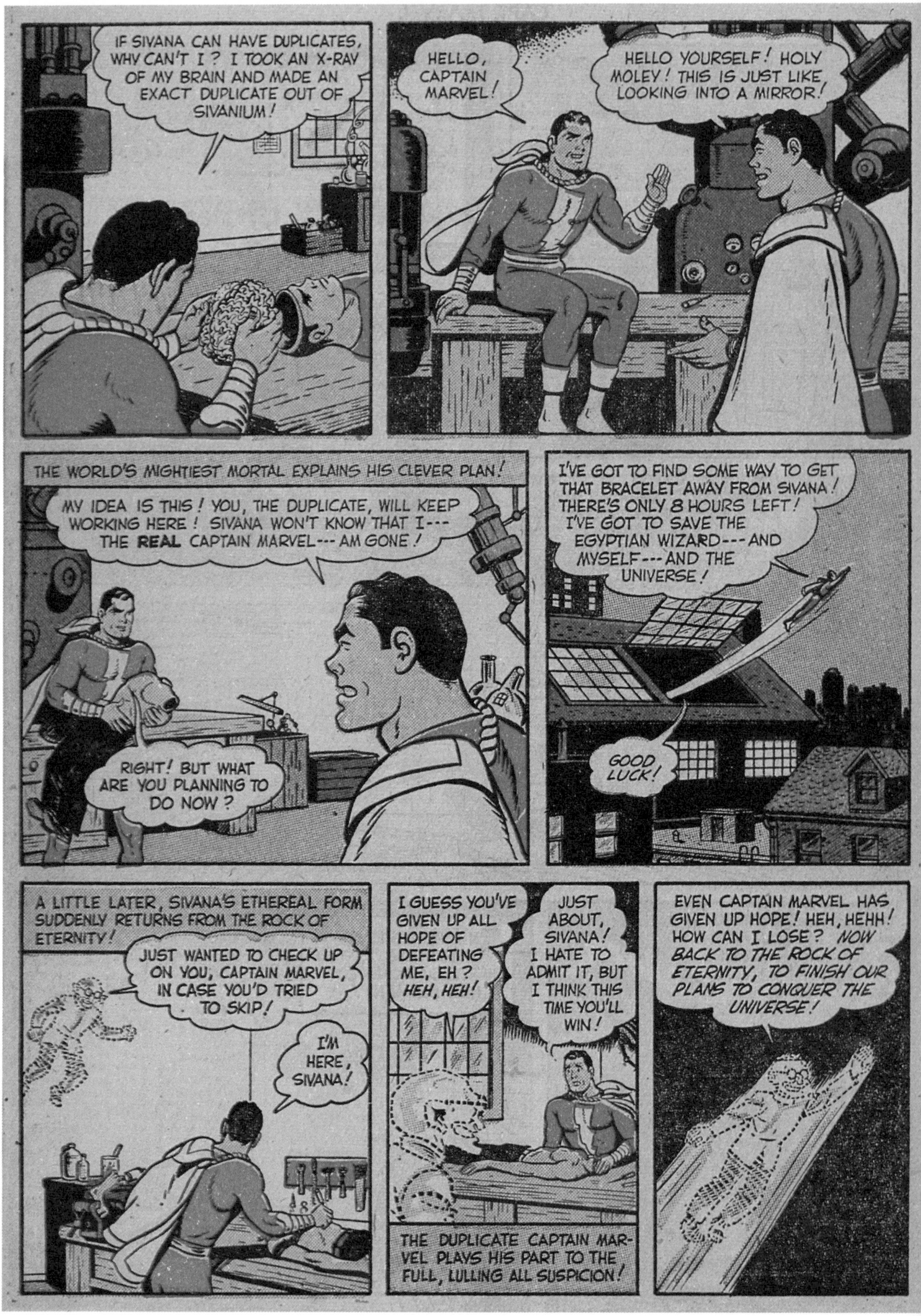
IF SIVANA CAN HAVE DUPLICATES, WHY CAN'T I ? I TOOK AN X-RAY OF MY BRAIN AND MADE AN EXACT DUPLICATE OUT OF SIVANIUM!
HELLO, CAPTAIN MARVEL!
HELLO YOURSELF! HOLY MOLEY! THIS IS JUST LIKE LOOKING INTO A MIRROR!
THE WORLD'S MIGHTIEST MORTAL EXPLAINS HIS CLEVER PLAN!
MY IDEA IS THIS! YOU, THE DUPLICATE, WILL KEEP WORKING HERE! SIVANA WON'T KNOW THAT I--- THE REAL CAPTAIN MARVEL--- AM GONE!
RIGHT! BUT WHAT ARE YOU PLANNING TO DO NOW?
I'VE GOT TO FIND SOME WAY TO GET THAT BRACELET AWAY FROM SIVANA! THERE'S ONLY 8 HOURS LEFT! I'VE GOT TO SAVE THE EGYPTIAN WIZARD--- AND MYSELF--- AND THE UNIVERSE!
GOOD LUCK!
A LITTLE LATER, SIVANA'S ETHEREAL FORM SUDDENLY RETURNS FROM THE ROCK OF ETERNITY!
JUST WANTED TO CHECK UP ON YOU, CAPTAIN MARVEL, IN CASE YOU'D TRIED TO SKIP!
I'M HERE, SIVANA!
I GUESS YOU'VE GIVEN UP ALL HOPE OF DEFEATING ME, EH? HEH, HEH!
JUST ABOUT, SIVANA! I HATE TO ADMIT IT, BUT I THINK THIS TIME YOU'LL WIN!
THE DUPLICATE CAPTAIN MARVEL PLAYS HIS PART TO THE FULL, LULLING ALL SUSPICION!
EVEN CAPTAIN MARVEL HAS GIVEN UP HOPE! HEH, HEHH! HOW CAN I LOSE? NOW BACK TO THE ROCK OF ETERNITY, TO FINISH OUR PLANS TO CONQUER THE UNIVERSE!

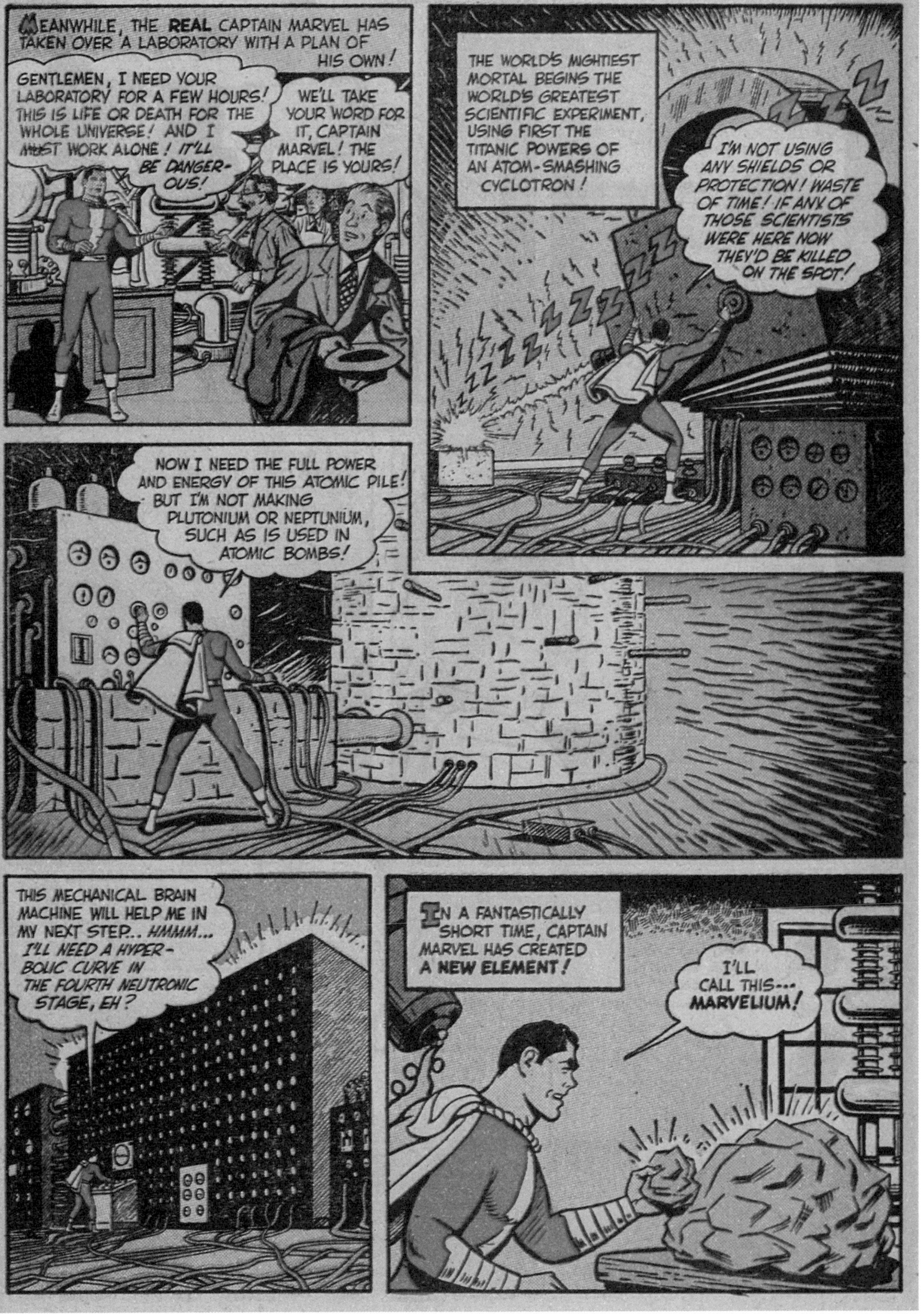
MEANWHILE, THE REAL CAPTAIN MARVEL HAS TAKEN OVER A LABORATORY WITH A PLAN OF HIS OWN!
GENTLEMEN, I NEED YOUR LABORATORY FOR A FEW HOURS! THIS IS LIFE OR DEATH FOR THE WHOLE UNIVERSE! AND I MUST WORK ALONE! IT'LL BE DANGER-OUS!
WE'LL TAKE YOUR WORD FOR IT, CAPTAIN MARVEL! THE PLACE IS YOURS!
THE WORLD'S MIGHTIEST MORTAL BEGINS THE WORLD'S GREATEST SCIENTIFIC EXPERIMENT, USING FIRST THE TITANIC POWERS OF AN ATOM-SMASHING CYCLOTRON!
I'M NOT USING ANY SHIELDS OR PROTECTION! WASTE OF TIME! IF ANY OF THOSE SCIENTISTS WERE HERE NOW THEY'D BE KILLED ON THE SPOT!
NOW I NEED THE FULL POWER AND ENERGY OF THIS ATOMIC PILE! BUT I'M NOT MAKING PLUTONIUM OR NEPTUNIUM, SUCH AS IS USED IN ATOMIC BOMBS!
THIS MECHANICAL BRAIN MACHINE WILL HELP ME IN MY NEXT STEP... HMMM... I'LL NEED A HYPER-BOLIC CURVE IN THE FOURTH NEUTRONIC STAGE, EH?
IN A FANTASTICALLY SHORT TIME, CAPTAIN MARVEL HAS CREATED A NEW ELEMENT!
I'LL CALL THIS--- MARVELIUM!

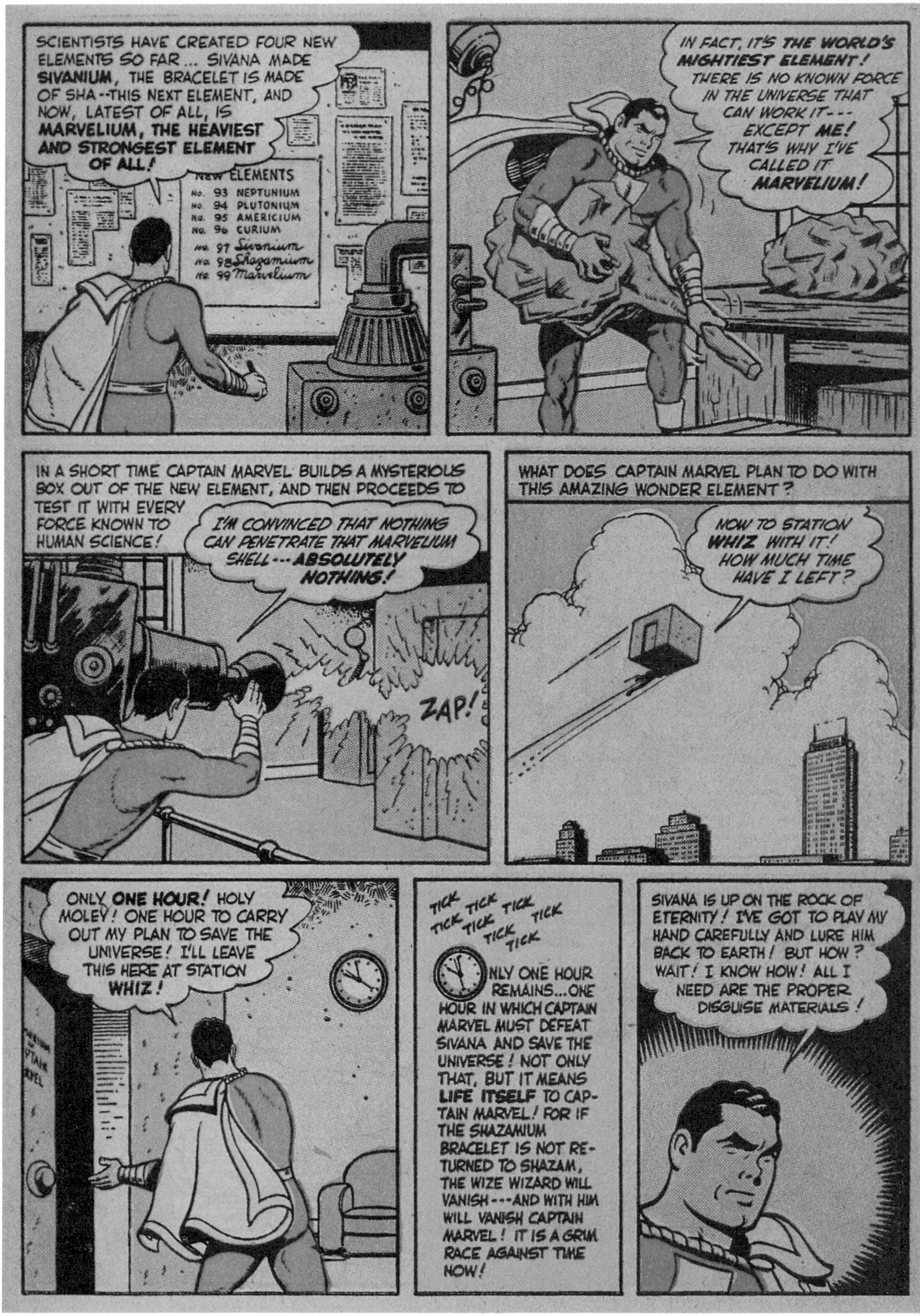
SCIENTISTS HAVE CREATED FOUR NEW ELEMENTS SO FAR ... SIVANA MADE SIVANIUM, THE BRACELET IS MADE OF SHA--THIS NEXT ELEMENT, AND NOW, LATEST OF ALL, IS MARVELIUM, THE HEAVIEST AND STRONGEST ELEMENT OF ALL!
NEW ELEMENTS
NO. 93 NEPTUNIUM
NO. 94 PLUTONIUM
NO. 95 AMERICIUM
NO. 96 CURIUM
NO. 97 Sivanium
NO. 98 Shazamium
NO. 99 Marvelium
IN FACT, IT'S THE WORLD'S MIGHTIEST ELEMENT! THERE IS NO KNOWN FORCE IN THE UNIVERSE THAT CAN WORK IT--- EXCEPT ME! THAT'S WHY I'VE CALLED IT MARVELIUM!
IN A SHORT TIME CAPTAIN MARVEL BUILDS A MYSTERIOUS BOX OUT OF THE NEW ELEMENT, AND THEN PROCEEDS TO TEST IT WITH EVERY FORCE KNOWN TO HUMAN SCIENCE!
I'M CONVINCED THAT NOTHING CAN PENETRATE THAT MARVELIUM SHELL --- ABSOLUTELY NOTHING!
ZAP!
WHAT DOES CAPTAIN MARVEL PLAN TO DO WITH THIS AMAZING WONDER ELEMENT?
NOW TO STATION WHIZ WITH IT! HOW MUCH TIME HAVE I LEFT?
ONLY ONE HOUR! HOLY MOLEY! ONE HOUR TO CARRY OUT MY PLAN TO SAVE THE UNIVERSE! I'LL LEAVE THIS HERE AT STATION WHIZ!
TICK TICK TICK TICK TICK TICK TICK TICK
ONLY ONE HOUR REMAINS...ONE HOUR IN WHICH CAPTAIN MARVEL MUST DEFEAT SIVANA AND SAVE THE UNIVERSE! NOT ONLY THAT, BUT IT MEANS LIFE ITSELF TO CAPTAIN MARVEL! FOR IF THE SHAZAMIUM BRACELET IS NOT RETURNED TO SHAZAM, THE WIZE WIZARD WILL VANISH---AND WITH HIM WILL VANISH CAPTAIN MARVEL! IT IS A GRIM RACE AGAINST TIME NOW!
SIVANA IS UP ON THE ROCK OF ETERNITY! I'VE GOT TO PLAY MY HAND CAREFULLY AND LURE HIM BACK TO EARTH! BUT HOW? WAIT! I KNOW HOW! ALL I NEED ARE THE PROPER DISGUISE MATERIALS!

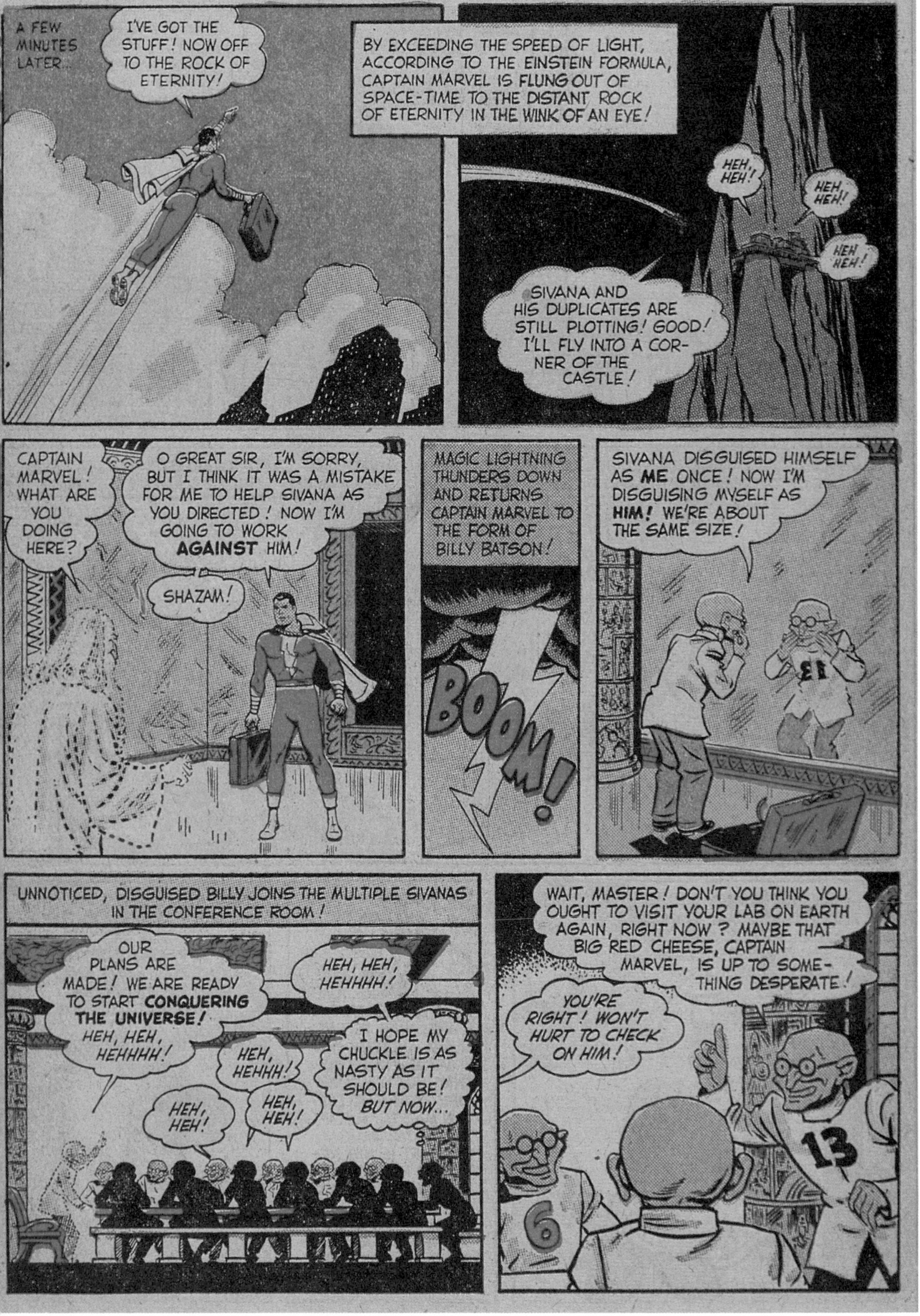
A FEW MINUTES LATER...
I'VE GOT THE STUFF! NOW OFF TO THE ROCK OF ETERNITY!
BY EXCEEDING THE SPEED OF LIGHT, ACCORDING TO THE EINSTEIN FORMULA, CAPTAIN MARVEL IS FLUNG OUT OF SPACE-TIME TO THE DISTANT ROCK OF ETERNITY IN THE WINK OF AN EYE!
HEH, HEH!
HEH, HEH!
HEH HEH!
SIVANA AND HIS DUPLICATES ARE STILL PLOTTING! GOOD! I'LL FLY INTO A CORNER OF THE CASTLE!
CAPTAIN MARVEL! WHAT ARE YOU DOING HERE?
O GREAT SIR, I'M SORRY, BUT I THINK IT WAS A MISTAKE FOR ME TO HELP SIVANA AS YOU DIRECTED! NOW I'M GOING TO WORK AGAINST HIM!
SHAZAM!
MAGIC LIGHTNING THUNDERS DOWN AND RETURNS CAPTAIN MARVEL TO THE FORM OF BILLY BATSON!
BOOOM!
SIVANA DISGUISED HIMSELF AS ME ONCE! NOW I'M DISGUISING MYSELF AS HIM! WE'RE ABOUT THE SAME SIZE!
UNNOTICED, DISGUISED BILLY JOINS THE MULTIPLE SIVANAS IN THE CONFERENCE ROOM!
OUR PLANS ARE MADE! WE ARE READY TO START CONQUERING THE UNIVERSE! HEH, HEH, HEHHHH!
HEH, HEH, HEHHHH!
I HOPE MY CHUCKLE IS AS NASTY AS IT SHOULD BE! BUT NOW...
HEH, HEHHH!
HEH, HEH!
HEH, HEH!
WAIT, MASTER! DON'T YOU THINK YOU OUGHT TO VISIT YOUR LAB ON EARTH AGAIN, RIGHT NOW? MAYBE THAT BIG RED CHEESE, CAPTAIN MARVEL, IS UP TO SOMETHING DESPERATE!
YOU'RE RIGHT! WON'T HURT TO CHECK ON HIM!
13
6

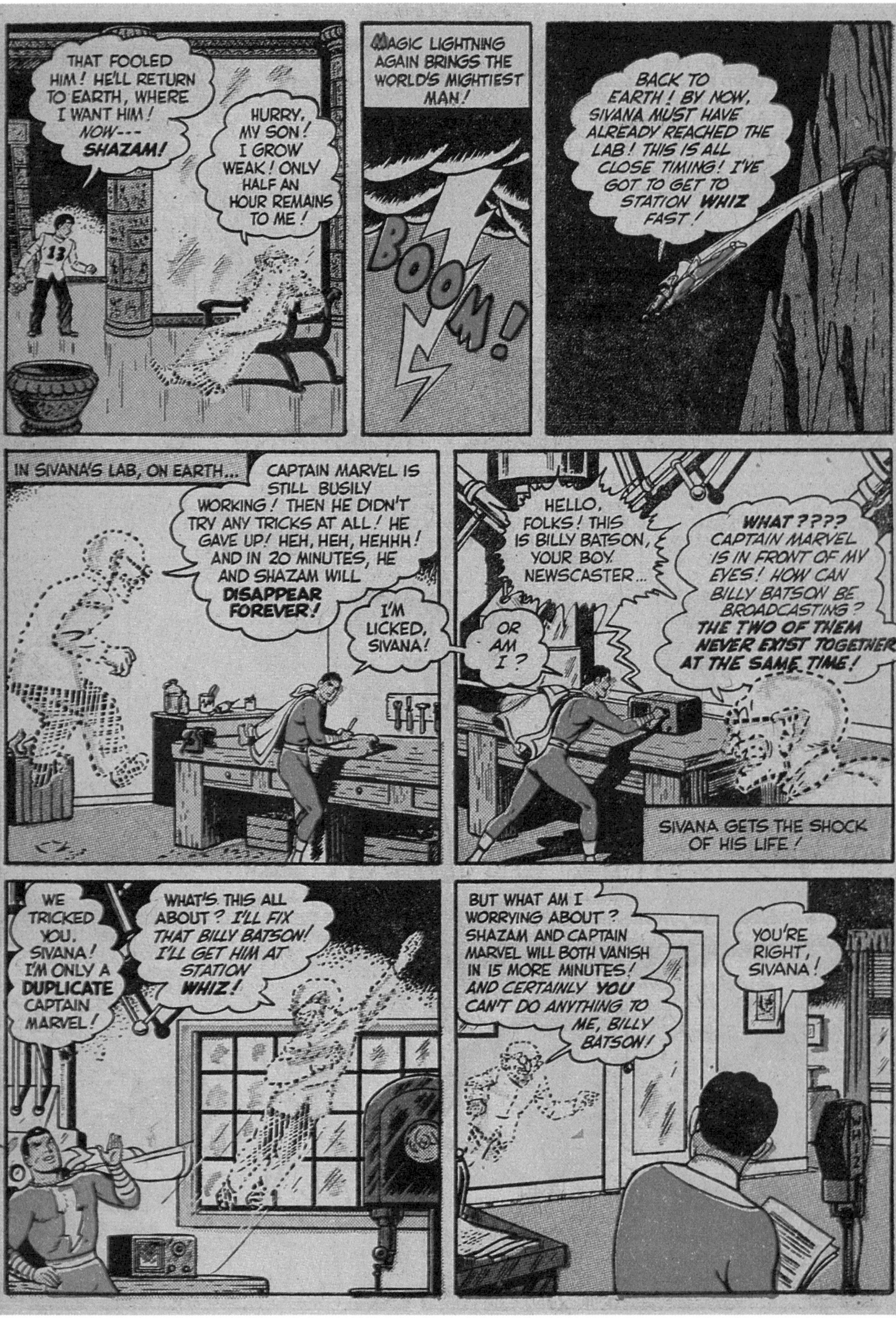

THAT FOOLED HIM! HE'LL RETURN TO EARTH, WHERE I WANT HIM! NOW--- SHAZAM!
HURRY, MY SON! I GROW WEAK! ONLY HALF AN HOUR REMAINS TO ME!
MAGIC LIGHTNING AGAIN BRINGS THE WORLD'S MIGHTIEST MAN!
BOOM!
BACK TO EARTH! BY NOW, SIVANA MUST HAVE ALREADY REACHED THE LAB! THIS IS ALL CLOSE TIMING! I'VE GOT TO GET TO STATION WHIZ FAST!
IN SIVANA'S LAB, ON EARTH...
CAPTAIN MARVEL IS STILL BUSILY WORKING! THEN HE DIDN'T TRY ANY TRICKS AT ALL! HE GAVE UP! HEH, HEH, HEHHH! AND IN 20 MINUTES, HE AND SHAZAM WILL DISAPPEAR FOREVER!
I'M LICKED, SIVANA!
OR AM I?
HELLO, FOLKS! THIS IS BILLY BATSON, YOUR BOY NEWSCASTER...
WHAT???? CAPTAIN MARVEL IS IN FRONT OF MY EYES! HOW CAN BILLY BATSON BE BROADCASTING? THE TWO OF THEM NEVER EXIST TOGETHER AT THE SAME TIME!
SIVANA GETS THE SHOCK OF HIS LIFE!
WE TRICKED YOU, SIVANA! I'M ONLY A DUPLICATE CAPTAIN MARVEL!
WHAT'S THIS ALL ABOUT? I'LL FIX THAT BILLY BATSON! I'LL GET HIM AT STATION WHIZ!
BUT WHAT AM I WORRYING ABOUT? SHAZAM AND CAPTAIN MARVEL WILL BOTH VANISH IN 15 MORE MINUTES! AND CERTAINLY YOU CAN'T DO ANYTHING TO ME, BILLY BATSON!
YOU'RE RIGHT, SIVANA!

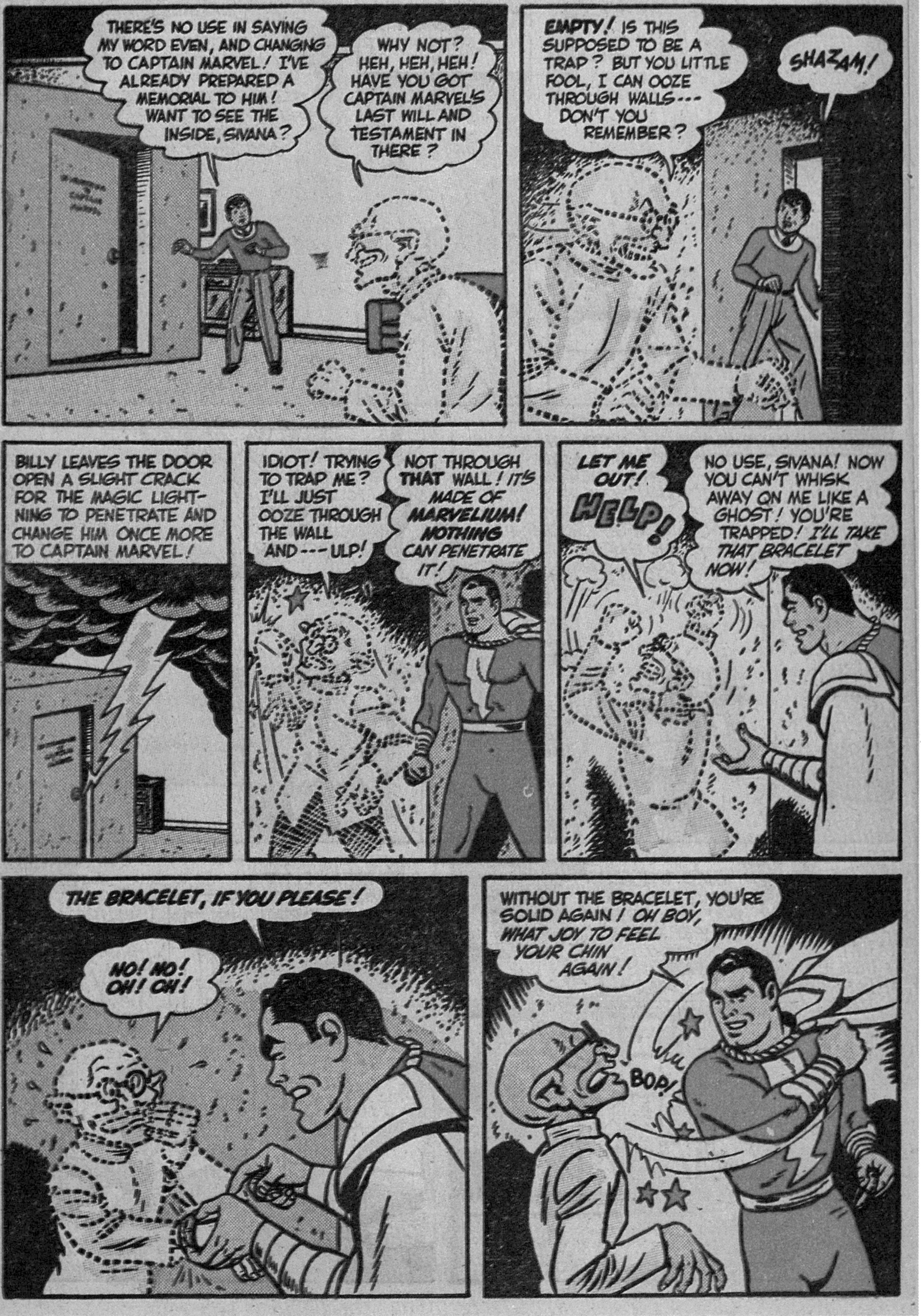
THERE'S NO USE IN SAYING MY WORD EVEN, AND CHANGING TO CAPTAIN MARVEL! I'VE ALREADY PREPARED A MEMORIAL TO HIM! WANT TO SEE THE INSIDE, SIVANA?
WHY NOT? HEH, HEH, HEH! HAVE YOU GOT CAPTAIN MARVEL'S LAST WILL AND TESTAMENT IN THERE?
EMPTY! IS THIS SUPPOSED TO BE A TRAP? BUT YOU LITTLE FOOL, I CAN OOZE THROUGH WALLS--- DON'T YOU REMEMBER?
SHAZAM!
BILLY LEAVES THE DOOR OPEN A SLIGHT CRACK FOR THE MAGIC LIGHTNING TO PENETRATE AND CHANGE HIM ONCE MORE TO CAPTAIN MARVEL!
IDIOT! TRYING TO TRAP ME? I'LL JUST OOZE THROUGH THE WALL AND---ULP!
NOT THROUGH THAT WALL! IT'S MADE OF MARVELIUM! NOTHING CAN PENETRATE IT!
LET ME OUT! HELP!
NO USE, SIVANA! NOW YOU CAN'T WHISK AWAY ON ME LIKE A GHOST! YOU'RE TRAPPED! I'LL TAKE THAT BRACELET NOW!
THE BRACELET, IF YOU PLEASE!
NO! NO! OH! OH!
WITHOUT THE BRACELET, YOU'RE SOLID AGAIN! OH BOY, WHAT JOY TO FEEL YOUR CHIN AGAIN!
BOP!

NOW TO GET THIS BRACELET TO THE WIZARD... HOLY MOLEY! ONLY A FEW SECONDS LEFT!

IN MEMORIUM TO CAPTAIN MARVEL

I'LL WEAR THE BRACELET MYSELF! IN ETHEREAL FORM I CAN WHISK TO THE ROCK OF ETERNITY INSTANTLY!

CAPTAIN MARVEL ARRIVES AT THE VERY ZERO MOMENT!

FAREWELL, MY SON......

NO! I'VE GOT THE BRACELET! PUT IT ON! HURRY!

MY STRENGTH IS BACK! ALL IS WELL! WE HAVE WON!

SHAZAM IS SAVED!

YES, BUT WHEW!--- THAT WAS CLOSE! I WISH YOU HADN'T ADVISED ME TO HELP SIVANA FIRST, SIR! I WOULD HAVE DEFEATED HIM SOONER!

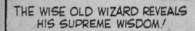

THE WISE OLD WIZARD REVEALS HIS SUPREME WISDOM!

NO, MY SON! YOU WOULD HAVE LOST! THINK BACK--- ONLY BY HELPING SIVANA DID YOU USE THE SIVANIUM AND THUS DISCOVER THE WAY TO MAKE A DUPLICATE OF YOURSELF, LEAVING YOU FREE TO MAKE MARVELIUM! OTHERWISE, OPPOSING SIVANA, YOU WOULD HAVE WASTED YOUR TIME IN USELESS DIRECT BATTLE!

FORGIVE ME, GREAT SIR! I SHOULD NEVER HAVE DOUBTED YOU FOR A MOMENT!

IT WAS SO WRITTEN--- AND SO IT CAME TO PASS!

BUT WAIT--- THOSE DUPLICATE SIVANAS! I MUST DESTROY THEM!

YOUR DUPLICATE ALSO CAME, AND IS TAKING CARE OF THAT, MY SON!

POW

BAM

SOK

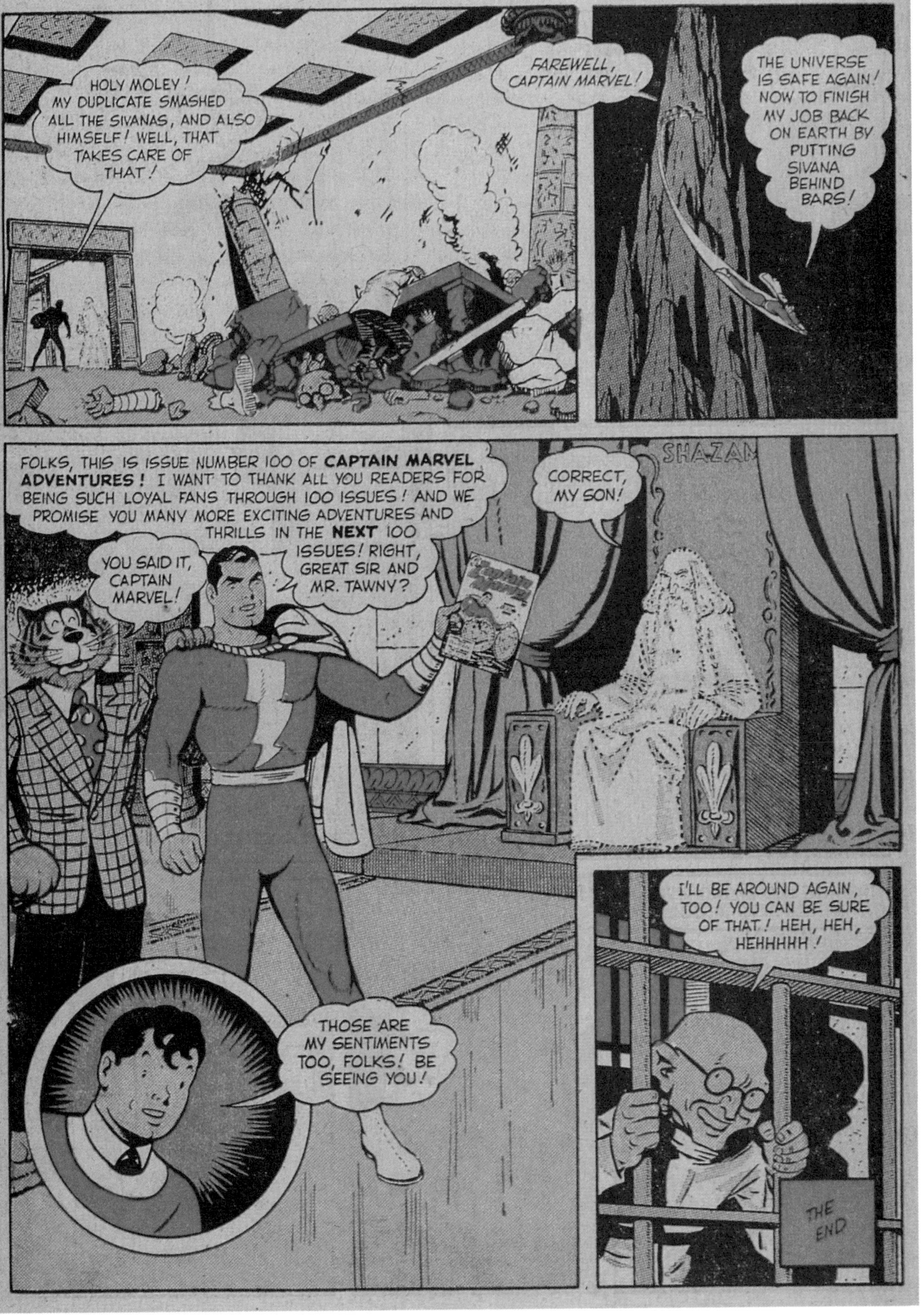
HOLY MOLEY! MY DUPLICATE SMASHED ALL THE SIVANAS, AND ALSO HIMSELF! WELL, THAT TAKES CARE OF THAT!
FAREWELL, CAPTAIN MARVEL!
THE UNIVERSE IS SAFE AGAIN! NOW TO FINISH MY JOB BACK ON EARTH BY PUTTING SIVANA BEHIND BARS!
FOLKS, THIS IS ISSUE NUMBER 100 OF CAPTAIN MARVEL ADVENTURES! I WANT TO THANK ALL YOU READERS FOR BEING SUCH LOYAL FANS THROUGH 100 ISSUES! AND WE PROMISE YOU MANY MORE EXCITING ADVENTURES AND THRILLS IN THE NEXT 100 ISSUES! RIGHT, GREAT SIR AND MR. TAWNY?
SHAZAM
CORRECT, MY SON!
YOU SAID IT, CAPTAIN MARVEL!
THOSE ARE MY SENTIMENTS TOO, FOLKS! BE SEEING YOU!
I'LL BE AROUND AGAIN, TOO! YOU CAN BE SURE OF THAT! HEH, HEH, HEHHHHH!
THE END

About Basil Wolverton

Powerhouse Pepper was the work of Basil Wolverton, who also produced one of the best known and most widely distributed caricatures ever drawn by an American. Only a few of the millions who saw that drawing bothered to retain its artist's name, however, and fewer still learned much about his other work. Finally, although Wolverton has a high reputation among the aficionados of the comic book, he produced at least two kinds of features, and thus his admirers have trouble deciding which represented the best Wolverton, or the "real" Wolverton.

Basil Wolverton (1909-1978) was born in the Oregon town of Central Point. With no formal art training, he sold his first cartoon to *America's Humor* in 1926. He was long established as a newspaper artist in the Northwest by the time he started contributing to comic books in 1938. His first regular feature was *Spacehawk,* an interplanetary adventure with a far-larger-than-life hero, begun in *Target* comics in mid-1940. Spacehawk's adventures were often brutal and violent, and (not uniquely) they tended to equate retribution with justice.

Wolverton's depictions of realistic figures in *Spacehawk* and his other space fantasies were often stiff and posturing, and his panels occasionally cramped. But his grasp of depth and perspective was almost uncanny, and resulted in one of the most compelling visual fantasies ever seen in the comics idiom. Indeed, Wolverton's 1940s drawings of space-suited figures, adrift, attached umbilically to their motherships, uncannily predict the realities of the space shots of the 1960s and 1970s.

Wolverton's most famous cartoon, mentioned earlier, appeared on a cover of *Life* in 1946. It came about as the result of a contest held by United Features Syndicate for the best depiction of a character alluded to but never seen in Al Capp's *Li'l Abner,* Lena the Hyena, "Lower Slobbovia's ugliest woman." Wolverton won with a drawing that managed to be ingeniously hideous and compellingly gleeful all at once. The drawing more or less established Wolverton as a master of comic grotesques and he contributed more of them to *Mad* in the 1950s and to the short-lived *Plop!* in the 1970s.

Beginning in 1942, meanwhile, Wolverton had contributed *Powerhouse Pepper,* an example of which we have chosen for inclusion here. Powerhouse Pepper was conceived, somewhat along the lines of Popeye or Alley Oop, as a relatively innocent comic hero who could outpunch anyone who pushed him too far. His adventures frequently involved him in the kind of broad burlesque of standard plots and situations depicted here.

In these explosive, low-comic stories, Wolverton's talent for grotesques was always there but always latent. His comparative ease with cartoon figures of keenly exaggerated anatomy, Wolverton's engaging silliness, his sight-gag ornamentation of his silliness in his drawings, his elementary energy in depicting comic attitudes—all of these resources thrived in *Powerhouse Pepper.* In addition, he sprinkled his *Powerhouse* dialogue with engaging doggerel rhymes and alliterations.

The feature lasted nearly a decade after Powerhouse's initial appearance in *Joker Comics,* and there were five intermittent issues of a *Powerhouse Pepper* comic book as well.

M.W.

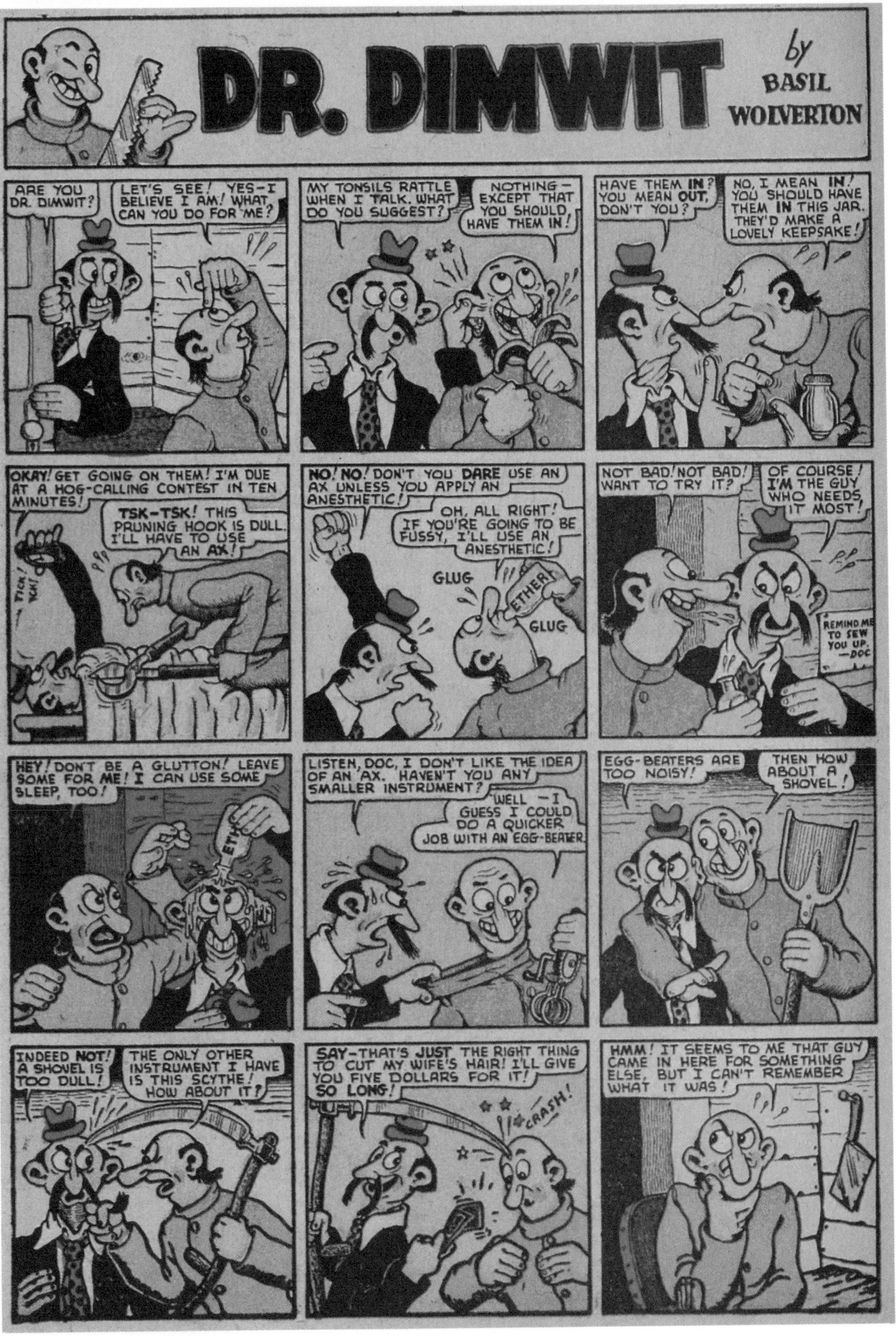
DR. DIMWIT
by BASIL WOLVERTON
ARE YOU DR. DIMWIT?
LET'S SEE! YES–I BELIEVE I AM! WHAT CAN YOU DO FOR ME?
MY TONSILS RATTLE WHEN I TALK. WHAT DO YOU SUGGEST?
NOTHING— EXCEPT THAT YOU SHOULD HAVE THEM IN!
HAVE THEM IN? YOU MEAN OUT, DON'T YOU?
NO, I MEAN IN! YOU SHOULD HAVE THEM IN THIS JAR. THEY'D MAKE A LOVELY KEEPSAKE!
OKAY! GET GOING ON THEM! I'M DUE AT A HOG-CALLING CONTEST IN TEN MINUTES!
TSK-TSK! THIS PRUNING HOOK IS DULL. I'LL HAVE TO USE AN AX!
NO! NO! DON'T YOU DARE USE AN AX UNLESS YOU APPLY AN ANESTHETIC!
OH, ALL RIGHT! IF YOU'RE GOING TO BE FUSSY, I'LL USE AN ANESTHETIC!
GLUG
ETHER
GLUG
NOT BAD! NOT BAD! WANT TO TRY IT?
OF COURSE! I'M THE GUY WHO NEEDS IT MOST!
REMIND ME TO SEW YOU UP. —DOC
HEY! DON'T BE A GLUTTON! LEAVE SOME FOR ME! I CAN USE SOME SLEEP, TOO!
LISTEN, DOC, I DON'T LIKE THE IDEA OF AN AX. HAVEN'T YOU ANY SMALLER INSTRUMENT?
WELL —I GUESS I COULD DO A QUICKER JOB WITH AN EGG-BEATER.
EGG-BEATERS ARE TOO NOISY!
THEN HOW ABOUT A SHOVEL!
INDEED NOT! A SHOVEL IS TOO DULL!
THE ONLY OTHER INSTRUMENT I HAVE IS THIS SCYTHE! HOW ABOUT IT?
SAY–THAT'S JUST THE RIGHT THING TO CUT MY WIFE'S HAIR! I'LL GIVE YOU FIVE DOLLARS FOR IT! SO LONG!
CRASH!
HMM! IT SEEMS TO ME THAT GUY CAME IN HERE FOR SOMETHING ELSE, BUT I CAN'T REMEMBER WHAT IT WAS!

From *Sub-Mariner* No. 4, 1942.

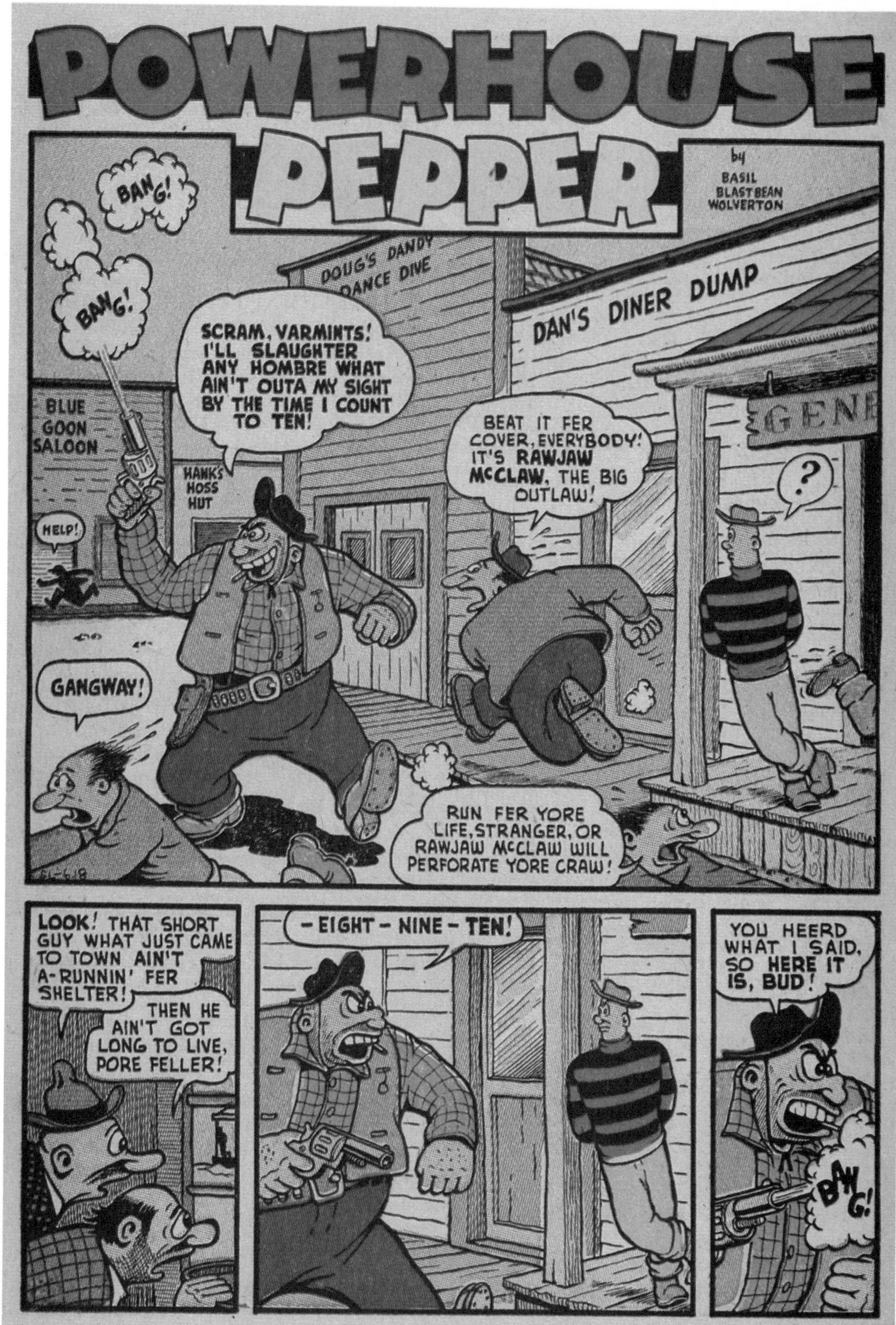
POWERHOUSE PEPPER
by BASIL BLASTBEAN WOLVERTON
BANG!
BANG!
DOUG'S DANDY DANCE DIVE
DAN'S DINER DUMP
SCRAM, VARMINTS! I'LL SLAUGHTER ANY HOMBRE WHAT AIN'T OUTA MY SIGHT BY THE TIME I COUNT TO TEN!
BLUE GOON SALOON
HANK'S HOSS HUT
HELP!
BEAT IT FER COVER, EVERYBODY! IT'S RAWJAW McCLAW, THE BIG OUTLAW!
GENE
?
GANGWAY!
RUN FER YORE LIFE, STRANGER, OR RAWJAW McCLAW WILL PERFORATE YORE CRAW!
LOOK! THAT SHORT GUY WHAT JUST CAME TO TOWN AIN'T A-RUNNIN' FER SHELTER!
THEN HE AIN'T GOT LONG TO LIVE, PORE FELLER!
- EIGHT - NINE - TEN!
YOU HEERD WHAT I SAID, SO HERE IT IS, BUD!
BANG!

From *Tessie the Typist* No. 8, January 1947.

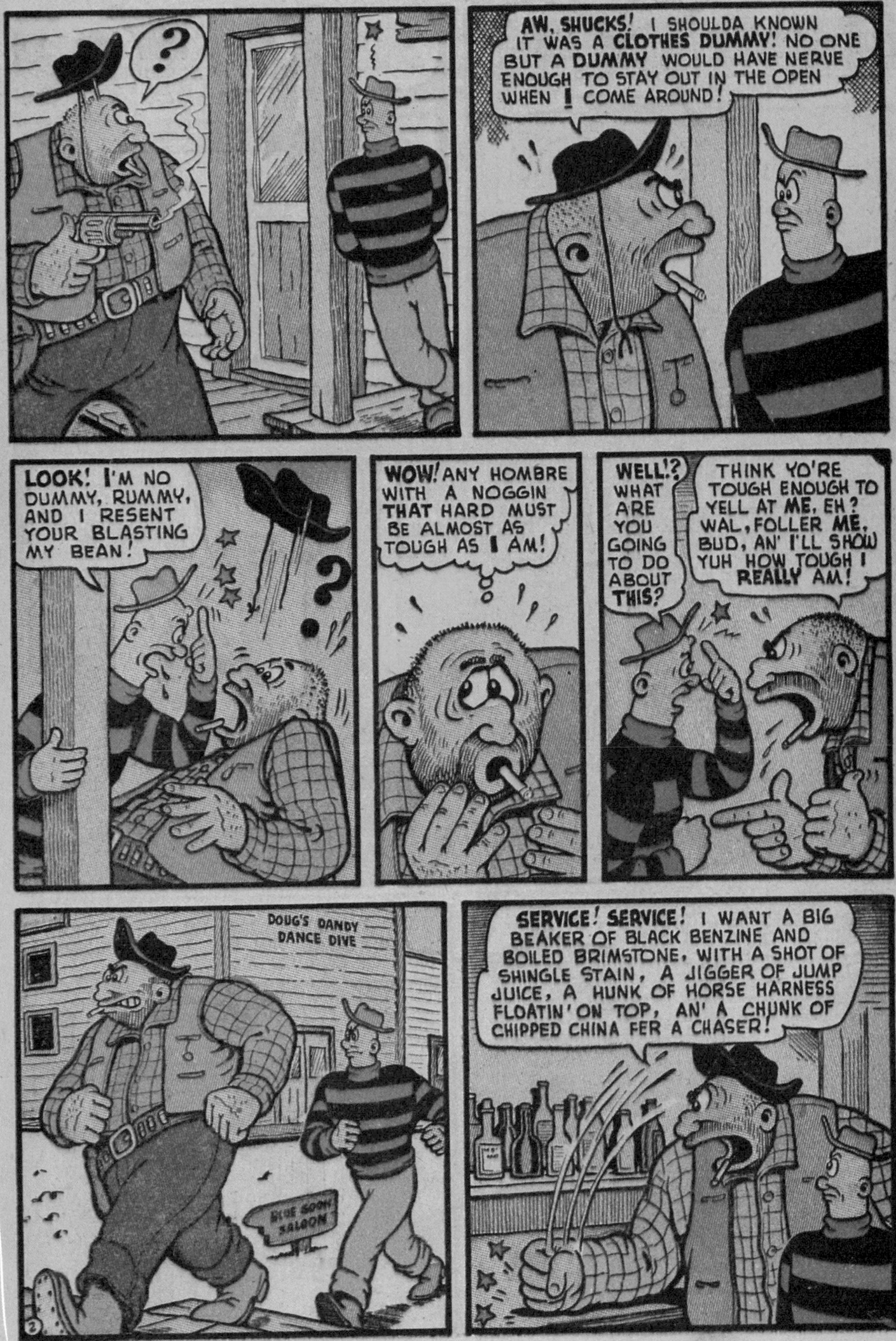
?
AW, SHUCKS! I SHOULDA KNOWN IT WAS A CLOTHES DUMMY! NO ONE BUT A DUMMY WOULD HAVE NERVE ENOUGH TO STAY OUT IN THE OPEN WHEN I COME AROUND!
LOOK! I'M NO DUMMY, RUMMY, AND I RESENT YOUR BLASTING MY BEAN!
?
WOW! ANY HOMBRE WITH A NOGGIN THAT HARD MUST BE ALMOST AS TOUGH AS I AM!
WELL!? WHAT ARE YOU GOING TO DO ABOUT THIS?
THINK YO'RE TOUGH ENOUGH TO YELL AT ME, EH? WAL, FOLLER ME, BUD, AN' I'LL SHOW YUH HOW TOUGH I REALLY AM!
DOUG'S DANDY DANCE DIVE
SALOON
SERVICE! SERVICE! I WANT A BIG BEAKER OF BLACK BENZINE AND BOILED BRIMSTONE, WITH A SHOT OF SHINGLE STAIN, A JIGGER OF JUMP JUICE, A HUNK OF HORSE HARNESS FLOATIN' ON TOP, AN' A CHUNK OF CHIPPED CHINA FER A CHASER!

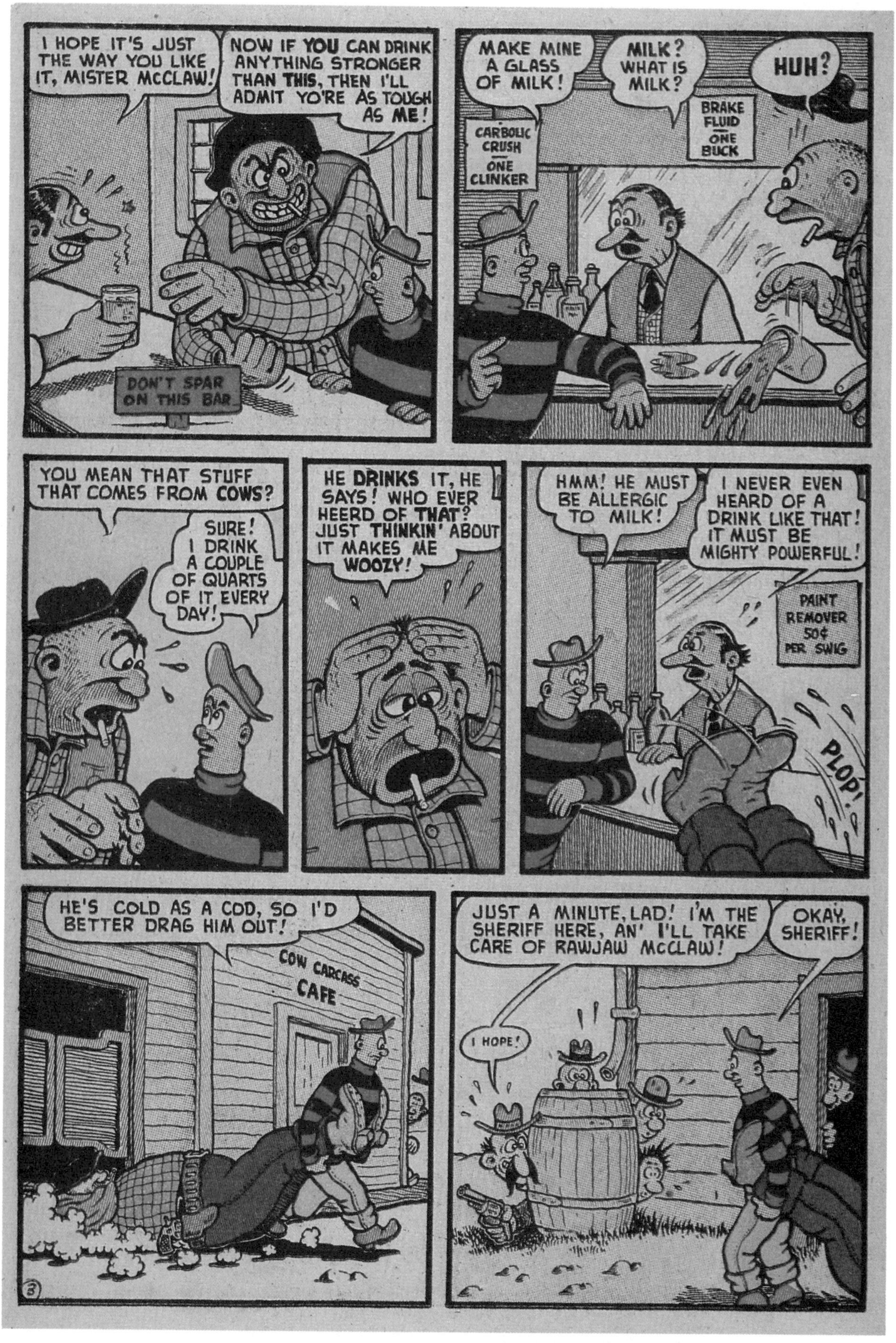

I HOPE IT'S JUST THE WAY YOU LIKE IT, MISTER McCLAW!
NOW IF YOU CAN DRINK ANYTHING STRONGER THAN THIS, THEN I'LL ADMIT YO'RE AS TOUGH AS ME!
DON'T SPAR ON THIS BAR
MAKE MINE A GLASS OF MILK!
MILK? WHAT IS MILK?
HUH?
CARBOLIC CRUSH — ONE CLINKER
BRAKE FLUID — ONE BUCK
YOU MEAN THAT STUFF THAT COMES FROM COWS?
SURE! I DRINK A COUPLE OF QUARTS OF IT EVERY DAY!
HE DRINKS IT, HE SAYS! WHO EVER HEERD OF THAT? JUST THINKIN' ABOUT IT MAKES ME WOOZY!
HMM! HE MUST BE ALLERGIC TO MILK!
I NEVER EVEN HEARD OF A DRINK LIKE THAT! IT MUST BE MIGHTY POWERFUL!
PAINT REMOVER 50¢ PER SWIG
PLOP!
HE'S COLD AS A COD, SO I'D BETTER DRAG HIM OUT!
COW CARCASS CAFE
3
JUST A MINUTE, LAD! I'M THE SHERIFF HERE, AN' I'LL TAKE CARE OF RAWJAW McCLAW!
OKAY, SHERIFF!
I HOPE!

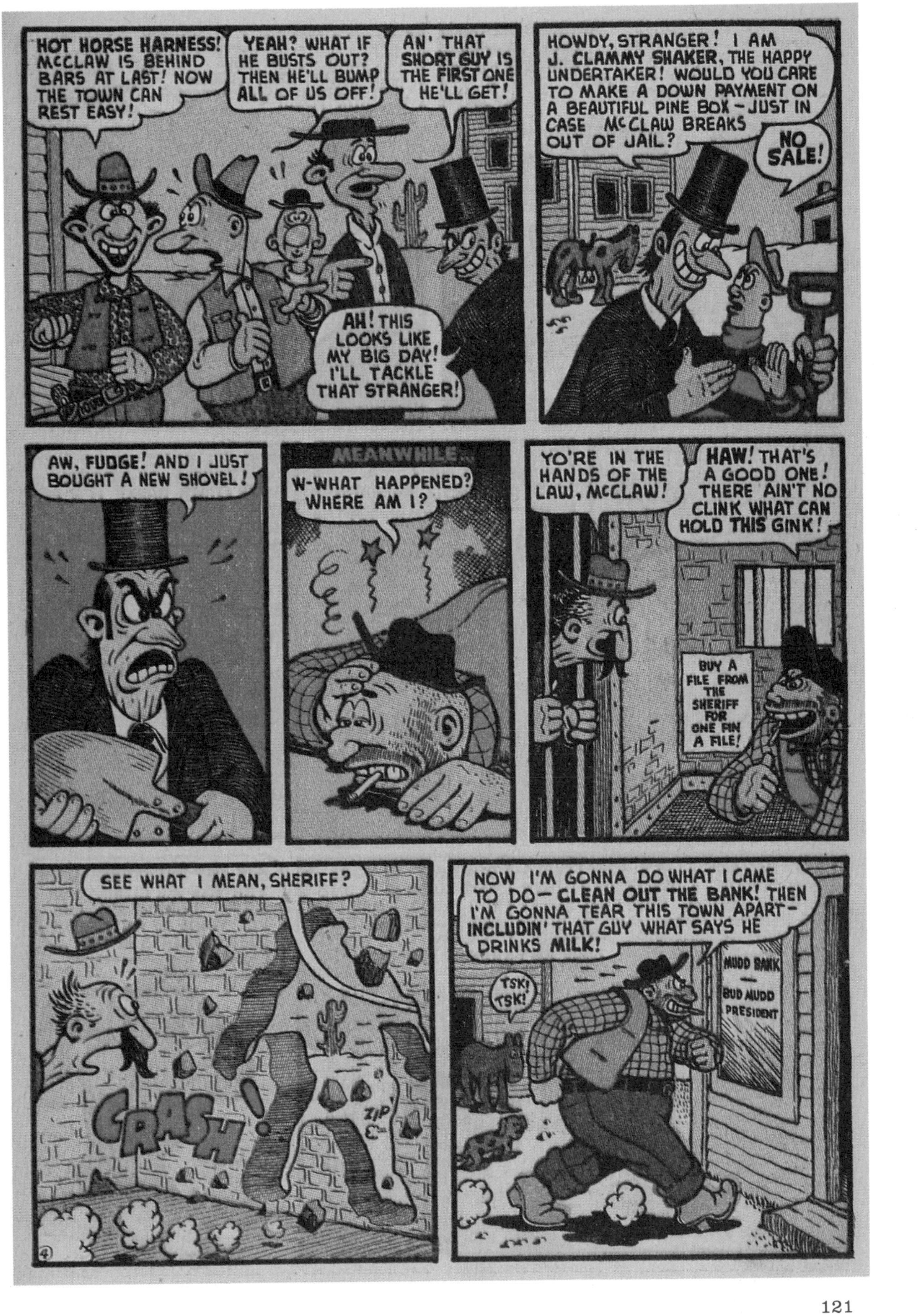
HOT HORSE HARNESS! McCLAW IS BEHIND BARS AT LAST! NOW THE TOWN CAN REST EASY!
YEAH? WHAT IF HE BUSTS OUT? THEN HE'LL BUMP ALL OF US OFF!
AN' THAT SHORT GUY IS THE FIRST ONE HE'LL GET!
AH! THIS LOOKS LIKE MY BIG DAY! I'LL TACKLE THAT STRANGER!
HOWDY, STRANGER! I AM J. CLAMMY SHAKER, THE HAPPY UNDERTAKER! WOULD YOU CARE TO MAKE A DOWN PAYMENT ON A BEAUTIFUL PINE BOX – JUST IN CASE McCLAW BREAKS OUT OF JAIL?
NO SALE!
AW, FUDGE! AND I JUST BOUGHT A NEW SHOVEL!
MEANWHILE...
W-WHAT HAPPENED? WHERE AM I?
YO'RE IN THE HANDS OF THE LAW, McCLAW!
HAW! THAT'S A GOOD ONE! THERE AIN'T NO CLINK WHAT CAN HOLD THIS GINK!
BUY A FILE FROM THE SHERIFF FOR ONE FIN A FILE!
SEE WHAT I MEAN, SHERIFF?
CRASH!
ZIP
4
NOW I'M GONNA DO WHAT I CAME TO DO– CLEAN OUT THE BANK! THEN I'M GONNA TEAR THIS TOWN APART– INCLUDIN' THAT GUY WHAT SAYS HE DRINKS MILK!
TSK! TSK!
MUDD BANK
BUD MUDD PRESIDENT

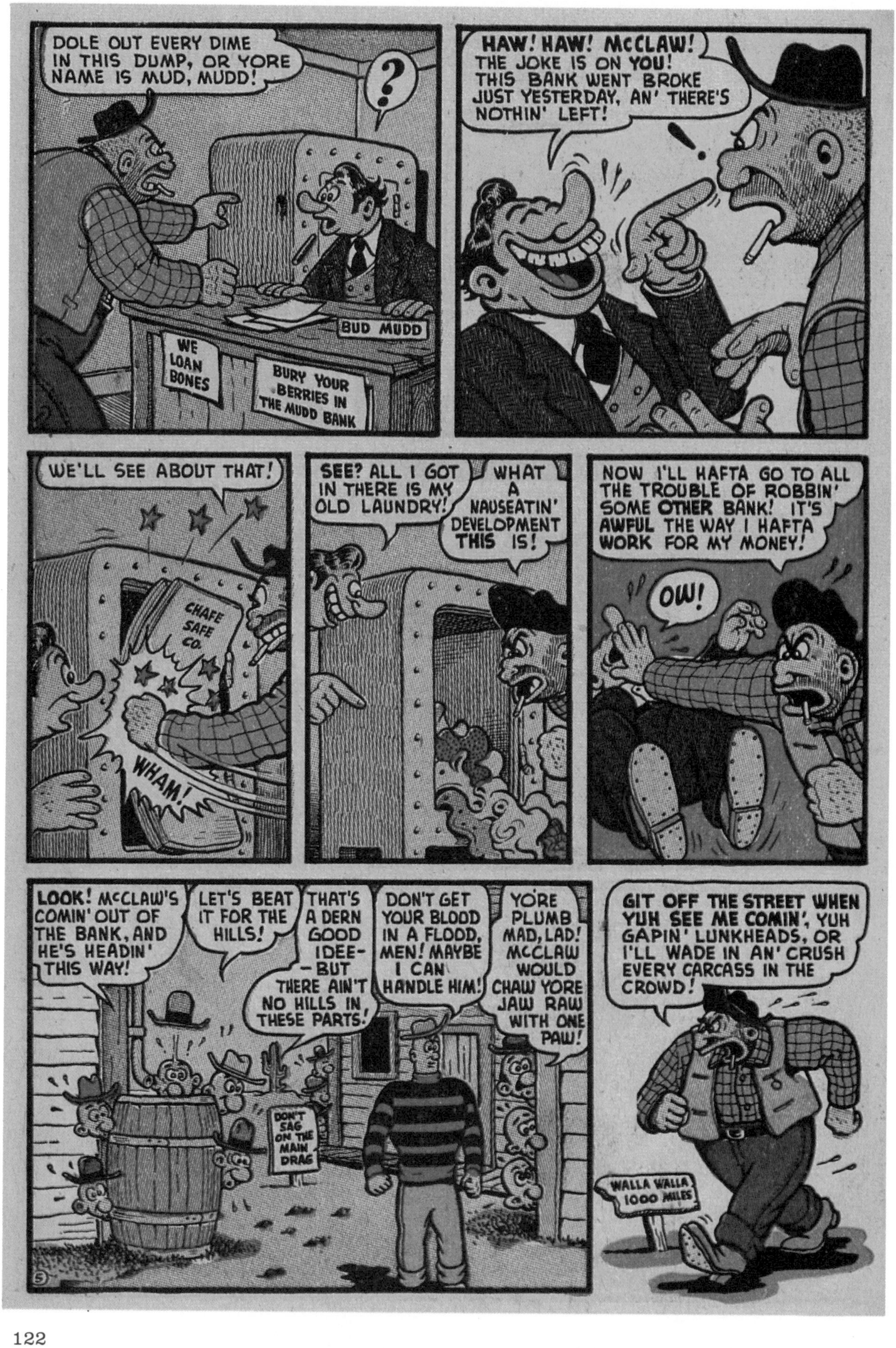
DOLE OUT EVERY DIME IN THIS DUMP, OR YORE NAME IS MUD, MUDD!
?
BUD MUDD
WE LOAN BONES
BURY YOUR BERRIES IN THE MUDD BANK
HAW! HAW! McCLAW! THE JOKE IS ON YOU! THIS BANK WENT BROKE JUST YESTERDAY, AN' THERE'S NOTHIN' LEFT!
!
WE'LL SEE ABOUT THAT!
CHAFE SAFE CO.
WHAM!
SEE? ALL I GOT IN THERE IS MY OLD LAUNDRY!
WHAT A NAUSEATIN' DEVELOPMENT THIS IS!
NOW I'LL HAFTA GO TO ALL THE TROUBLE OF ROBBIN' SOME OTHER BANK! IT'S AWFUL THE WAY I HAFTA WORK FOR MY MONEY!
OW!
LOOK! McCLAW'S COMIN' OUT OF THE BANK, AND HE'S HEADIN' THIS WAY!
LET'S BEAT IT FOR THE HILLS!
THAT'S A DERN GOOD IDEE- —BUT THERE AIN'T NO HILLS IN THESE PARTS!
DON'T GET YOUR BLOOD IN A FLOOD, MEN! MAYBE I CAN HANDLE HIM!
YO'RE PLUMB MAD, LAD! McCLAW WOULD CHAW YORE JAW RAW WITH ONE PAW!
DON'T SAG ON THE MAIN DRAG
GIT OFF THE STREET WHEN YUH SEE ME COMIN', YUH GAPIN' LUNKHEADS, OR I'LL WADE IN AN' CRUSH EVERY CARCASS IN THE CROWD!
WALLA WALLA 1000 MILES

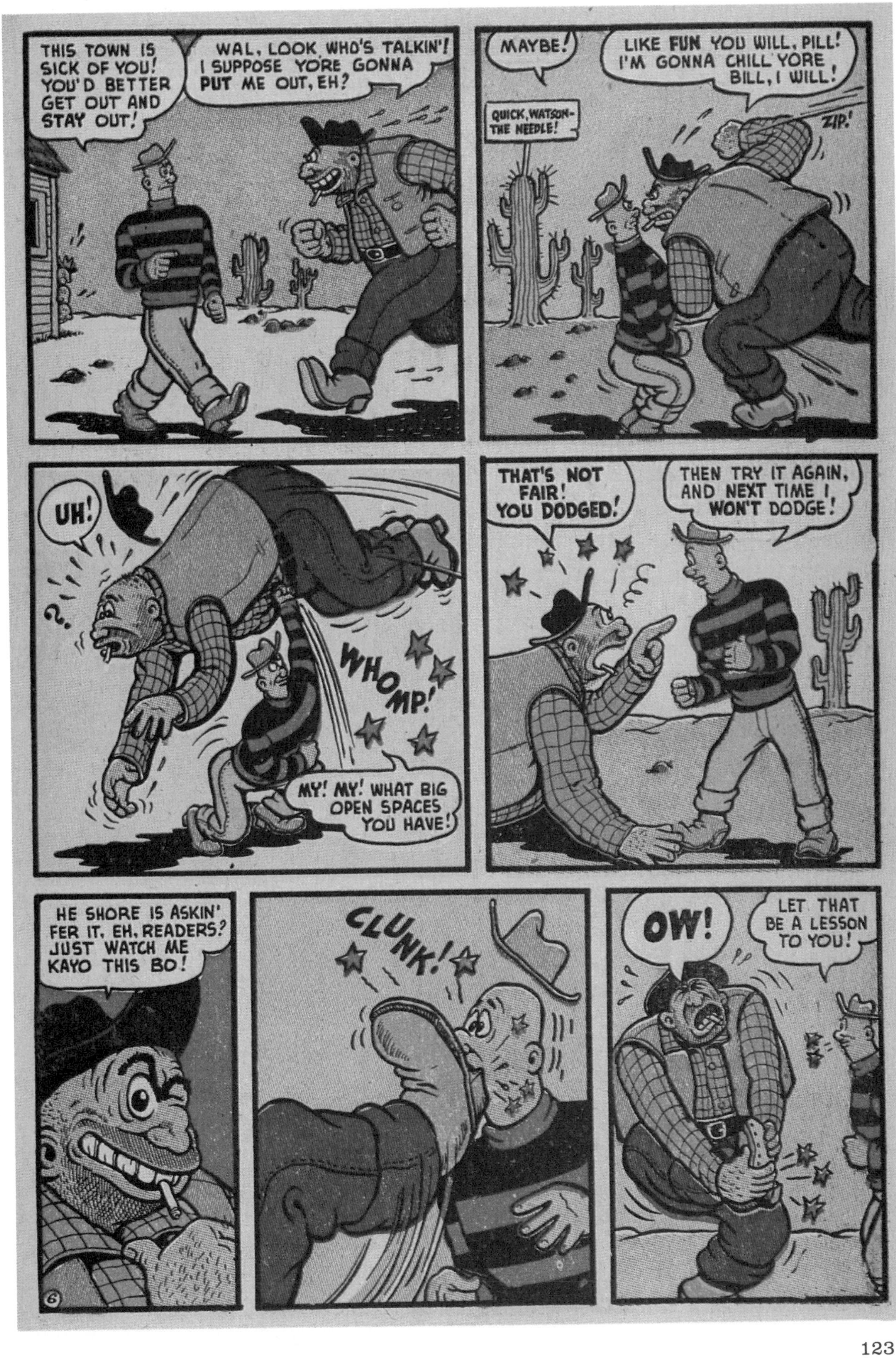
THIS TOWN IS SICK OF YOU! YOU'D BETTER GET OUT AND STAY OUT!
WAL, LOOK WHO'S TALKIN'! I SUPPOSE YO'RE GONNA PUT ME OUT, EH?
MAYBE!
QUICK, WATSON-THE NEEDLE!
LIKE FUN YOU WILL, PILL! I'M GONNA CHILL YORE BILL, I WILL!
ZIP!
UH!
?
WHOMP!
MY! MY! WHAT BIG OPEN SPACES YOU HAVE!
THAT'S NOT FAIR! YOU DODGED!
THEN TRY IT AGAIN, AND NEXT TIME I WON'T DODGE!
HE SHORE IS ASKIN' FER IT, EH, READERS? JUST WATCH ME KAYO THIS BO!
6
CLUNK!
OW!
LET THAT BE A LESSON TO YOU!

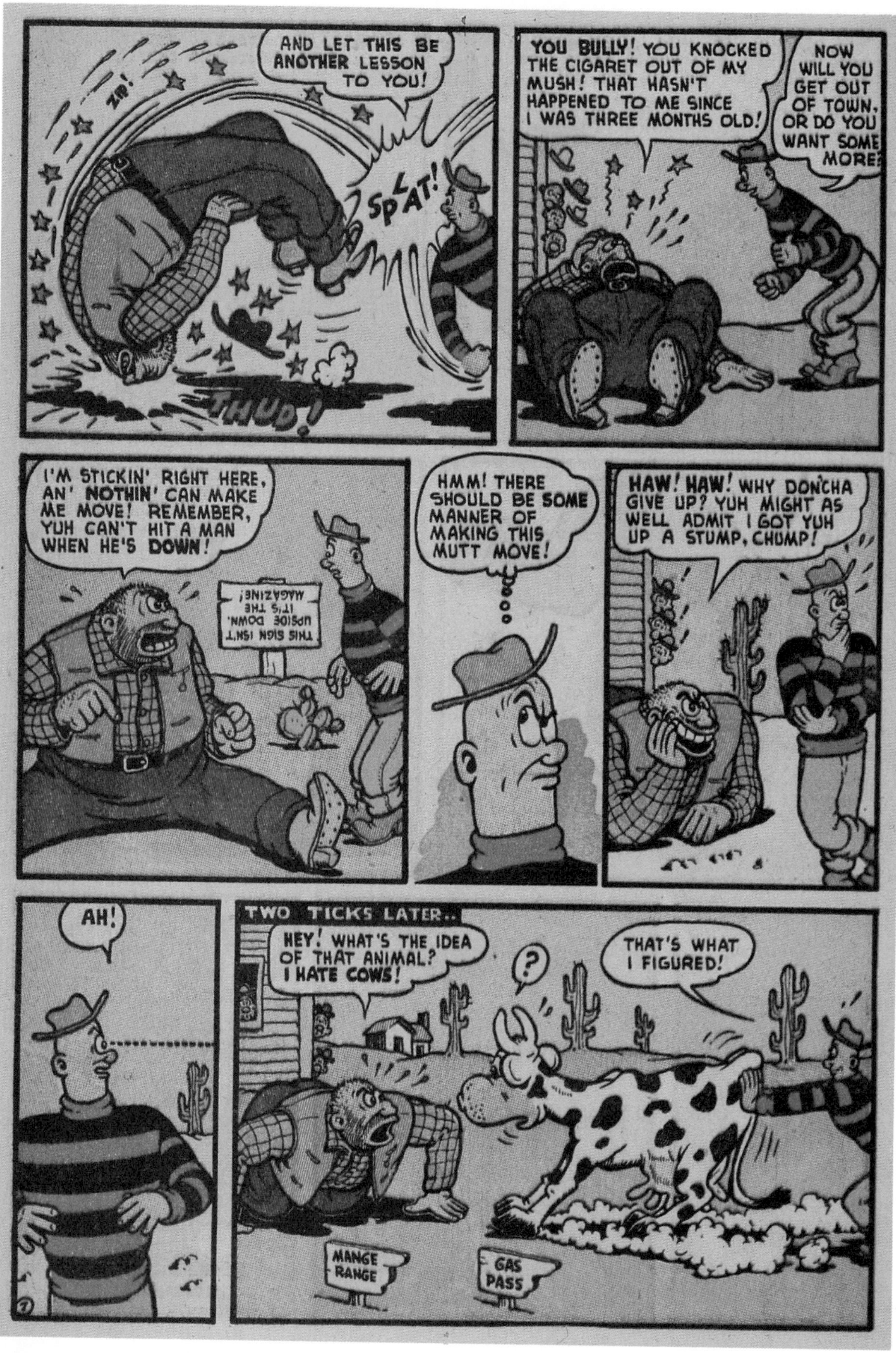

ZIP!
AND LET THIS BE ANOTHER LESSON TO YOU!
SPLAT!
THUD!
YOU BULLY! YOU KNOCKED THE CIGARET OUT OF MY MUSH! THAT HASN'T HAPPENED TO ME SINCE I WAS THREE MONTHS OLD!
NOW WILL YOU GET OUT OF TOWN, OR DO YOU WANT SOME MORE?
I'M STICKIN' RIGHT HERE, AN' NOTHIN' CAN MAKE ME MOVE! REMEMBER, YUH CAN'T HIT A MAN WHEN HE'S DOWN!
THIS SIGN ISN'T UPSIDE DOWN, IT'S THE MAGAZINE!
HMM! THERE SHOULD BE SOME MANNER OF MAKING THIS MUTT MOVE!
HAW! HAW! WHY DON'CHA GIVE UP? YUH MIGHT AS WELL ADMIT I GOT YUH UP A STUMP, CHUMP!
AH!
TWO TICKS LATER..
HEY! WHAT'S THE IDEA OF THAT ANIMAL? I HATE COWS!
?
THAT'S WHAT I FIGURED!
MANGE RANGE
GAS PASS
7

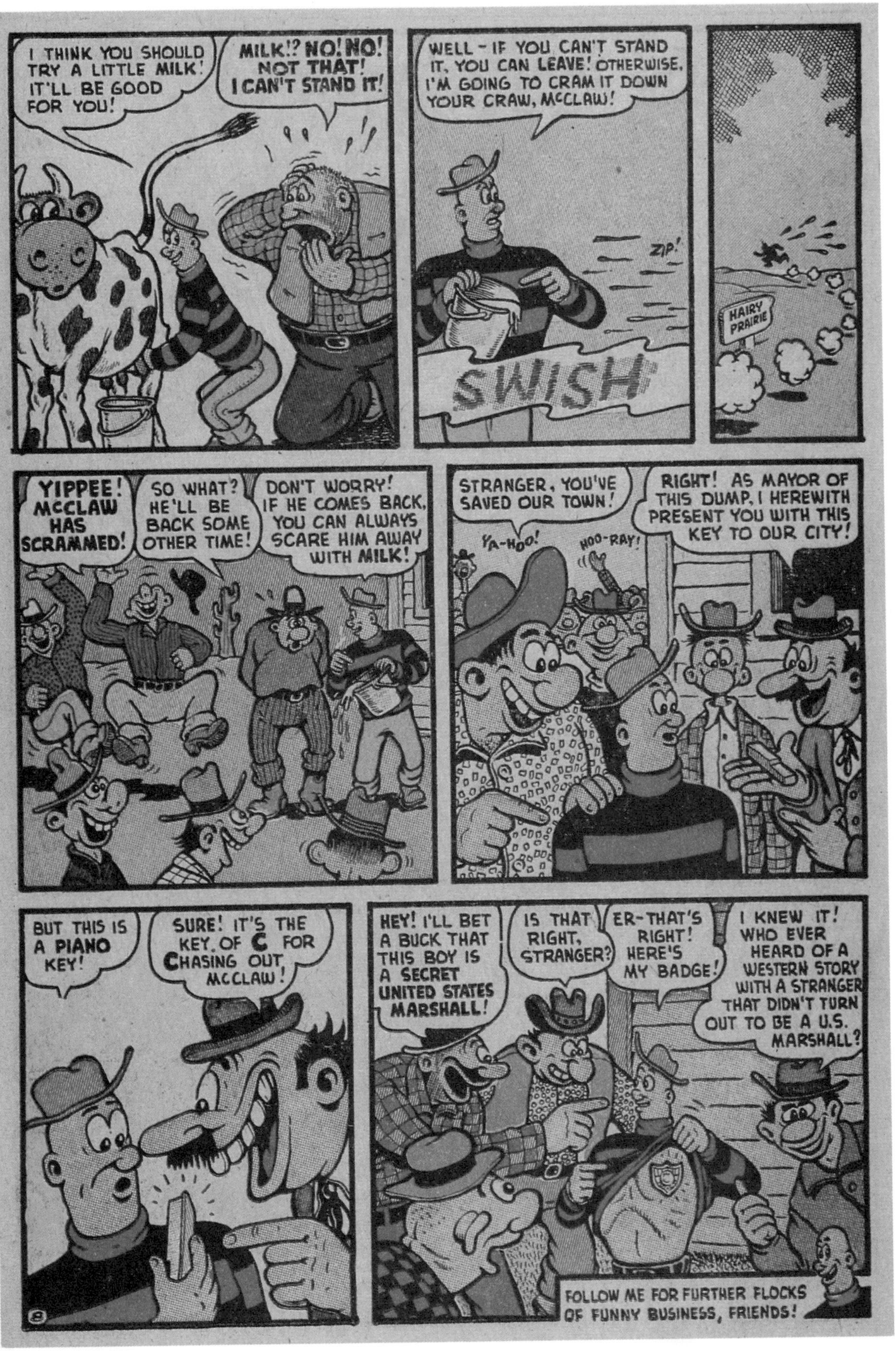
I THINK YOU SHOULD TRY A LITTLE MILK! IT'LL BE GOOD FOR YOU!
MILK!? NO! NO! NOT THAT! I CAN'T STAND IT!
WELL - IF YOU CAN'T STAND IT, YOU CAN LEAVE! OTHERWISE, I'M GOING TO CRAM IT DOWN YOUR CRAW, McCLAW!
ZIP!
SWISH
HAIRY PRAIRIE
YIPPEE! McCLAW HAS SCRAMMED!
SO WHAT? HE'LL BE BACK SOME OTHER TIME!
DON'T WORRY! IF HE COMES BACK, YOU CAN ALWAYS SCARE HIM AWAY WITH MILK!
STRANGER, YOU'VE SAVED OUR TOWN!
YA-HOO!
HOO-RAY!
RIGHT! AS MAYOR OF THIS DUMP, I HEREWITH PRESENT YOU WITH THIS KEY TO OUR CITY!
BUT THIS IS A PIANO KEY!
SURE! IT'S THE KEY OF C FOR CHASING OUT McCLAW!
HEY! I'LL BET A BUCK THAT THIS BOY IS A SECRET UNITED STATES MARSHALL!
IS THAT RIGHT, STRANGER?
ER-THAT'S RIGHT! HERE'S MY BADGE!
I KNEW IT! WHO EVER HEARD OF A WESTERN STORY WITH A STRANGER THAT DIDN'T TURN OUT TO BE A U.S. MARSHALL?
FOLLOW ME FOR FURTHER FLOCKS OF FUNNY BUSINESS, FRIENDS!
8

About George Carlson

The first thing that strikes one about George Carlson is the uniqueness of his drawing style, all curves and circles and flow, all boldness in its comic figures. The second is his swirling ingenuity in designing and filling the individual comic-book page. And the third, which comes as one begins to read him, is the apparently absolute sureness Carlson has in what he is doing—whatever that may turn out to be.

In 1970, Harlan Ellison (science-fiction author, screen-writer) offered an appreciation of Carlson's work as a "comic of the absurd," and in the course of his essay he invoked most of those modern writers whose work is apt to involve and move us before we are quite sure what they are up to—Pirandello, Kafka, Genêt, Beckett, Pinter, Ionesco.

Ellison was writing in the anthology *All in Color for a Dime,* and both his subject and his approach must have come as a surprise to the book's readers and some of its other contributors, preoccupied as most of them evidently were with the *sock-baram-powie-shoosh* of the super-heroes. Ellison's awe, his enthusiasm, and his careful recounting of one of Carlson's best strip episodes could, of course, have been no substitute for the real thing, and most of the book's readers probably had not seen the real thing.

George Carlson (1887-1962) came to comics rather late in a long and varied career. In the 1930s and 1940s he was a prolific illustrator of popular children's books, chiefly for the Platt and Munk company (he illustrated eight collections of Uncle Wiggily stories). He also did the illustration for the original dust jacket for *Gone With the Wind,* and he was puzzle editor for the *National Girl Scouts Magazine* (that later aspect of his career was revived for the short-lived *Puzzle Fun Comics*).

Between the February 1942 and December 1949 issues, the full life of *Jingle Jangle Comics,* George Carlson worked on that magazine. He contributed the plotting and drawing to one *Jingle Jangle Tale* and one adventure of *The Pie-Face Prince of Pretzelburg,* Dimwitri by name, in almost every issue.

Jingle Jangle Comics, like its contemporary *Animal Comics* (and like our contemporary *Casper the Friendly Ghost*), was a comic book intended for small children, and I expect that the virtues of Carlson's work will not occur to us unless we remember that fact. Carlson's wonderful silliness and follow-your-nose whimsy functioned best when it was uninhibited by any demands of a well-rounded plot (which he did occasionally set for himself). Like another American tale-spinner/illustrator for small children, Johnny Gruelle, the creator of Raggedy Ann, Carlson functioned best when he improvised—that is, free-associated—incident upon incident to an ending, rather in the manner of small children playing an adventure game among themselves, and making it up as they go along.

All of which leads me here to invoke another name. Enough of litterateurs and playwrights of the absurd. George Carlson was a kind of George Herriman for little children, and the achievement of his work in *Jingle Jangle Comics* is like Herriman's *Krazy Kat,* but on the level of a small child.

I realize that this is praise indeed. And if it is valid praise, then surely what is called for next is a book collection of Carlson's best comics work—a book all to himself.

M.W.

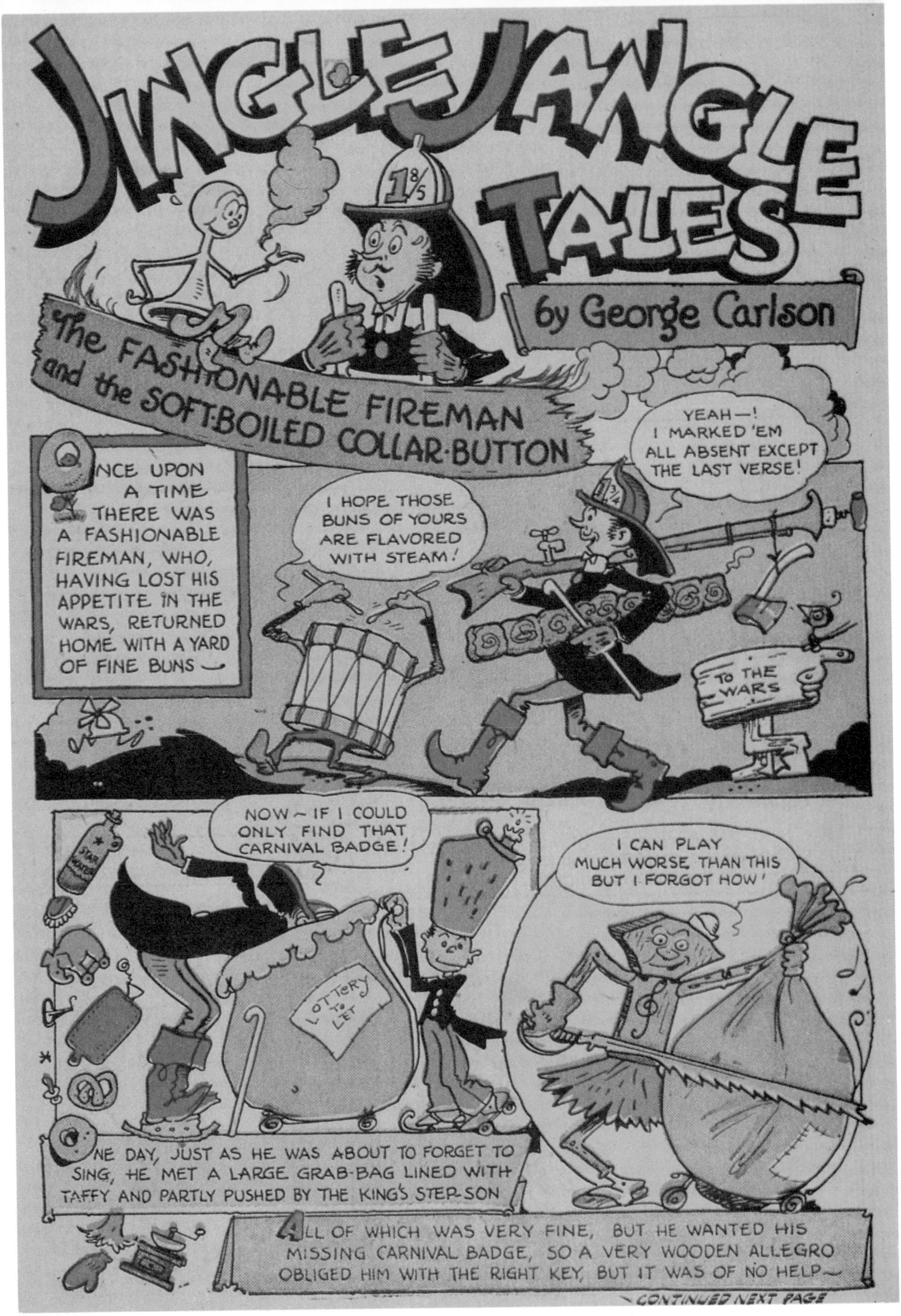
JINGLE JANGLE TALES
by George Carlson
The FASHIONABLE FIREMAN and the SOFT-BOILED COLLAR-BUTTON
1 8/5
ONCE UPON A TIME THERE WAS A FASHIONABLE FIREMAN, WHO, HAVING LOST HIS APPETITE IN THE WARS, RETURNED HOME WITH A YARD OF FINE BUNS —
I HOPE THOSE BUNS OF YOURS ARE FLAVORED WITH STEAM!
YEAH—! I MARKED 'EM ALL ABSENT EXCEPT THE LAST VERSE!
1 3/4
TO THE WARS
NOW ~ IF I COULD ONLY FIND THAT CARNIVAL BADGE!
STAR WATER
LOTTERY TO LET
I CAN PLAY MUCH WORSE THAN THIS BUT I FORGOT HOW!
ONE DAY, JUST AS HE WAS ABOUT TO FORGET TO SING, HE MET A LARGE GRAB-BAG LINED WITH TAFFY AND PARTLY PUSHED BY THE KING'S STEP-SON
ALL OF WHICH WAS VERY FINE, BUT HE WANTED HIS MISSING CARNIVAL BADGE, SO A VERY WOODEN ALLEGRO OBLIGED HIM WITH THE RIGHT KEY, BUT IT WAS OF NO HELP—
~ CONTINUED NEXT PAGE

From *Jingle Jangle Comics* No. 5, October 1943.

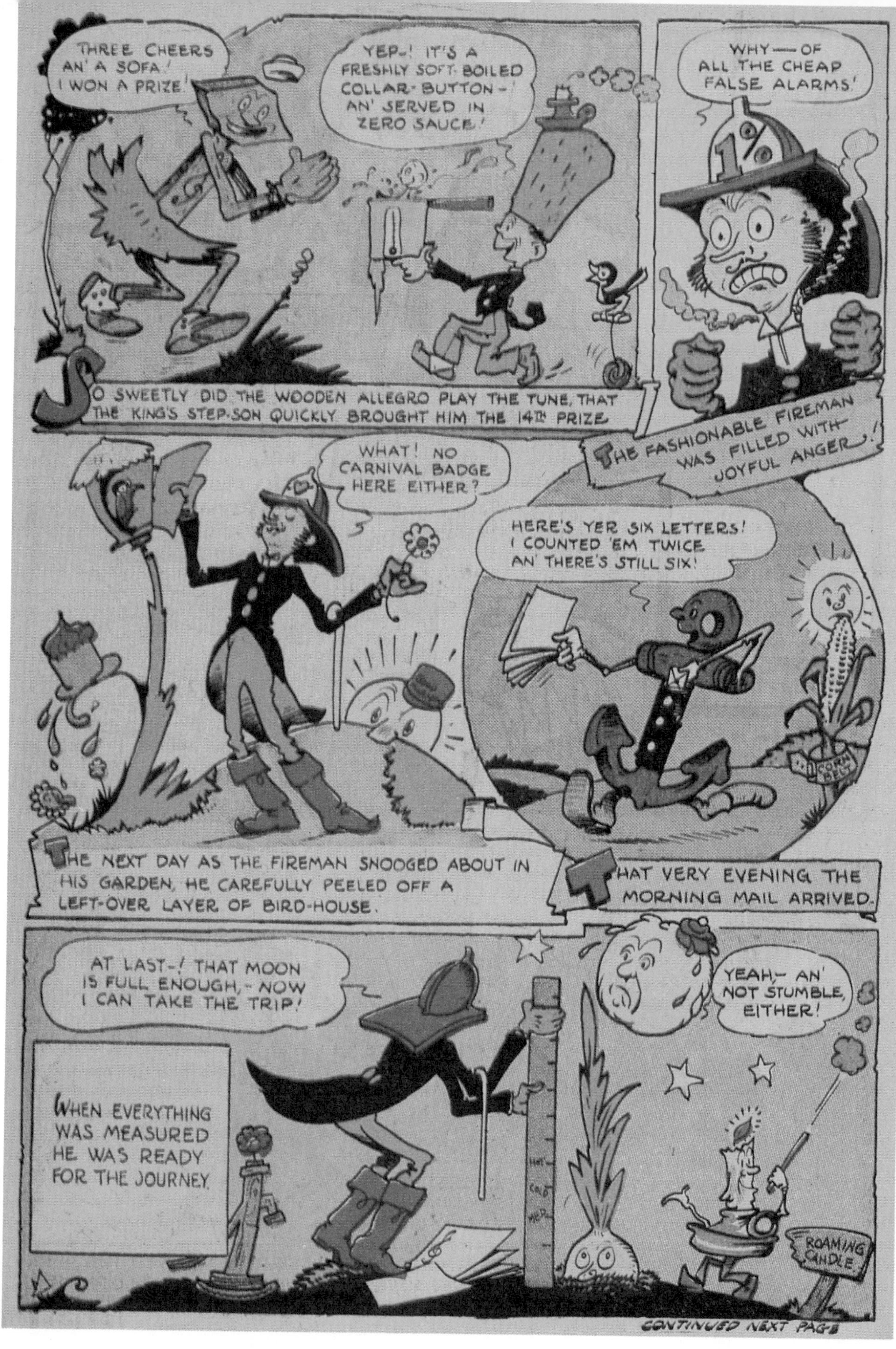
THREE CHEERS AN' A SOFA! I WON A PRIZE!
YEP-! IT'S A FRESHLY SOFT-BOILED COLLAR-BUTTON-! AN' SERVED IN ZERO SAUCE!
WHY—OF ALL THE CHEAP FALSE ALARMS!
SO SWEETLY DID THE WOODEN ALLEGRO PLAY THE TUNE, THAT THE KING'S STEP-SON QUICKLY BROUGHT HIM THE 14TH PRIZE
THE FASHIONABLE FIREMAN WAS FILLED WITH JOYFUL ANGER!
WHAT! NO CARNIVAL BADGE HERE EITHER?
HERE'S YER SIX LETTERS! I COUNTED 'EM TWICE AN' THERE'S STILL SIX!
CORN BELT
THE NEXT DAY AS THE FIREMAN SNOOGED ABOUT IN HIS GARDEN, HE CAREFULLY PEELED OFF A LEFT-OVER LAYER OF BIRD-HOUSE.
THAT VERY EVENING THE MORNING MAIL ARRIVED.
AT LAST-! THAT MOON IS FULL ENOUGH,-NOW I CAN TAKE THE TRIP!
YEAH,-AN' NOT STUMBLE, EITHER!
WHEN EVERYTHING WAS MEASURED HE WAS READY FOR THE JOURNEY.
ROAMING CANDLE

CONTINUED NEXT PAGE

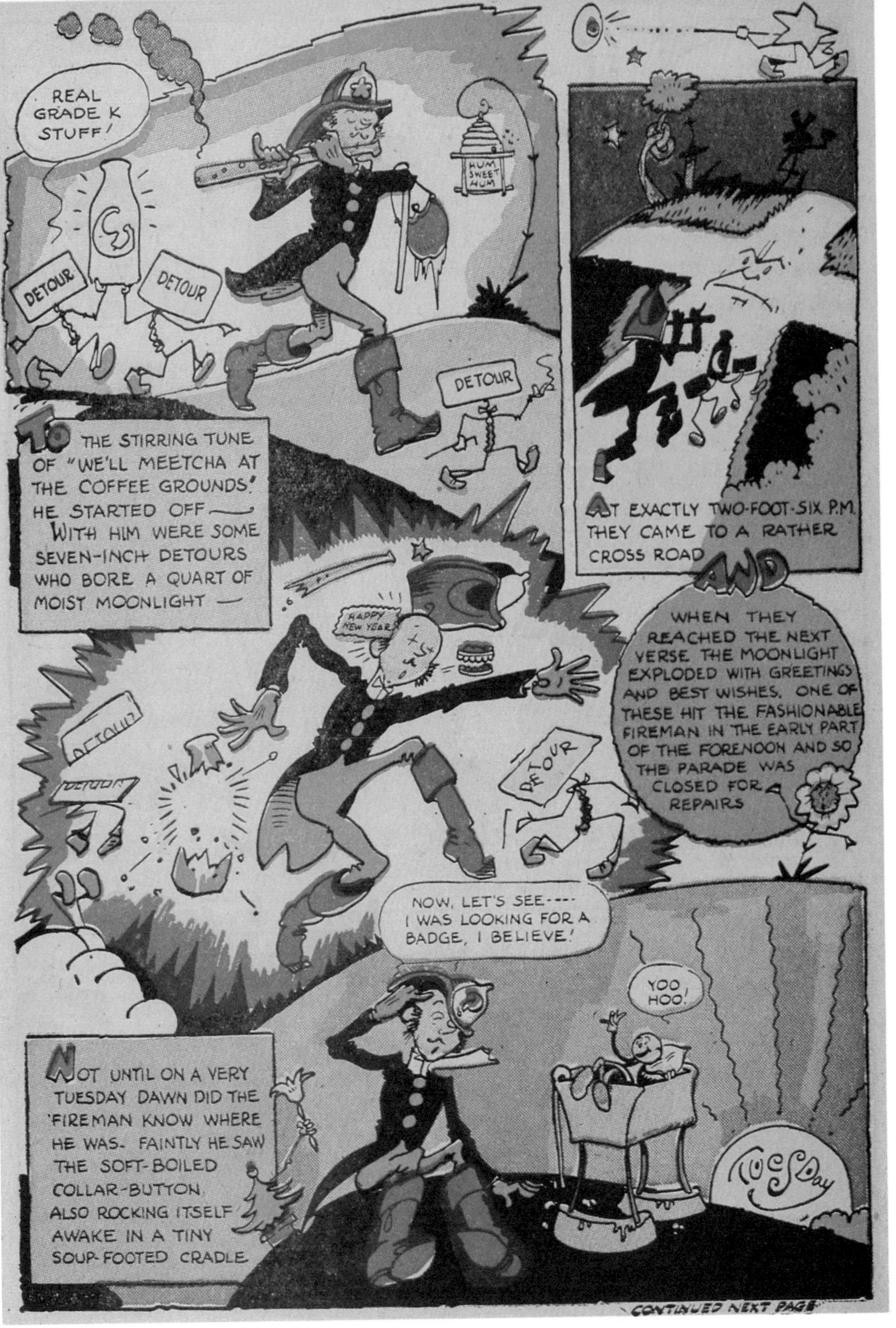
REAL GRADE K STUFF!
HUM SWEET HUM
DETOUR
DETOUR
DETOUR
TO THE STIRRING TUNE OF "WE'LL MEETCHA AT THE COFFEE GROUNDS." HE STARTED OFF — WITH HIM WERE SOME SEVEN-INCH DETOURS WHO BORE A QUART OF MOIST MOONLIGHT —
AT EXACTLY TWO-FOOT-SIX P.M. THEY CAME TO A RATHER CROSS ROAD
HAPPY NEW YEAR
DETOUR
DETOUR
DETOUR
AND WHEN THEY REACHED THE NEXT VERSE THE MOONLIGHT EXPLODED WITH GREETINGS AND BEST WISHES. ONE OF THESE HIT THE FASHIONABLE FIREMAN IN THE EARLY PART OF THE FORENOON AND SO THE PARADE WAS CLOSED FOR REPAIRS
NOW, LET'S SEE---- I WAS LOOKING FOR A BADGE, I BELIEVE!
YOO HOO!
NOT UNTIL ON A VERY TUESDAY DAWN DID THE 'FIREMAN KNOW WHERE HE WAS. FAINTLY HE SAW THE SOFT-BOILED COLLAR-BUTTON ALSO ROCKING ITSELF AWAKE IN A TINY SOUP-FOOTED CRADLE
TUESDAY
CONTINUED NEXT PAGE

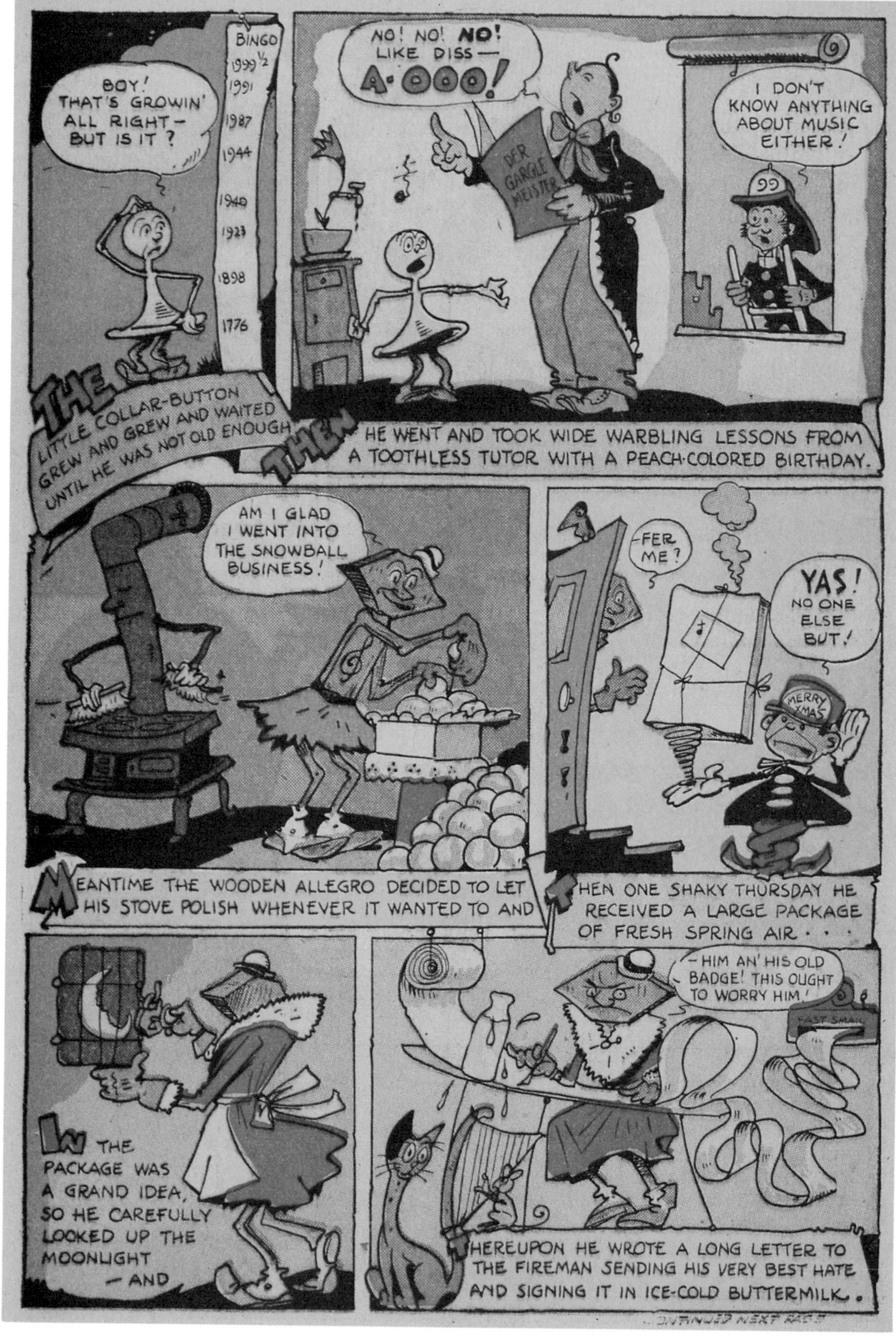
BINGO
1999 1/2
1991
1987
1944
1940
1923
1898
1776
BOY! THAT'S GROWIN' ALL RIGHT— BUT IS IT?
THE LITTLE COLLAR-BUTTON GREW AND GREW AND WAITED UNTIL HE WAS NOT OLD ENOUGH
NO! NO! NO! LIKE DISS— A-OOO!
DER GARGLE MEISTER
I DON'T KNOW ANYTHING ABOUT MUSIC EITHER!
99
THEN HE WENT AND TOOK WIDE WARBLING LESSONS FROM A TOOTHLESS TUTOR WITH A PEACH-COLORED BIRTHDAY.
AM I GLAD I WENT INTO THE SNOWBALL BUSINESS!
MEANTIME THE WOODEN ALLEGRO DECIDED TO LET HIS STOVE POLISH WHENEVER IT WANTED TO AND
-FER ME?
YAS! NO ONE ELSE BUT!
MERRY XMAS
THEN ONE SHAKY THURSDAY HE RECEIVED A LARGE PACKAGE OF FRESH SPRING AIR · · ·
IN THE PACKAGE WAS A GRAND IDEA, SO HE CAREFULLY LOOKED UP THE MOONLIGHT —AND
-HIM AN' HIS OLD BADGE! THIS OUGHT TO WORRY HIM!
FAST SMAIL
WHEREUPON HE WROTE A LONG LETTER TO THE FIREMAN SENDING HIS VERY BEST HATE AND SIGNING IT IN ICE-COLD BUTTERMILK.
CONTINUED NEXT PAGE

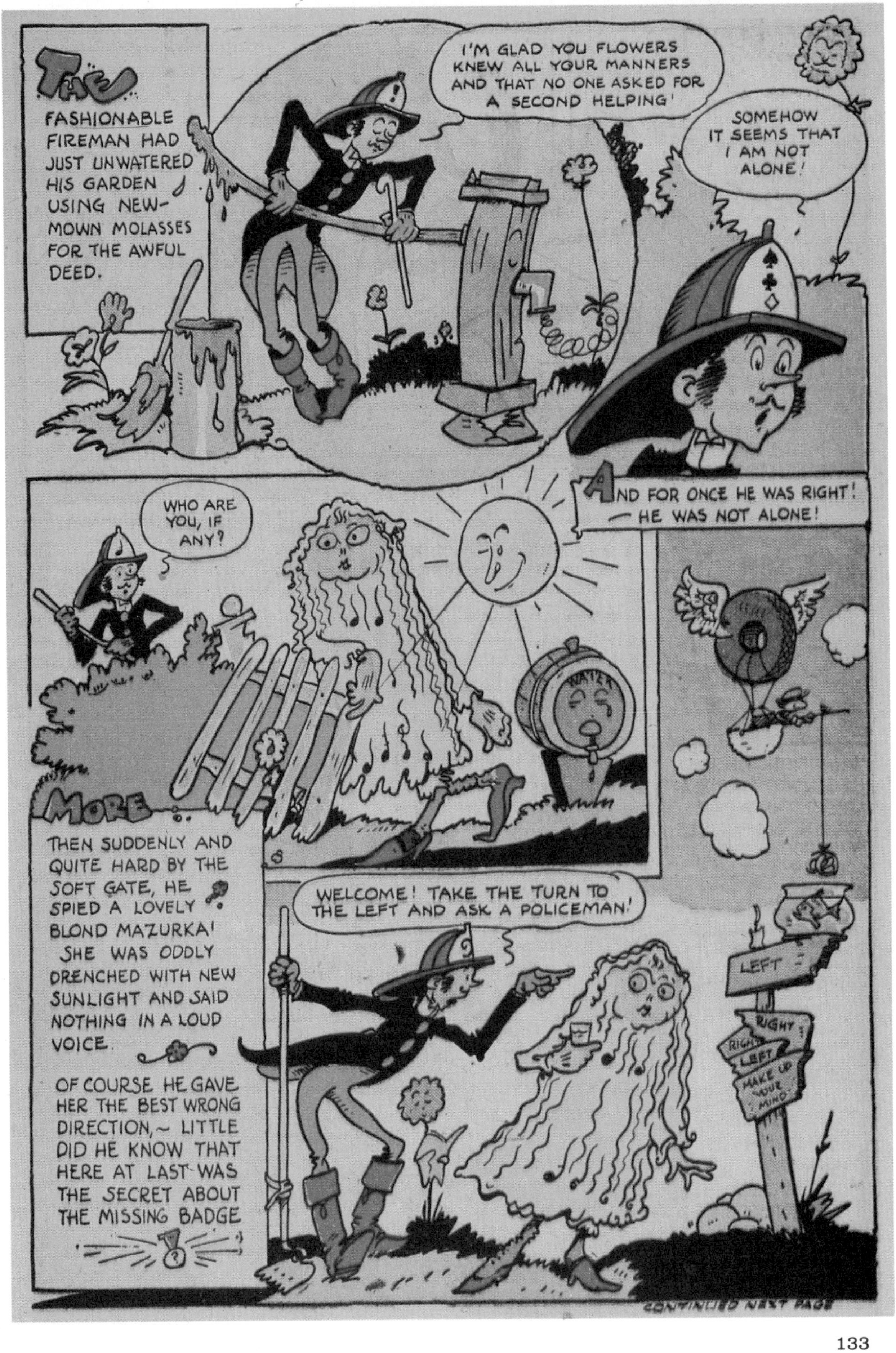
THE
FASHIONABLE FIREMAN HAD JUST UNWATERED HIS GARDEN USING NEW-MOWN MOLASSES FOR THE AWFUL DEED.
I'M GLAD YOU FLOWERS KNEW ALL YOUR MANNERS AND THAT NO ONE ASKED FOR A SECOND HELPING!
SOMEHOW IT SEEMS THAT I AM NOT ALONE!
AND FOR ONCE HE WAS RIGHT! — HE WAS NOT ALONE!
WHO ARE YOU, IF ANY?
WATER
MORE
THEN SUDDENLY AND QUITE HARD BY THE SOFT GATE, HE SPIED A LOVELY BLOND MAZURKA! SHE WAS ODDLY DRENCHED WITH NEW SUNLIGHT AND SAID NOTHING IN A LOUD VOICE.
OF COURSE HE GAVE HER THE BEST WRONG DIRECTION,~ LITTLE DID HE KNOW THAT HERE AT LAST WAS THE SECRET ABOUT THE MISSING BADGE
WELCOME! TAKE THE TURN TO THE LEFT AND ASK A POLICEMAN!
LEFT
RIGHT
RIGHT
LEFT
MAKE UP YOUR MIND
CONTINUED NEXT PAGE

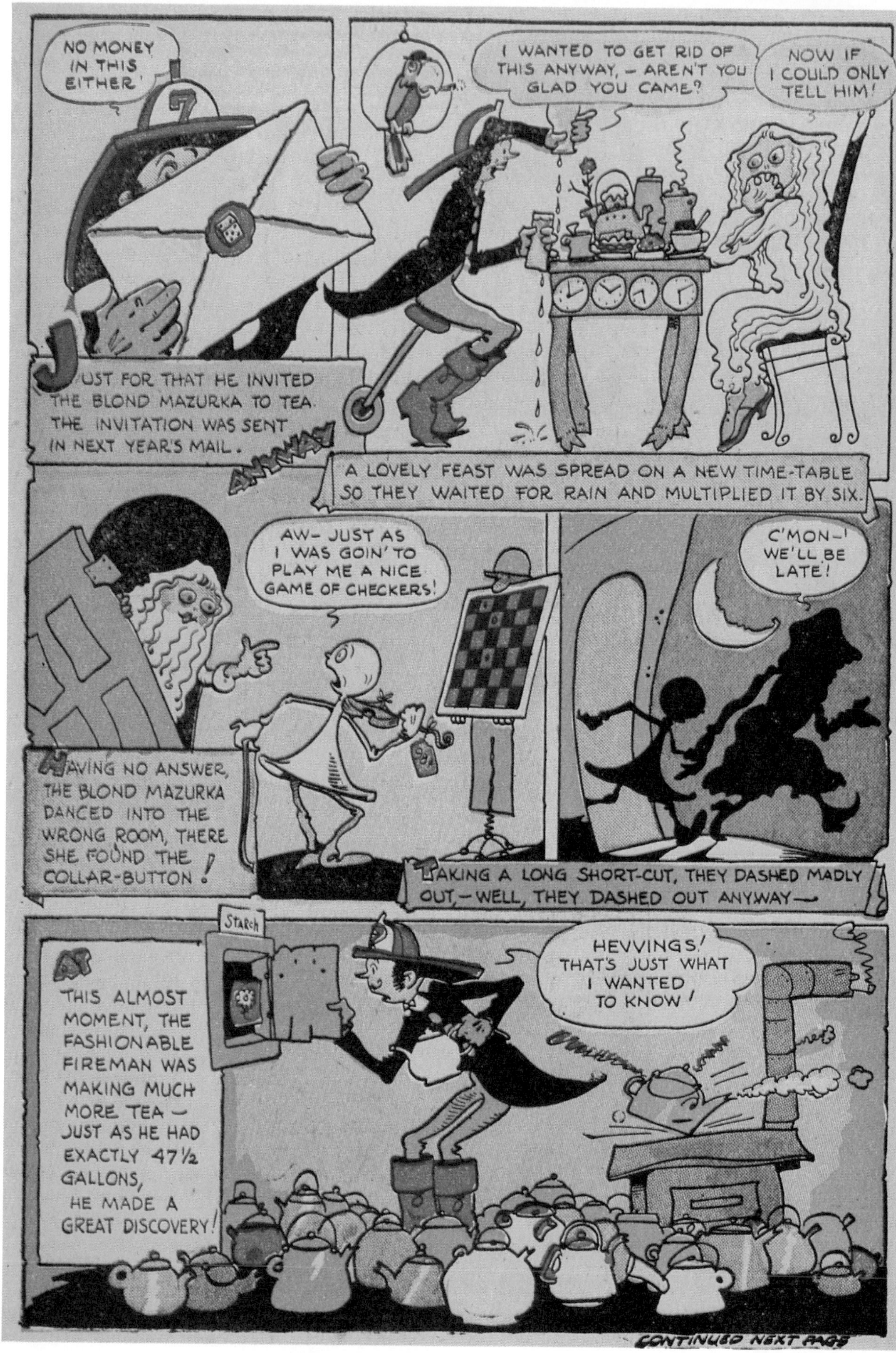
NO MONEY IN THIS EITHER!
JUST FOR THAT HE INVITED THE BLOND MAZURKA TO TEA. THE INVITATION WAS SENT IN NEXT YEAR'S MAIL.
ANYWAY
I WANTED TO GET RID OF THIS ANYWAY, - AREN'T YOU GLAD YOU CAME?
NOW IF I COULD ONLY TELL HIM!
A LOVELY FEAST WAS SPREAD ON A NEW TIME-TABLE SO THEY WAITED FOR RAIN AND MULTIPLIED IT BY SIX.
AW- JUST AS I WAS GOIN' TO PLAY ME A NICE GAME OF CHECKERS!
HAVING NO ANSWER, THE BLOND MAZURKA DANCED INTO THE WRONG ROOM, THERE SHE FOUND THE COLLAR-BUTTON!
C'MON-! WE'LL BE LATE!
TAKING A LONG SHORT-CUT, THEY DASHED MADLY OUT, - WELL, THEY DASHED OUT ANYWAY—
STARCH
AT THIS ALMOST MOMENT, THE FASHIONABLE FIREMAN WAS MAKING MUCH MORE TEA — JUST AS HE HAD EXACTLY 47½ GALLONS, HE MADE A GREAT DISCOVERY!
HEVVINGS! THAT'S JUST WHAT I WANTED TO KNOW!
CONTINUED NEXT PAGE

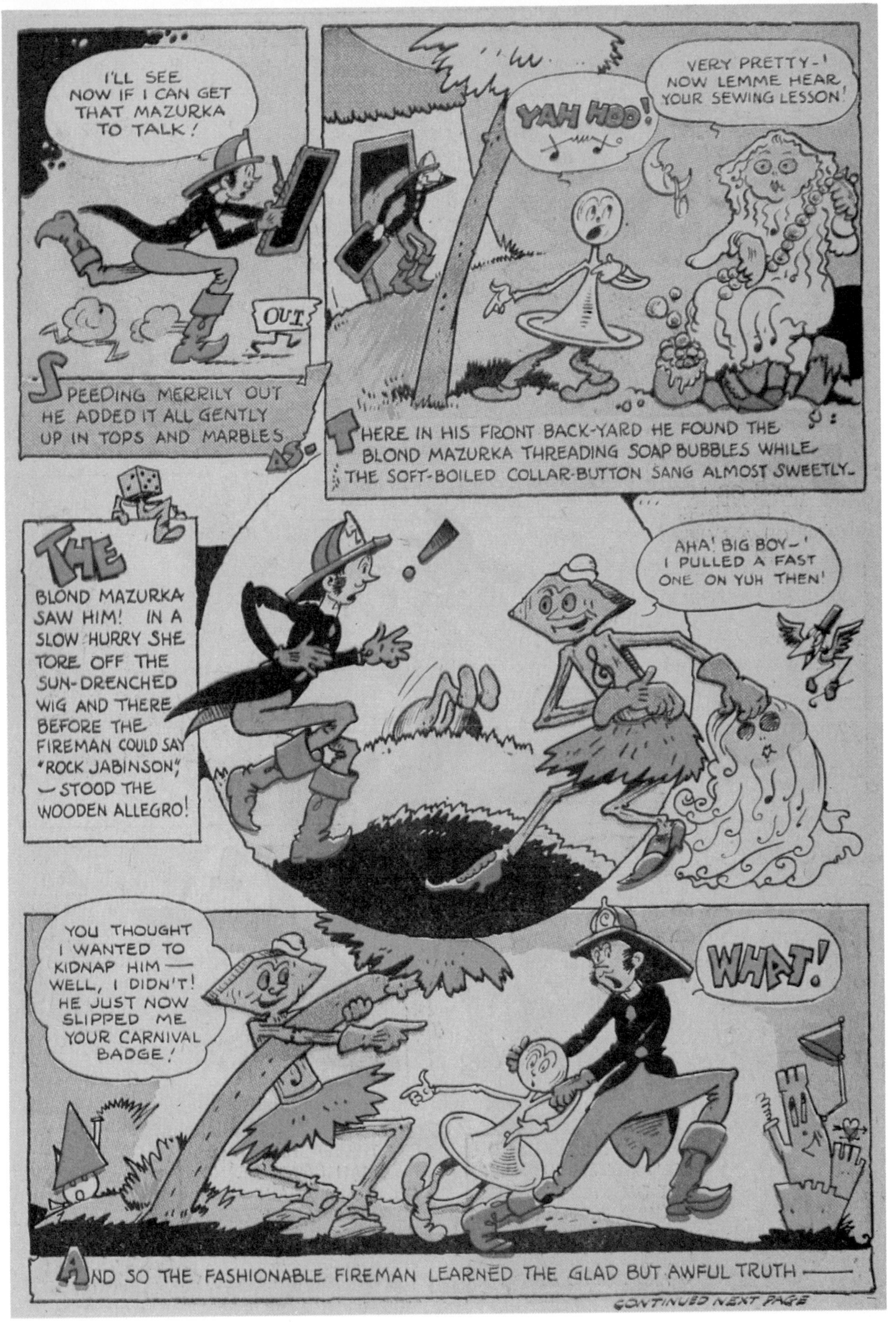
I'LL SEE NOW IF I CAN GET THAT MAZURKA TO TALK!
OUT
SPEEDING MERRILY OUT HE ADDED IT ALL GENTLY UP IN TOPS AND MARBLES.
YAH HOO!
VERY PRETTY-! NOW LEMME HEAR YOUR SEWING LESSON!
THERE IN HIS FRONT BACK-YARD HE FOUND THE BLOND MAZURKA THREADING SOAP BUBBLES WHILE THE SOFT-BOILED COLLAR-BUTTON SANG ALMOST SWEETLY.
THE BLOND MAZURKA SAW HIM! IN A SLOW HURRY SHE TORE OFF THE SUN-DRENCHED WIG AND THERE BEFORE THE FIREMAN COULD SAY "ROCK JABINSON", —STOOD THE WOODEN ALLEGRO!
AHA! BIG BOY-! I PULLED A FAST ONE ON YUH THEN!
YOU THOUGHT I WANTED TO KIDNAP HIM— WELL, I DIDN'T! HE JUST NOW SLIPPED ME YOUR CARNIVAL BADGE!
WHAT!
AND SO THE FASHIONABLE FIREMAN LEARNED THE GLAD BUT AWFUL TRUTH——
CONTINUED NEXT PAGE

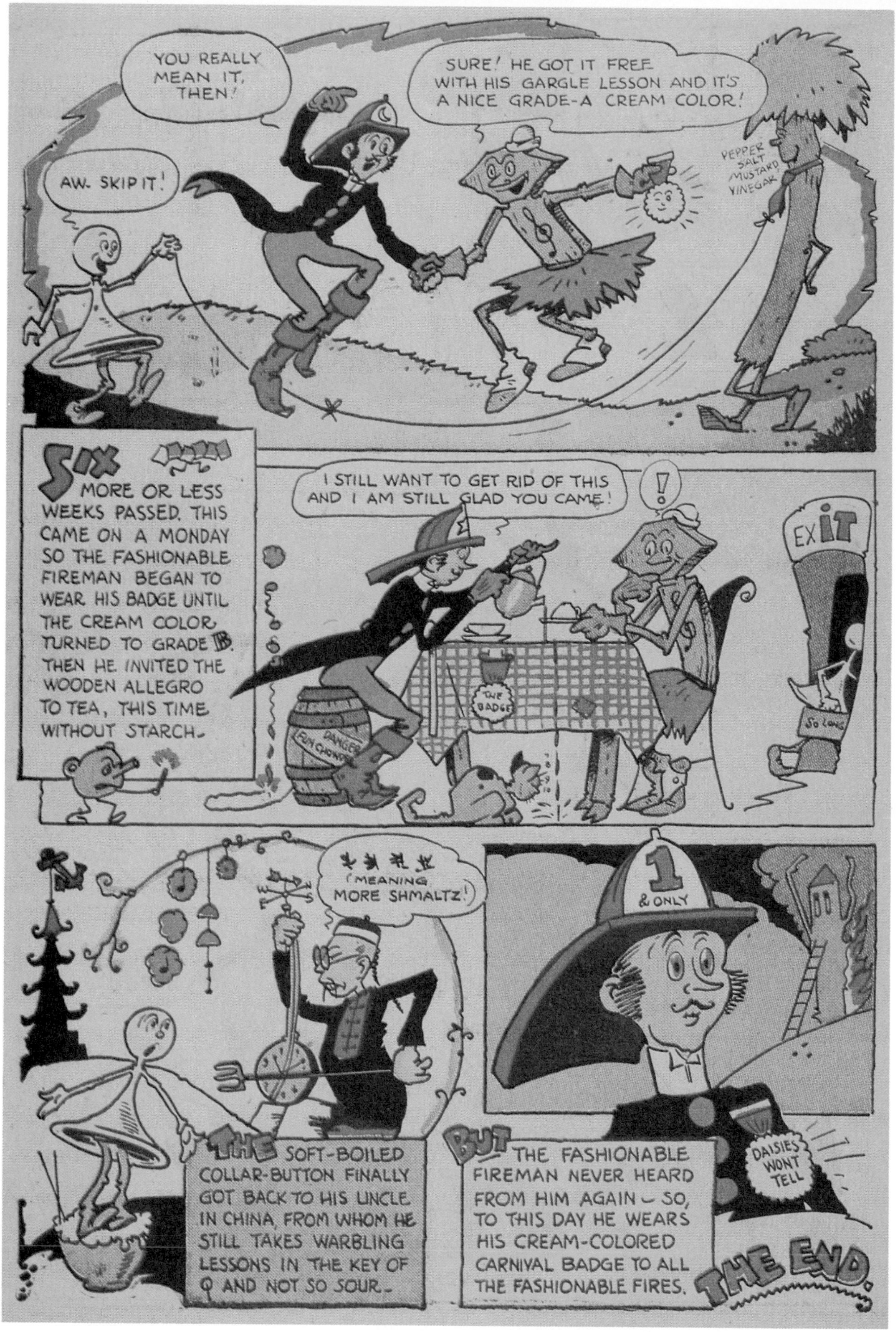
YOU REALLY MEAN IT, THEN!
SURE! HE GOT IT FREE WITH HIS GARGLE LESSON AND IT'S A NICE GRADE-A CREAM COLOR!
AW. SKIP IT!
PEPPER SALT MUSTARD VINEGAR
SIX MORE OR LESS WEEKS PASSED. THIS CAME ON A MONDAY SO THE FASHIONABLE FIREMAN BEGAN TO WEAR HIS BADGE UNTIL THE CREAM COLOR TURNED TO GRADE B. THEN HE INVITED THE WOODEN ALLEGRO TO TEA, THIS TIME WITHOUT STARCH.
I STILL WANT TO GET RID OF THIS AND I AM STILL GLAD YOU CAME!
!
EXIT
THE BADGE
DANGER FUM CHOWDER
SO LONG
(MEANING MORE SHMALTZ!)
1 & ONLY
THE SOFT-BOILED COLLAR-BUTTON FINALLY GOT BACK TO HIS UNCLE IN CHINA, FROM WHOM HE STILL TAKES WARBLING LESSONS IN THE KEY OF Q AND NOT SO SOUR.
BUT THE FASHIONABLE FIREMAN NEVER HEARD FROM HIM AGAIN — SO, TO THIS DAY HE WEARS HIS CREAM-COLORED CARNIVAL BADGE TO ALL THE FASHIONABLE FIRES.
DAISIES WONT TELL
THE END.

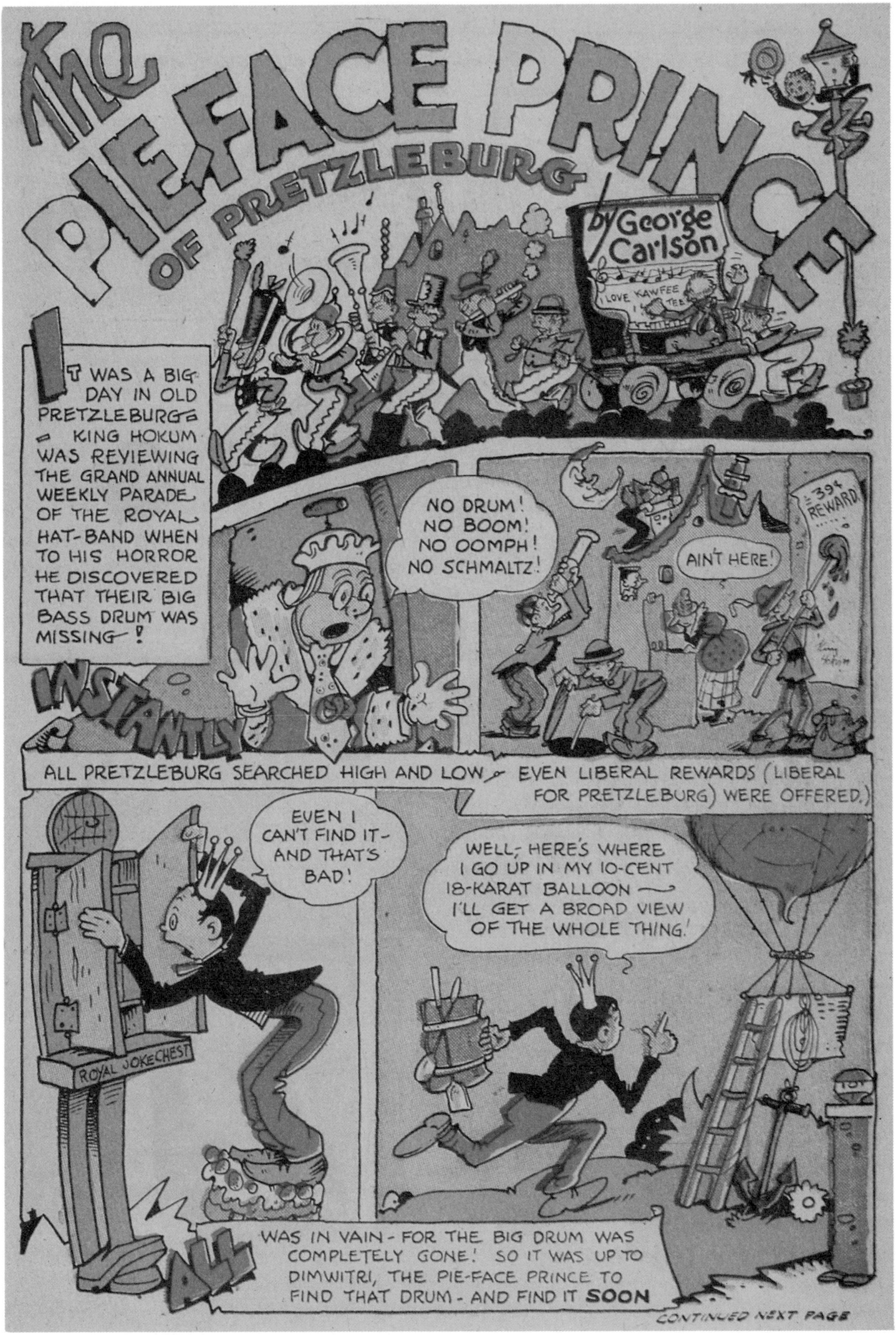

The PIE-FACE PRINCE OF PRETZLEBURG
by George Carlson
I LOVE KAWFEE
IT WAS A BIG DAY IN OLD PRETZLEBURG — KING HOKUM WAS REVIEWING THE GRAND ANNUAL WEEKLY PARADE OF THE ROYAL HAT-BAND WHEN TO HIS HORROR HE DISCOVERED THAT THEIR BIG BASS DRUM WAS MISSING!
NO DRUM! NO BOOM! NO OOMPH! NO SCHMALTZ!
AIN'T HERE!
REWARD
INSTANTLY
ALL PRETZLEBURG SEARCHED HIGH AND LOW — EVEN LIBERAL REWARDS (LIBERAL FOR PRETZLEBURG) WERE OFFERED.
EVEN I CAN'T FIND IT - AND THAT'S BAD!
ROYAL JOKECHEST
WELL, HERE'S WHERE I GO UP IN MY 10-CENT 18-KARAT BALLOON — I'LL GET A BROAD VIEW OF THE WHOLE THING!
ALL WAS IN VAIN - FOR THE BIG DRUM WAS COMPLETELY GONE! SO IT WAS UP TO DIMWITRI, THE PIE-FACE PRINCE TO FIND THAT DRUM - AND FIND IT SOON
CONTINUED NEXT PAGE

From *Jingle Jangle Comics* No. 5, October 1943.

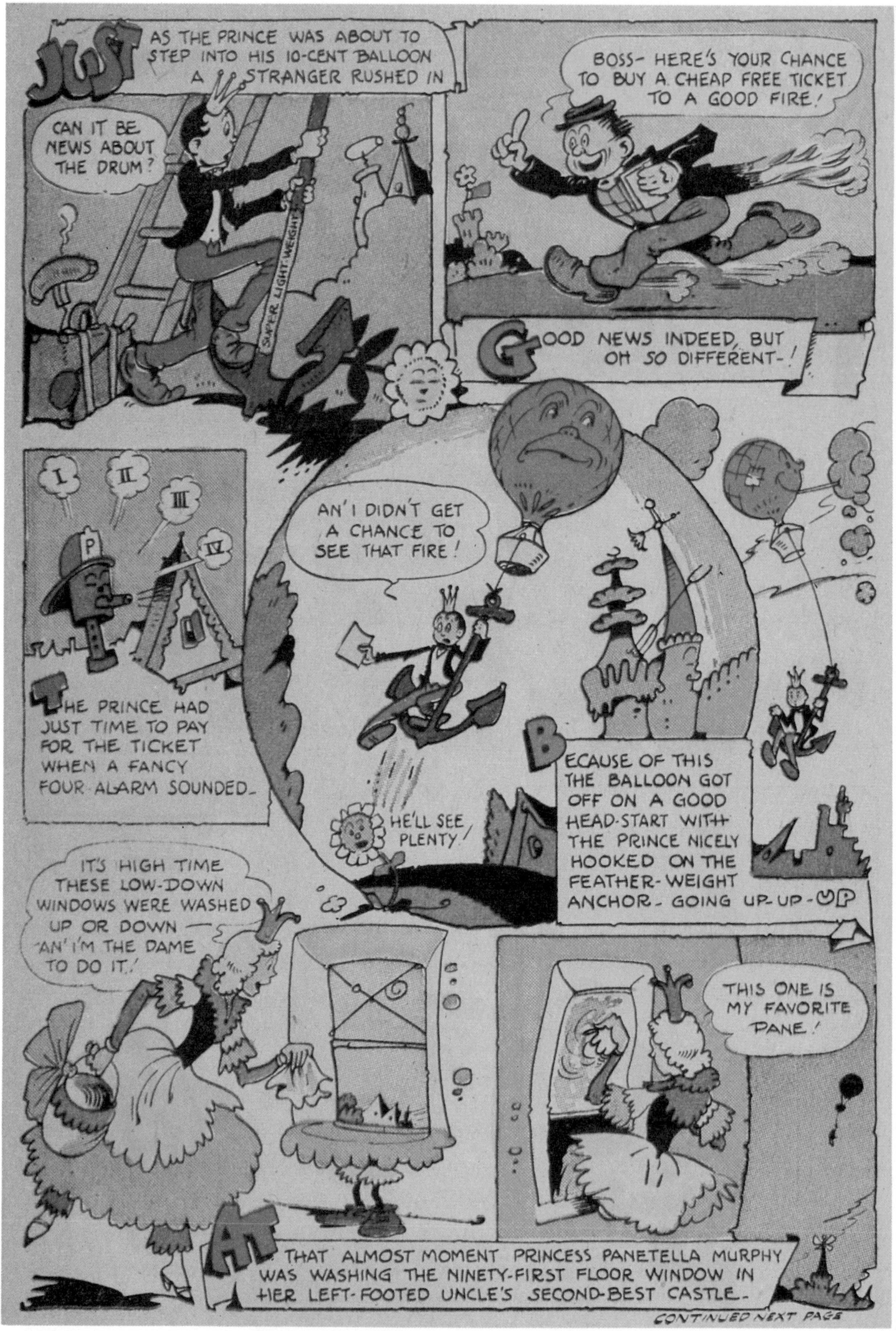
JUST AS THE PRINCE WAS ABOUT TO STEP INTO HIS 10-CENT BALLOON A STRANGER RUSHED IN
CAN IT BE NEWS ABOUT THE DRUM?
SUPER LIGHT WEIGHT
BOSS- HERE'S YOUR CHANCE TO BUY A CHEAP FREE TICKET TO A GOOD FIRE!
GOOD NEWS INDEED, BUT OH SO DIFFERENT-!
I
II
III
IV
P
THE PRINCE HAD JUST TIME TO PAY FOR THE TICKET WHEN A FANCY FOUR-ALARM SOUNDED-
AN' I DIDN'T GET A CHANCE TO SEE THAT FIRE!
HE'LL SEE PLENTY!
BECAUSE OF THIS THE BALLOON GOT OFF ON A GOOD HEAD-START WITH THE PRINCE NICELY HOOKED ON THE FEATHER-WEIGHT ANCHOR- GOING UP-UP-UP
IT'S HIGH TIME THESE LOW-DOWN WINDOWS WERE WASHED UP OR DOWN — AN' I'M THE DAME TO DO IT!
THIS ONE IS MY FAVORITE PANE!
AT THAT ALMOST MOMENT PRINCESS PANETELLA MURPHY WAS WASHING THE NINETY-FIRST FLOOR WINDOW IN HER LEFT-FOOTED UNCLE'S SECOND-BEST CASTLE-
CONTINUED NEXT PAGE

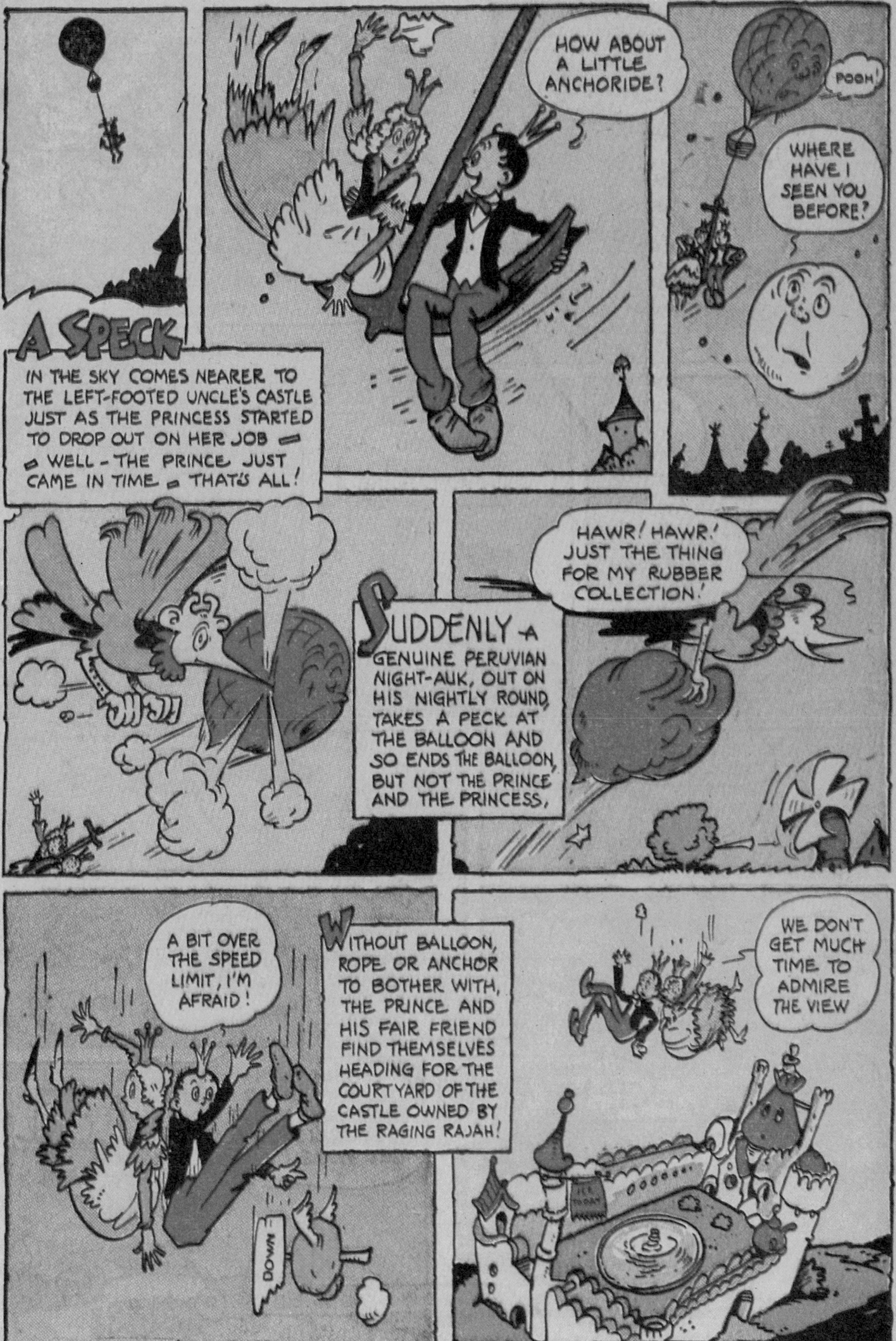
HOW ABOUT A LITTLE ANCHORIDE?
POOH!
WHERE HAVE I SEEN YOU BEFORE?
A SPECK IN THE SKY COMES NEARER TO THE LEFT-FOOTED UNCLE'S CASTLE JUST AS THE PRINCESS STARTED TO DROP OUT ON HER JOB — WELL - THE PRINCE JUST CAME IN TIME — THAT'S ALL!
SUDDENLY - A GENUINE PERUVIAN NIGHT-AUK, OUT ON HIS NIGHTLY ROUND, TAKES A PECK AT THE BALLOON AND SO ENDS THE BALLOON, BUT NOT THE PRINCE AND THE PRINCESS,
HAWR! HAWR! JUST THE THING FOR MY RUBBER COLLECTION!
A BIT OVER THE SPEED LIMIT, I'M AFRAID!
WITHOUT BALLOON, ROPE OR ANCHOR TO BOTHER WITH, THE PRINCE AND HIS FAIR FRIEND FIND THEMSELVES HEADING FOR THE COURTYARD OF THE CASTLE OWNED BY THE RAGING RAJAH!
DOWN
WE DON'T GET MUCH TIME TO ADMIRE THE VIEW
CONTINUED NEXT PAGE

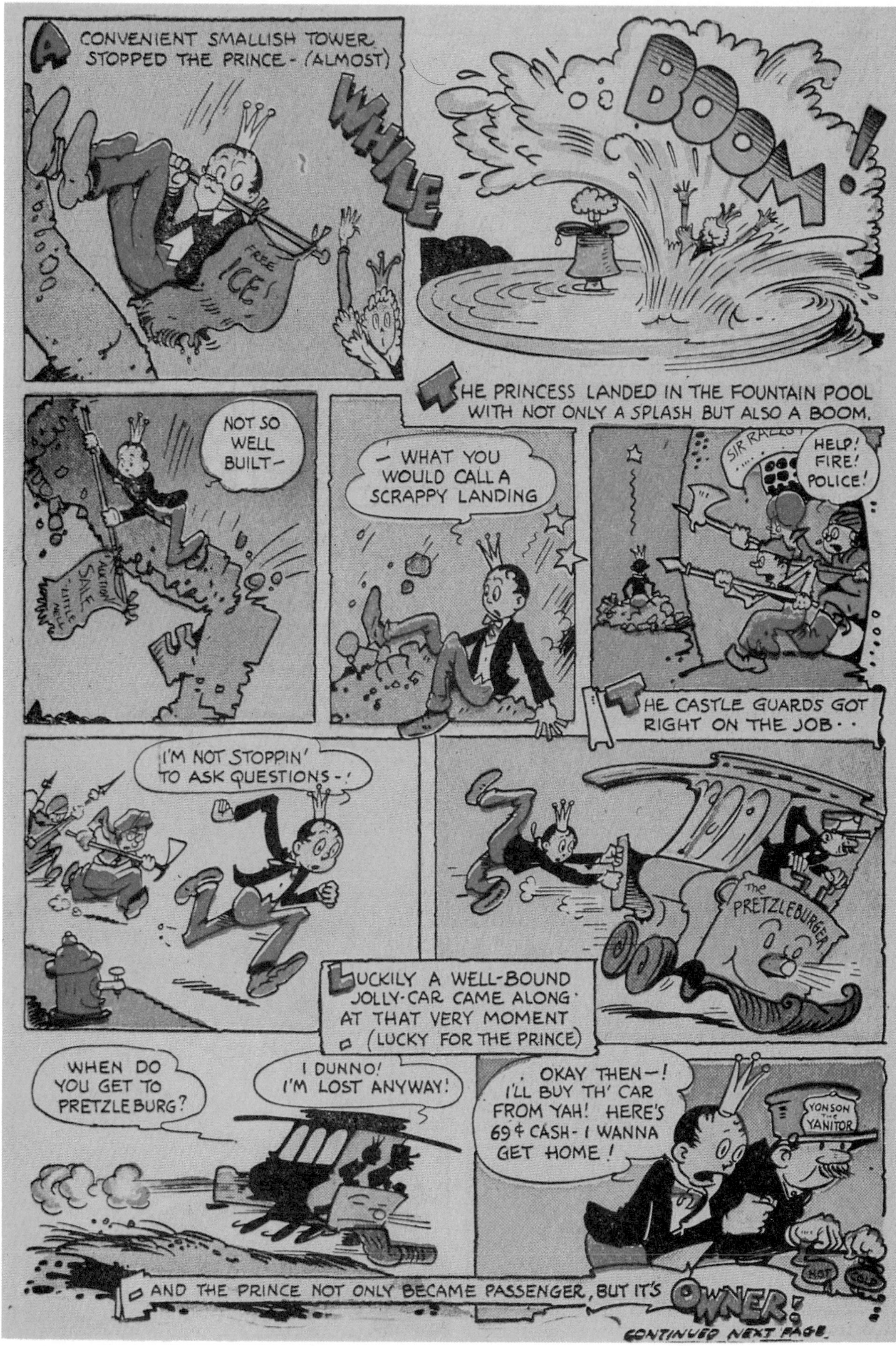
A CONVENIENT SMALLISH TOWER STOPPED THE PRINCE - (ALMOST)
WHILE
FREE ICES
BOOM!
THE PRINCESS LANDED IN THE FOUNTAIN POOL WITH NOT ONLY A SPLASH BUT ALSO A BOOM.
NOT SO WELL BUILT-
AUCTION SALE LITTLE NELL
- WHAT YOU WOULD CALL A SCRAPPY LANDING
HELP! FIRE! POLICE!
THE CASTLE GUARDS GOT RIGHT ON THE JOB . .
I'M NOT STOPPIN' TO ASK QUESTIONS -!
The PRETZLEBURGER
LUCKILY A WELL-BOUND JOLLY-CAR CAME ALONG AT THAT VERY MOMENT (LUCKY FOR THE PRINCE)
WHEN DO YOU GET TO PRETZLEBURG?
I DUNNO! I'M LOST ANYWAY!
OKAY THEN-! I'LL BUY TH' CAR FROM YAH! HERE'S 69¢ CASH- I WANNA GET HOME!
YONSON THE YANITOR
HOT COLA
AND THE PRINCE NOT ONLY BECAME PASSENGER, BUT IT'S OWNER!
CONTINUED NEXT PAGE.

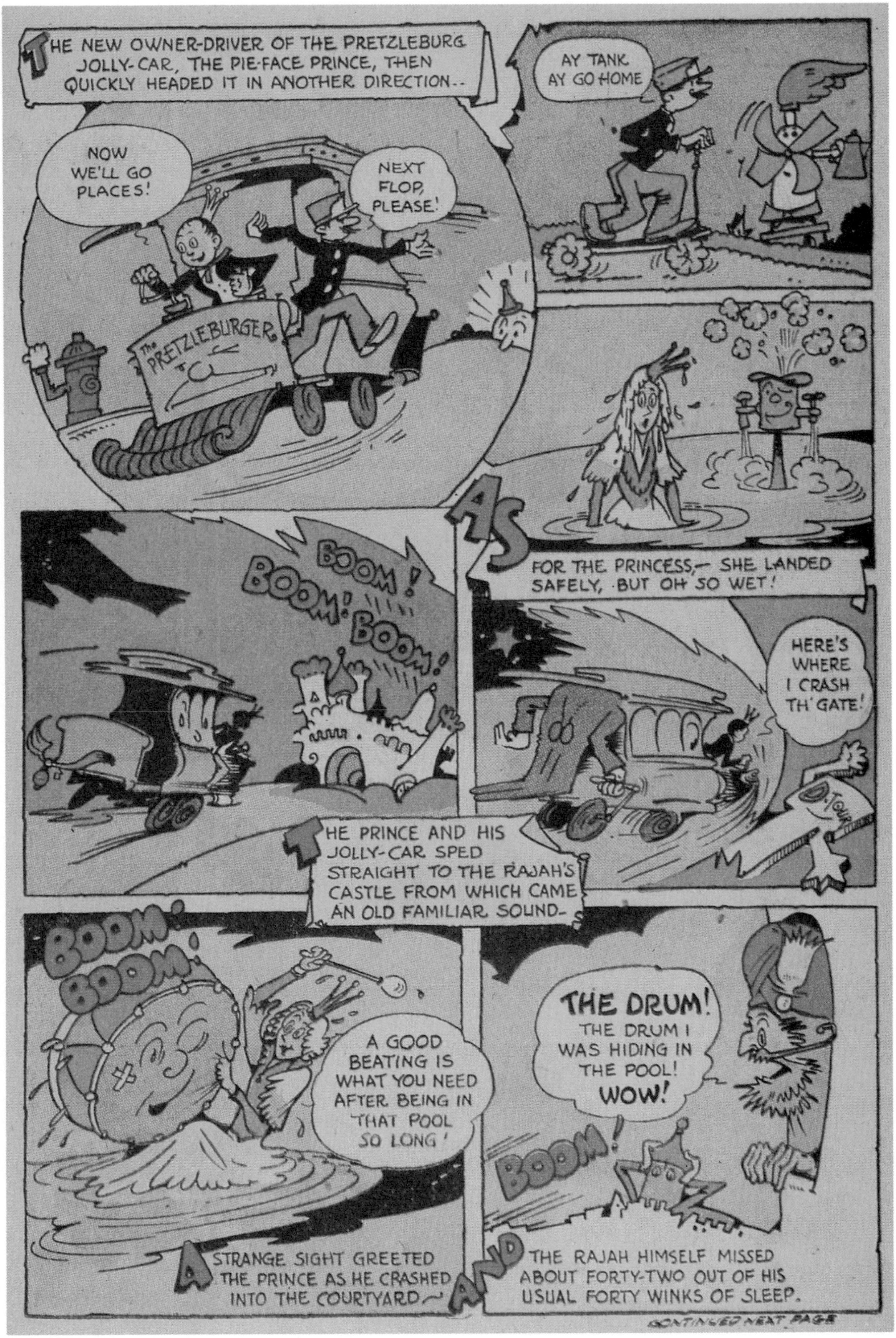
THE NEW OWNER-DRIVER OF THE PRETZLEBURG JOLLY-CAR, THE PIE-FACE PRINCE, THEN QUICKLY HEADED IT IN ANOTHER DIRECTION..
NOW WE'LL GO PLACES!
NEXT FLOP, PLEASE!
The PRETZLEBURGER
AY TANK AY GO HOME
AS FOR THE PRINCESS,— SHE LANDED SAFELY, BUT OH SO WET!
BOOM! BOOM! BOOM!
HERE'S WHERE I CRASH TH' GATE!
D-TOUR
THE PRINCE AND HIS JOLLY-CAR SPED STRAIGHT TO THE RAJAH'S CASTLE FROM WHICH CAME AN OLD FAMILIAR SOUND—
BOOM! BOOM!
A GOOD BEATING IS WHAT YOU NEED AFTER BEING IN THAT POOL SO LONG!
A STRANGE SIGHT GREETED THE PRINCE AS HE CRASHED INTO THE COURTYARD—
THE DRUM! THE DRUM I WAS HIDING IN THE POOL! WOW!
BOOM!
AND THE RAJAH HIMSELF MISSED ABOUT FORTY-TWO OUT OF HIS USUAL FORTY WINKS OF SLEEP.
CONTINUED NEXT PAGE

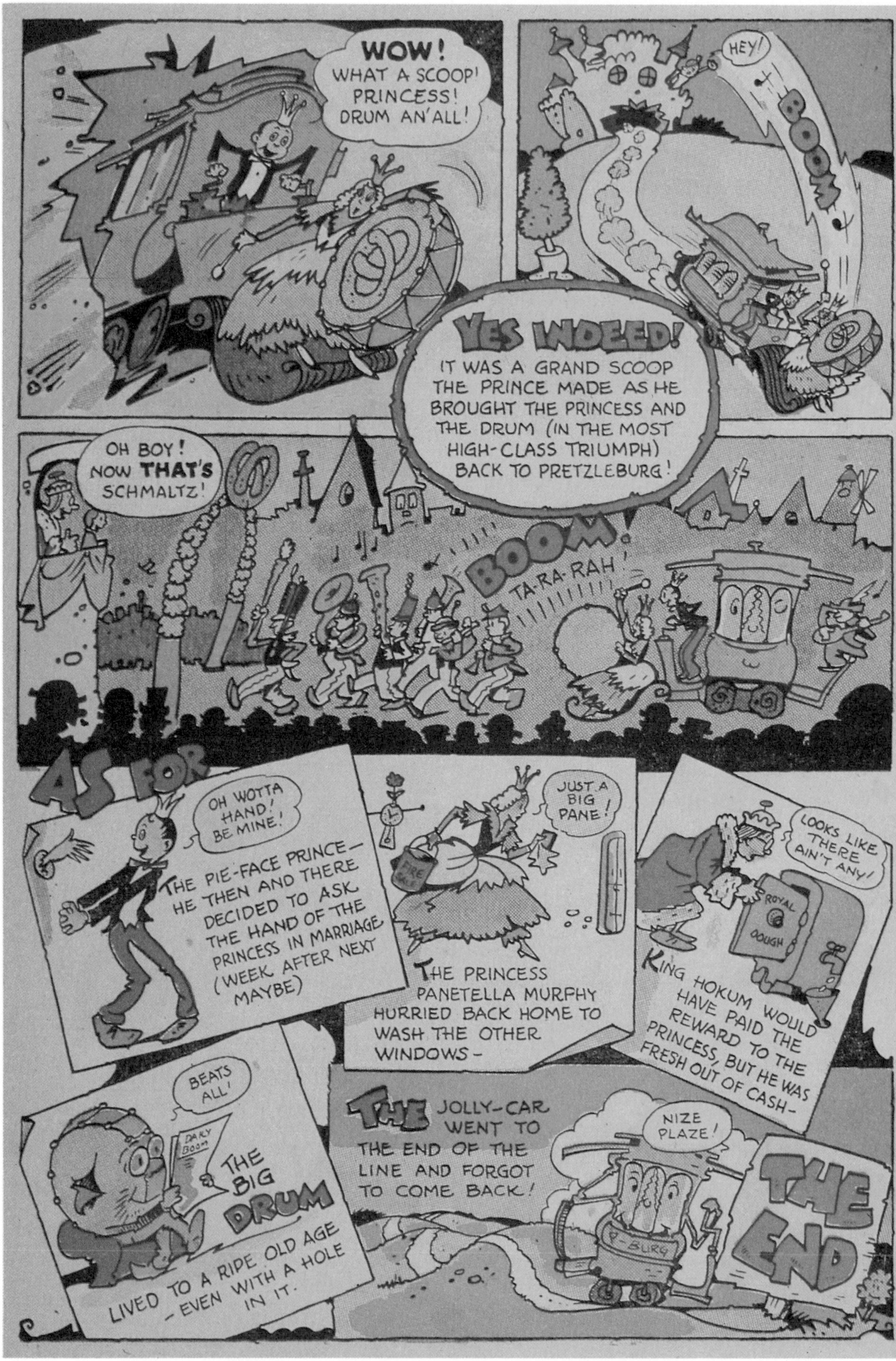

WOW! WHAT A SCOOP! PRINCESS! DRUM AN'ALL!
HEY!
BOOM
YES INDEED! IT WAS A GRAND SCOOP THE PRINCE MADE AS HE BROUGHT THE PRINCESS AND THE DRUM (IN THE MOST HIGH-CLASS TRIUMPH) BACK TO PRETZLEBURG!
OH BOY! NOW THAT'S SCHMALTZ!
BOOM!
TA-RA-RAH!
AS FOR
OH WOTTA HAND! BE MINE!
THE PIE-FACE PRINCE— HE THEN AND THERE DECIDED TO ASK THE HAND OF THE PRINCESS IN MARRIAGE (WEEK AFTER NEXT MAYBE)
JUST A BIG PANE!
THE PRINCESS PANETELLA MURPHY HURRIED BACK HOME TO WASH THE OTHER WINDOWS—
LOOKS LIKE THERE AIN'T ANY!
ROYAL DOUGH
KING HOKUM WOULD HAVE PAID THE REWARD TO THE PRINCESS, BUT HE WAS FRESH OUT OF CASH—
BEATS ALL!
THE BIG DRUM
LIVED TO A RIPE OLD AGE —EVEN WITH A HOLE IN IT.
THE JOLLY-CAR WENT TO THE END OF THE LINE AND FORGOT TO COME BACK!
NIZE PLAZE!
P-BURG
THE END

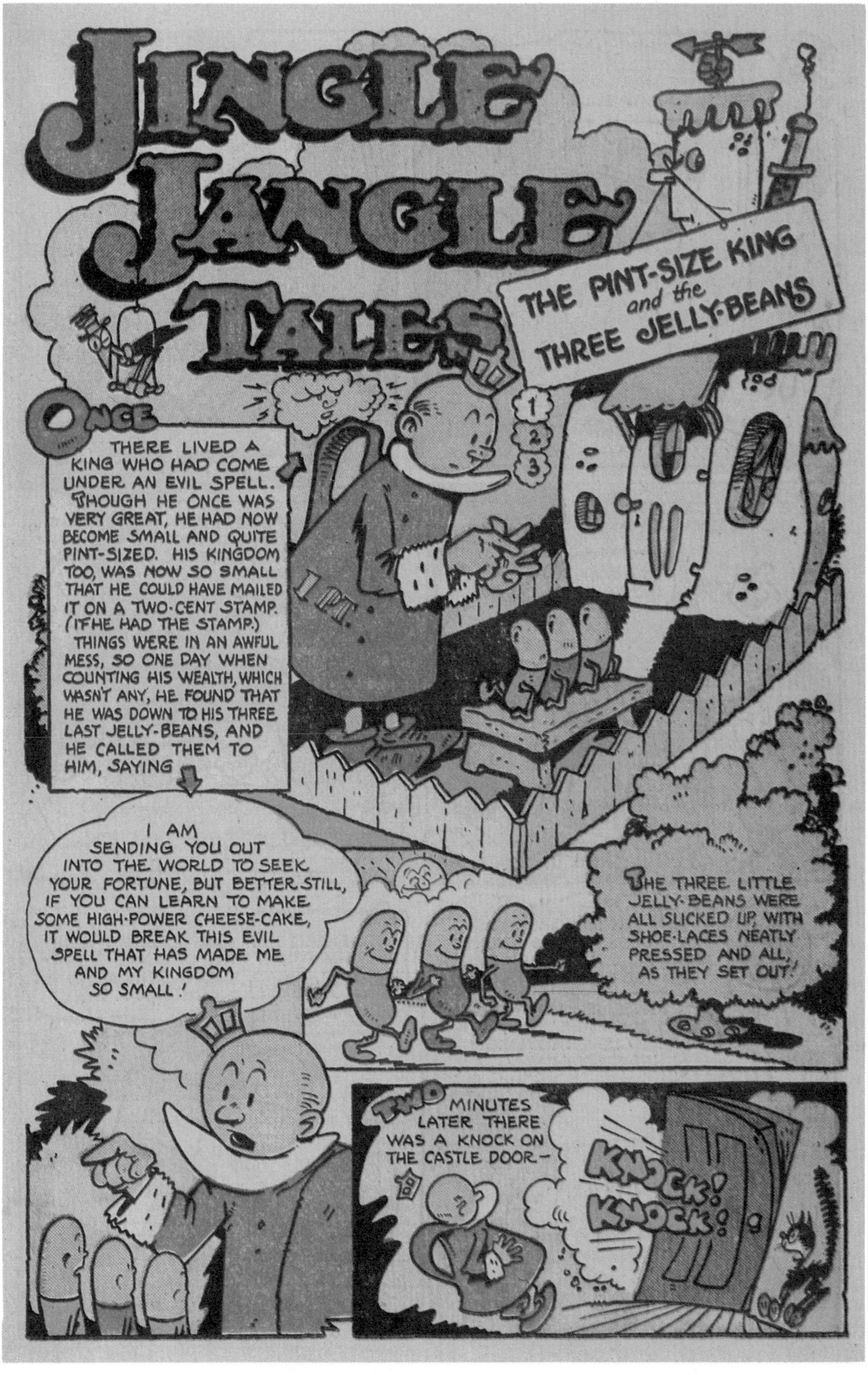
JINGLE JANGLE TALES
THE PINT-SIZE KING and the THREE JELLY-BEANS
1 2 3
ONCE THERE LIVED A KING WHO HAD COME UNDER AN EVIL SPELL. THOUGH HE ONCE WAS VERY GREAT, HE HAD NOW BECOME SMALL AND QUITE PINT-SIZED. HIS KINGDOM TOO, WAS NOW SO SMALL THAT HE COULD HAVE MAILED IT ON A TWO-CENT STAMP. (IF HE HAD THE STAMP.) THINGS WERE IN AN AWFUL MESS, SO ONE DAY WHEN COUNTING HIS WEALTH, WHICH WASN'T ANY, HE FOUND THAT HE WAS DOWN TO HIS THREE LAST JELLY-BEANS, AND HE CALLED THEM TO HIM, SAYING
1 PT.
I AM SENDING YOU OUT INTO THE WORLD TO SEEK YOUR FORTUNE, BUT BETTER STILL, IF YOU CAN LEARN TO MAKE SOME HIGH-POWER CHEESE-CAKE, IT WOULD BREAK THIS EVIL SPELL THAT HAS MADE ME AND MY KINGDOM SO SMALL!
THE THREE LITTLE JELLY-BEANS WERE ALL SLICKED UP, WITH SHOE-LACES NEATLY PRESSED AND ALL, AS THEY SET OUT!
TWO MINUTES LATER THERE WAS A KNOCK ON THE CASTLE DOOR—
KNOCK! KNOCK!

From *Jingle Jangle Comics* No. 24, December 1946.

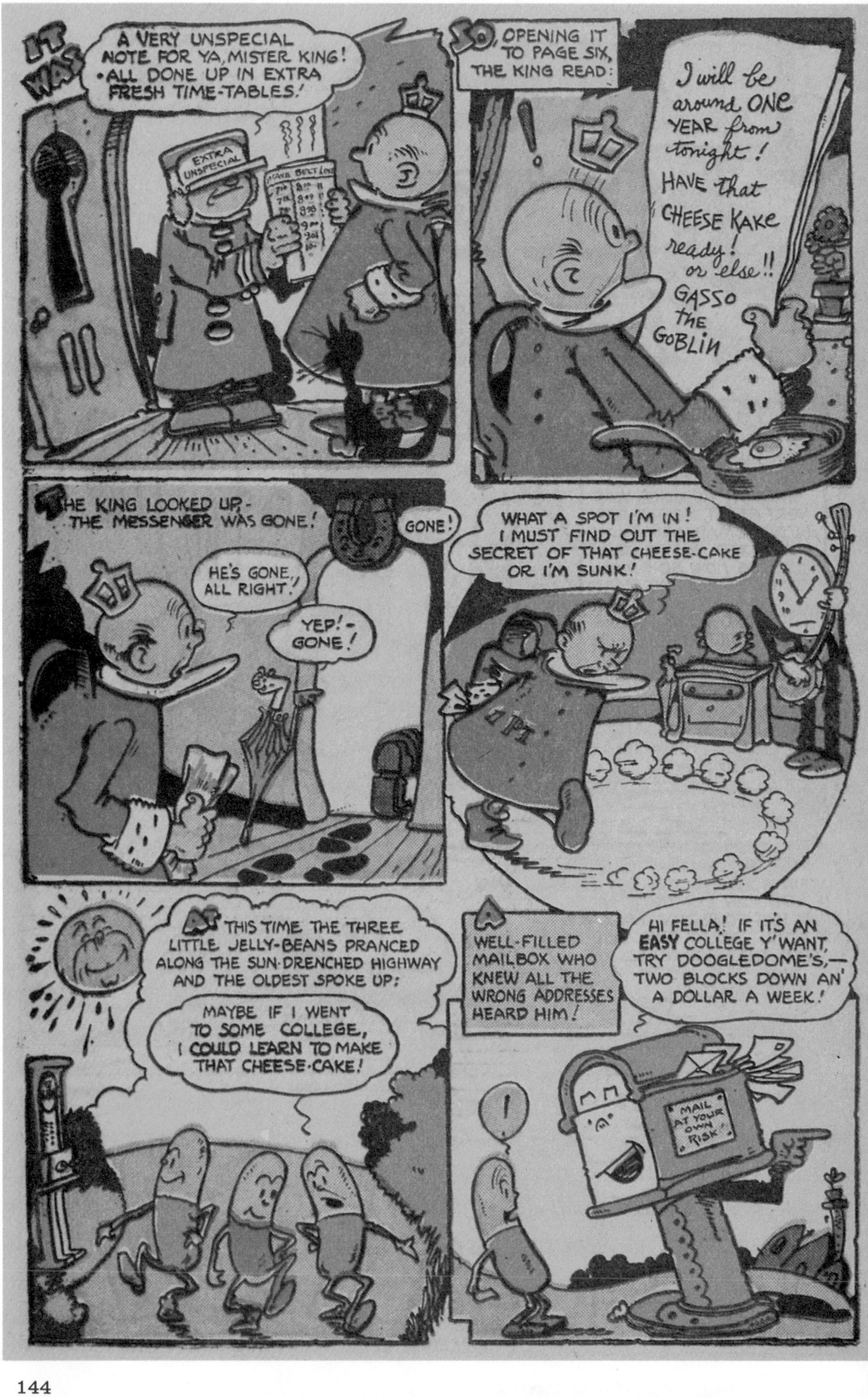

IT WAS
A VERY UNSPECIAL NOTE FOR YA, MISTER KING! • ALL DONE UP IN EXTRA FRESH TIME-TABLES!
EXTRA UNSPECIAL
SO, OPENING IT TO PAGE SIX, THE KING READ:
I will be around ONE YEAR from tonight! HAVE that CHEESE KAKE ready! or else!! GASSO THE GOBLIN
!
THE KING LOOKED UP - THE MESSENGER WAS GONE!
GONE!
HE'S GONE, ALL RIGHT.
YEP! - GONE!
WHAT A SPOT I'M IN! I MUST FIND OUT THE SECRET OF THAT CHEESE-CAKE OR I'M SUNK!
AS THIS TIME THE THREE LITTLE JELLY-BEANS PRANCED ALONG THE SUN-DRENCHED HIGHWAY AND THE OLDEST SPOKE UP:
MAYBE IF I WENT TO SOME COLLEGE, I COULD LEARN TO MAKE THAT CHEESE-CAKE!
A WELL-FILLED MAILBOX WHO KNEW ALL THE WRONG ADDRESSES HEARD HIM!
HI FELLA! IF IT'S AN EASY COLLEGE Y'WANT, TRY DOOGLEDOME'S,— TWO BLOCKS DOWN AN' A DOLLAR A WEEK!
!
MAIL AT YOUR OWN RISK

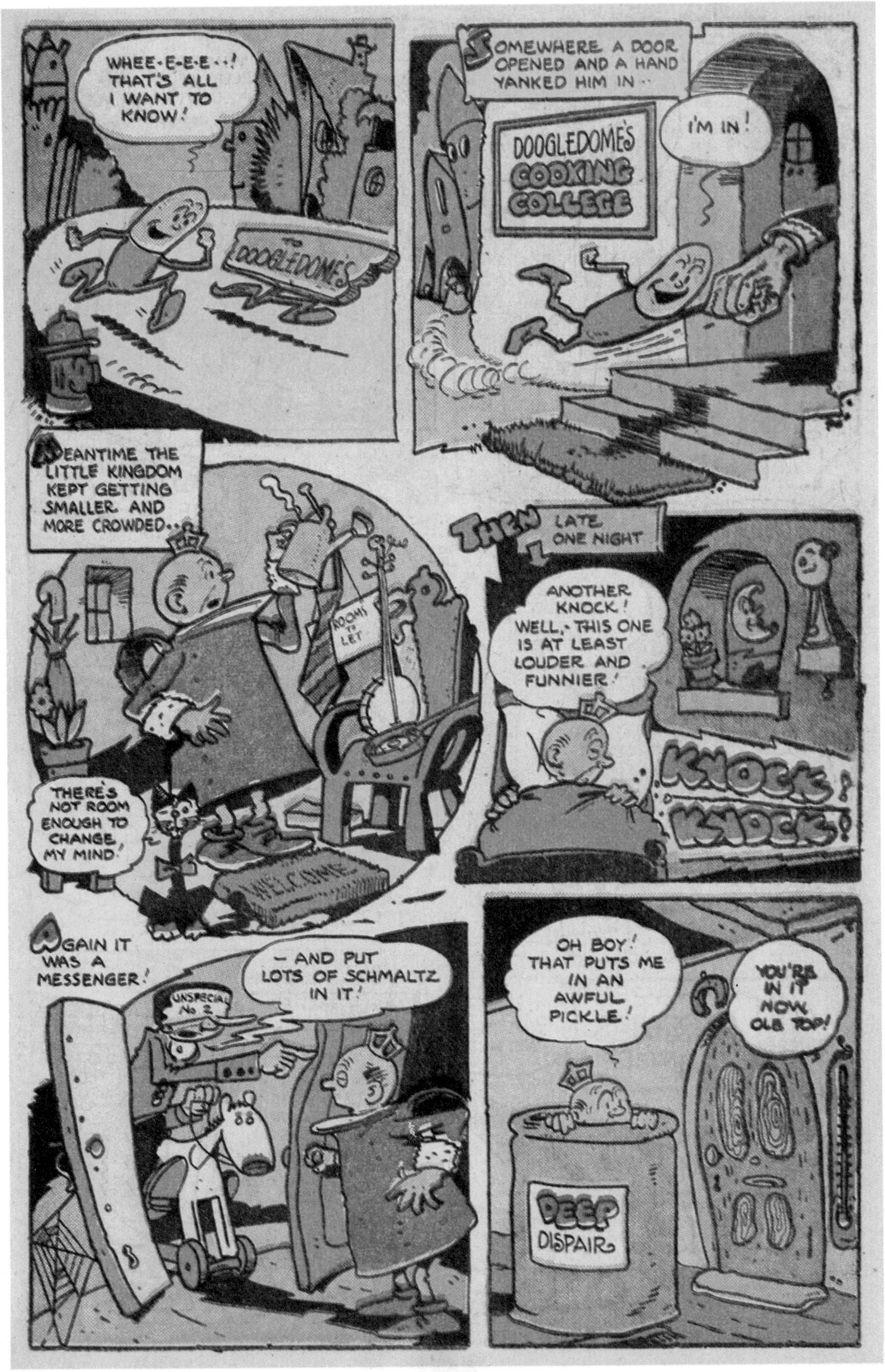
WHEE-E-E-E--! THAT'S ALL I WANT TO KNOW!
DOOGLEDOME'S
SOMEWHERE A DOOR OPENED AND A HAND YANKED HIM IN--
DOOGLEDOME'S COOKING COLLEGE
I'M IN!
MEANTIME THE LITTLE KINGDOM KEPT GETTING SMALLER AND MORE CROWDED--
ROOMS TO LET
THERE'S NOT ROOM ENOUGH TO CHANGE MY MIND!
WELCOME
THEN LATE ONE NIGHT
ANOTHER KNOCK! WELL,- THIS ONE IS AT LEAST LOUDER AND FUNNIER!
KNOCK! KNOCK!
AGAIN IT WAS A MESSENGER!
UNSPECIAL No. 2
- AND PUT LOTS OF SCHMALTZ IN IT!
OH BOY! THAT PUTS ME IN AN AWFUL PICKLE!
YOU'RE IN IT NOW, OLD TOP!
DEEP DISPAIR

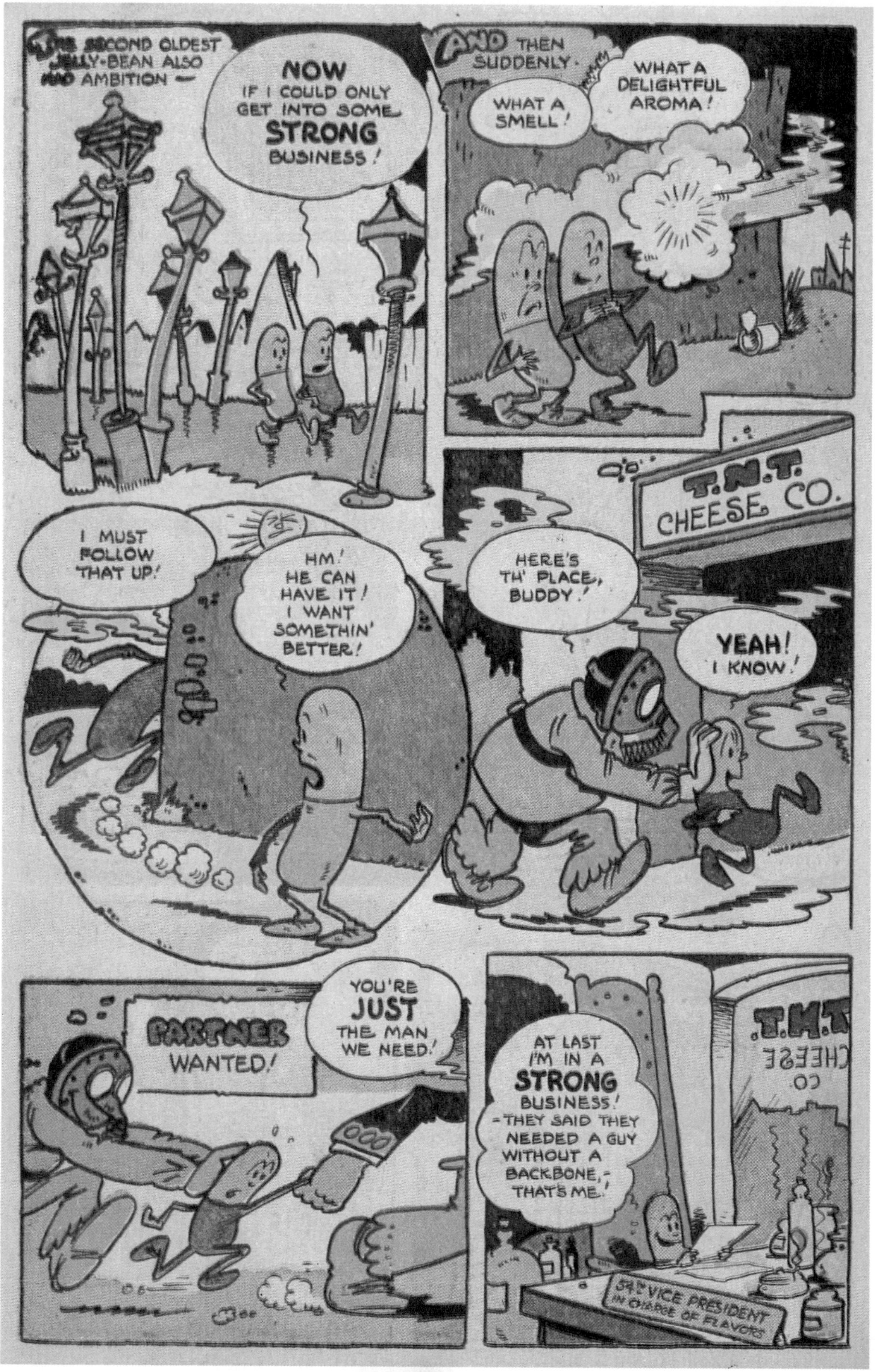
THE SECOND OLDEST JELLY-BEAN ALSO HAD AMBITION —
NOW IF I COULD ONLY GET INTO SOME STRONG BUSINESS!
AND THEN SUDDENLY.
WHAT A SMELL!
WHAT A DELIGHTFUL AROMA!
I MUST FOLLOW THAT UP!
HM! HE CAN HAVE IT! I WANT SOMETHIN' BETTER!
T.N.T. CHEESE CO.
HERE'S TH' PLACE, BUDDY!
YEAH! I KNOW!
PARTNER WANTED!
YOU'RE JUST THE MAN WE NEED!
T.N.T. CHEESE CO.
AT LAST I'M IN A STRONG BUSINESS! -THEY SAID THEY NEEDED A GUY WITHOUT A BACKBONE,- THAT'S ME!
54th VICE PRESIDENT IN CHARGE OF FLAVORS

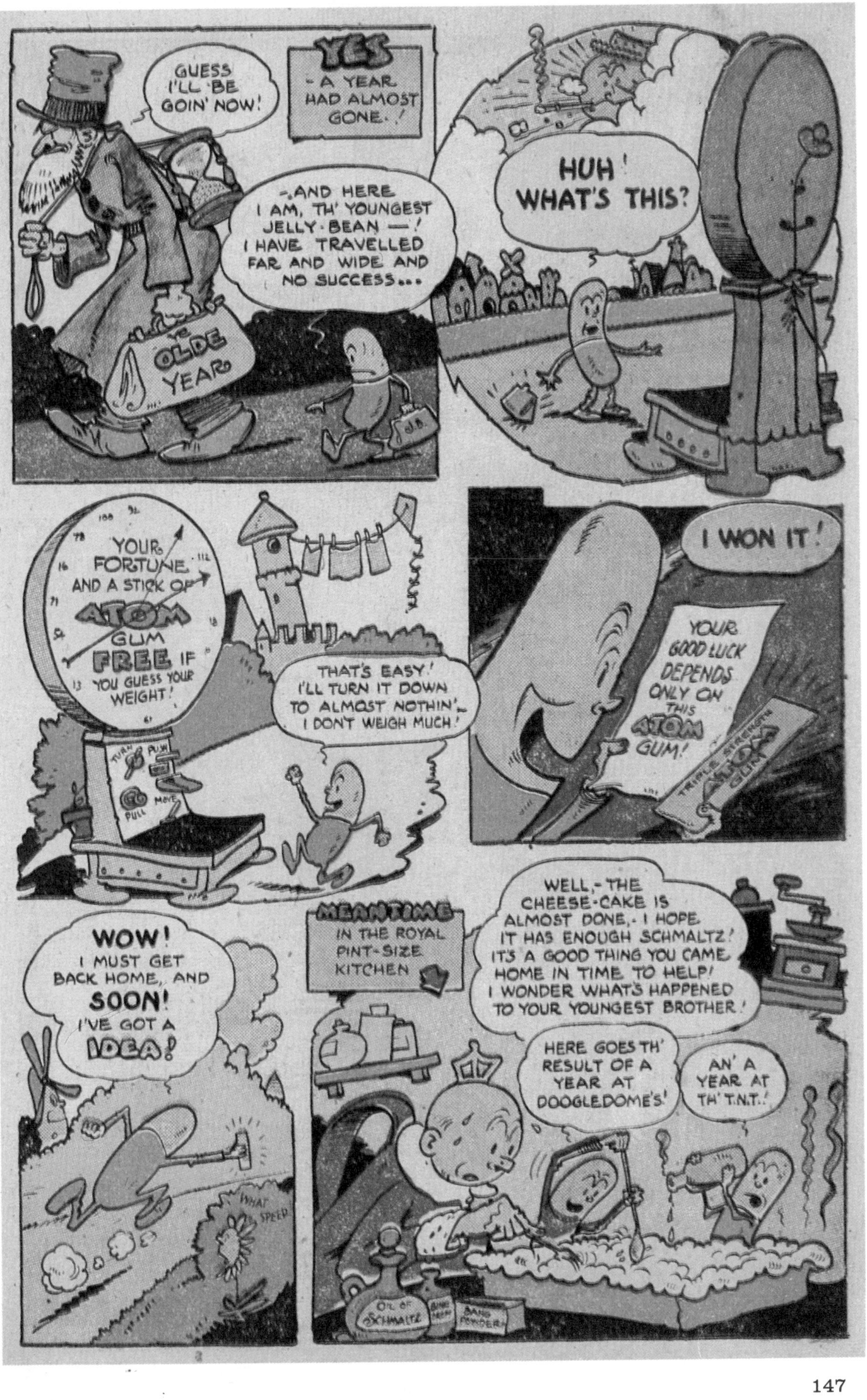
GUESS I'LL BE GOIN' NOW!
YES - A YEAR HAD ALMOST GONE!
YE OLDE YEAR
-AND HERE I AM, TH' YOUNGEST JELLY-BEAN —! I HAVE TRAVELLED FAR AND WIDE AND NO SUCCESS...
HUH! WHAT'S THIS?
YOUR FORTUNE AND A STICK OF ATOM GUM FREE IF YOU GUESS YOUR WEIGHT!
TURN PUSH PULL MOVE
THAT'S EASY! I'LL TURN IT DOWN TO ALMOST NOTHIN' — I DON'T WEIGH MUCH!
I WON IT!
YOUR GOOD LUCK DEPENDS ONLY ON THIS ATOM GUM!
TRIPLE STRENGTH ATOM GUM
WOW! I MUST GET BACK HOME, AND SOON! I'VE GOT A IDEA!
WHAT SPEED
MEANTIME IN THE ROYAL PINT-SIZE KITCHEN
WELL,- THE CHEESE-CAKE IS ALMOST DONE,- I HOPE IT HAS ENOUGH SCHMALTZ! IT'S A GOOD THING YOU CAME HOME IN TIME TO HELP! I WONDER WHAT'S HAPPENED TO YOUR YOUNGEST BROTHER!
HERE GOES TH' RESULT OF A YEAR AT DOOGLEDOME'S!
AN' A YEAR AT TH' T.N.T.!
OIL OF SCHMALTZ
BANG POWDER

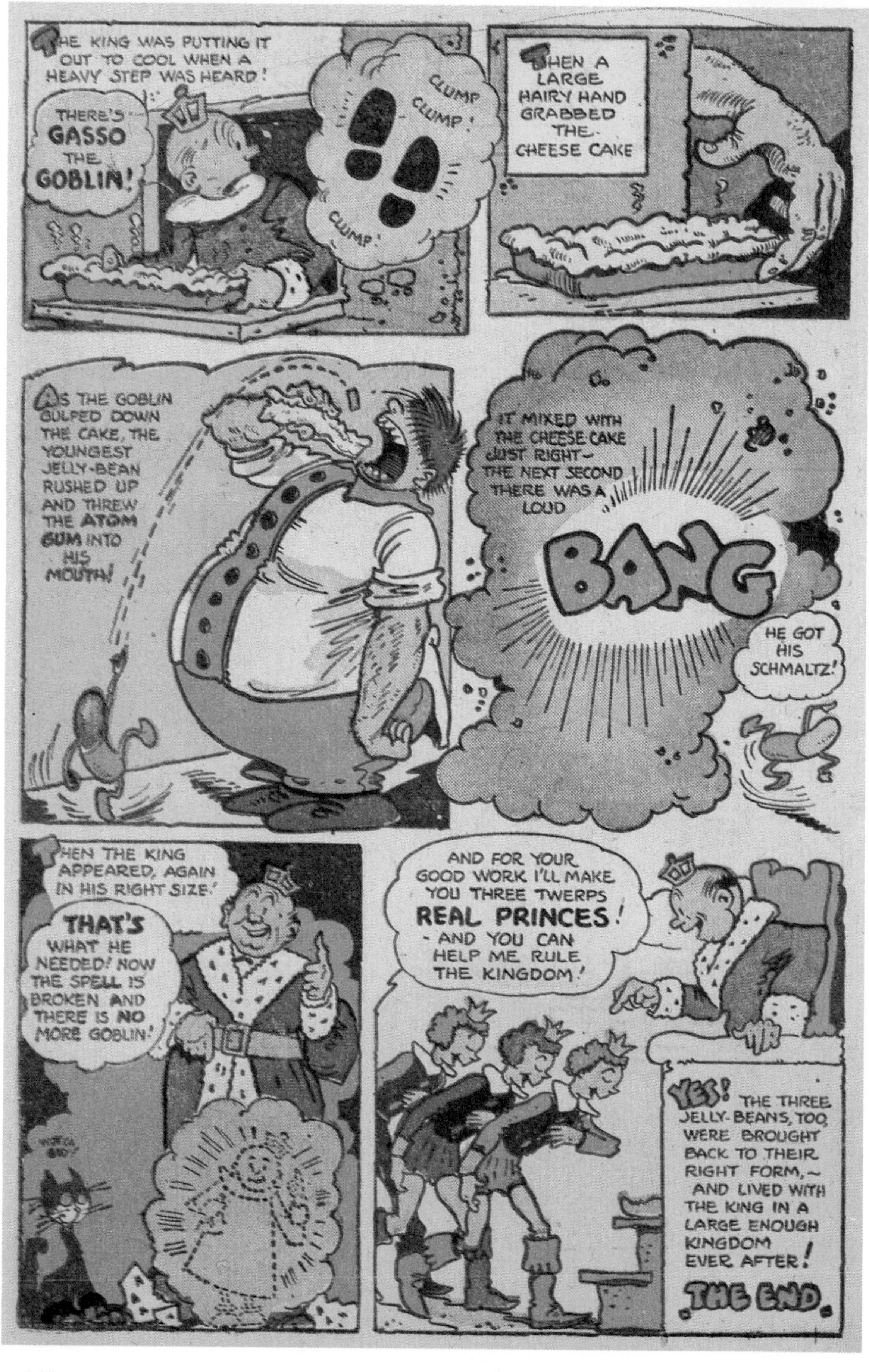
THE KING WAS PUTTING IT OUT TO COOL WHEN A HEAVY STEP WAS HEARD!
THERE'S GASSO THE GOBLIN!
CLUMP CLUMP! CLUMP!
THEN A LARGE HAIRY HAND GRABBED THE CHEESE CAKE
AS THE GOBLIN GULPED DOWN THE CAKE, THE YOUNGEST JELLY-BEAN RUSHED UP AND THREW THE ATOM GUM INTO HIS MOUTH!
IT MIXED WITH THE CHEESE CAKE JUST RIGHT— THE NEXT SECOND THERE WAS A LOUD
BANG
HE GOT HIS SCHMALTZ!
THEN THE KING APPEARED, AGAIN IN HIS RIGHT SIZE!
THAT'S WHAT HE NEEDED! NOW THE SPELL IS BROKEN AND THERE IS NO MORE GOBLIN!
AND FOR YOUR GOOD WORK I'LL MAKE YOU THREE TWERPS REAL PRINCES! - AND YOU CAN HELP ME RULE THE KINGDOM!
YES! THE THREE JELLY-BEANS, TOO, WERE BROUGHT BACK TO THEIR RIGHT FORM,— AND LIVED WITH THE KING IN A LARGE ENOUGH KINGDOM EVER AFTER!
THE END

About "Little Lulu" and John Stanley

Late in 1934, there was a small crisis at the *Saturday Evening Post*. The magazine was losing Carl Anderson's popular weekly panel cartoon, *Henry,* to King Features Syndicate. An editor at the *Post* asked a regular contributor to the magazine, Marjorie Henderson Buell—she signed her cartoons "Marge"—for help in coming up with a replacement for *Henry.* The *Post* wanted a child like Henry, but a girl this time. "The editors noodled out the name," Mrs. Buell told an interviewer more than thirty years later. "I was too busy thinking about how she'd look and what she'd do."

The name the editors "noodled out" was "Little Lulu." For a design, Mrs. Buell essentially added a skirt and corkscrew curls to Henry's shoe-button eyes and up-turned nose. The new character was a devilish child, heiress to a long line of such characters that in newspaper comics extended back to the Yellow Kid, Buster Brown, and the Katzenjammer Kids. Like theirs, her mischief, as displayed in a weekly panel, often bordered on the malicious.

Lulu first appeared in the *Post* for February 23, 1935, and ran there until the end of 1944. By that time, Lulu was also appearing in animated cartoons and in ads for Kleenex tissues. "The *Post* didn't want me to go into large-scale business with Lulu," Mrs. Buell has said, "but I wanted to see what she could do in all forms. We parted amicably."

A few months after Lulu left the *Post,* she made her debut in a comic book. That first issue of *Little Lulu* was written and drawn by a cartoonist named John Stanley. (*At the Beach,* the first of the four stories we have chosen for his book, is from that issue.) Stanley also wrote and illustrated the second issue of *Little Lulu.* After that, he drew only the covers, but he wrote everything in each issue for thirteen or fourteen years—about 150 issues, all told—and his writing made *Little Lulu* an extraordinary comic book.

John Stanley was born on March 22, 1914, in New York City, and he worked briefly at the Max Fleischer animation studios, made drawings for Disney merchandise, and held down other jobs before he began writing and drawing stories for Western Printing and Lithographing Company (which produced comic books for publication by another company, Dell) in the early 1940s. At that time, Western produced many comic books for small children, most of them edited by Oskar Lebeck. Lebeck ruled with a light hand, and cartoonists like Walt Kelly, Dan Noonan, Morris Gollub, and, of course, John Stanley did charming and funny work for him. It was Lebeck who assigned Stanley to *Little Lulu.* "I'm sure it was due to no special form of brilliance he thought I'd lend to it," Stanley told Don Phelps. "It could have been handed to Dan Noonan, Kelly, or anyone else. I just happened to be available at the time."

To say that Stanley "wrote" *Little Lulu* is actually a little deceptive, since he was responsible for more than the plots and the dialogue. He sketched each story in rough form, so that he controlled the staging within each panel and the appearance and the attitudes of the characters. The finished drawings were made by other cartoonists (the three later stories in this book were illustrated by Irving Tripp). Stanley himself disliked the published drawings—"too static for me"—but in fact, the "static" style seems appropriate for such highly stylized characters.

Like the panel cartoons, Stanley's stories had a strong flavor of the 1930s. Most obviously, the children—especially the boys—dressed in styles of that decade (knickers, shorts, and so on). Lulu's home town was not suburban, but looked like an eastern city of the Depression years: small, plain houses, with tiny yards or none at all (many front doors opened directly onto the sidewalk). Families were small—one or two children—and the parents usually middle-aged or close to it. Like the *Archie* stories, whose trappings were similarly dated, Stanley's *Lulu* stories remained frozen in time, with only a few concessions to postwar changes. The anachronisms seem never to have been bothered *Little Lulu*'s readers.

At first, Stanley's conception of Lulu herself owed quite a bit to Marge's. But Stanley's Lulu was not so much mischievous as single-minded. She had a very clear idea of what was important to *her,* and she wasn't distracted by irrelevancies like what adults thought was important. Children are, after all, very serious about their own concerns, and Stanley's stories abound in collisions between adults and children all of whom are behaving reasonably— on their own terms.

For the first few years, Stanley worked mainly with Lulu herself and her friend Tubby (who was, like Lulu, inherited from the magazine cartoons). Other children appeared in more or less interchangeable roles until, around 1950, Stanley gave Tubby a group of friends—Willie, Eddie, and Iggy—and a clubhouse, and gave Lulu some other girls to play with, including a buck-toothed gamine named Annie. The rivalry between boys and girls—an element in the series from the start—was magnified by the presence of so many children from both sexes. Lulu herself became a "good little girl" who outsmarted the boys, instead of triumphing through sheer brass as she had in the past. Many of the stories built around the rivalry theme are ingenious and funny, and the best of them spiral upward until the boys become the victims of a comic catastrophe like the one at the climax of *Five Little Babies,* which follows here.

Stanley found other ideas that could be nursed into comic life and exploited in one story after another. For example, Tubby assumed Lulu's old role as the serenely egocentric child, resenting all adult efforts to deflect him from his course; he played that role brilliantly in a string of stories in which he became "the Spider," a detective wreaking all the havoc necessary to solve a case. (Lulu's father was invariably the culprit—although he was of course no culprit at all by adult standards.)

Stanley's most striking departure from the feature he inherited from Marge was in the stories that Lulu told to Alvin, a vicious little next-door neighbor whose personality was not far removed from that of the magazine-cartoon Lulu. Beneath the laughter, Stanley's mock fairy tales could be as strong as real fairy tales. Lulu was the featured player, as well as the narrator, and she often took the part of a cheerful Candide in a world otherwise filled with greedy and stupid people. In *The Little Rich Boy,* a story we have chosen for this book, the fairy-tale Lulu is an ingénue indeed—until she gets rich. Then she takes revenge, with a chilling thoroughness, on the boy who has scorned her love.

While he was writing *Little Lulu,* Stanley contributed scripts to many other Dell comic books, and in the 1960s, after leaving *Lulu,* he both wrote and illustrated a few, like *Melvin Monster.* But he left comic books years ago (his comments on comic books—even his own work—have become rather sour), and he has worked recently for a silk-screening company in upstate New York.

M.B.

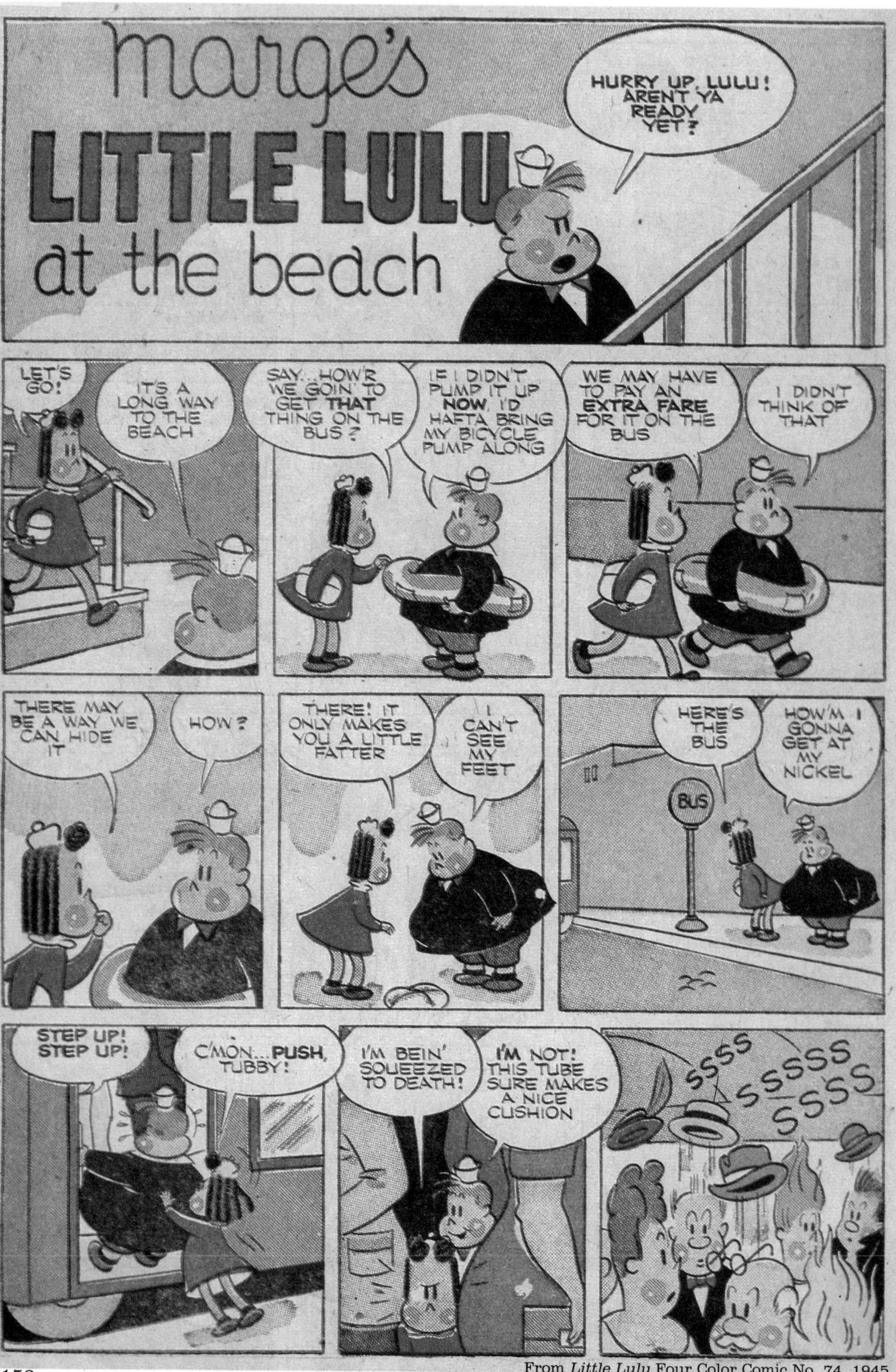
marge's
LITTLE LULU
at the beach
HURRY UP, LULU! AREN'T YA READY YET?
LET'S GO!
IT'S A LONG WAY TO THE BEACH
SAY...HOW'R WE GOIN' TO GET THAT THING ON THE BUS?
IF I DIDN'T PUMP IT UP NOW, I'D HAFTA BRING MY BICYCLE PUMP ALONG
WE MAY HAVE TO PAY AN EXTRA FARE FOR IT ON THE BUS
I DIDN'T THINK OF THAT
THERE MAY BE A WAY WE CAN HIDE IT
HOW?
THERE! IT ONLY MAKES YOU A LITTLE FATTER
I CAN'T SEE MY FEET
HERE'S THE BUS
HOW'M I GONNA GET AT MY NICKEL
BUS
STEP UP! STEP UP!
C'MON...PUSH, TUBBY!
I'M BEIN' SQUEEZED TO DEATH!
I'M NOT! THIS TUBE SURE MAKES A NICE CUSHION
SSSS SSSSS SSSS

From *Little Lulu* Four Color Comic No. 74, 1945.

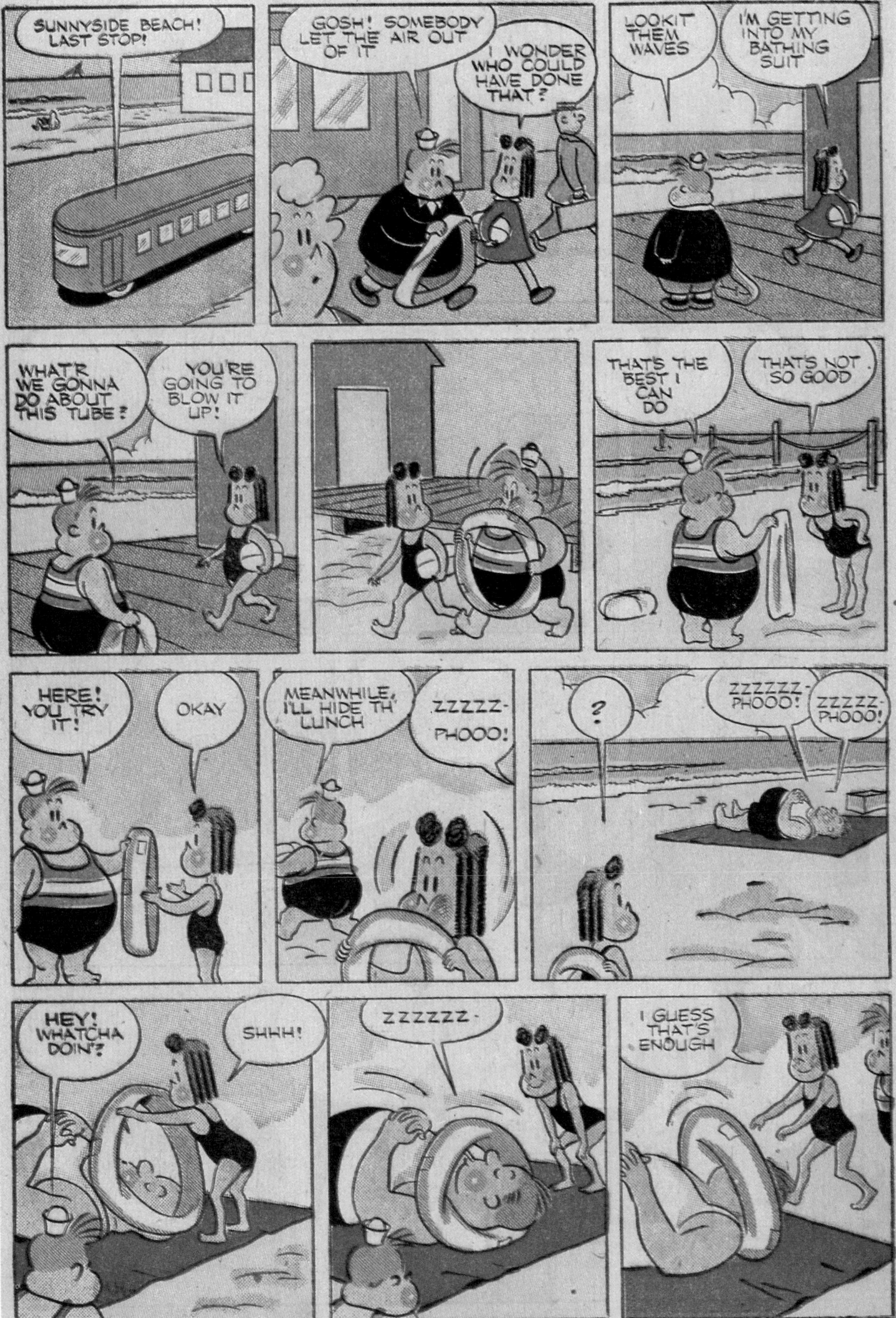
SUNNYSIDE BEACH! LAST STOP!
GOSH! SOMEBODY LET THE AIR OUT OF IT
I WONDER WHO COULD HAVE DONE THAT?
LOOKIT THEM WAVES
I'M GETTING INTO MY BATHING SUIT
WHAT'R WE GONNA DO ABOUT THIS TUBE?
YOU'RE GOING TO BLOW IT UP!
THAT'S THE BEST I CAN DO
THAT'S NOT SO GOOD
HERE! YOU TRY IT!
OKAY
MEANWHILE, I'LL HIDE TH' LUNCH
ZZZZZ-PHOOO!
?
ZZZZZZ-PHOOO!
ZZZZZ-PHOOO!
HEY! WHATCHA DOIN'?
SHHH!
ZZZZZZ-
I GUESS THAT'S ENOUGH

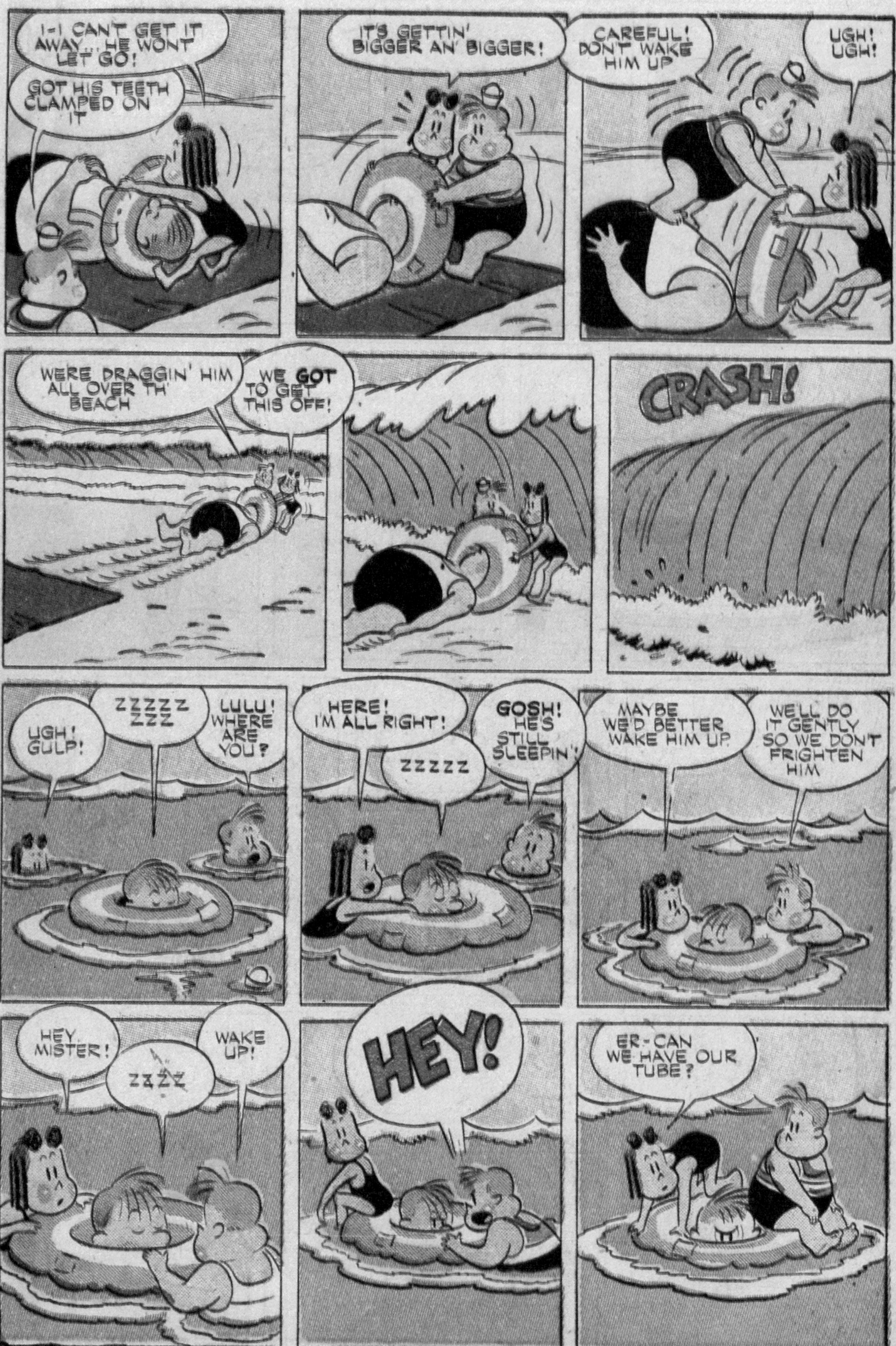
I-I CAN'T GET IT AWAY... HE WON'T LET GO!
GOT HIS TEETH CLAMPED ON IT
IT'S GETTIN' BIGGER AN' BIGGER!
CAREFUL! DON'T WAKE HIM UP
UGH! UGH!
WE'RE DRAGGIN' HIM ALL OVER TH' BEACH
WE GOT TO GET THIS OFF!
CRASH!
UGH! GULP!
ZZZZZ ZZZ
LULU! WHERE ARE YOU?
HERE! I'M ALL RIGHT!
ZZZZZ
GOSH! HE'S STILL SLEEPIN'!
MAYBE WE'D BETTER WAKE HIM UP.
WE'LL DO IT GENTLY SO WE DON'T FRIGHTEN HIM
HEY, MISTER!
ZZZZ
WAKE UP!
HEY!
ER-CAN WE HAVE OUR TUBE?

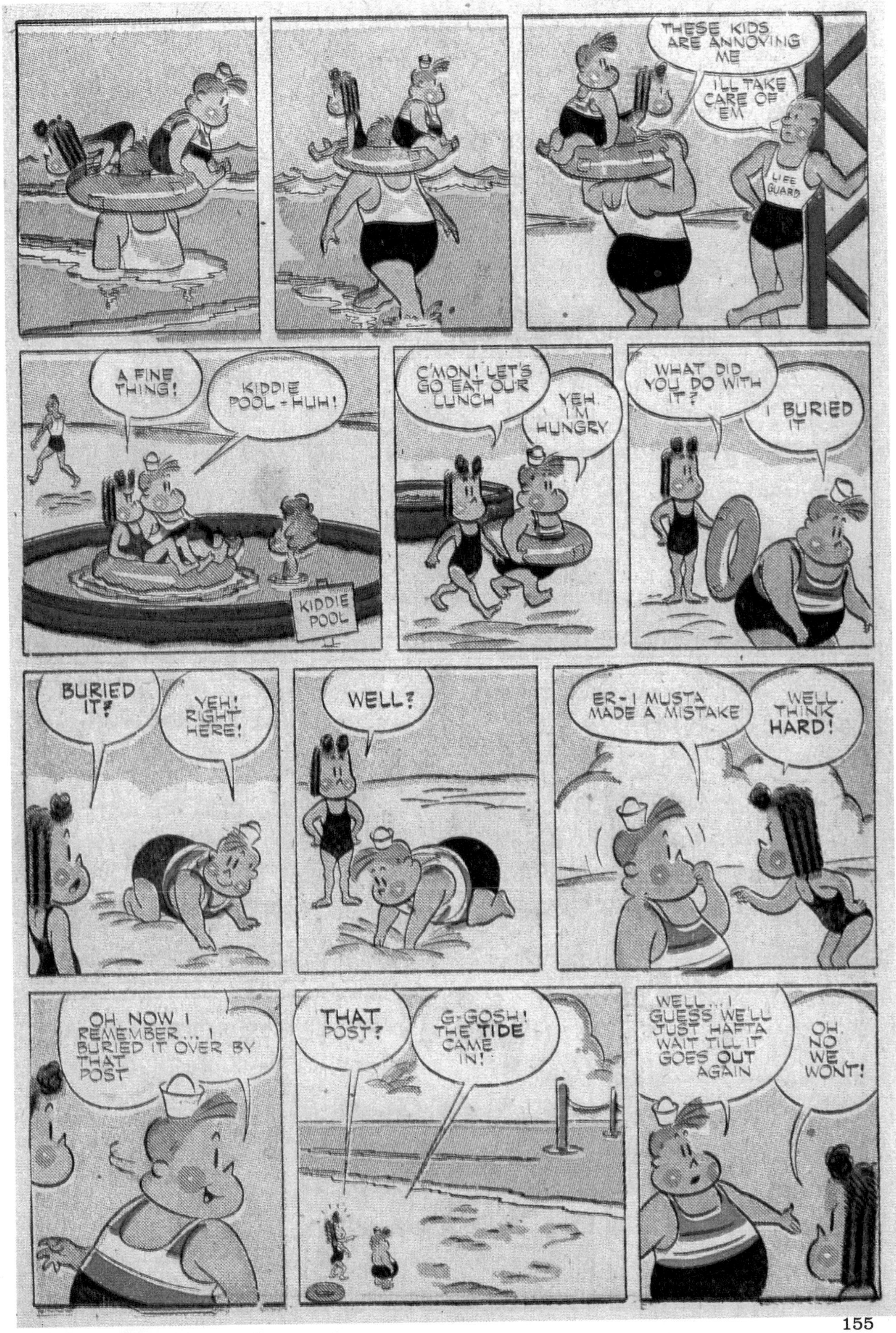

THESE KIDS ARE ANNOYING ME
I'LL TAKE CARE OF 'EM
LIFE GUARD
A FINE THING!
KIDDIE POOL - HUH!
KIDDIE POOL
C'MON! LET'S GO EAT OUR LUNCH
YEH. I'M HUNGRY
WHAT DID YOU DO WITH IT?
I BURIED IT
BURIED IT?
YEH! RIGHT HERE!
WELL?
ER - I MUSTA MADE A MISTAKE
WELL, THINK HARD!
OH NOW I REMEMBER... I BURIED IT OVER BY THAT POST
THAT POST?
G-GOSH! THE TIDE CAME IN!
WELL... I GUESS WE'LL JUST HAFTA WAIT TILL IT GOES OUT AGAIN
OH, NO WE WON'T!

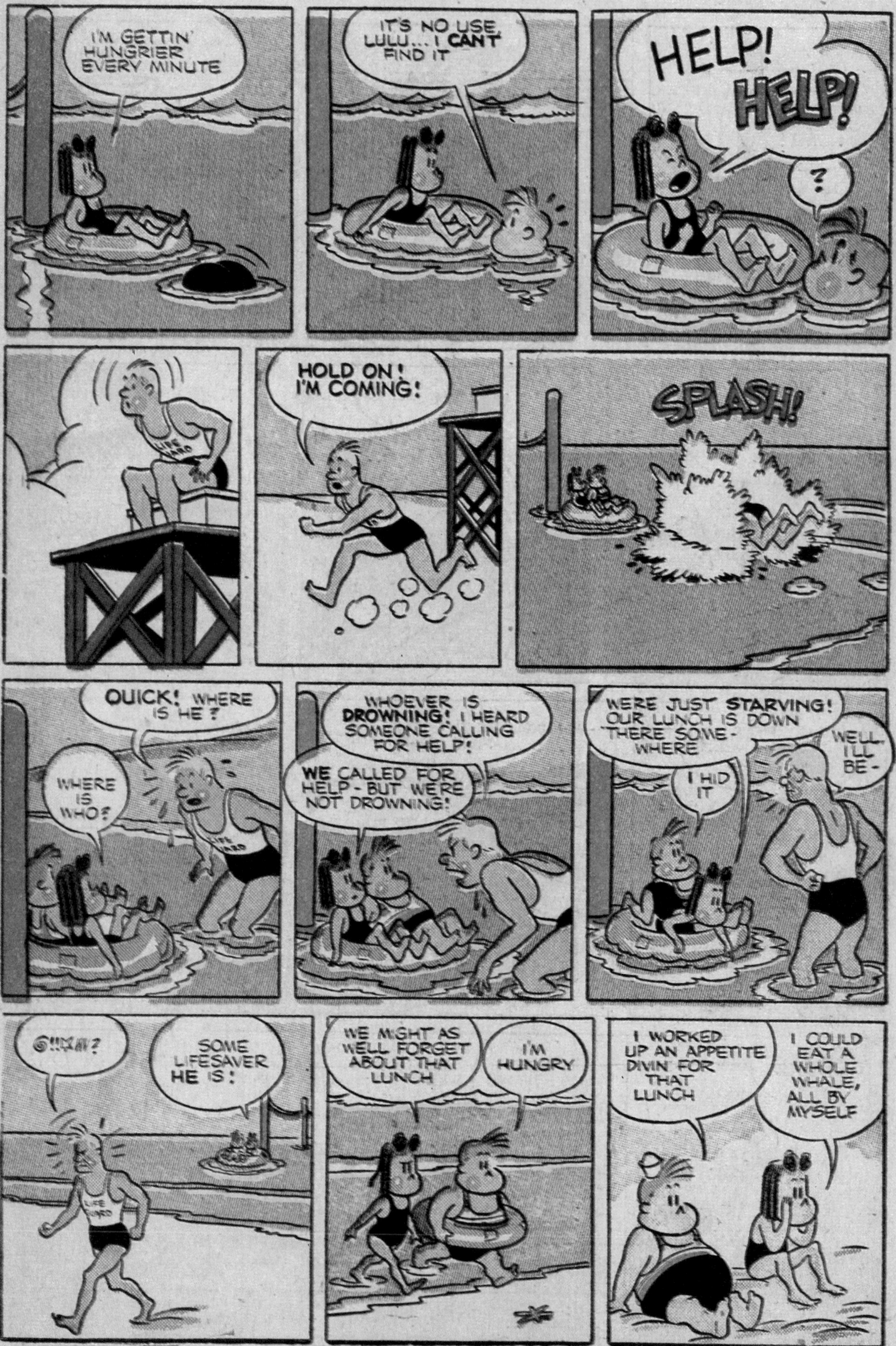

I'M GETTIN' HUNGRIER EVERY MINUTE
IT'S NO USE, LULU... I **CAN'T** FIND IT
HELP!
HELP!
?
HOLD ON! I'M COMING!
SPLASH!
QUICK! WHERE IS HE?
WHERE IS WHO?
WHOEVER IS **DROWNING!** I HEARD SOMEONE CALLING FOR HELP!
WE CALLED FOR HELP - BUT WE'RE NOT DROWNING!
WE'RE JUST **STARVING!** OUR LUNCH IS DOWN THERE SOME-WHERE
I HID IT
WELL, I'LL BE-
SOME LIFESAVER **HE** IS!
WE MIGHT AS WELL FORGET ABOUT THAT LUNCH
I'M HUNGRY
I WORKED UP AN APPETITE DIVIN' FOR THAT LUNCH
I COULD EAT A WHOLE WHALE, ALL BY MYSELF

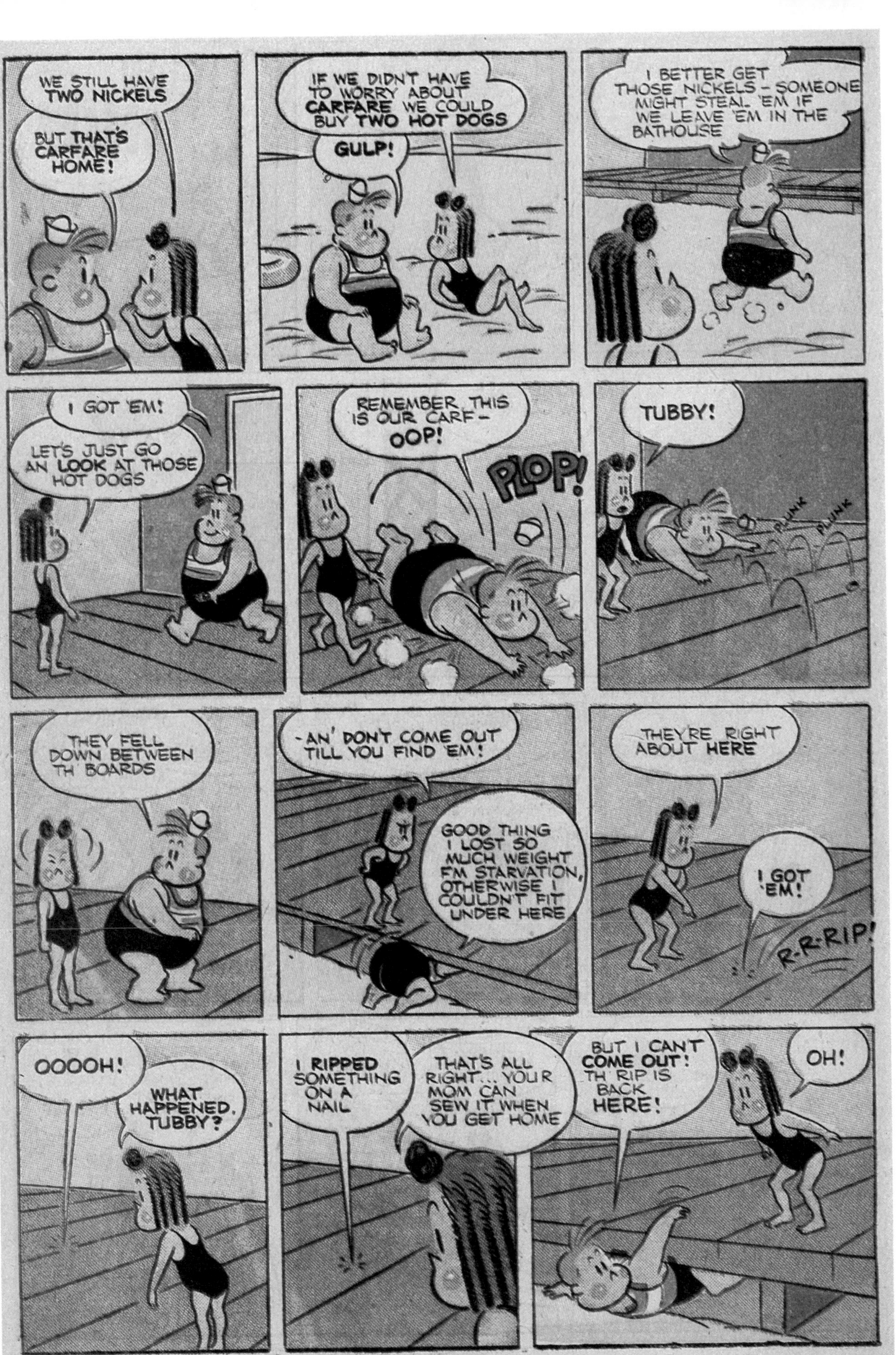

WE STILL HAVE TWO NICKELS
BUT THAT'S CARFARE HOME!
IF WE DIDN'T HAVE TO WORRY ABOUT CARFARE WE COULD BUY TWO HOT DOGS
GULP!
I BETTER GET THOSE NICKELS - SOMEONE MIGHT STEAL 'EM IF WE LEAVE 'EM IN THE BATHOUSE
I GOT 'EM!
LET'S JUST GO AN LOOK AT THOSE HOT DOGS
REMEMBER THIS IS OUR CARF- OOP!
PLOP!
TUBBY!
PLINK
PLINK
THEY FELL DOWN BETWEEN TH' BOARDS
-AN' DON'T COME OUT TILL YOU FIND 'EM!
GOOD THING I LOST SO MUCH WEIGHT F'M STARVATION, OTHERWISE I COULDN'T FIT UNDER HERE
THEY'RE RIGHT ABOUT HERE
I GOT 'EM!
R-R-RIP!
OOOOH!
WHAT HAPPENED, TUBBY?
I RIPPED SOMETHING ON A NAIL
THAT'S ALL RIGHT... YOUR MOM CAN SEW IT WHEN YOU GET HOME
BUT I CAN'T COME OUT! TH' RIP IS BACK HERE!
OH!

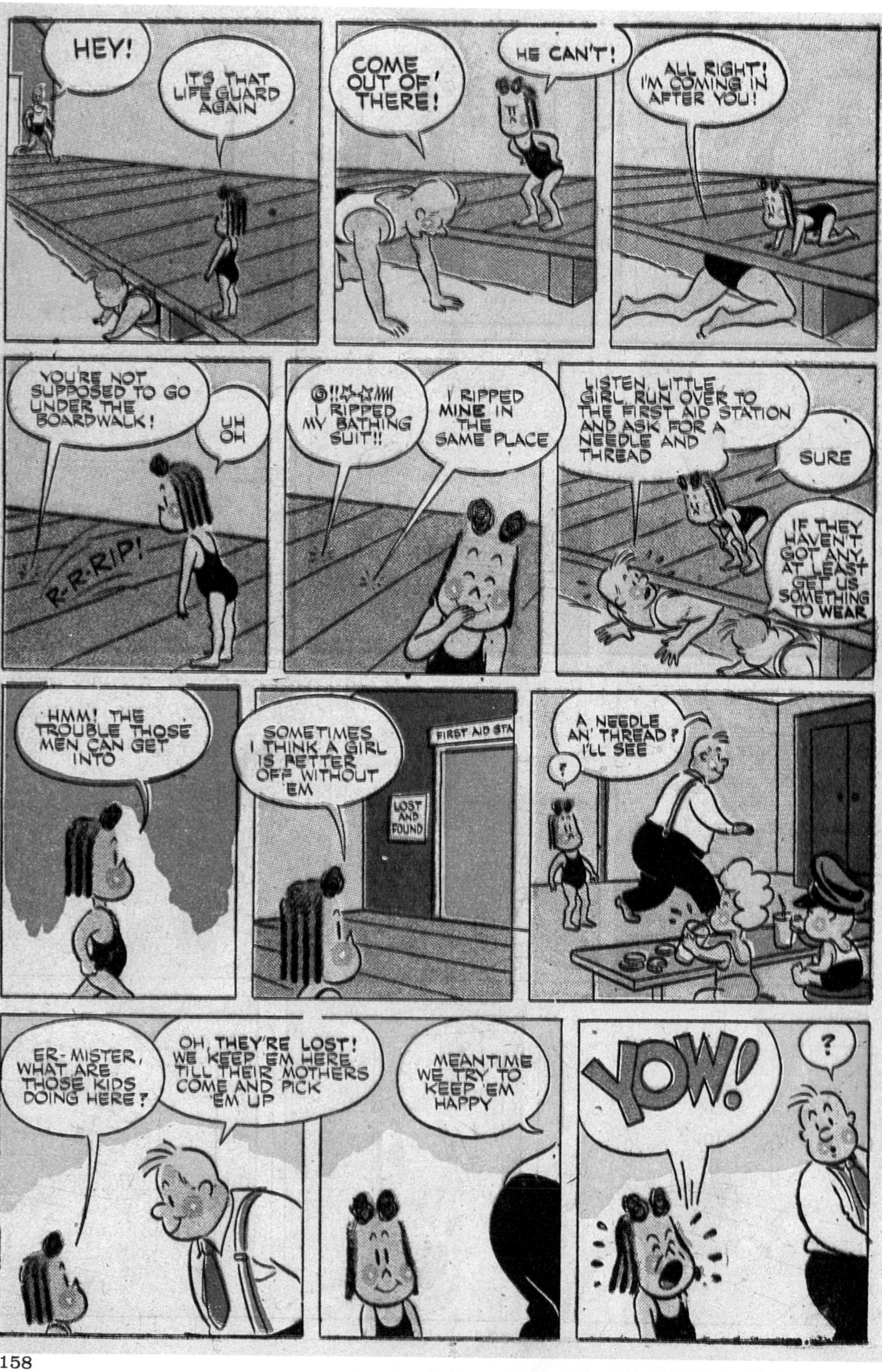
HEY!
IT'S THAT LIFE GUARD AGAIN
COME OUT OF THERE!
HE CAN'T!
ALL RIGHT! I'M COMING IN AFTER YOU!
YOU'RE NOT SUPPOSED TO GO UNDER THE BOARDWALK!
UH OH
R-R-RIP!
I RIPPED MY BATHING SUIT!!
I RIPPED MINE IN THE SAME PLACE
LISTEN, LITTLE GIRL, RUN OVER TO THE FIRST AID STATION AND ASK FOR A NEEDLE AND THREAD
SURE
IF THEY HAVEN'T GOT ANY, AT LEAST GET US SOMETHING TO WEAR
HMM! THE TROUBLE THOSE MEN CAN GET INTO
SOMETIMES I THINK A GIRL IS BETTER OFF WITHOUT 'EM
FIRST AID STA
LOST AND FOUND
A NEEDLE AN' THREAD? I'LL SEE
?
ER-MISTER, WHAT ARE THOSE KIDS DOING HERE?
OH THEY'RE LOST! WE KEEP 'EM HERE TILL THEIR MOTHERS COME AND PICK 'EM UP
MEANTIME WE TRY TO KEEP 'EM HAPPY
YOW!
?

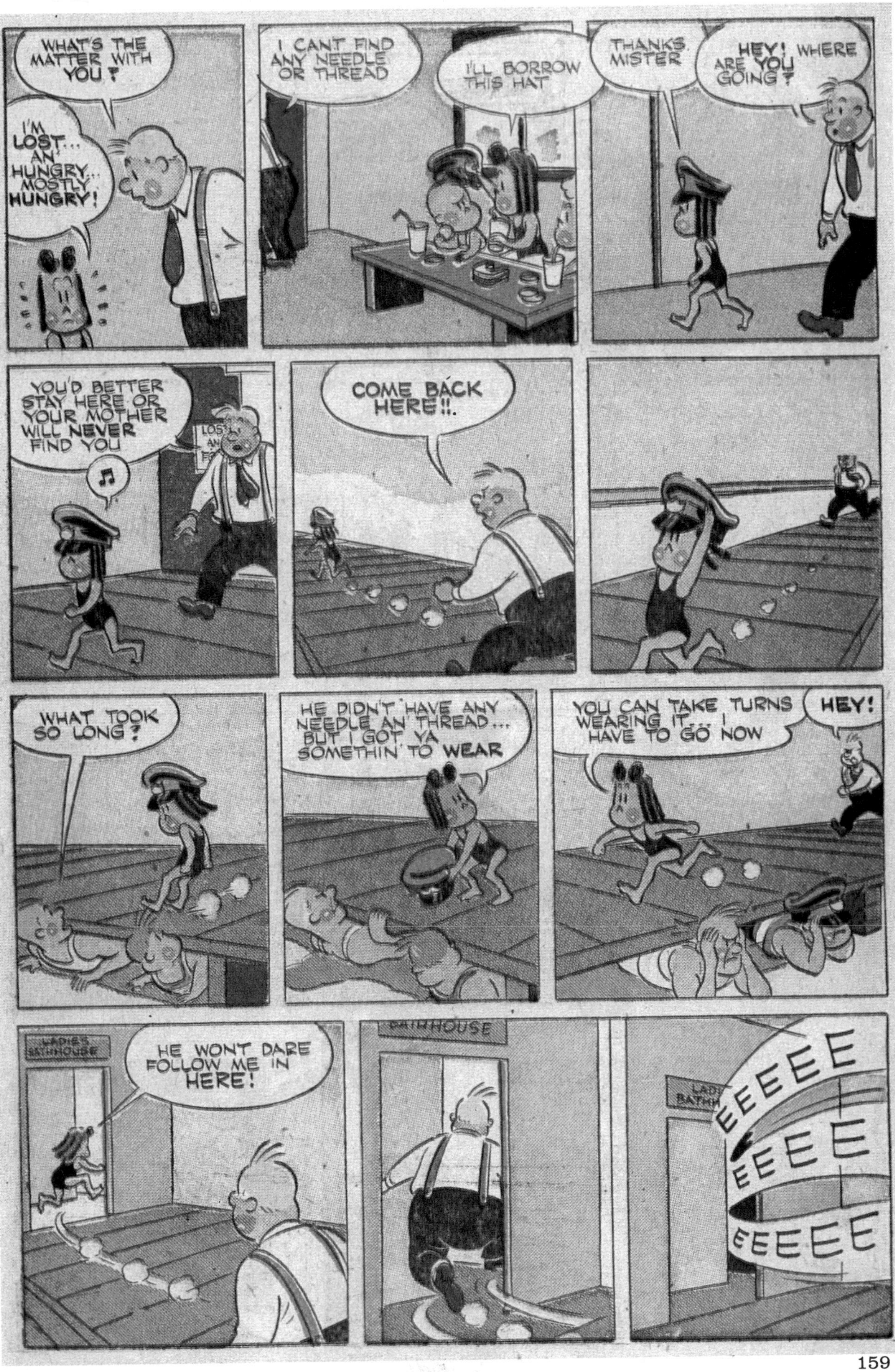

WHAT'S THE MATTER WITH YOU ?
I'M LOST... AN' HUNGRY... MOSTLY HUNGRY!
I CAN'T FIND ANY NEEDLE OR THREAD
I'LL BORROW THIS HAT
THANKS, MISTER
HEY! WHERE ARE YOU GOING ?
YOU'D BETTER STAY HERE OR YOUR MOTHER WILL NEVER FIND YOU
COME BACK HERE!!
WHAT TOOK SO LONG ?
HE DIDN'T HAVE ANY NEEDLE AN' THREAD... BUT I GOT YA SOMETHIN' TO WEAR
YOU CAN TAKE TURNS WEARING IT... I HAVE TO GO NOW
HEY!
LADIES BATHHOUSE
HE WON'T DARE FOLLOW ME IN HERE!
BATHHOUSE
EEEEE EEEEE EEEEE

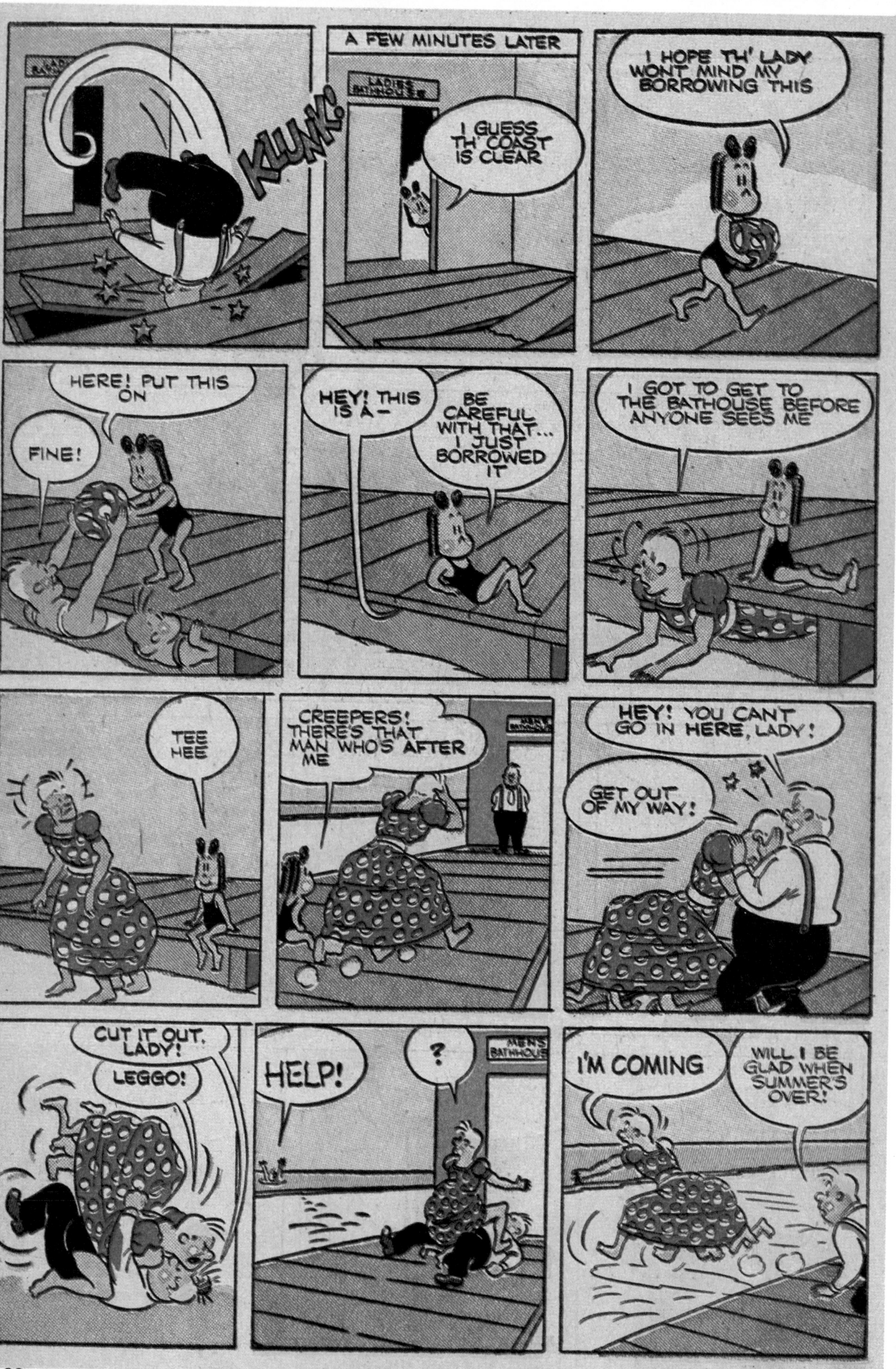
KLUNK!
A FEW MINUTES LATER
LADIES BATHHOUSE
I GUESS TH' COAST IS CLEAR
I HOPE TH' LADY WONT MIND MY BORROWING THIS
HERE! PUT THIS ON
FINE!
HEY! THIS IS A—
BE CAREFUL WITH THAT... I JUST BORROWED IT
I GOT TO GET TO THE BATHHOUSE BEFORE ANYONE SEES ME
TEE HEE
CREEPERS! THERE'S THAT MAN WHO'S AFTER ME
HEY! YOU CANT GO IN HERE, LADY!
GET OUT OF MY WAY!
CUT IT OUT, LADY!
LEGGO!
HELP!
?
MENS BATHHOUSE
I'M COMING
WILL I BE GLAD WHEN SUMMER'S OVER!

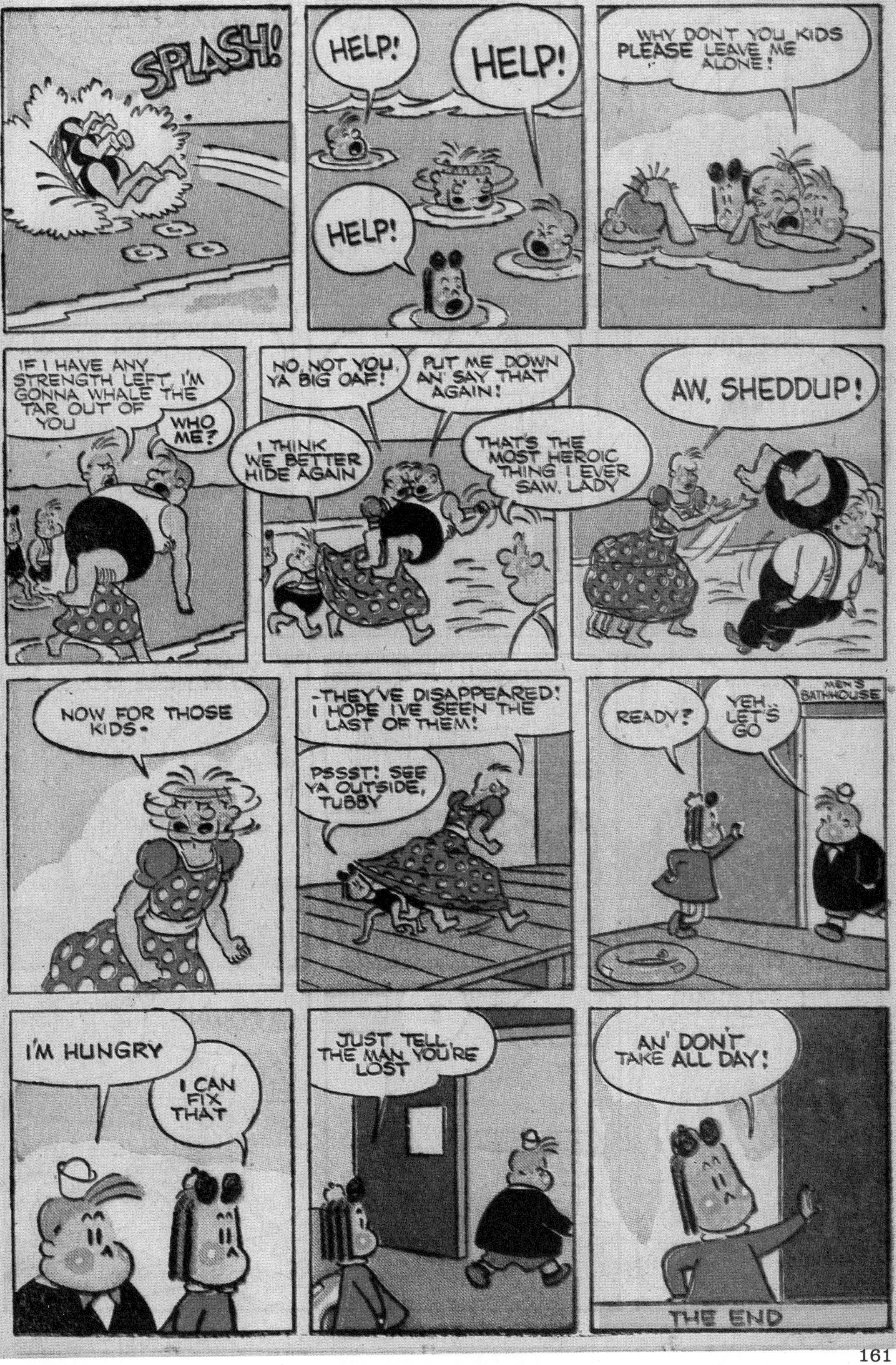
SPLASH!
HELP!
HELP!
HELP!
WHY DON'T YOU KIDS PLEASE LEAVE ME ALONE!
IF I HAVE ANY STRENGTH LEFT, I'M GONNA WHALE THE TAR OUT OF YOU
WHO ME?
NO, NOT YOU, YA BIG OAF!
PUT ME DOWN AN' SAY THAT AGAIN!
I THINK WE BETTER HIDE AGAIN
THAT'S THE MOST HEROIC THING I EVER SAW, LADY
AW, SHEDDUP!
NOW FOR THOSE KIDS-
-THEY'VE DISAPPEARED! I HOPE I'VE SEEN THE LAST OF THEM!
PSSST! SEE YA OUTSIDE, TUBBY
READY?
YEH. LET'S GO
MEN'S BATHHOUSE
I'M HUNGRY
I CAN FIX THAT
JUST TELL THE MAN YOU'RE LOST
AN' DON'T TAKE ALL DAY!
THE END

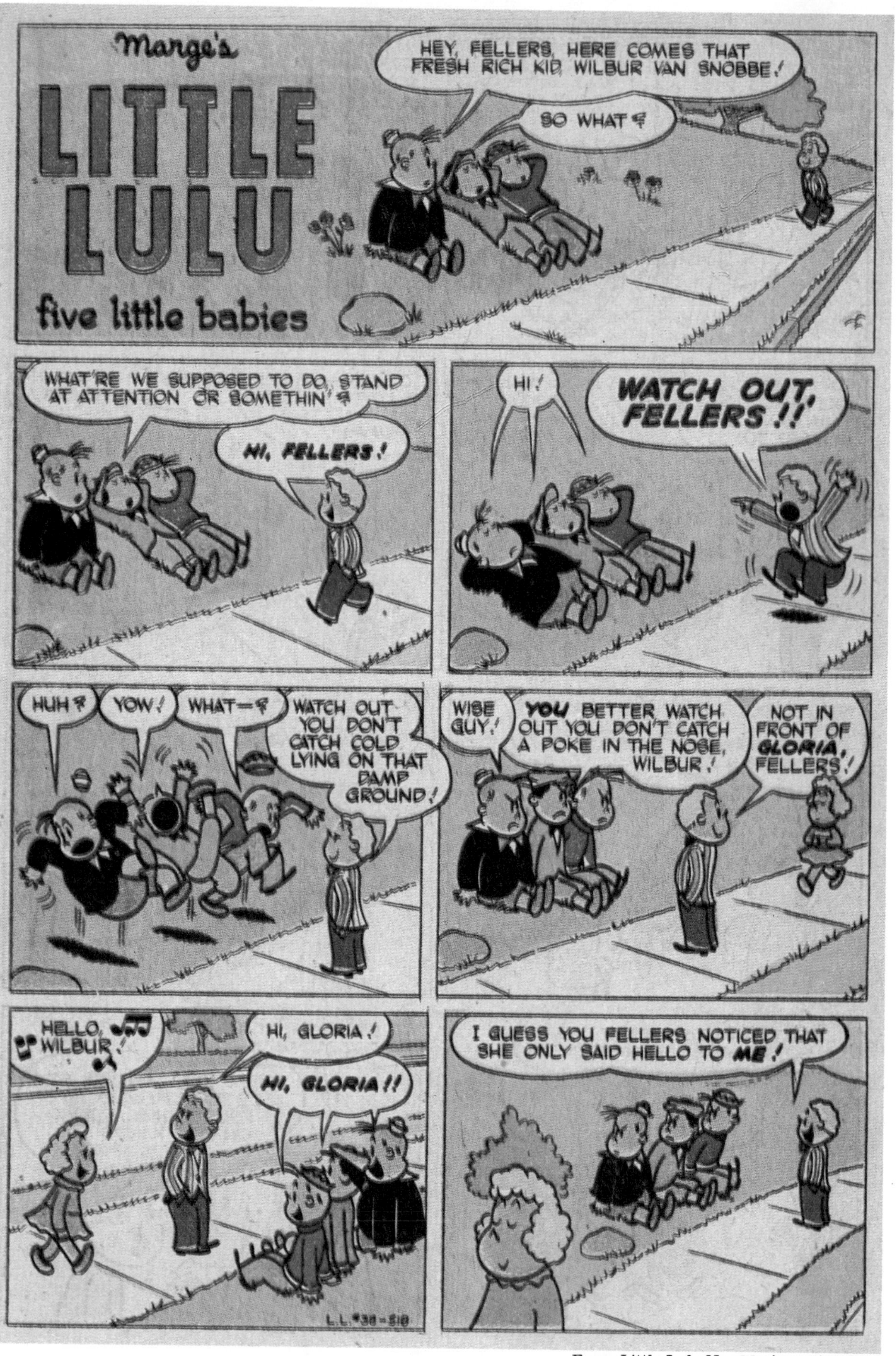
Marge's
LITTLE LULU
five little babies
HEY, FELLERS, HERE COMES THAT FRESH RICH KID, WILBUR VAN SNOBBE!
SO WHAT?
WHAT'RE WE SUPPOSED TO DO, STAND AT ATTENTION OR SOMETHIN'?
HI, FELLERS!
HI!
WATCH OUT, FELLERS!!
HUH?
YOW!
WHAT—?
WATCH OUT YOU DON'T CATCH COLD LYING ON THAT DAMP GROUND!
WISE GUY!
YOU BETTER WATCH OUT YOU DON'T CATCH A POKE IN THE NOSE, WILBUR!
NOT IN FRONT OF GLORIA, FELLERS!
HELLO, WILBUR!
HI, GLORIA!
HI, GLORIA!!
I GUESS YOU FELLERS NOTICED THAT SHE ONLY SAID HELLO TO ME!
L.L. #38-S18

From *Little Lulu* No. 38, August 1951.

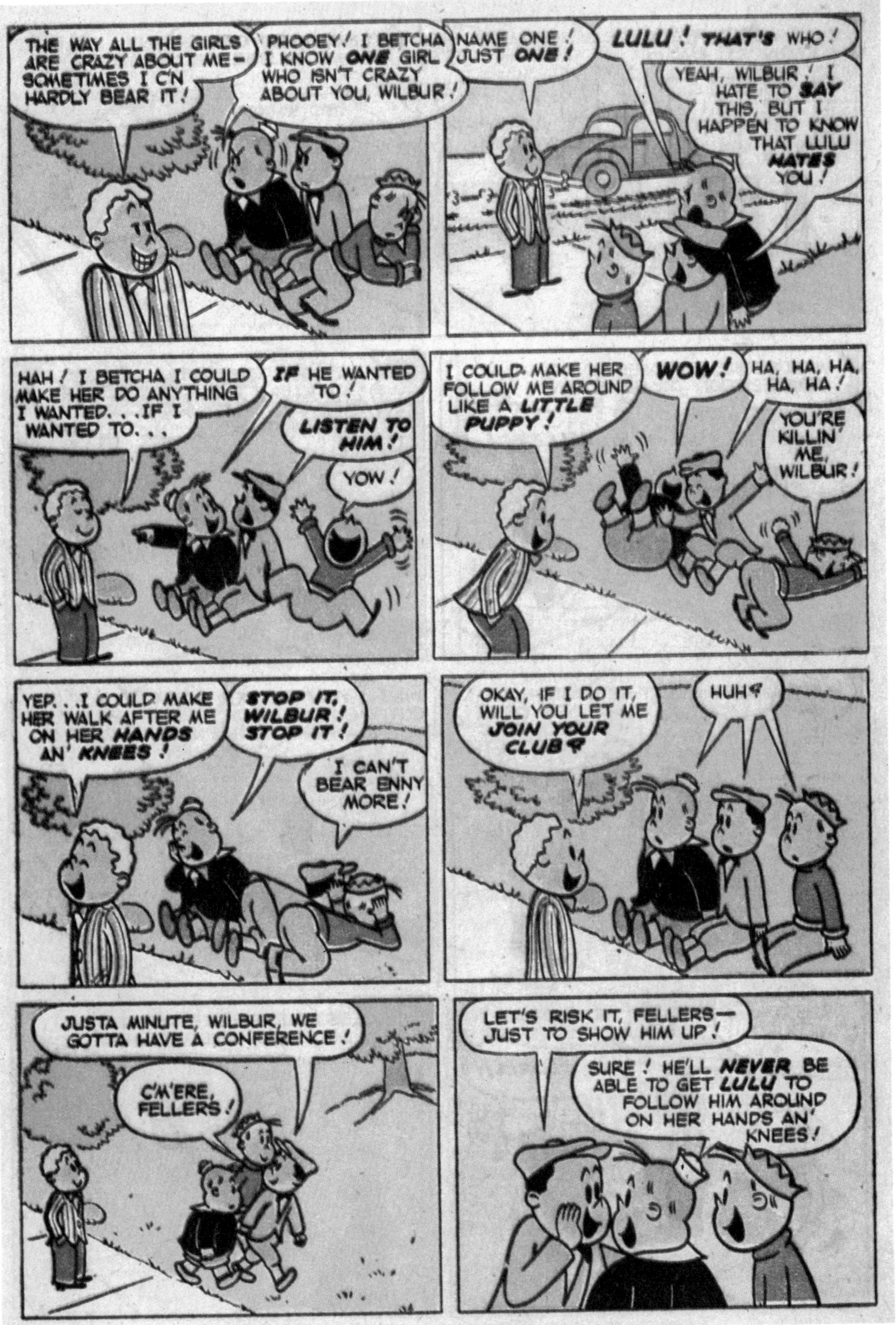
THE WAY ALL THE GIRLS ARE CRAZY ABOUT ME— SOMETIMES I C'N HARDLY BEAR IT!
PHOOEY! I BETCHA I KNOW ONE GIRL WHO ISN'T CRAZY ABOUT YOU, WILBUR!
NAME ONE! JUST ONE!
LULU! THAT'S WHO!
YEAH, WILBUR! I HATE TO SAY THIS, BUT I HAPPEN TO KNOW THAT LULU HATES YOU!
HAH! I BETCHA I COULD MAKE HER DO ANYTHING I WANTED. . .IF I WANTED TO. . .
IF HE WANTED TO!
LISTEN TO HIM!
YOW!
I COULD MAKE HER FOLLOW ME AROUND LIKE A LITTLE PUPPY!
WOW!
HA, HA, HA, HA, HA!
YOU'RE KILLIN' ME, WILBUR!
YEP. . .I COULD MAKE HER WALK AFTER ME ON HER HANDS AN' KNEES!
STOP IT, WILBUR! STOP IT!
I CAN'T BEAR ENNY MORE!
OKAY, IF I DO IT, WILL YOU LET ME JOIN YOUR CLUB?
HUH?
JUSTA MINUTE, WILBUR, WE GOTTA HAVE A CONFERENCE!
C'M'ERE, FELLERS!
LET'S RISK IT, FELLERS— JUST TO SHOW HIM UP!
SURE! HE'LL NEVER BE ABLE TO GET LULU TO FOLLOW HIM AROUND ON HER HANDS AN' KNEES!

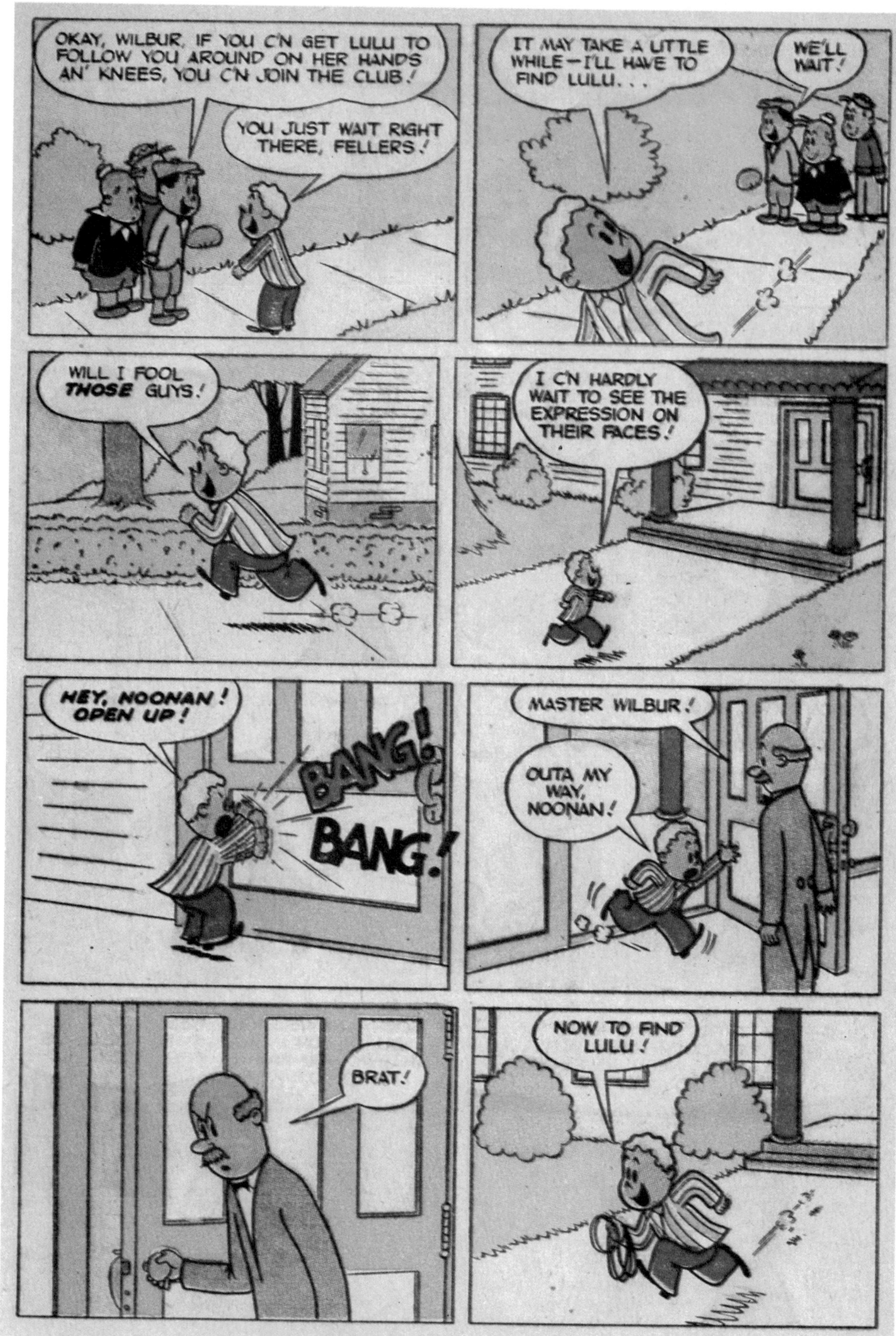
OKAY, WILBUR, IF YOU C'N GET LULU TO FOLLOW YOU AROUND ON HER HANDS AN' KNEES, YOU C'N JOIN THE CLUB!
YOU JUST WAIT RIGHT THERE, FELLERS!
IT MAY TAKE A LITTLE WHILE—I'LL HAVE TO FIND LULU...
WE'LL WAIT!
WILL I FOOL THOSE GUYS!
I C'N HARDLY WAIT TO SEE THE EXPRESSION ON THEIR FACES!
HEY, NOONAN! OPEN UP!
BANG!
BANG!
MASTER WILBUR!
OUTA MY WAY, NOONAN!
BRAT!
NOW TO FIND LULU!

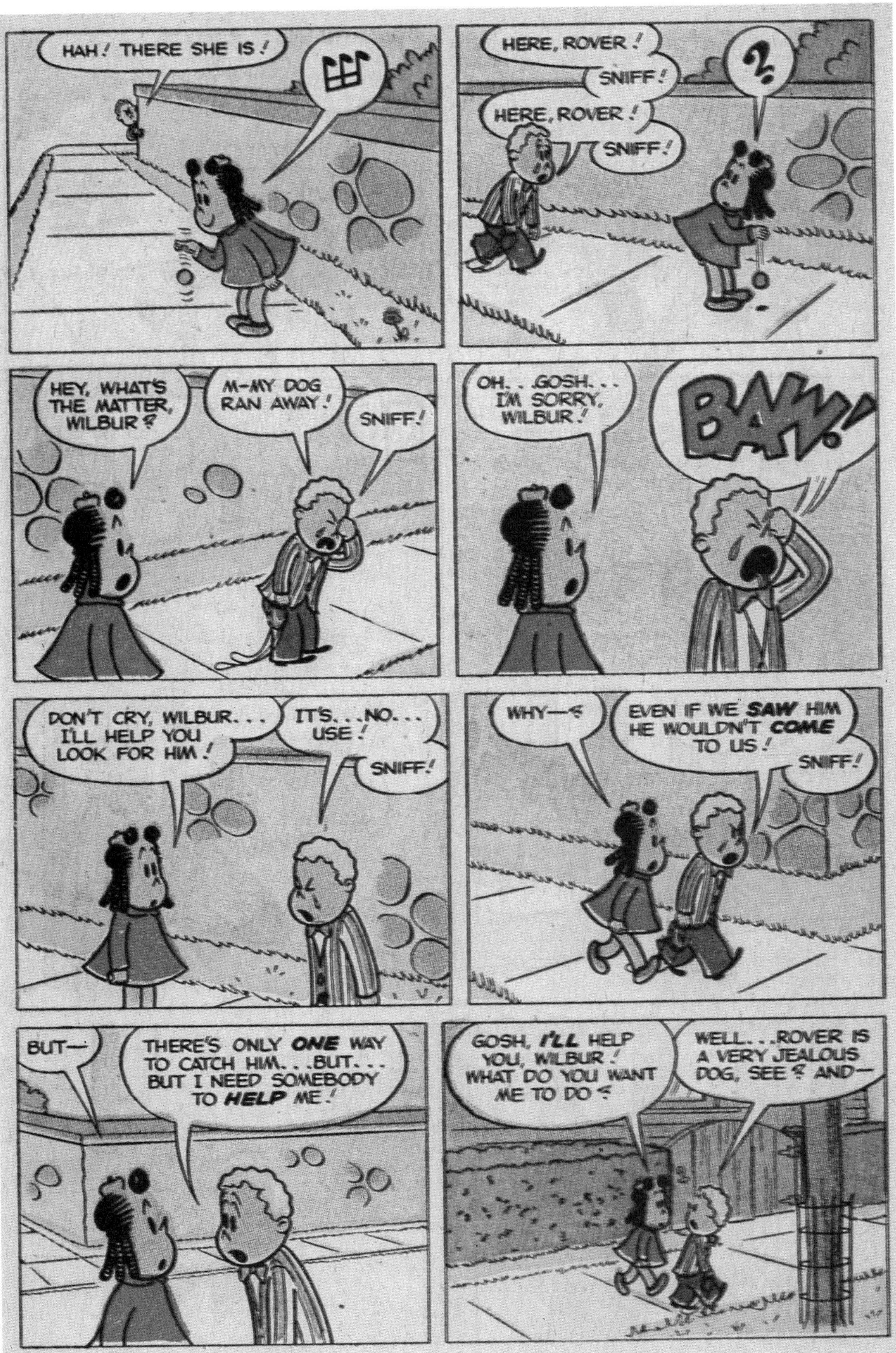

HAH! THERE SHE IS!
HERE, ROVER!
SNIFF!
HERE, ROVER!
SNIFF!
?
HEY, WHAT'S THE MATTER, WILBUR?
M-MY DOG RAN AWAY!
SNIFF!
OH. . .GOSH. . . I'M SORRY, WILBUR!
BAW!
DON'T CRY, WILBUR. . . I'LL HELP YOU LOOK FOR HIM!
IT'S. . .NO. . . USE!
SNIFF!
WHY—?
EVEN IF WE SAW HIM HE WOULDN'T COME TO US!
SNIFF!
BUT—
THERE'S ONLY ONE WAY TO CATCH HIM. . .BUT. . . BUT I NEED SOMEBODY TO HELP ME!
GOSH, I'LL HELP YOU, WILBUR! WHAT DO YOU WANT ME TO DO?
WELL. . .ROVER IS A VERY JEALOUS DOG, SEE? AND—

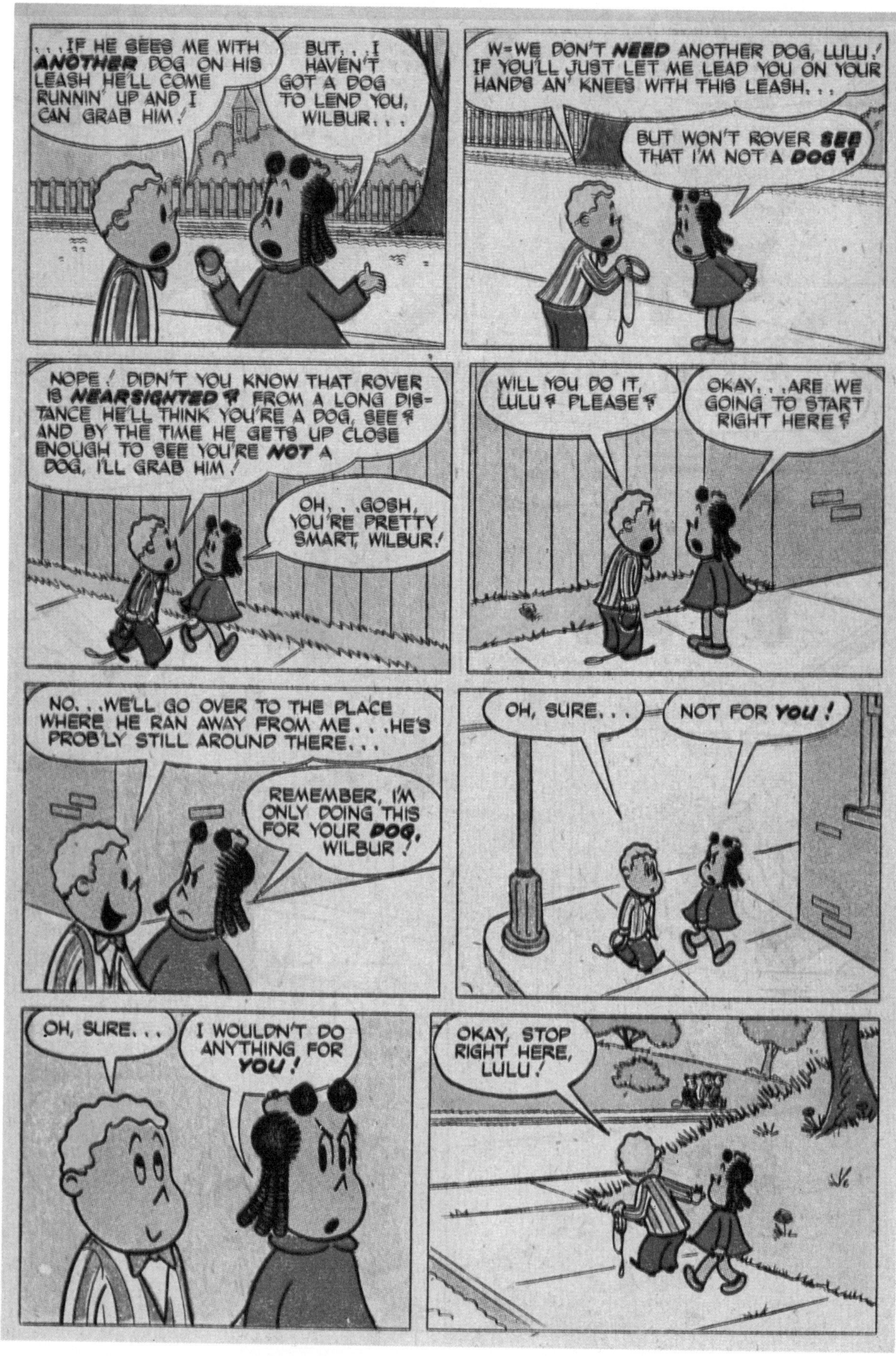
. . .IF HE SEES ME WITH ANOTHER DOG ON HIS LEASH HE'LL COME RUNNIN' UP AND I CAN GRAB HIM!
BUT. . .I HAVEN'T GOT A DOG TO LEND YOU, WILBUR. . .
W-WE DON'T NEED ANOTHER DOG, LULU! IF YOU'LL JUST LET ME LEAD YOU ON YOUR HANDS AN' KNEES WITH THIS LEASH. . .
BUT WON'T ROVER SEE THAT I'M NOT A DOG?
NOPE! DIDN'T YOU KNOW THAT ROVER IS NEARSIGHTED? FROM A LONG DISTANCE HE'LL THINK YOU'RE A DOG, SEE? AND BY THE TIME HE GETS UP CLOSE ENOUGH TO SEE YOU'RE NOT A DOG, I'LL GRAB HIM!
OH. . .GOSH, YOU'RE PRETTY SMART, WILBUR!
WILL YOU DO IT, LULU? PLEASE?
OKAY. . .ARE WE GOING TO START RIGHT HERE?
NO. . .WE'LL GO OVER TO THE PLACE WHERE HE RAN AWAY FROM ME. . .HE'S PROB'LY STILL AROUND THERE. . .
REMEMBER, I'M ONLY DOING THIS FOR YOUR DOG, WILBUR!
OH, SURE. . .
NOT FOR YOU!
OH, SURE. . .
I WOULDN'T DO ANYTHING FOR YOU!
OKAY, STOP RIGHT HERE, LULU!

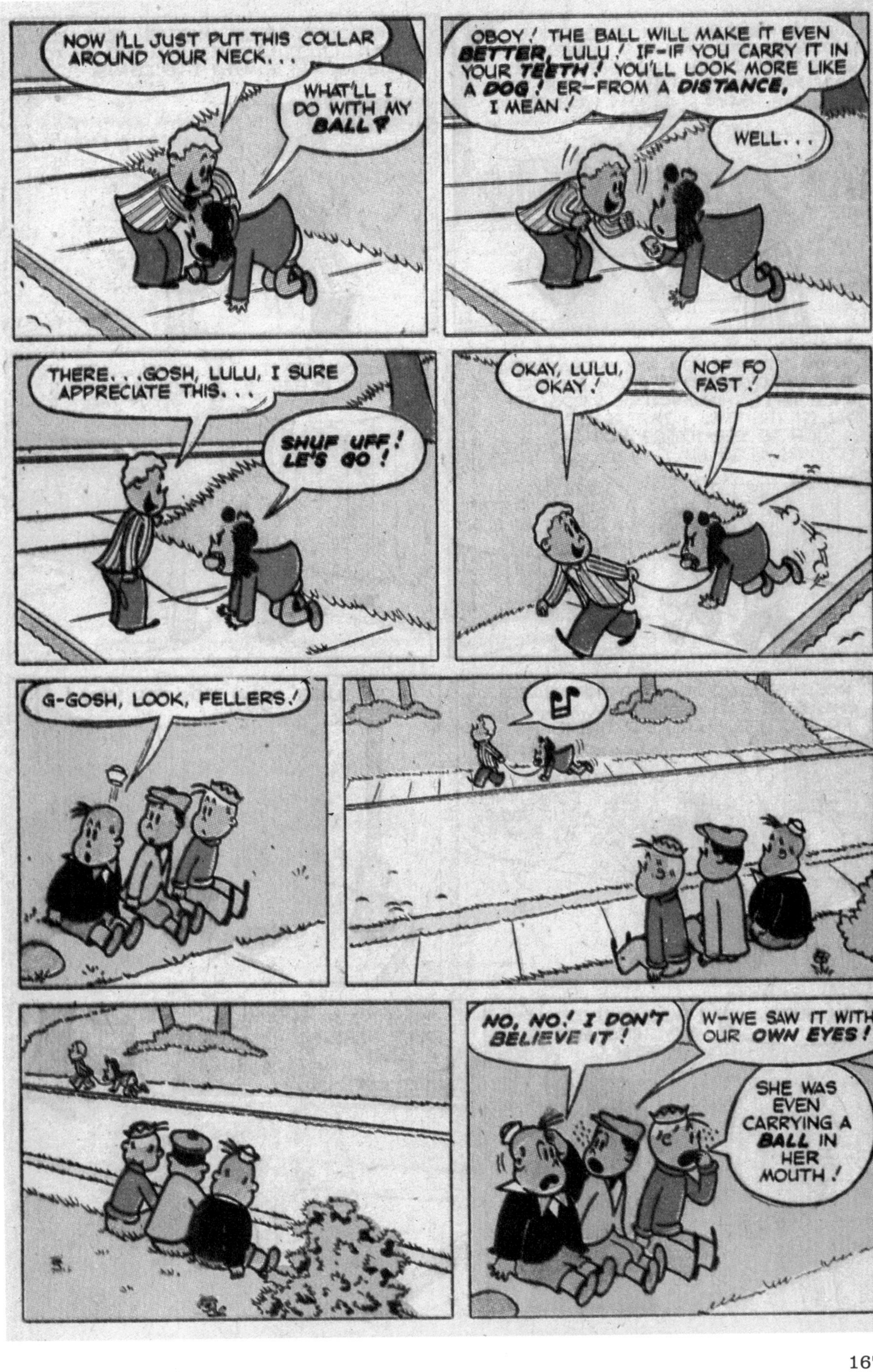
NOW I'LL JUST PUT THIS COLLAR AROUND YOUR NECK...
WHAT'LL I DO WITH MY BALL?
OBOY! THE BALL WILL MAKE IT EVEN BETTER, LULU! IF-IF YOU CARRY IT IN YOUR TEETH! YOU'LL LOOK MORE LIKE A DOG! ER—FROM A DISTANCE, I MEAN!
WELL...
THERE...GOSH, LULU, I SURE APPRECIATE THIS...
SHUF UFF! LE'S GO!
OKAY, LULU, OKAY!
NOF FO FAST!
G-GOSH, LOOK, FELLERS!
NO, NO! I DON'T BELIEVE IT!
W-WE SAW IT WITH OUR OWN EYES!
SHE WAS EVEN CARRYING A BALL IN HER MOUTH!

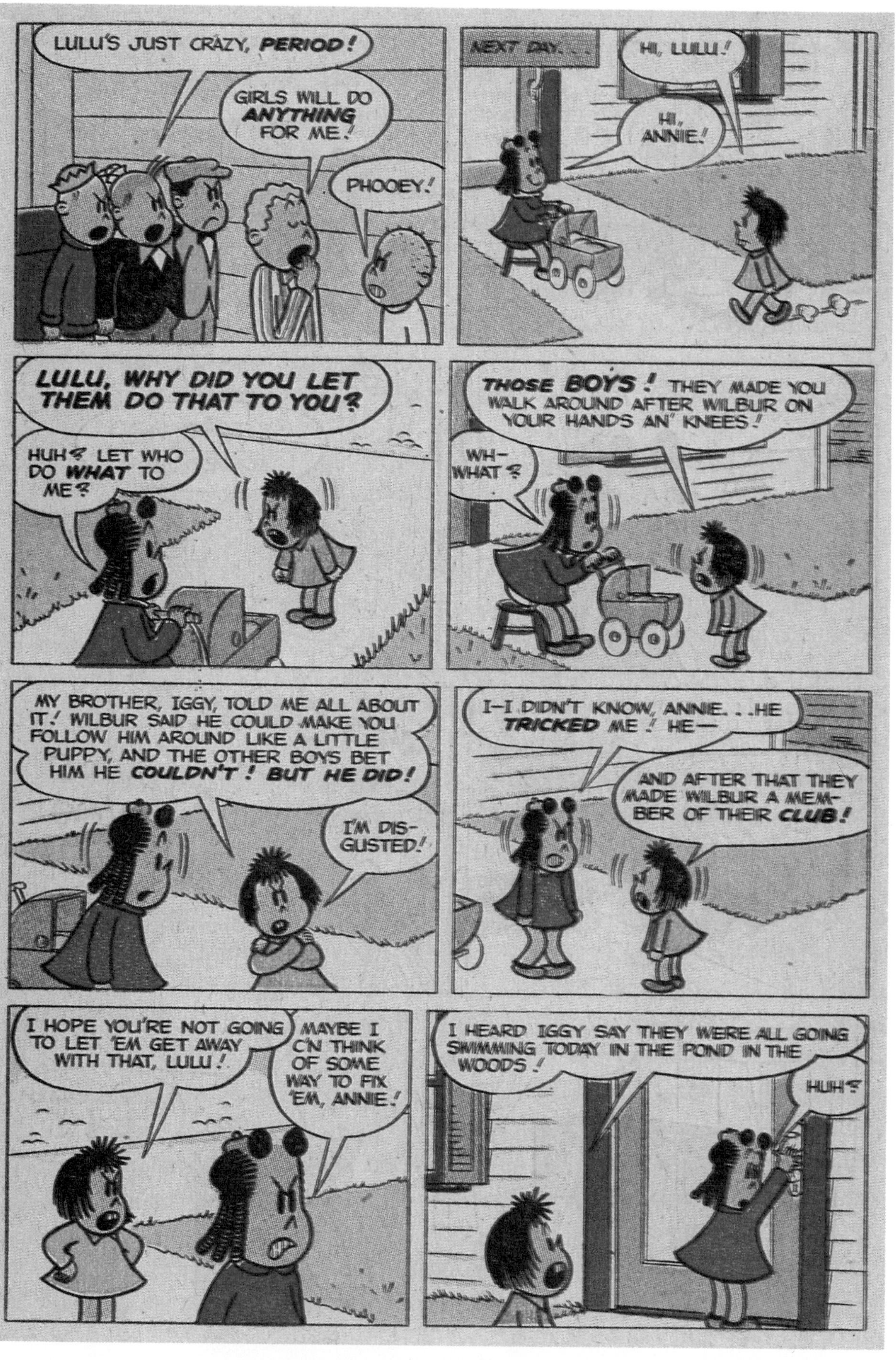
LULU'S JUST CRAZY, PERIOD!
GIRLS WILL DO ANYTHING FOR ME.!
PHOOEY!
NEXT DAY. . .
HI, LULU!
HI, ANNIE!
LULU, WHY DID YOU LET THEM DO THAT TO YOU?
HUH? LET WHO DO WHAT TO ME?
THOSE BOYS! THEY MADE YOU WALK AROUND AFTER WILBUR ON YOUR HANDS AN' KNEES!
WH-WHAT?
MY BROTHER, IGGY, TOLD ME ALL ABOUT IT! WILBUR SAID HE COULD MAKE YOU FOLLOW HIM AROUND LIKE A LITTLE PUPPY, AND THE OTHER BOYS BET HIM HE COULDN'T! BUT HE DID!
I'M DISGUSTED!
I-I DIDN'T KNOW, ANNIE. . .HE TRICKED ME! HE—
AND AFTER THAT THEY MADE WILBUR A MEMBER OF THEIR CLUB!
I HOPE YOU'RE NOT GOING TO LET 'EM GET AWAY WITH THAT, LULU!
MAYBE I C'N THINK OF SOME WAY TO FIX 'EM, ANNIE!
I HEARD IGGY SAY THEY WERE ALL GOING SWIMMING TODAY IN THE POND IN THE WOODS!
HUH?

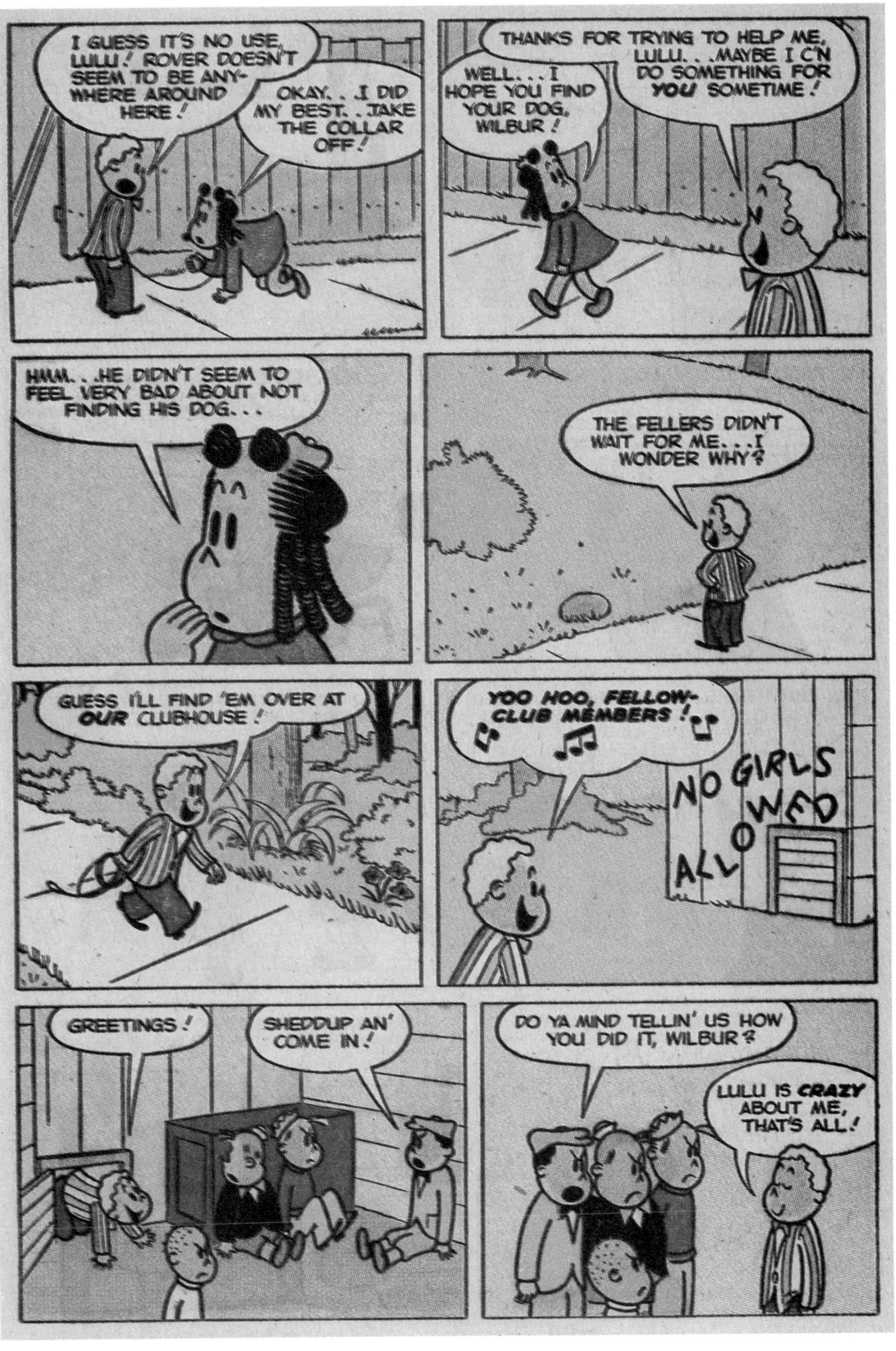
I GUESS IT'S NO USE, LULU! ROVER DOESN'T SEEM TO BE ANYWHERE AROUND HERE!
OKAY. . .I DID MY BEST. . .TAKE THE COLLAR OFF!
THANKS FOR TRYING TO HELP ME, LULU. . .MAYBE I C'N DO SOMETHING FOR YOU SOMETIME!
WELL. . . I HOPE YOU FIND YOUR DOG, WILBUR!
HMM. . .HE DIDN'T SEEM TO FEEL VERY BAD ABOUT NOT FINDING HIS DOG. . .
THE FELLERS DIDN'T WAIT FOR ME. . .I WONDER WHY?
GUESS I'LL FIND 'EM OVER AT OUR CLUBHOUSE!
YOO HOO, FELLOW-CLUB MEMBERS!
NO GIRLS ALLOWED
GREETINGS!
SHEDDUP AN' COME IN!
DO YA MIND TELLIN' US HOW YOU DID IT, WILBUR?
LULU IS CRAZY ABOUT ME, THAT'S ALL!

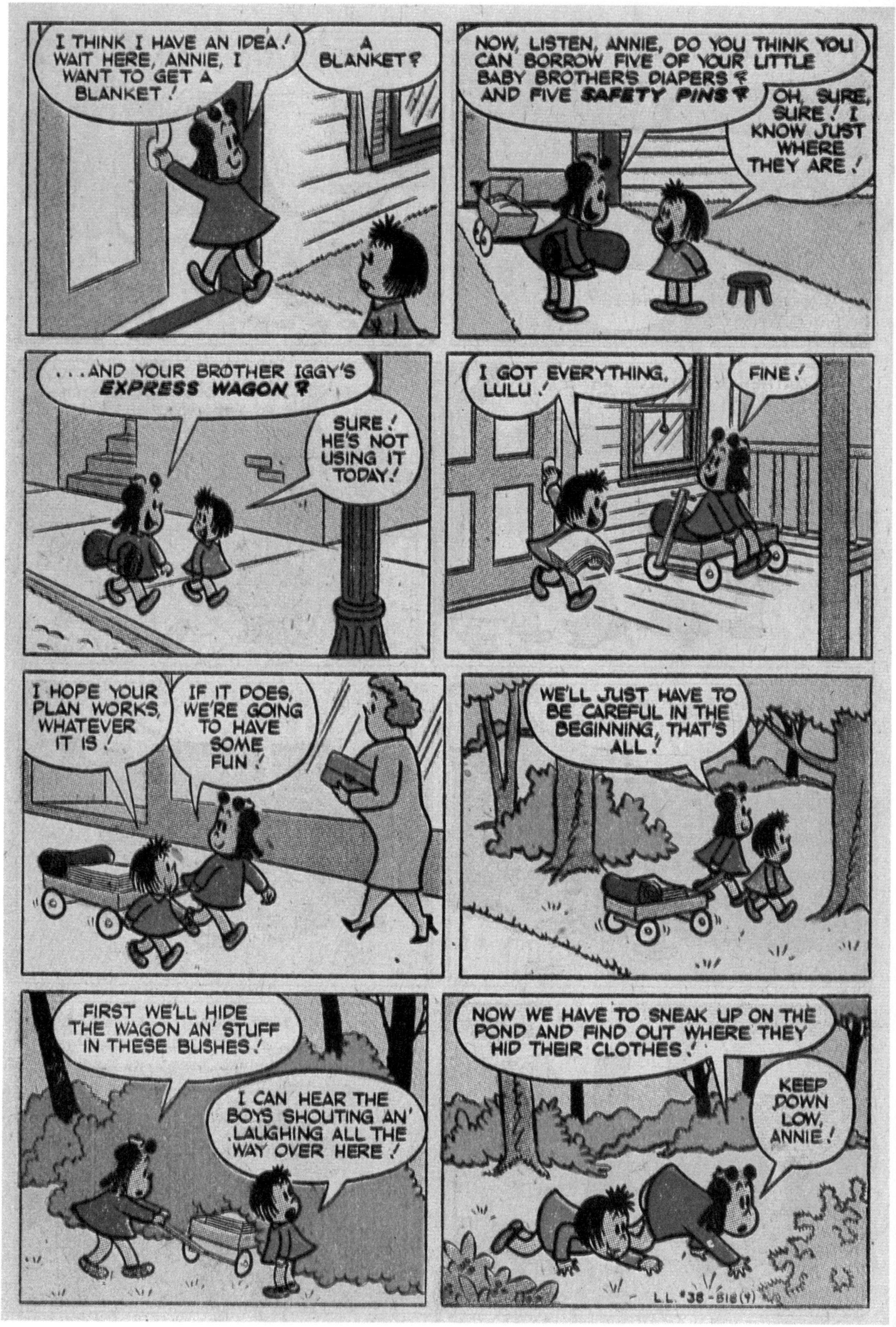
I THINK I HAVE AN IDEA! WAIT HERE, ANNIE, I WANT TO GET A BLANKET!
A BLANKET?
NOW, LISTEN, ANNIE, DO YOU THINK YOU CAN BORROW FIVE OF YOUR LITTLE BABY BROTHER'S DIAPERS? AND FIVE SAFETY PINS?
OH, SURE, SURE! I KNOW JUST WHERE THEY ARE!
...AND YOUR BROTHER IGGY'S EXPRESS WAGON?
SURE! HE'S NOT USING IT TODAY!
I GOT EVERYTHING, LULU!
FINE!
I HOPE YOUR PLAN WORKS, WHATEVER IT IS!
IF IT DOES, WE'RE GOING TO HAVE SOME FUN!
WE'LL JUST HAVE TO BE CAREFUL IN THE BEGINNING, THAT'S ALL!
FIRST WE'LL HIDE THE WAGON AN' STUFF IN THESE BUSHES!
I CAN HEAR THE BOYS SHOUTING AN' LAUGHING ALL THE WAY OVER HERE!
NOW WE HAVE TO SNEAK UP ON THE POND AND FIND OUT WHERE THEY HID THEIR CLOTHES!
KEEP DOWN LOW, ANNIE!
L.L. #38-518 (9)

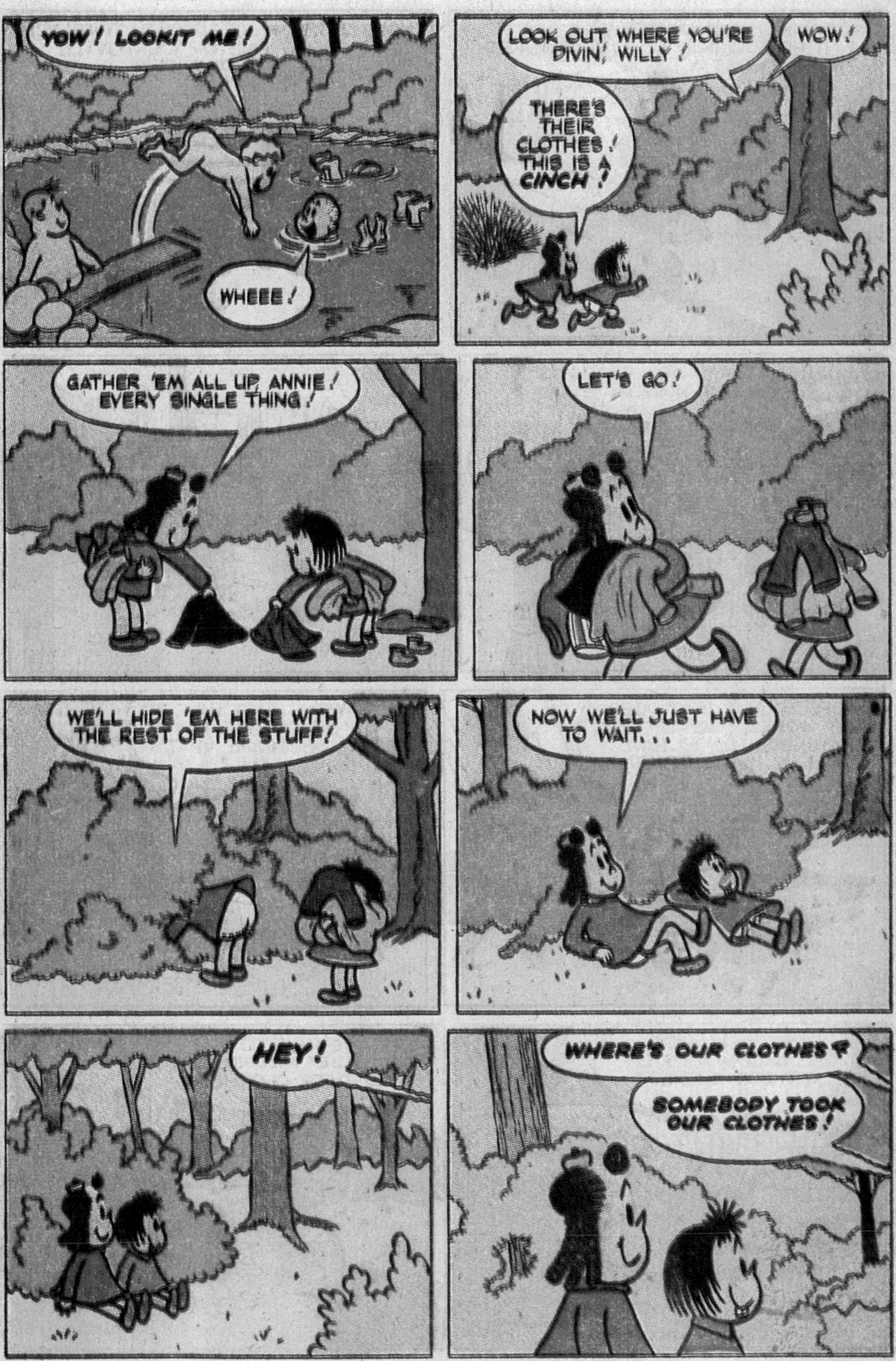
YOW! LOOKIT ME!
WHEEE!
LOOK OUT WHERE YOU'RE DIVIN', WILLY!
WOW!
THERE'S THEIR CLOTHES! THIS IS A CINCH!
GATHER 'EM ALL UP, ANNIE! EVERY SINGLE THING!
LET'S GO!
WE'LL HIDE 'EM HERE WITH THE REST OF THE STUFF!
NOW WE'LL JUST HAVE TO WAIT...
HEY!
WHERE'S OUR CLOTHES?
SOMEBODY TOOK OUR CLOTHES!

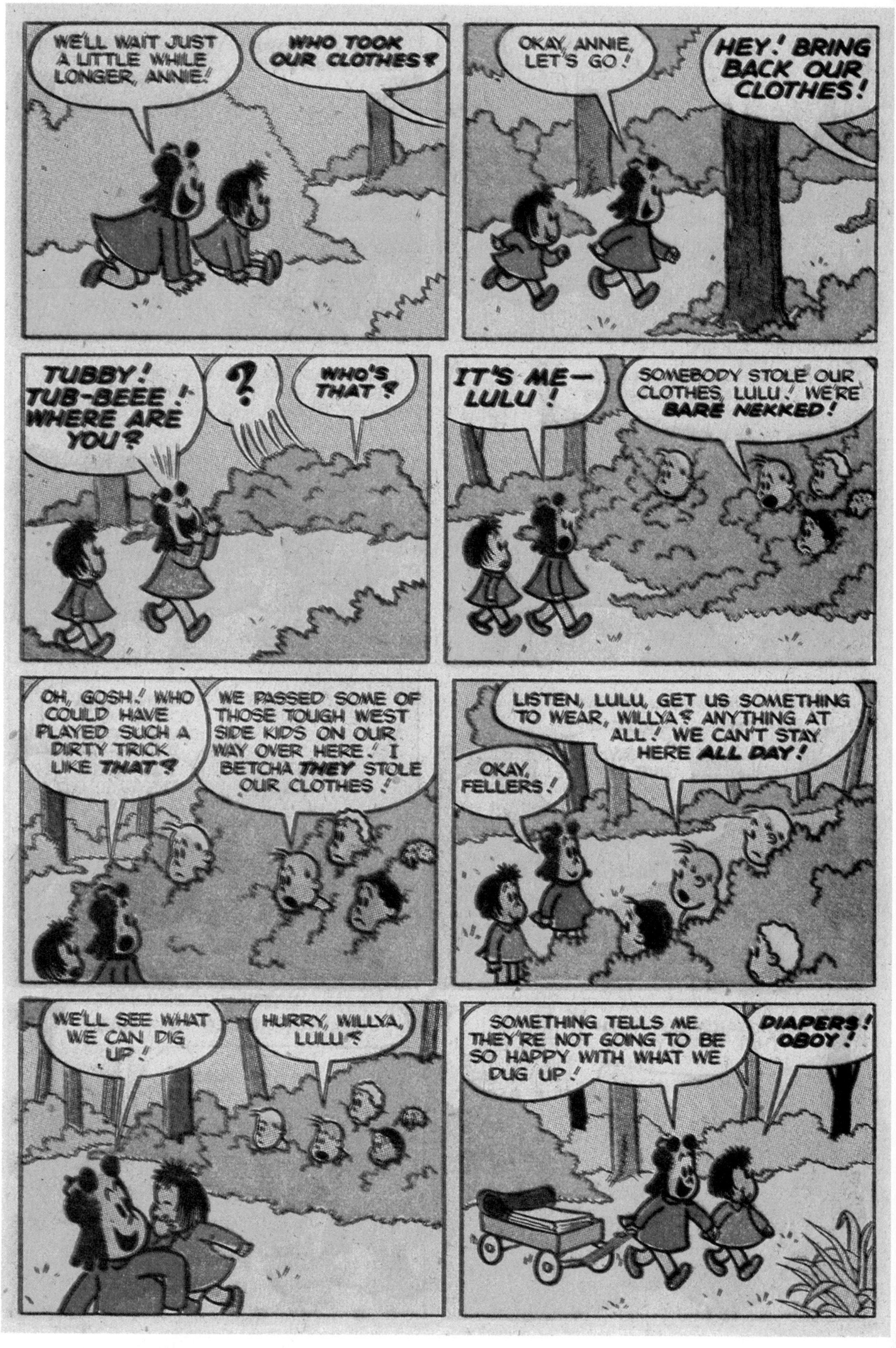
WE'LL WAIT JUST A LITTLE WHILE LONGER, ANNIE!
WHO TOOK OUR CLOTHES?
OKAY, ANNIE, LET'S GO!
HEY! BRING BACK OUR CLOTHES!
TUBBY! TUB-BEEE! WHERE ARE YOU?
?
WHO'S THAT?
IT'S ME— LULU!
SOMEBODY STOLE OUR CLOTHES, LULU! WE'RE BARE NEKKED!
OH, GOSH! WHO COULD HAVE PLAYED SUCH A DIRTY TRICK LIKE THAT?
WE PASSED SOME OF THOSE TOUGH WEST SIDE KIDS ON OUR WAY OVER HERE! I BETCHA THEY STOLE OUR CLOTHES!
LISTEN, LULU, GET US SOMETHING TO WEAR, WILLYA? ANYTHING AT ALL! WE CAN'T STAY HERE ALL DAY!
OKAY, FELLERS!
WE'LL SEE WHAT WE CAN DIG UP!
HURRY, WILLYA, LULU!
SOMETHING TELLS ME THEY'RE NOT GOING TO BE SO HAPPY WITH WHAT WE DUG UP!
DIAPERS! OBOY!

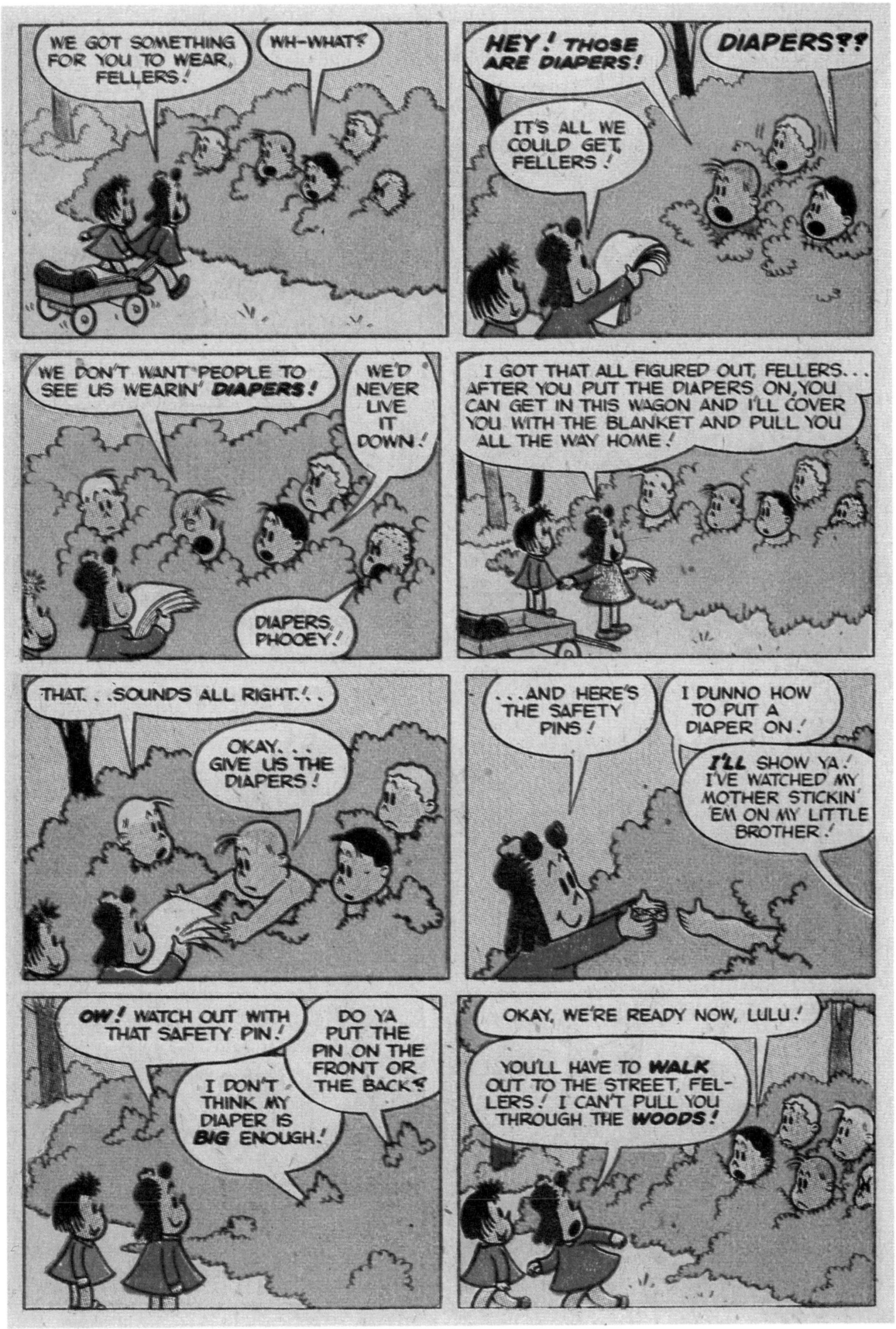
WE GOT SOMETHING FOR YOU TO WEAR, FELLERS!
WH-WHAT?
HEY! THOSE ARE DIAPERS!
DIAPERS?!
IT'S ALL WE COULD GET, FELLERS!
WE DON'T WANT PEOPLE TO SEE US WEARIN' DIAPERS!
WE'D NEVER LIVE IT DOWN!
DIAPERS, PHOOEY!
I GOT THAT ALL FIGURED OUT, FELLERS... AFTER YOU PUT THE DIAPERS ON, YOU CAN GET IN THIS WAGON AND I'LL COVER YOU WITH THE BLANKET AND PULL YOU ALL THE WAY HOME!
THAT...SOUNDS ALL RIGHT!..
OKAY... GIVE US THE DIAPERS!
...AND HERE'S THE SAFETY PINS!
I DUNNO HOW TO PUT A DIAPER ON!
I'LL SHOW YA! I'VE WATCHED MY MOTHER STICKIN' 'EM ON MY LITTLE BROTHER!
OW! WATCH OUT WITH THAT SAFETY PIN!
DO YA PUT THE PIN ON THE FRONT OR THE BACK?
I DON'T THINK MY DIAPER IS BIG ENOUGH!
OKAY, WE'RE READY NOW, LULU!
YOU'LL HAVE TO WALK OUT TO THE STREET, FELLERS! I CAN'T PULL YOU THROUGH THE WOODS!

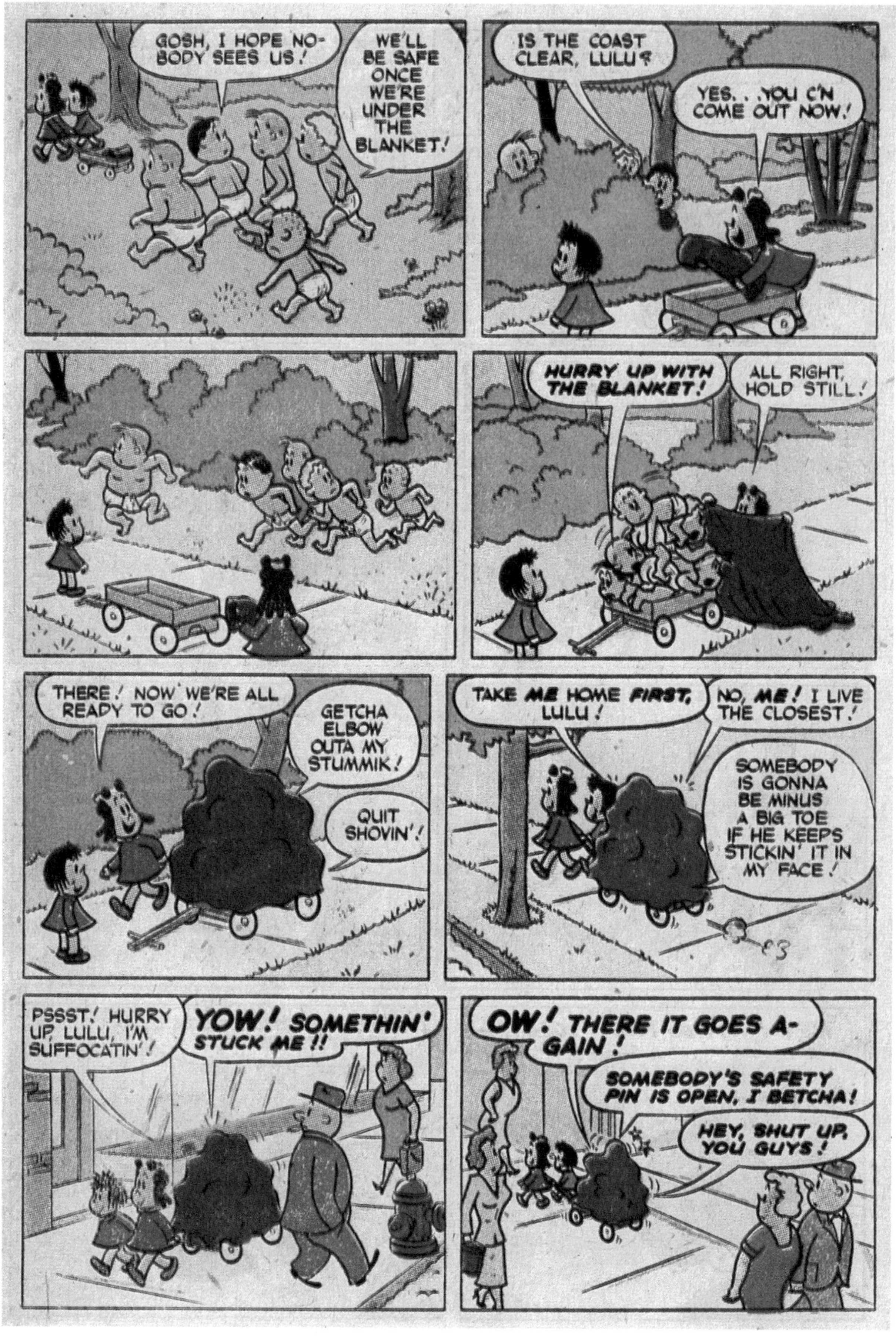
GOSH, I HOPE NOBODY SEES US!
WE'LL BE SAFE ONCE WE'RE UNDER THE BLANKET!
IS THE COAST CLEAR, LULU?
YES. . .YOU C'N COME OUT NOW!
HURRY UP WITH THE BLANKET!
ALL RIGHT, HOLD STILL!
THERE! NOW WE'RE ALL READY TO GO!
GETCHA ELBOW OUTA MY STUMMIK!
QUIT SHOVIN'!
TAKE ME HOME FIRST, LULU!
NO, ME! I LIVE THE CLOSEST!
SOMEBODY IS GONNA BE MINUS A BIG TOE IF HE KEEPS STICKIN' IT IN MY FACE!
PSSST! HURRY UP, LULU, I'M SUFFOCATIN'!
YOW! SOMETHIN' STUCK ME!!
OW! THERE IT GOES A-GAIN!
SOMEBODY'S SAFETY PIN IS OPEN, I BETCHA!
HEY, SHUT UP, YOU GUYS!

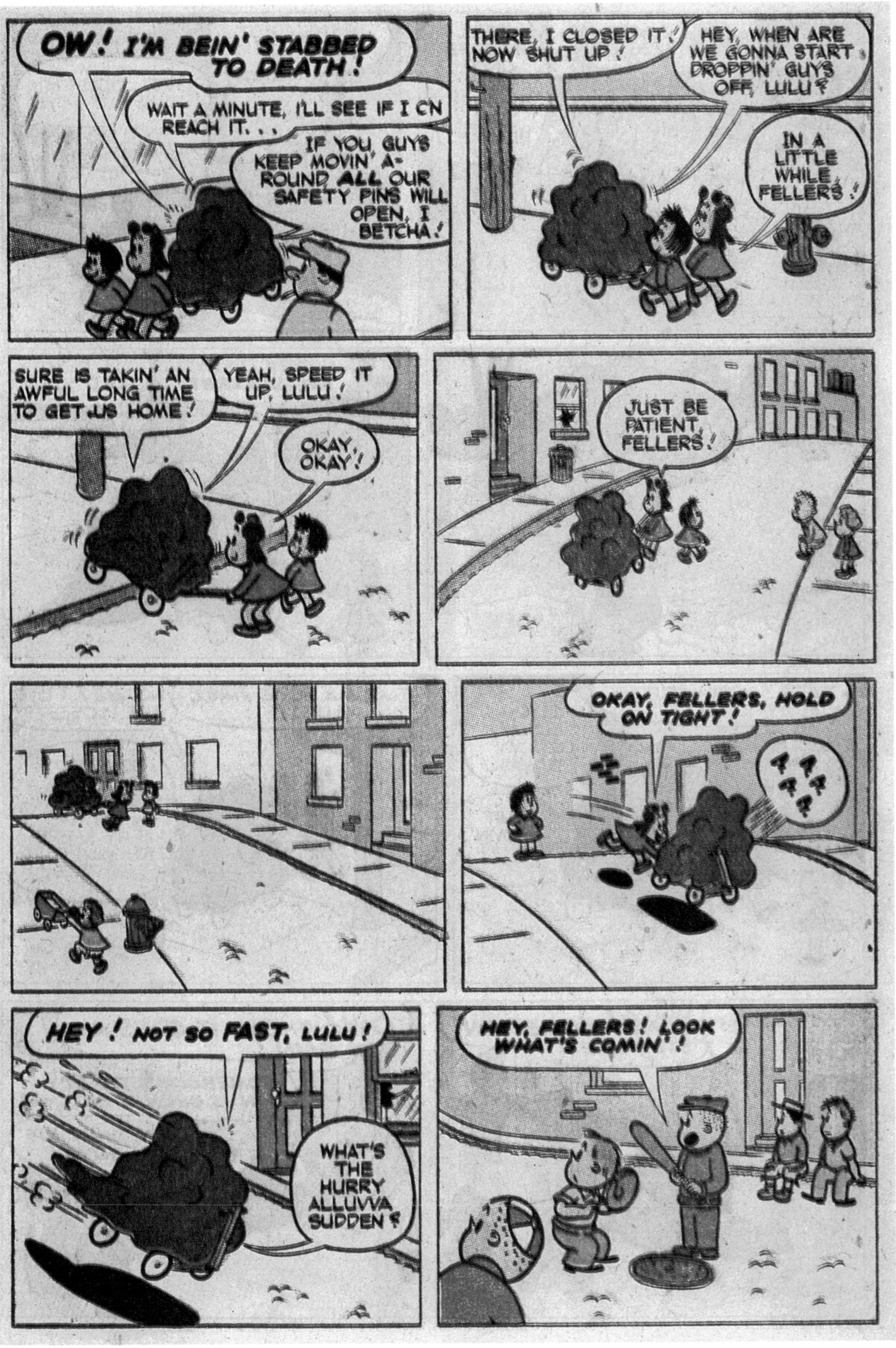
OW! I'M BEIN' STABBED TO DEATH!
WAIT A MINUTE, I'LL SEE IF I C'N REACH IT. . .
IF YOU GUYS KEEP MOVIN' A-ROUND ALL OUR SAFETY PINS WILL OPEN, I BETCHA!
THERE, I CLOSED IT! NOW SHUT UP!
HEY, WHEN ARE WE GONNA START DROPPIN' GUYS OFF, LULU?
IN A LITTLE WHILE, FELLERS!
SURE IS TAKIN' AN AWFUL LONG TIME TO GET US HOME!
YEAH, SPEED IT UP, LULU!
OKAY, OKAY!
JUST BE PATIENT, FELLERS!
OKAY, FELLERS, HOLD ON TIGHT!
? ? ? ? ?
HEY! NOT SO FAST, LULU!
WHAT'S THE HURRY ALLUVVA SUDDEN?
HEY, FELLERS! LOOK WHAT'S COMIN'!

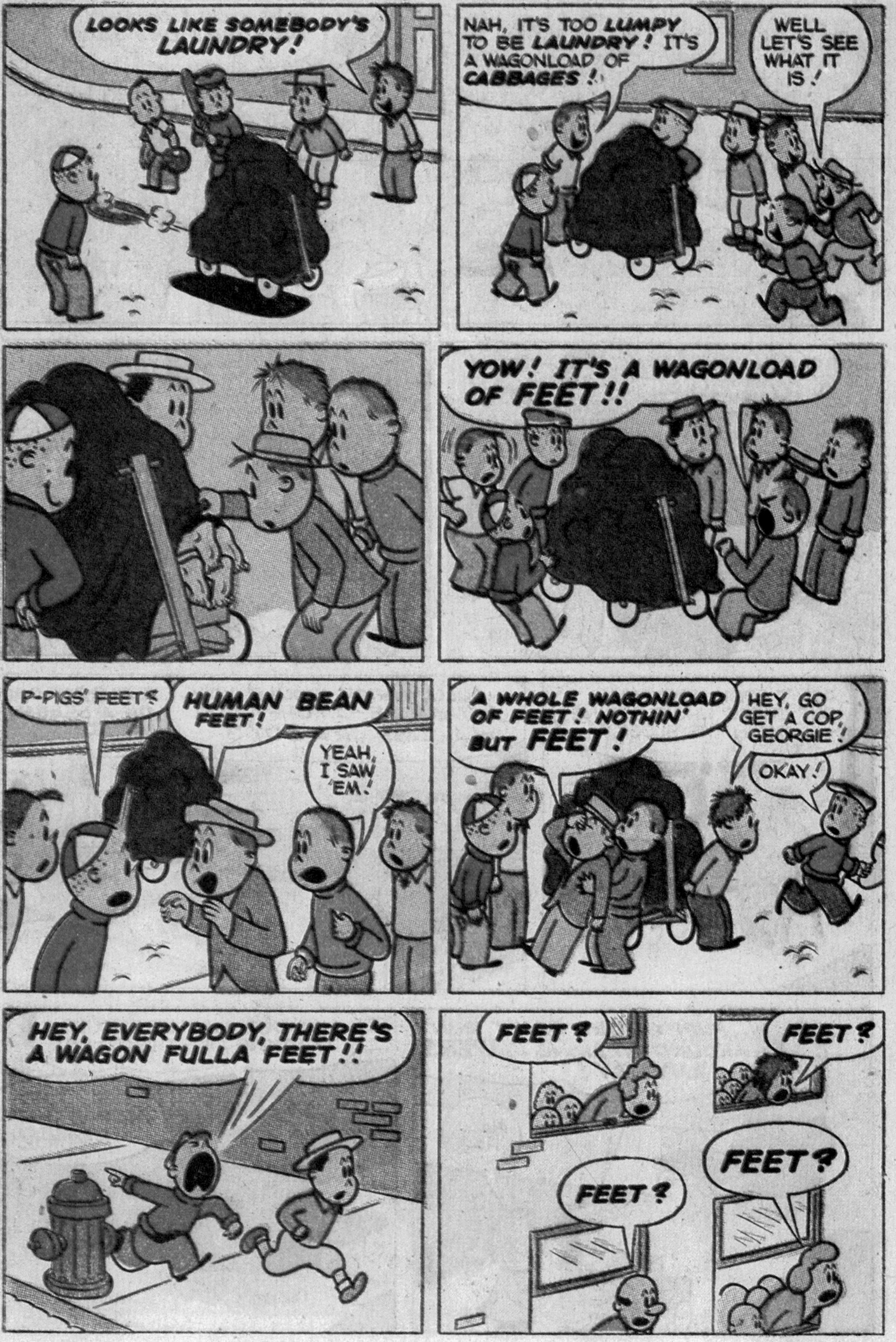
LOOKS LIKE SOMEBODY'S LAUNDRY!
NAH, IT'S TOO LUMPY TO BE LAUNDRY! IT'S A WAGONLOAD OF CABBAGES!
WELL LET'S SEE WHAT IT IS!
YOW! IT'S A WAGONLOAD OF FEET!!
P-PIGS' FEET?
HUMAN BEAN FEET!
YEAH, I SAW 'EM!
A WHOLE WAGONLOAD OF FEET! NOTHIN' BUT FEET!
HEY, GO GET A COP, GEORGIE!
OKAY!
HEY, EVERYBODY, THERE'S A WAGON FULLA FEET!!
FEET?
FEET?
FEET?
FEET?

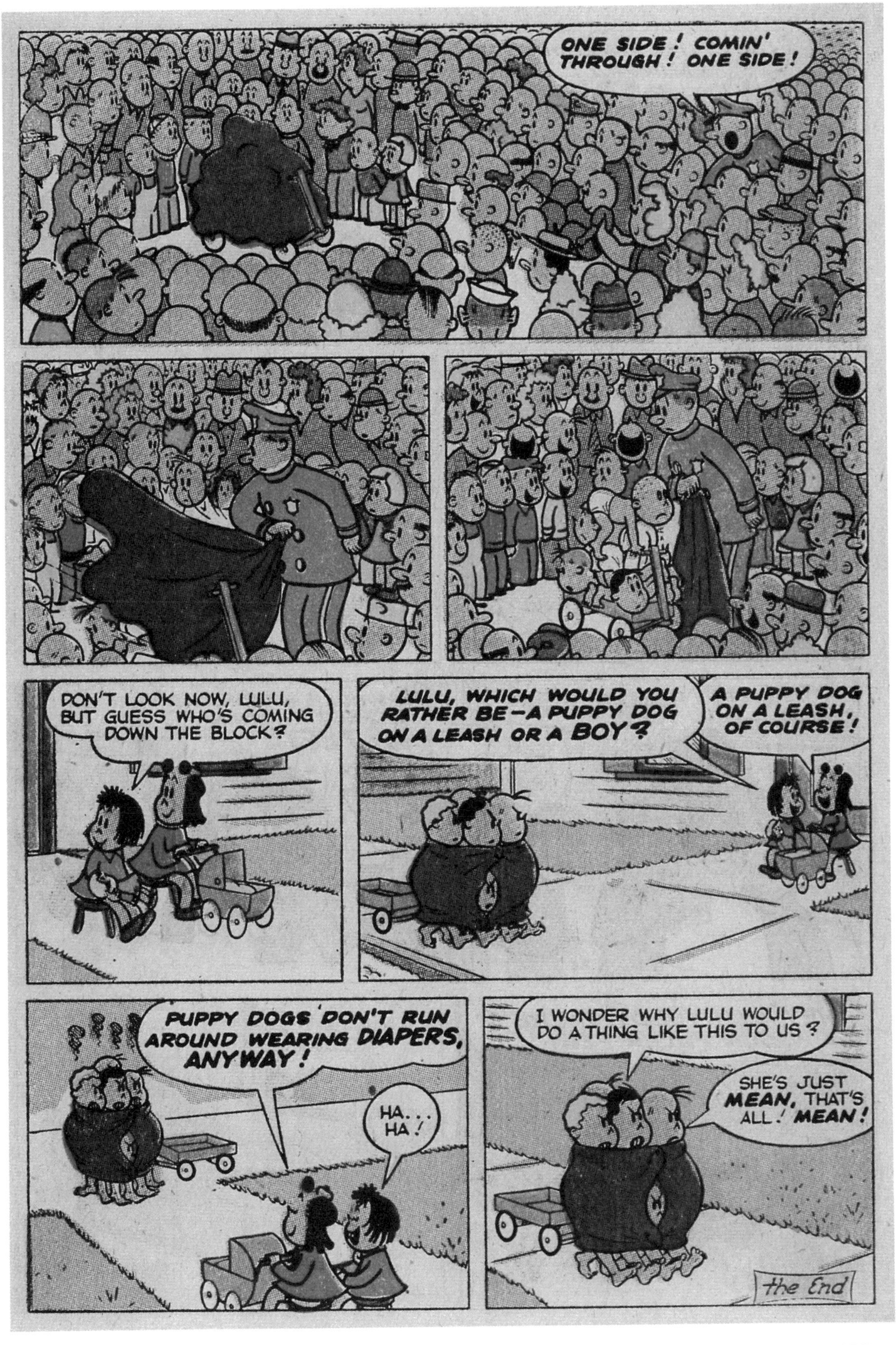
ONE SIDE! COMIN' THROUGH! ONE SIDE!
DON'T LOOK NOW, LULU, BUT GUESS WHO'S COMING DOWN THE BLOCK?
LULU, WHICH WOULD YOU RATHER BE—A PUPPY DOG ON A LEASH OR A BOY?
A PUPPY DOG ON A LEASH, OF COURSE!
PUPPY DOGS DON'T RUN AROUND WEARING DIAPERS, ANYWAY!
HA... HA!
I WONDER WHY LULU WOULD DO A THING LIKE THIS TO US?
SHE'S JUST MEAN, THAT'S ALL! MEAN!
the End

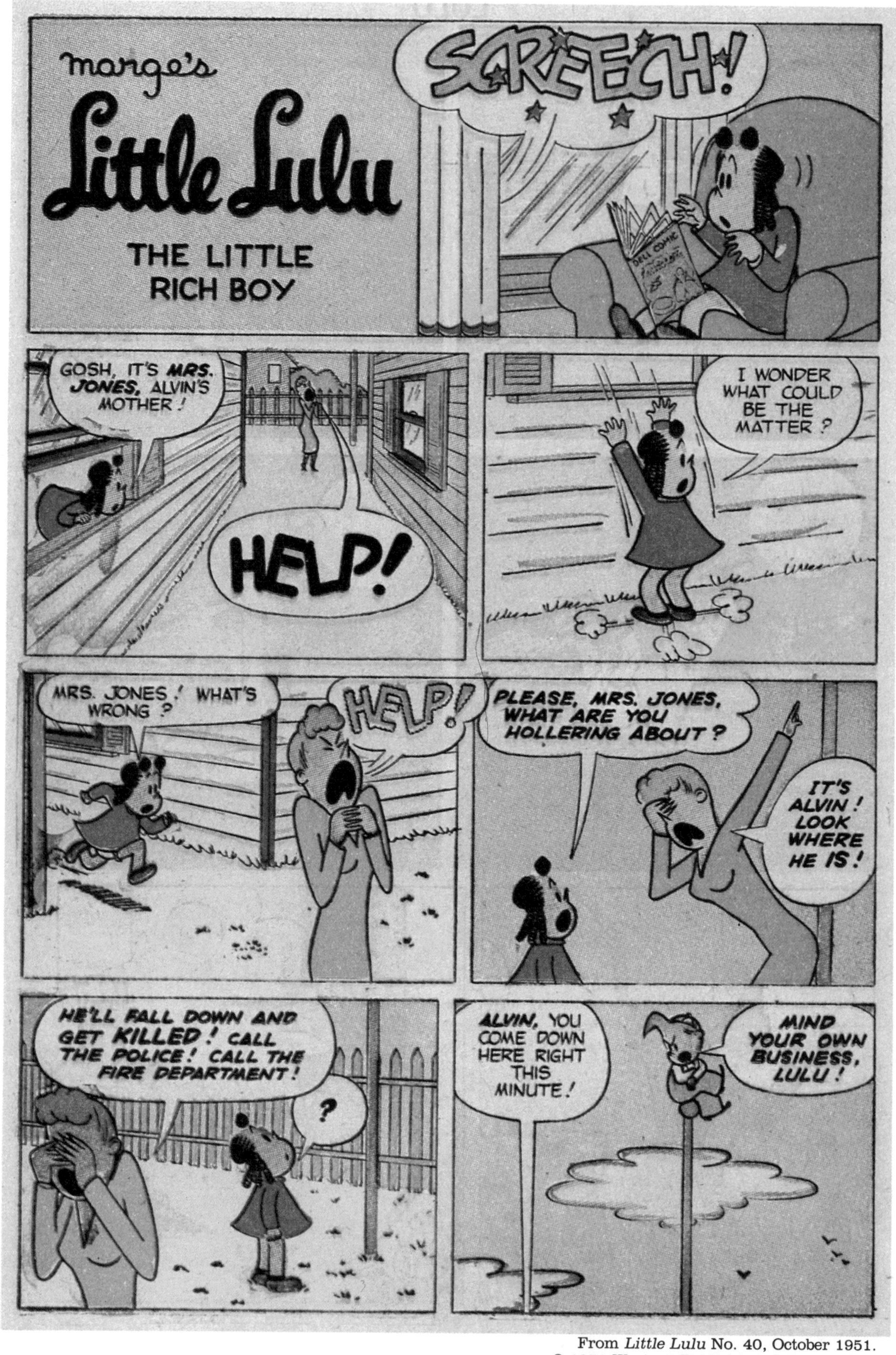
marge's
Little Lulu
THE LITTLE RICH BOY
SCREECH!
GOSH, IT'S MRS. JONES, ALVIN'S MOTHER!
HELP!
I WONDER WHAT COULD BE THE MATTER?
MRS. JONES! WHAT'S WRONG?
HELP!
PLEASE, MRS. JONES, WHAT ARE YOU HOLLERING ABOUT?
IT'S ALVIN! LOOK WHERE HE IS!
HE'LL FALL DOWN AND GET KILLED! CALL THE POLICE! CALL THE FIRE DEPARTMENT!
?
ALVIN, YOU COME DOWN HERE RIGHT THIS MINUTE!
MIND YOUR OWN BUSINESS, LULU!

From *Little Lulu* No. 40, October 1951.

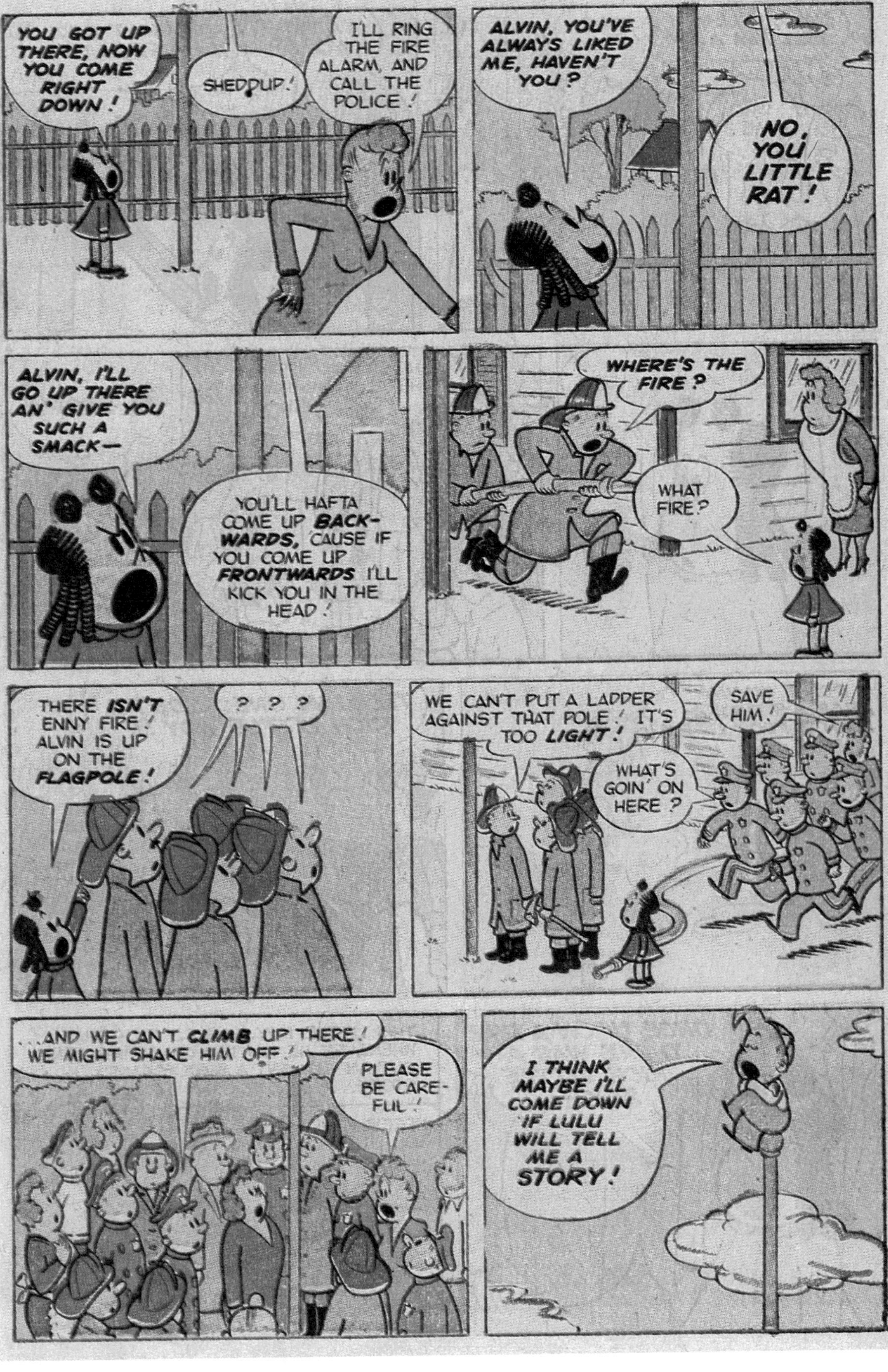
YOU GOT UP THERE, NOW YOU COME RIGHT DOWN!
SHEDDUP!
I'LL RING THE FIRE ALARM, AND CALL THE POLICE!
ALVIN, YOU'VE ALWAYS LIKED ME, HAVEN'T YOU?
NO, YOU LITTLE RAT!
ALVIN, I'LL GO UP THERE AN' GIVE YOU SUCH A SMACK—
YOU'LL HAFTA COME UP BACK-WARDS, CAUSE IF YOU COME UP FRONTWARDS I'LL KICK YOU IN THE HEAD!
WHERE'S THE FIRE?
WHAT FIRE?
THERE ISN'T ENNY FIRE! ALVIN IS UP ON THE FLAGPOLE!
? ? ?
WE CAN'T PUT A LADDER AGAINST THAT POLE! IT'S TOO LIGHT!
SAVE HIM!
WHAT'S GOIN' ON HERE?
...AND WE CAN'T CLIMB UP THERE! WE MIGHT SHAKE HIM OFF!
PLEASE BE CARE-FUL!
I THINK MAYBE I'LL COME DOWN IF LULU WILL TELL ME A STORY!

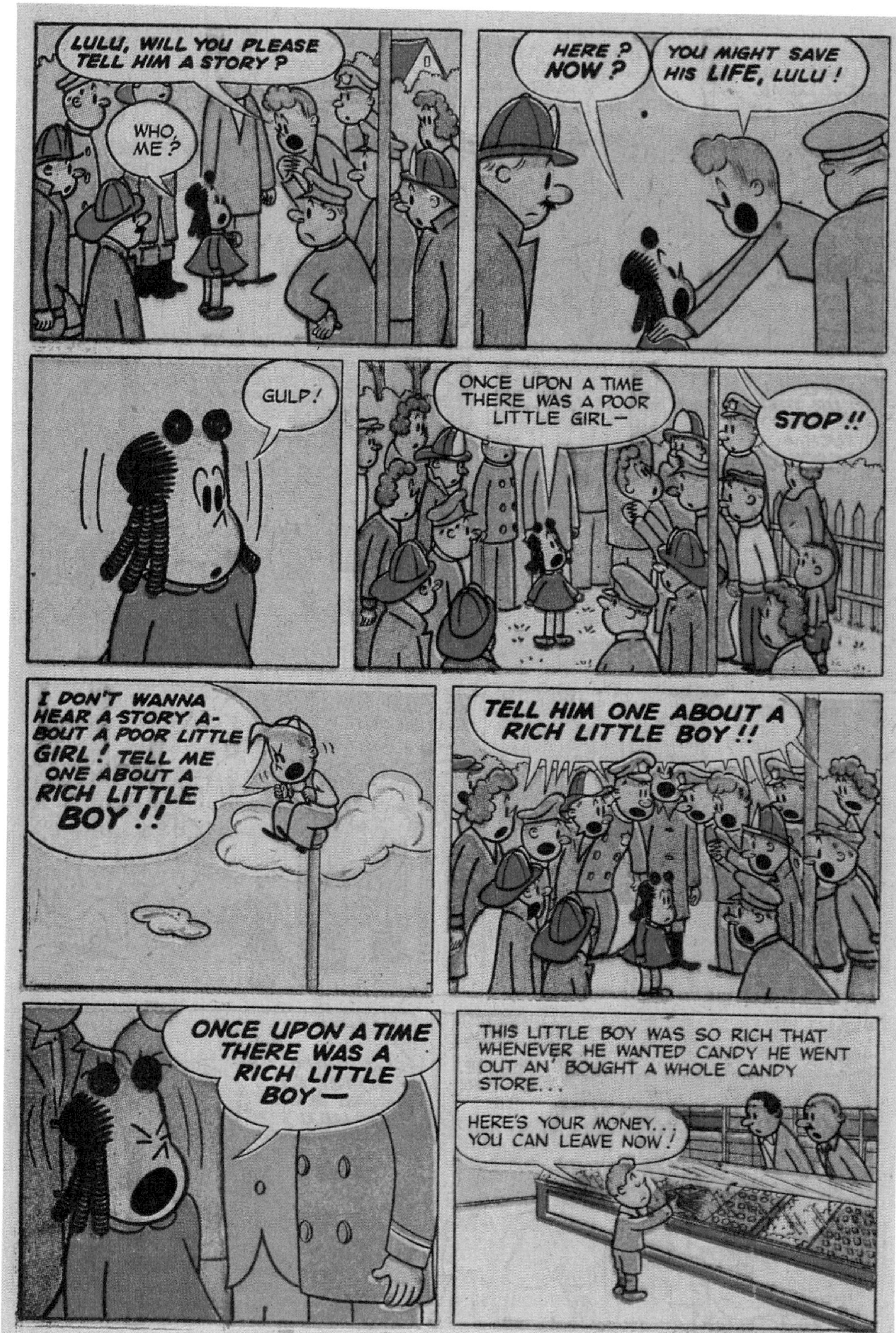
LULU, WILL YOU PLEASE TELL HIM A STORY?
WHO, ME?
HERE? NOW?
YOU MIGHT SAVE HIS LIFE, LULU!
GULP!
ONCE UPON A TIME THERE WAS A POOR LITTLE GIRL—
STOP!!
I DON'T WANNA HEAR A STORY ABOUT A POOR LITTLE GIRL! TELL ME ONE ABOUT A RICH LITTLE BOY!!
TELL HIM ONE ABOUT A RICH LITTLE BOY!!
ONCE UPON A TIME THERE WAS A RICH LITTLE BOY—
THIS LITTLE BOY WAS SO RICH THAT WHENEVER HE WANTED CANDY HE WENT OUT AN' BOUGHT A WHOLE CANDY STORE...
HERE'S YOUR MONEY... YOU CAN LEAVE NOW!

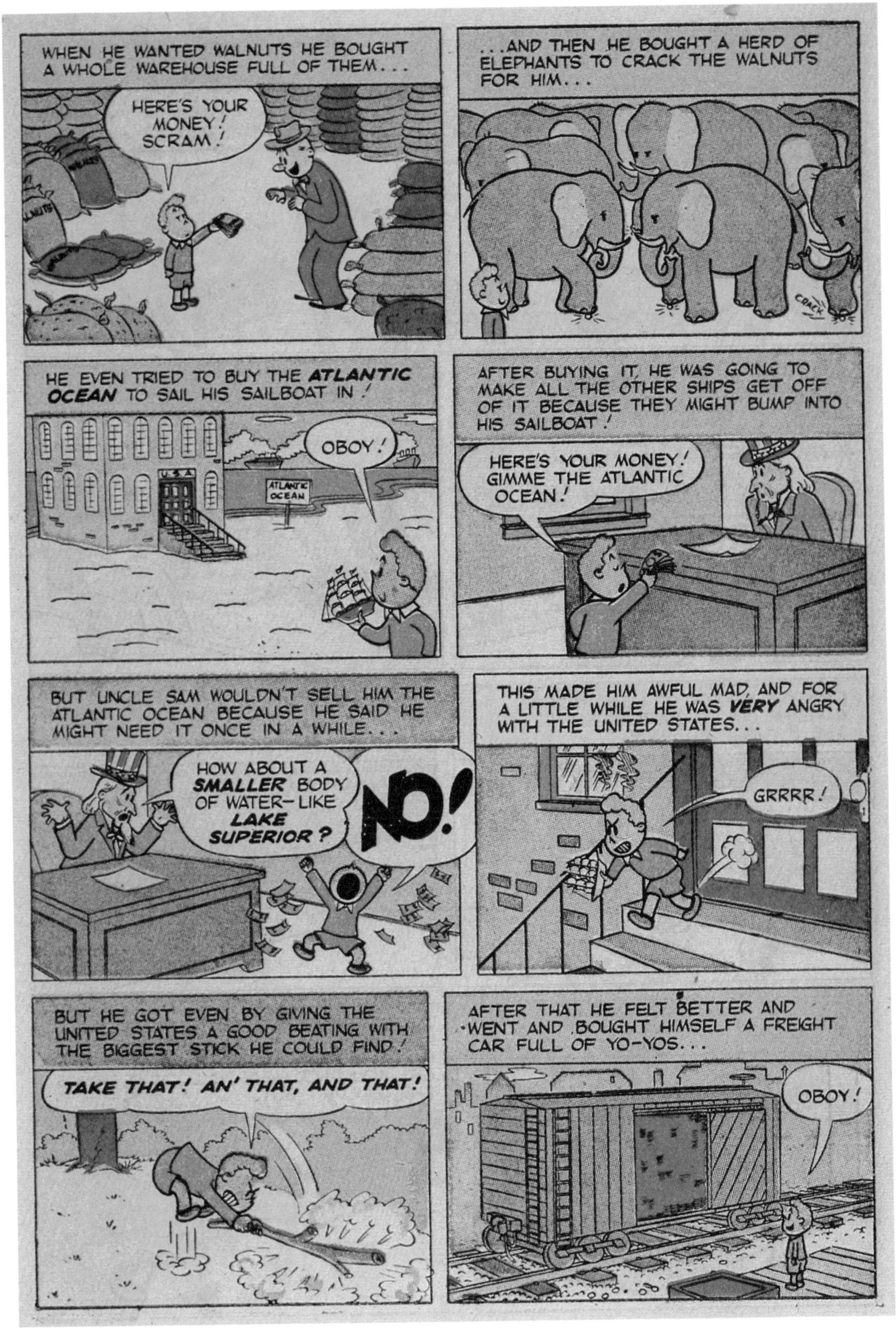
WHEN HE WANTED WALNUTS HE BOUGHT A WHOLE WAREHOUSE FULL OF THEM...
HERE'S YOUR MONEY! SCRAM!
...AND THEN HE BOUGHT A HERD OF ELEPHANTS TO CRACK THE WALNUTS FOR HIM...
CRACK
HE EVEN TRIED TO BUY THE ATLANTIC OCEAN TO SAIL HIS SAILBOAT IN!
U.S.A.
ATLANTIC OCEAN
OBOY!
AFTER BUYING IT, HE WAS GOING TO MAKE ALL THE OTHER SHIPS GET OFF OF IT BECAUSE THEY MIGHT BUMP INTO HIS SAILBOAT!
HERE'S YOUR MONEY! GIMME THE ATLANTIC OCEAN!
BUT UNCLE SAM WOULDN'T SELL HIM THE ATLANTIC OCEAN BECAUSE HE SAID HE MIGHT NEED IT ONCE IN A WHILE...
HOW ABOUT A SMALLER BODY OF WATER—LIKE LAKE SUPERIOR?
NO!
THIS MADE HIM AWFUL MAD, AND FOR A LITTLE WHILE HE WAS VERY ANGRY WITH THE UNITED STATES...
GRRRR!
BUT HE GOT EVEN BY GIVING THE UNITED STATES A GOOD BEATING WITH THE BIGGEST STICK HE COULD FIND!
TAKE THAT! AN' THAT, AND THAT!
AFTER THAT HE FELT BETTER AND WENT AND BOUGHT HIMSELF A FREIGHT CAR FULL OF YO-YOS...
OBOY!

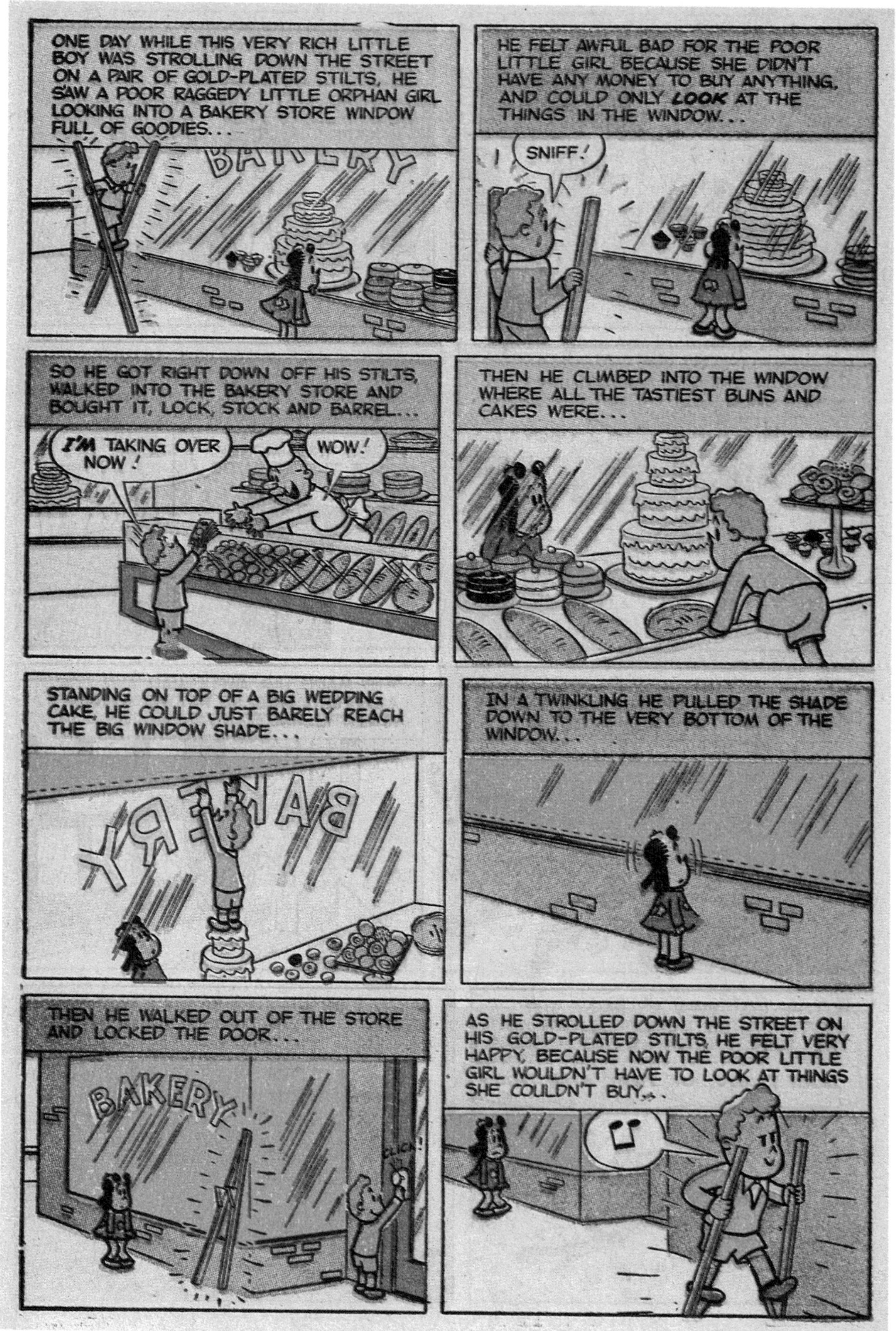

ONE DAY WHILE THIS VERY RICH LITTLE BOY WAS STROLLING DOWN THE STREET ON A PAIR OF GOLD-PLATED STILTS, HE SAW A POOR RAGGEDY LITTLE ORPHAN GIRL LOOKING INTO A BAKERY STORE WINDOW FULL OF GOODIES...
BAKERY
HE FELT AWFUL BAD FOR THE POOR LITTLE GIRL BECAUSE SHE DIDN'T HAVE ANY MONEY TO BUY ANYTHING, AND COULD ONLY **LOOK** AT THE THINGS IN THE WINDOW...
SNIFF!
SO HE GOT RIGHT DOWN OFF HIS STILTS, WALKED INTO THE BAKERY STORE AND BOUGHT IT, LOCK, STOCK AND BARREL...
I'M TAKING OVER NOW!
WOW!
THEN HE CLIMBED INTO THE WINDOW WHERE ALL THE TASTIEST BUNS AND CAKES WERE...
STANDING ON TOP OF A BIG WEDDING CAKE, HE COULD JUST BARELY REACH THE BIG WINDOW SHADE...
IN A TWINKLING HE PULLED THE SHADE DOWN TO THE VERY BOTTOM OF THE WINDOW...
THEN HE WALKED OUT OF THE STORE AND LOCKED THE DOOR...
BAKERY
CLICK!
AS HE STROLLED DOWN THE STREET ON HIS GOLD-PLATED STILTS, HE FELT VERY HAPPY, BECAUSE NOW THE POOR LITTLE GIRL WOULDN'T HAVE TO LOOK AT THINGS SHE COULDN'T BUY...

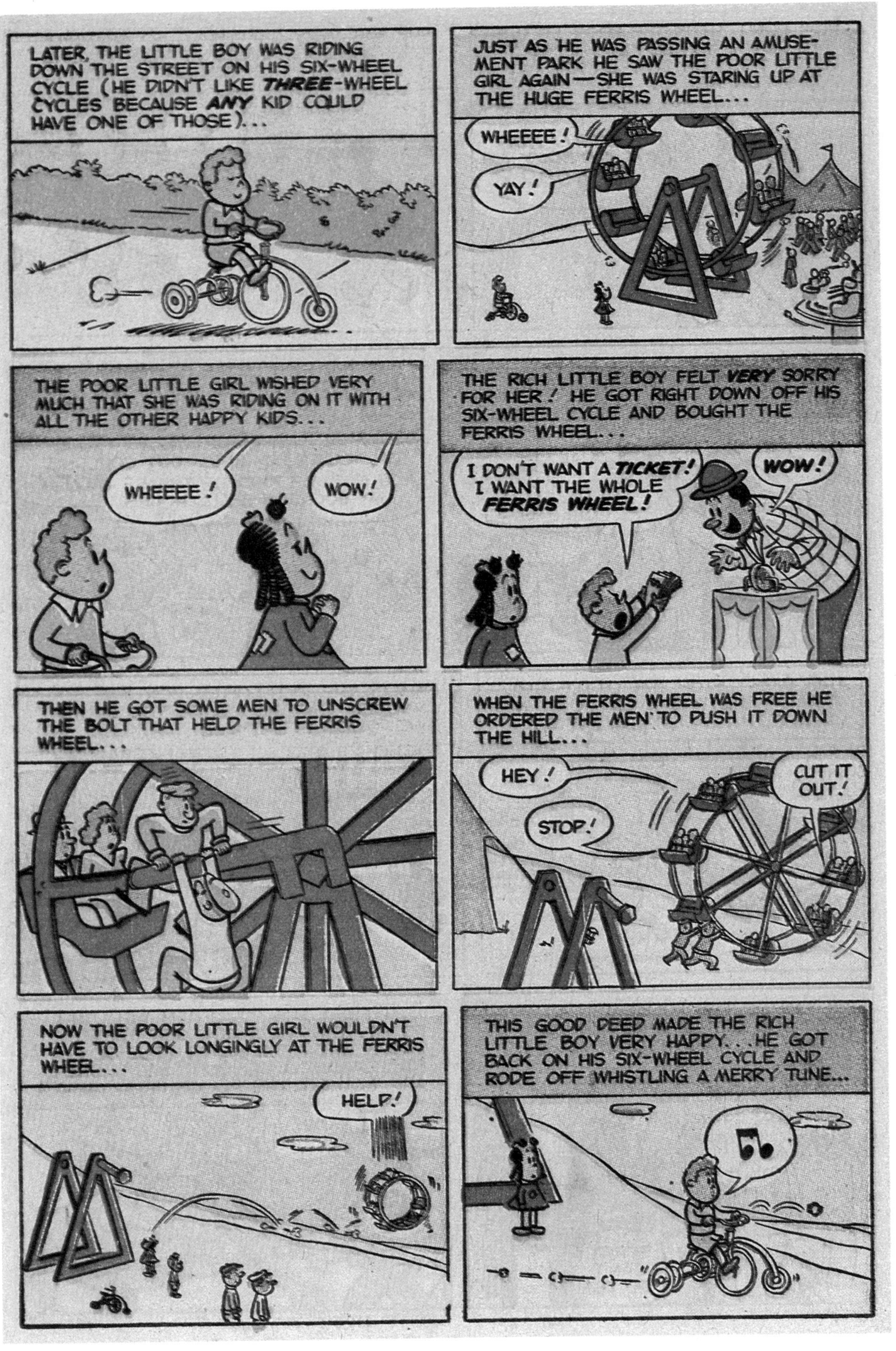

LATER, THE LITTLE BOY WAS RIDING DOWN THE STREET ON HIS SIX-WHEEL CYCLE (HE DIDN'T LIKE THREE-WHEEL CYCLES BECAUSE ANY KID COULD HAVE ONE OF THOSE)...
JUST AS HE WAS PASSING AN AMUSEMENT PARK HE SAW THE POOR LITTLE GIRL AGAIN—SHE WAS STARING UP AT THE HUGE FERRIS WHEEL...
WHEEEE!
YAY!
THE POOR LITTLE GIRL WISHED VERY MUCH THAT SHE WAS RIDING ON IT WITH ALL THE OTHER HAPPY KIDS...
WHEEEE!
WOW!
THE RICH LITTLE BOY FELT VERY SORRY FOR HER! HE GOT RIGHT DOWN OFF HIS SIX-WHEEL CYCLE AND BOUGHT THE FERRIS WHEEL...
I DON'T WANT A TICKET! I WANT THE WHOLE FERRIS WHEEL!
WOW!
THEN HE GOT SOME MEN TO UNSCREW THE BOLT THAT HELD THE FERRIS WHEEL...
WHEN THE FERRIS WHEEL WAS FREE HE ORDERED THE MEN TO PUSH IT DOWN THE HILL...
HEY!
STOP!
CUT IT OUT!
NOW THE POOR LITTLE GIRL WOULDN'T HAVE TO LOOK LONGINGLY AT THE FERRIS WHEEL...
HELP!
THIS GOOD DEED MADE THE RICH LITTLE BOY VERY HAPPY... HE GOT BACK ON HIS SIX-WHEEL CYCLE AND RODE OFF WHISTLING A MERRY TUNE...

Panel 1: NOW DON'T THINK THE POOR LITTLE GIRL DIDN'T NOTICE ALL THE GOOD DEEDS THE RICH LITTLE BOY WAS DOING FOR HER...

GOSH! HOW C'N ANYBODY BE SO GOOD?

Panel 2: SHE WAS VERY GRATEFUL...SO GRATEFUL, THAT SHE JUST COULDN'T HELP FALLING IN LOVE WITH THE RICH LITTLE BOY...

?

Panel 3: SHE FELL SO MUCH IN LOVE WITH HIM THAT SHE FOLLOWED HIM AROUND WHEREVER HE WENT...

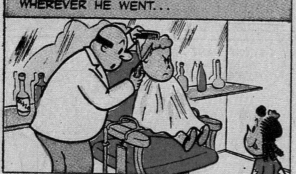

Panel 4: BUT THE RICH LITTLE BOY WAS VERY ANNOYED...HE TOLD HER IF SHE DIDN'T STOP FOLLOWING HIM AROUND HE'D GIVE HER SUCH A SOCK—

OH, YOU'RE SO KIND! BUT COULDN'T YOU GIVE ME TWO OF THEM? BOTH MY SOCKS ARE ALL HOLES!

Panel 5: THIS DIDN'T STOP THE LITTLE GIRL AT ALL—SHE WAS EVEN MORE IN LOVE WITH HIM THAN BEFORE!

Panel 6: FINALLY THE RICH LITTLE BOY WAS SO ANNOYED THAT HE DECIDED TO GO TO THE POLICE STATION...

Panel 7: HE WANTED THE POLICEMEN TO ARREST THE LITTLE GIRL AND PUT HER IN JAIL FOR THE REST OF HER LIFE...

SORRY, CAN'T DO IT!

Panel 8: ...AT FIRST THE POLICEMEN WOULDN'T DO IT...BUT THEY CHANGED THEIR MINDS WHEN THE RICH LITTLE BOY PULLED OUT A BIG BUNDLE OF MONEY AND BOUGHT THE POLICE DEPARTMENT!

WOW!

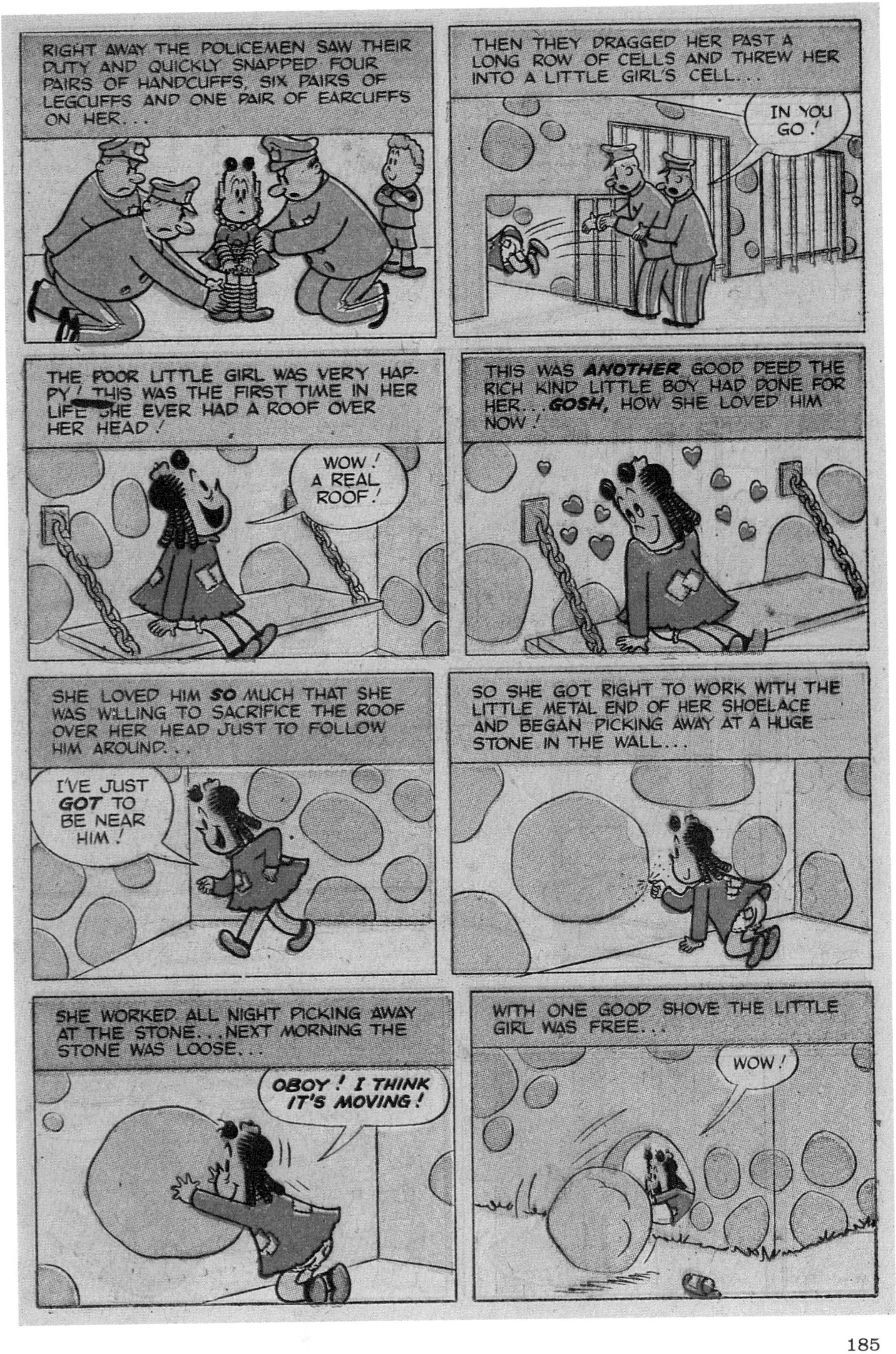
RIGHT AWAY THE POLICEMEN SAW THEIR DUTY AND QUICKLY SNAPPED FOUR PAIRS OF HANDCUFFS, SIX PAIRS OF LEGCUFFS AND ONE PAIR OF EARCUFFS ON HER...
THEN THEY DRAGGED HER PAST A LONG ROW OF CELLS AND THREW HER INTO A LITTLE GIRL'S CELL...
IN YOU GO!
THE POOR LITTLE GIRL WAS VERY HAPPY! THIS WAS THE FIRST TIME IN HER LIFE SHE EVER HAD A ROOF OVER HER HEAD!
WOW! A REAL ROOF!
THIS WAS **ANOTHER** GOOD DEED THE RICH KIND LITTLE BOY HAD DONE FOR HER... **GOSH,** HOW SHE LOVED HIM NOW!
SHE LOVED HIM **SO** MUCH THAT SHE WAS WILLING TO SACRIFICE THE ROOF OVER HER HEAD JUST TO FOLLOW HIM AROUND...
I'VE JUST **GOT** TO BE NEAR HIM!
SO SHE GOT RIGHT TO WORK WITH THE LITTLE METAL END OF HER SHOELACE AND BEGAN PICKING AWAY AT A HUGE STONE IN THE WALL...
SHE WORKED ALL NIGHT PICKING AWAY AT THE STONE... NEXT MORNING THE STONE WAS LOOSE...
OBOY! I THINK IT'S MOVING!
WITH ONE GOOD SHOVE THE LITTLE GIRL WAS FREE...
WOW!

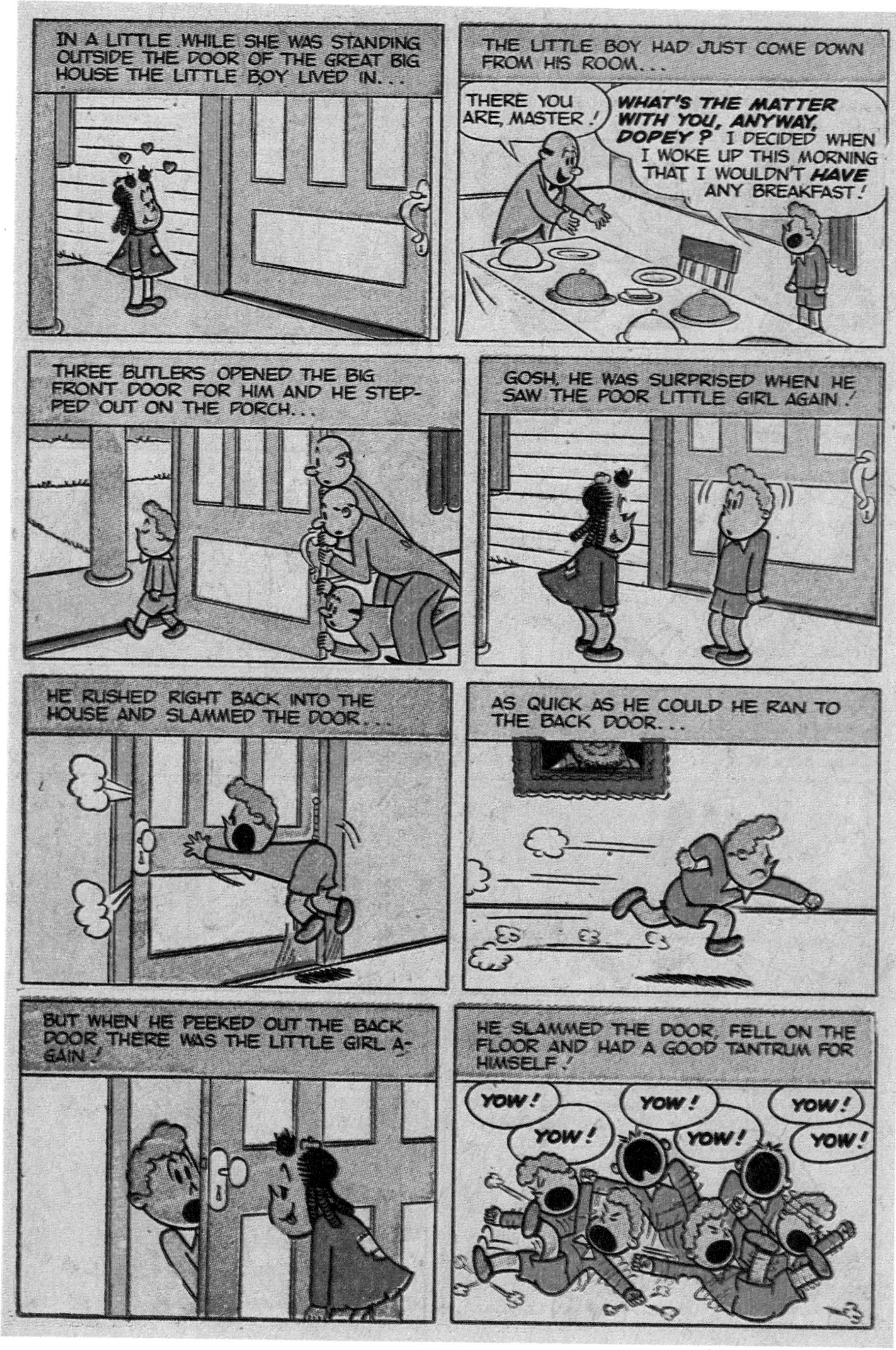
IN A LITTLE WHILE SHE WAS STANDING OUTSIDE THE DOOR OF THE GREAT BIG HOUSE THE LITTLE BOY LIVED IN...
THE LITTLE BOY HAD JUST COME DOWN FROM HIS ROOM...
THERE YOU ARE, MASTER!
WHAT'S THE MATTER WITH YOU, ANYWAY, DOPEY? I DECIDED WHEN I WOKE UP THIS MORNING THAT I WOULDN'T HAVE ANY BREAKFAST!
THREE BUTLERS OPENED THE BIG FRONT DOOR FOR HIM AND HE STEPPED OUT ON THE PORCH...
GOSH, HE WAS SURPRISED WHEN HE SAW THE POOR LITTLE GIRL AGAIN!
HE RUSHED RIGHT BACK INTO THE HOUSE AND SLAMMED THE DOOR...
AS QUICK AS HE COULD HE RAN TO THE BACK DOOR...
BUT WHEN HE PEEKED OUT THE BACK DOOR THERE WAS THE LITTLE GIRL AGAIN!
HE SLAMMED THE DOOR, FELL ON THE FLOOR AND HAD A GOOD TANTRUM FOR HIMSELF!
YOW!
YOW!
YOW!
YOW!
YOW!
YOW!

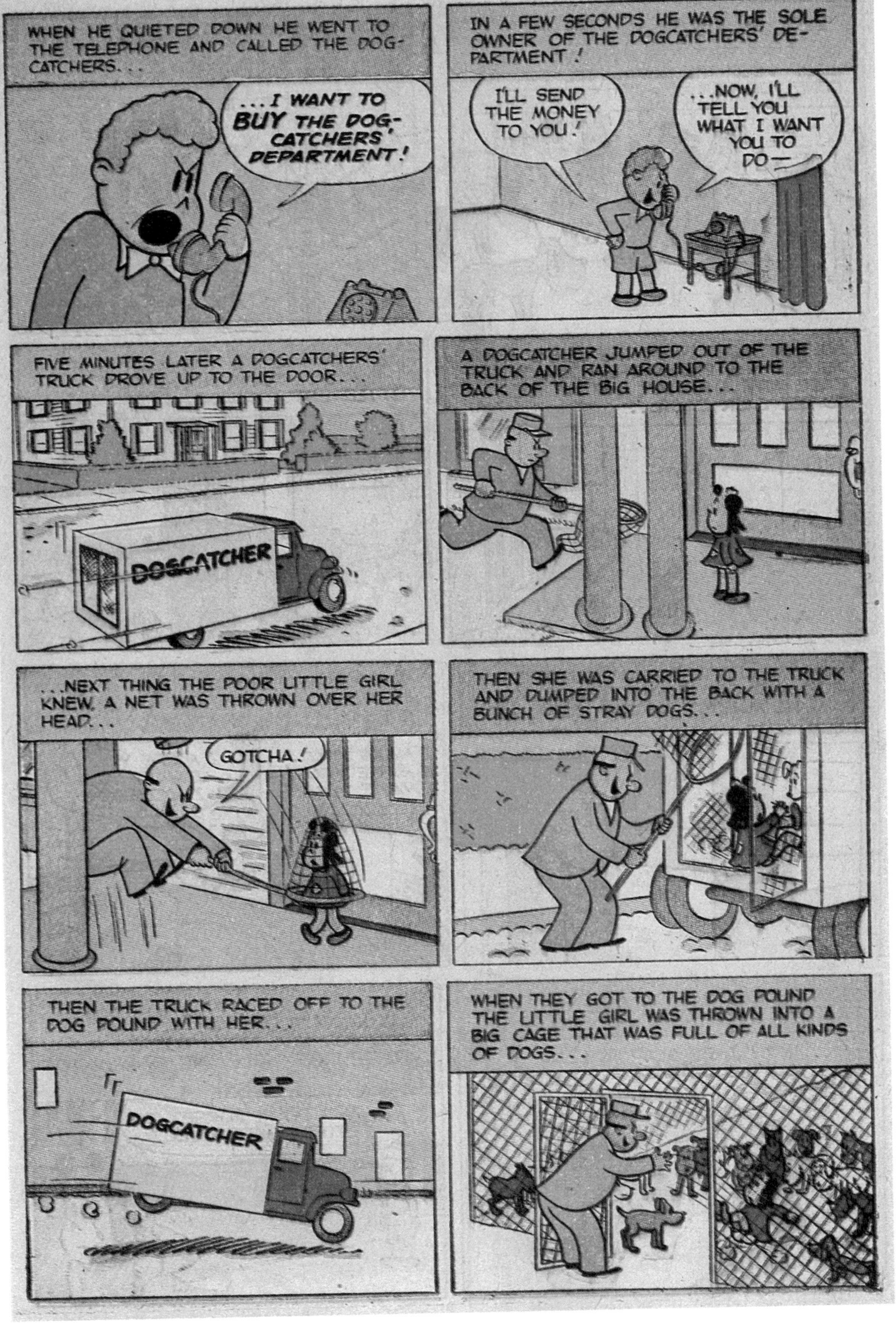
WHEN HE QUIETED DOWN HE WENT TO THE TELEPHONE AND CALLED THE DOG-CATCHERS...
...I WANT TO BUY THE DOG-CATCHERS' DEPARTMENT!
IN A FEW SECONDS HE WAS THE SOLE OWNER OF THE DOGCATCHERS' DE-PARTMENT!
I'LL SEND THE MONEY TO YOU!
...NOW, I'LL TELL YOU WHAT I WANT YOU TO DO—
FIVE MINUTES LATER A DOGCATCHERS' TRUCK DROVE UP TO THE DOOR...
DOGCATCHER
A DOGCATCHER JUMPED OUT OF THE TRUCK AND RAN AROUND TO THE BACK OF THE BIG HOUSE...
...NEXT THING THE POOR LITTLE GIRL KNEW, A NET WAS THROWN OVER HER HEAD...
GOTCHA!
THEN SHE WAS CARRIED TO THE TRUCK AND DUMPED INTO THE BACK WITH A BUNCH OF STRAY DOGS...
THEN THE TRUCK RACED OFF TO THE DOG POUND WITH HER...
DOGCATCHER
WHEN THEY GOT TO THE DOG POUND THE LITTLE GIRL WAS THROWN INTO A BIG CAGE THAT WAS FULL OF ALL KINDS OF DOGS...

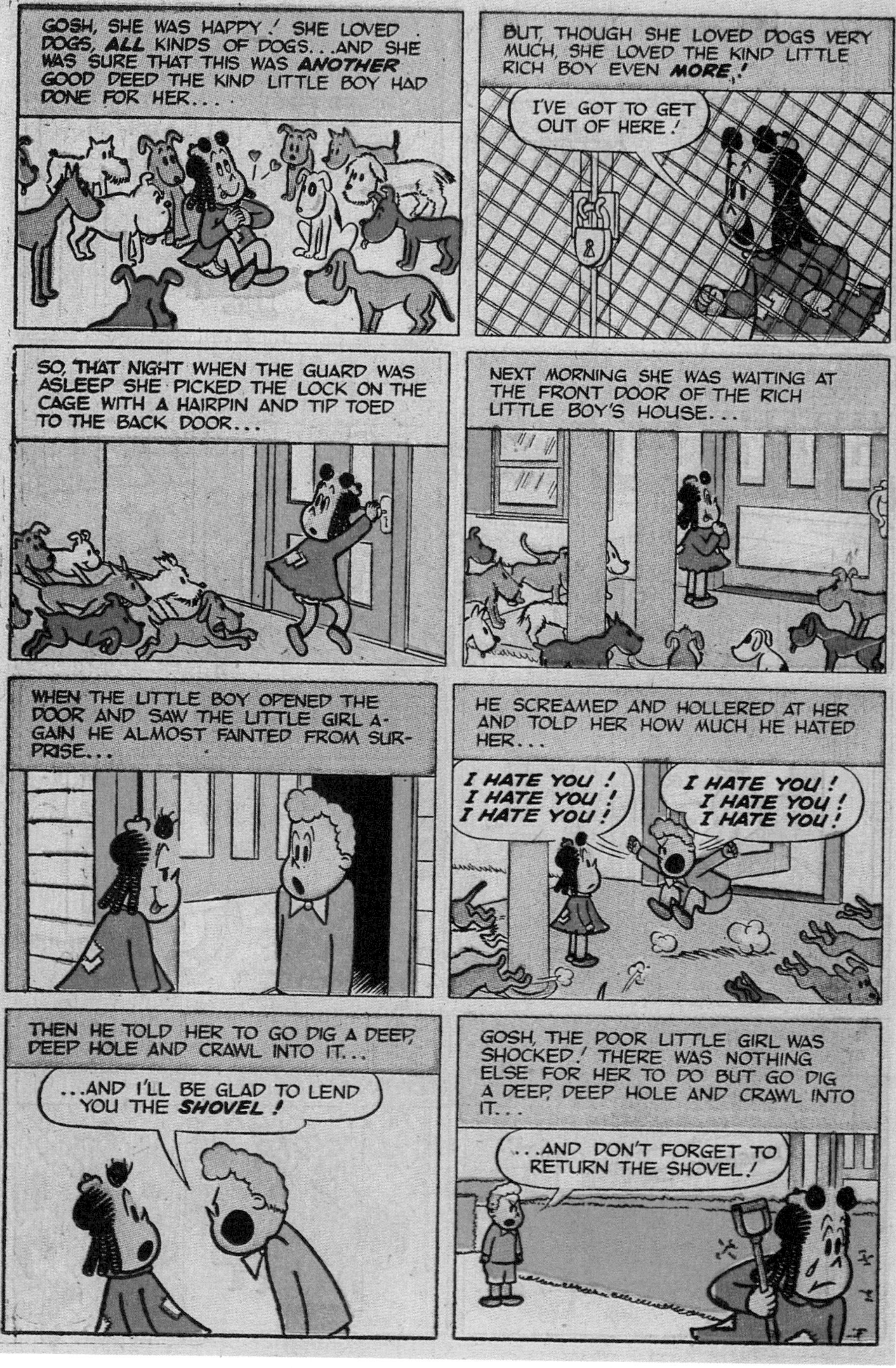
GOSH, SHE WAS HAPPY! SHE LOVED DOGS, ALL KINDS OF DOGS...AND SHE WAS SURE THAT THIS WAS ANOTHER GOOD DEED THE KIND LITTLE BOY HAD DONE FOR HER...
BUT, THOUGH SHE LOVED DOGS VERY MUCH, SHE LOVED THE KIND LITTLE RICH BOY EVEN MORE!
I'VE GOT TO GET OUT OF HERE!
SO, THAT NIGHT WHEN THE GUARD WAS ASLEEP SHE PICKED THE LOCK ON THE CAGE WITH A HAIRPIN AND TIP TOED TO THE BACK DOOR...
NEXT MORNING SHE WAS WAITING AT THE FRONT DOOR OF THE RICH LITTLE BOY'S HOUSE...
WHEN THE LITTLE BOY OPENED THE DOOR AND SAW THE LITTLE GIRL AGAIN HE ALMOST FAINTED FROM SURPRISE...
HE SCREAMED AND HOLLERED AT HER AND TOLD HER HOW MUCH HE HATED HER...
I HATE YOU! I HATE YOU! I HATE YOU!
I HATE YOU! I HATE YOU! I HATE YOU!
THEN HE TOLD HER TO GO DIG A DEEP, DEEP HOLE AND CRAWL INTO IT...
...AND I'LL BE GLAD TO LEND YOU THE SHOVEL!
GOSH, THE POOR LITTLE GIRL WAS SHOCKED! THERE WAS NOTHING ELSE FOR HER TO DO BUT GO DIG A DEEP, DEEP HOLE AND CRAWL INTO IT...
...AND DON'T FORGET TO RETURN THE SHOVEL!

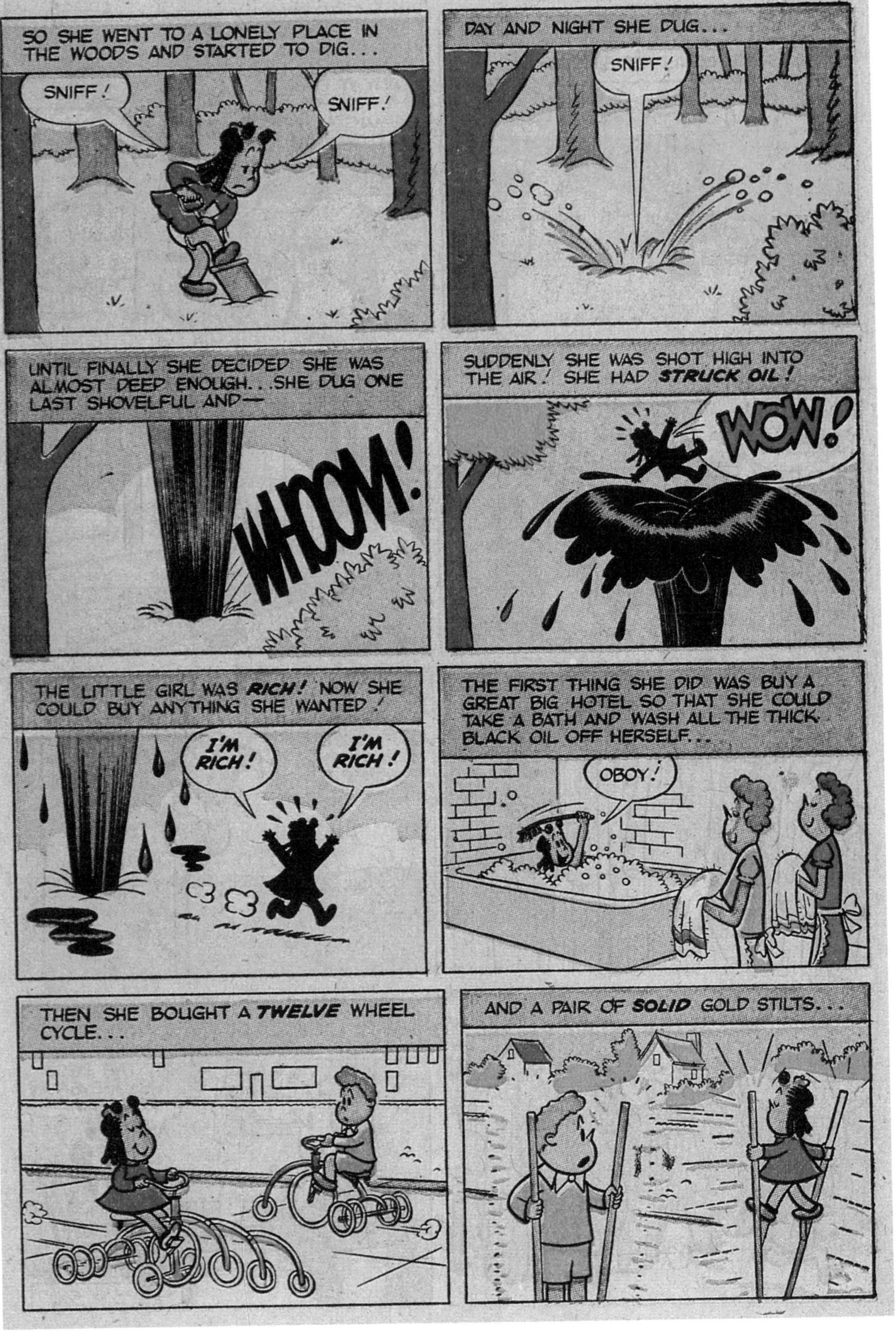
SO SHE WENT TO A LONELY PLACE IN THE WOODS AND STARTED TO DIG...
SNIFF!
SNIFF!
DAY AND NIGHT SHE DUG...
SNIFF!
UNTIL FINALLY SHE DECIDED SHE WAS ALMOST DEEP ENOUGH...SHE DUG ONE LAST SHOVELFUL AND—
WHOOM!
SUDDENLY SHE WAS SHOT HIGH INTO THE AIR! SHE HAD STRUCK OIL!
WOW!
THE LITTLE GIRL WAS RICH! NOW SHE COULD BUY ANYTHING SHE WANTED!
I'M RICH!
I'M RICH!
THE FIRST THING SHE DID WAS BUY A GREAT BIG HOTEL SO THAT SHE COULD TAKE A BATH AND WASH ALL THE THICK BLACK OIL OFF HERSELF...
OBOY!
THEN SHE BOUGHT A TWELVE WHEEL CYCLE...
AND A PAIR OF SOLID GOLD STILTS...

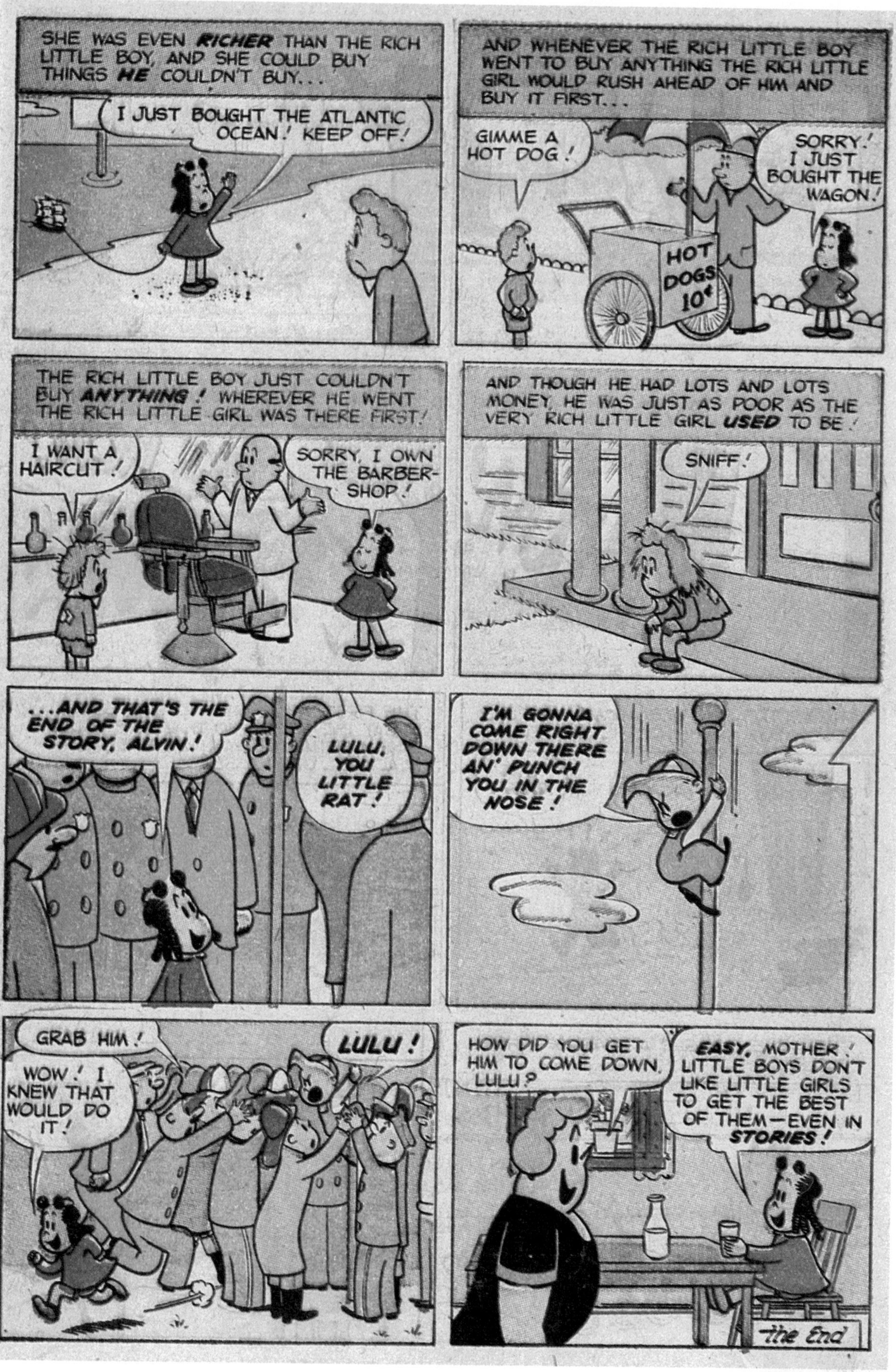
SHE WAS EVEN RICHER THAN THE RICH LITTLE BOY, AND SHE COULD BUY THINGS HE COULDN'T BUY...
I JUST BOUGHT THE ATLANTIC OCEAN! KEEP OFF!
AND WHENEVER THE RICH LITTLE BOY WENT TO BUY ANYTHING THE RICH LITTLE GIRL WOULD RUSH AHEAD OF HIM AND BUY IT FIRST...
GIMME A HOT DOG!
SORRY! I JUST BOUGHT THE WAGON!
HOT DOGS 10¢
THE RICH LITTLE BOY JUST COULDN'T BUY ANYTHING! WHEREVER HE WENT THE RICH LITTLE GIRL WAS THERE FIRST!
I WANT A HAIRCUT!
SORRY, I OWN THE BARBER-SHOP!
AND THOUGH HE HAD LOTS AND LOTS MONEY, HE WAS JUST AS POOR AS THE VERY RICH LITTLE GIRL USED TO BE!
SNIFF!
...AND THAT'S THE END OF THE STORY, ALVIN!
LULU, YOU LITTLE RAT!
I'M GONNA COME RIGHT DOWN THERE AN' PUNCH YOU IN THE NOSE!
GRAB HIM!
LULU!
WOW! I KNEW THAT WOULD DO IT!
HOW DID YOU GET HIM TO COME DOWN, LULU?
EASY, MOTHER! LITTLE BOYS DON'T LIKE LITTLE GIRLS TO GET THE BEST OF THEM—EVEN IN STORIES!
The End

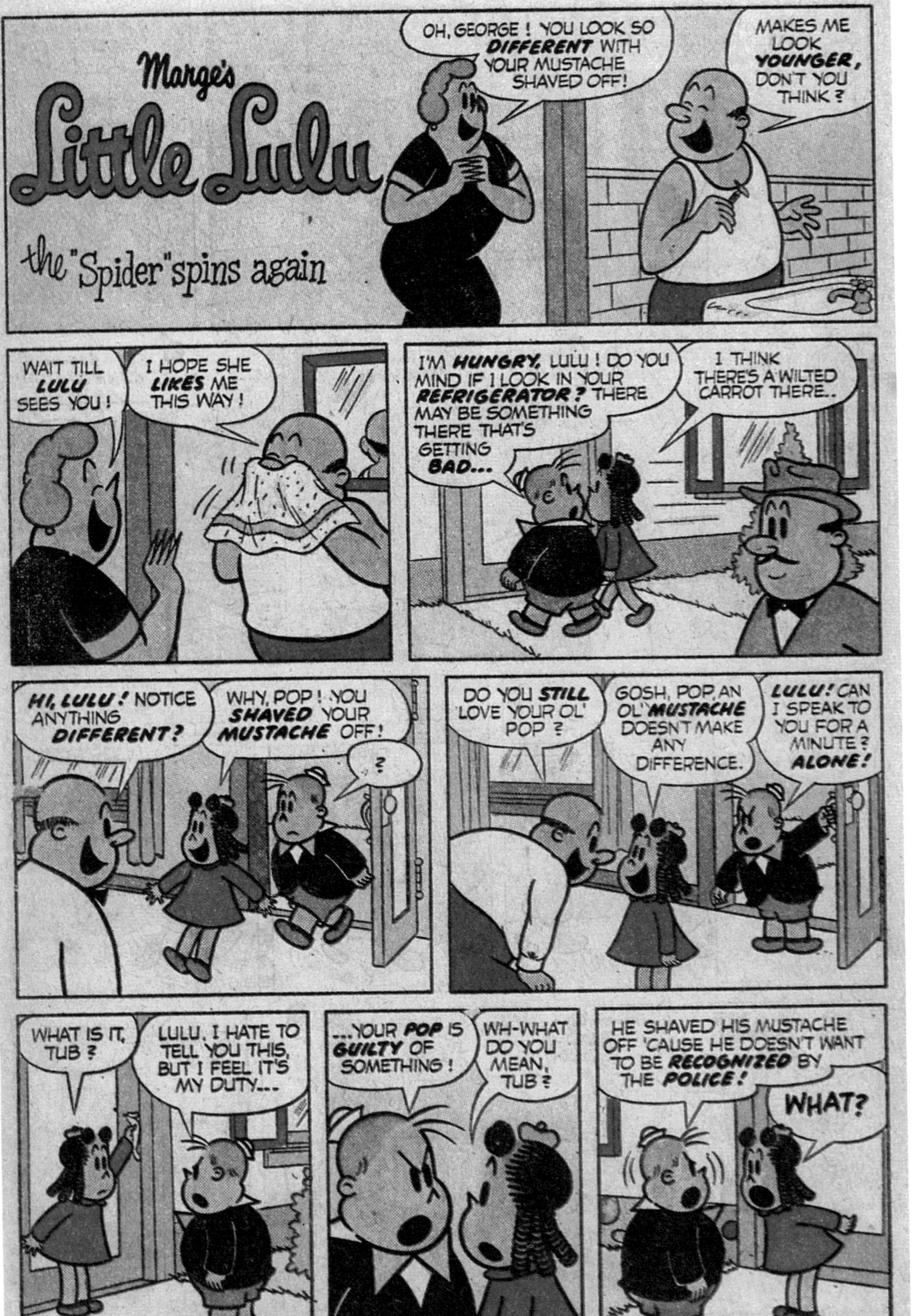
Marge's
Little Lulu
the "Spider" spins again
OH, GEORGE! YOU LOOK SO DIFFERENT WITH YOUR MUSTACHE SHAVED OFF!
MAKES ME LOOK YOUNGER, DON'T YOU THINK?
WAIT TILL LULU SEES YOU!
I HOPE SHE LIKES ME THIS WAY!
I'M HUNGRY, LULU! DO YOU MIND IF I LOOK IN YOUR REFRIGERATOR? THERE MAY BE SOMETHING THERE THAT'S GETTING BAD...
I THINK THERE'S A WILTED CARROT THERE..
HI, LULU! NOTICE ANYTHING DIFFERENT?
WHY, POP! YOU SHAVED YOUR MUSTACHE OFF!
?
DO YOU STILL LOVE YOUR OL' POP?
GOSH, POP, AN OL' MUSTACHE DOESN'T MAKE ANY DIFFERENCE.
LULU! CAN I SPEAK TO YOU FOR A MINUTE? ALONE!
WHAT IS IT, TUB?
LULU, I HATE TO TELL YOU THIS, BUT I FEEL IT'S MY DUTY...
...YOUR POP IS GUILTY OF SOMETHING!
WH-WHAT DO YOU MEAN, TUB?
HE SHAVED HIS MUSTACHE OFF 'CAUSE HE DOESN'T WANT TO BE RECOGNIZED BY THE POLICE!
WHAT?

From *Little Lulu* No. 81, March 1955.

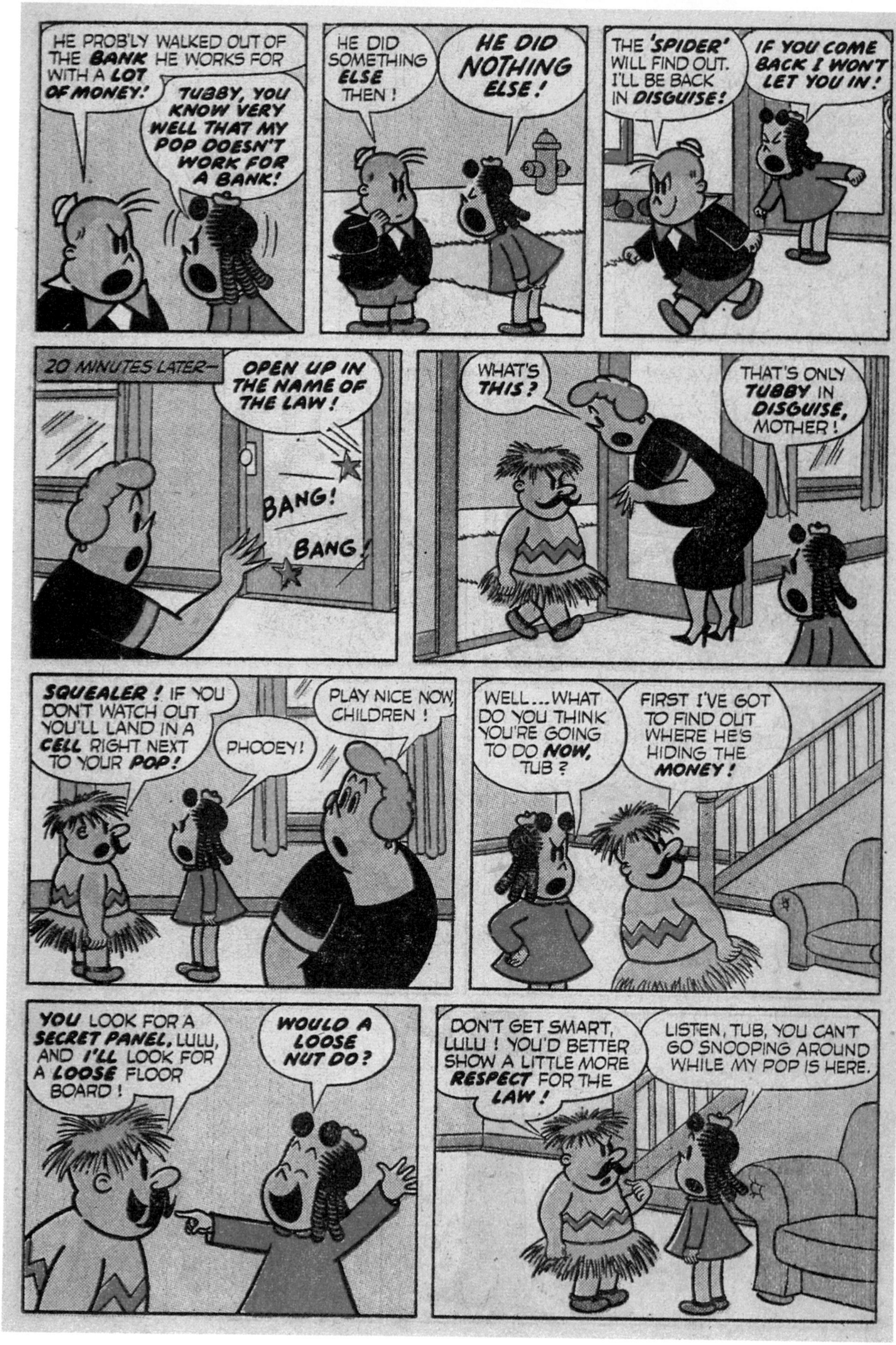
HE PROB'LY WALKED OUT OF THE BANK HE WORKS FOR WITH A LOT OF MONEY!
TUBBY, YOU KNOW VERY WELL THAT MY POP DOESN'T WORK FOR A BANK!
HE DID SOMETHING ELSE THEN!
HE DID NOTHING ELSE!
THE 'SPIDER' WILL FIND OUT. I'LL BE BACK IN DISGUISE!
IF YOU COME BACK I WON'T LET YOU IN!
20 MINUTES LATER—
OPEN UP IN THE NAME OF THE LAW!
BANG!
BANG!
WHAT'S THIS?
THAT'S ONLY TUBBY IN DISGUISE, MOTHER!
SQUEALER! IF YOU DON'T WATCH OUT YOU'LL LAND IN A CELL RIGHT NEXT TO YOUR POP!
PHOOEY!
PLAY NICE NOW, CHILDREN!
WELL... WHAT DO YOU THINK YOU'RE GOING TO DO NOW, TUB?
FIRST I'VE GOT TO FIND OUT WHERE HE'S HIDING THE MONEY!
YOU LOOK FOR A SECRET PANEL, LULU, AND I'LL LOOK FOR A LOOSE FLOOR BOARD!
WOULD A LOOSE NUT DO?
DON'T GET SMART, LULU! YOU'D BETTER SHOW A LITTLE MORE RESPECT FOR THE LAW!
LISTEN, TUB, YOU CAN'T GO SNOOPING AROUND WHILE MY POP IS HERE.

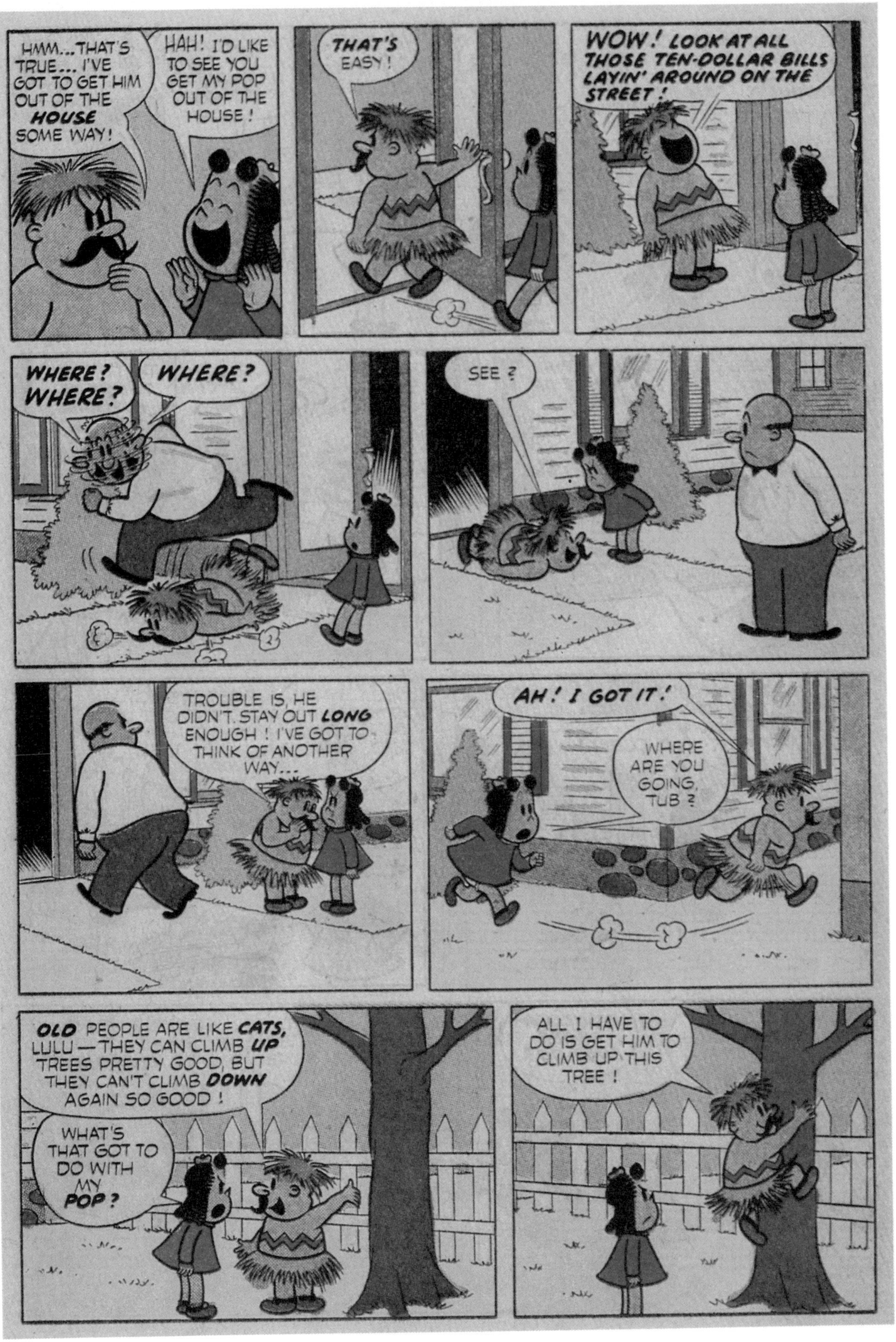
HMM...THAT'S TRUE... I'VE GOT TO GET HIM OUT OF THE HOUSE SOME WAY!
HAH! I'D LIKE TO SEE YOU GET MY POP OUT OF THE HOUSE!
THAT'S EASY!
WOW! LOOK AT ALL THOSE TEN-DOLLAR BILLS LAYIN' AROUND ON THE STREET!
WHERE? WHERE?
WHERE?
SEE ?
TROUBLE IS, HE DIDN'T STAY OUT LONG ENOUGH! I'VE GOT TO THINK OF ANOTHER WAY...
AH! I GOT IT!
WHERE ARE YOU GOING, TUB ?
OLD PEOPLE ARE LIKE CATS, LULU — THEY CAN CLIMB UP TREES PRETTY GOOD, BUT THEY CAN'T CLIMB DOWN AGAIN SO GOOD!
WHAT'S THAT GOT TO DO WITH MY POP?
ALL I HAVE TO DO IS GET HIM TO CLIMB UP THIS TREE!

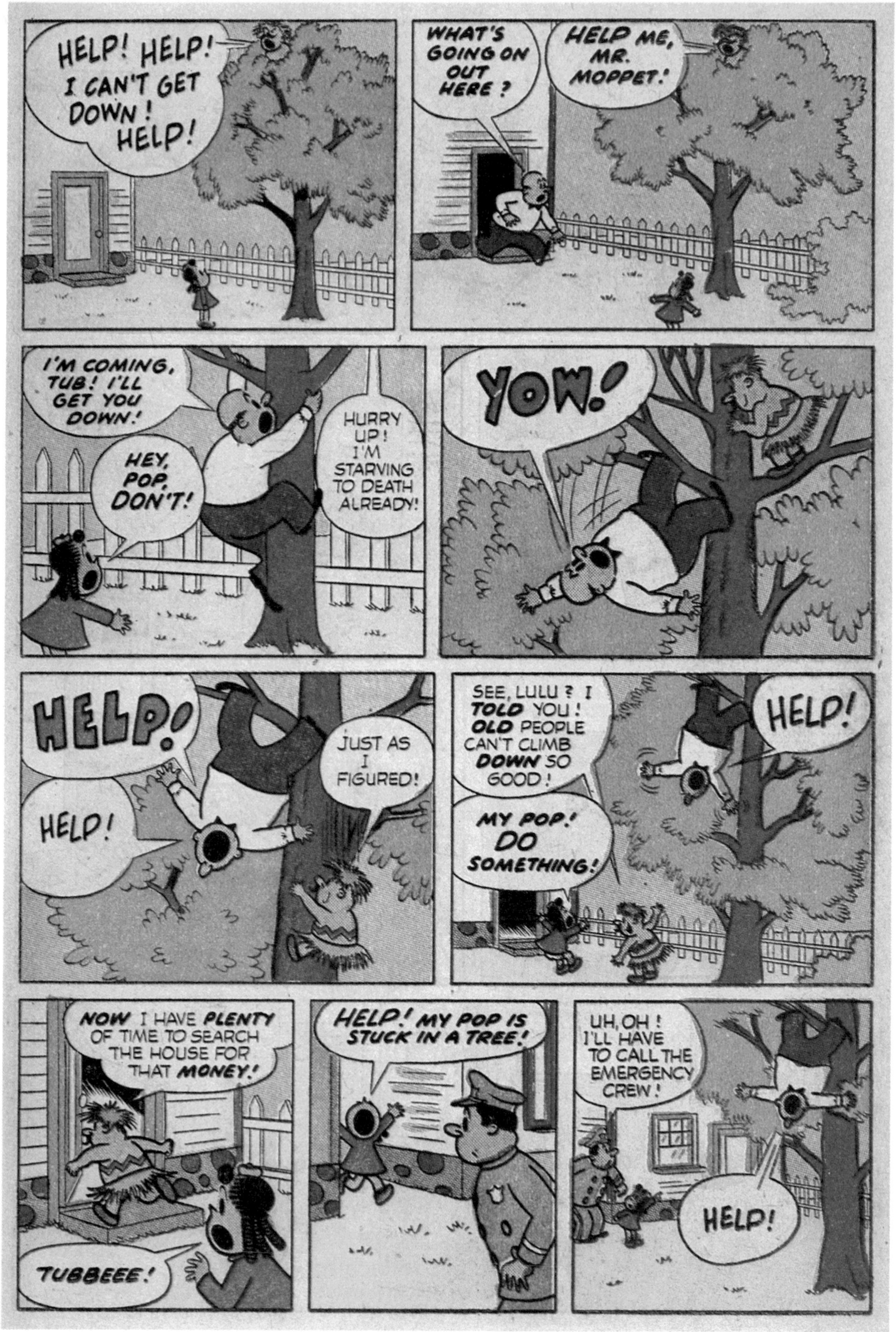

HELP! HELP! I CAN'T GET DOWN! HELP!
WHAT'S GOING ON OUT HERE?
HELP ME, MR. MOPPET!
I'M COMING, TUB! I'LL GET YOU DOWN!
HEY, POP, DON'T!
HURRY UP! I'M STARVING TO DEATH ALREADY!
YOW!
HELP!
HELP!
JUST AS I FIGURED!
SEE, LULU? I TOLD YOU! OLD PEOPLE CAN'T CLIMB DOWN SO GOOD!
HELP!
MY POP! DO SOMETHING!
NOW I HAVE PLENTY OF TIME TO SEARCH THE HOUSE FOR THAT MONEY!
TUBBEEE!
HELP! MY POP IS STUCK IN A TREE!
UH, OH! I'LL HAVE TO CALL THE EMERGENCY CREW!
HELP!

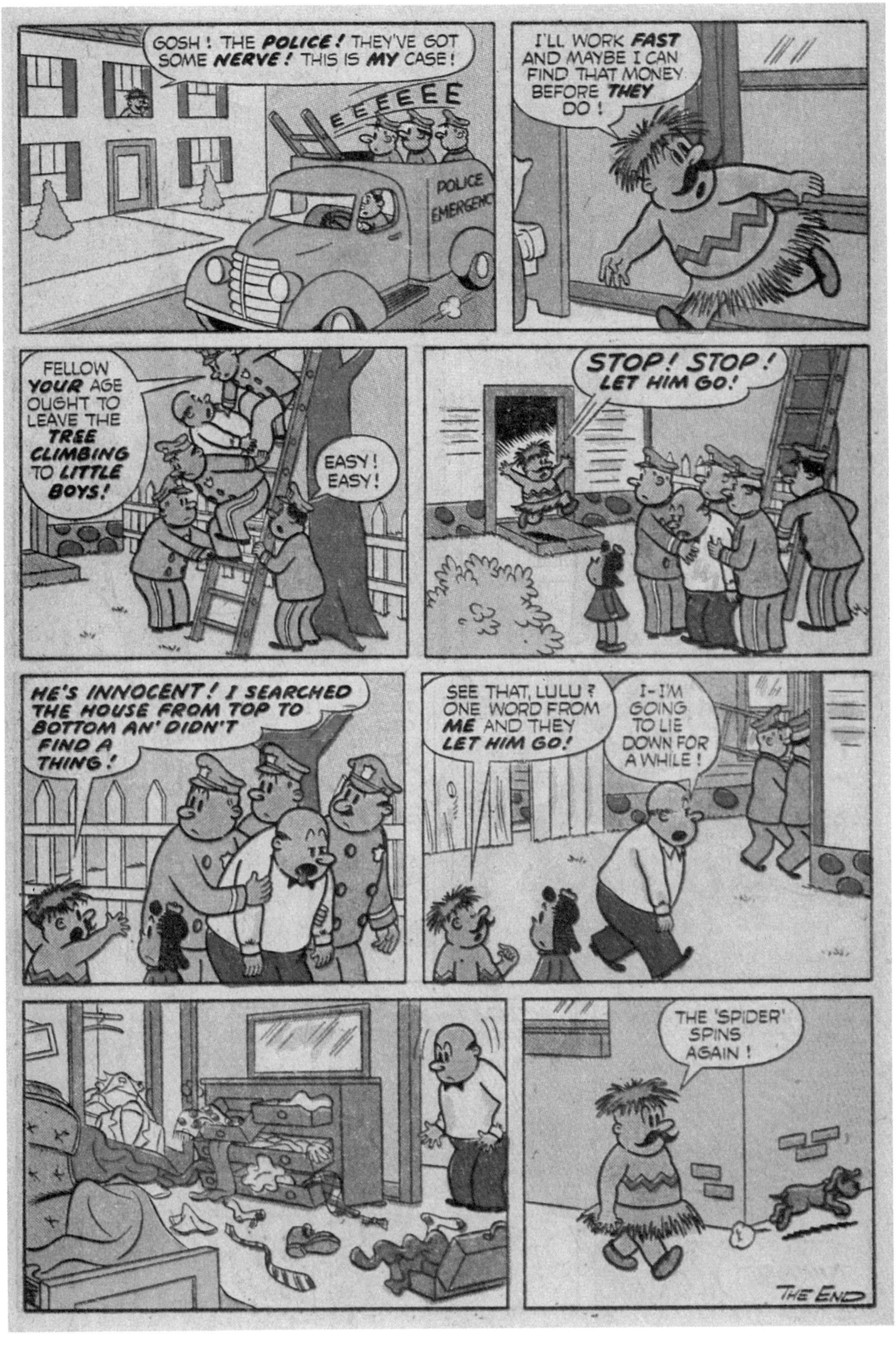
GOSH! THE POLICE! THEY'VE GOT SOME NERVE! THIS IS MY CASE!
EEEEEEE
POLICE EMERGENC
I'LL WORK FAST AND MAYBE I CAN FIND THAT MONEY BEFORE THEY DO!
FELLOW YOUR AGE OUGHT TO LEAVE THE TREE CLIMBING TO LITTLE BOYS!
EASY! EASY!
STOP! STOP! LET HIM GO!
HE'S INNOCENT! I SEARCHED THE HOUSE FROM TOP TO BOTTOM AN' DIDN'T FIND A THING!
SEE THAT, LULU? ONE WORD FROM ME AND THEY LET HIM GO!
I-I'M GOING TO LIE DOWN FOR A WHILE!
THE 'SPIDER' SPINS AGAIN!
THE END

About "Donald Duck" and Carl Barks

In the late 1930s, the Walt Disney characters were appearing not in a comic book but in a children's magazine called the *Mickey Mouse Magazine.* In 1940, this magazine was converted into a monthly comic book called *Walt Disney's Comics and Stories;* it was the first of dozens of comic books based on animated-cartoon characters. The comic books with major characters like Donald Duck, Bugs Bunny, Woody Woodpecker, and Tom and Jerry were produced by Western Printing and Lithographing Company and published under the Dell label. Other publishers used less popular characters, like Mighty Mouse and the Fox and the Crow, or invented their own. The "funny animal" comic books, as they were often called, remained consistently popular throughout the 1940s and 1950s. They faded only in the 1960s, when the super-heroes made a comeback. The Disney comic books were always the most popular of the "funny animal" comic books; and of the Disney comic books, the most popular—and easily the best—were written and drawn by Carl Barks.

Barks was born in Oregon on March 27, 1901, and he passed through a variety of jobs—heating rivets in a railroad yard, editing a men's humor magazine in Minneapolis—before going to work for the Disney Studios in 1935. He was a "story man," thinking up gags for Donald Duck cartoons, until he left Disney in 1942 to work as a free-lance cartoonist. He started his new career by illustrating the ten-page *Donald Duck* feature for the April 1943 issue of *Walt Disney's Comics and Stories;* for the next issue, he wrote, as well as illustrated, *Donald Duck* and he continued to write and illustrate that feature in almost every issue of *Walt Disney's Comics* for the next twenty-three years.

Barks of course never signed his work, but his crisp, precise drawing style was so distinctive—in comic books otherwise filled with soft, broad drawings—that he was recognized by many children as "the good artist." Barks's *Donald Duck*—the lead story in each issue of *Walt Disney's Comics*—was so popular that when Barks was taken off the feature in 1950 to handle stories in other Disney comic books, reader protests quickly led to his reinstatement. At one point in the early 1950s, *Walt Disney's Comics* was selling three million copies per issue, making it one of the most successful comic books ever published; and a very large part of that success was due to Barks.

During his first ten years in comic books, Barks also wrote and illustrated longer stories—usually thirty-two pages—for the *Donald Duck* comic book. Most of these stories were comic adventures—mixtures of laughter and thrills. Barks sent Donald and his three nephews, Huey,

Dewey, and Louie, to many exotic places, like the jungles of Africa, the outback of Australia, and the desolate moors of Scotland. The best-remembered of these stories is probably *Lost in the Andes,* in which Donald and his nephews went to South America in search of mysterious square eggs. Deep in the Andes, they found not only the eggs but a block-shaped race of people who spoke in the accents of the American Deep South and called their homeland "Plain Awful."

When he started writing and drawing *Donald Duck,* Barks had only Donald and his nephews (and occasionally Donald's girlfriend, Daisy) to work with. For one 1947 story in *Donald Duck,* Barks gave Donald a wealthy, miserly uncle, Scrooge McDuck. Scrooge was a supporting character in the *Donald Duck* stories for the next few years; he was always trying to get more money or protect what he had, and this made him a fertile source of plot ideas. Scrooge finally became so popular that he was given his own comic book in 1952. Like the Barks issues of *Donald Duck,* the quarterly *Uncle Scrooge* combined comedy and adventure; Scrooge's money could—and did—take the ducks any place, from the sunken continent of Atlantis to outer space. *Uncle Scrooge* was tremendously successful, outselling those Disney comic books with characters—like Mickey Mouse—who were more famous but who did not have the good fortune to have their adventures recounted by Carl Barks.

Along the way, Barks created other characters who became more or less established residents of the Disney universe: Donald's incredibly lucky cousin, Gladstone Gander; the eccentric inventor, Gyro Gearloose (a chicken); the Junior Woodchucks of the World (a spoof of the Boy Scouts); the villainous Beagle Boys; the sorceress Magica de Spell.

Barks's stories were so popular, and so good, because he took pains where most writers and cartoonists for "funny animal" comic books did not. He used the ducks in everything from purest slapstick to hair-raising adventures that had only a light flavoring of comedy—but always, he worked to give his stories plausibility. Plausibility in the way the plots and gags were constructed, in the detailed and accurately drawn settings (he made sure that an ancient Persian city *looked* like an ancient Persian city), and above all, in the way his characters talked and behaved. Barks's characters were never puppets; the ducks were always propelled by passions so comically powerful that they could scarcely be contained even within exaggerated faces and bodies. In Barks's stories, the world is very different from the one we know—it is a world of talking ducks, and of huge

"money bins" filled with Scrooge's coins and greenbacks—
but "duck nature" is really human nature, and very much
the same as in our own world. It was by making his characters
so completely recognizable as people, despite their orange
beaks and webbed feet, that Barks won the devotion of so
many readers.

Barks's work was at its richest and funniest in the late
1940s and early 1950s. *Letter to Santa,* the story we have
included here, was published in 1949, in the first issue of a
"giant" comic book—it cost twenty-five cents, instead of the
usual dime—called *Walt Disney's Christmas Parade. Letter* is
a rarity among Barks's longer stories because it is not a
mixture of comedy and adventure but is instead completely
comic from start to finish, like most of the ten-page stories
in *Walt Disney's Comics.*

Letter to Santa was the first story with the "classic"
version of Uncle Scrooge—the cranky old capitalist who is
bursting with energy, and who has so much cash that it
spills around his desk. In the earlier stories, Scrooge was not
as rich or as egomaniacal; in later stories, after he had
gotten his own comic book, Scrooge became a bit more
likable but a bit less funny.

Santa Claus himself appears in *Letter to Santa,* and this
is unusual, because Barks usually avoided characters who
were wholly fanciful even on the terms set by the ducks'
fanciful universe. But when Barks did use such characters—
Santa Claus, or a witch, or a dragon—he presented them
with the same care, the same concern for plausibility,
that he gave to the other elements in his stories; Barks's
Santa is one we can almost believe in. For one thing,
Barks has figured out a way to get his Santa down even
narrow chimneys. Note too that this Santa is a very practical
fellow; he gives the nephews exactly what they want, but
only that—there's no flood of unrequested gifts. And,
typically for Barks, this Santa, by his very existence, creates
more problems than he solves.

Carl Barks retired from comic-book work in 1966,
although he wrote a few stories for the *Junior Woodchucks*
comic book until 1973. He lives now in southern California,
where he has carved out a new (and successful) career as a
painter in oils and water colors.

M.B.

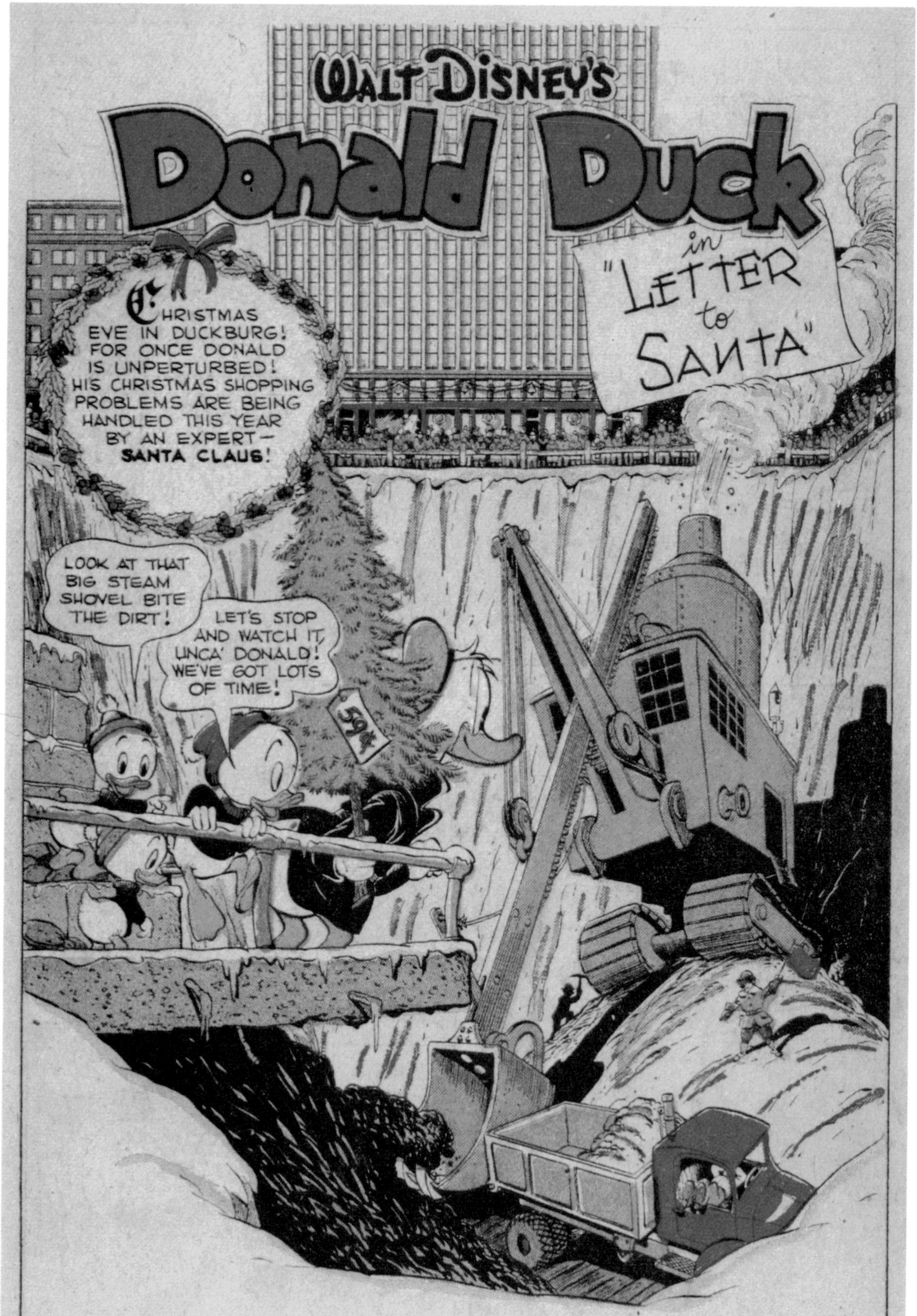
WALT DISNEY'S
Donald Duck
in "LETTER to SANTA"
CHRISTMAS EVE IN DUCKBURG! FOR ONCE DONALD IS UNPERTURBED! HIS CHRISTMAS SHOPPING PROBLEMS ARE BEING HANDLED THIS YEAR BY AN EXPERT— SANTA CLAUS!
LOOK AT THAT BIG STEAM SHOVEL BITE THE DIRT!
LET'S STOP AND WATCH IT, UNCA' DONALD! WE'VE GOT LOTS OF TIME!
59¢

From *Walt Disney's Christmas Parade* No. 1, 1949.

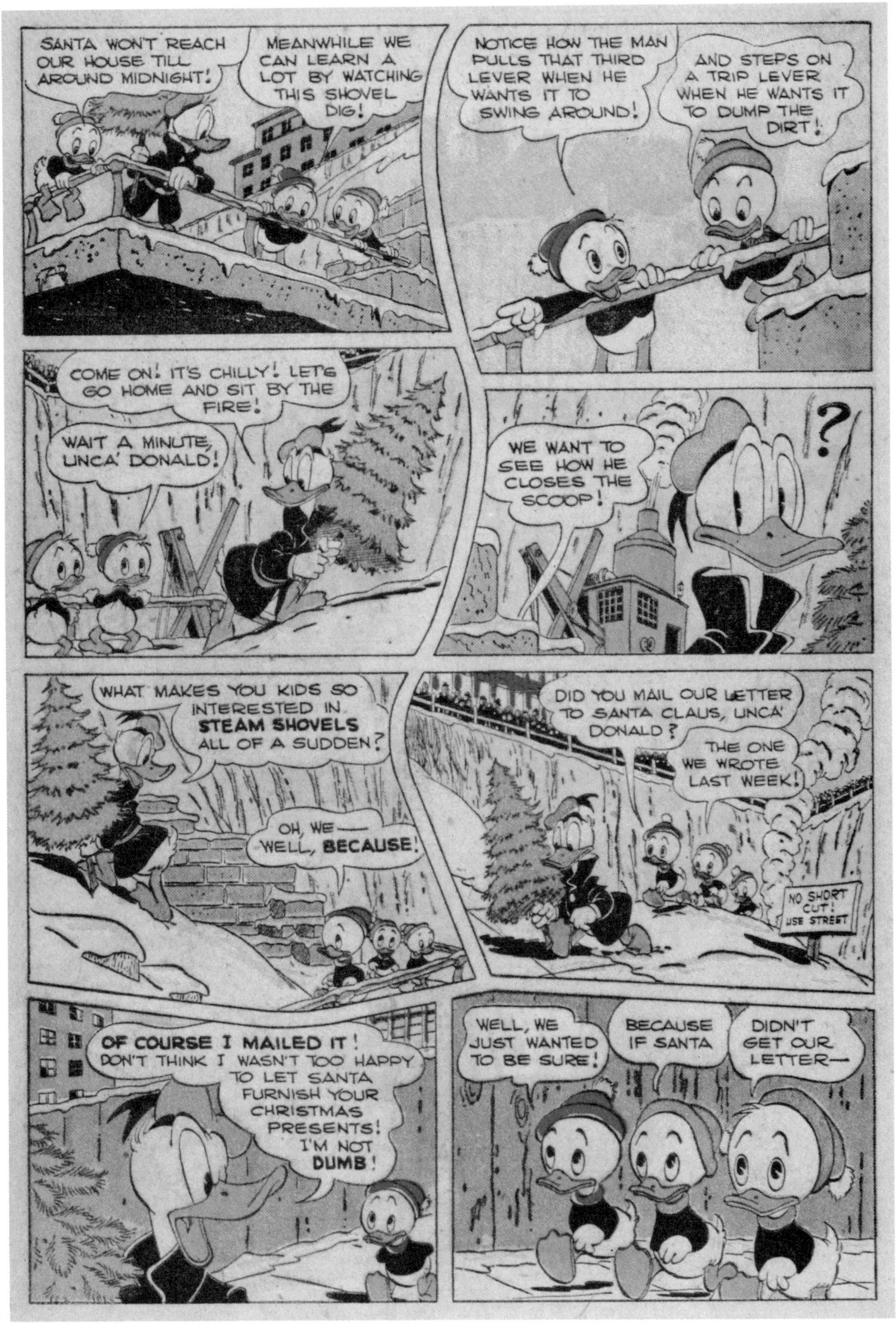
SANTA WON'T REACH OUR HOUSE TILL AROUND MIDNIGHT!
MEANWHILE WE CAN LEARN A LOT BY WATCHING THIS SHOVEL DIG!
NOTICE HOW THE MAN PULLS THAT THIRD LEVER WHEN HE WANTS IT TO SWING AROUND!
AND STEPS ON A TRIP LEVER WHEN HE WANTS IT TO DUMP THE DIRT!
COME ON! IT'S CHILLY! LET'S GO HOME AND SIT BY THE FIRE!
WAIT A MINUTE, UNCA' DONALD!
WE WANT TO SEE HOW HE CLOSES THE SCOOP!
?
WHAT MAKES YOU KIDS SO INTERESTED IN **STEAM SHOVELS** ALL OF A SUDDEN?
OH, WE— WELL, **BECAUSE**!
DID YOU MAIL OUR LETTER TO SANTA CLAUS, UNCA' DONALD?
THE ONE WE WROTE LAST WEEK!
NO SHORT CUT! USE STREET
OF COURSE I MAILED IT! DON'T THINK I WASN'T TOO HAPPY TO LET SANTA FURNISH YOUR CHRISTMAS PRESENTS! I'M NOT **DUMB**!
WELL, WE JUST WANTED TO BE SURE!
BECAUSE IF SANTA
DIDN'T GET OUR LETTER—

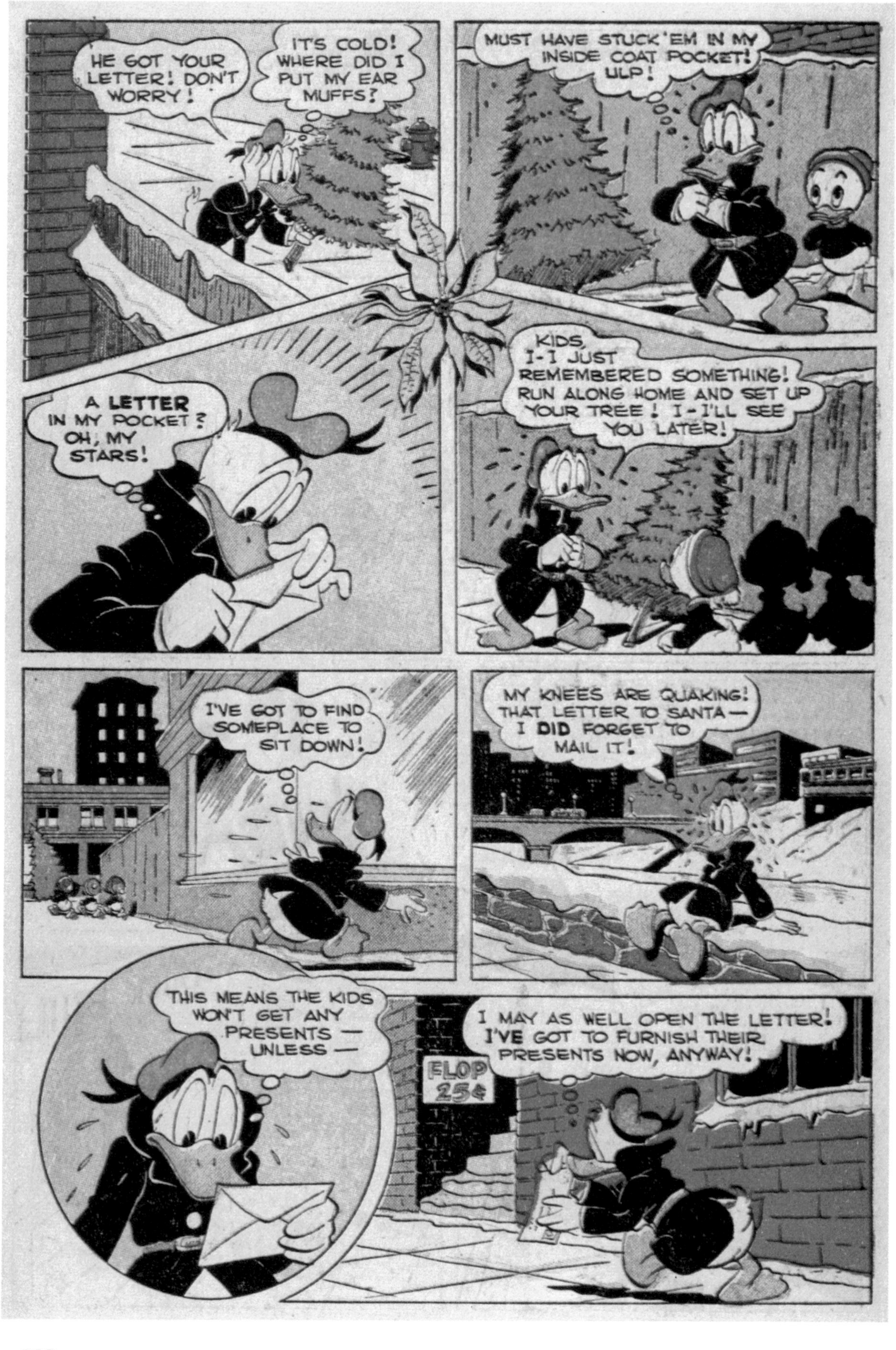
HE GOT YOUR LETTER! DON'T WORRY!
IT'S COLD! WHERE DID I PUT MY EAR MUFFS?
MUST HAVE STUCK 'EM IN MY INSIDE COAT POCKET! ULP!
A LETTER IN MY POCKET? OH, MY STARS!
KIDS, I-I JUST REMEMBERED SOMETHING! RUN ALONG HOME AND SET UP YOUR TREE! I-I'LL SEE YOU LATER!
I'VE GOT TO FIND SOMEPLACE TO SIT DOWN!
MY KNEES ARE QUAKING! THAT LETTER TO SANTA — I DID FORGET TO MAIL IT!
THIS MEANS THE KIDS WON'T GET ANY PRESENTS — UNLESS —
FLOP 25¢
I MAY AS WELL OPEN THE LETTER! I'VE GOT TO FURNISH THEIR PRESENTS NOW, ANYWAY!

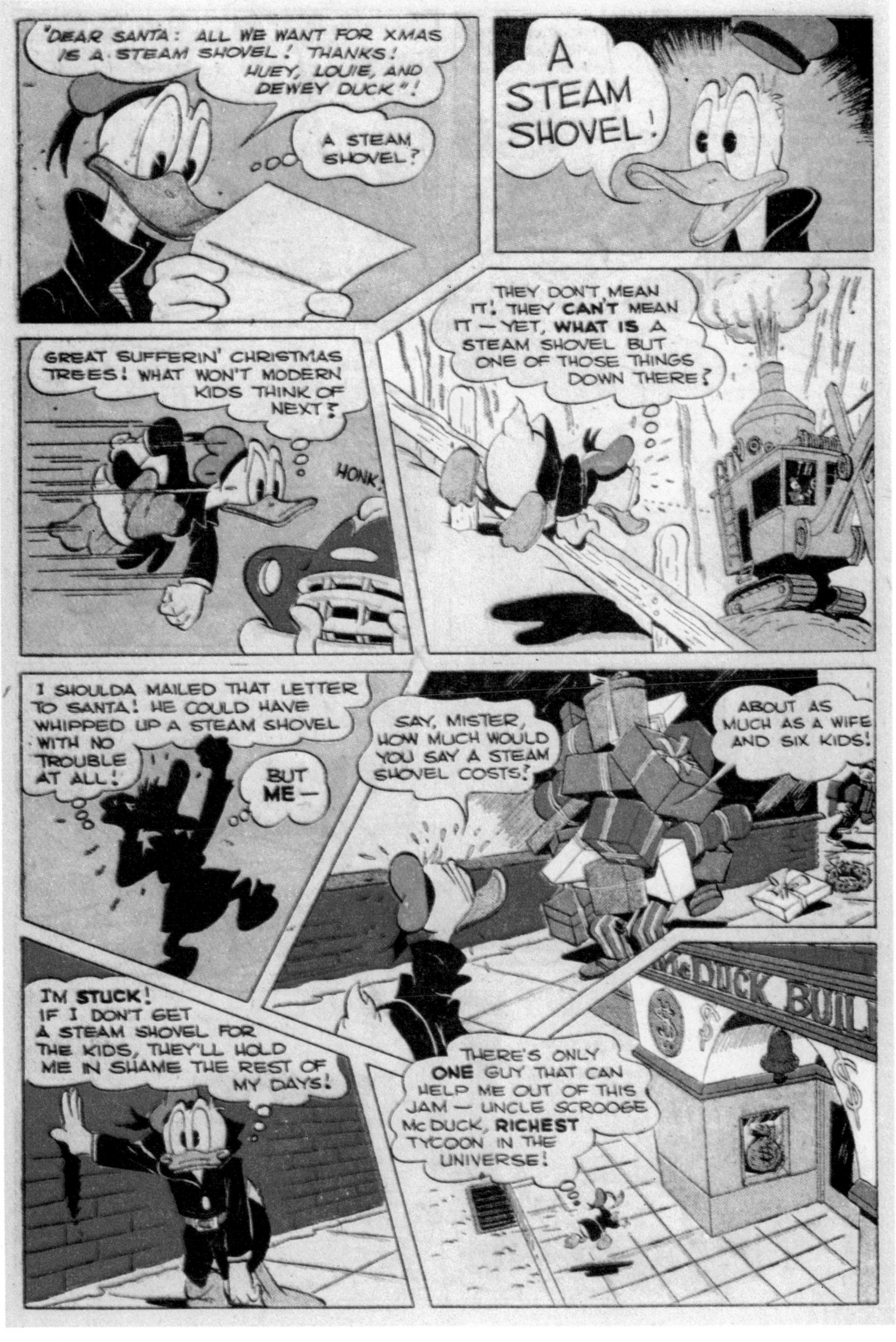
"DEAR SANTA: ALL WE WANT FOR XMAS IS A STEAM SHOVEL! THANKS! HUEY, LOUIE, AND DEWEY DUCK"!
A STEAM SHOVEL?
A STEAM SHOVEL!
GREAT SUFFERIN' CHRISTMAS TREES! WHAT WON'T MODERN KIDS THINK OF NEXT?
HONK!
THEY DON'T MEAN IT! THEY CAN'T MEAN IT — YET, WHAT IS A STEAM SHOVEL BUT ONE OF THOSE THINGS DOWN THERE?
I SHOULDA MAILED THAT LETTER TO SANTA! HE COULD HAVE WHIPPED UP A STEAM SHOVEL WITH NO TROUBLE AT ALL!
BUT ME—
SAY, MISTER, HOW MUCH WOULD YOU SAY A STEAM SHOVEL COSTS?
ABOUT AS MUCH AS A WIFE AND SIX KIDS!
I'M STUCK! IF I DON'T GET A STEAM SHOVEL FOR THE KIDS, THEY'LL HOLD ME IN SHAME THE REST OF MY DAYS!
THERE'S ONLY ONE GUY THAT CAN HELP ME OUT OF THIS JAM — UNCLE SCROOGE McDUCK, RICHEST TYCOON IN THE UNIVERSE!
McDUCK BUIL

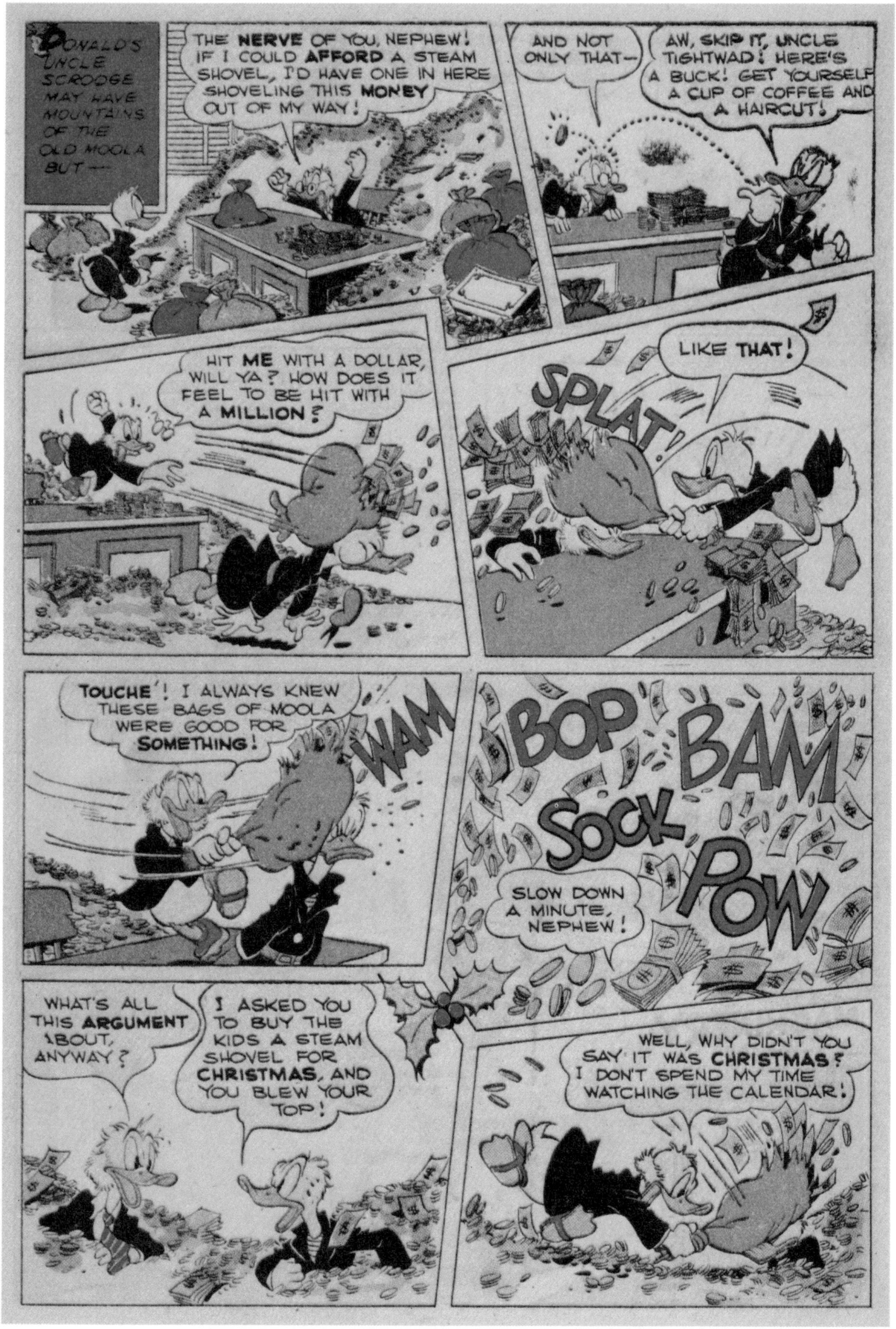
DONALD'S UNCLE SCROOGE MAY HAVE MOUNTAINS OF THE OLD MOOLA BUT---
THE NERVE OF YOU, NEPHEW! IF I COULD AFFORD A STEAM SHOVEL, I'D HAVE ONE IN HERE SHOVELING THIS MONEY OUT OF MY WAY!
AND NOT ONLY THAT--
AW, SKIP IT, UNCLE TIGHTWAD! HERE'S A BUCK! GET YOURSELF A CUP OF COFFEE AND A HAIRCUT!
HIT ME WITH A DOLLAR, WILL YA? HOW DOES IT FEEL TO BE HIT WITH A MILLION?
SPLAT!
LIKE THAT!
TOUCHE'! I ALWAYS KNEW THESE BAGS OF MOOLA WERE GOOD FOR SOMETHING!
WAM
BOP
BAM
SOCK
POW
SLOW DOWN A MINUTE, NEPHEW!
WHAT'S ALL THIS ARGUMENT ABOUT, ANYWAY?
I ASKED YOU TO BUY THE KIDS A STEAM SHOVEL FOR CHRISTMAS, AND YOU BLEW YOUR TOP!
WELL, WHY DIDN'T YOU SAY IT WAS CHRISTMAS? I DON'T SPEND MY TIME WATCHING THE CALENDAR!

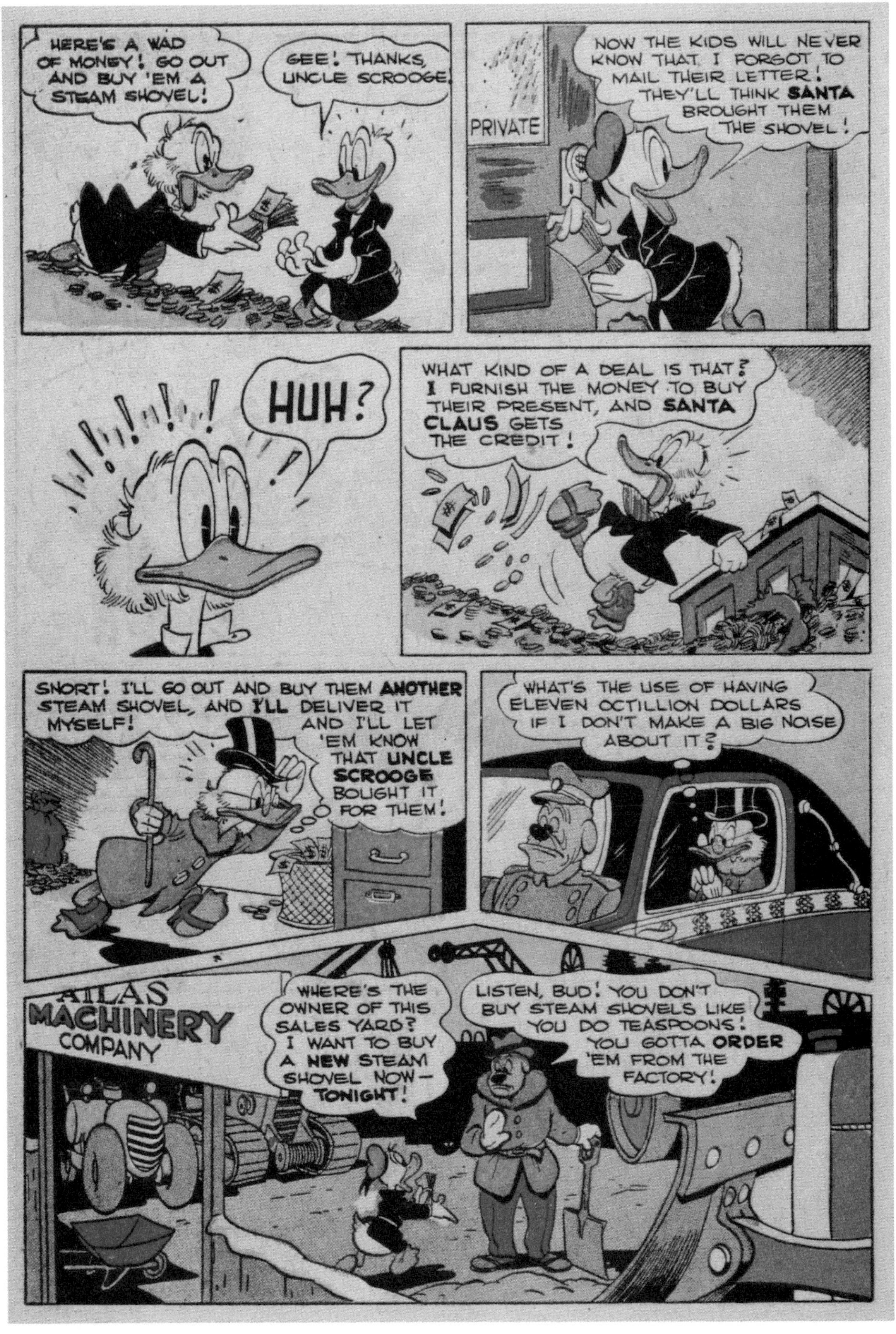
HERE'S A WAD OF MONEY! GO OUT AND BUY 'EM A STEAM SHOVEL!
GEE! THANKS, UNCLE SCROOGE!
PRIVATE
NOW THE KIDS WILL NEVER KNOW THAT I FORGOT TO MAIL THEIR LETTER! THEY'LL THINK SANTA BROUGHT THEM THE SHOVEL!
HUH?
WHAT KIND OF A DEAL IS THAT? I FURNISH THE MONEY TO BUY THEIR PRESENT, AND SANTA CLAUS GETS THE CREDIT!
SNORT! I'LL GO OUT AND BUY THEM ANOTHER STEAM SHOVEL, AND I'LL DELIVER IT MYSELF!
AND I'LL LET 'EM KNOW THAT UNCLE SCROOGE BOUGHT IT FOR THEM!
WHAT'S THE USE OF HAVING ELEVEN OCTILLION DOLLARS IF I DON'T MAKE A BIG NOISE ABOUT IT?
ATLAS MACHINERY COMPANY
WHERE'S THE OWNER OF THIS SALES YARD? I WANT TO BUY A NEW STEAM SHOVEL NOW—TONIGHT!
LISTEN, BUD! YOU DON'T BUY STEAM SHOVELS LIKE YOU DO TEASPOONS! YOU GOTTA ORDER 'EM FROM THE FACTORY!

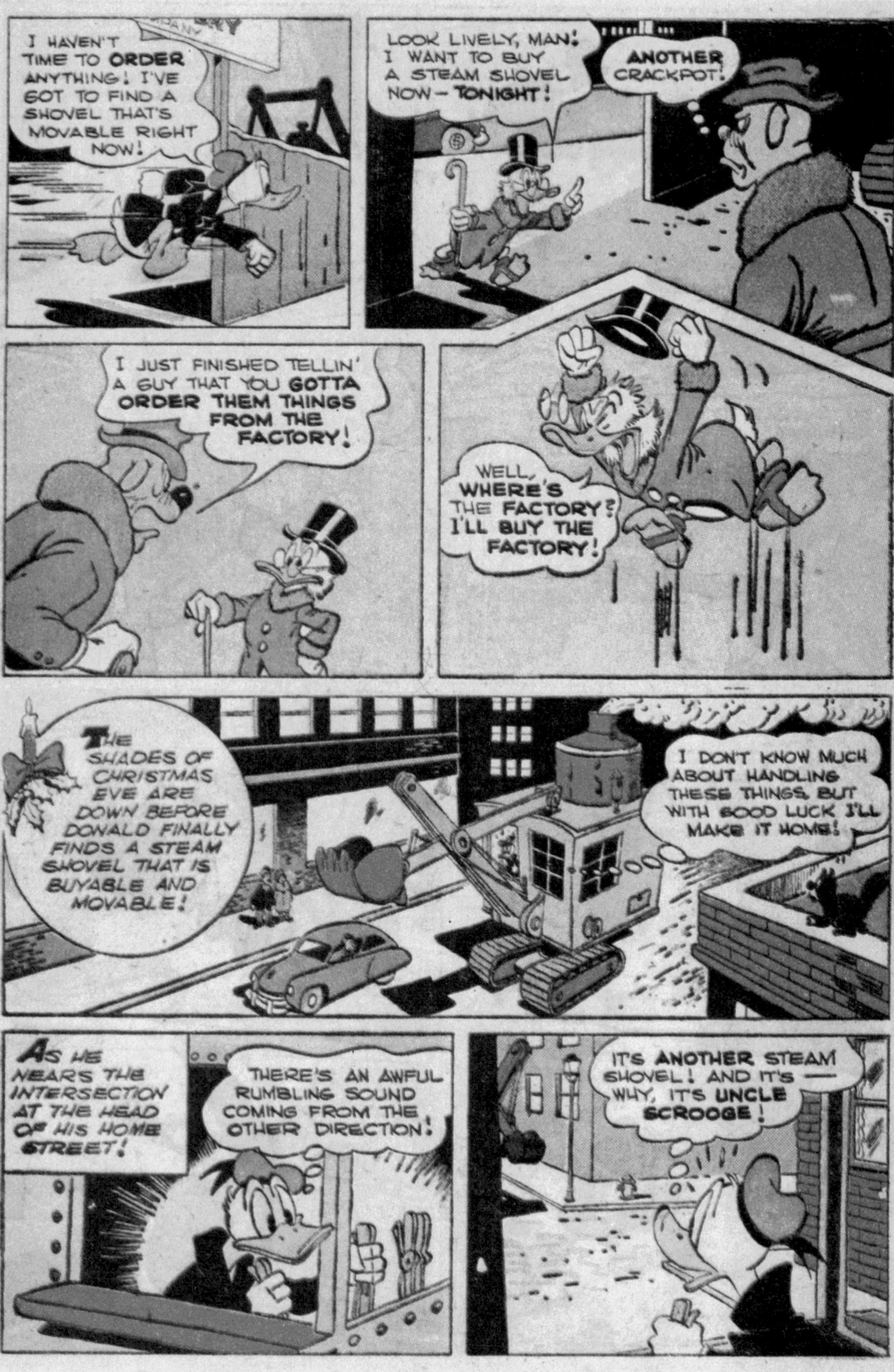
I HAVEN'T TIME TO **ORDER** ANYTHING! I'VE GOT TO FIND A SHOVEL THAT'S MOVABLE RIGHT NOW!
LOOK LIVELY, MAN! I WANT TO BUY A STEAM SHOVEL NOW—**TONIGHT**!
ANOTHER CRACKPOT!
I JUST FINISHED TELLIN' A GUY THAT YOU **GOTTA ORDER THEM THINGS FROM THE FACTORY**!
WELL, **WHERE'S** THE **FACTORY**? **I'LL BUY THE FACTORY**!
THE SHADES OF CHRISTMAS EVE ARE DOWN BEFORE DONALD FINALLY FINDS A STEAM SHOVEL THAT IS BUYABLE AND MOVABLE!
I DON'T KNOW MUCH ABOUT HANDLING THESE THINGS, BUT WITH GOOD LUCK **I'LL** MAKE IT HOME!
AS HE NEARS THE INTERSECTION AT THE HEAD OF HIS HOME STREET!
THERE'S AN AWFUL RUMBLING SOUND COMING FROM THE OTHER DIRECTION!
IT'S **ANOTHER** STEAM SHOVEL! AND IT'S — WHY, IT'S **UNCLE SCROOGE**!

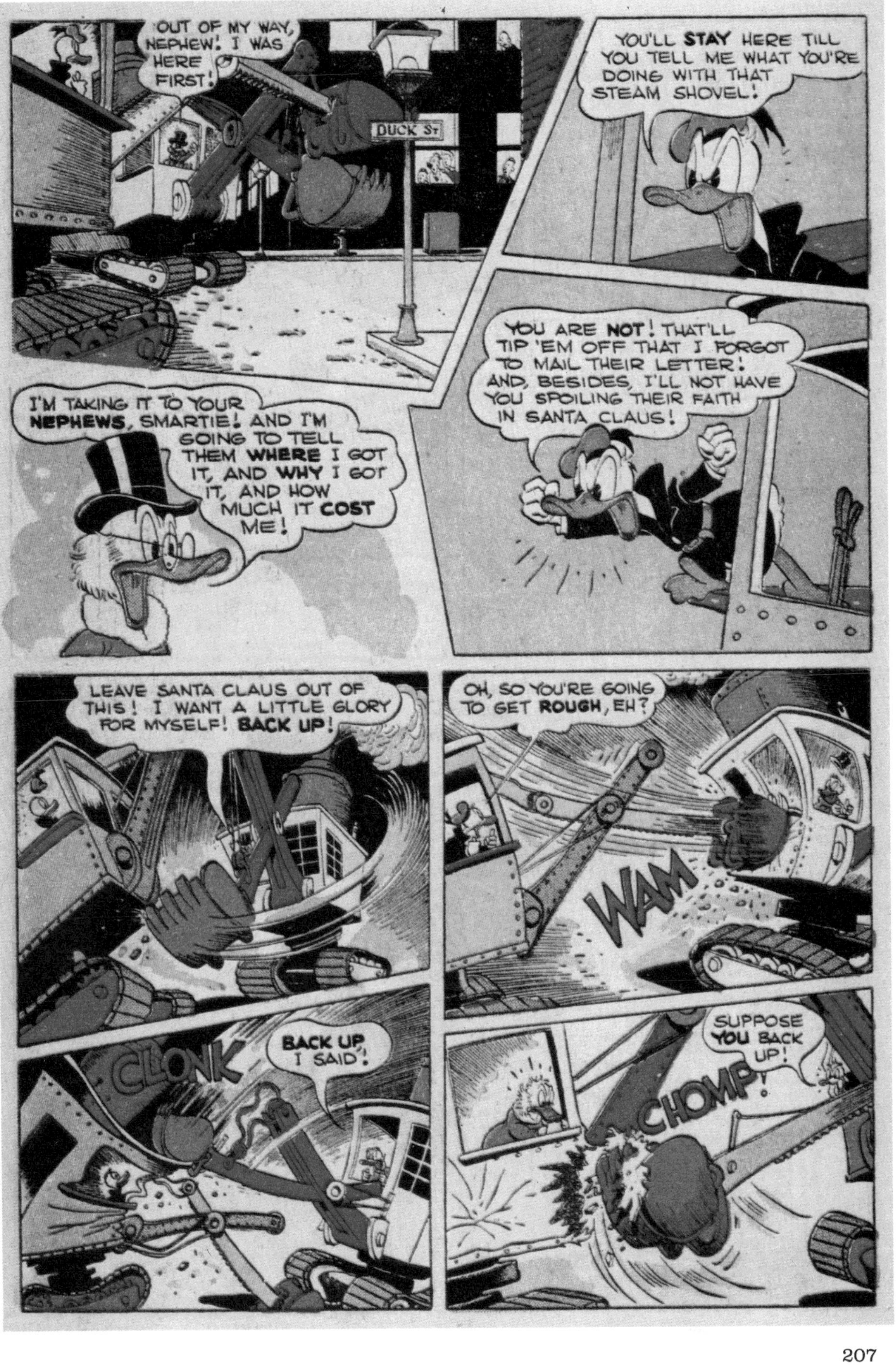

OUT OF MY WAY, NEPHEW! I WAS HERE FIRST!
DUCK St
YOU'LL STAY HERE TILL YOU TELL ME WHAT YOU'RE DOING WITH THAT STEAM SHOVEL!
I'M TAKING IT TO YOUR NEPHEWS, SMARTIE! AND I'M GOING TO TELL THEM WHERE I GOT IT, AND WHY I GOT IT, AND HOW MUCH IT COST ME!
YOU ARE NOT! THAT'LL TIP 'EM OFF THAT I FORGOT TO MAIL THEIR LETTER! AND, BESIDES, I'LL NOT HAVE YOU SPOILING THEIR FAITH IN SANTA CLAUS!
LEAVE SANTA CLAUS OUT OF THIS! I WANT A LITTLE GLORY FOR MYSELF! BACK UP!
OH, SO YOU'RE GOING TO GET ROUGH, EH?
WAM
CLONK
BACK UP I SAID!
SUPPOSE YOU BACK UP!
CHOMP!

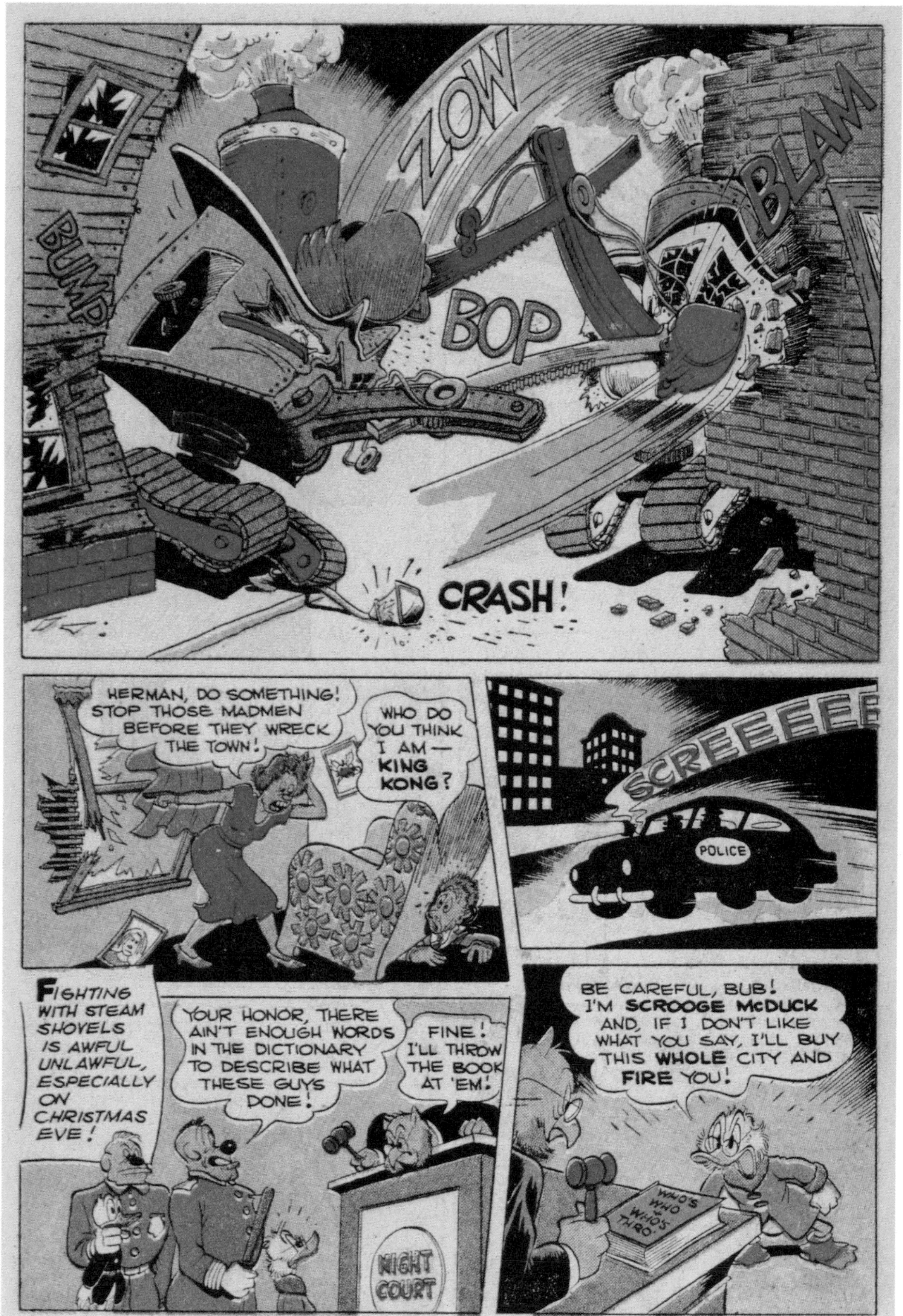
BUMP
ZOW
BLAM
BOP
CRASH!
HERMAN, DO SOMETHING! STOP THOSE MADMEN BEFORE THEY WRECK THE TOWN!
WHO DO YOU THINK I AM— KING KONG?
SCREEEEEE
POLICE
FIGHTING WITH STEAM SHOVELS IS AWFUL UNLAWFUL, ESPECIALLY ON CHRISTMAS EVE!
YOUR HONOR, THERE AIN'T ENOUGH WORDS IN THE DICTIONARY TO DESCRIBE WHAT THESE GUYS DONE!
FINE! I'LL THROW THE BOOK AT 'EM!
NIGHT COURT
BE CAREFUL, BUB! I'M SCROOGE McDUCK AND, IF I DON'T LIKE WHAT YOU SAY, I'LL BUY THIS WHOLE CITY AND FIRE YOU!
WHO'S WHO WHO'S THRO'

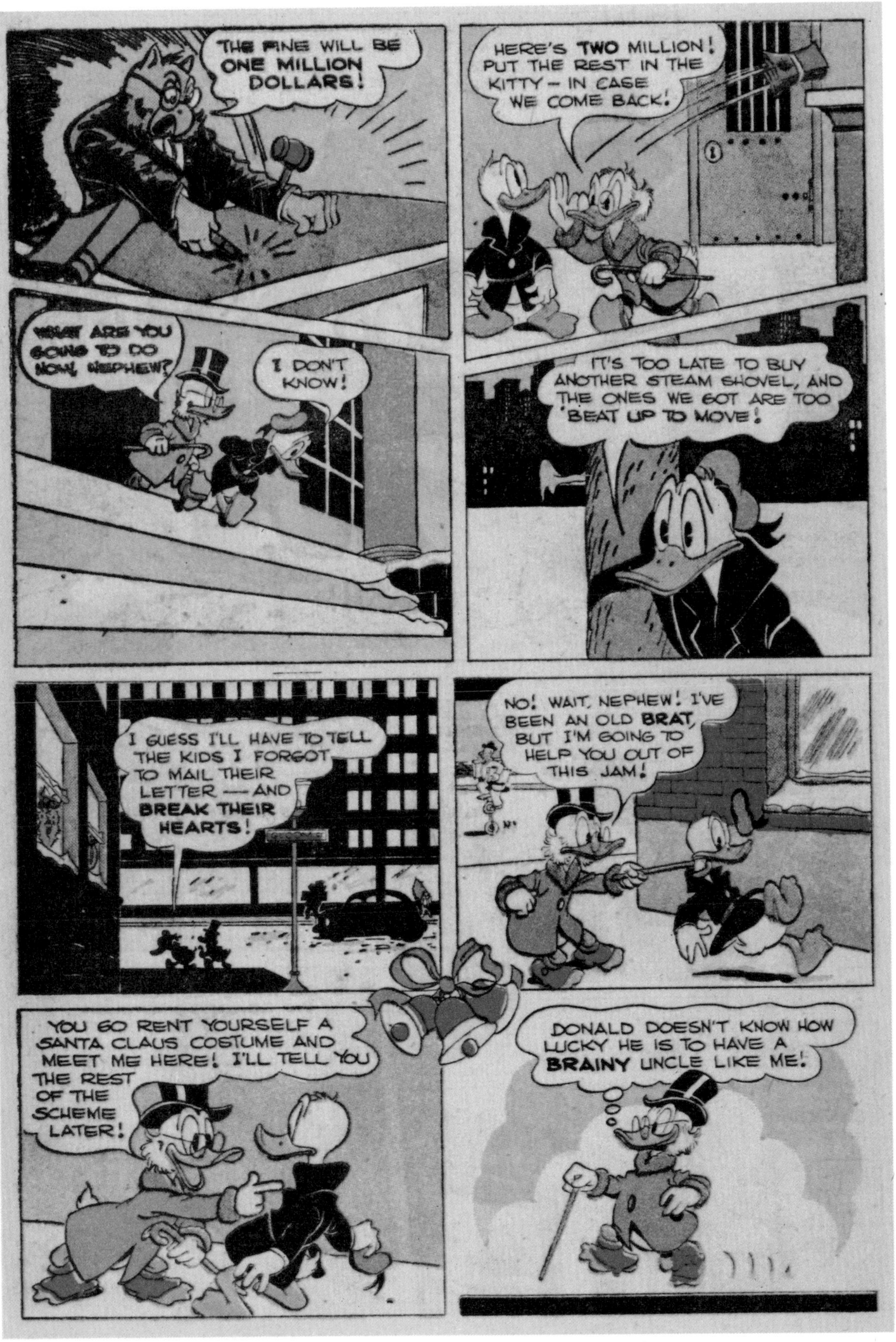
THE FINE WILL BE ONE MILLION DOLLARS!
HERE'S TWO MILLION! PUT THE REST IN THE KITTY — IN CASE WE COME BACK!
WHAT ARE YOU GOING TO DO NOW, NEPHEW?
I DON'T KNOW!
IT'S TOO LATE TO BUY ANOTHER STEAM SHOVEL, AND THE ONES WE GOT ARE TOO BEAT UP TO MOVE!
I GUESS I'LL HAVE TO TELL THE KIDS I FORGOT TO MAIL THEIR LETTER — AND BREAK THEIR HEARTS!
NO! WAIT, NEPHEW! I'VE BEEN AN OLD BRAT, BUT I'M GOING TO HELP YOU OUT OF THIS JAM!
YOU GO RENT YOURSELF A SANTA CLAUS COSTUME AND MEET ME HERE! I'LL TELL YOU THE REST OF THE SCHEME LATER!
DONALD DOESN'T KNOW HOW LUCKY HE IS TO HAVE A BRAINY UNCLE LIKE ME!

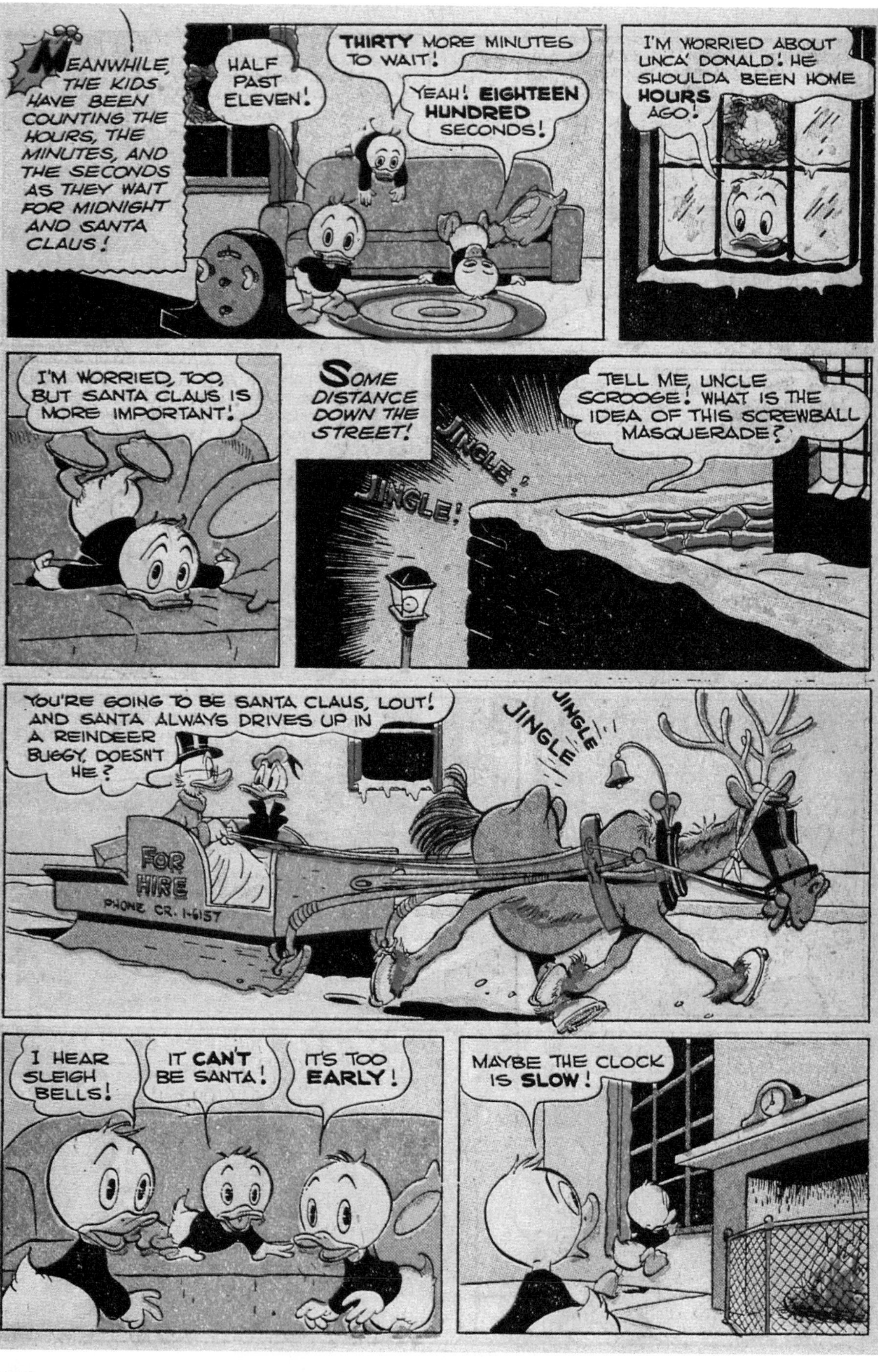
MEANWHILE, THE KIDS HAVE BEEN COUNTING THE HOURS, THE MINUTES, AND THE SECONDS AS THEY WAIT FOR MIDNIGHT AND SANTA CLAUS!
HALF PAST ELEVEN!
THIRTY MORE MINUTES TO WAIT!
YEAH! EIGHTEEN HUNDRED SECONDS!
I'M WORRIED ABOUT UNCA' DONALD! HE SHOULDA BEEN HOME HOURS AGO!
I'M WORRIED, TOO, BUT SANTA CLAUS IS MORE IMPORTANT!
SOME DISTANCE DOWN THE STREET!
JINGLE!
JINGLE!
TELL ME, UNCLE SCROOGE! WHAT IS THE IDEA OF THIS SCREWBALL MASQUERADE?
YOU'RE GOING TO BE SANTA CLAUS, LOUT! AND SANTA ALWAYS DRIVES UP IN A REINDEER BUGGY, DOESN'T HE?
JINGLE
JINGLE
FOR HIRE
PHONE CR. 1-6157
I HEAR SLEIGH BELLS!
IT CAN'T BE SANTA!
IT'S TOO EARLY!
MAYBE THE CLOCK IS SLOW!

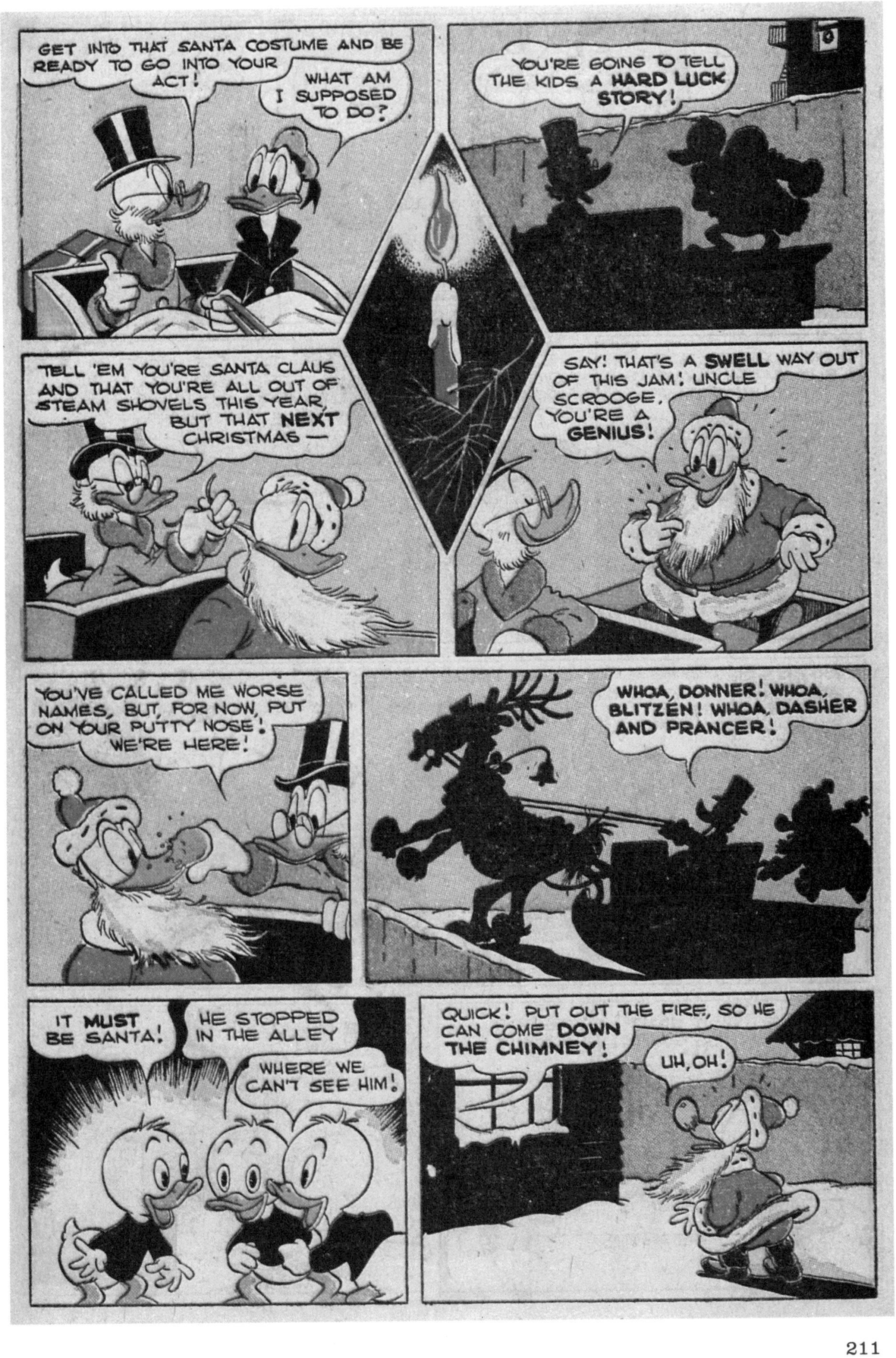
GET INTO THAT SANTA COSTUME AND BE READY TO GO INTO YOUR ACT!
WHAT AM I SUPPOSED TO DO?
YOU'RE GOING TO TELL THE KIDS A **HARD LUCK STORY**!
TELL 'EM YOU'RE SANTA CLAUS AND THAT YOU'RE ALL OUT OF STEAM SHOVELS THIS YEAR, BUT THAT **NEXT** CHRISTMAS —
SAY! THAT'S A **SWELL** WAY OUT OF THIS JAM! UNCLE SCROOGE, YOU'RE A **GENIUS**!
YOU'VE CALLED ME WORSE NAMES, BUT, FOR NOW, PUT ON YOUR PUTTY NOSE! WE'RE HERE!
WHOA, DONNER! WHOA, BLITZEN! WHOA, DASHER AND PRANCER!
IT **MUST** BE SANTA!
HE STOPPED IN THE ALLEY
WHERE WE CAN'T SEE HIM!
QUICK! PUT OUT THE FIRE, SO HE CAN COME **DOWN THE CHIMNEY**!
UH, OH!

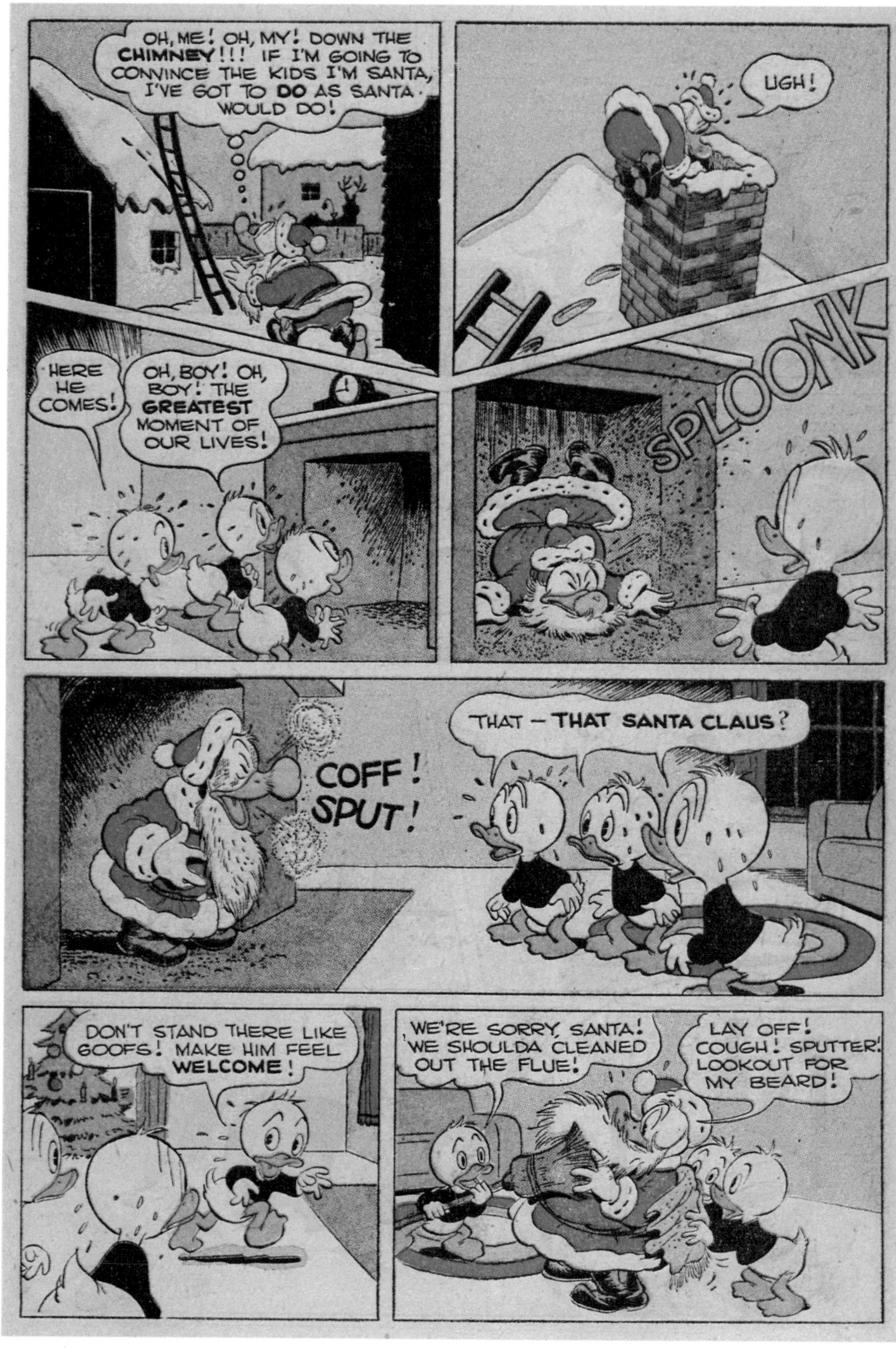
OH, ME! OH, MY! DOWN THE CHIMNEY!!! IF I'M GOING TO CONVINCE THE KIDS I'M SANTA, I'VE GOT TO DO AS SANTA WOULD DO!
UGH!
HERE HE COMES!
OH, BOY! OH, BOY! THE GREATEST MOMENT OF OUR LIVES!
SPLOONK
THAT — THAT SANTA CLAUS?
COFF! SPUT!
DON'T STAND THERE LIKE GOOFS! MAKE HIM FEEL WELCOME!
WE'RE SORRY, SANTA! WE SHOULDA CLEANED OUT THE FLUE!
LAY OFF! COUGH! SPUTTER! LOOKOUT FOR MY BEARD!

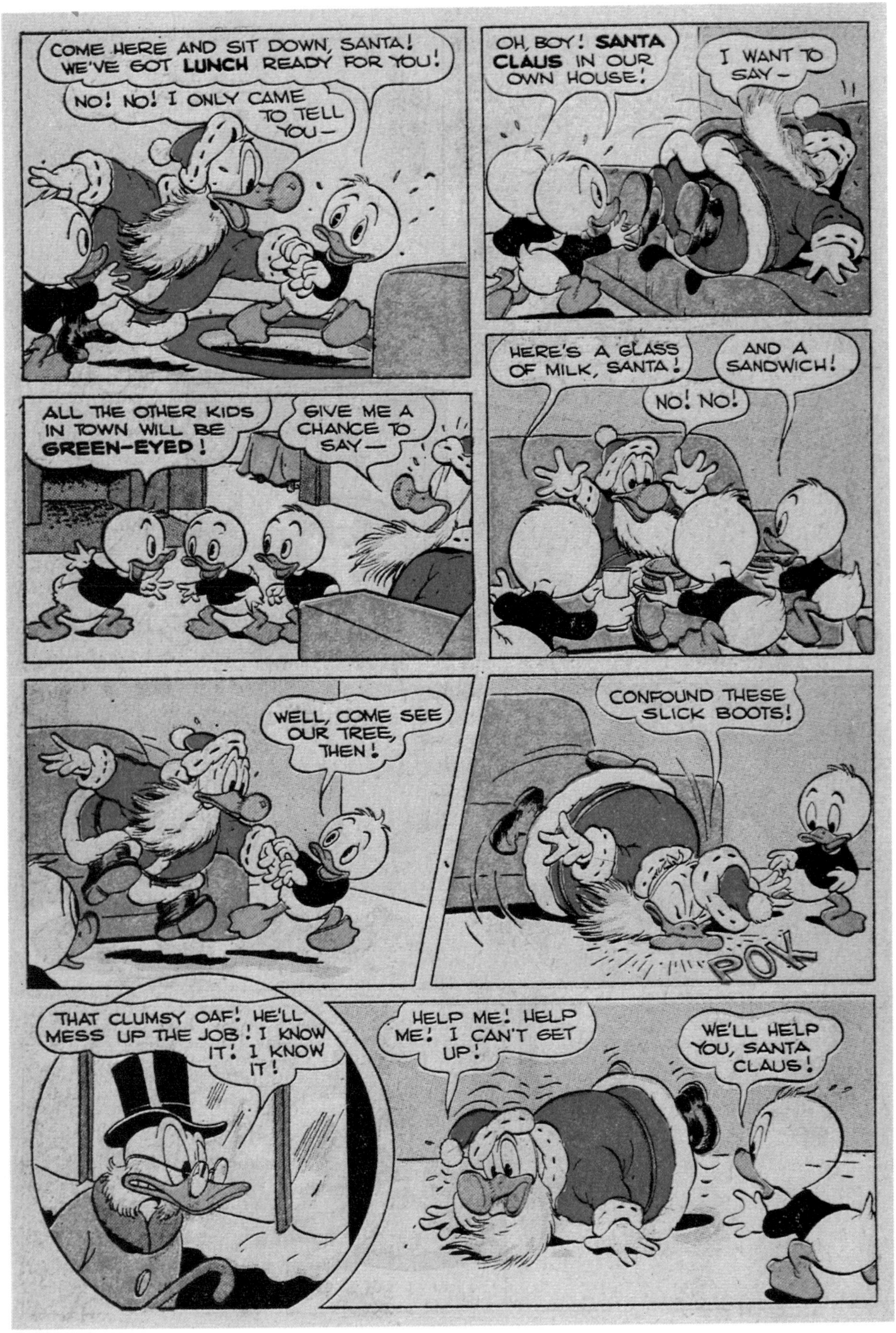

COME HERE AND SIT DOWN, SANTA! WE'VE GOT LUNCH READY FOR YOU!
NO! NO! I ONLY CAME TO TELL YOU—
OH, BOY! SANTA CLAUS IN OUR OWN HOUSE!
I WANT TO SAY—
ALL THE OTHER KIDS IN TOWN WILL BE GREEN-EYED!
GIVE ME A CHANCE TO SAY—
HERE'S A GLASS OF MILK, SANTA!
AND A SANDWICH!
NO! NO!
WELL, COME SEE OUR TREE, THEN!
CONFOUND THESE SLICK BOOTS!
POK
THAT CLUMSY OAF! HE'LL MESS UP THE JOB! I KNOW IT! I KNOW IT!
HELP ME! HELP ME! I CAN'T GET UP!
WE'LL HELP YOU, SANTA CLAUS!

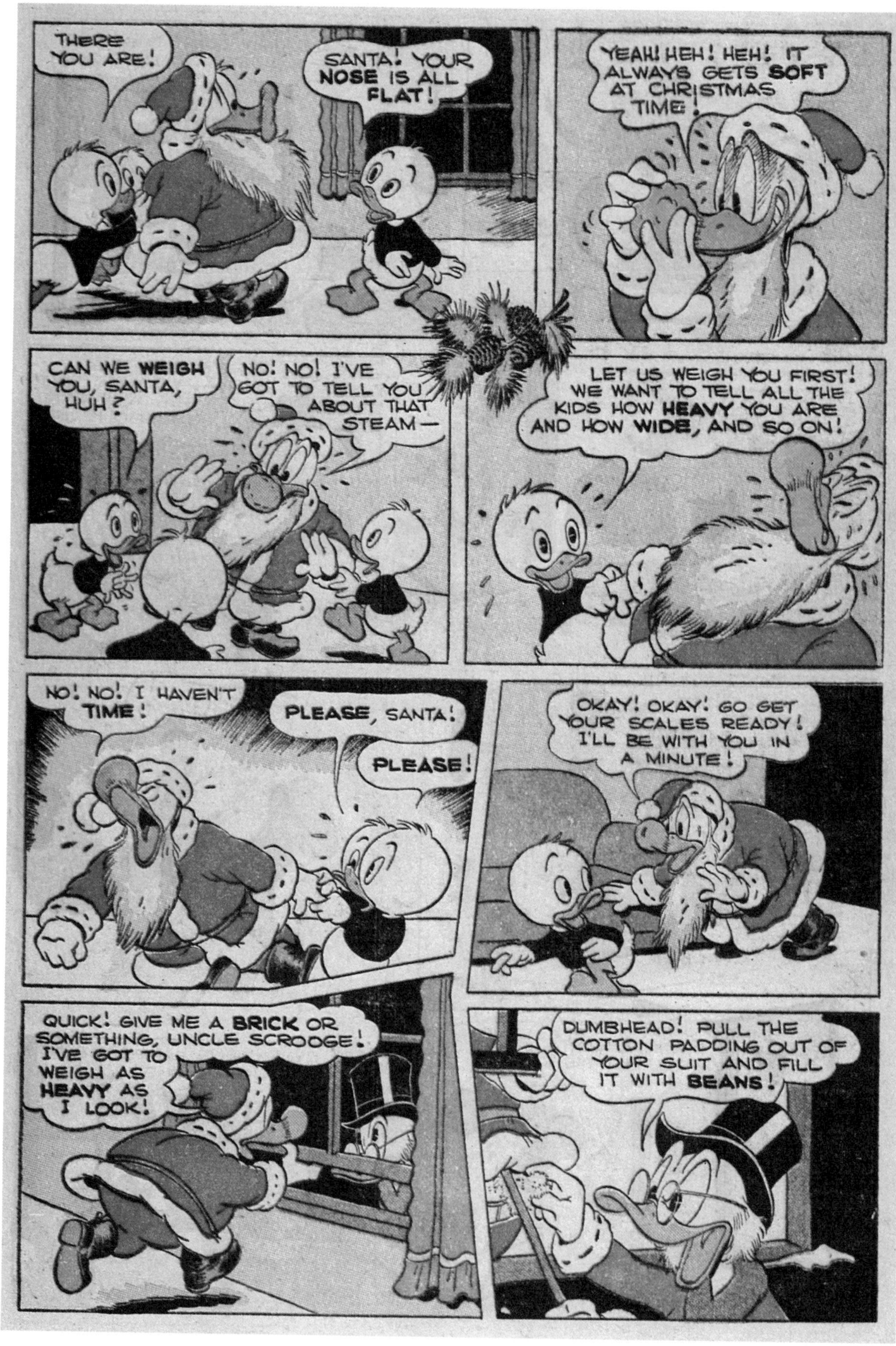
THERE YOU ARE!
SANTA! YOUR NOSE IS ALL FLAT!
YEAH! HEH! HEH! IT ALWAYS GETS SOFT AT CHRISTMAS TIME!
CAN WE WEIGH YOU, SANTA, HUH?
NO! NO! I'VE GOT TO TELL YOU ABOUT THAT STEAM—
LET US WEIGH YOU FIRST! WE WANT TO TELL ALL THE KIDS HOW HEAVY YOU ARE AND HOW WIDE, AND SO ON!
NO! NO! I HAVEN'T TIME!
PLEASE, SANTA!
PLEASE!
OKAY! OKAY! GO GET YOUR SCALES READY! I'LL BE WITH YOU IN A MINUTE!
QUICK! GIVE ME A BRICK OR SOMETHING, UNCLE SCROOGE! I'VE GOT TO WEIGH AS HEAVY AS I LOOK!
DUMBHEAD! PULL THE COTTON PADDING OUT OF YOUR SUIT AND FILL IT WITH BEANS!

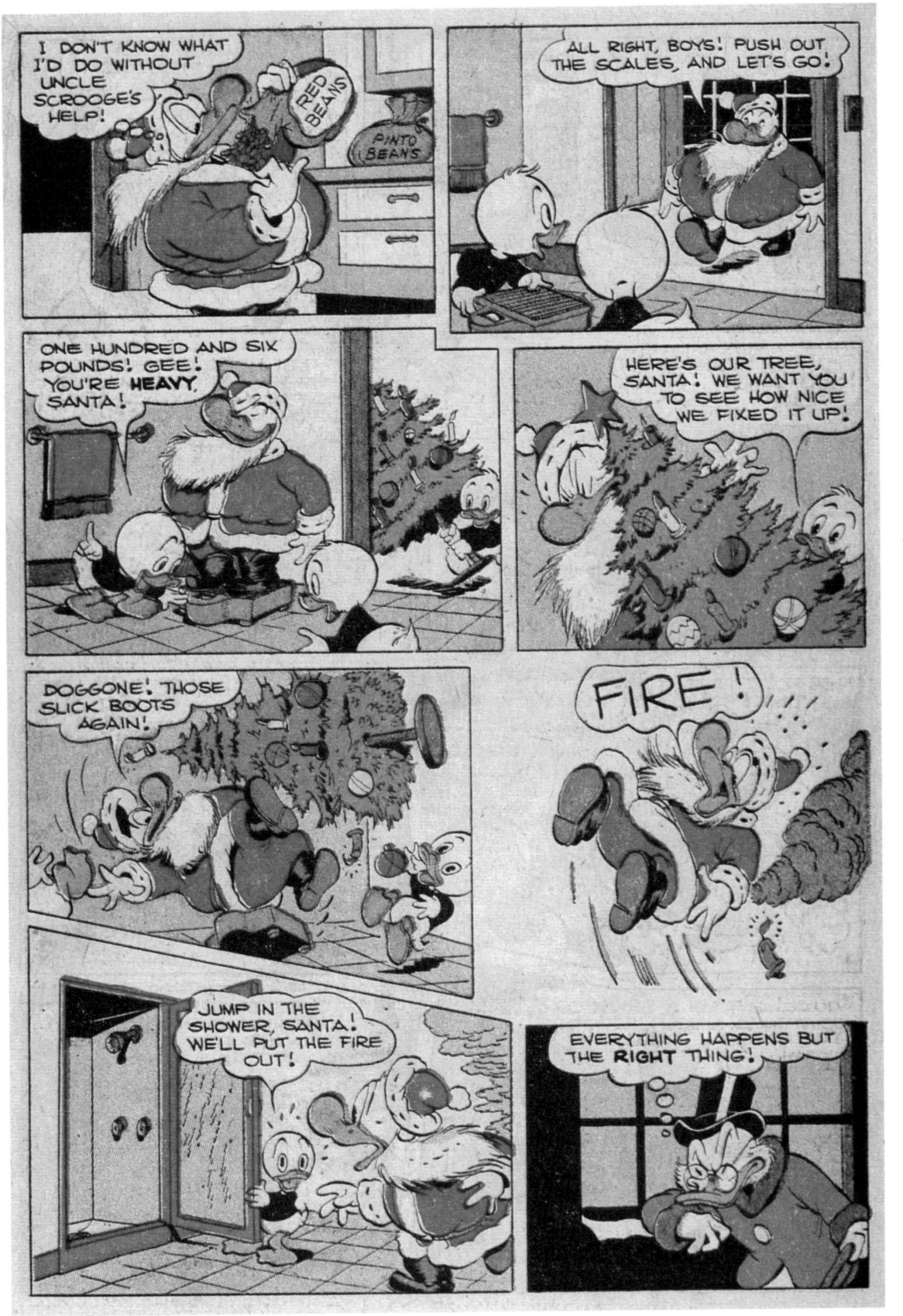
I DON'T KNOW WHAT I'D DO WITHOUT UNCLE SCROOGE'S HELP!
RED BEANS
PINTO BEANS
ALL RIGHT, BOYS! PUSH OUT THE SCALES, AND LET'S GO!
ONE HUNDRED AND SIX POUNDS! GEE! YOU'RE **HEAVY**, SANTA!
HERE'S OUR TREE, SANTA! WE WANT YOU TO SEE HOW NICE WE FIXED IT UP!
DOGGONE! THOSE SLICK BOOTS AGAIN!
FIRE!
JUMP IN THE SHOWER, SANTA! WE'LL PUT THE FIRE OUT!
EVERYTHING HAPPENS BUT THE **RIGHT** THING!

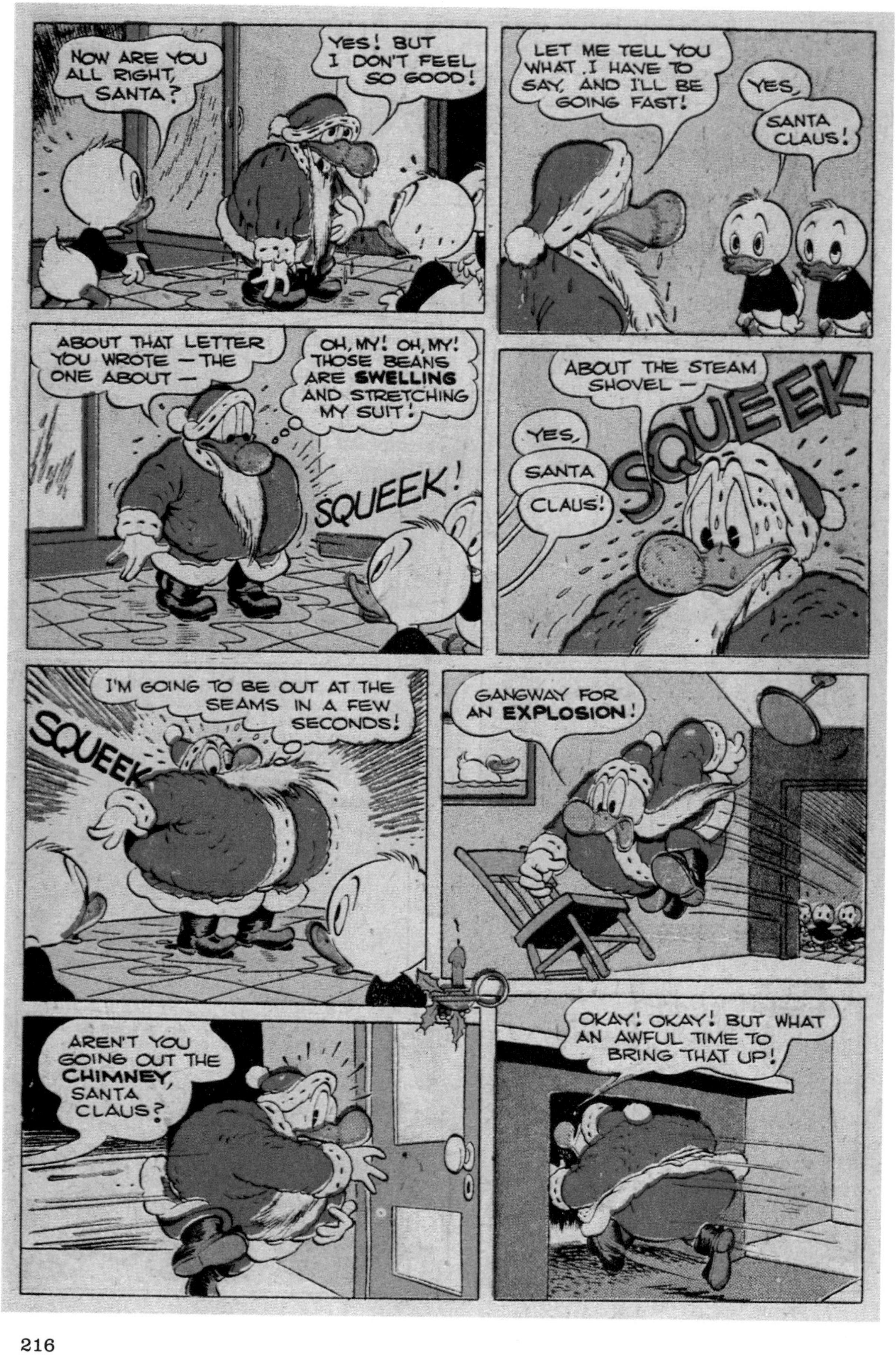

NOW ARE YOU ALL RIGHT, SANTA?
YES! BUT I DON'T FEEL SO GOOD!
LET ME TELL YOU WHAT I HAVE TO SAY, AND I'LL BE GOING FAST!
YES,
SANTA CLAUS!
ABOUT THAT LETTER YOU WROTE — THE ONE ABOUT —
OH, MY! OH, MY! THOSE BEANS ARE **SWELLING** AND STRETCHING MY SUIT!
SQUEEK!
ABOUT THE STEAM SHOVEL —
YES,
SANTA
CLAUS!
SQUEEK
I'M GOING TO BE OUT AT THE SEAMS IN A FEW SECONDS!
SQUEEK
GANGWAY FOR AN **EXPLOSION**!
AREN'T YOU GOING OUT THE **CHIMNEY**, SANTA CLAUS?
OKAY! OKAY! BUT WHAT AN AWFUL TIME TO BRING THAT UP!

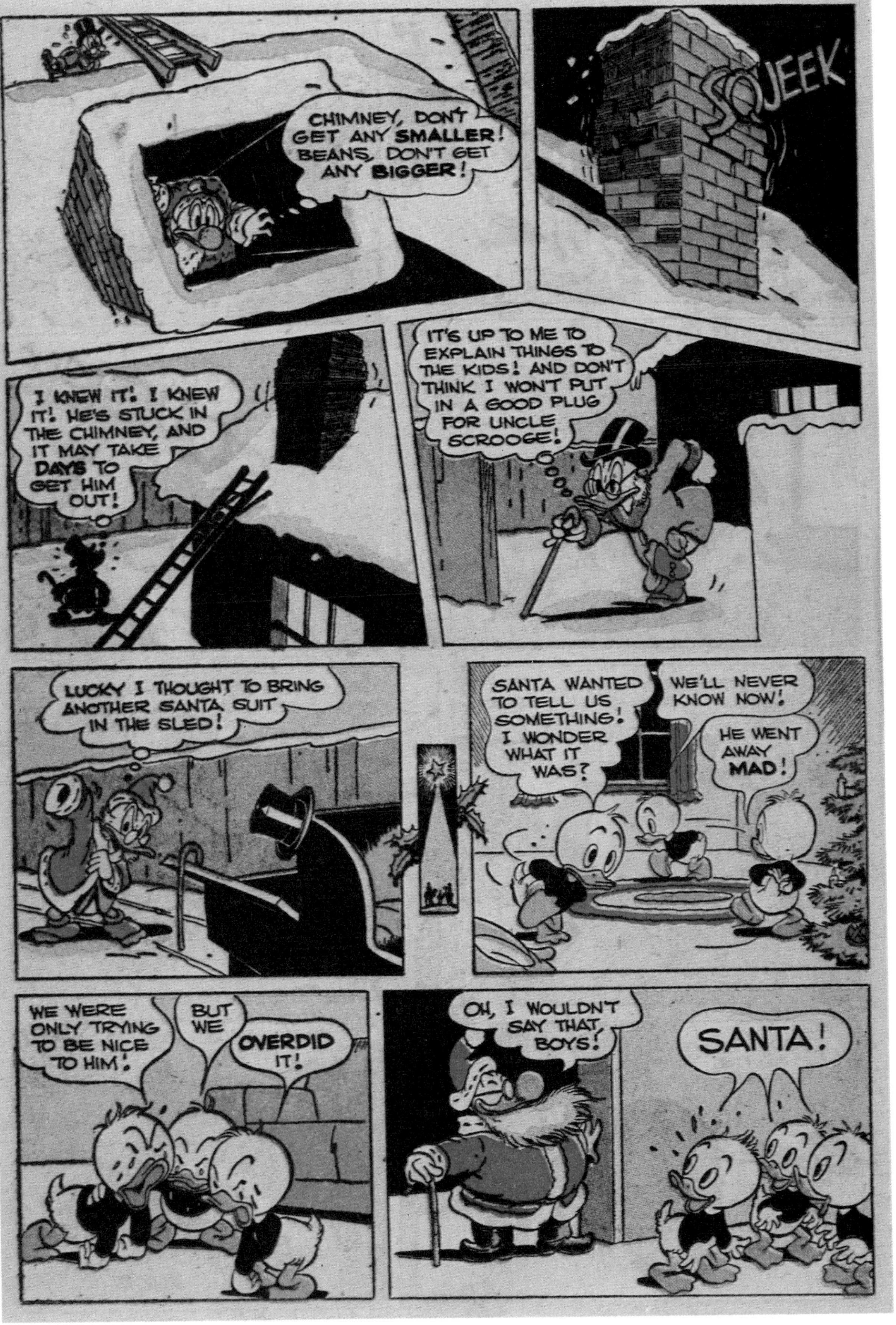

CHIMNEY, DON'T GET ANY SMALLER! BEANS, DON'T GET ANY BIGGER!
SQUEEK
I KNEW IT! I KNEW IT! HE'S STUCK IN THE CHIMNEY, AND IT MAY TAKE DAYS TO GET HIM OUT!
IT'S UP TO ME TO EXPLAIN THINGS TO THE KIDS! AND DON'T THINK I WON'T PUT IN A GOOD PLUG FOR UNCLE SCROOGE!
LUCKY I THOUGHT TO BRING ANOTHER SANTA SUIT IN THE SLED!
SANTA WANTED TO TELL US SOMETHING! I WONDER WHAT IT WAS?
WE'LL NEVER KNOW NOW!
HE WENT AWAY MAD!
WE WERE ONLY TRYING TO BE NICE TO HIM!
BUT WE
OVERDID IT!
OH, I WOULDN'T SAY THAT, BOYS!
SANTA!

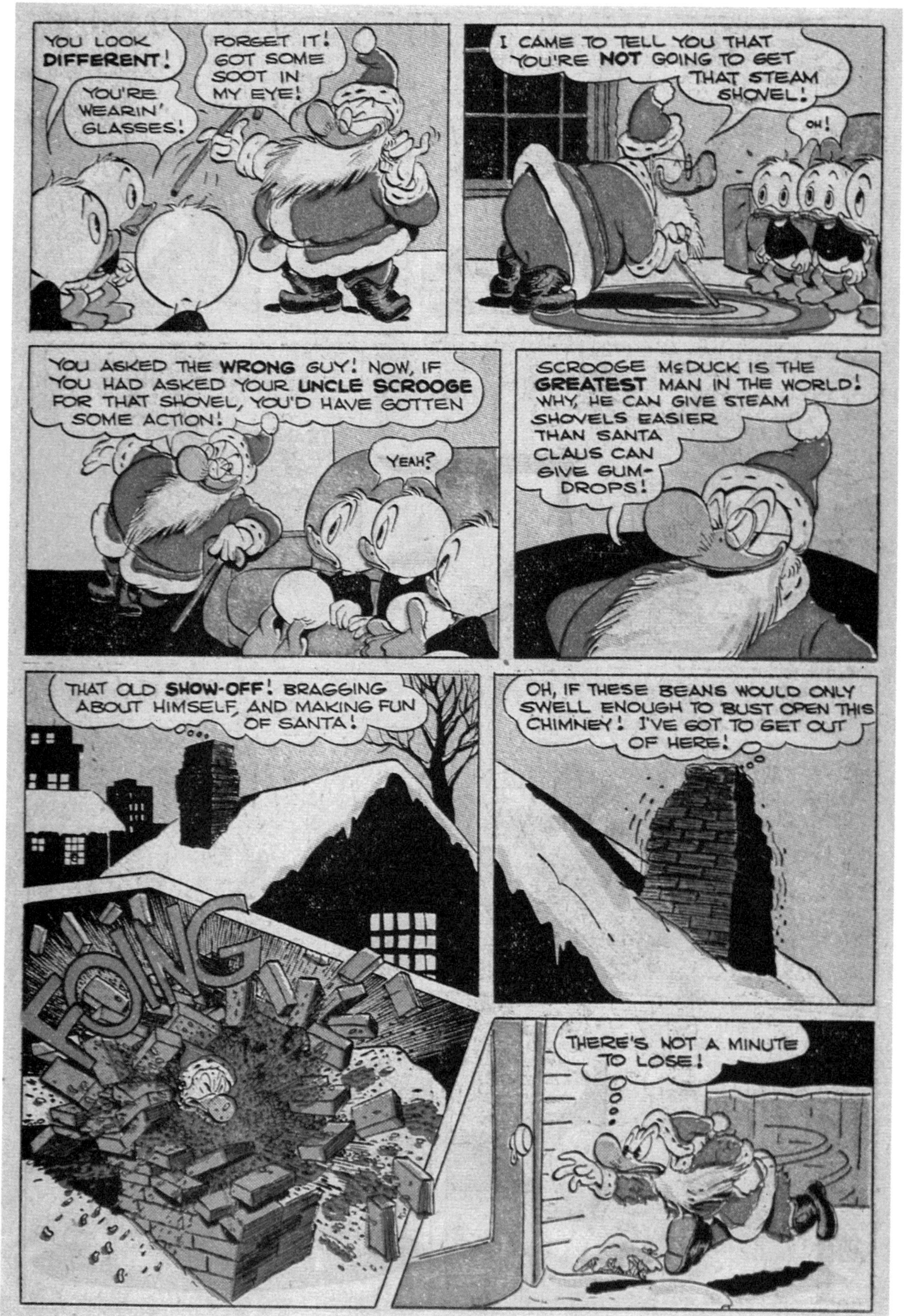
YOU LOOK DIFFERENT!
YOU'RE WEARIN' GLASSES!
FORGET IT! GOT SOME SOOT IN MY EYE!
I CAME TO TELL YOU THAT YOU'RE NOT GOING TO GET THAT STEAM SHOVEL!
OH!
YOU ASKED THE WRONG GUY! NOW, IF YOU HAD ASKED YOUR UNCLE SCROOGE FOR THAT SHOVEL, YOU'D HAVE GOTTEN SOME ACTION!
YEAH?
SCROOGE McDUCK IS THE GREATEST MAN IN THE WORLD! WHY, HE CAN GIVE STEAM SHOVELS EASIER THAN SANTA CLAUS CAN GIVE GUM-DROPS!
THAT OLD SHOW-OFF! BRAGGING ABOUT HIMSELF, AND MAKING FUN OF SANTA!
OH, IF THESE BEANS WOULD ONLY SWELL ENOUGH TO BUST OPEN THIS CHIMNEY! I'VE GOT TO GET OUT OF HERE!
FOING
THERE'S NOT A MINUTE TO LOSE!

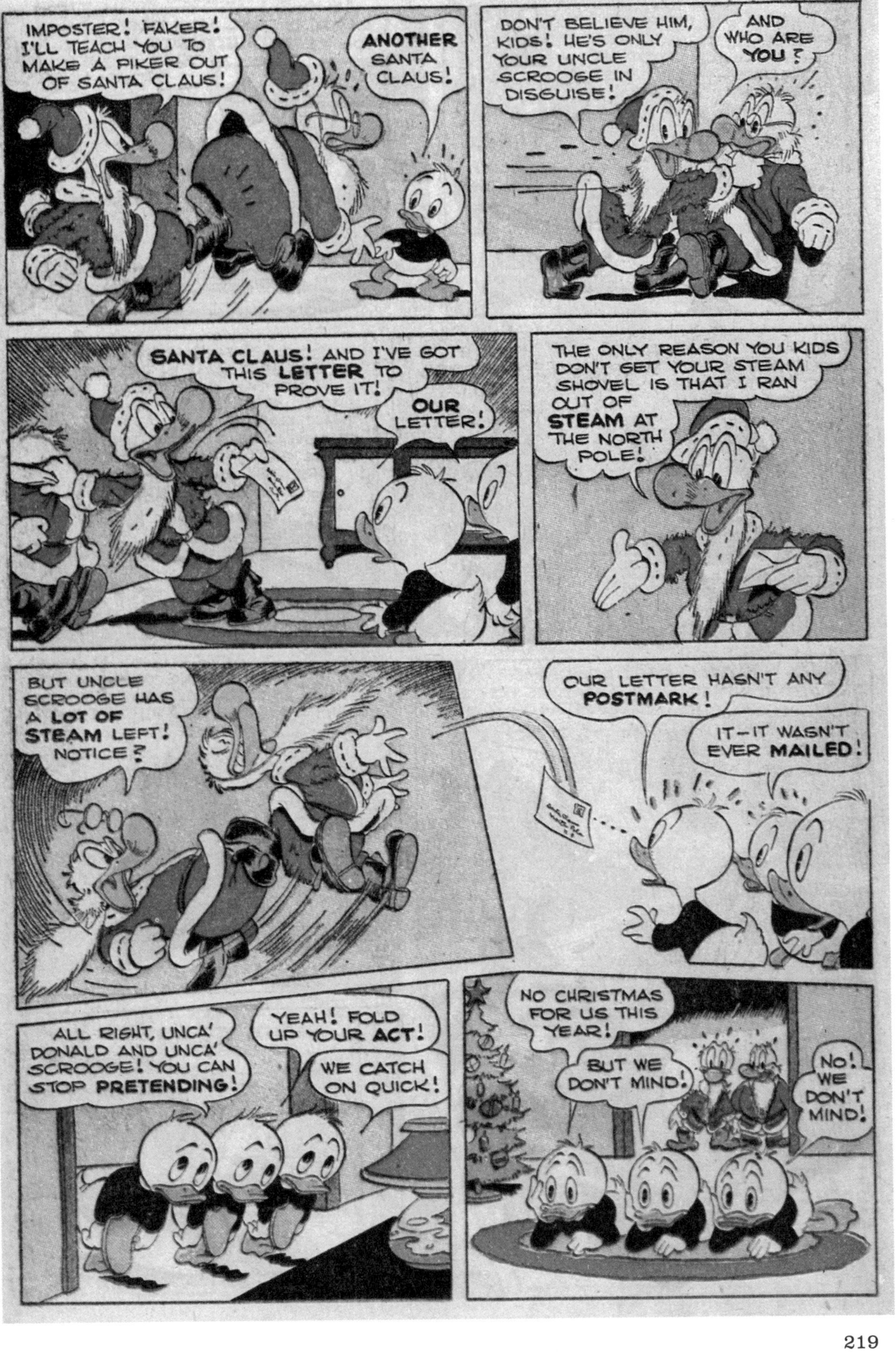

IMPOSTER! FAKER! I'LL TEACH YOU TO MAKE A PIKER OUT OF SANTA CLAUS!
ANOTHER SANTA CLAUS!
DON'T BELIEVE HIM, KIDS! HE'S ONLY YOUR UNCLE SCROOGE IN DISGUISE!
AND WHO ARE YOU?
SANTA CLAUS! AND I'VE GOT THIS LETTER TO PROVE IT!
OUR LETTER!
THE ONLY REASON YOU KIDS DON'T GET YOUR STEAM SHOVEL IS THAT I RAN OUT OF STEAM AT THE NORTH POLE!
BUT UNCLE SCROOGE HAS A LOT OF STEAM LEFT! NOTICE?
OUR LETTER HASN'T ANY POSTMARK!
IT—IT WASN'T EVER MAILED!
ALL RIGHT, UNCA' DONALD AND UNCA' SCROOGE! YOU CAN STOP PRETENDING!
YEAH! FOLD UP YOUR ACT!
WE CATCH ON QUICK!
NO CHRISTMAS FOR US THIS YEAR!
BUT WE DON'T MIND!
NO! WE DON'T MIND!

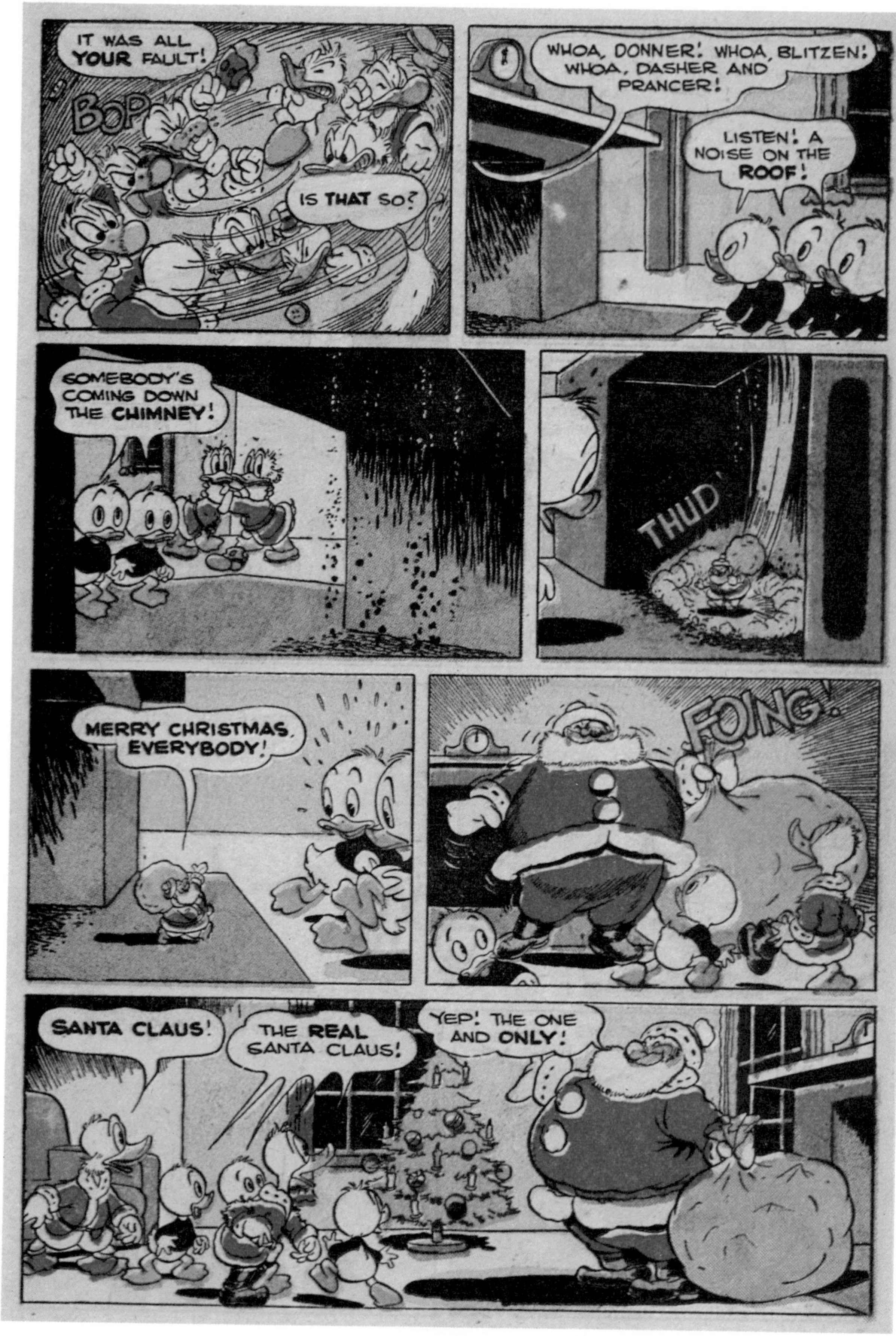
IT WAS ALL YOUR FAULT!
BOP
IS THAT SO?
WHOA, DONNER! WHOA, BLITZEN! WHOA, DASHER AND PRANCER!
LISTEN! A NOISE ON THE ROOF!
SOMEBODY'S COMING DOWN THE CHIMNEY!
THUD
MERRY CHRISTMAS, EVERYBODY!
FOING!
SANTA CLAUS!
THE REAL SANTA CLAUS!
YEP! THE ONE AND ONLY!

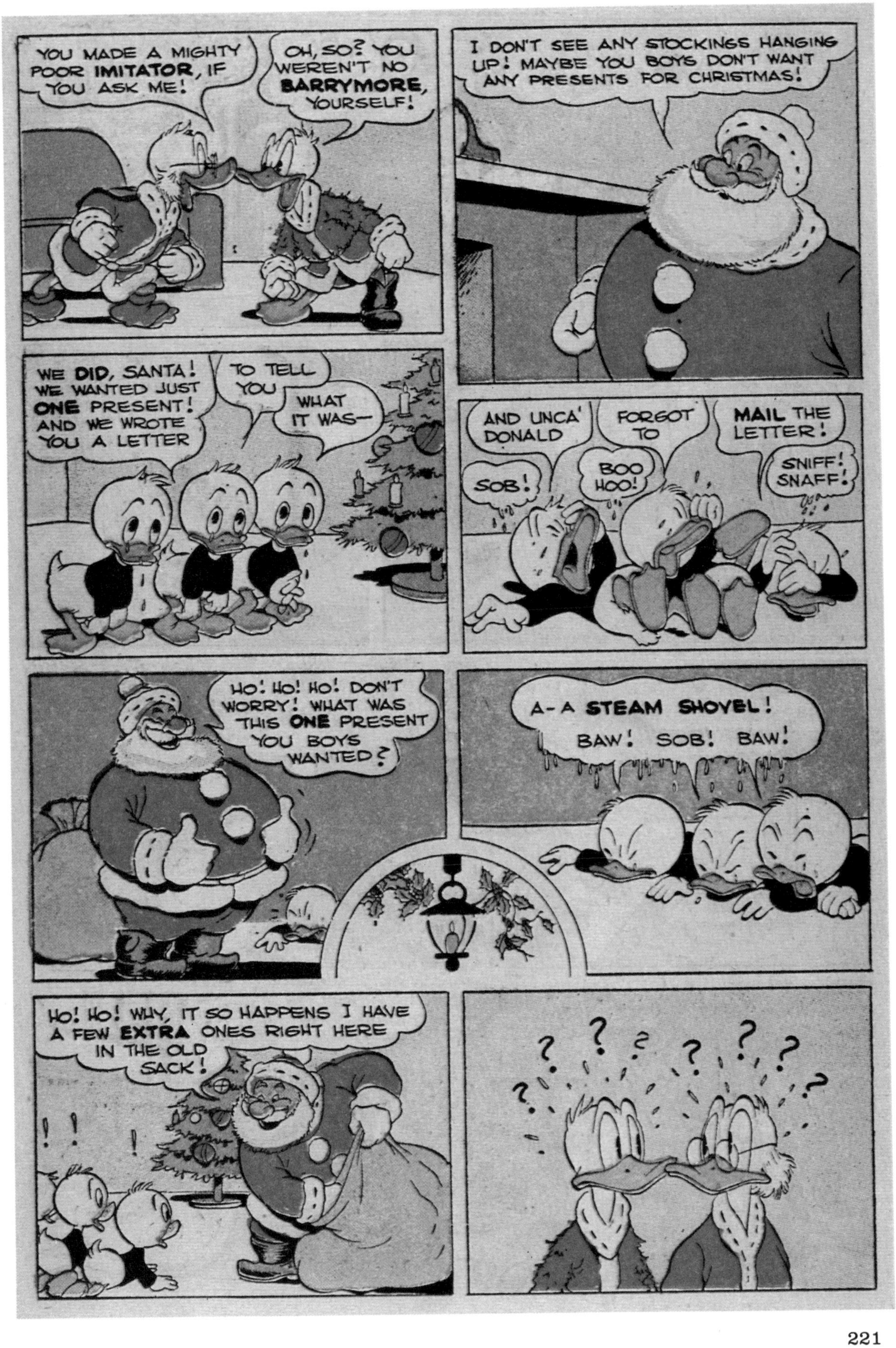
YOU MADE A MIGHTY POOR IMITATOR, IF YOU ASK ME!
OH, SO? YOU WEREN'T NO BARRYMORE, YOURSELF!
I DON'T SEE ANY STOCKINGS HANGING UP! MAYBE YOU BOYS DON'T WANT ANY PRESENTS FOR CHRISTMAS!
WE DID, SANTA! WE WANTED JUST ONE PRESENT! AND WE WROTE YOU A LETTER
TO TELL YOU
WHAT IT WAS—
AND UNCA' DONALD
FORGOT TO
MAIL THE LETTER!
SOB!
BOO HOO!
SNIFF! SNAFF!
HO! HO! HO! DON'T WORRY! WHAT WAS THIS ONE PRESENT YOU BOYS WANTED?
A-A STEAM SHOVEL!
BAW! SOB! BAW!
HO! HO! WHY, IT SO HAPPENS I HAVE A FEW EXTRA ONES RIGHT HERE IN THE OLD SACK!
! ! !
? ? ? ? ? ? ? ?

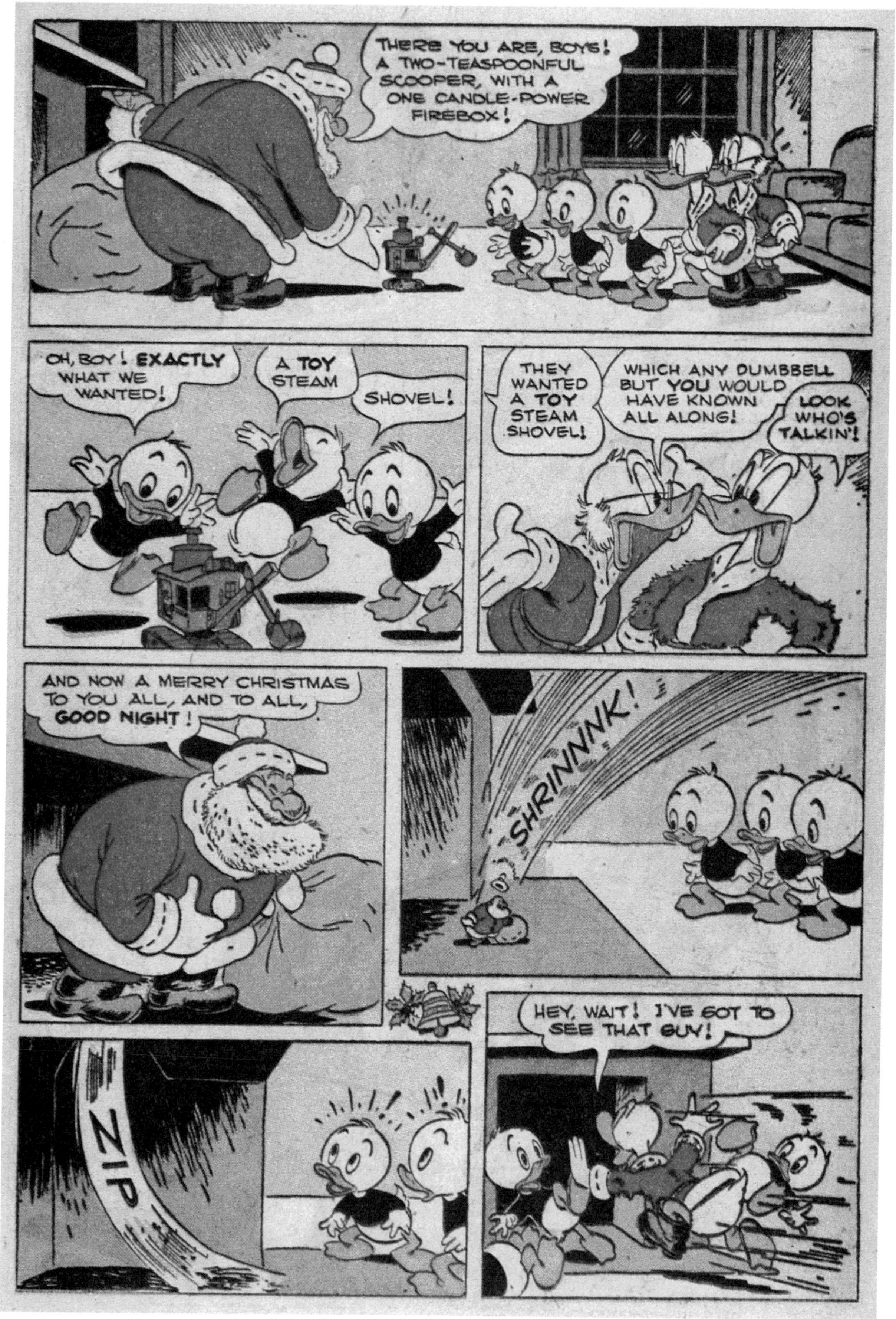
THERE YOU ARE, BOYS! A TWO-TEASPOONFUL SCOOPER, WITH A ONE CANDLE-POWER FIREBOX!
OH, BOY! EXACTLY WHAT WE WANTED!
A TOY STEAM
SHOVEL!
THEY WANTED A TOY STEAM SHOVEL!
WHICH ANY DUMBBELL BUT YOU WOULD HAVE KNOWN ALL ALONG!
LOOK WHO'S TALKIN'!
AND NOW A MERRY CHRISTMAS TO YOU ALL, AND TO ALL, GOOD NIGHT!
SHRINNNK!
ZIP
HEY, WAIT! I'VE GOT TO SEE THAT GUY!

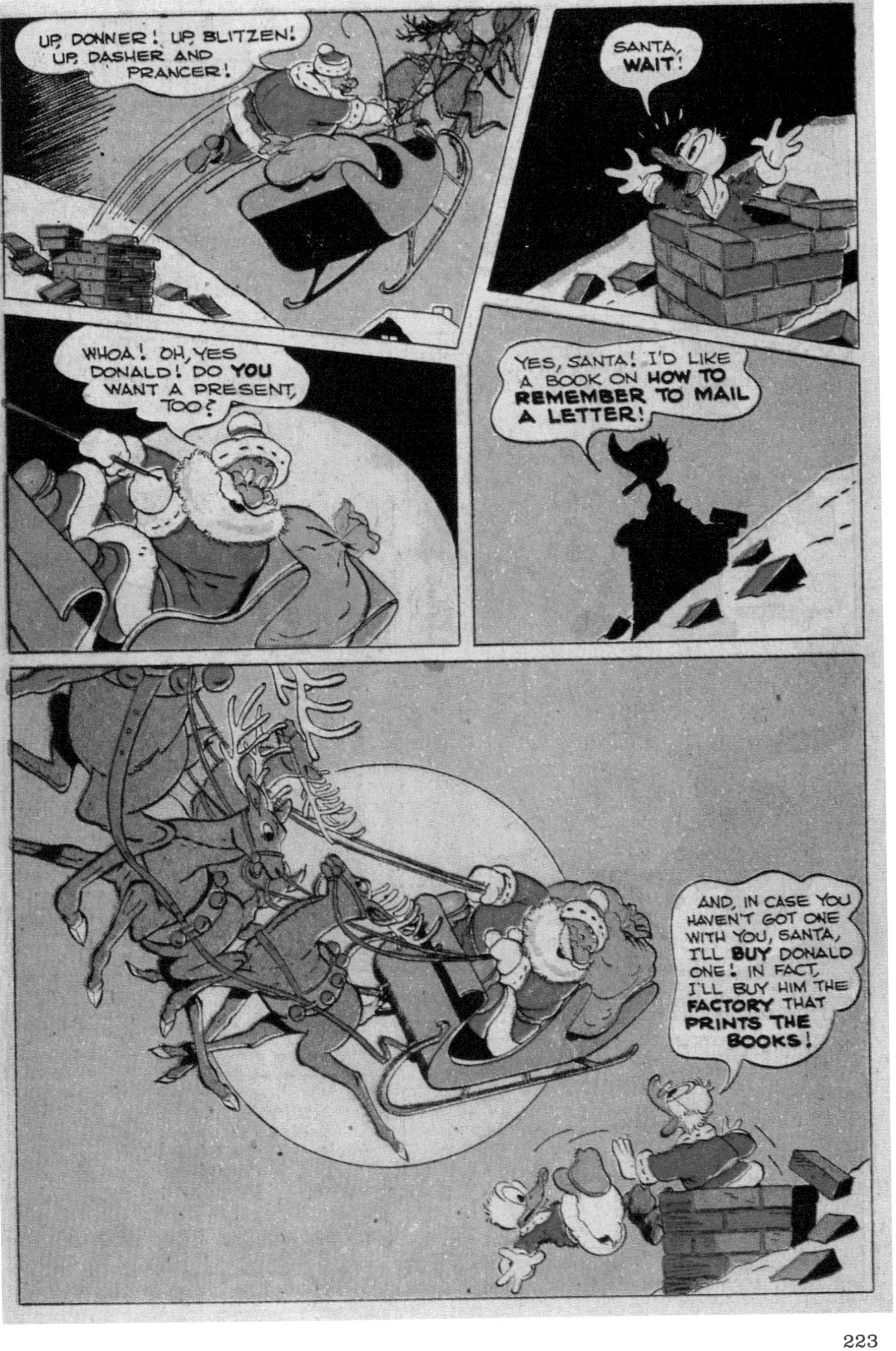
UP, DONNER! UP, BLITZEN! UP, DASHER AND PRANCER!
SANTA, WAIT!
WHOA! OH, YES DONALD! DO YOU WANT A PRESENT, TOO?
YES, SANTA! I'D LIKE A BOOK ON HOW TO REMEMBER TO MAIL A LETTER!
AND, IN CASE YOU HAVEN'T GOT ONE WITH YOU, SANTA, I'LL BUY DONALD ONE! IN FACT, I'LL BUY HIM THE FACTORY THAT PRINTS THE BOOKS!

About "Pogo" and Walt Kelly

It will probably come as a surprise to some readers to find Pogo and Walt Kelly in this collection. It will probably come as a surprise to more readers to learn that Kelly actually began Pogo as a comic-book character, first in *Animal Comics* from 1942 to 1947, and then in the *Pogo Possum* comic book, which ran for sixteen issues between 1949 and 1954. By the time that the fine, farcical adventures presented here first appeared in *Pogo Possum,* Kelly's *Pogo* had already become a widely syndicated, much-loved newspaper feature, and softcover collections of those newspaper strips were best sellers.

In discussing his own past, Walt Kelly sometimes indulged in the same talent for whimsy that he brought to the animal adventures in the Okefenokee. So it has become difficult to be sure of the biographical details. But the main facts seem clear enough. Kelly was born August 25, 1913, in Philadelphia, but his family had moved to Bridgeport, Connecticut, within two years. Kelly on occasion described his father as a painter of theatrical scenery, but that seems doubtful, particularly as the profession of a citizen of Bridgeport in the 1930s. In any case, Walt contributed drawings to his high school newspaper (which he also edited) and yearbook. On graduation, he went to work for the Bridgeport *Post.*

By 1935, Walt Kelly had been hired by the Walt Disney Studios, where he animated parts of *Fantasia* and *Dumbo.* In 1941, Kelly moved to New York, where he worked for Western Printing and Lithographing Company on Dell comic books, chiefly *Animal Comics* and *Our Gang.*

For the former he created a feature that was probably derived to some extent from the Uncle Remus stories. At first it had no continuing title but it centered around a comically ravenous alligator named Albert and a black youngster named Bumbazine who visited with Albert and the animals in a southern swamp. The swamp's anthropomorphic inhabitants included a Pogo Possum whose role became gradually more prominent as Bumbazine's waned. (Incidentally, the drawing of Pogo that appears in the collection *Ten Ever-Lovin' Blue-Eyed Years with Pogo* captioned, "Pogo circa 1943," is another example of Kelly whimsy, circa 1959. Pogo did look different in his early appearances but he didn't look like that.)

During World War II, Kelly worked as a civilian employee for the Army, contributing drawings to language manuals. He continued to work for Western Printing, too, contributing to comic books like *Raggedy Ann and Andy, Santa Claus Funnies,* and *Easter with Mother Goose*—along with *Animal Comics* and *Our Gang*—well into the postwar years. The charming illustrated parodies of standard nursery rhymes and nursery tales that were later featured in Kelly's books were first tried out in *Raggedy Ann and Andy* and other comic books.

In 1949, Kelly became art editor for the idealistic enterprise known as the New York *Star,* a newspaper for which he did editorial cartoons and spot drawings, and for which he revived Pogo in a daily comic strip. When the *Star* died, *Pogo* was taken over by the New York *Post* and its Post-Hall Syndicate, then by Field Enterprises. The success of that strip was rapid and book collections of *Pogo* strips quickly followed. Kelly remained the steward of the strip until his death on October 18, 1973.

Walt Kelly's work in *Animal Comics,* with its audience of small children, is particularly interesting in retrospect. The early Albert Alligator was a comic villain who actually intended to make his lunches of the swamp's other inhabitants. That fact gives another dimension to one of the adventures that follows: the one about Albert's accidental cannibalism. Many fine variations on that idea appeared in Kelly's daily and Sunday *Pogo* strips.

Kelly found himself and found the nature of his talent when *Pogo* became a four-panel, daily comic strip. But the *Pogo* Sunday feature gave Kelly's improvisational fancy a larger yard to play in, and the contemporaneous comic book, so unduly neglected as it was, gave him virtually an open field.

The comic-book treatment of *Pogo* was curiously different. Despite more panels and more panels, the characters dominate the strip and the backgrounds are sparser. (Incidentally, Kelly's comic-book stories, like those of John Stanley's *Little Lulu,* would thus make superb storyboards for cartoons—particularly TV cartoons—just as they are.)

The three vaudeville-like comic-book sketches that follow, with their comic delight in the humanized attitudes and reactions of their characters, their verbal games and fun, and their detached but passionate observations on us all—these *Pogo* sketches suggest that Walt Kelly's sensibility was perhaps closest to that of another gifted and whimsical twentieth-century Irishman, James Joyce.

In addition to the three stories from *Pogo Possum,* we have included the very first Pogo story, published in *Animal Comics* in 1942.

M.W.

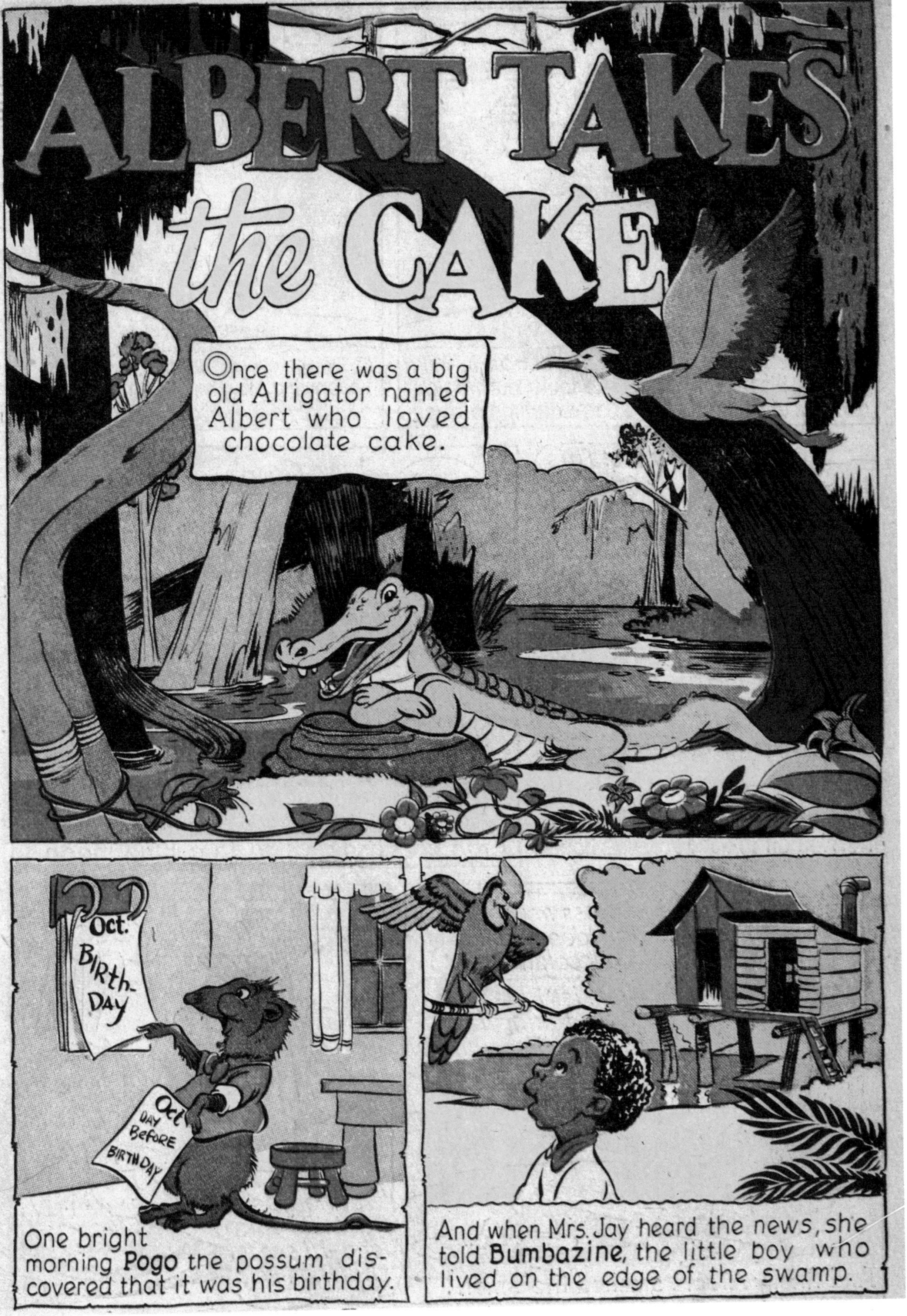
ALBERT TAKES the CAKE
Once there was a big old Alligator named Albert who loved chocolate cake.
Oct. BIRTH-DAY
Oct DAY BEFORE BIRTHDAY
One bright morning Pogo the possum discovered that it was his birthday.
And when Mrs. Jay heard the news, she told Bumbazine, the little boy who lived on the edge of the swamp.

From *Animal Comics* No. 1, 1942.

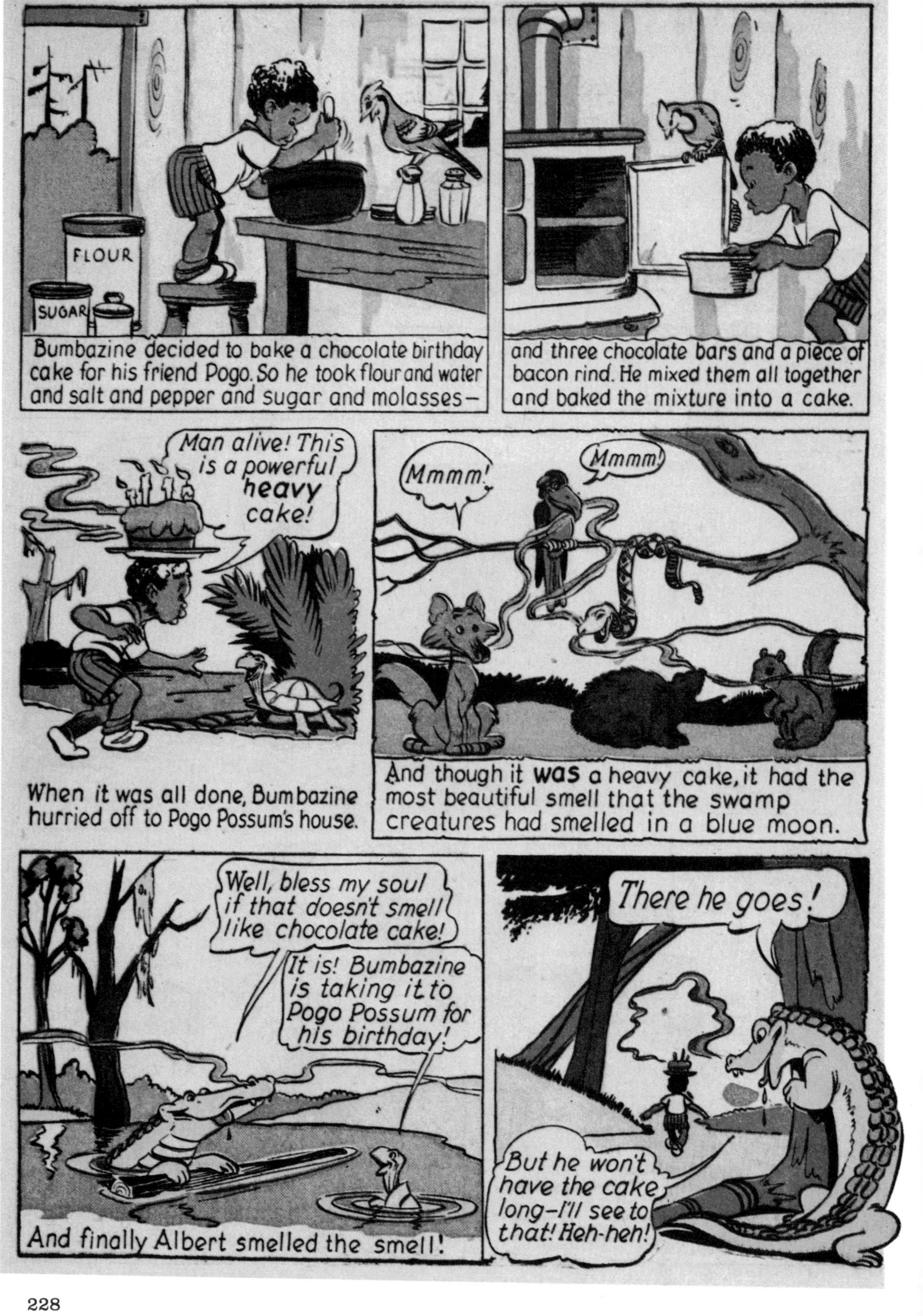
FLOUR
SUGAR
Bumbazine decided to bake a chocolate birthday cake for his friend Pogo. So he took flour and water and salt and pepper and sugar and molasses—
and three chocolate bars and a piece of bacon rind. He mixed them all together and baked the mixture into a cake.
Man alive! This is a powerful heavy cake!
When it was all done, Bumbazine hurried off to Pogo Possum's house.
Mmmm!
Mmmm!
And though it was a heavy cake, it had the most beautiful smell that the swamp creatures had smelled in a blue moon.
Well, bless my soul if that doesn't smell like chocolate cake!
It is! Bumbazine is taking it to Pogo Possum for his birthday!
And finally Albert smelled the smell!
There he goes!
But he won't have the cake long—I'll see to that! Heh-heh!

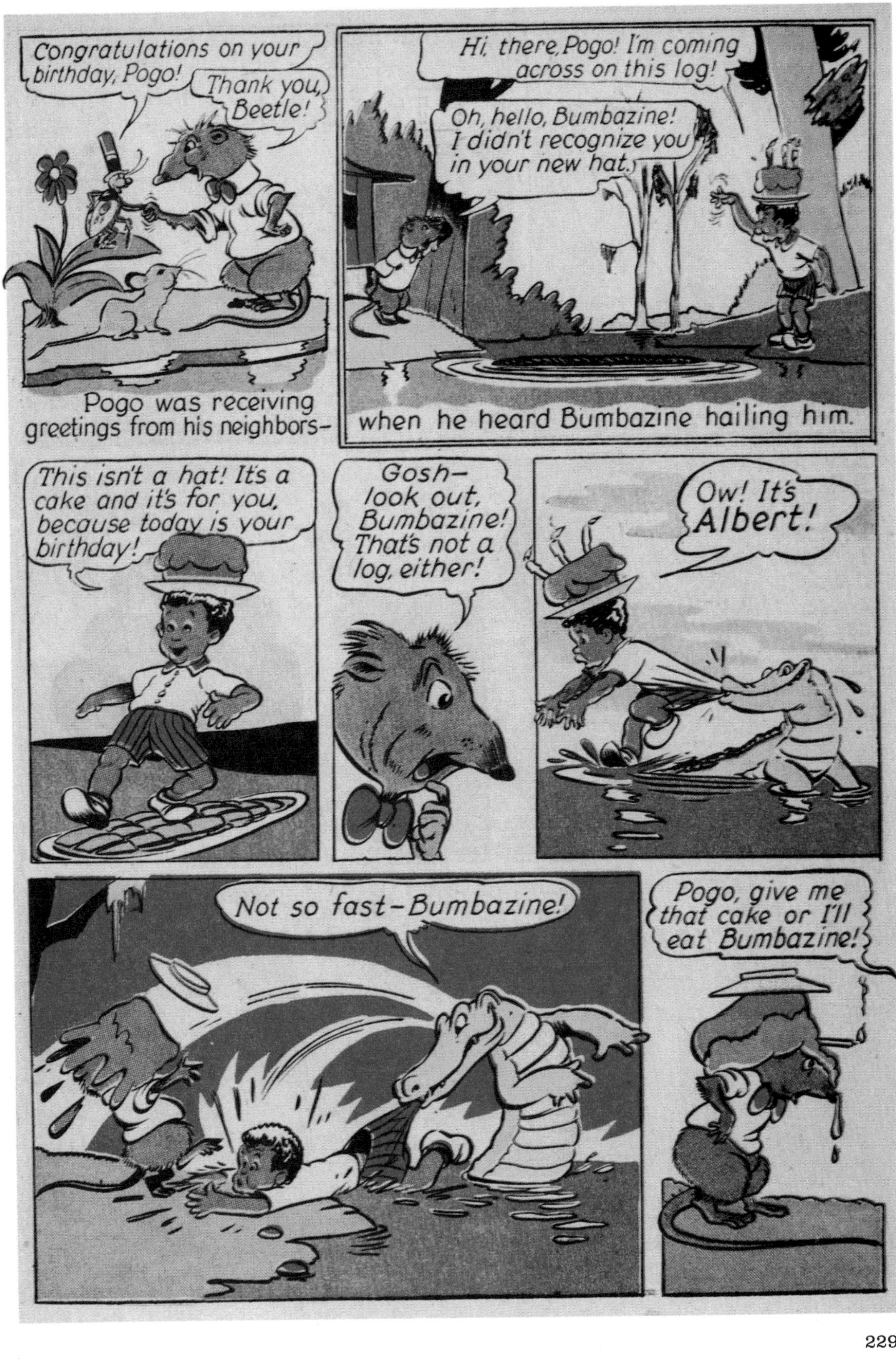
Congratulations on your birthday, Pogo!
Thank you, Beetle!
Pogo was receiving greetings from his neighbors-
Hi, there, Pogo! I'm coming across on this log!
Oh, hello, Bumbazine! I didn't recognize you in your new hat.
when he heard Bumbazine hailing him.
This isn't a hat! It's a cake and it's for you, because today is your birthday!
Gosh- look out, Bumbazine! That's not a log, either!
Ow! It's Albert!
Not so fast-Bumbazine!
Pogo, give me that cake or I'll eat Bumbazine!

Yum-yum!

Don't eat Bumbazine because **that** is me!

Now you're caught too, Pogo! Looks like this is going to be **quite** a meal!

Now, I'll eat Pogo first, then Bumbazine, and for dessert I'll eat this beautiful and delicious chocolate cake with candles!

Oh, don't eat **me** first—I don't deserve the honor. Besides, I had crabapples, pickles, persimmons, lemons and fourteen cups of vinegar for breakfast— so I would sour up your whole dinner!

Then I'll eat Bumbazine first!

Oh, no, I still have on my winter underwear and I'll just itch up your insides— How would you get in there to scratch?

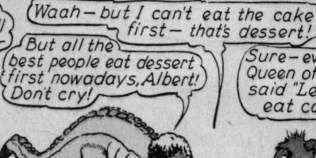

Waah—but I can't eat the cake first—that's dessert!

But all the best people eat dessert first nowadays, Albert! Don't cry!

Sure—even the Queen of France said "Let 'em eat cake!"

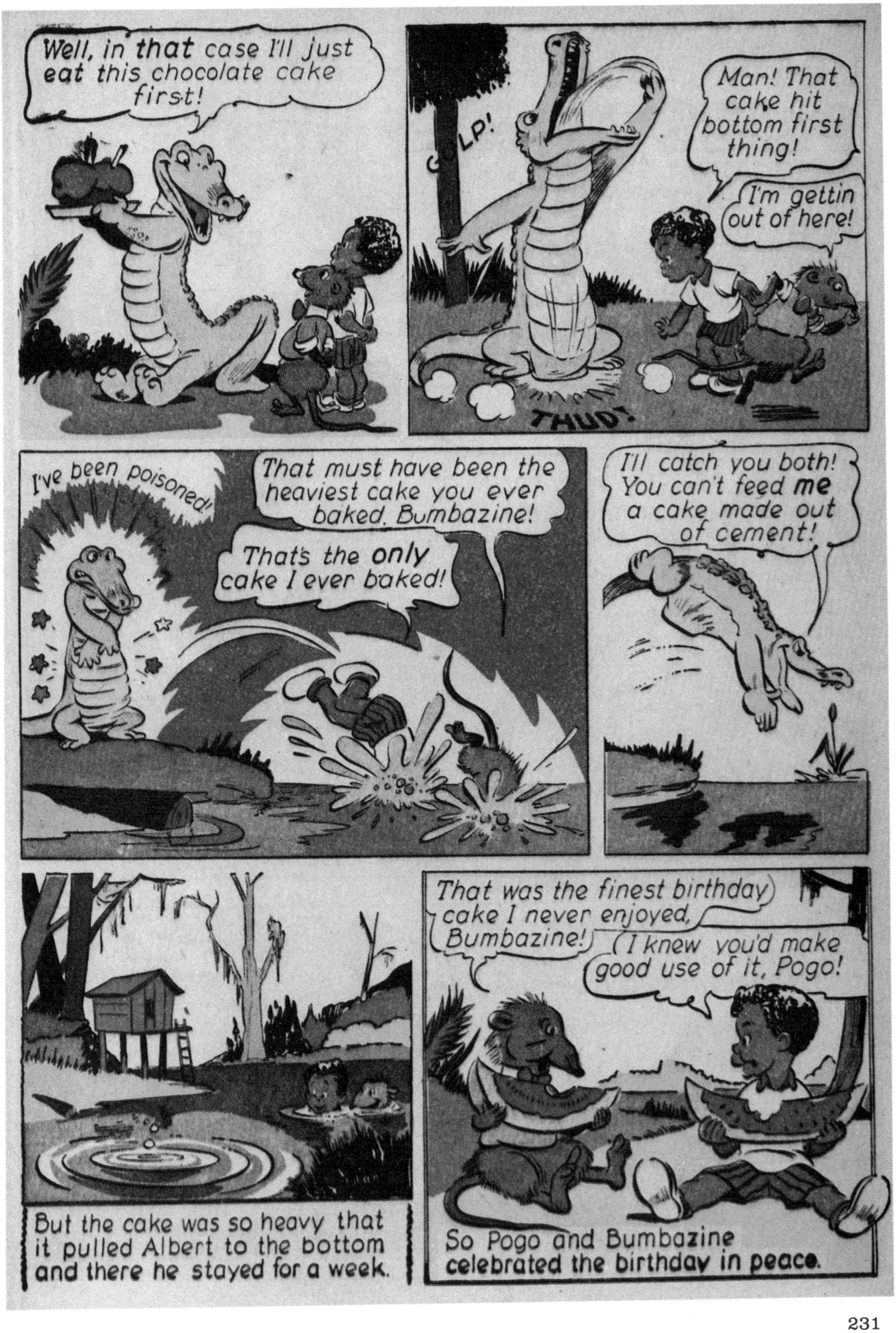
Well, in that case I'll just eat this chocolate cake first!
GULP!
Man! That cake hit bottom first thing!
I'm gettin out of here!
THUD!
I've been poisoned!
That must have been the heaviest cake you ever baked, Bumbazine!
That's the only cake I ever baked!
I'll catch you both! You can't feed me a cake made out of cement!
But the cake was so heavy that it pulled Albert to the bottom and there he stayed for a week.
That was the finest birthday cake I never enjoyed, Bumbazine!
I knew you'd make good use of it, Pogo!
So Pogo and Bumbazine celebrated the birthday in peace.

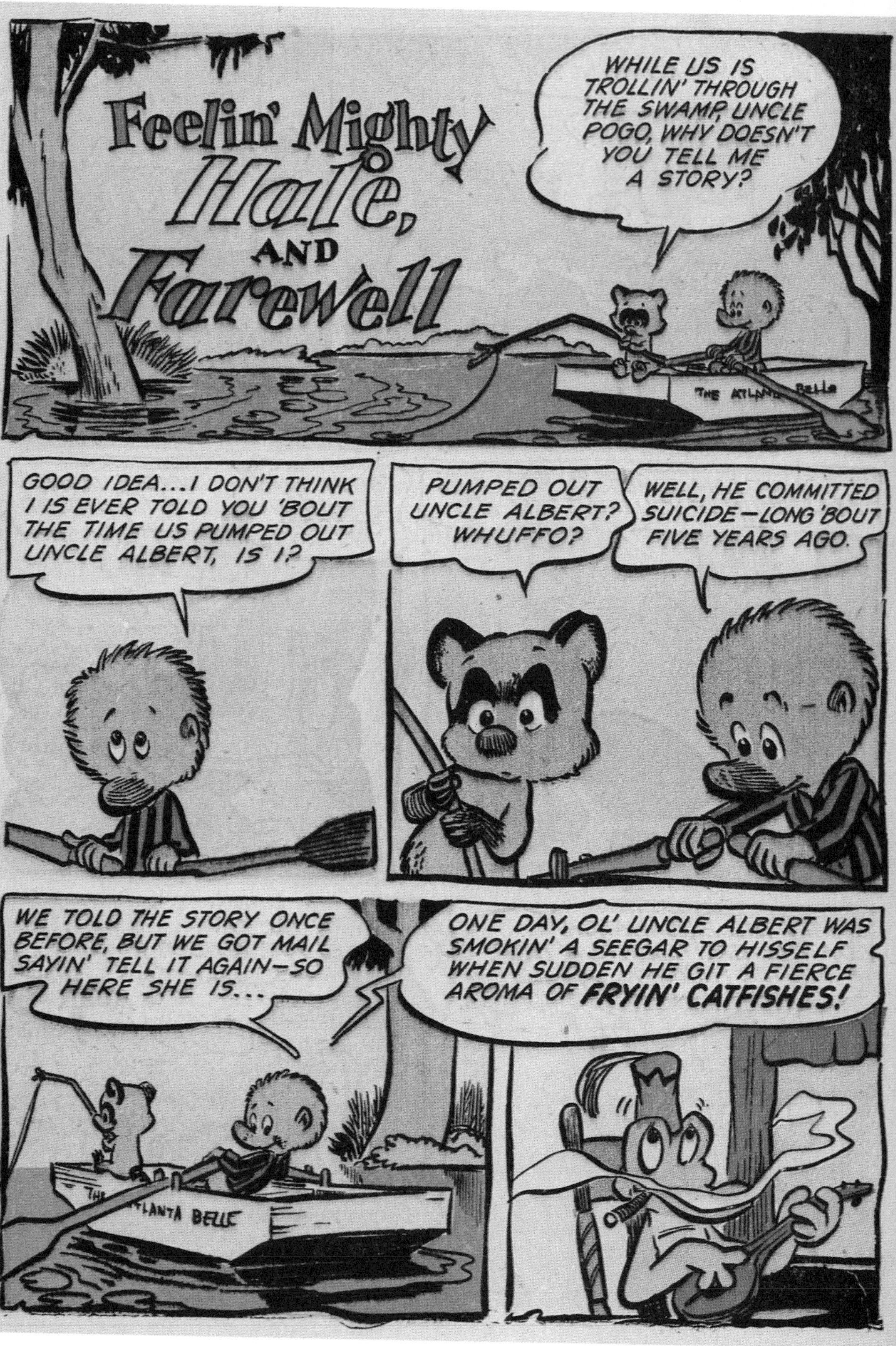

Feelin' Mighty Hale, AND Farewell
WHILE US IS TROLLIN' THROUGH THE SWAMP, UNCLE POGO, WHY DOESN'T YOU TELL ME A STORY?
GOOD IDEA...I DON'T THINK I IS EVER TOLD YOU 'BOUT THE TIME US PUMPED OUT UNCLE ALBERT, IS I?
PUMPED OUT UNCLE ALBERT? WHUFFO?
WELL, HE COMMITTED SUICIDE—LONG 'BOUT FIVE YEARS AGO.
WE TOLD THE STORY ONCE BEFORE, BUT WE GOT MAIL SAYIN' TELL IT AGAIN—SO HERE SHE IS...
ONE DAY, OL' UNCLE ALBERT WAS SMOKIN' A SEEGAR TO HISSELF WHEN SUDDEN HE GIT A FIERCE AROMA OF **FRYIN' CATFISHES!**

From *Pogo Possum* No. 3, Aug.-Oct. 1950

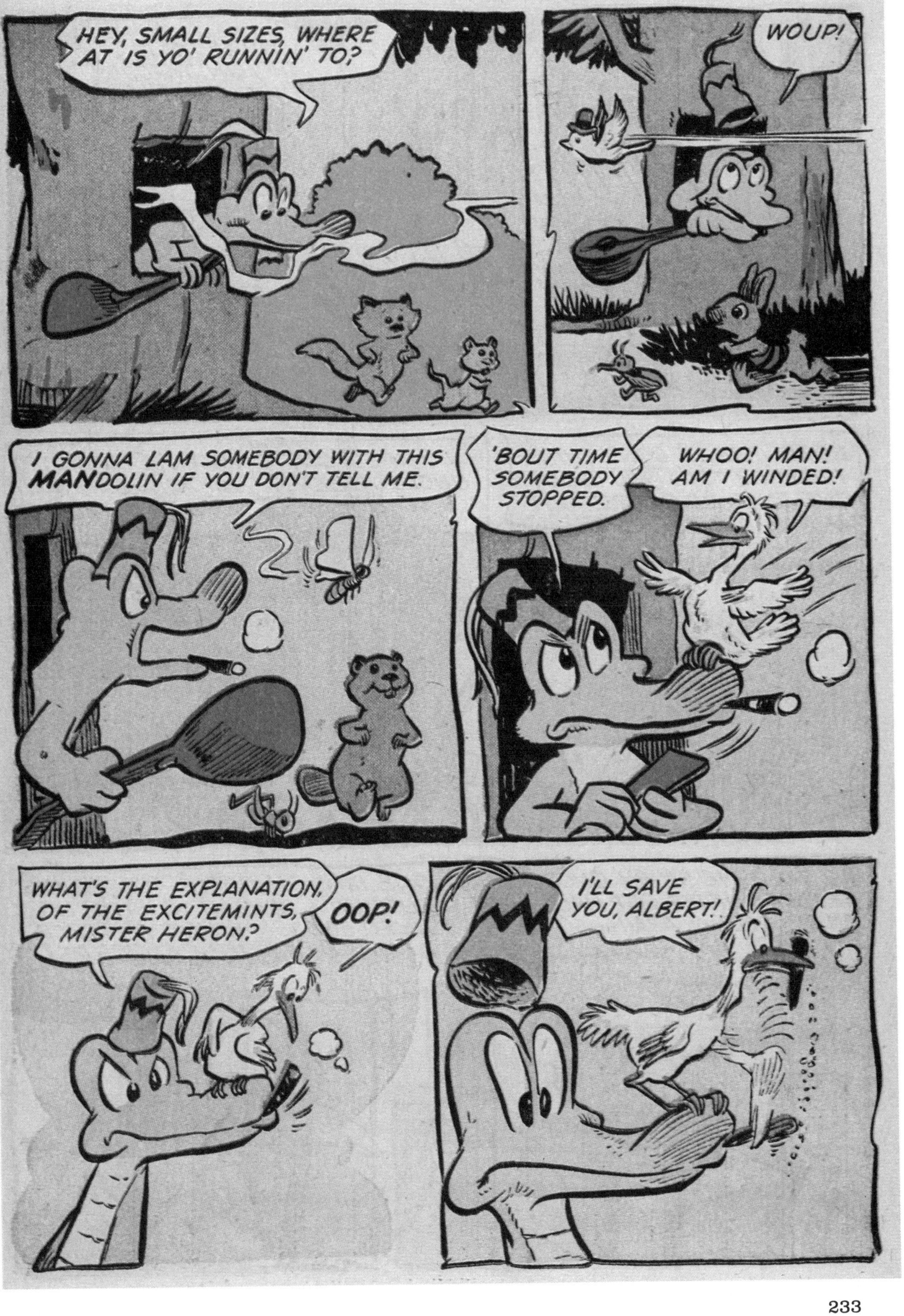
HEY, SMALL SIZES, WHERE AT IS YO' RUNNIN' TO?
WOUP!
I GONNA LAM SOMEBODY WITH THIS MANDOLIN IF YOU DON'T TELL ME.
'BOUT TIME SOMEBODY STOPPED.
WHOO! MAN! AM I WINDED!
WHAT'S THE EXPLANATION, OF THE EXCITEMINTS, MISTER HERON?
OOP!
I'LL SAVE YOU, ALBERT!

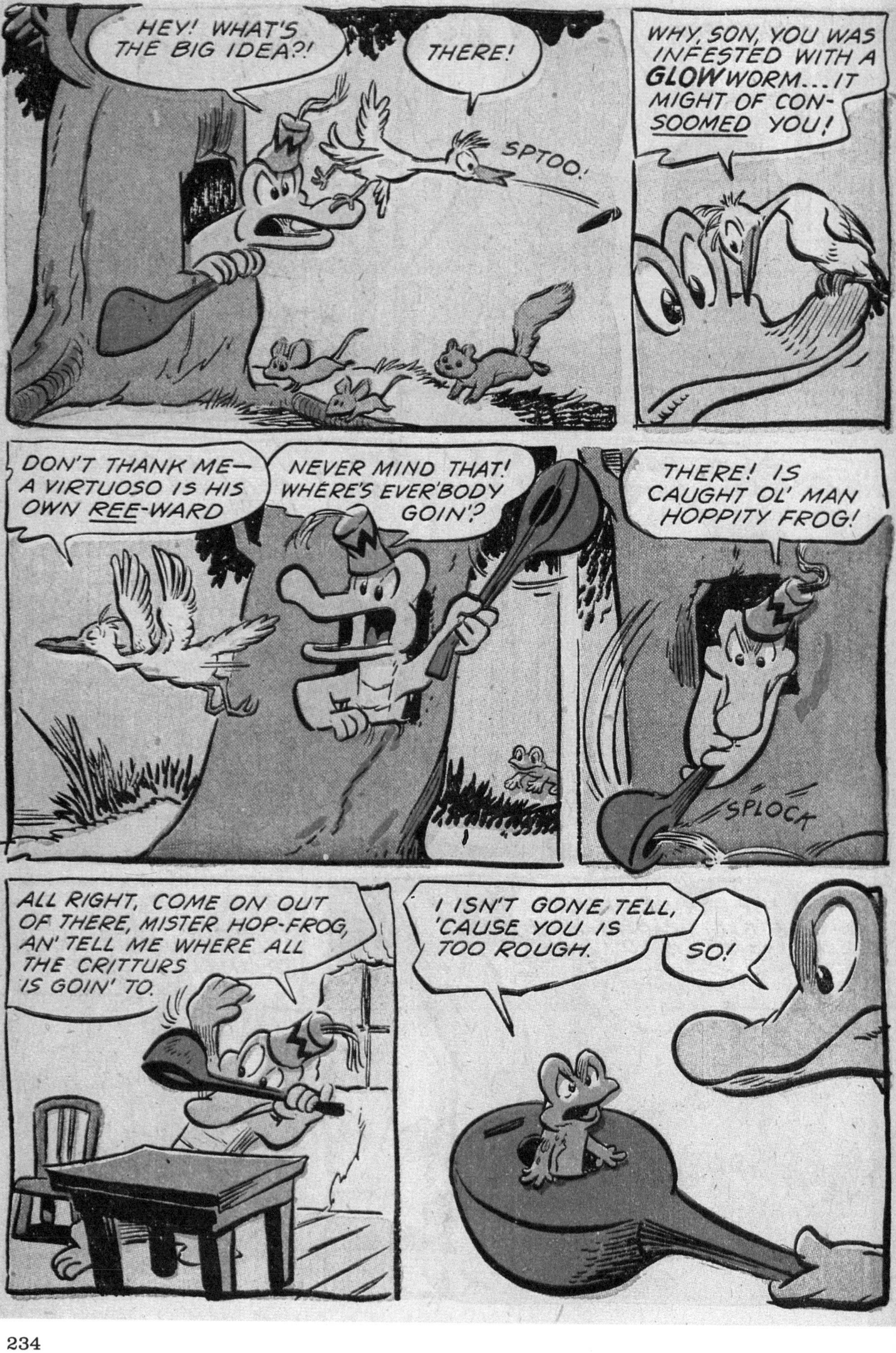
HEY! WHAT'S THE BIG IDEA?!
THERE!
SPTOO!
WHY, SON, YOU WAS INFESTED WITH A GLOW WORM... IT MIGHT OF CON-SOOMED YOU!
DON'T THANK ME— A VIRTUOSO IS HIS OWN REE-WARD
NEVER MIND THAT! WHERE'S EVER'BODY GOIN'?
THERE! IS CAUGHT OL' MAN HOPPITY FROG!
SPLOCK
ALL RIGHT, COME ON OUT OF THERE, MISTER HOP-FROG, AN' TELL ME WHERE ALL THE CRITTURS IS GOIN' TO.
I ISN'T GONE TELL, 'CAUSE YOU IS TOO ROUGH.
SO!

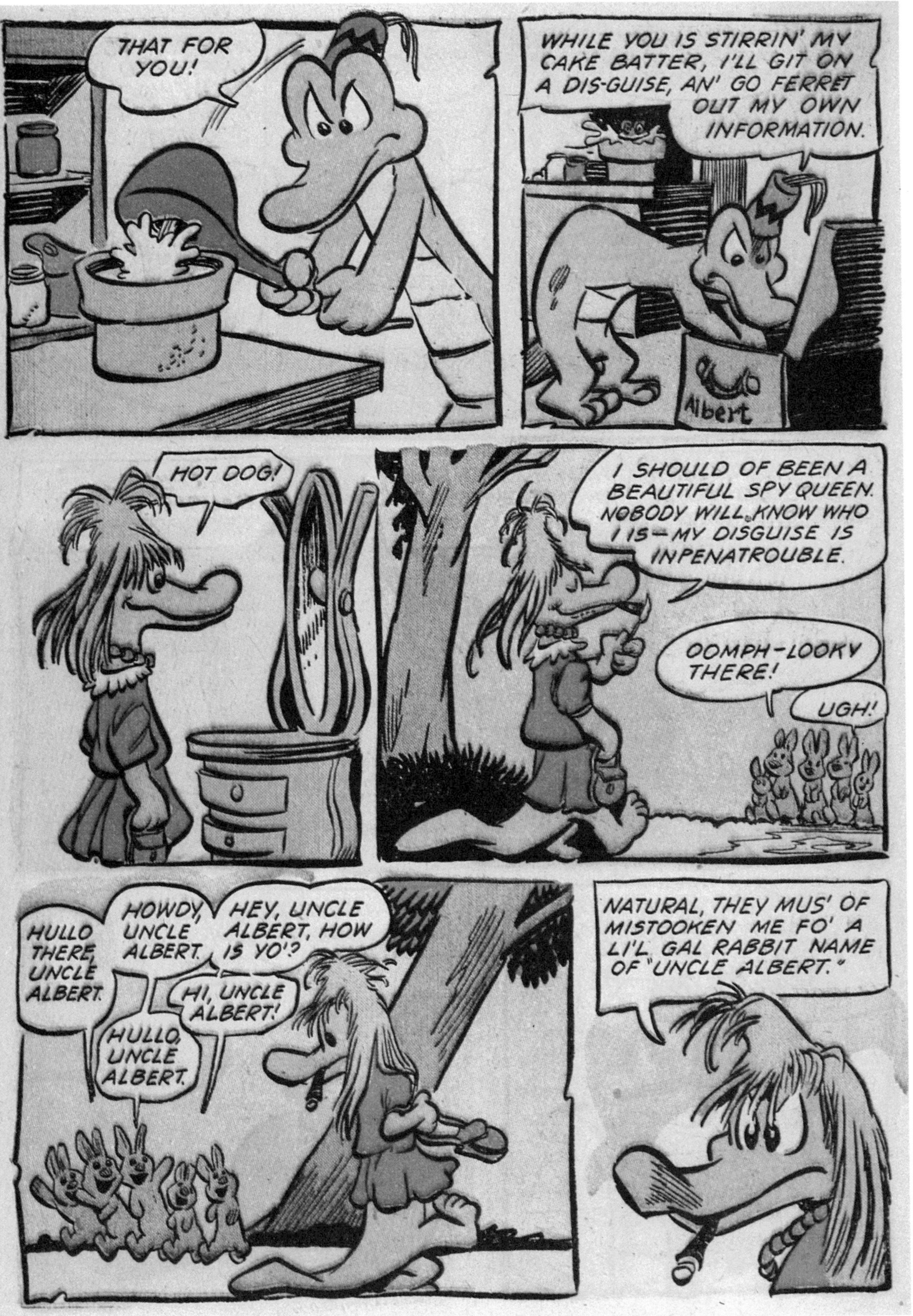

THAT FOR YOU!
WHILE YOU IS STIRRIN' MY CAKE BATTER, I'LL GIT ON A DIS-GUISE, AN' GO FERRET OUT MY OWN INFORMATION.
Albert
HOT DOG!
I SHOULD OF BEEN A BEAUTIFUL SPY QUEEN. NOBODY WILL KNOW WHO I IS—MY DISGUISE IS INPENATROUBLE.
OOMPH—LOOKY THERE!
UGH!
HULLO THERE, UNCLE ALBERT.
HOWDY, UNCLE ALBERT.
HEY, UNCLE ALBERT, HOW IS YO'?
HI, UNCLE ALBERT!
HULLO, UNCLE ALBERT.
NATURAL, THEY MUS' OF MISTOOKEN ME FO' A LI'L GAL RABBIT NAME OF "UNCLE ALBERT."

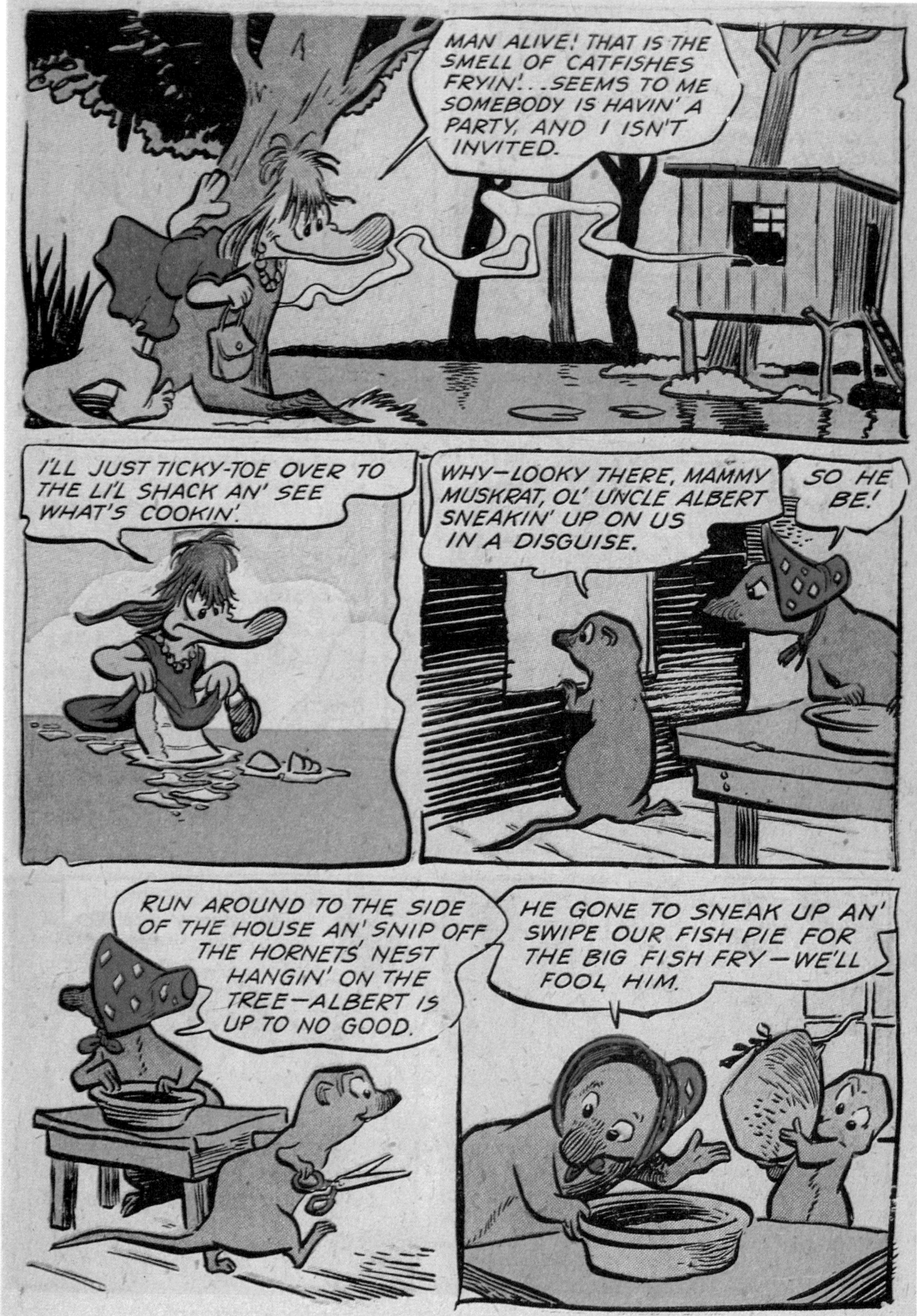
MAN ALIVE! THAT IS THE SMELL OF CATFISHES FRYIN'. . .SEEMS TO ME SOMEBODY IS HAVIN' A PARTY, AND I ISN'T INVITED.
I'LL JUST TICKY-TOE OVER TO THE LI'L SHACK AN' SEE WHAT'S COOKIN'.
WHY—LOOKY THERE, MAMMY MUSKRAT, OL' UNCLE ALBERT SNEAKIN' UP ON US IN A DISGUISE.
SO HE BE!
RUN AROUND TO THE SIDE OF THE HOUSE AN' SNIP OFF THE HORNETS' NEST HANGIN' ON THE TREE—ALBERT IS UP TO NO GOOD.
HE GONE TO SNEAK UP AN' SWIPE OUR FISH PIE FOR THE BIG FISH FRY—WE'LL FOOL HIM.

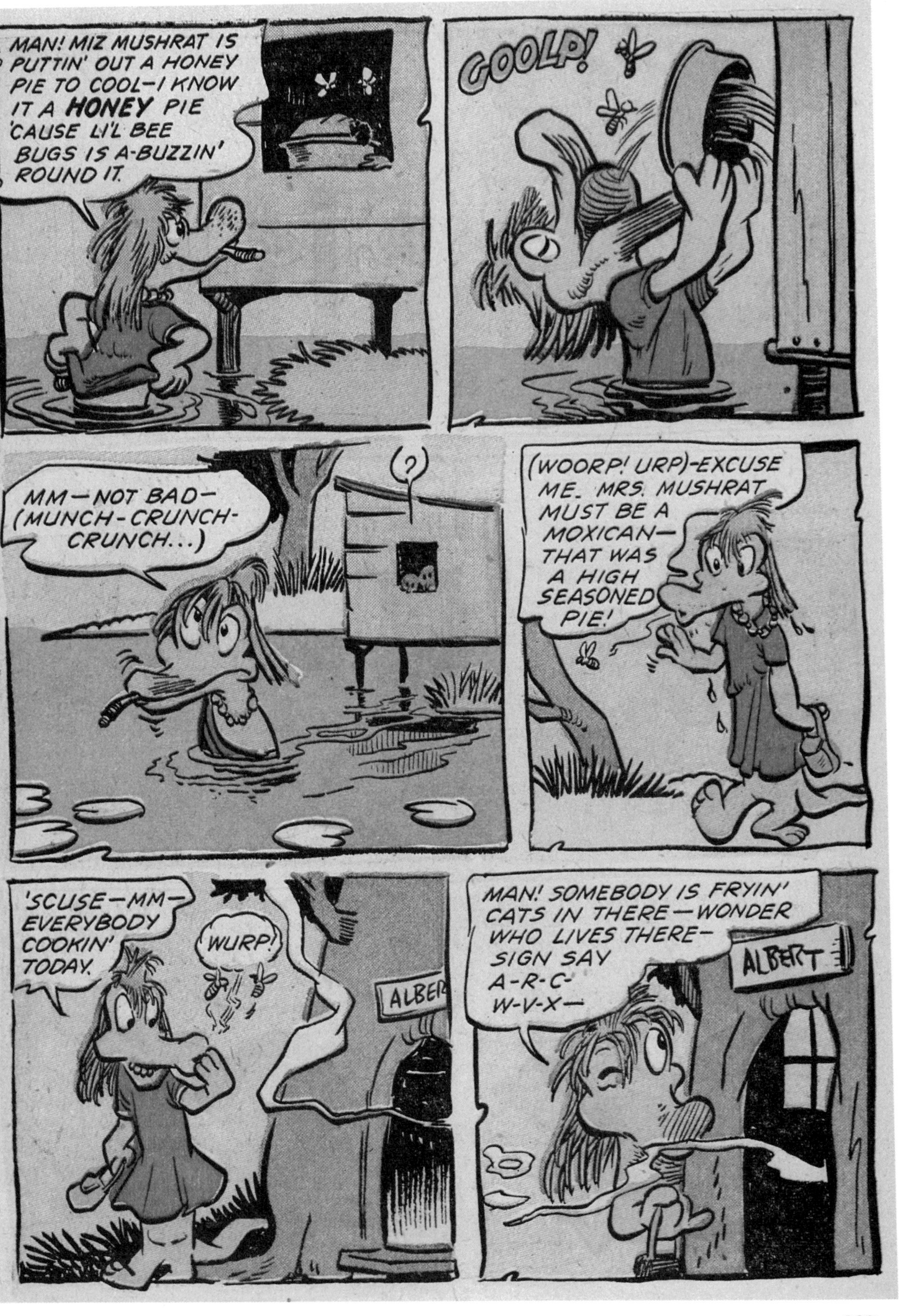
MAN! MIZ MUSHRAT IS PUTTIN' OUT A HONEY PIE TO COOL—I KNOW IT A **HONEY** PIE 'CAUSE LI'L BEE BUGS IS A-BUZZIN' ROUND IT.
GOOLP!
MM—NOT BAD—(MUNCH-CRUNCH-CRUNCH...)
(?)
(WOORP! URP)-EXCUSE ME. MRS. MUSHRAT MUST BE A MOXICAN—THAT WAS A HIGH SEASONED PIE!
'SCUSE—MM—EVERYBODY COOKIN' TODAY.
WURP!
ALBER
MAN! SOMEBODY IS FRYIN' CATS IN THERE—WONDER WHO LIVES THERE—SIGN SAY A-R-C-W-V-X—
ALBERT

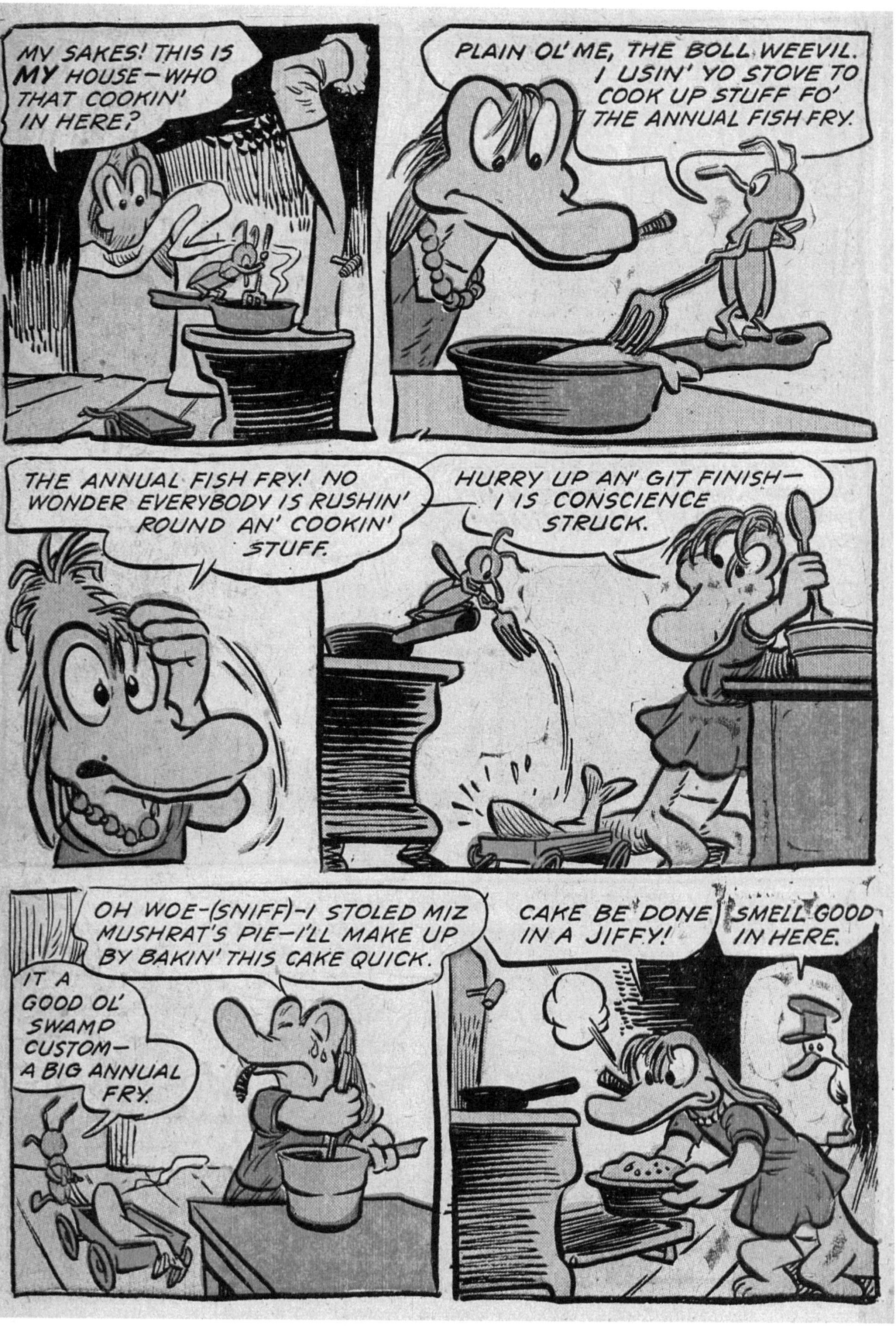
MY SAKES! THIS IS MY HOUSE—WHO THAT COOKIN' IN HERE?
PLAIN OL' ME, THE BOLL WEEVIL. I USIN' YO STOVE TO COOK UP STUFF FO' THE ANNUAL FISH FRY.
THE ANNUAL FISH FRY! NO WONDER EVERYBODY IS RUSHIN' ROUND AN' COOKIN' STUFF.
HURRY UP AN' GIT FINISH— I IS CONSCIENCE STRUCK.
OH WOE-(SNIFF)-I STOLED MIZ MUSHRAT'S PIE—I'LL MAKE UP BY BAKIN' THIS CAKE QUICK.
IT A GOOD OL' SWAMP CUSTOM— A BIG ANNUAL FRY.
CAKE BE DONE IN A JIFFY!
SMELL GOOD IN HERE.

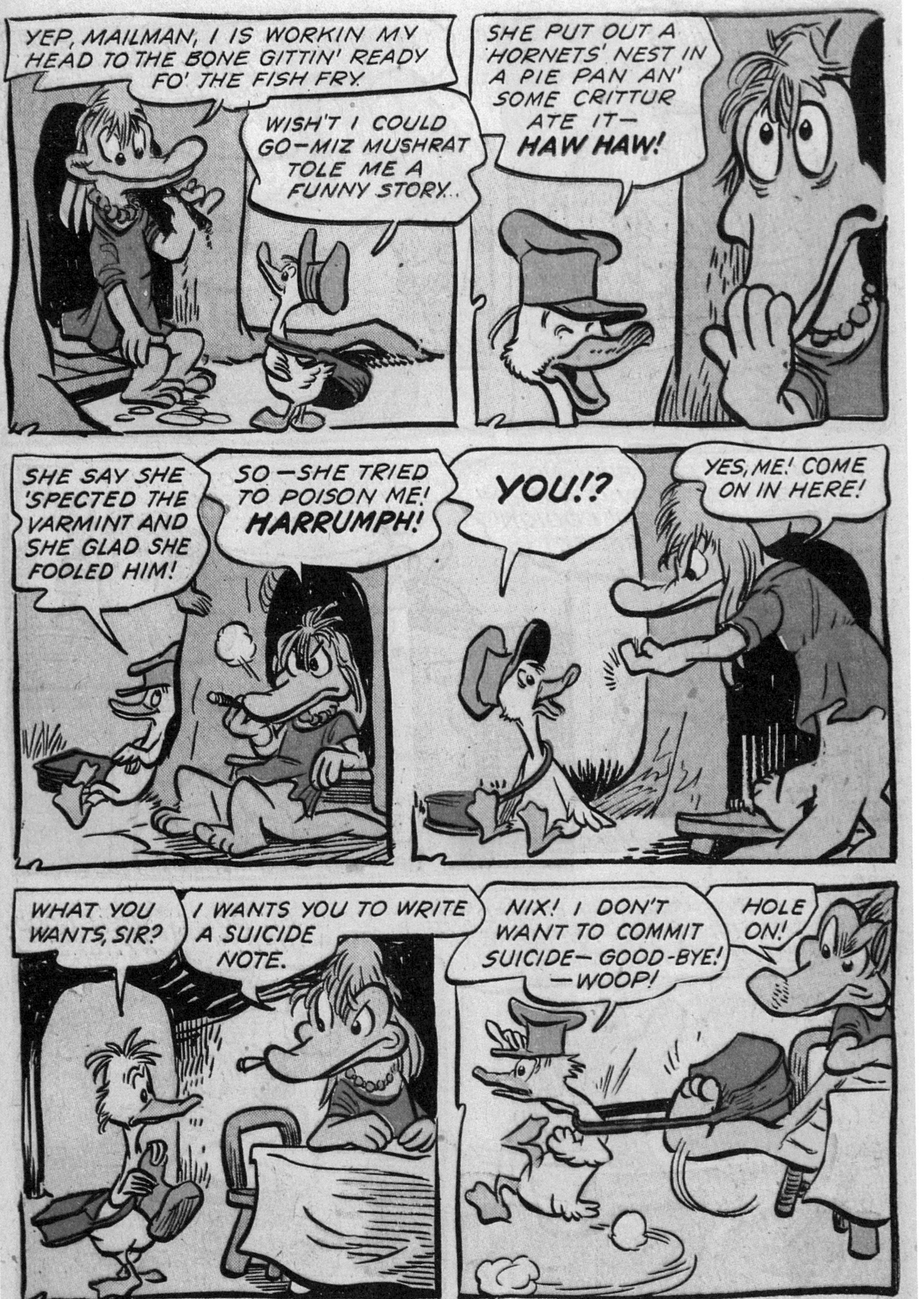

YEP, MAILMAN, I IS WORKIN MY HEAD TO THE BONE GITTIN' READY FO' THE FISH FRY.
WISH'T I COULD GO—MIZ MUSHRAT TOLE ME A FUNNY STORY..
SHE PUT OUT A HORNETS' NEST IN A PIE PAN AN' SOME CRITTUR ATE IT— HAW HAW!
SHE SAY SHE 'SPECTED THE VARMINT AND SHE GLAD SHE FOOLED HIM!
SO—SHE TRIED TO POISON ME! HARRUMPH!
YOU!?
YES, ME! COME ON IN HERE!
WHAT YOU WANTS, SIR?
I WANTS YOU TO WRITE A SUICIDE NOTE.
NIX! I DON'T WANT TO COMMIT SUICIDE— GOOD-BYE! —WOOP!
HOLE ON!

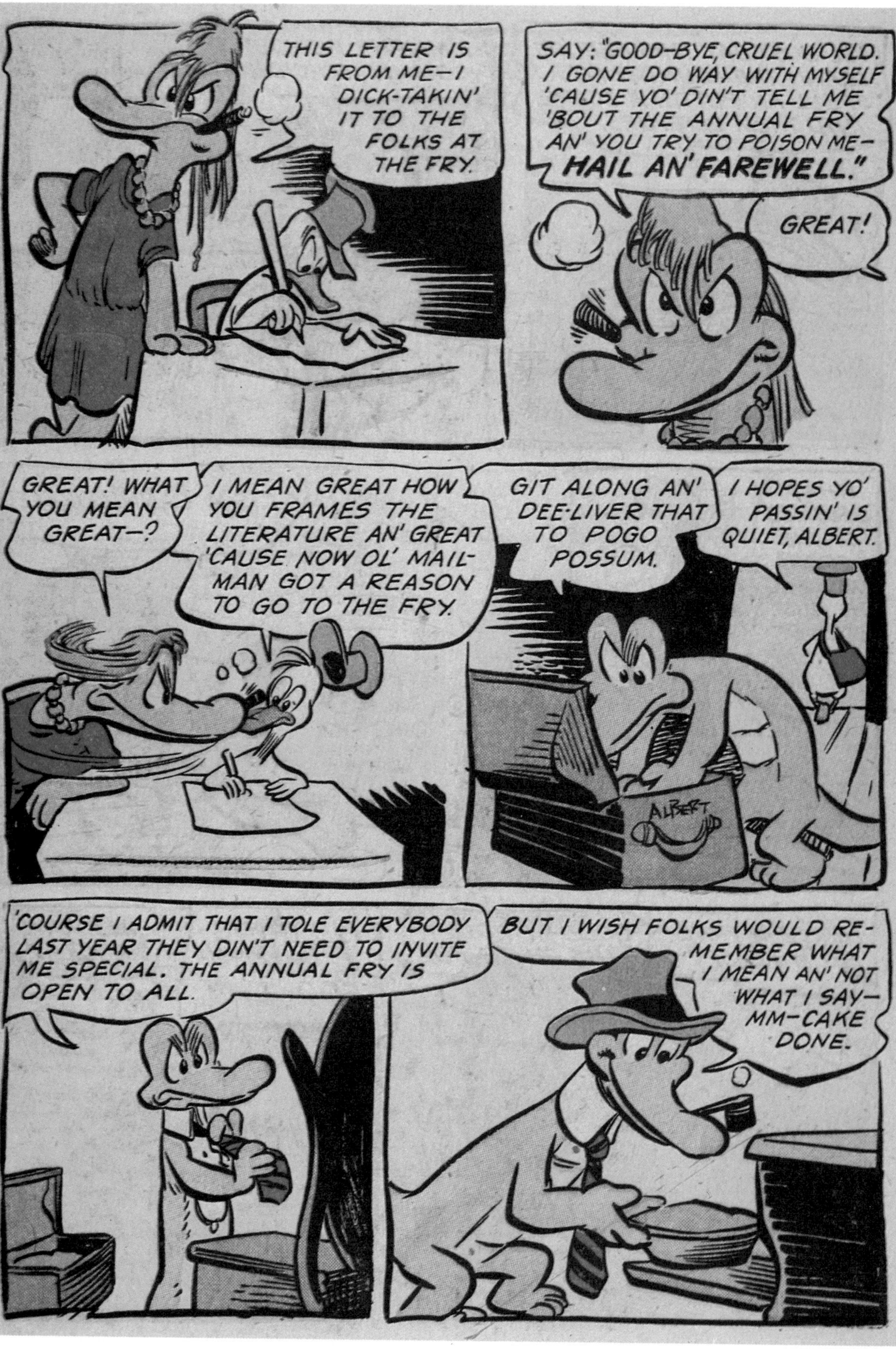

THIS LETTER IS FROM ME—I DICK-TAKIN' IT TO THE FOLKS AT THE FRY.
SAY: "GOOD-BYE, CRUEL WORLD. I GONE DO WAY WITH MYSELF 'CAUSE YO' DIN'T TELL ME 'BOUT THE ANNUAL FRY AN' YOU TRY TO POISON ME— HAIL AN' FAREWELL."
GREAT!
GREAT! WHAT YOU MEAN GREAT—?
I MEAN GREAT HOW YOU FRAMES THE LITERATURE AN' GREAT 'CAUSE NOW OL' MAIL-MAN GOT A REASON TO GO TO THE FRY.
GIT ALONG AN' DEE-LIVER THAT TO POGO POSSUM.
I HOPES YO' PASSIN' IS QUIET, ALBERT.
ALBERT
'COURSE I ADMIT THAT I TOLE EVERYBODY LAST YEAR THEY DIN'T NEED TO INVITE ME SPECIAL. THE ANNUAL FRY IS OPEN TO ALL.
BUT I WISH FOLKS WOULD RE-MEMBER WHAT I MEAN AN' NOT WHAT I SAY— MM-CAKE DONE.

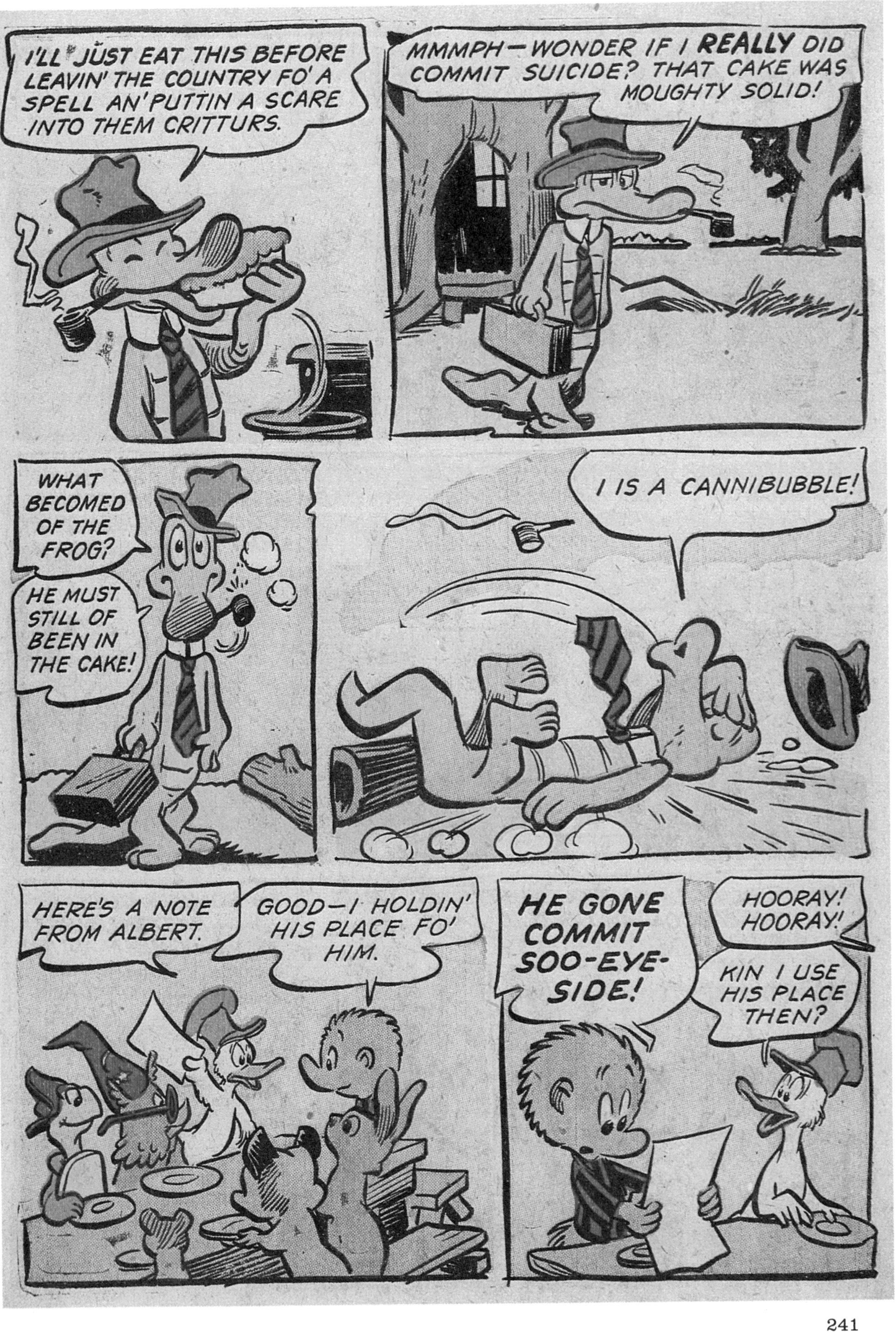

I'LL JUST EAT THIS BEFORE LEAVIN' THE COUNTRY FO' A SPELL AN' PUTTIN A SCARE INTO THEM CRITTURS.
MMMPH—WONDER IF I **REALLY** DID COMMIT SUICIDE? THAT CAKE WAS MOUGHTY SOLID!
WHAT BECOMED OF THE FROG?
HE MUST STILL OF BEEN IN THE CAKE!
I IS A CANNIBUBBLE!
HERE'S A NOTE FROM ALBERT.
GOOD—I HOLDIN' HIS PLACE FO' HIM.
HE GONE COMMIT SOO-EYE-SIDE!
HOORAY! HOORAY!
KIN I USE HIS PLACE THEN?

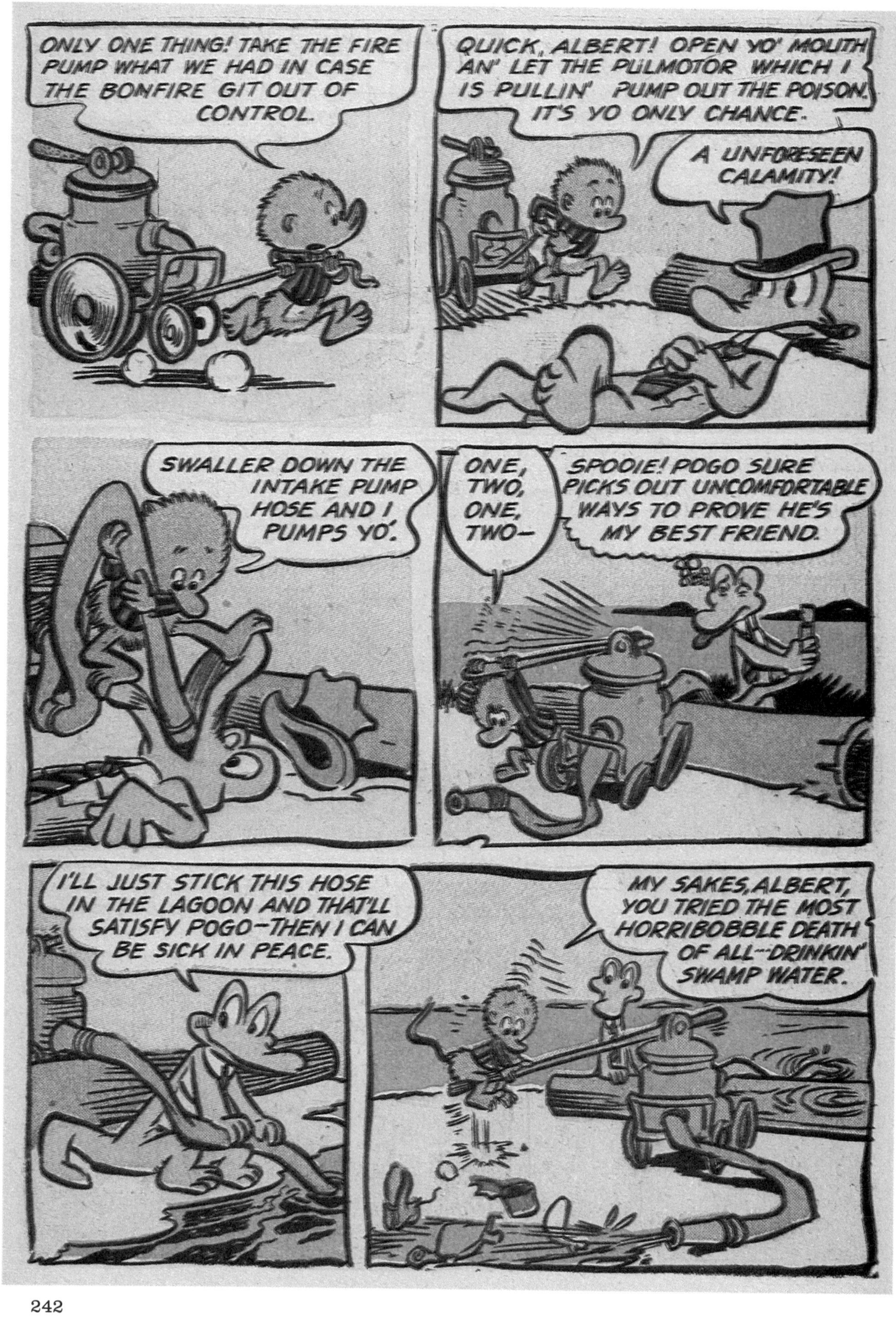
ONLY ONE THING! TAKE THE FIRE PUMP WHAT WE HAD IN CASE THE BONFIRE GIT OUT OF CONTROL.
QUICK, ALBERT! OPEN YO' MOUTH AN' LET THE PULMOTOR WHICH I IS PULLIN' PUMP OUT THE POISON. IT'S YO ONLY CHANCE.
A UNFORESEEN CALAMITY!
SWALLER DOWN THE INTAKE PUMP HOSE AND I PUMPS YO'.
ONE, TWO, ONE, TWO—
SPOOIE! POGO SURE PICKS OUT UNCOMFORTABLE WAYS TO PROVE HE'S MY BEST FRIEND.
I'LL JUST STICK THIS HOSE IN THE LAGOON AND THAT'LL SATISFY POGO—THEN I CAN BE SICK IN PEACE.
MY SAKES, ALBERT, YOU TRIED THE MOST HORRIBOBBLE DEATH OF ALL—DRINKIN' SWAMP WATER.

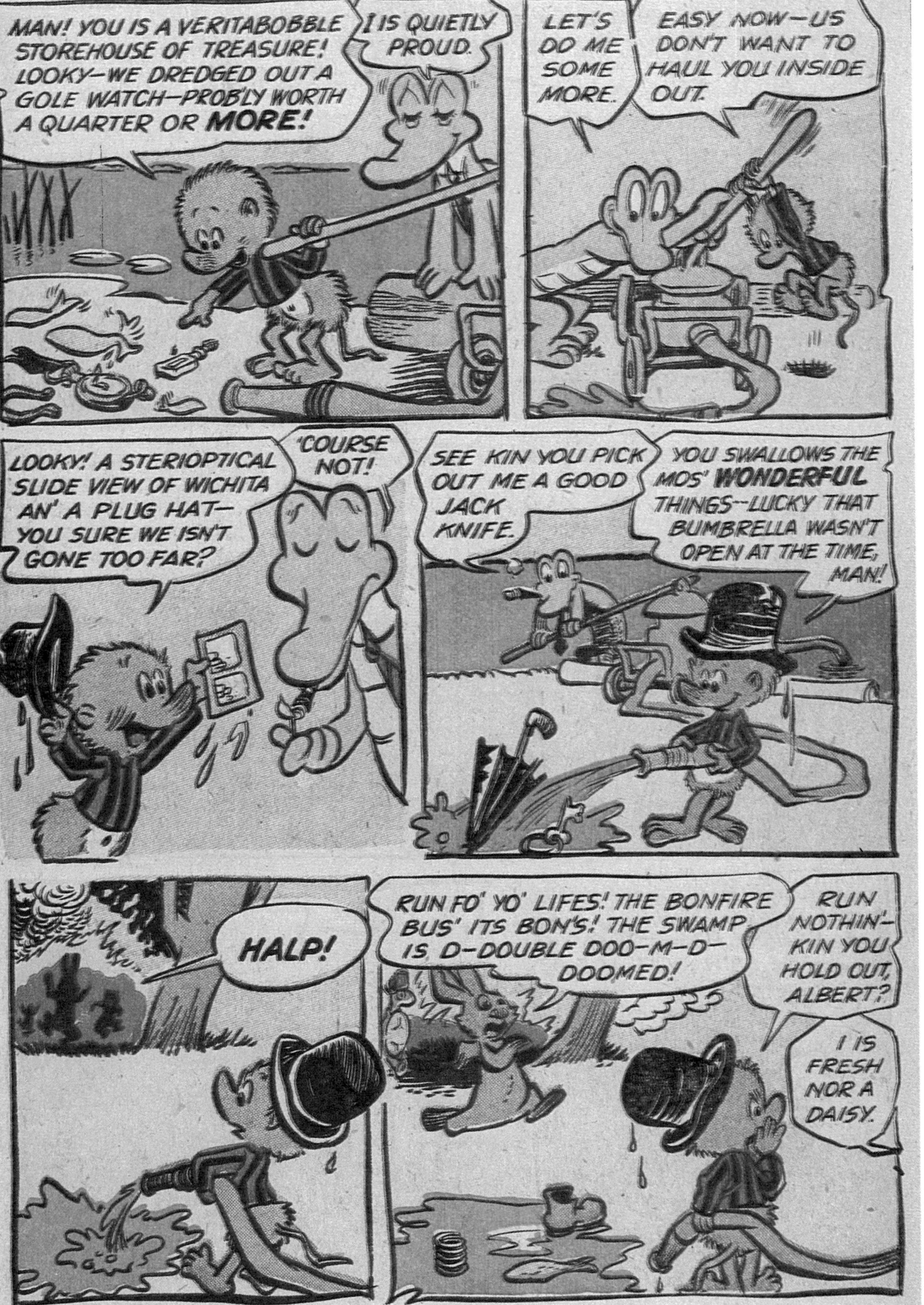
MAN! YOU IS A VERITABOBBLE STOREHOUSE OF TREASURE! LOOKY—WE DREDGED OUT A GOLE WATCH—PROB'LY WORTH A QUARTER OR MORE!
I IS QUIETLY PROUD.
LET'S DO ME SOME MORE.
EASY NOW—US DON'T WANT TO HAUL YOU INSIDE OUT.
LOOKY! A STERIOPTICAL SLIDE VIEW OF WICHITA AN' A PLUG HAT—YOU SURE WE ISN'T GONE TOO FAR?
'COURSE NOT!
SEE KIN YOU PICK OUT ME A GOOD JACK KNIFE.
YOU SWALLOWS THE MOS' WONDERFUL THINGS--LUCKY THAT BUMBRELLA WASN'T OPEN AT THE TIME, MAN!
HALP!
RUN FO' YO' LIFES! THE BONFIRE BUS' ITS BON'S! THE SWAMP IS D-DOUBLE DOO-M-D-DOOMED!
RUN NOTHIN'-KIN YOU HOLD OUT, ALBERT?
I IS FRESH NOR A DAISY.

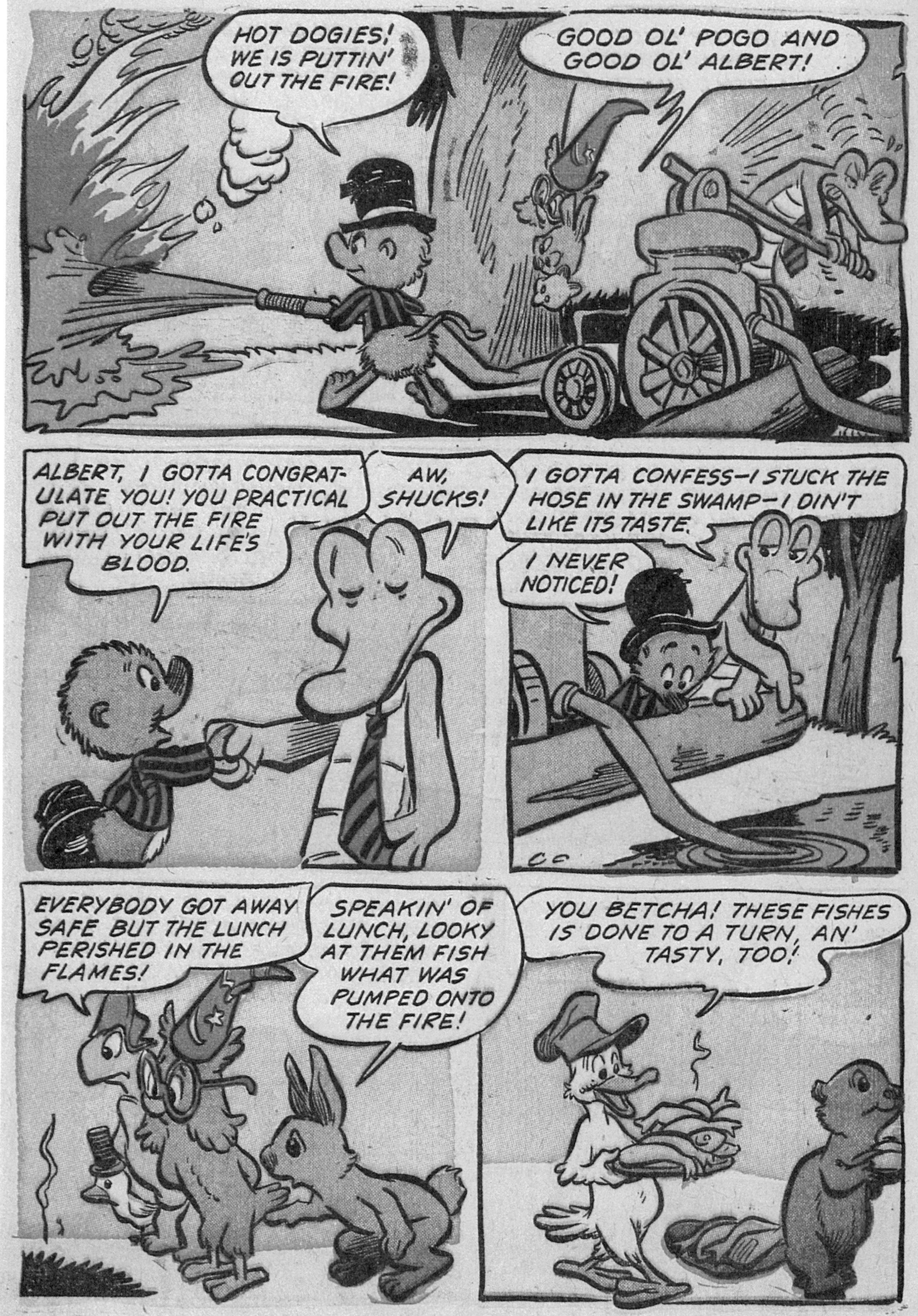
HOT DOGIES! WE IS PUTTIN' OUT THE FIRE!
GOOD OL' POGO AND GOOD OL' ALBERT!
ALBERT, I GOTTA CONGRAT-ULATE YOU! YOU PRACTICAL PUT OUT THE FIRE WITH YOUR LIFE'S BLOOD.
AW, SHUCKS!
I GOTTA CONFESS—I STUCK THE HOSE IN THE SWAMP—I DIN'T LIKE ITS TASTE.
I NEVER NOTICED!
EVERYBODY GOT AWAY SAFE BUT THE LUNCH PERISHED IN THE FLAMES!
SPEAKIN' OF LUNCH, LOOKY AT THEM FISH WHAT WAS PUMPED ONTO THE FIRE!
YOU BETCHA! THESE FISHES IS DONE TO A TURN, AN' TASTY, TOO!

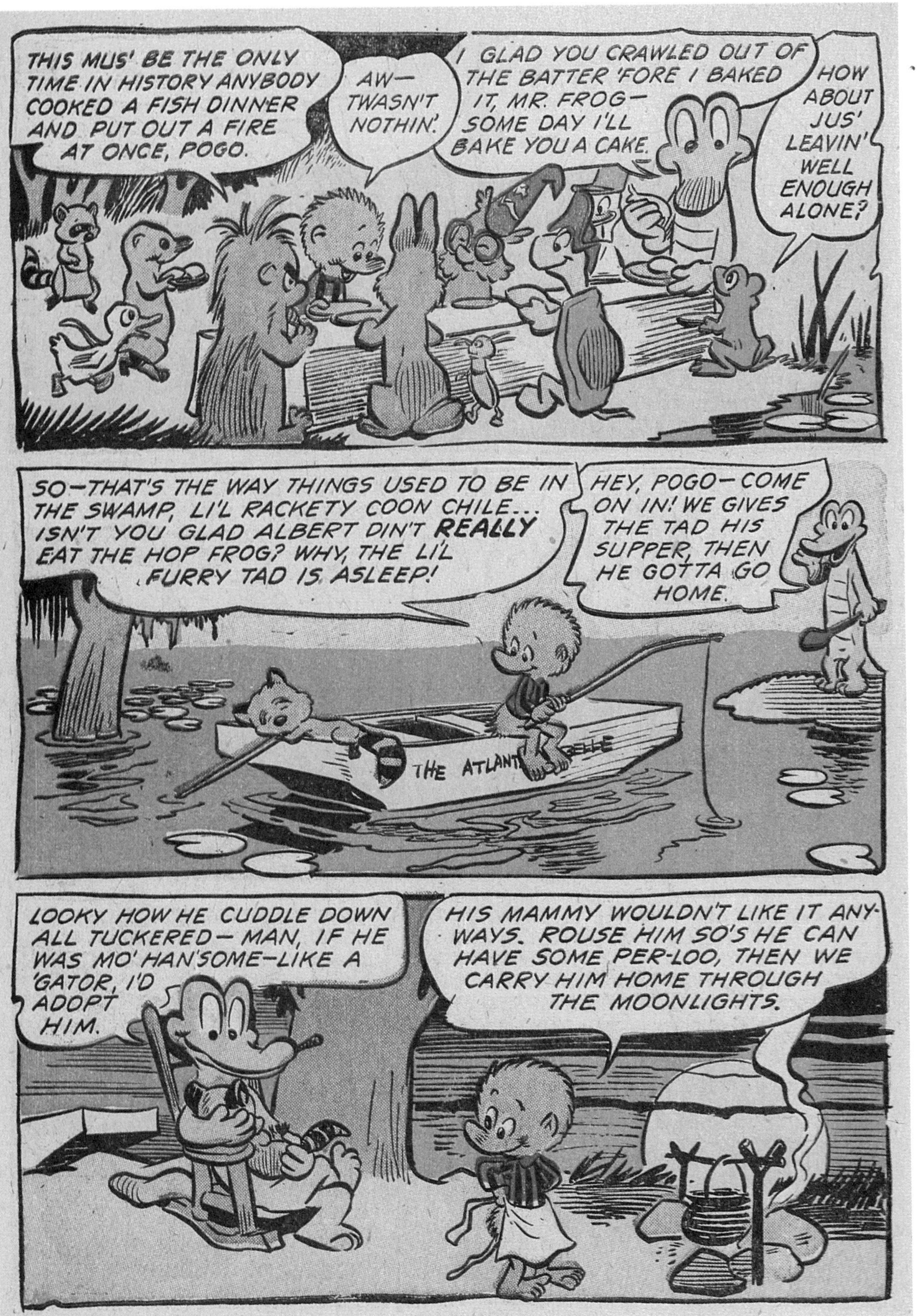
THIS MUS' BE THE ONLY TIME IN HISTORY ANYBODY COOKED A FISH DINNER AND PUT OUT A FIRE AT ONCE, POGO.
AW— TWASN'T NOTHIN'.
I GLAD YOU CRAWLED OUT OF THE BATTER 'FORE I BAKED IT, MR. FROG— SOME DAY I'LL BAKE YOU A CAKE.
HOW ABOUT JUS' LEAVIN' WELL ENOUGH ALONE?
SO—THAT'S THE WAY THINGS USED TO BE IN THE SWAMP, LI'L RACKETY COON CHILE... ISN'T YOU GLAD ALBERT DIN'T REALLY EAT THE HOP FROG? WHY, THE LI'L FURRY TAD IS ASLEEP!
HEY, POGO—COME ON IN! WE GIVES THE TAD HIS SUPPER, THEN HE GOTTA GO HOME.
THE ATLANT BELLE
LOOKY HOW HE CUDDLE DOWN ALL TUCKERED—MAN, IF HE WAS MO' HAN'SOME—LIKE A 'GATOR, I'D ADOPT HIM.
HIS MAMMY WOULDN'T LIKE IT ANY-WAYS. ROUSE HIM SO'S HE CAN HAVE SOME PER-LOO, THEN WE CARRY HIM HOME THROUGH THE MOONLIGHTS.

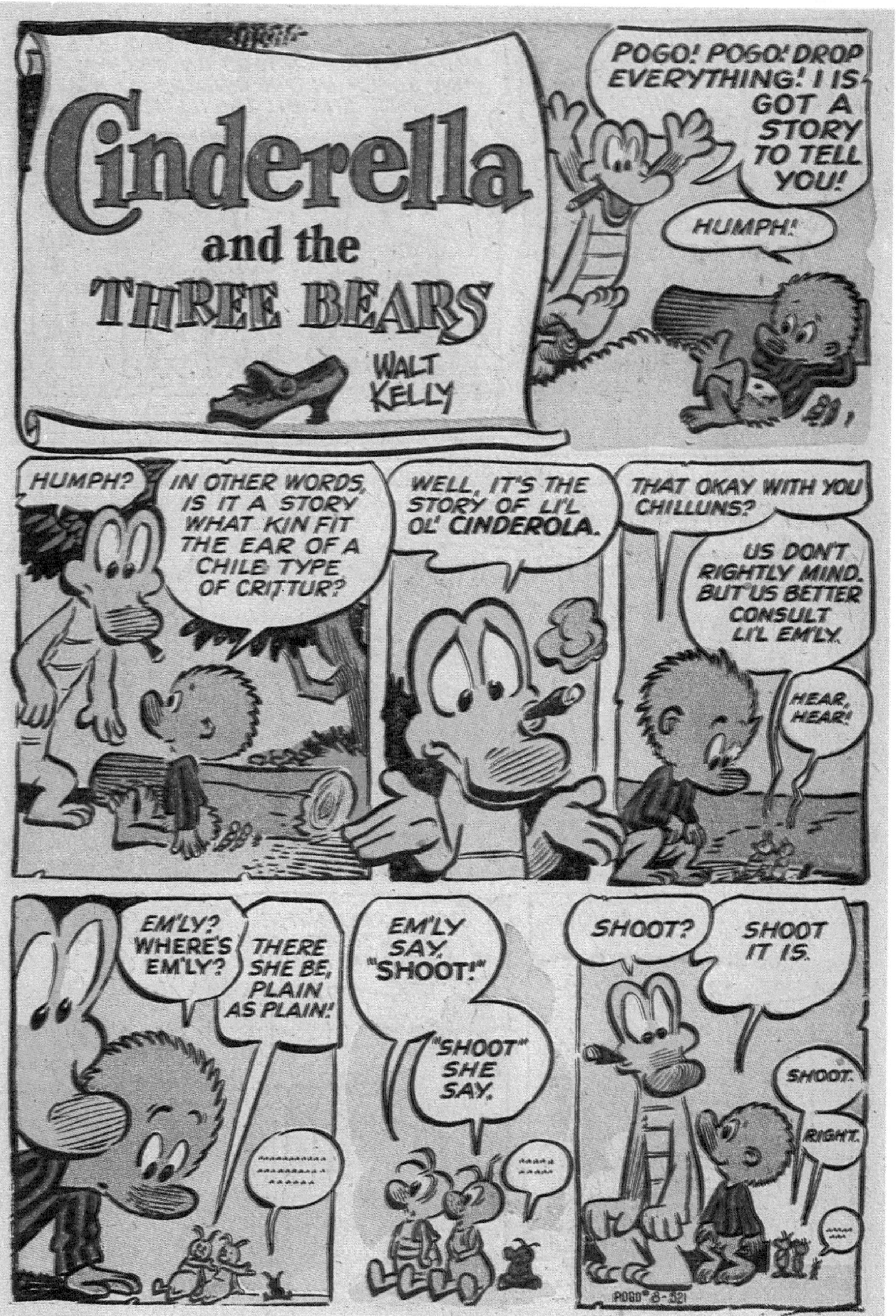
Cinderella
and the
THREE BEARS
WALT KELLY
POGO! POGO! DROP EVERYTHING! I IS GOT A STORY TO TELL YOU!
HUMPH!
HUMPH?
IN OTHER WORDS, IS IT A STORY WHAT KIN FIT THE EAR OF A CHILE TYPE OF CRITTUR?
WELL, IT'S THE STORY OF LI'L OL' CINDEROLA.
THAT OKAY WITH YOU CHILLUNS?
US DON'T RIGHTLY MIND. BUT US BETTER CONSULT LI'L EM'LY.
HEAR, HEAR!
EM'LY? WHERE'S EM'LY?
THERE SHE BE, PLAIN AS PLAIN!
EM'LY SAY, "SHOOT!"
"SHOOT" SHE SAY.
SHOOT?
SHOOT IT IS.
SHOOT.
RIGHT.
POGO® 8-521

From *Pogo Possum* No. 8, Jan.-Mar. 1952.

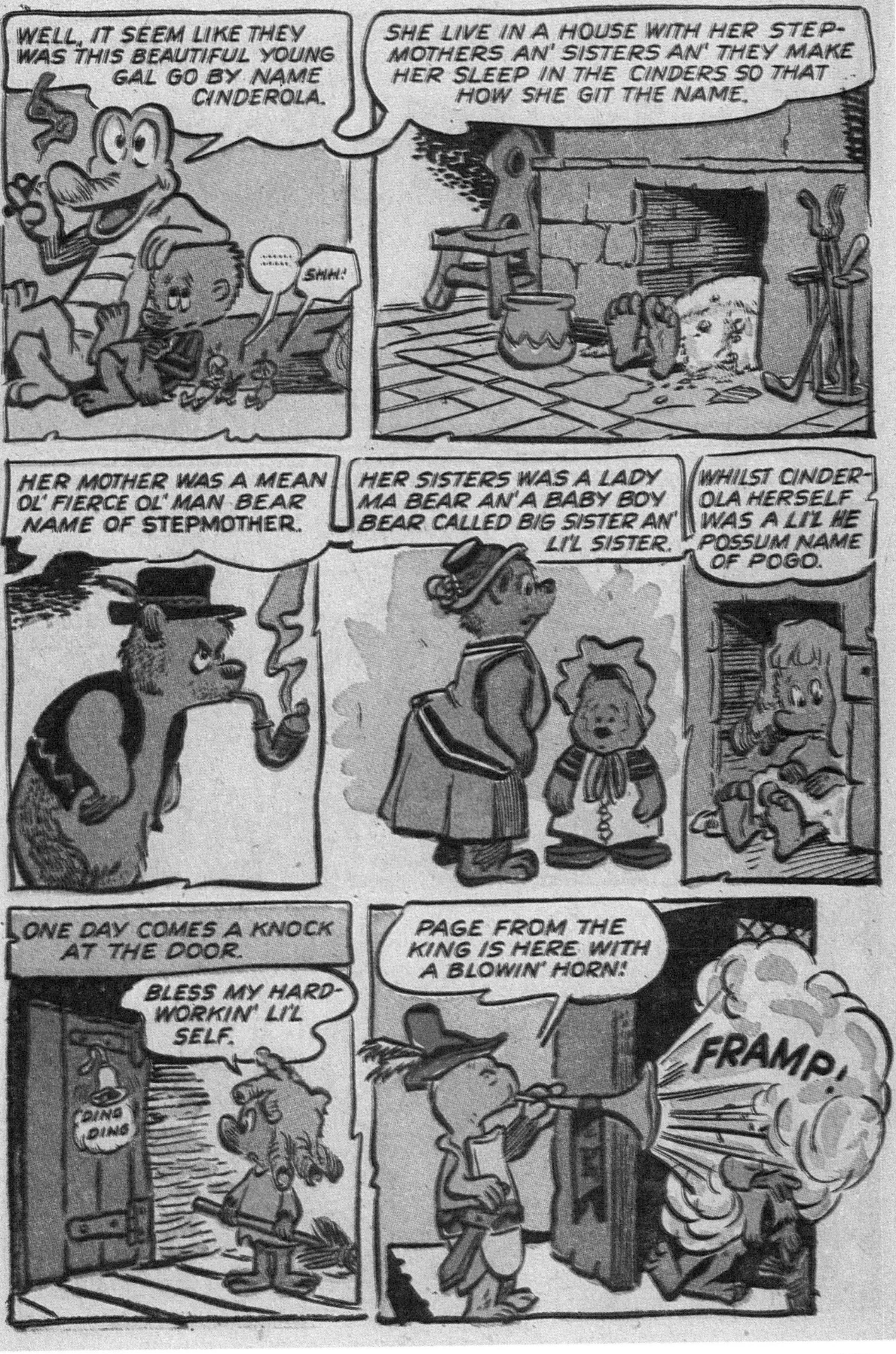
WELL, IT SEEM LIKE THEY WAS THIS BEAUTIFUL YOUNG GAL GO BY NAME CINDEROLA.
SHH!
SHE LIVE IN A HOUSE WITH HER STEP-MOTHERS AN' SISTERS AN' THEY MAKE HER SLEEP IN THE CINDERS SO THAT HOW SHE GIT THE NAME.
HER MOTHER WAS A MEAN OL' FIERCE OL' MAN BEAR NAME OF STEPMOTHER.
HER SISTERS WAS A LADY MA BEAR AN' A BABY BOY BEAR CALLED BIG SISTER AN' LI'L SISTER.
WHILST CINDER-OLA HERSELF WAS A LI'L HE POSSUM NAME OF POGO.
ONE DAY COMES A KNOCK AT THE DOOR.
DING DING
BLESS MY HARD-WORKIN' LI'L SELF.
PAGE FROM THE KING IS HERE WITH A BLOWIN' HORN!
FRAMP!

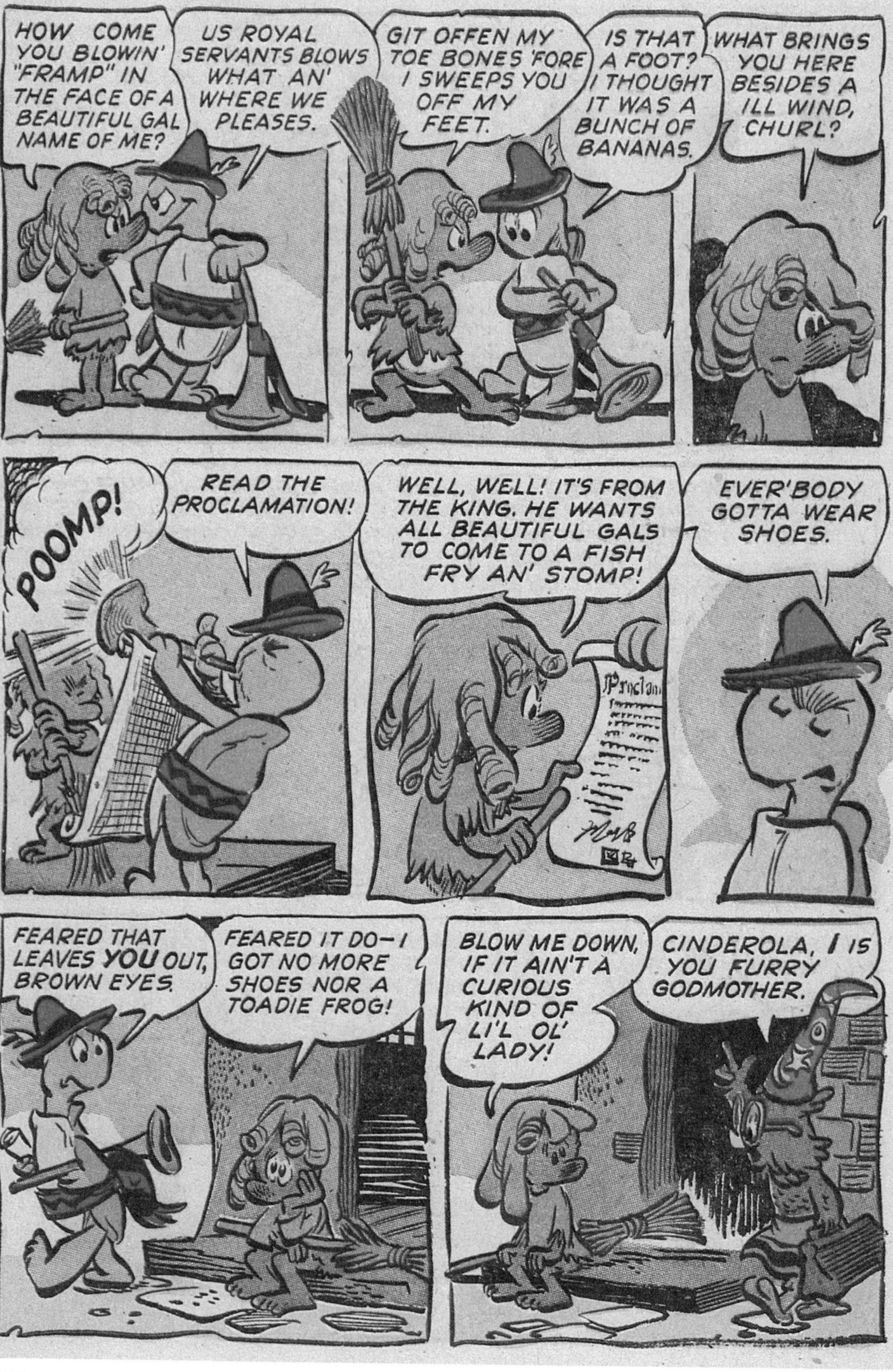

HOW COME YOU BLOWIN' "FRAMP" IN THE FACE OF A BEAUTIFUL GAL NAME OF ME?
US ROYAL SERVANTS BLOWS WHAT AN' WHERE WE PLEASES.
GIT OFFEN MY TOE BONES 'FORE I SWEEPS YOU OFF MY FEET.
IS THAT A FOOT? I THOUGHT IT WAS A BUNCH OF BANANAS.
WHAT BRINGS YOU HERE BESIDES A ILL WIND, CHURL?
POOMP!
READ THE PROCLAMATION!
WELL, WELL! IT'S FROM THE KING. HE WANTS ALL BEAUTIFUL GALS TO COME TO A FISH FRY AN' STOMP!
EVER'BODY GOTTA WEAR SHOES.
FEARED THAT LEAVES YOU OUT, BROWN EYES.
FEARED IT DO—I GOT NO MORE SHOES NOR A TOADIE FROG!
BLOW ME DOWN, IF IT AIN'T A CURIOUS KIND OF LI'L OL' LADY!
CINDEROLA, I IS YOU FURRY GODMOTHER.

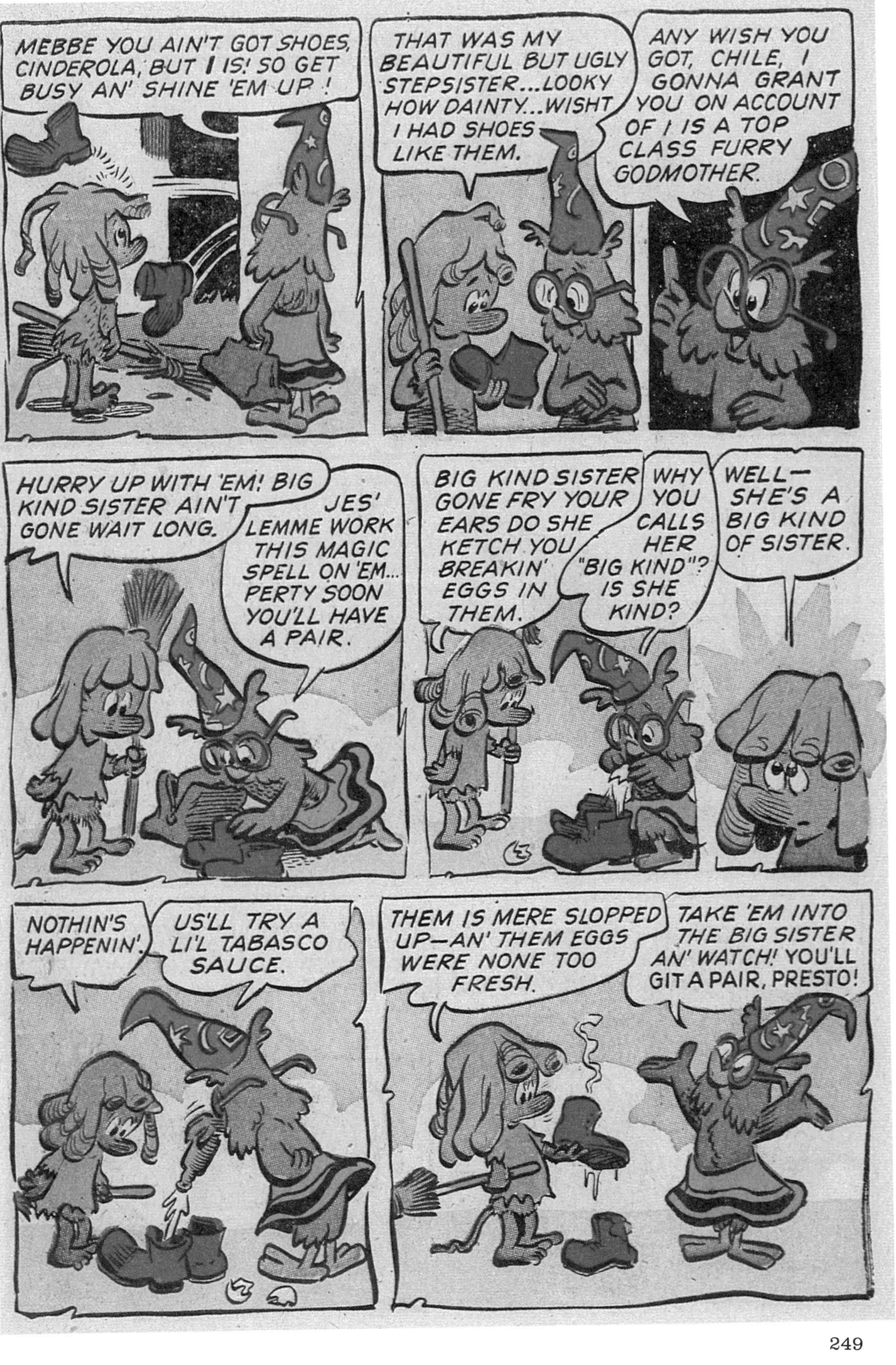
MEBBE YOU AIN'T GOT SHOES, CINDEROLA, BUT I IS! SO GET BUSY AN' SHINE 'EM UP!
THAT WAS MY BEAUTIFUL BUT UGLY STEPSISTER...LOOKY HOW DAINTY...WISHT I HAD SHOES LIKE THEM.
ANY WISH YOU GOT, CHILE, I GONNA GRANT YOU ON ACCOUNT OF I IS A TOP CLASS FURRY GODMOTHER.
HURRY UP WITH 'EM! BIG KIND SISTER AIN'T GONE WAIT LONG.
JES' LEMME WORK THIS MAGIC SPELL ON 'EM... PERTY SOON YOU'LL HAVE A PAIR.
BIG KIND SISTER GONE FRY YOUR EARS DO SHE KETCH YOU BREAKIN' EGGS IN THEM.
WHY YOU CALLS HER "BIG KIND"? IS SHE KIND?
WELL— SHE'S A BIG KIND OF SISTER.
NOTHIN'S HAPPENIN'.
US'LL TRY A LI'L TABASCO SAUCE.
THEM IS MERE SLOPPED UP—AN' THEM EGGS WERE NONE TOO FRESH.
TAKE 'EM INTO THE BIG SISTER AN' WATCH! YOU'LL GIT A PAIR, PRESTO!

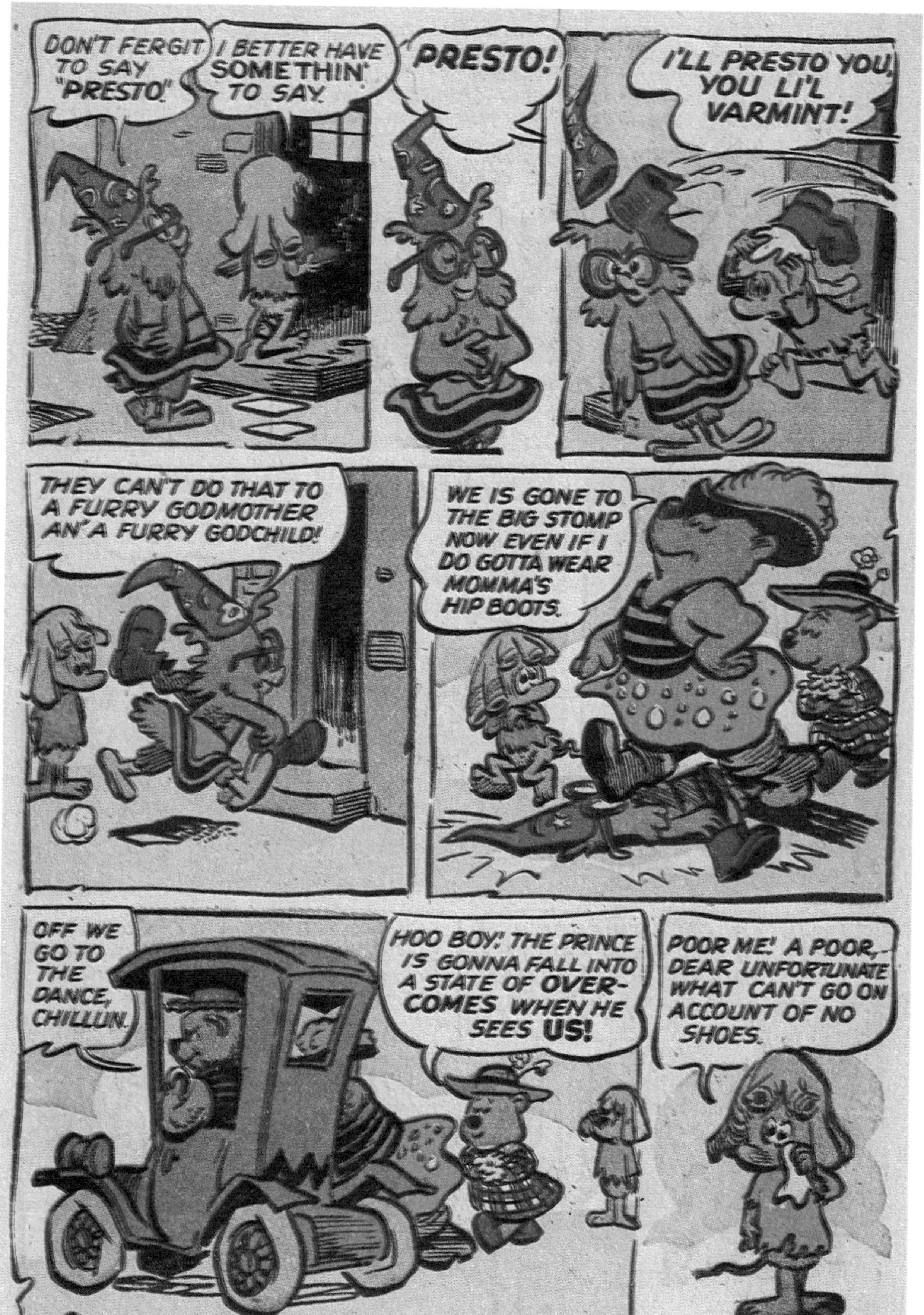
DON'T FERGIT TO SAY "PRESTO!"
I BETTER HAVE SOMETHIN' TO SAY.
PRESTO!
I'LL PRESTO YOU, YOU LI'L VARMINT!
THEY CAN'T DO THAT TO A FURRY GODMOTHER AN' A FURRY GODCHILD!
WE IS GONE TO THE BIG STOMP NOW EVEN IF I DO GOTTA WEAR MOMMA'S HIP BOOTS.
OFF WE GO TO THE DANCE, CHILLUN.
HOO BOY! THE PRINCE IS GONNA FALL INTO A STATE OF OVER-COMES WHEN HE SEES US!
POOR ME! A POOR, DEAR UNFORTUNATE WHAT CAN'T GO ON ACCOUNT OF NO SHOES.

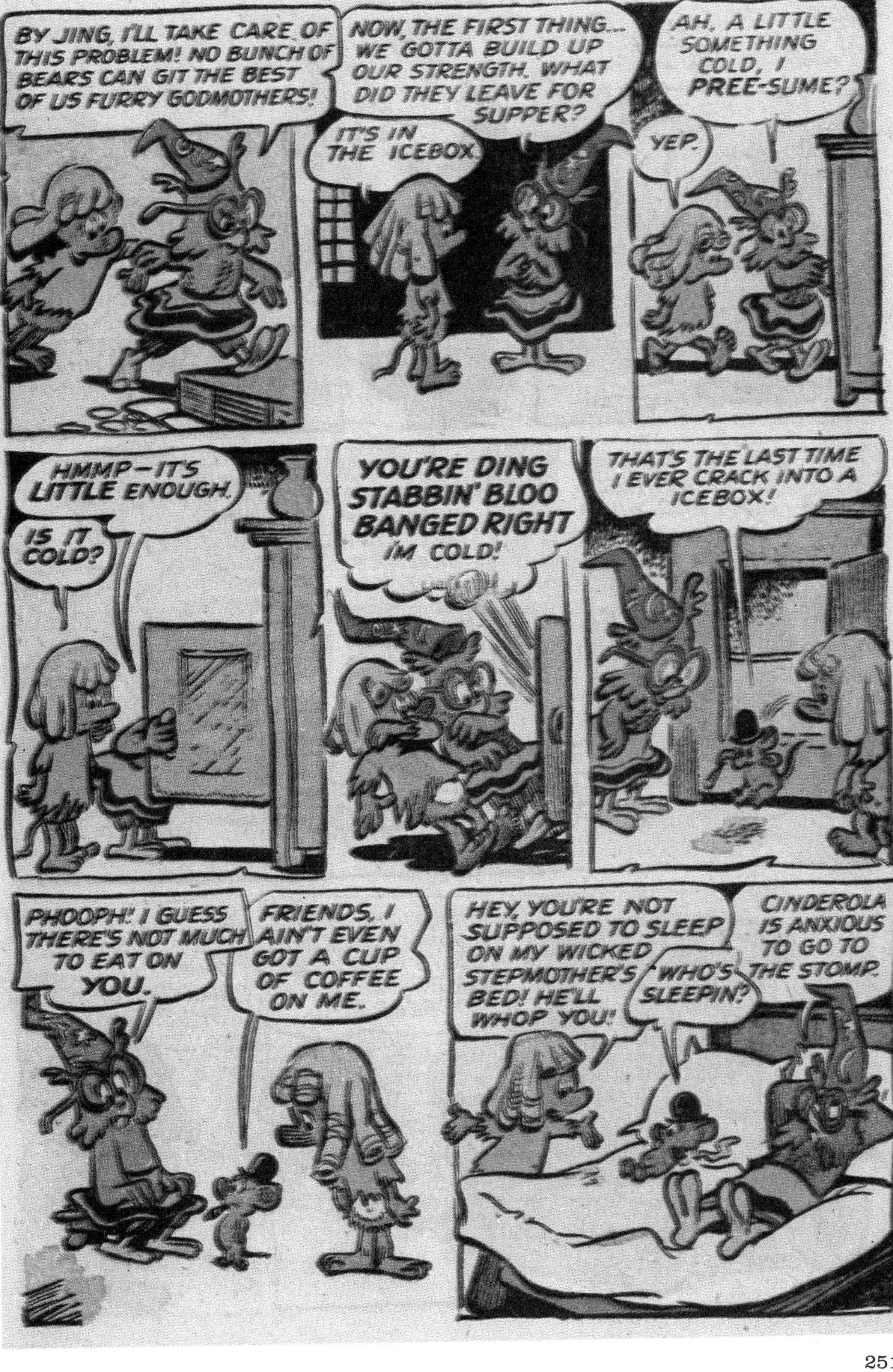
BY JING, I'LL TAKE CARE OF THIS PROBLEM! NO BUNCH OF BEARS CAN GIT THE BEST OF US FURRY GODMOTHERS!
NOW, THE FIRST THING... WE GOTTA BUILD UP OUR STRENGTH. WHAT DID THEY LEAVE FOR SUPPER?
IT'S IN THE ICEBOX.
AH, A LITTLE SOMETHING COLD, I PREE-SUME?
YEP.
HMMP—IT'S LITTLE ENOUGH.
IS IT COLD?
YOU'RE DING STABBIN' BLOO BANGED RIGHT I'M COLD!
THAT'S THE LAST TIME I EVER CRACK INTO A ICEBOX!
PHOOPH! I GUESS THERE'S NOT MUCH TO EAT ON YOU.
FRIENDS, I AIN'T EVEN GOT A CUP OF COFFEE ON ME.
HEY, YOU'RE NOT SUPPOSED TO SLEEP ON MY WICKED STEPMOTHER'S BED! HE'LL WHOP YOU!
WHO'S SLEEPIN?
CINDEROLA IS ANXIOUS TO GO TO THE STOMP.

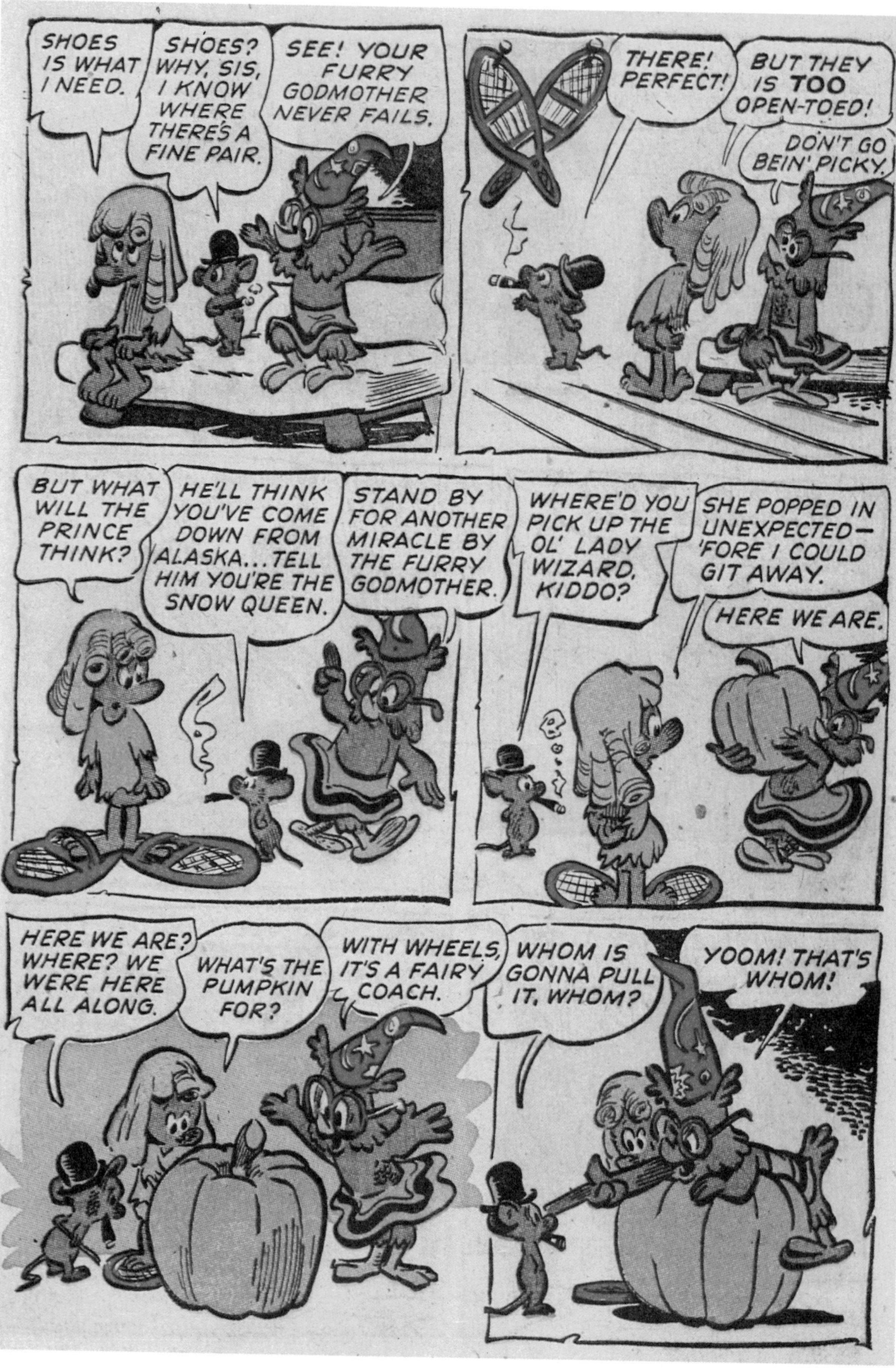
SHOES IS WHAT I NEED.
SHOES? WHY, SIS, I KNOW WHERE THERE'S A FINE PAIR.
SEE! YOUR FURRY GODMOTHER NEVER FAILS.
THERE! PERFECT!
BUT THEY IS **TOO** OPEN-TOED!
DON'T GO BEIN' PICKY.
BUT WHAT WILL THE PRINCE THINK?
HE'LL THINK YOU'VE COME DOWN FROM ALASKA...TELL HIM YOU'RE THE SNOW QUEEN.
STAND BY FOR ANOTHER MIRACLE BY THE FURRY GODMOTHER.
WHERE'D YOU PICK UP THE OL' LADY WIZARD, KIDDO?
SHE POPPED IN UNEXPECTED—'FORE I COULD GIT AWAY.
HERE WE ARE.
HERE WE ARE? WHERE? WE WERE HERE ALL ALONG.
WHAT'S THE PUMPKIN FOR?
WITH WHEELS, IT'S A FAIRY COACH.
WHOM IS GONNA PULL IT, WHOM?
YOOM! THAT'S WHOM!

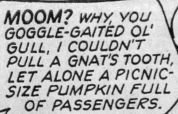

MOOM? WHY, YOU GOGGLE-GAITED OL' GULL, I COULDN'T PULL A GNAT'S TOOTH, LET ALONE A PICNIC-SIZE PUMPKIN FULL OF PASSENGERS.

ALA-GA-ROO-GA-ZAM! THERE! YOU'RE A HORSE!

IF I'M A HORSE, HE'S A BEAUTIFUL GAL!

THAT SETTLES THAT.

IN JUS' A WUFFY THIS COACH WILL BE READY FOR YOU, CINDEROLA.

IF I'M PULLIN', LADY, **YOU** IS PUSHIN'!

THINK ANYBODY WILL NOTICE MY SHOES IS STICKIN' OUT?

YOU WANT THE FRONT DOOR OR THE BACK, MISS?

LET'S TRY TO SNEAK IN A WINDOW.

POORADE! POO-RADE!

YOU SHOULD BE HOME IN BED!

ME, TOO.

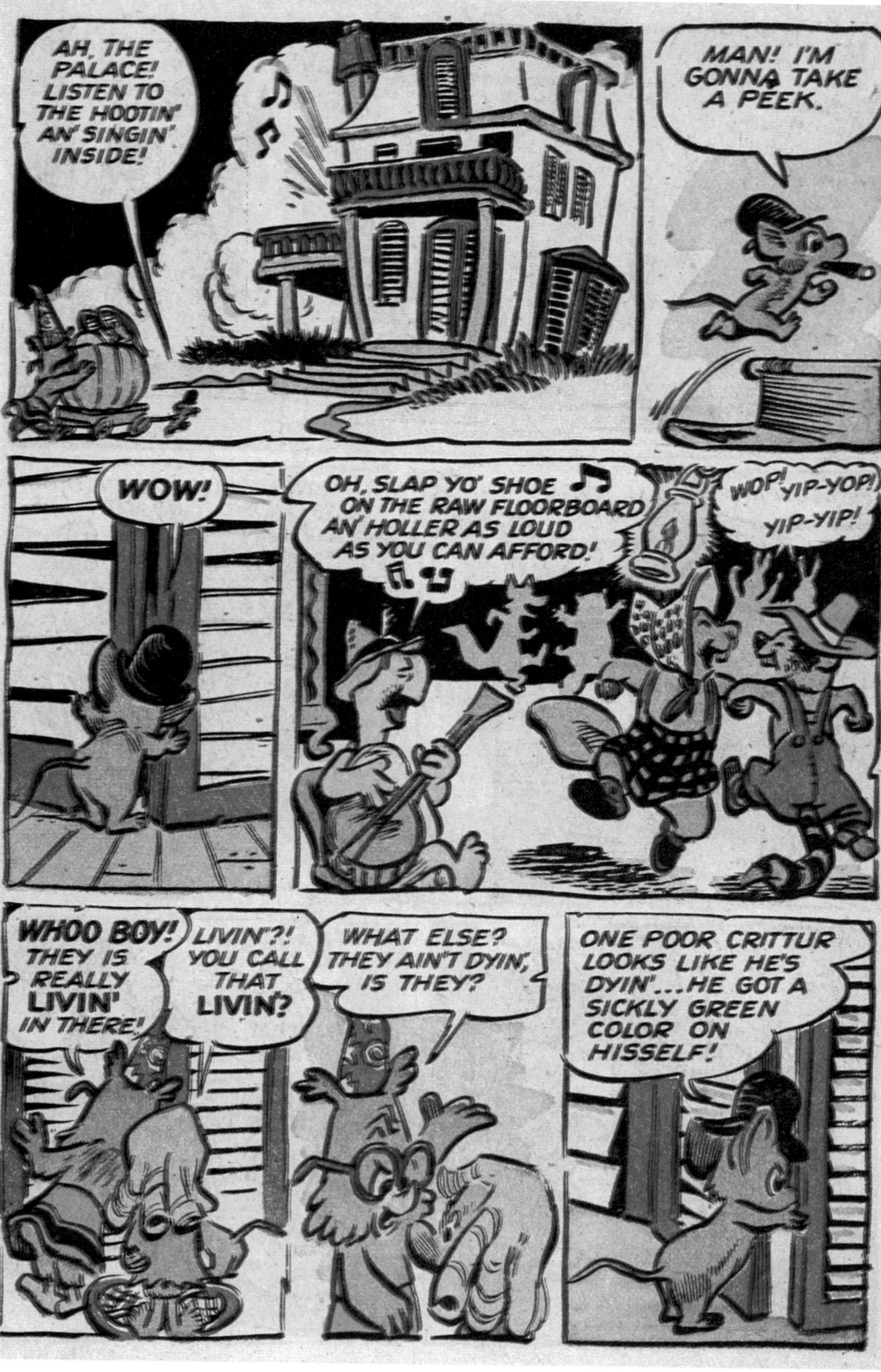
AH, THE PALACE! LISTEN TO THE HOOTIN' AN' SINGIN' INSIDE!
MAN! I'M GONNA TAKE A PEEK.
WOW!
OH, SLAP YO' SHOE ON THE RAW FLOORBOARD AN' HOLLER AS LOUD AS YOU CAN AFFORD!
WOP! YIP-YOP! YIP-YIP!
WHOO BOY! THEY IS REALLY LIVIN' IN THERE!
LIVIN'"?! YOU CALL THAT LIVIN'?
WHAT ELSE? THEY AIN'T DYIN', IS THEY?
ONE POOR CRITTUR LOOKS LIKE HE'S DYIN'...HE GOT A SICKLY GREEN COLOR ON HISSELF!

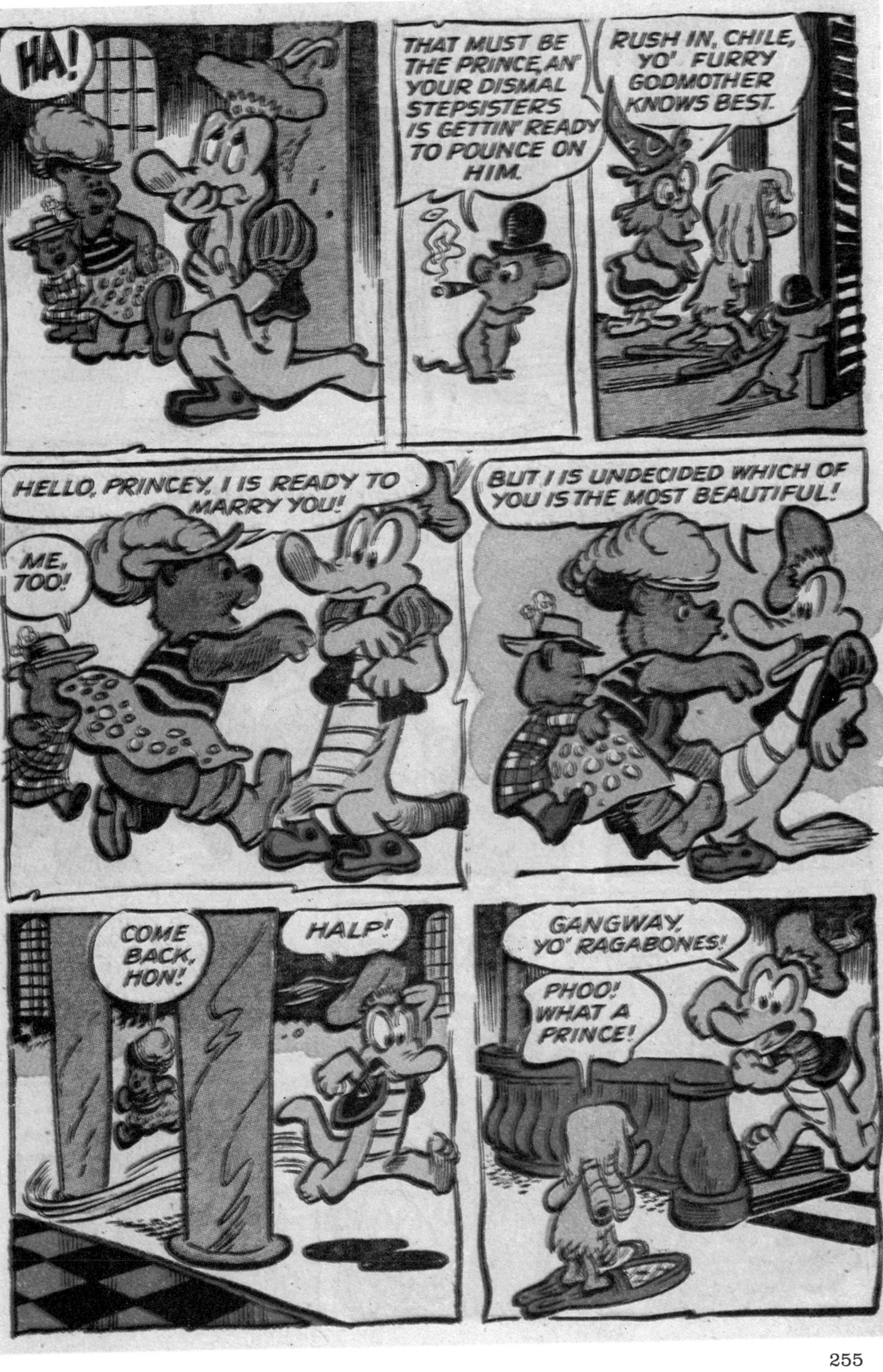
HA!
THAT MUST BE THE PRINCE, AN' YOUR DISMAL STEPSISTERS IS GETTIN' READY TO POUNCE ON HIM.
RUSH IN, CHILE, YO' FURRY GODMOTHER KNOWS BEST.
HELLO, PRINCEY, I IS READY TO MARRY YOU!
ME, TOO!
BUT I IS UNDECIDED WHICH OF YOU IS THE MOST BEAUTIFUL!
COME BACK, HON!
HALP!
GANGWAY, YO' RAGABONES!
PHOO! WHAT A PRINCE!

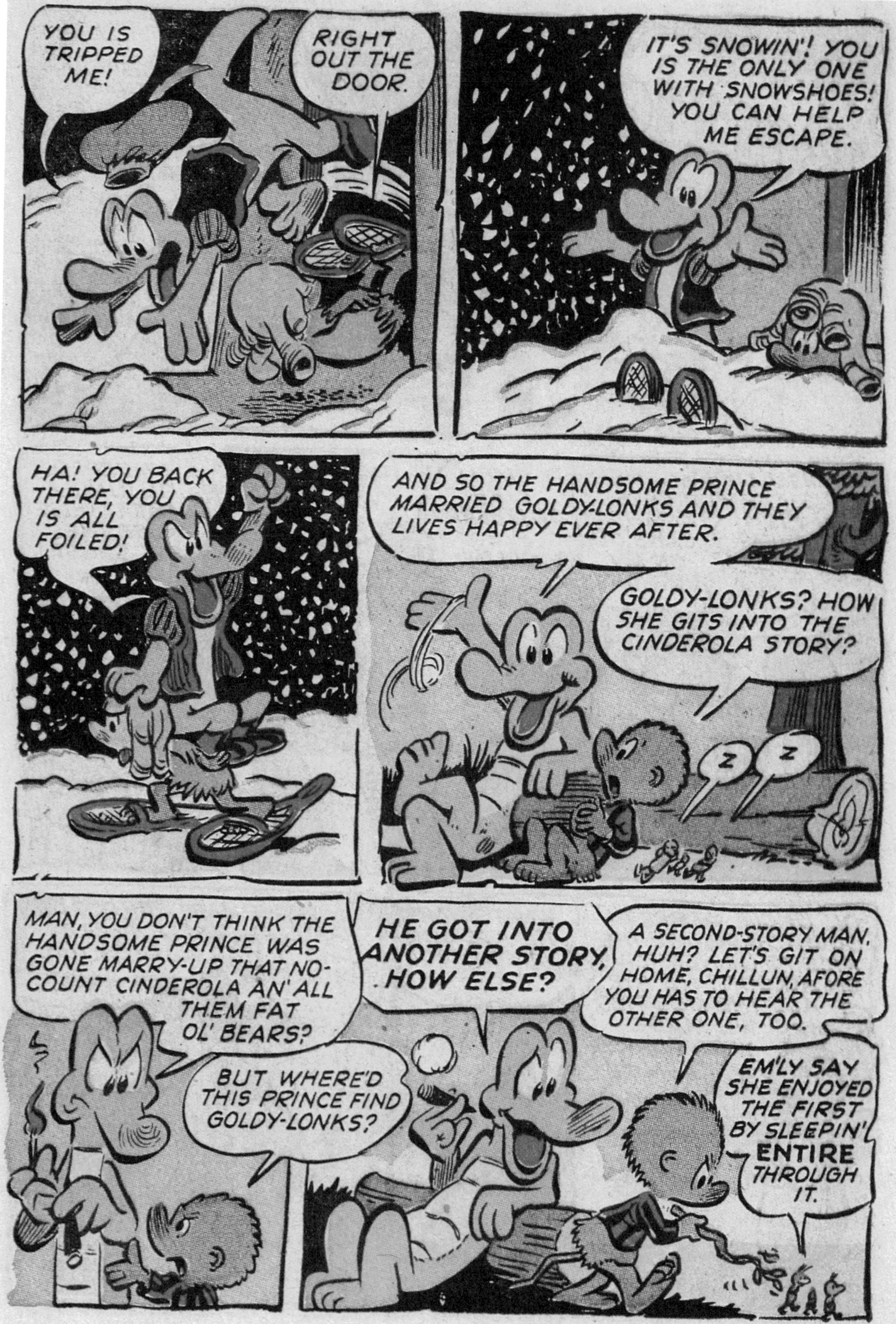
YOU IS TRIPPED ME!
RIGHT OUT THE DOOR.
IT'S SNOWIN'! YOU IS THE ONLY ONE WITH SNOWSHOES! YOU CAN HELP ME ESCAPE.
HA! YOU BACK THERE, YOU IS ALL FOILED!
AND SO THE HANDSOME PRINCE MARRIED GOLDY-LONKS AND THEY LIVES HAPPY EVER AFTER.
GOLDY-LONKS? HOW SHE GITS INTO THE CINDEROLA STORY?
Z
Z
MAN, YOU DON'T THINK THE HANDSOME PRINCE WAS GONE MARRY-UP THAT NO-COUNT CINDEROLA AN' ALL THEM FAT OL' BEARS?
BUT WHERE'D THIS PRINCE FIND GOLDY-LONKS?
HE GOT INTO ANOTHER STORY, HOW ELSE?
A SECOND-STORY MAN, HUH? LET'S GIT ON HOME, CHILLUN, AFORE YOU HAS TO HEAR THE OTHER ONE, TOO.
EM'LY SAY SHE ENJOYED THE FIRST BY SLEEPIN' ENTIRE THROUGH IT.

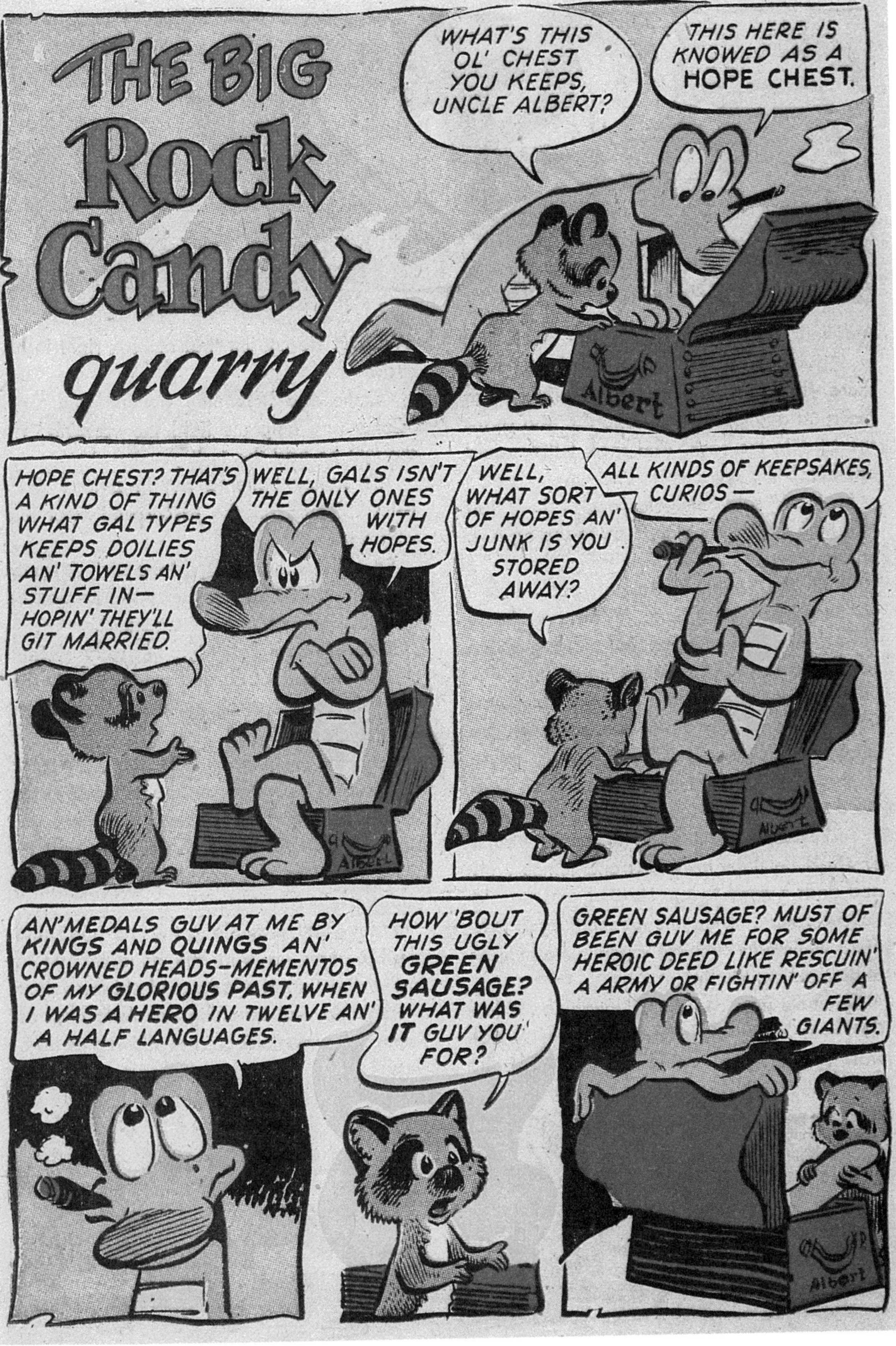
THE BIG Rock Candy quarry
WHAT'S THIS OL' CHEST YOU KEEPS, UNCLE ALBERT?
THIS HERE IS KNOWED AS A HOPE CHEST.
Albert
HOPE CHEST? THAT'S A KIND OF THING WHAT GAL TYPES KEEPS DOILIES AN' TOWELS AN' STUFF IN— HOPIN' THEY'LL GIT MARRIED.
WELL, GALS ISN'T THE ONLY ONES WITH HOPES.
WELL, WHAT SORT OF HOPES AN' JUNK IS YOU STORED AWAY?
ALL KINDS OF KEEPSAKES, CURIOS —
AN' MEDALS GUV AT ME BY KINGS AND QUINGS AN' CROWNED HEADS—MEMENTOS OF MY GLORIOUS PAST, WHEN I WAS A HERO IN TWELVE AN' A HALF LANGUAGES.
HOW 'BOUT THIS UGLY GREEN SAUSAGE? WHAT WAS IT GUV YOU FOR?
GREEN SAUSAGE? MUST OF BEEN GUV ME FOR SOME HEROIC DEED LIKE RESCUIN' A ARMY OR FIGHTIN' OFF A FEW GIANTS.
Albert

From *Pogo Possum* No. 8, Jan.-Mar. 1952.

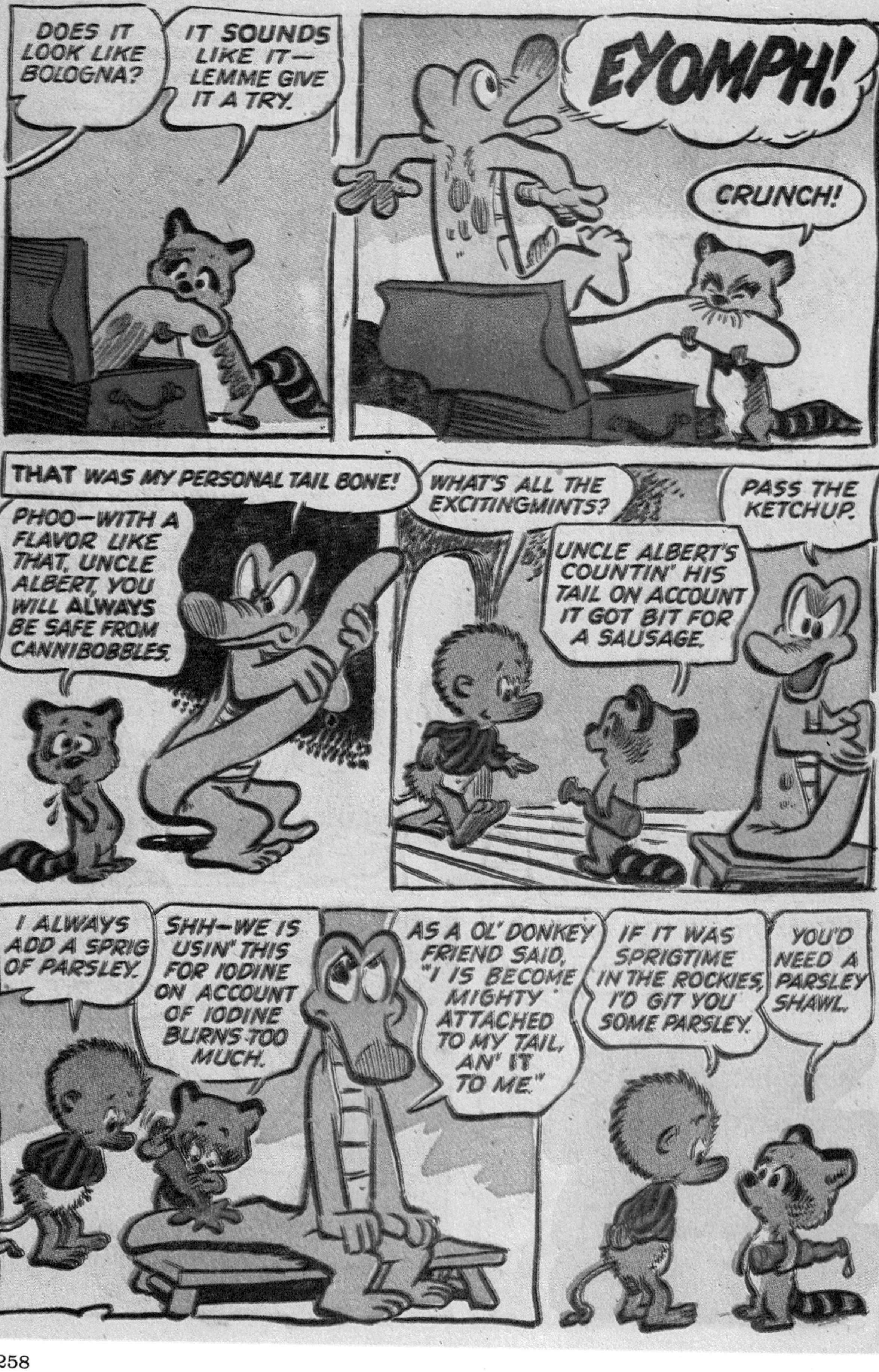
DOES IT LOOK LIKE BOLOGNA?
IT SOUNDS LIKE IT— LEMME GIVE IT A TRY.
EYOMPH!
CRUNCH!
THAT WAS MY PERSONAL TAIL BONE!
PHOO—WITH A FLAVOR LIKE THAT, UNCLE ALBERT, YOU WILL ALWAYS BE SAFE FROM CANNIBOBBLES.
WHAT'S ALL THE EXCITINGMINTS?
UNCLE ALBERT'S COUNTIN' HIS TAIL ON ACCOUNT IT GOT BIT FOR A SAUSAGE.
PASS THE KETCHUP.
I ALWAYS ADD A SPRIG OF PARSLEY.
SHH—WE IS USIN' THIS FOR IODINE ON ACCOUNT OF IODINE BURNS TOO MUCH.
AS A OL' DONKEY FRIEND SAID, "I IS BECOME MIGHTY ATTACHED TO MY TAIL, AN' IT TO ME."
IF IT WAS SPRIGTIME IN THE ROCKIES, I'D GIT YOU SOME PARSLEY.
YOU'D NEED A PARSLEY SHAWL.

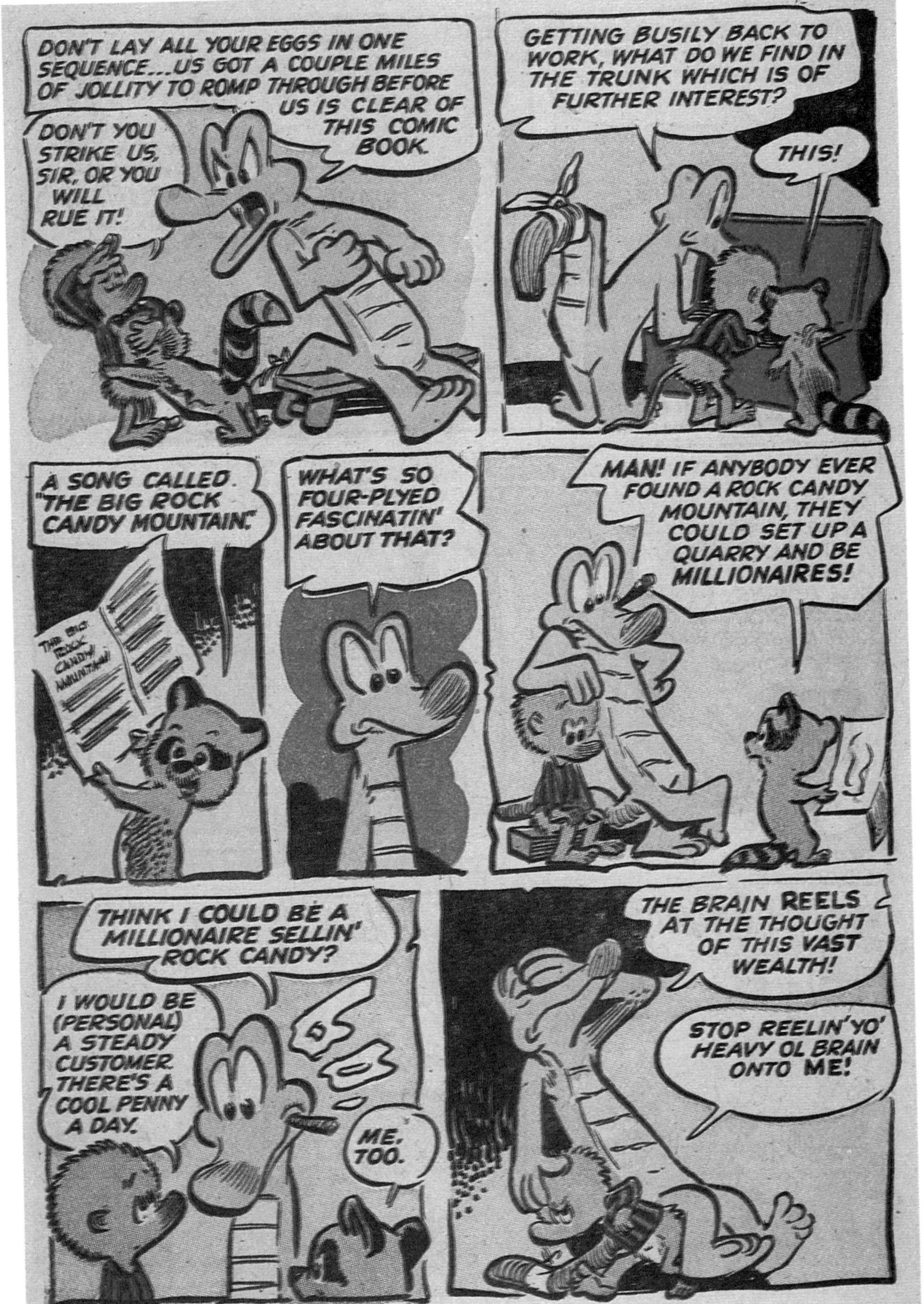
DON'T LAY ALL YOUR EGGS IN ONE SEQUENCE...US GOT A COUPLE MILES OF JOLLITY TO ROMP THROUGH BEFORE US IS CLEAR OF THIS COMIC BOOK.
DON'T YOU STRIKE US, SIR, OR YOU WILL RUE IT!
GETTING BUSILY BACK TO WORK, WHAT DO WE FIND IN THE TRUNK WHICH IS OF FURTHER INTEREST?
THIS!
A SONG CALLED "THE BIG ROCK CANDY MOUNTAIN."
WHAT'S SO FOUR-PLYED FASCINATIN' ABOUT THAT?
MAN! IF ANYBODY EVER FOUND A ROCK CANDY MOUNTAIN, THEY COULD SET UP A QUARRY AND BE MILLIONAIRES!
THINK I COULD BE A MILLIONAIRE SELLIN' ROCK CANDY?
I WOULD BE (PERSONAL) A STEADY CUSTOMER. THERE'S A COOL PENNY A DAY.
ME, TOO.
THE BRAIN REELS AT THE THOUGHT OF THIS VAST WEALTH!
STOP REELIN' YO' HEAVY OL BRAIN ONTO ME!

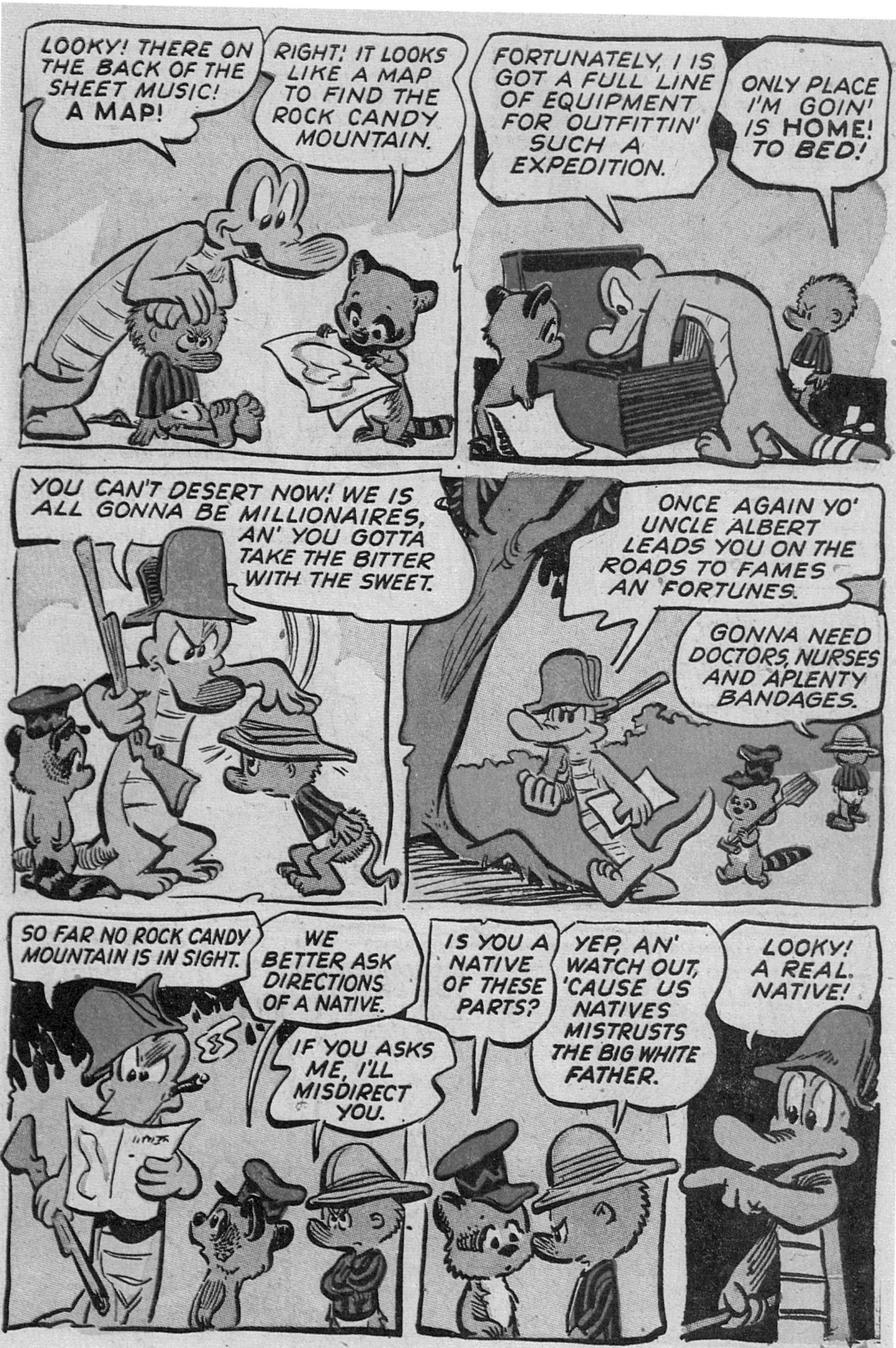
LOOKY! THERE ON THE BACK OF THE SHEET MUSIC! A MAP!
RIGHT! IT LOOKS LIKE A MAP TO FIND THE ROCK CANDY MOUNTAIN.
FORTUNATELY, I IS GOT A FULL LINE OF EQUIPMENT FOR OUTFITTIN' SUCH A EXPEDITION.
ONLY PLACE I'M GOIN' IS HOME! TO BED!
YOU CAN'T DESERT NOW! WE IS ALL GONNA BE MILLIONAIRES, AN' YOU GOTTA TAKE THE BITTER WITH THE SWEET.
ONCE AGAIN YO' UNCLE ALBERT LEADS YOU ON THE ROADS TO FAMES AN FORTUNES.
GONNA NEED DOCTORS, NURSES AND APLENTY BANDAGES.
SO FAR NO ROCK CANDY MOUNTAIN IS IN SIGHT.
WE BETTER ASK DIRECTIONS OF A NATIVE.
IF YOU ASKS ME, I'LL MISDIRECT YOU.
IS YOU A NATIVE OF THESE PARTS?
YEP, AN' WATCH OUT, 'CAUSE US NATIVES MISTRUSTS THE BIG WHITE FATHER.
LOOKY! A REAL NATIVE!

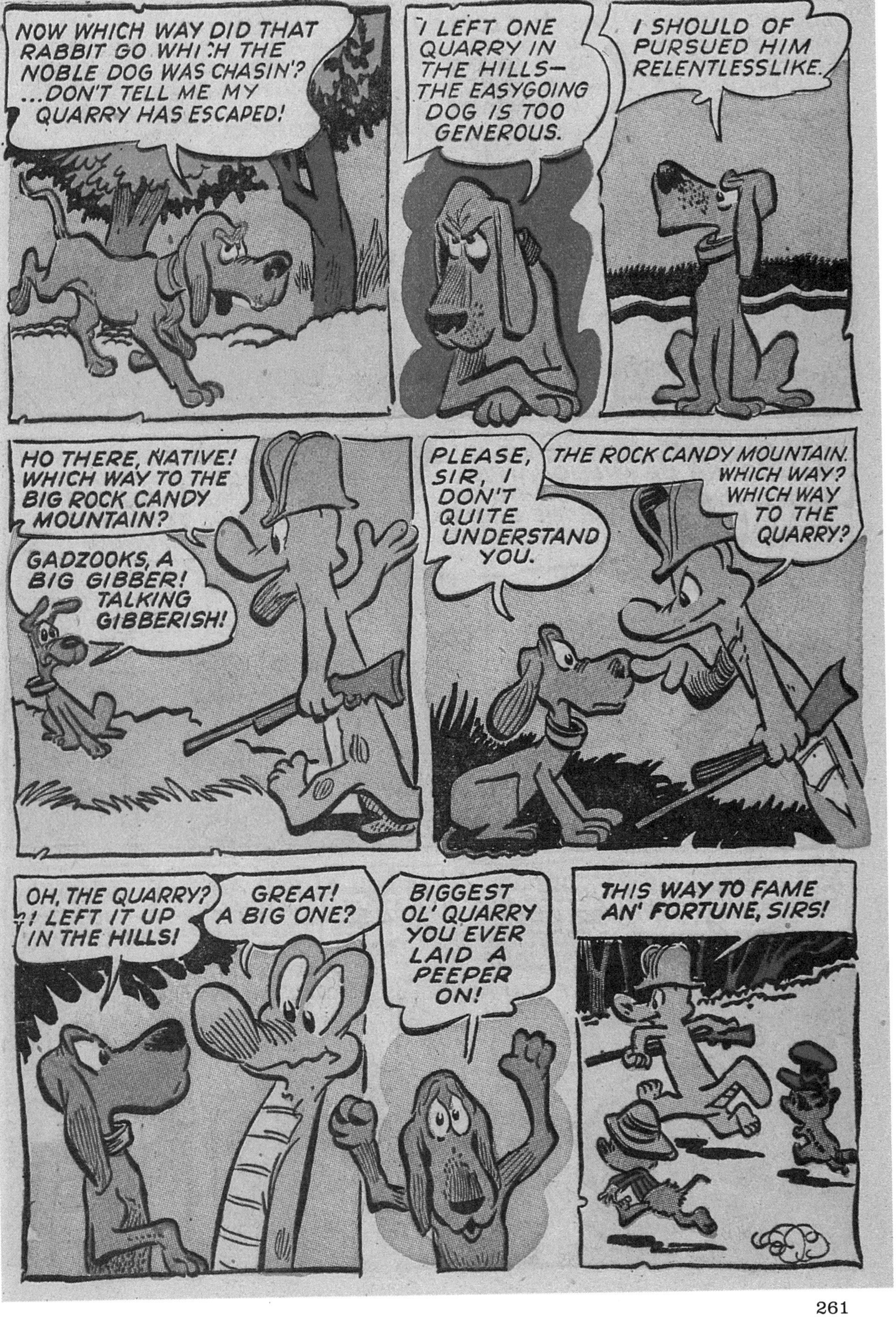
NOW WHICH WAY DID THAT RABBIT GO WHICH THE NOBLE DOG WAS CHASIN'? ...DON'T TELL ME MY QUARRY HAS ESCAPED!
I LEFT ONE QUARRY IN THE HILLS— THE EASYGOING DOG IS TOO GENEROUS.
I SHOULD OF PURSUED HIM RELENTLESSLIKE.
HO THERE, NATIVE! WHICH WAY TO THE BIG ROCK CANDY MOUNTAIN?
GADZOOKS, A BIG GIBBER! TALKING GIBBERISH!
PLEASE, SIR, I DON'T QUITE UNDERSTAND YOU.
THE ROCK CANDY MOUNTAIN. WHICH WAY? WHICH WAY TO THE QUARRY?
OH, THE QUARRY? I LEFT IT UP IN THE HILLS!
GREAT! A BIG ONE?
BIGGEST OL' QUARRY YOU EVER LAID A PEEPER ON!
THIS WAY TO FAME AN' FORTUNE, SIRS!

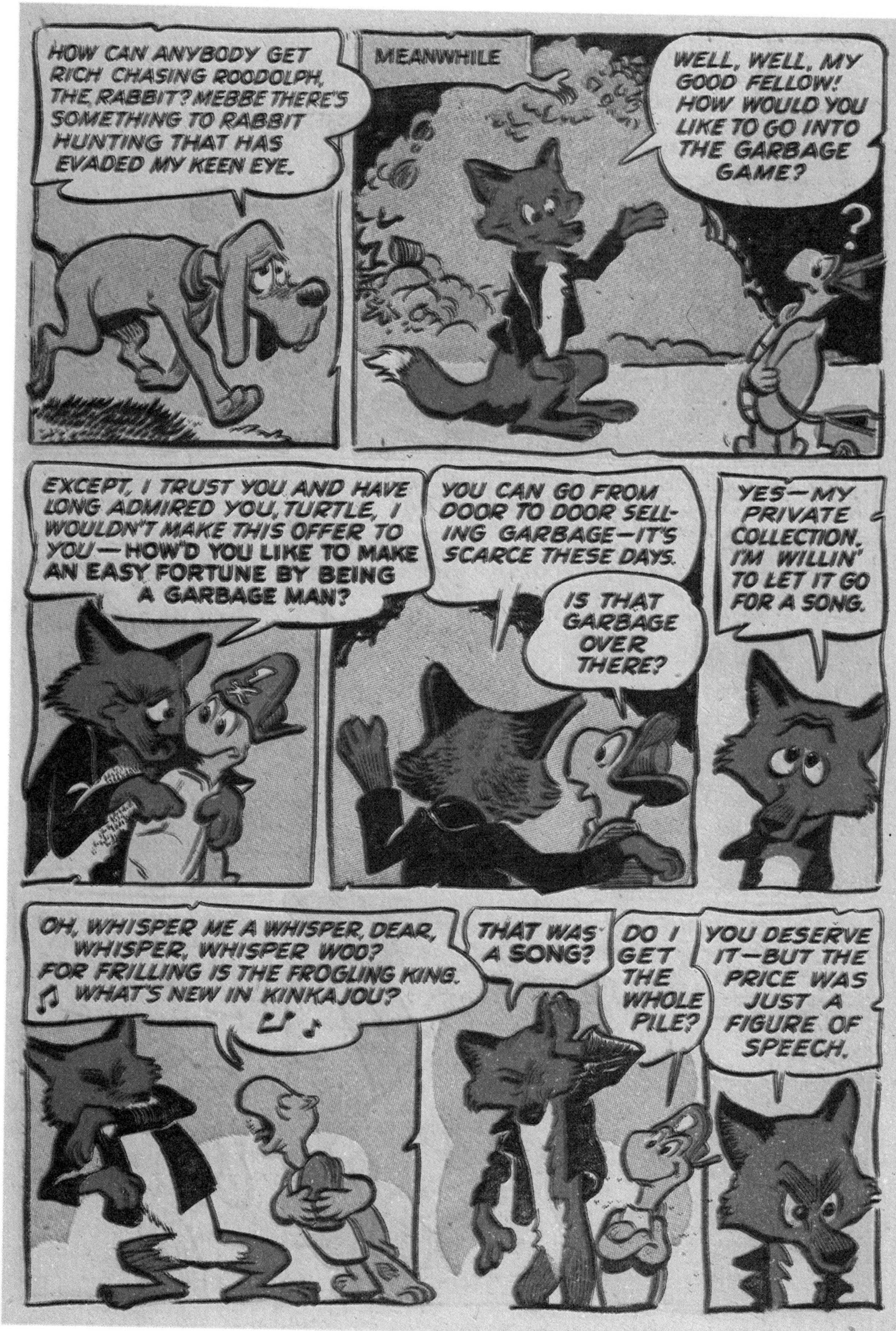
HOW CAN ANYBODY GET RICH CHASING ROODOLPH, THE RABBIT? MEBBE THERE'S SOMETHING TO RABBIT HUNTING THAT HAS EVADED MY KEEN EYE.
MEANWHILE
WELL, WELL, MY GOOD FELLOW! HOW WOULD YOU LIKE TO GO INTO THE GARBAGE GAME?
?
EXCEPT, I TRUST YOU AND HAVE LONG ADMIRED YOU, TURTLE, I WOULDN'T MAKE THIS OFFER TO YOU—HOW'D YOU LIKE TO MAKE AN EASY FORTUNE BY BEING A GARBAGE MAN?
YOU CAN GO FROM DOOR TO DOOR SELLING GARBAGE—IT'S SCARCE THESE DAYS.
IS THAT GARBAGE OVER THERE?
YES—MY PRIVATE COLLECTION. I'M WILLIN' TO LET IT GO FOR A SONG.
OH, WHISPER ME A WHISPER, DEAR, WHISPER, WHISPER WOO? FOR FRILLING IS THE FROGLING KING. WHAT'S NEW IN KINKAJOU?
THAT WAS A SONG?
DO I GET THE WHOLE PILE?
YOU DESERVE IT—BUT THE PRICE WAS JUST A FIGURE OF SPEECH.

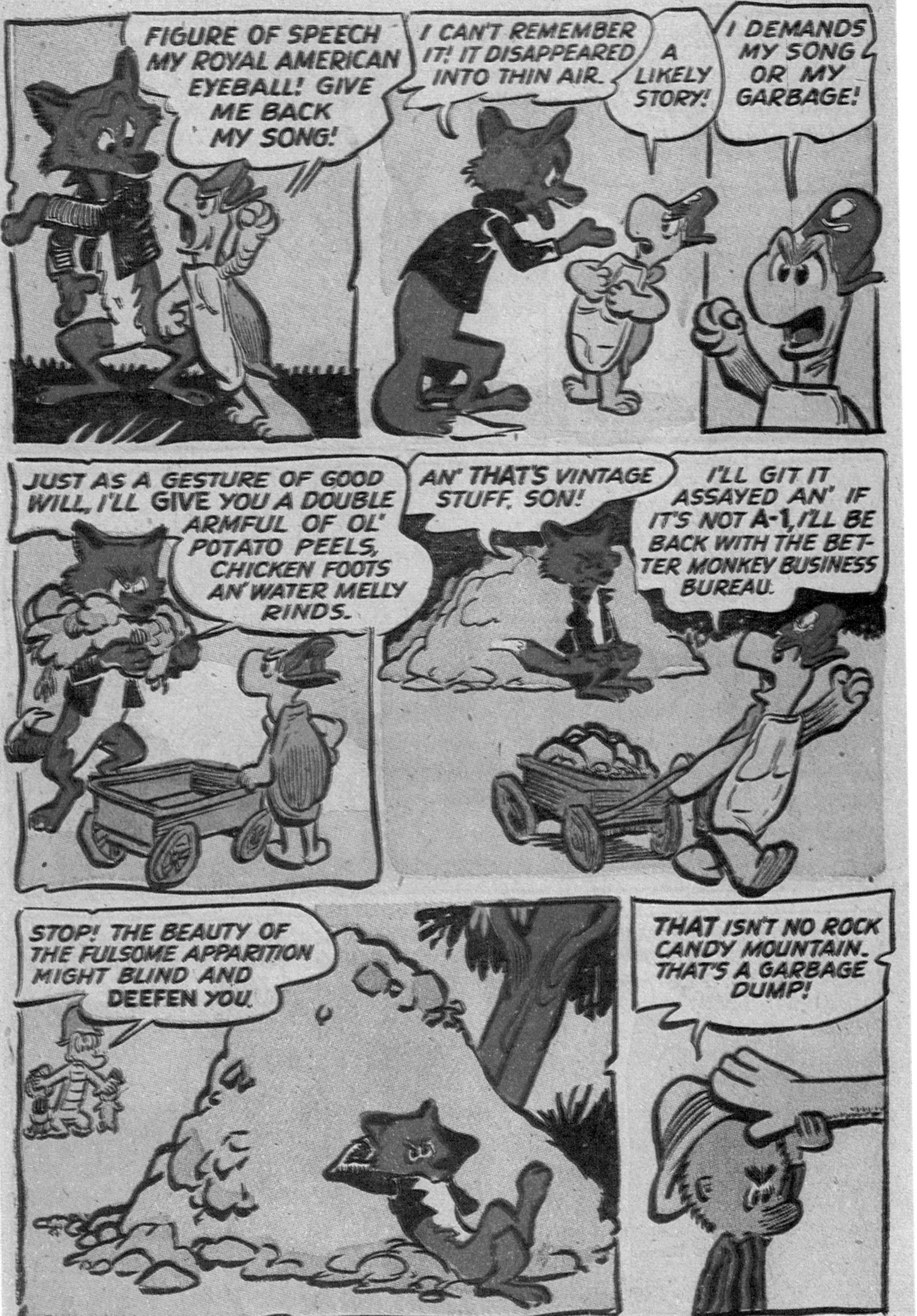
FIGURE OF SPEECH MY ROYAL AMERICAN EYEBALL! GIVE ME BACK MY SONG!
I CAN'T REMEMBER IT! IT DISAPPEARED INTO THIN AIR.
A LIKELY STORY!
I DEMANDS MY SONG OR MY GARBAGE!
JUST AS A GESTURE OF GOOD WILL, I'LL GIVE YOU A DOUBLE ARMFUL OF OL' POTATO PEELS, CHICKEN FOOTS AN' WATER MELLY RINDS.
AN' THAT'S VINTAGE STUFF, SON!
I'LL GIT IT ASSAYED AN' IF IT'S NOT A-1, I'LL BE BACK WITH THE BETTER MONKEY BUSINESS BUREAU.
STOP! THE BEAUTY OF THE FULSOME APPARITION MIGHT BLIND AND DEEFEN YOU.
THAT ISN'T NO ROCK CANDY MOUNTAIN. THAT'S A GARBAGE DUMP!

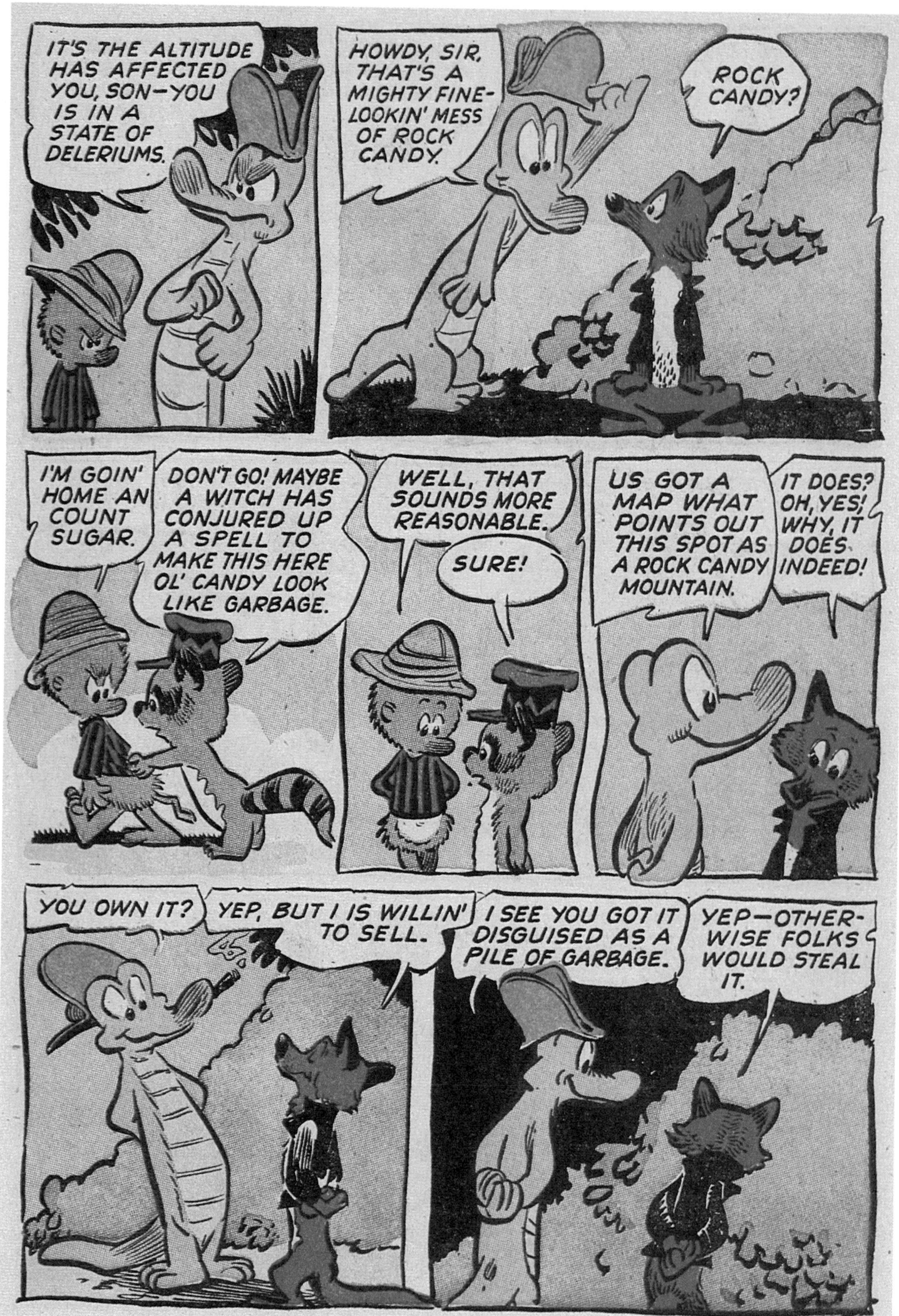

IT'S THE ALTITUDE HAS AFFECTED YOU, SON—YOU IS IN A STATE OF DELERIUMS.
HOWDY, SIR, THAT'S A MIGHTY FINE-LOOKIN' MESS OF ROCK CANDY.
ROCK CANDY?
I'M GOIN' HOME AN COUNT SUGAR.
DON'T GO! MAYBE A WITCH HAS CONJURED UP A SPELL TO MAKE THIS HERE OL' CANDY LOOK LIKE GARBAGE.
WELL, THAT SOUNDS MORE REASONABLE.
SURE!
US GOT A MAP WHAT POINTS OUT THIS SPOT AS A ROCK CANDY MOUNTAIN.
IT DOES? OH, YES! WHY, IT DOES INDEED!
YOU OWN IT?
YEP, BUT I IS WILLIN' TO SELL.
I SEE YOU GOT IT DISGUISED AS A PILE OF GARBAGE.
YEP—OTHERWISE FOLKS WOULD STEAL IT.

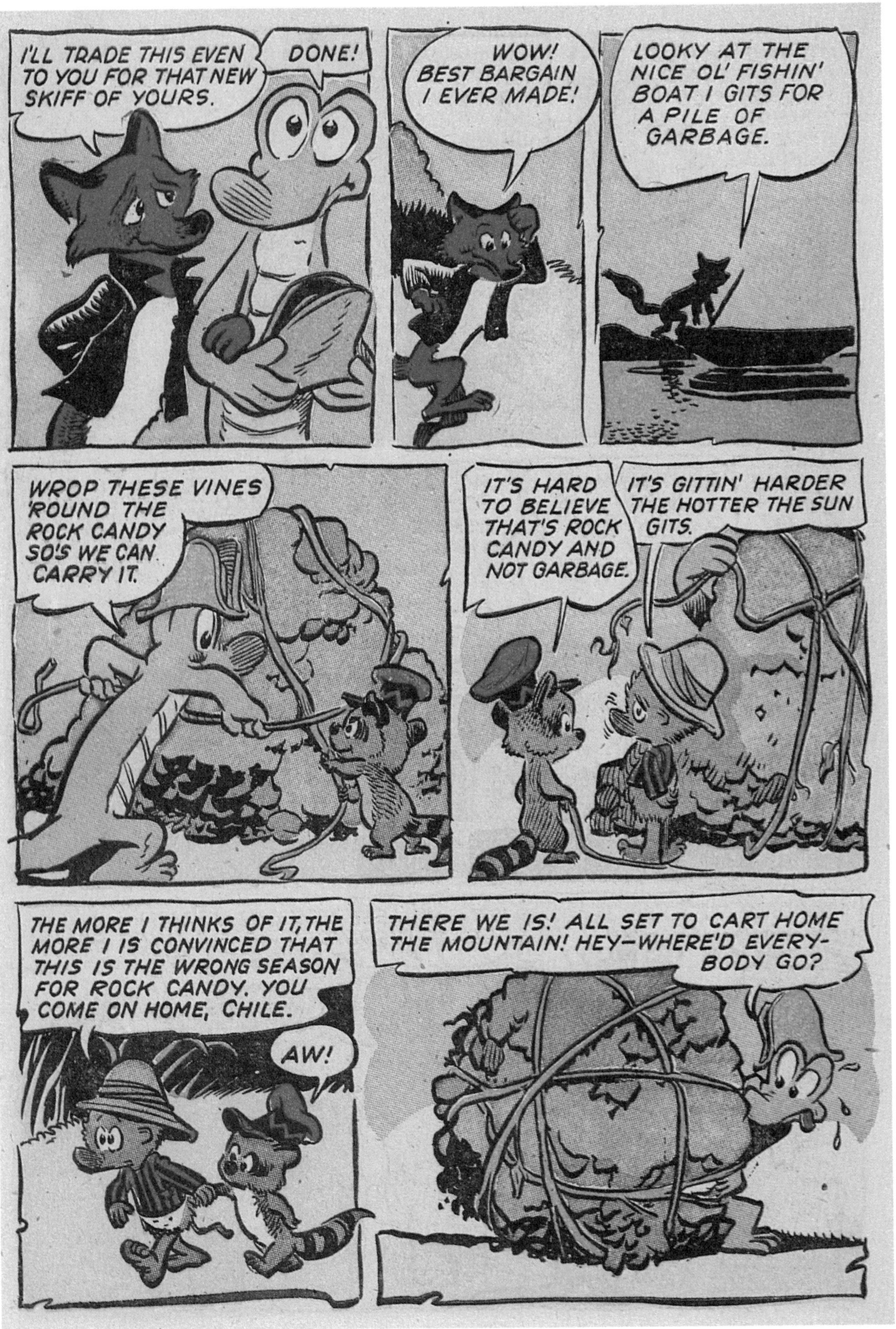

I'LL TRADE THIS EVEN TO YOU FOR THAT NEW SKIFF OF YOURS.
DONE!
WOW! BEST BARGAIN I EVER MADE!
LOOKY AT THE NICE OL' FISHIN' BOAT I GITS FOR A PILE OF GARBAGE.
WROP THESE VINES 'ROUND THE ROCK CANDY SO'S WE CAN CARRY IT.
IT'S HARD TO BELIEVE THAT'S ROCK CANDY AND NOT GARBAGE.
IT'S GITTIN' HARDER THE HOTTER THE SUN GITS.
THE MORE I THINKS OF IT, THE MORE I IS CONVINCED THAT THIS IS THE WRONG SEASON FOR ROCK CANDY. YOU COME ON HOME, CHILE.
AW!
THERE WE IS! ALL SET TO CART HOME THE MOUNTAIN! HEY—WHERE'D EVERY-BODY GO?

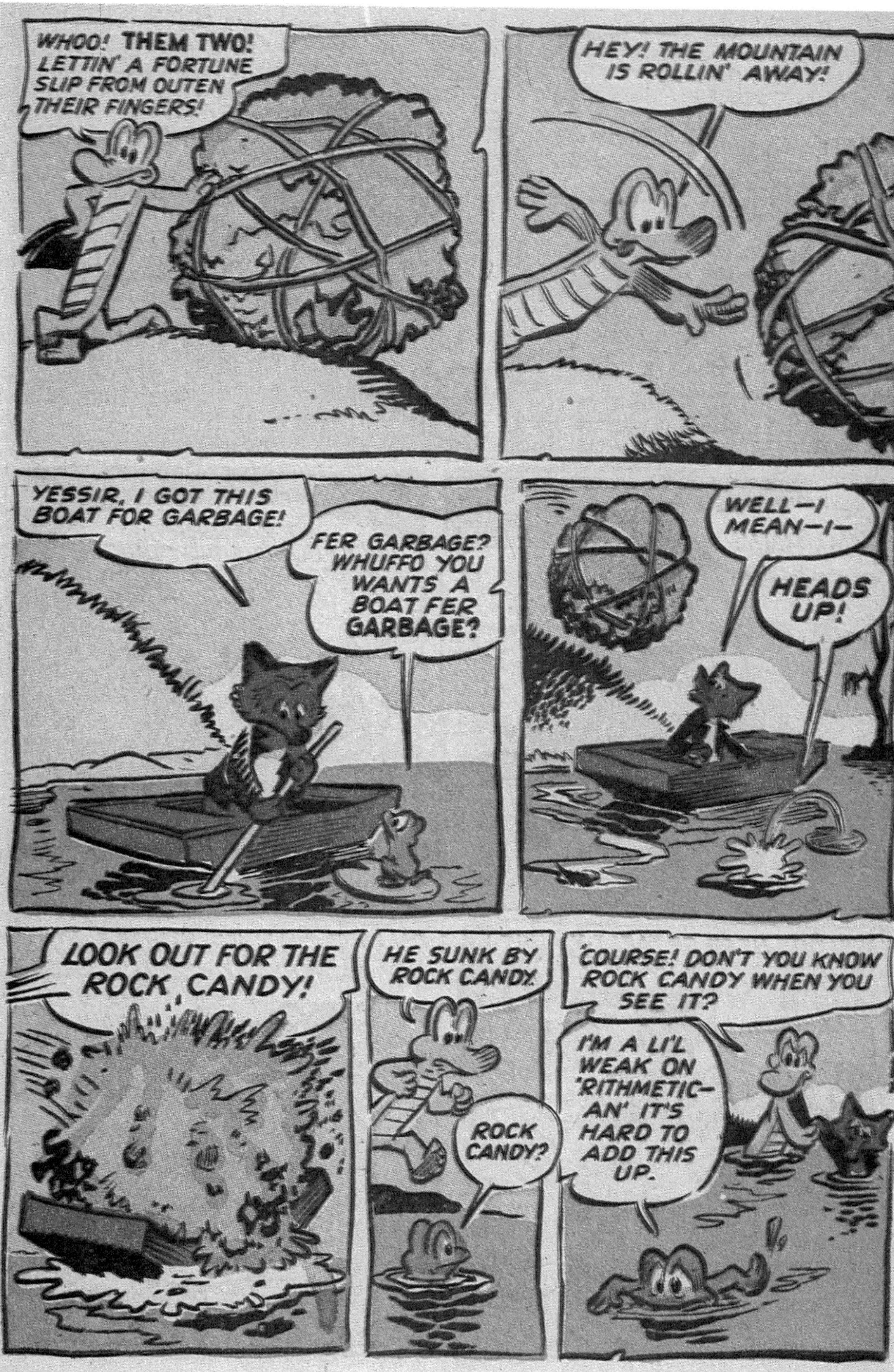
WHOO! THEM TWO! LETTIN' A FORTUNE SLIP FROM OUTEN THEIR FINGERS!
HEY! THE MOUNTAIN IS ROLLIN' AWAY!
YESSIR, I GOT THIS BOAT FOR GARBAGE!
FER GARBAGE? WHUFFO YOU WANTS A BOAT FER GARBAGE?
WELL—I MEAN—I—
HEADS UP!
LOOK OUT FOR THE ROCK CANDY!
HE SUNK BY ROCK CANDY.
ROCK CANDY?
'COURSE! DON'T YOU KNOW ROCK CANDY WHEN YOU SEE IT?
I'M A LI'L WEAK ON 'RITHMETIC— AN' IT'S HARD TO ADD THIS UP.

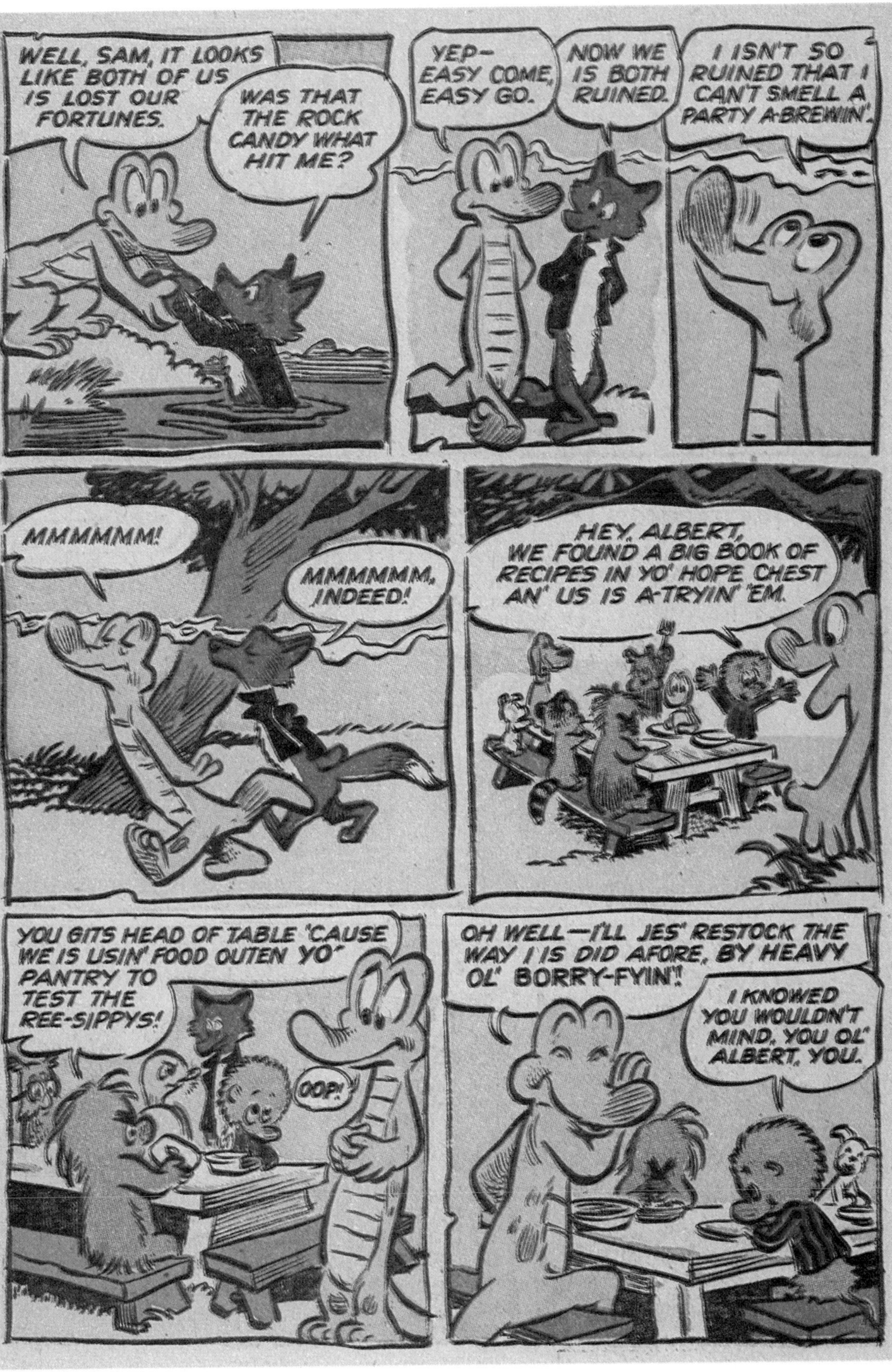
WELL, SAM, IT LOOKS LIKE BOTH OF US IS LOST OUR FORTUNES.
WAS THAT THE ROCK CANDY WHAT HIT ME?
YEP— EASY COME, EASY GO.
NOW WE IS BOTH RUINED.
I ISN'T SO RUINED THAT I CAN'T SMELL A PARTY A-BREWIN'.
MMMMMM!
MMMMMM, INDEED!
HEY, ALBERT, WE FOUND A BIG BOOK OF RECIPES IN YO' HOPE CHEST AN' US IS A-TRYIN' 'EM.
YOU GITS HEAD OF TABLE 'CAUSE WE IS USIN' FOOD OUTEN YO' PANTRY TO TEST THE REE-SIPPYS!
OOP!
OH WELL—I'LL JES' RESTOCK THE WAY I IS DID AFORE, BY HEAVY OL' BORRY-FYIN'!
I KNOWED YOU WOULDN'T MIND, YOU OL' ALBERT, YOU.

About "The Spirit" and Will Eisner

As comic books boomed in the prewar years, some newspaper syndicates began trying to take advantage of their popularity. The Register and Tribune Syndicate of Des Moines offered a sixteen-page (later eight-page) comic book that newspapers could distribute along with their Sunday comics sections. The comic book first appeared on June 2, 1940, and ran for a little more than twelve years, until October 5, 1952; it appeared in relatively few newspapers, mostly in large eastern cities.

The comic book's lead feature, *The Spirit,* was written and drawn by Will Eisner (with some help from other writers and cartoonists). Eisner was one of the principals in the small firm that assembled the comic book every week; unlike most comic-book creators, Eisner has always owned at least part of his feature.

Eisner, who was born in New York City on March 6, 1917, had already spent several years producing comic books—complete packages, ready to print—for several publishers by the time he started *The Spirit.* A number of well-known features, like *Sheena, Queen of the Jungle,* had been originated by Eisner and the men who worked for him. As Eisner told John Benson, "I was running a shop in which we made comic-book features pretty much the way Ford turned out cars. So perhaps the reason that the Register and Tribune consented to distribute *The Spirit* in the first place was because I had demonstrated my ability as a producer...." Throughout his career in comic books, Eisner remained that rare combination: an artist who was also a capable businessman.

The Spirit himself was a hero from the vigilante mold. His costume, however, amounted to nothing more than a mask and gloves. Eisner resisted pressure from his business partners to make the Spirit a costumed hero of the Batman variety, and so the Spirit remained a cross between a super-hero and a pulp-fiction detective. He was a criminologist named Denny Colt—supposedly dead, but actually living in a hideout in Wildwood Cemetery.

The Spirit, in its first year or so, was not far removed from conventional comic-book stuff of the period. But in 1941, Eisner started making very free and inventive use of the comics medium, as in the first of the three stories included here, and the emphasis began to shift away from the title character.

More than most comics creators, Eisner had the freedom to strike out in new directions; his partners and his syndicate made few demands on him, except that he meet his deadlines. Eisner explained the evolution of *The Spirit* to Benson: "I began to realize who I was writing for"—that is, an audience dominated by adults, rather than children—and "I suddenly found an opportunity to do what I had really always wanted to do, which was to write 'seriously' or write good material, and at the same time stay within the medium I knew and had developed skills for."

Eisner was drafted in 1942, and *The Spirit* was left in the hands of other cartoonists during the war. When Eisner returned to *The Spirit,* he became pre-eminently a short-story writer who wrote mostly with pictures instead of entirely with words. Probably no other cartoonist has ever made such fluent use of his medium. John Benson, writing in *Panels* magazine, speaks of Eisner's "effortless visual narrative style, which is so unlabored that most readers are unaware of how much more his pictures tell us than do the pages of most comic books. Like Alfred Hitchcock, Eisner *shows* his stories instead of telling them. And Eisner's pictorial sense, like Hitchcock's, is so integral to his sense of narrative that it's often overlooked: the type of story favored by the artist is more likely to be recognized—the 'Hitchcock story' or the 'Eisner story'."

Eisner is, for one thing, a master of the "silent panel" (a panel without dialogue or captions), placing each such panel at the point where its dramatic effect is greatest. And Benson cites as an example of Eisner's virtuosity his use of "indirect portrayal: we are shown a reaction, or the aftermath of an action, rather than the action itself—and are thereby forced, usually without being aware of it, to imagine bits of action and story elements that Eisner has not actually shown."

The "Eisner story" could be playful, or serious, or sentimental—or all three at once, like the 1948 story about Gerhard Shnobble that we have included here. But it was always a big-city story (in its atmosphere if not in its setting) and, like city life, it was always flavored with the grotesque.

The other postwar episode that follows originated in a script by Jules Feiffer, who was one of Eisner's assistants before beginning his own highly successful career as a newspaper and magazine cartoonist; Feiffer told John Benson that the script was "an autobiographical fantasy based on my Bronx upbringing." (It is also one of the many comic-book stories that shows the influence of radio drama; Feiffer cites *Suspense* as a source.) Eisner always remained the dominant partner in such collaborations, of course, often rewriting a script until it was mostly his own work.

The Spirit himself is not much to be seen in the two postwar stories we have included, and that is true of many of the best postwar *Spirit* stories. Sometimes Eisner had to shoehorn the Spirit into what could have been complete and satisfying short stories without him. Although Eisner depicted his hero in an appealingly tongue-in-cheek manner, the Spirit remained a conventional character in many ways (he was, for example, preternaturally resilient when shot or beaten), and the postwar stories tended to be more interesting the less of the Spirit himself there was in them. Richard Kyle has said of Eisner, "He remained bound to a hero smaller than the truth he had to tell."

Eisner gave less and less of his time to *The Spirit* in the early 1950s, finally abandoning the feature to produce comics for the educational market. But in recent years *The Spirit* has been revived in a bimonthly magazine, now published by Kitchen Sink Enterprises. *The Spirit* magazine includes new material by Eisner as well as reprints of old stories.

M.B.

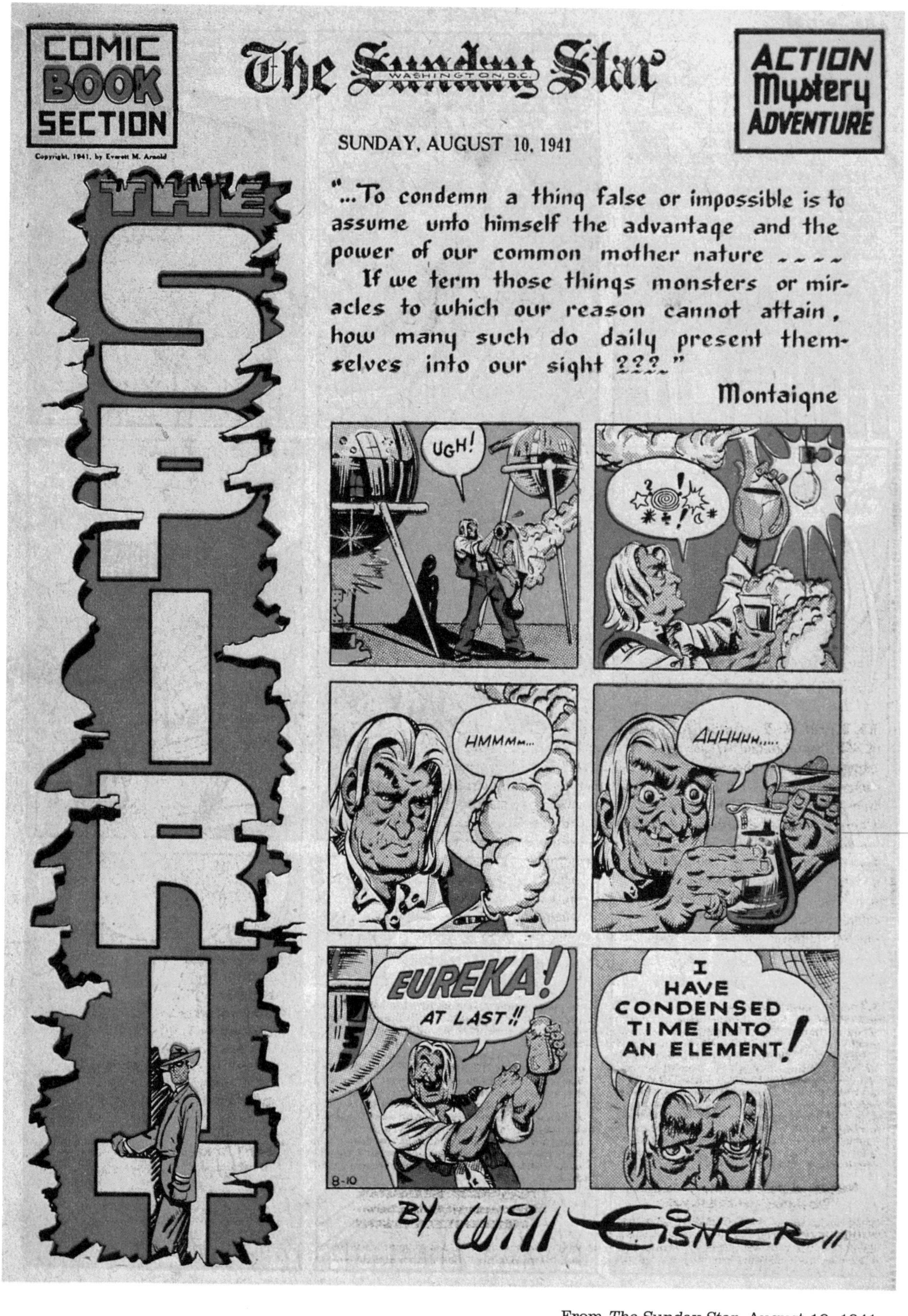
COMIC BOOK SECTION
Copyright, 1941, by Everett M. Arnold
The Sunday Star
WASHINGTON, D.C.
ACTION Mystery ADVENTURE
SUNDAY, AUGUST 10, 1941
THE SPIRIT
"...To condemn a thing false or impossible is to assume unto himself the advantage and the power of our common mother nature ----
If we term those things monsters or miracles to which our reason cannot attain, how many such do daily present themselves into our sight ???."
Montaigne
UGH!
HMMMM...
AHHHHH.....
EUREKA! AT LAST!!
I HAVE CONDENSED TIME INTO AN ELEMENT!
8-10
BY Will Eisner

From *The Sunday Star*, August 10, 1941.

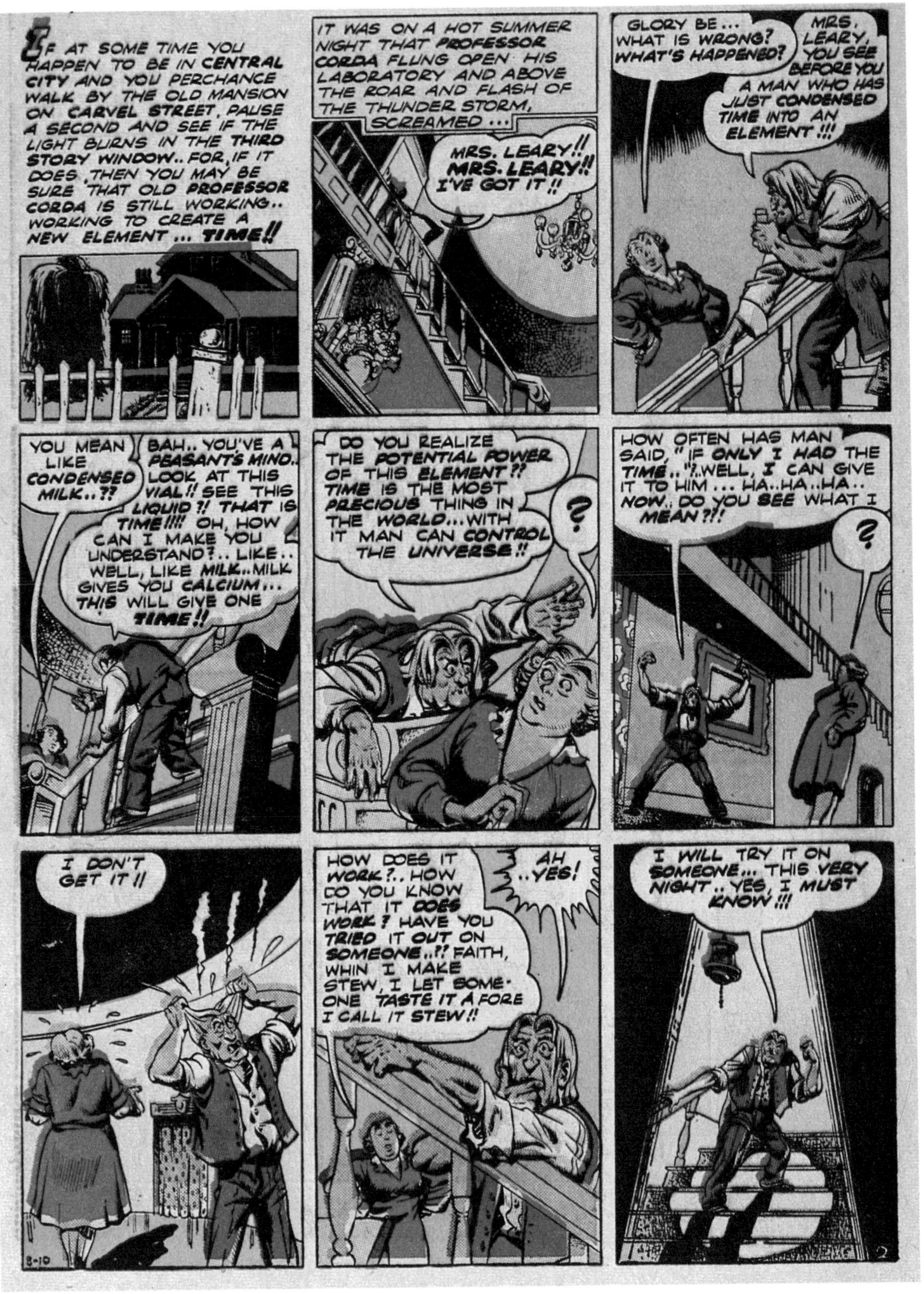
IF AT SOME TIME YOU HAPPEN TO BE IN CENTRAL CITY AND YOU PERCHANCE WALK BY THE OLD MANSION ON CARVEL STREET, PAUSE A SECOND AND SEE IF THE LIGHT BURNS IN THE THIRD STORY WINDOW.. FOR, IF IT DOES, THEN YOU MAY BE SURE THAT OLD PROFESSOR CORDA IS STILL WORKING.. WORKING TO CREATE A NEW ELEMENT ... TIME!!
IT WAS ON A HOT SUMMER NIGHT THAT PROFESSOR CORDA FLUNG OPEN HIS LABORATORY AND ABOVE THE ROAR AND FLASH OF THE THUNDER STORM, SCREAMED ...
MRS. LEARY!! MRS. LEARY!! I'VE GOT IT !!
GLORY BE ... WHAT IS WRONG? WHAT'S HAPPENED?
MRS. LEARY, YOU SEE BEFORE YOU A MAN WHO HAS JUST CONDENSED TIME INTO AN ELEMENT !!!
YOU MEAN LIKE CONDENSED MILK..??
BAH.. YOU'VE A PEASANT'S MIND.. LOOK AT THIS VIAL!! SEE THIS LIQUID?! THAT IS TIME!!!! OH, HOW CAN I MAKE YOU UNDERSTAND?.. LIKE.. WELL, LIKE MILK..MILK GIVES YOU CALCIUM... THIS WILL GIVE ONE TIME!!
DO YOU REALIZE THE POTENTIAL POWER OF THIS ELEMENT?? TIME IS THE MOST PRECIOUS THING IN THE WORLD...WITH IT MAN CAN CONTROL THE UNIVERSE!!
?
HOW OFTEN HAS MAN SAID, "IF ONLY I HAD THE TIME.."?..WELL, I CAN GIVE IT TO HIM ... HA..HA..HA.. NOW.. DO YOU SEE WHAT I MEAN?!!
?
I DON'T GET IT !!
HOW DOES IT WORK?.. HOW DO YOU KNOW THAT IT DOES WORK? HAVE YOU TRIED IT OUT ON SOMEONE..?? FAITH, WHIN I MAKE STEW, I LET SOME-ONE TASTE IT A FORE I CALL IT STEW!!
AH ..YES!
I WILL TRY IT ON SOMEONE... THIS VERY NIGHT.. YES, I MUST KNOW !!!
8-10
2

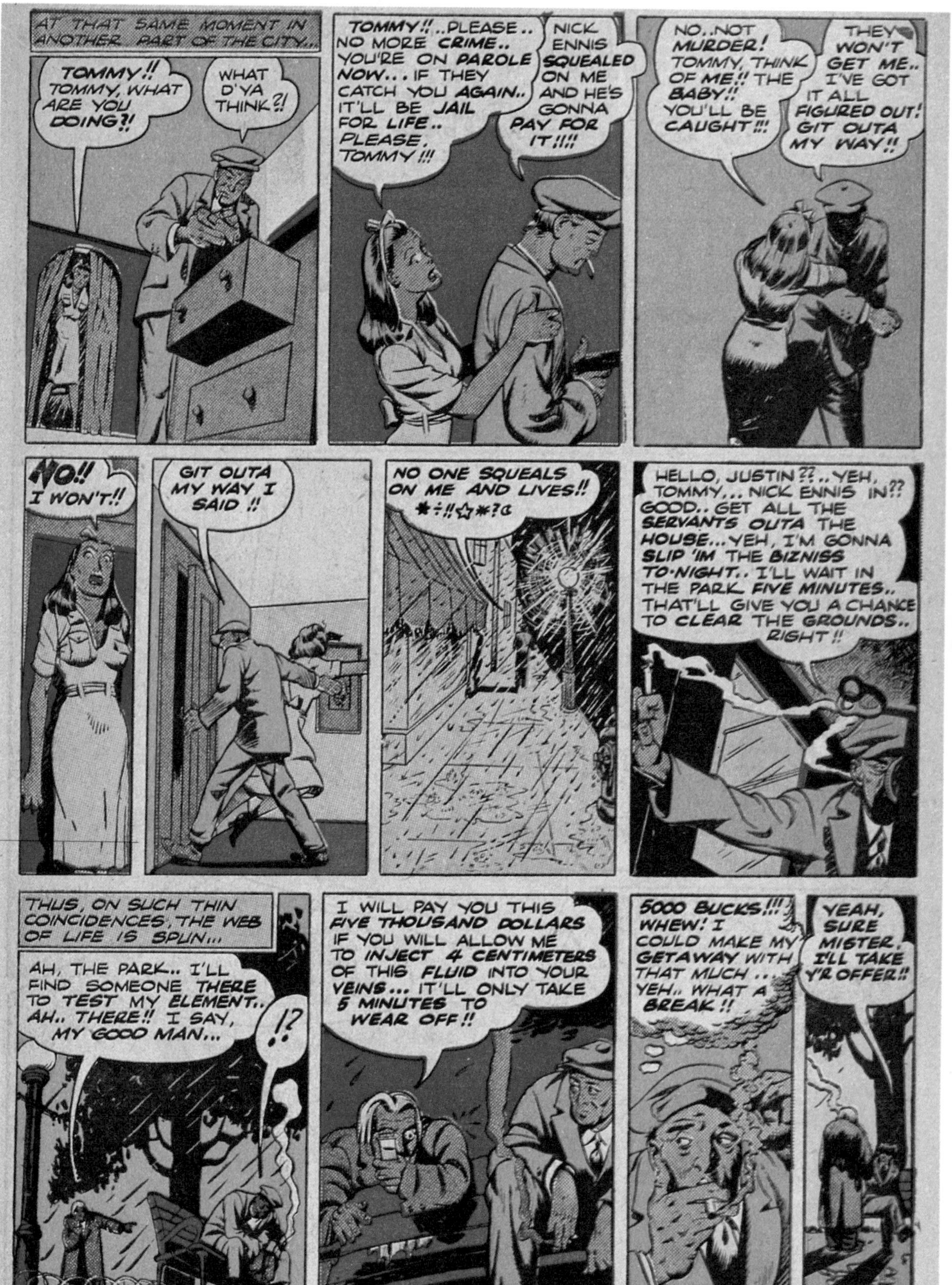

AT THAT SAME MOMENT IN ANOTHER PART OF THE CITY...
TOMMY!! TOMMY, WHAT ARE YOU DOING?!
WHAT D'YA THINK?!
TOMMY!! ..PLEASE.. NO MORE CRIME.. YOU'RE ON PAROLE NOW... IF THEY CATCH YOU AGAIN.. IT'LL BE JAIL FOR LIFE.. PLEASE, TOMMY!!!
NICK ENNIS SQUEALED ON ME AND HE'S GONNA PAY FOR IT!!!!
NO..NOT MURDER! TOMMY, THINK OF ME!! THE BABY!! YOU'LL BE CAUGHT!!!
THEY WON'T GET ME.. I'VE GOT IT ALL FIGURED OUT! GIT OUTA MY WAY!!
NO!! I WON'T!!
GIT OUTA MY WAY I SAID !!
NO ONE SQUEALS ON ME AND LIVES!!
HELLO, JUSTIN??..YEH, TOMMY... NICK ENNIS IN?? GOOD.. GET ALL THE SERVANTS OUTA THE HOUSE...YEH, I'M GONNA SLIP 'IM THE BIZNISS TO-NIGHT.. I'LL WAIT IN THE PARK FIVE MINUTES.. THAT'LL GIVE YOU A CHANCE TO CLEAR THE GROUNDS.. RIGHT!!
THUS, ON SUCH THIN COINCIDENCES, THE WEB OF LIFE IS SPUN...
AH, THE PARK.. I'LL FIND SOMEONE THERE TO TEST MY ELEMENT.. AH.. THERE!! I SAY, MY GOOD MAN...
!?
I WILL PAY YOU THIS FIVE THOUSAND DOLLARS IF YOU WILL ALLOW ME TO INJECT 4 CENTIMETERS OF THIS FLUID INTO YOUR VEINS... IT'LL ONLY TAKE 5 MINUTES TO WEAR OFF!!
5000 BUCKS!!! WHEW! I COULD MAKE MY GETAWAY WITH THAT MUCH... YEH.. WHAT A BREAK!!
YEAH, SURE MISTER, I'LL TAKE Y'R OFFER!!

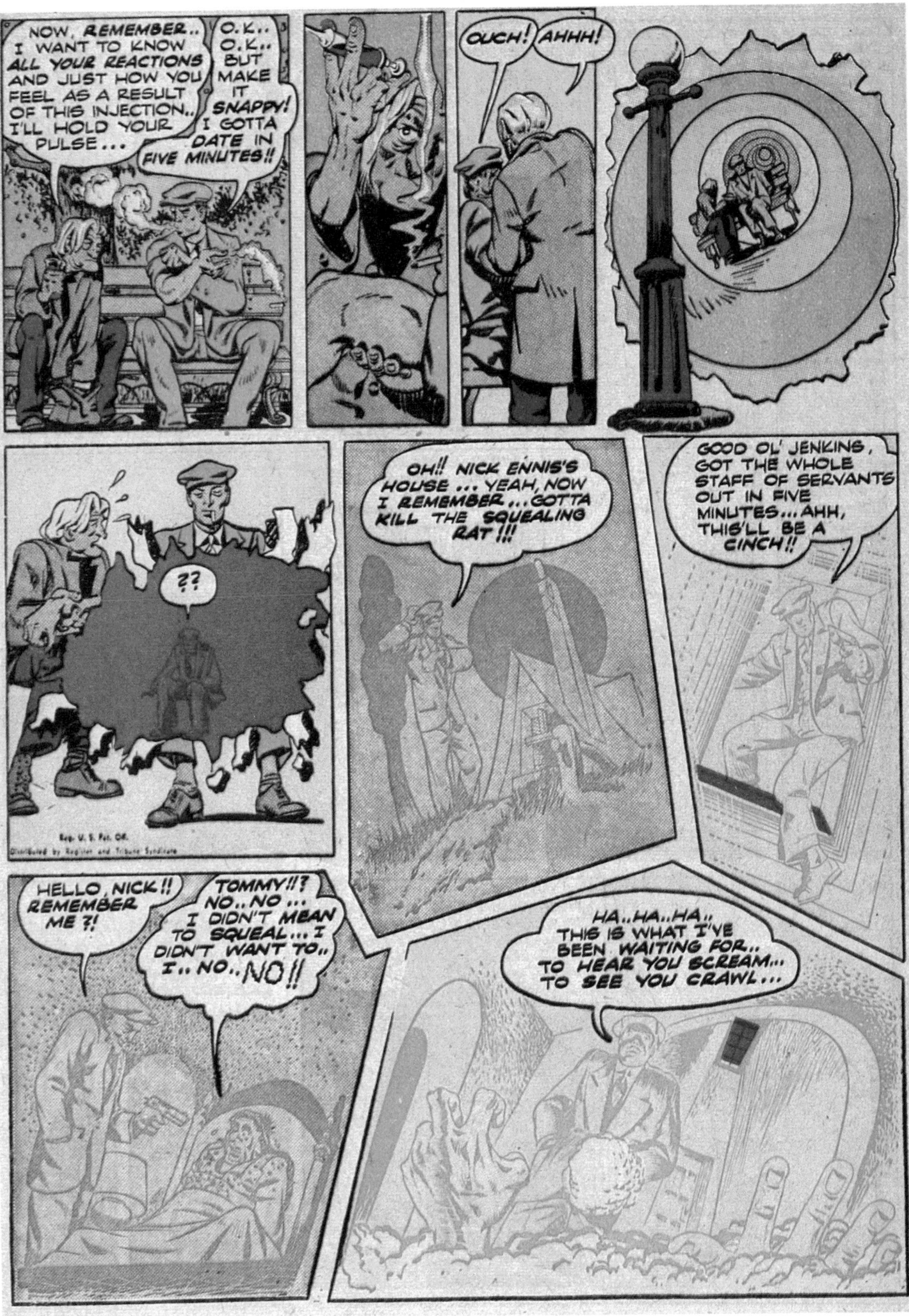

NOW, REMEMBER.. I WANT TO KNOW ALL YOUR REACTIONS AND JUST HOW YOU FEEL AS A RESULT OF THIS INJECTION.. I'LL HOLD YOUR PULSE...
O.K.. O.K.. BUT MAKE IT SNAPPY! I GOTTA DATE IN FIVE MINUTES!!
OUCH!
AHHH!
??
OH!! NICK ENNIS'S HOUSE ... YEAH, NOW I REMEMBER ... GOTTA KILL THE SQUEALING RAT!!!
GOOD OL' JENKINS, GOT THE WHOLE STAFF OF SERVANTS OUT IN FIVE MINUTES... AHH, THIS'LL BE A CINCH!!
HELLO, NICK!! REMEMBER ME ?!
TOMMY!!? NO.. NO ... I DIDN'T MEAN TO SQUEAL... I DIDN'T WANT TO.. I.. NO.. NO!!
HA..HA..HA.. THIS IS WHAT I'VE BEEN WAITING FOR.. TO HEAR YOU SCREAM... TO SEE YOU CRAWL...

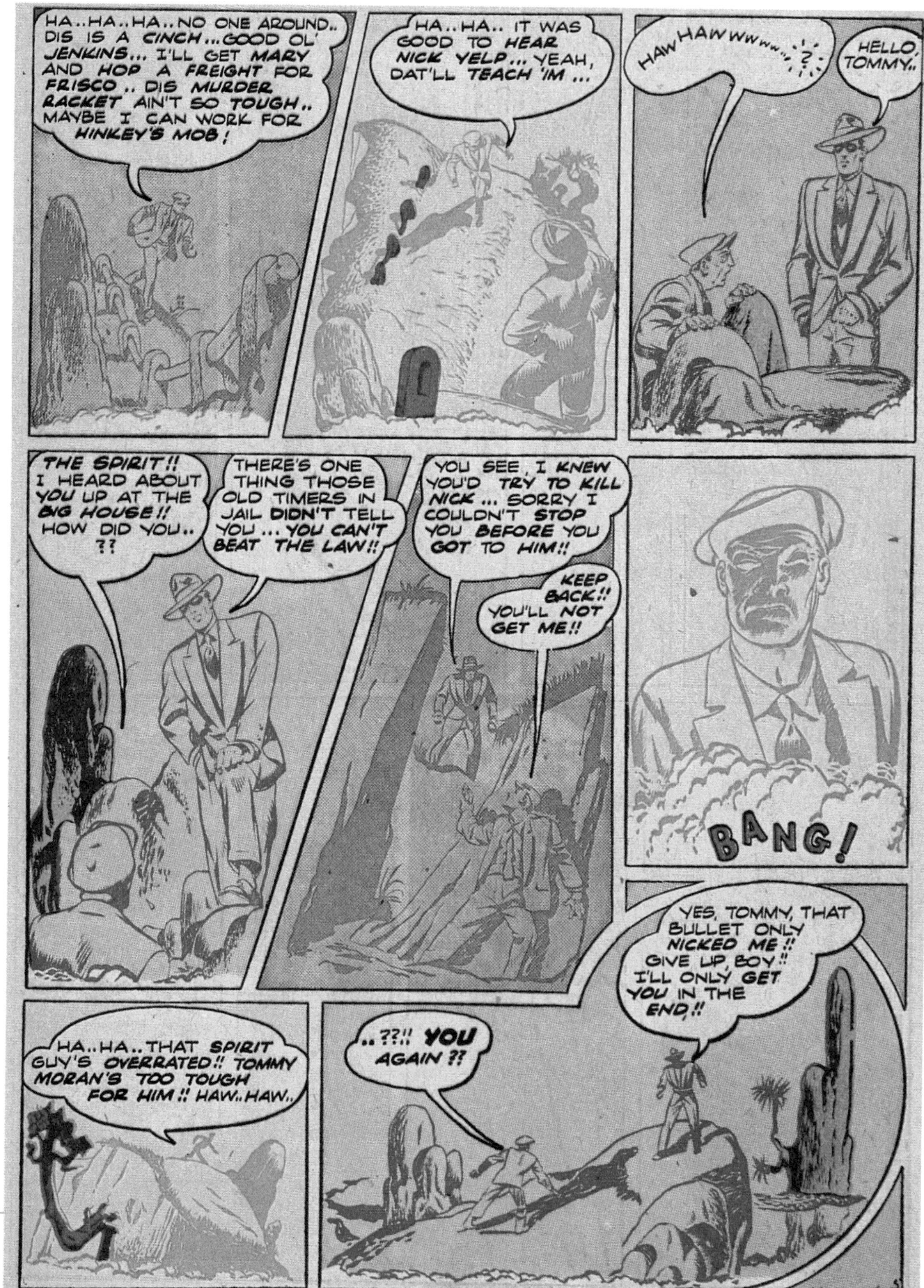
HA..HA..HA..NO ONE AROUND.. DIS IS A CINCH...GOOD OL' JENKINS... I'LL GET MARY AND HOP A FREIGHT FOR FRISCO.. DIS MURDER RACKET AIN'T SO TOUGH.. MAYBE I CAN WORK FOR HINKEY'S MOB!
HA..HA.. IT WAS GOOD TO HEAR NICK YELP... YEAH, DAT'LL TEACH 'IM...
HAW HAW WWwww...
?
HELLO, TOMMY..
THE SPIRIT!! I HEARD ABOUT YOU UP AT THE BIG HOUSE!! HOW DID YOU.. ??
THERE'S ONE THING THOSE OLD TIMERS IN JAIL DIDN'T TELL YOU... YOU CAN'T BEAT THE LAW!!
YOU SEE, I KNEW YOU'D TRY TO KILL NICK... SORRY I COULDN'T STOP YOU BEFORE YOU GOT TO HIM!!
KEEP BACK!! YOU'LL NOT GET ME!!
BANG!
HA..HA..THAT SPIRIT GUY'S OVERRATED!! TOMMY MORAN'S TOO TOUGH FOR HIM!! HAW..HAW..
..??!! YOU AGAIN??
YES, TOMMY, THAT BULLET ONLY NICKED ME!! GIVE UP, BOY!! I'LL ONLY GET YOU IN THE END!!

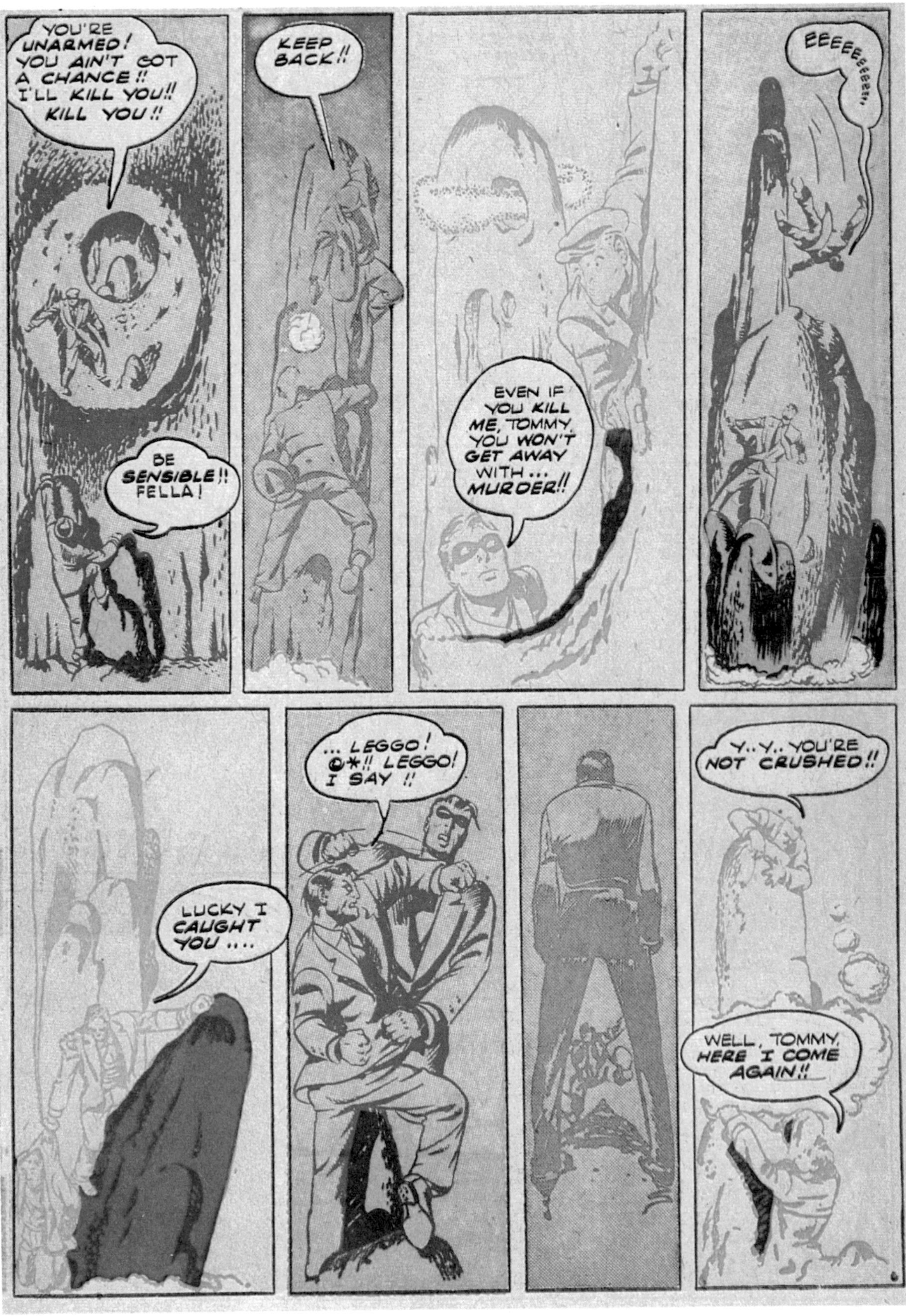
YOU'RE UNARMED! YOU AIN'T GOT A CHANCE!! I'LL KILL YOU!! KILL YOU!!
BE SENSIBLE!! FELLA!
KEEP BACK!!
EVEN IF YOU KILL ME, TOMMY, YOU WON'T GET AWAY WITH ... MURDER!!
EEEEEEEEEE...
LUCKY I CAUGHT YOU ....
... LEGGO! ©*!! LEGGO! I SAY !!
Y..Y.. YOU'RE NOT CRUSHED!!
WELL, TOMMY, HERE I COME AGAIN!!

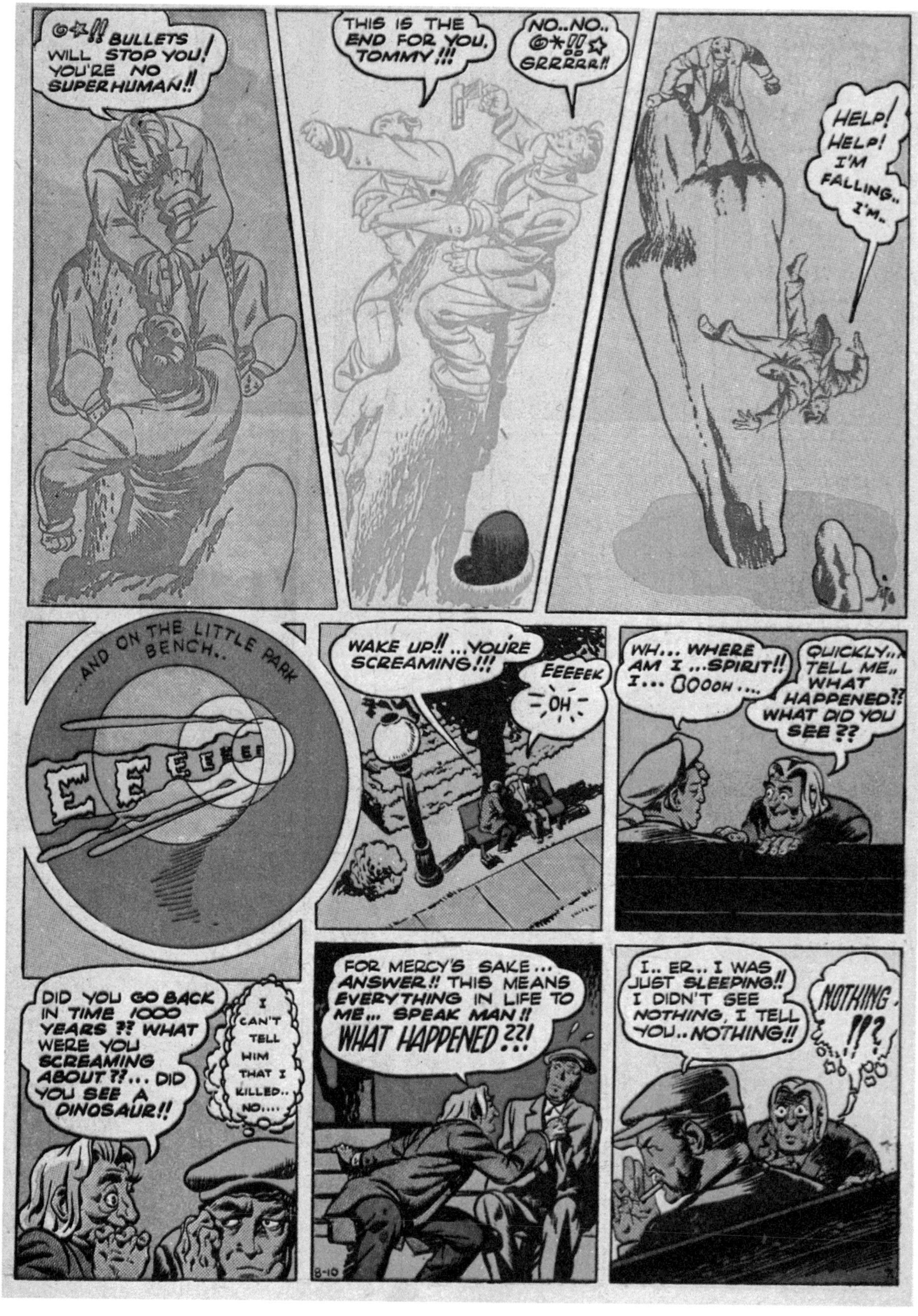
BULLETS WILL STOP YOU! YOU'RE NO SUPERHUMAN!!
THIS IS THE END FOR YOU, TOMMY!!!
NO..NO.. GRRRRRR!!
HELP! HELP! I'M FALLING.. I'M..
...AND ON THE LITTLE PARK BENCH..
EEEEEEE
WAKE UP!! ...YOU'RE SCREAMING!!!
EEEEEK
OH
WH... WHERE AM I ...SPIRIT!! I... OOOOH....
QUICKLY.. TELL ME.. WHAT HAPPENED?? WHAT DID YOU SEE??
DID YOU GO BACK IN TIME 1000 YEARS ?? WHAT WERE YOU SCREAMING ABOUT??... DID YOU SEE A DINOSAUR!!
I CAN'T TELL HIM THAT I KILLED.. NO....
FOR MERCY'S SAKE... ANSWER!! THIS MEANS EVERYTHING IN LIFE TO ME... SPEAK MAN!! WHAT HAPPENED ??!
8-10
I.. ER.. I WAS JUST SLEEPING!! I DIDN'T SEE NOTHING, I TELL YOU.. NOTHING!!
NOTHING.
!!?

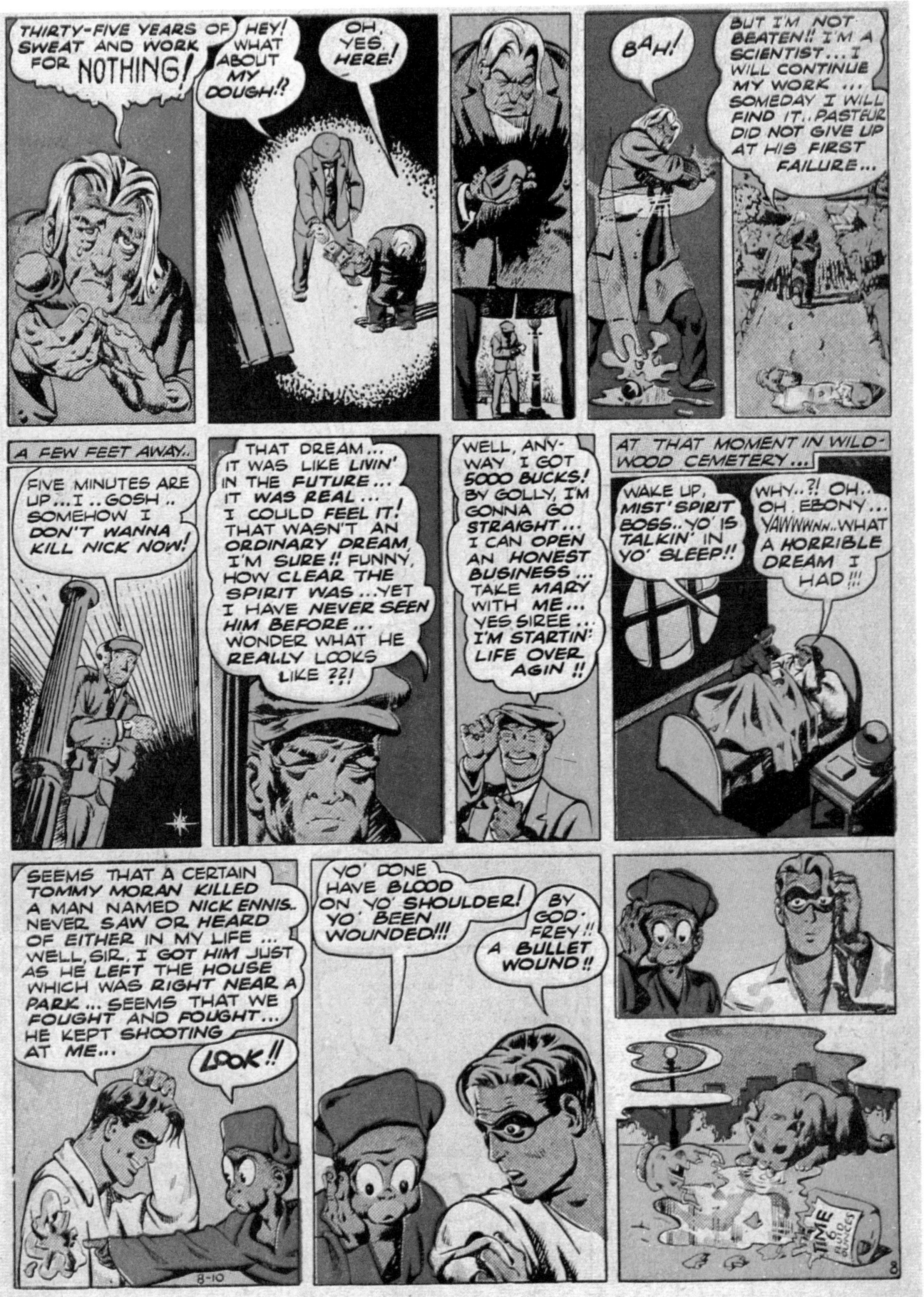

THIRTY-FIVE YEARS OF SWEAT AND WORK FOR NOTHING!
HEY! WHAT ABOUT MY DOUGH!?
OH, YES. HERE!
BAH!
BUT I'M NOT BEATEN!! I'M A SCIENTIST... I WILL CONTINUE MY WORK ... SOMEDAY I WILL FIND IT.. PASTEUR DID NOT GIVE UP AT HIS FIRST FAILURE...
A FEW FEET AWAY..
FIVE MINUTES ARE UP...I..GOSH.. SOMEHOW I DON'T WANNA KILL NICK NOW!
THAT DREAM... IT WAS LIKE LIVIN' IN THE FUTURE... IT WAS REAL... I COULD FEEL IT! THAT WASN'T AN ORDINARY DREAM, I'M SURE!! FUNNY, HOW CLEAR THE SPIRIT WAS...YET I HAVE NEVER SEEN HIM BEFORE... WONDER WHAT HE REALLY LOOKS LIKE ??!
WELL, ANY-WAY I GOT 5000 BUCKS! BY GOLLY, I'M GONNA GO STRAIGHT... I CAN OPEN AN HONEST BUSINESS... TAKE MARY WITH ME... YES SIREE... I'M STARTIN' LIFE OVER AGIN !!
AT THAT MOMENT IN WILD-WOOD CEMETERY...
WAKE UP, MIST' SPIRIT BOSS.. YO' IS TALKIN' IN YO' SLEEP!!
WHY..?! OH.. OH, EBONY... YAWWWNN.. WHAT A HORRIBLE DREAM I HAD!!!
SEEMS THAT A CERTAIN TOMMY MORAN KILLED A MAN NAMED NICK ENNIS.. NEVER SAW OR HEARD OF EITHER IN MY LIFE... WELL, SIR, I GOT HIM JUST AS HE LEFT THE HOUSE WHICH WAS RIGHT NEAR A PARK... SEEMS THAT WE FOUGHT AND FOUGHT... HE KEPT SHOOTING AT ME...
LOOK!!
YO' DONE HAVE BLOOD ON YO' SHOULDER! YO' BEEN WOUNDED!!!
BY GOD-FREY!! A BULLET WOUND!!
TIME
8-10
8

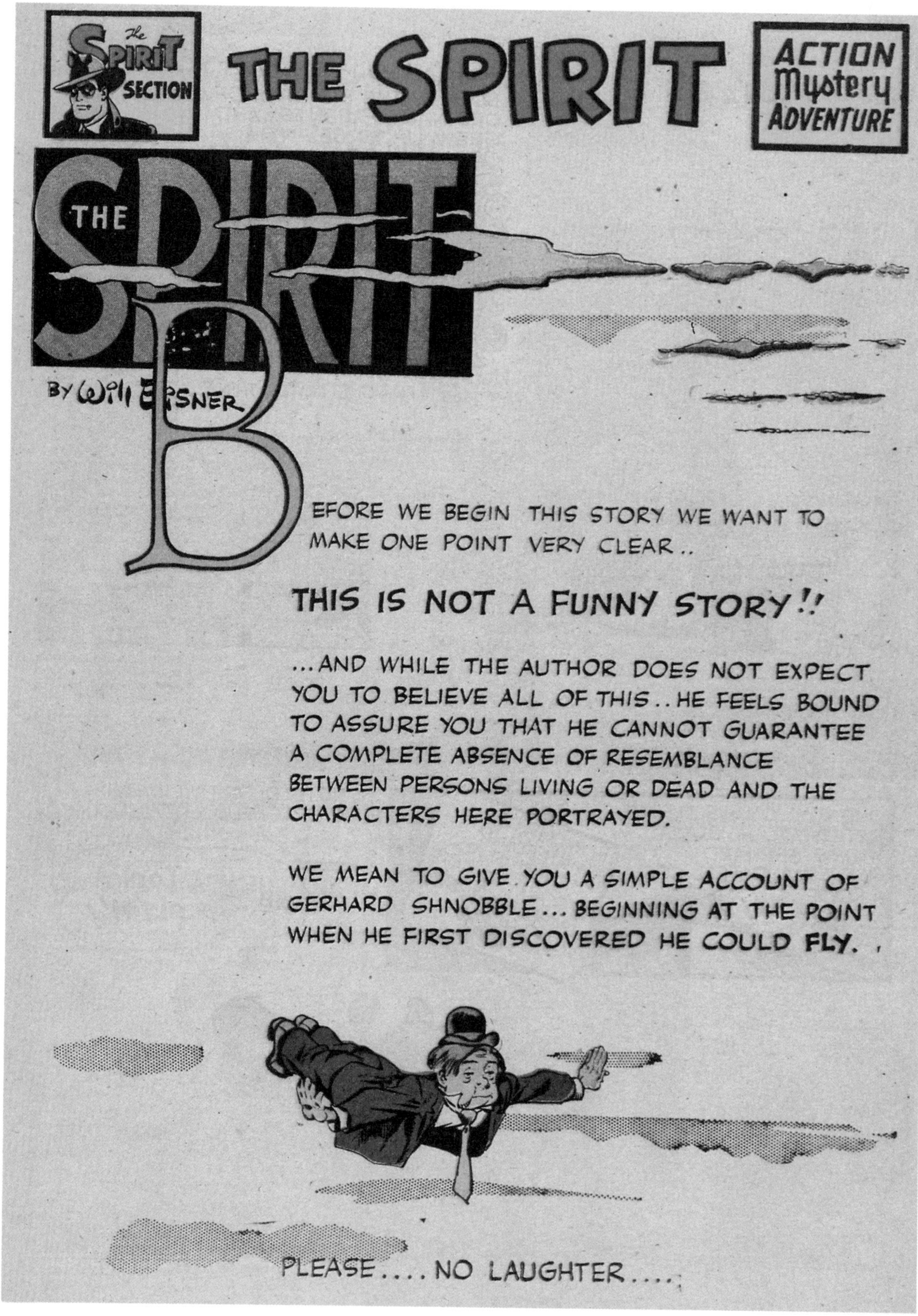

The SPIRIT SECTION
THE SPIRIT
ACTION Mystery ADVENTURE
THE SPIRIT
BY Will Eisner
BEFORE WE BEGIN THIS STORY WE WANT TO MAKE ONE POINT VERY CLEAR..
THIS IS NOT A FUNNY STORY!!
...AND WHILE THE AUTHOR DOES NOT EXPECT YOU TO BELIEVE ALL OF THIS..HE FEELS BOUND TO ASSURE YOU THAT HE CANNOT GUARANTEE A COMPLETE ABSENCE OF RESEMBLANCE BETWEEN PERSONS LIVING OR DEAD AND THE CHARACTERS HERE PORTRAYED.
WE MEAN TO GIVE YOU A SIMPLE ACCOUNT OF GERHARD SHNOBBLE... BEGINNING AT THE POINT WHEN HE FIRST DISCOVERED HE COULD FLY.
PLEASE.... NO LAUGHTER....

From the *Philadelphia Inquirer*, September 5, 1948.

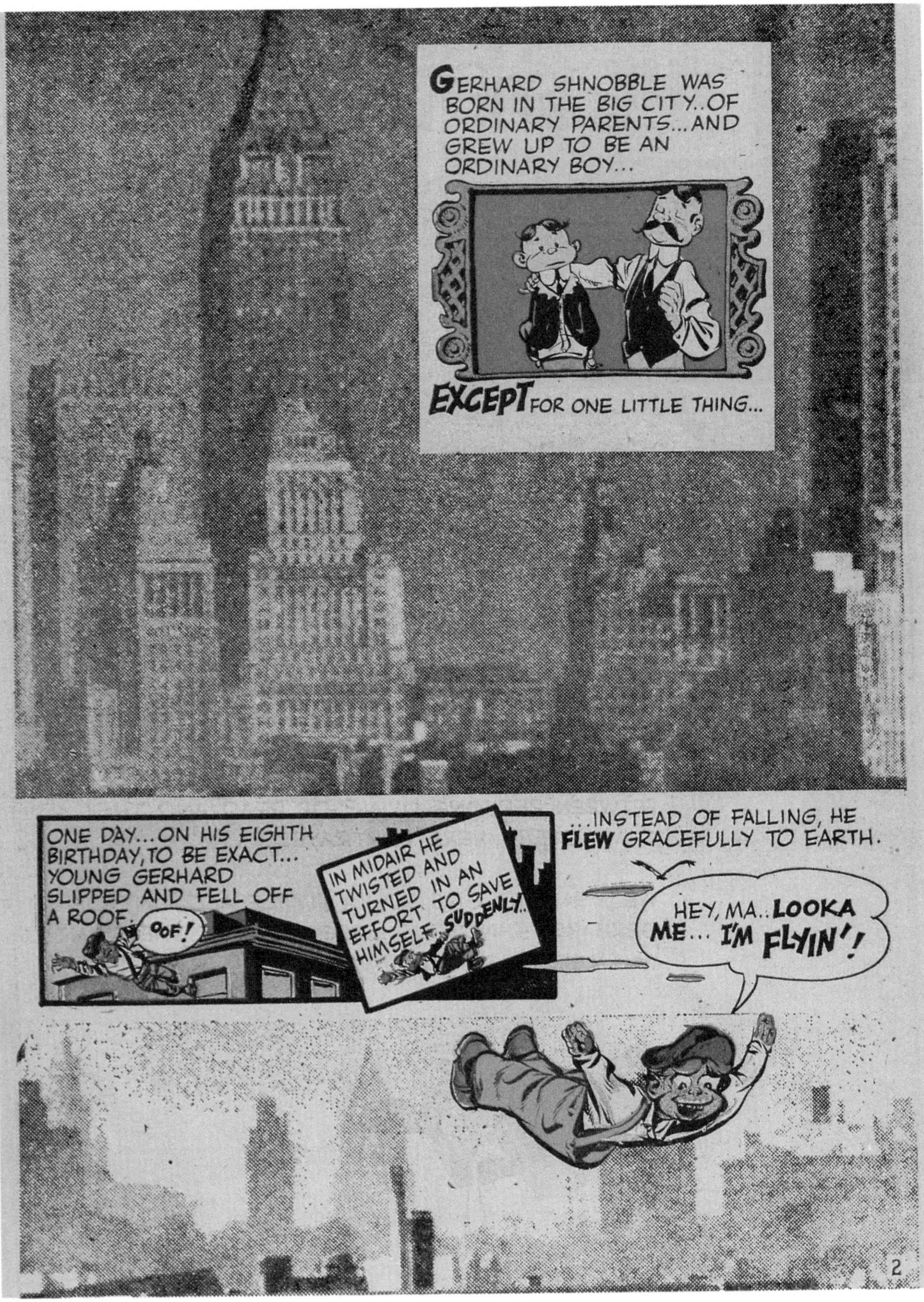
GERHARD SHNOBBLE WAS BORN IN THE BIG CITY..OF ORDINARY PARENTS...AND GREW UP TO BE AN ORDINARY BOY...
EXCEPT FOR ONE LITTLE THING...
ONE DAY...ON HIS EIGHTH BIRTHDAY, TO BE EXACT... YOUNG GERHARD SLIPPED AND FELL OFF A ROOF.
OOF!
IN MIDAIR HE TWISTED AND TURNED IN AN EFFORT TO SAVE HIMSELF... SUDDENLY..
...INSTEAD OF FALLING, HE FLEW GRACEFULLY TO EARTH.
HEY, MA.. LOOKA ME... I'M FLYIN'!
2

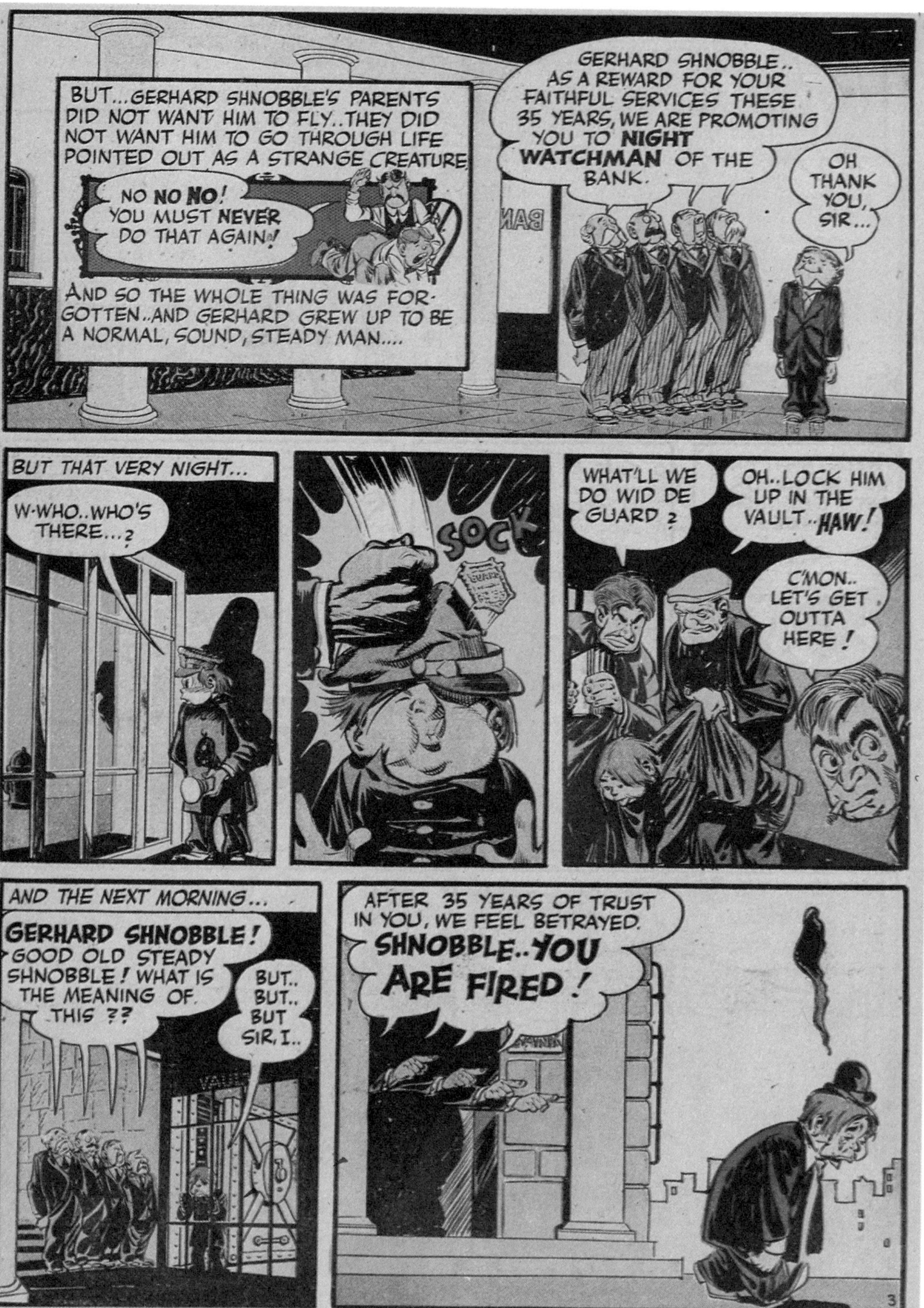

BUT...GERHARD SHNOBBLE'S PARENTS DID NOT WANT HIM TO FLY..THEY DID NOT WANT HIM TO GO THROUGH LIFE POINTED OUT AS A STRANGE CREATURE.
NO NO NO! YOU MUST NEVER DO THAT AGAIN!
AND SO THE WHOLE THING WAS FORGOTTEN..AND GERHARD GREW UP TO BE A NORMAL, SOUND, STEADY MAN....
GERHARD SHNOBBLE.. AS A REWARD FOR YOUR FAITHFUL SERVICES THESE 35 YEARS, WE ARE PROMOTING YOU TO NIGHT WATCHMAN OF THE BANK.
OH THANK YOU, SIR...
BUT THAT VERY NIGHT...
W-WHO..WHO'S THERE...?
SOCK
WHAT'LL WE DO WID DE GUARD?
OH..LOCK HIM UP IN THE VAULT..HAW!
C'MON.. LET'S GET OUTTA HERE!
AND THE NEXT MORNING...
GERHARD SHNOBBLE! GOOD OLD STEADY SHNOBBLE! WHAT IS THE MEANING OF THIS??
BUT.. BUT.. BUT SIR, I..
AFTER 35 YEARS OF TRUST IN YOU, WE FEEL BETRAYED. SHNOBBLE..YOU ARE FIRED!
3

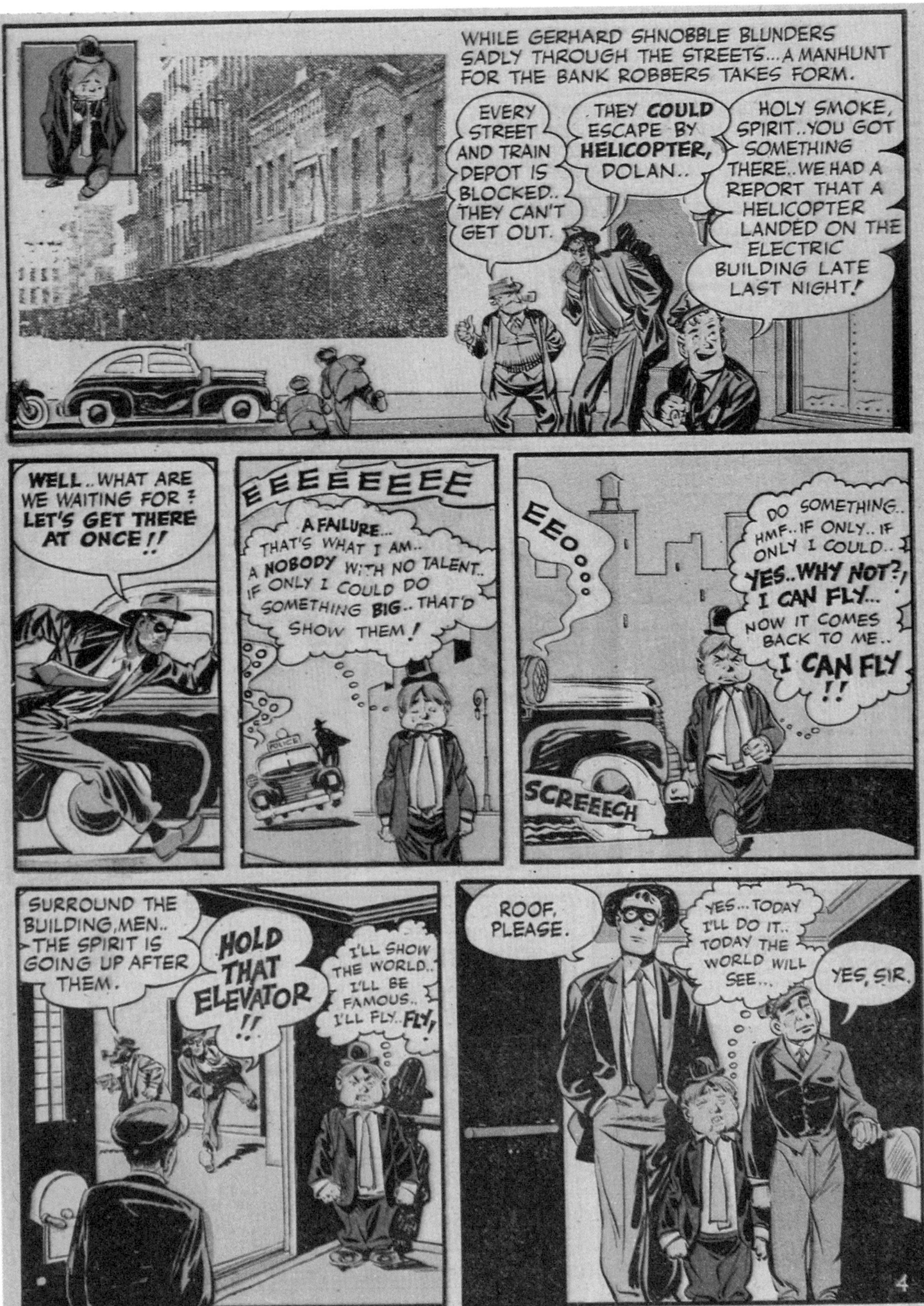
WHILE GERHARD SHNOBBLE BLUNDERS SADLY THROUGH THE STREETS... A MANHUNT FOR THE BANK ROBBERS TAKES FORM.
EVERY STREET AND TRAIN DEPOT IS BLOCKED.. THEY CAN'T GET OUT.
. THEY COULD ESCAPE BY HELICOPTER, DOLAN..
HOLY SMOKE, SPIRIT..YOU GOT SOMETHING THERE..WE HAD A REPORT THAT A HELICOPTER LANDED ON THE ELECTRIC BUILDING LATE LAST NIGHT!
WELL..WHAT ARE WE WAITING FOR? LET'S GET THERE AT ONCE!!
EEEEEEEEE
A FAILURE... THAT'S WHAT I AM.. A NOBODY WITH NO TALENT.. IF ONLY I COULD DO SOMETHING BIG.. THAT'D SHOW THEM!
POLICE
EEO
DO SOMETHING.. HMF.. IF ONLY.. IF ONLY I COULD..
YES..WHY NOT? I CAN FLY... NOW IT COMES BACK TO ME.. I CAN FLY !!
SCREEECH
SURROUND THE BUILDING, MEN.. THE SPIRIT IS GOING UP AFTER THEM.
HOLD THAT ELEVATOR !!
I'LL SHOW THE WORLD.. I'LL BE FAMOUS.. I'LL FLY.. FLY
ROOF, PLEASE.
YES... TODAY I'LL DO IT.. TODAY THE WORLD WILL SEE...
YES, SIR.
4

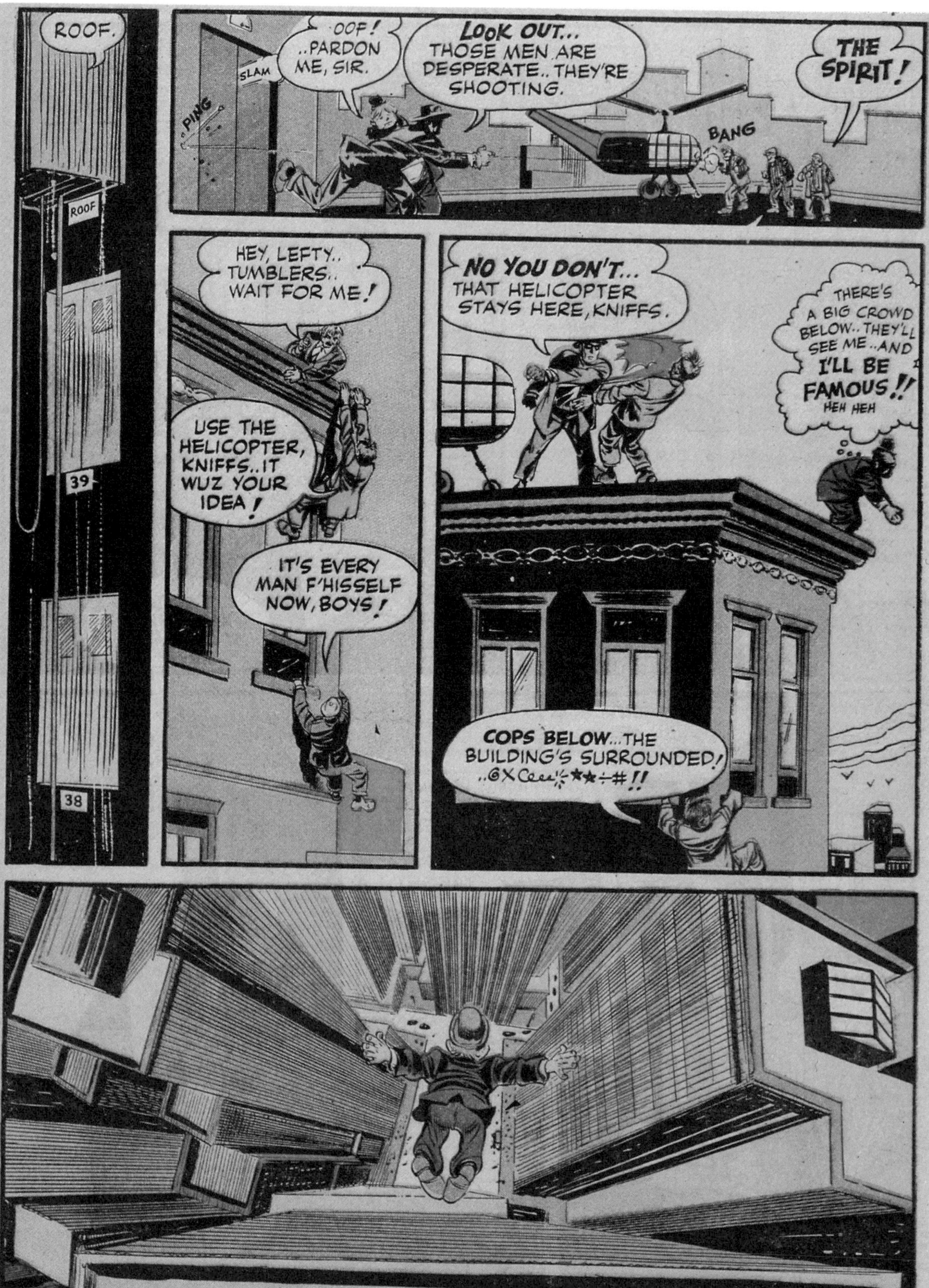
ROOF.
ROOF
39
38
SLAM
PING
OOF! ..PARDON ME, SIR.
LOOK OUT... THOSE MEN ARE DESPERATE.. THEY'RE SHOOTING.
BANG
THE SPIRIT!
HEY, LEFTY.. TUMBLERS.. WAIT FOR ME!
USE THE HELICOPTER, KNIFFS..IT WUZ YOUR IDEA!
IT'S EVERY MAN F'HISSELF NOW, BOYS!
NO YOU DON'T... THAT HELICOPTER STAYS HERE, KNIFFS.
THERE'S A BIG CROWD BELOW.. THEY'LL SEE ME..AND I'LL BE FAMOUS!! HEH HEH
COPS BELOW...THE BUILDING'S SURROUNDED!
5

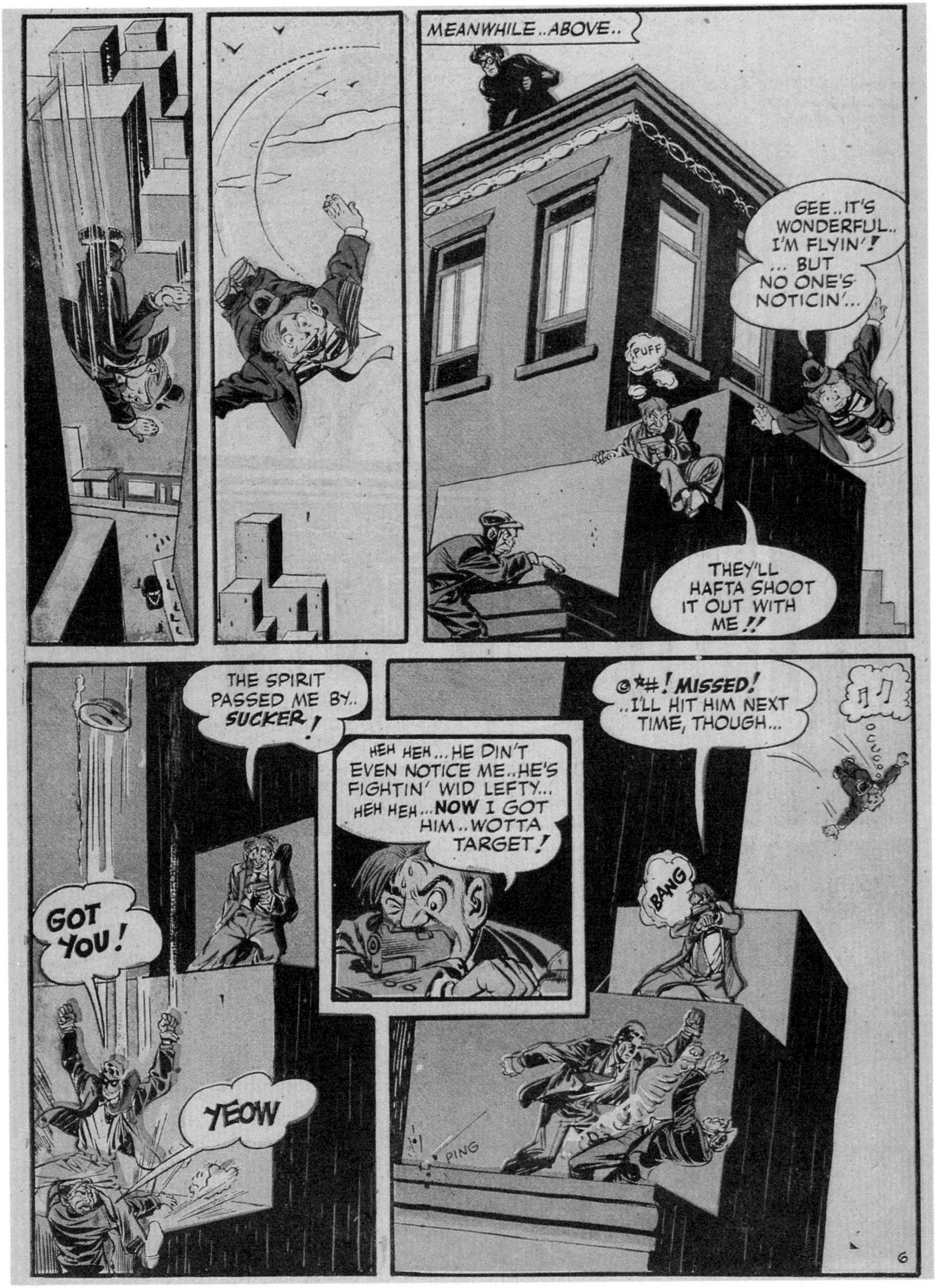
MEANWHILE..ABOVE..
GEE..IT'S WONDERFUL.. I'M FLYIN'! ... BUT NO ONE'S NOTICIN'...
PUFF
THEY'LL HAFTA SHOOT IT OUT WITH ME!!
THE SPIRIT PASSED ME BY.. SUCKER!
GOT YOU!
YEOW
HEH HEH... HE DIN'T EVEN NOTICE ME..HE'S FIGHTIN' WID LEFTY... HEH HEH...NOW I GOT HIM..WOTTA TARGET!
@*#! MISSED! ..I'LL HIT HIM NEXT TIME, THOUGH...
BANG
PING
6

BANG
BANG
BANG
BANG
IT'S JAIL FOR YOU...
POW
AND SO... LIFELESS...GERHARD SHNOBBLE FLUTTERED EARTHWARD..BUT DO NOT WEEP FOR SHNOBBLE...
RATHER SHED A TEAR FOR ALL MANKIND...
FOR NOT ONE PERSON IN THE ENTIRE CROWD THAT WATCHED HIS BODY BEING CARTED AWAY...
NOT ONE OF THEM KNEW OR EVEN SUSPECTED THAT ON THIS DAY GERHARD SHNOBBLE HAD FLOWN.

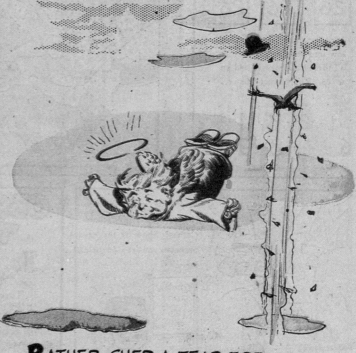

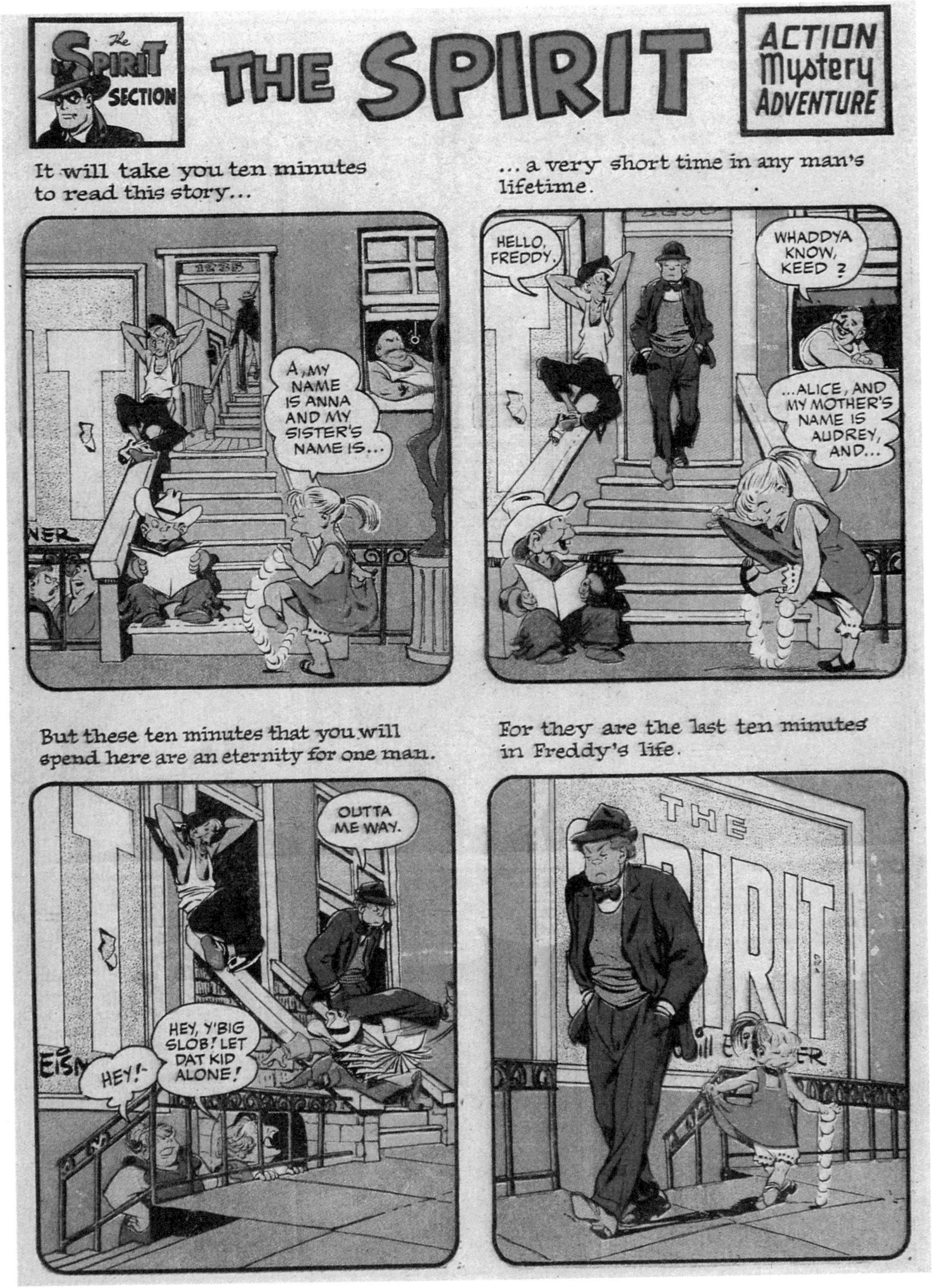
The Spirit Section
THE SPIRIT
ACTION Mystery ADVENTURE
It will take you ten minutes to read this story...
A, MY NAME IS ANNA AND MY SISTER'S NAME IS...
... a very short time in any man's lifetime.
HELLO, FREDDY.
WHADDYA KNOW, KEED ?
...ALICE, AND MY MOTHER'S NAME IS AUDREY, AND...
But these ten minutes that you will spend here are an eternity for one man.
OUTTA ME WAY.
HEY, Y'BIG SLOB! LET DAT KID ALONE!
HEY!-
For they are the last ten minutes in Freddy's life.
THE SPIRIT

From the *Philadelphia Inquirer*, September 11, 1949.

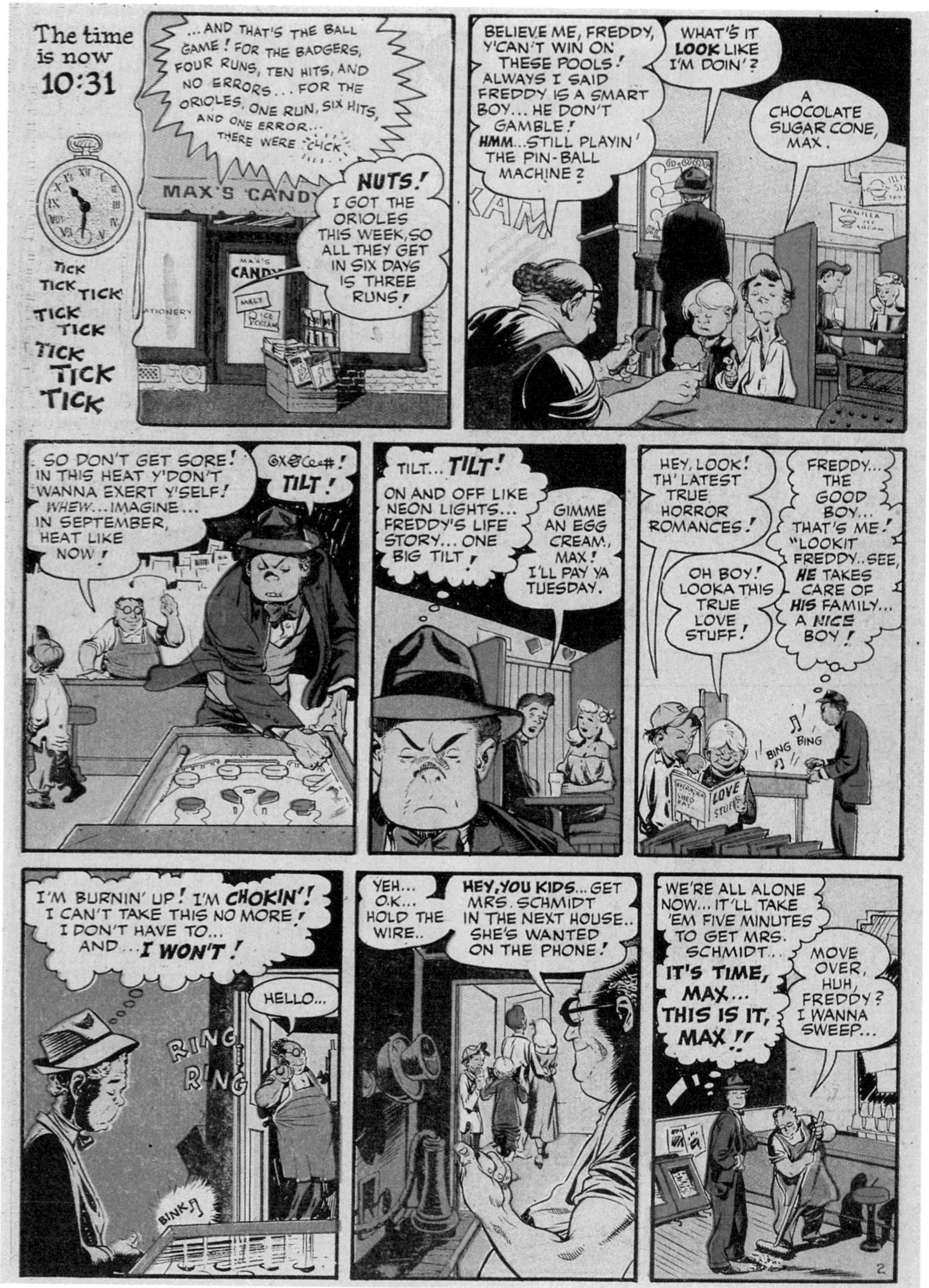
The time is now 10:31
TICK TICK TICK TICK TICK TICK TICK TICK
...AND THAT'S THE BALL GAME! FOR THE BADGERS, FOUR RUNS, TEN HITS, AND NO ERRORS... FOR THE ORIOLES, ONE RUN, SIX HITS, AND ONE ERROR... THERE WERE CLICK
MAX'S CANDY
NUTS! I GOT THE ORIOLES THIS WEEK, SO ALL THEY GET IN SIX DAYS IS THREE RUNS!
BELIEVE ME, FREDDY, Y'CAN'T WIN ON THESE POOLS! ALWAYS I SAID FREDDY IS A SMART BOY... HE DON'T GAMBLE! HMM... STILL PLAYIN' THE PIN-BALL MACHINE?
WHAT'S IT LOOK LIKE I'M DOIN'?
A CHOCOLATE SUGAR CONE, MAX.
SO DON'T GET SORE! IN THIS HEAT Y'DON'T WANNA EXERT Y'SELF! WHEW... IMAGINE... IN SEPTEMBER, HEAT LIKE NOW!
TILT!
TILT... TILT! ON AND OFF LIKE NEON LIGHTS... FREDDY'S LIFE STORY... ONE BIG TILT!
GIMME AN EGG CREAM, MAX! I'LL PAY YA TUESDAY.
HEY, LOOK! TH' LATEST TRUE HORROR ROMANCES!
OH BOY! LOOKA THIS TRUE LOVE STUFF!
FREDDY... THE GOOD BOY... THAT'S ME! "LOOKIT FREDDY.. SEE, HE TAKES CARE OF HIS FAMILY... A NICE BOY!
BING BING
I'M BURNIN' UP! I'M CHOKIN'! I CAN'T TAKE THIS NO MORE! I DON'T HAVE TO... AND... I WON'T!
HELLO...
RING RING
BINK
YEH... O.K... HOLD THE WIRE..
HEY, YOU KIDS... GET MRS. SCHMIDT IN THE NEXT HOUSE.. SHE'S WANTED ON THE PHONE!
WE'RE ALL ALONE NOW... IT'LL TAKE 'EM FIVE MINUTES TO GET MRS. SCHMIDT... IT'S TIME, MAX... THIS IS IT, MAX!!
MOVE OVER, HUH, FREDDY? I WANNA SWEEP...
2

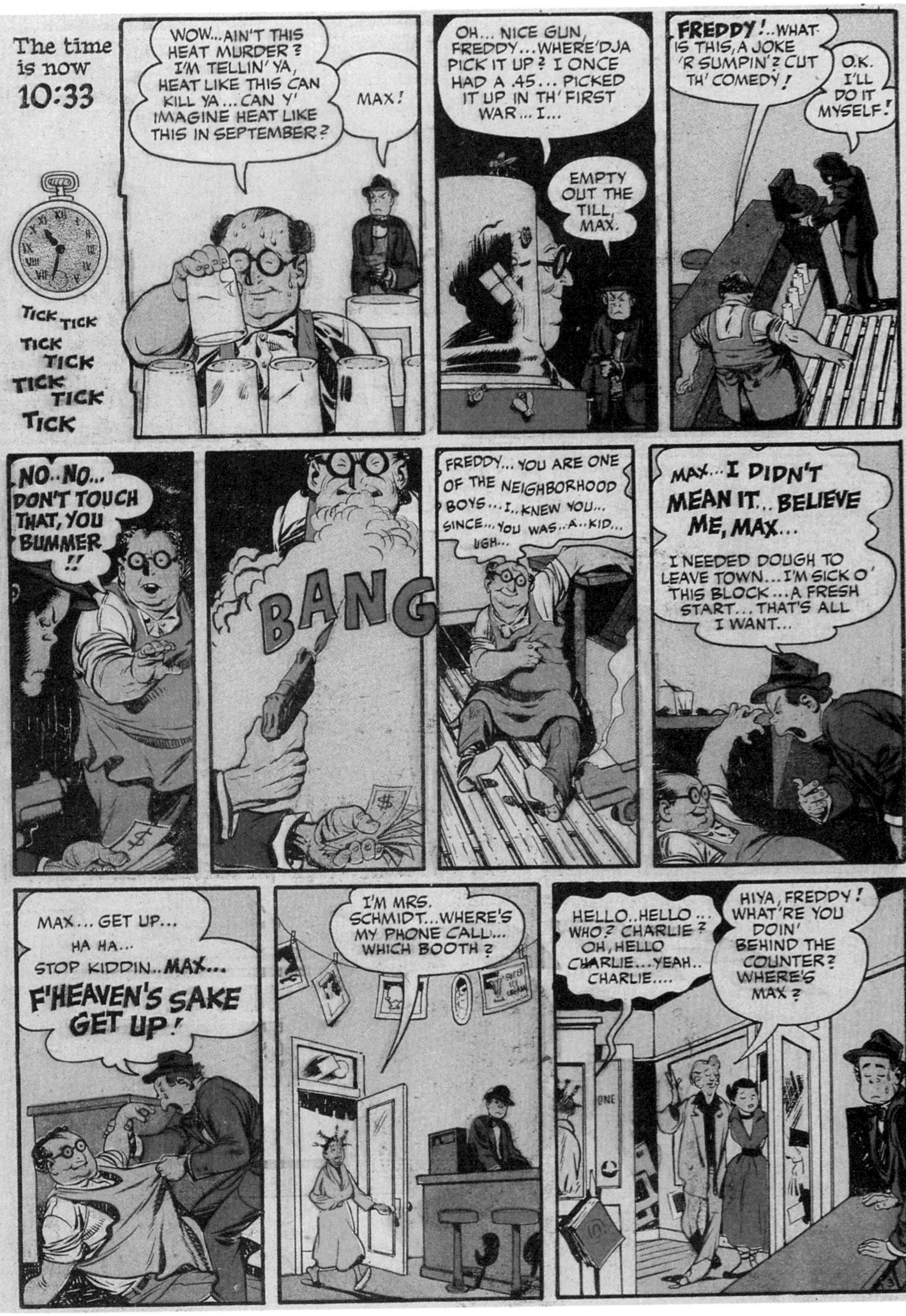
The time is now 10:33
TICK TICK TICK TICK TICK TICK TICK
WOW...AIN'T THIS HEAT MURDER? I'M TELLIN' YA, HEAT LIKE THIS CAN KILL YA...CAN Y' IMAGINE HEAT LIKE THIS IN SEPTEMBER?
MAX!
OH... NICE GUN, FREDDY...WHERE'DJA PICK IT UP? I ONCE HAD A .45... PICKED IT UP IN TH' FIRST WAR... I...
EMPTY OUT THE TILL, MAX.
FREDDY!..WHAT IS THIS, A JOKE 'R SUMPIN'? CUT TH' COMEDY!
O.K. I'LL DO IT MYSELF!
NO..NO... DON'T TOUCH THAT, YOU BUMMER!!
BANG
FREDDY... YOU ARE ONE OF THE NEIGHBORHOOD BOYS...I..KNEW YOU... SINCE...YOU WAS..A..KID... UGH...
MAX...I DIDN'T MEAN IT... BELIEVE ME, MAX...
I NEEDED DOUGH TO LEAVE TOWN...I'M SICK O' THIS BLOCK...A FRESH START...THAT'S ALL I WANT...
MAX... GET UP... HA HA... STOP KIDDIN..MAX... F'HEAVEN'S SAKE GET UP!
I'M MRS. SCHMIDT...WHERE'S MY PHONE CALL... WHICH BOOTH?
HELLO..HELLO... WHO? CHARLIE? OH, HELLO CHARLIE...YEAH.. CHARLIE....
HIYA, FREDDY! WHAT'RE YOU DOIN' BEHIND THE COUNTER? WHERE'S MAX?

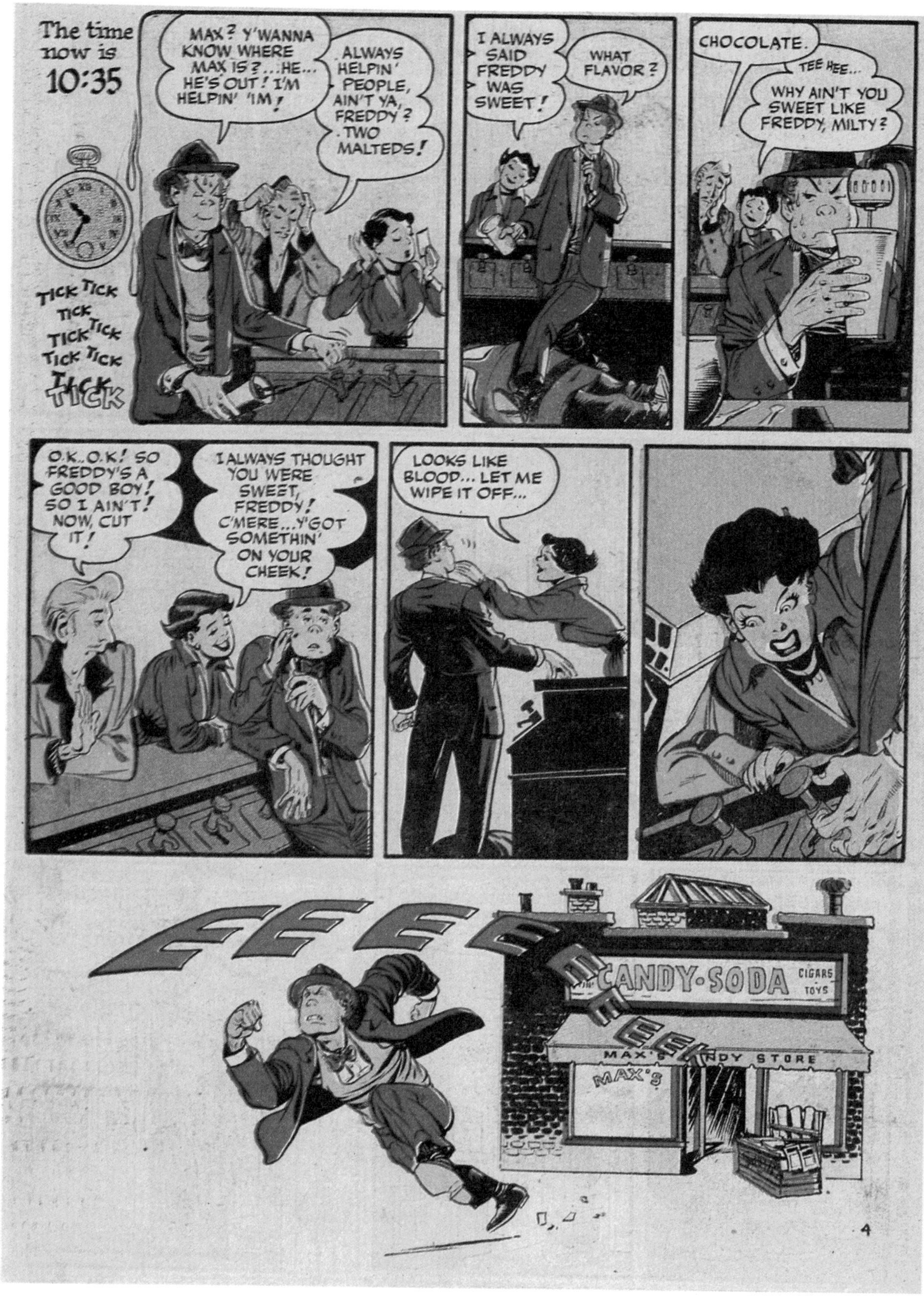
The time now is 10:35
MAX? Y'WANNA KNOW WHERE MAX IS?...HE... HE'S OUT! I'M HELPIN' 'IM!
ALWAYS HELPIN' PEOPLE, AIN'T YA, FREDDY? TWO MALTEDS!
TICK TICK TICK TICK TICK TICK TICK TICK
I ALWAYS SAID FREDDY WAS SWEET!
WHAT FLAVOR?
CHOCOLATE.
TEE HEE...
WHY AIN'T YOU SWEET LIKE FREDDY, MILTY?
O.K..O.K.! SO FREDDY'S A GOOD BOY! SO I AIN'T! NOW, CUT IT!
I ALWAYS THOUGHT YOU WERE SWEET, FREDDY! C'MERE...Y'GOT SOMETHIN' ON YOUR CHEEK!
LOOKS LIKE BLOOD... LET ME WIPE IT OFF...
EEEEEEEE
CANDY·SODA
CIGARS TOYS
MAX'S
4

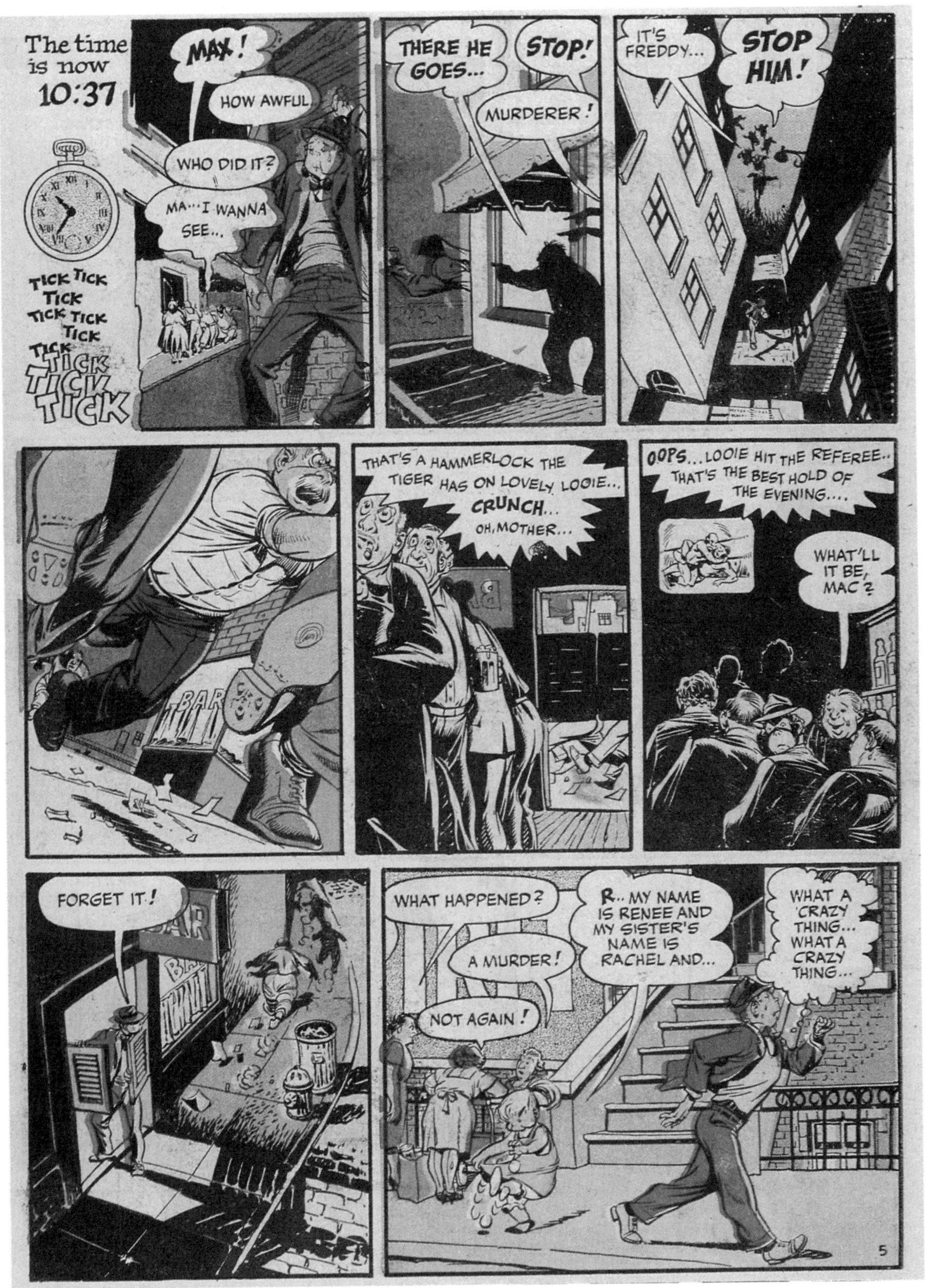

The time is now 10:37
TICK TICK TICK TICK TICK TICK TICK TICK TICK TICK
MAX!
HOW AWFUL
WHO DID IT?
MA... I WANNA SEE...
THERE HE GOES...
STOP!
MURDERER!
IT'S FREDDY...
STOP HIM!
THAT'S A HAMMERLOCK THE TIGER HAS ON LOVELY LOOIE... CRUNCH... OH, MOTHER...
OOPS... LOOIE HIT THE REFEREE.. THAT'S THE BEST HOLD OF THE EVENING....
WHAT'LL IT BE, MAC?
FORGET IT!
BAR
WHAT HAPPENED?
A MURDER!
NOT AGAIN!
R.. MY NAME IS RENEE AND MY SISTER'S NAME IS RACHEL AND...
WHAT A CRAZY THING... WHAT A CRAZY THING...
5

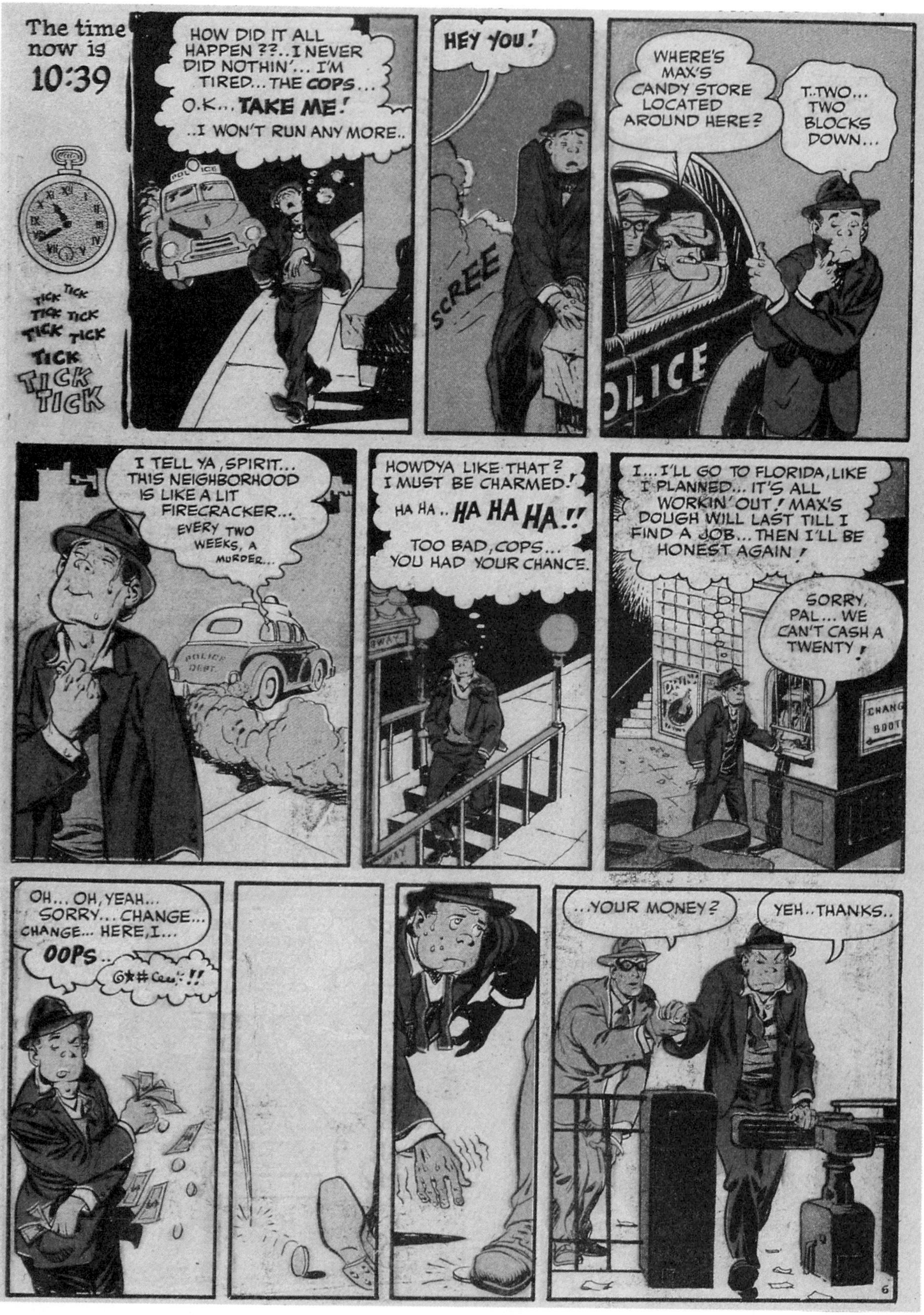
The time now is 10:39
TICK TICK TICK TICK TICK TICK TICK TICK TICK
HOW DID IT ALL HAPPEN ??.. I NEVER DID NOTHIN'... I'M TIRED... THE COPS... O.K... TAKE ME! ..I WON'T RUN ANY MORE..
POLICE
HEY YOU!
SCREE
WHERE'S MAX'S CANDY STORE LOCATED AROUND HERE?
T..TWO... TWO BLOCKS DOWN...
POLICE
I TELL YA, SPIRIT... THIS NEIGHBORHOOD IS LIKE A LIT FIRECRACKER... EVERY TWO WEEKS, A MURDER...
POLICE DEPT.
HOWDYA LIKE THAT? I MUST BE CHARMED! HA HA.. HA HA HA!!
TOO BAD, COPS... YOU HAD YOUR CHANCE.
I... I'LL GO TO FLORIDA, LIKE I PLANNED... IT'S ALL WORKIN' OUT! MAX'S DOUGH WILL LAST TILL I FIND A JOB... THEN I'LL BE HONEST AGAIN!
SORRY, PAL... WE CAN'T CASH A TWENTY!
OH... OH, YEAH... SORRY... CHANGE... CHANGE... HERE, I... OOPS.. G*#Cee!!
...YOUR MONEY?
YEH.. THANKS..
6

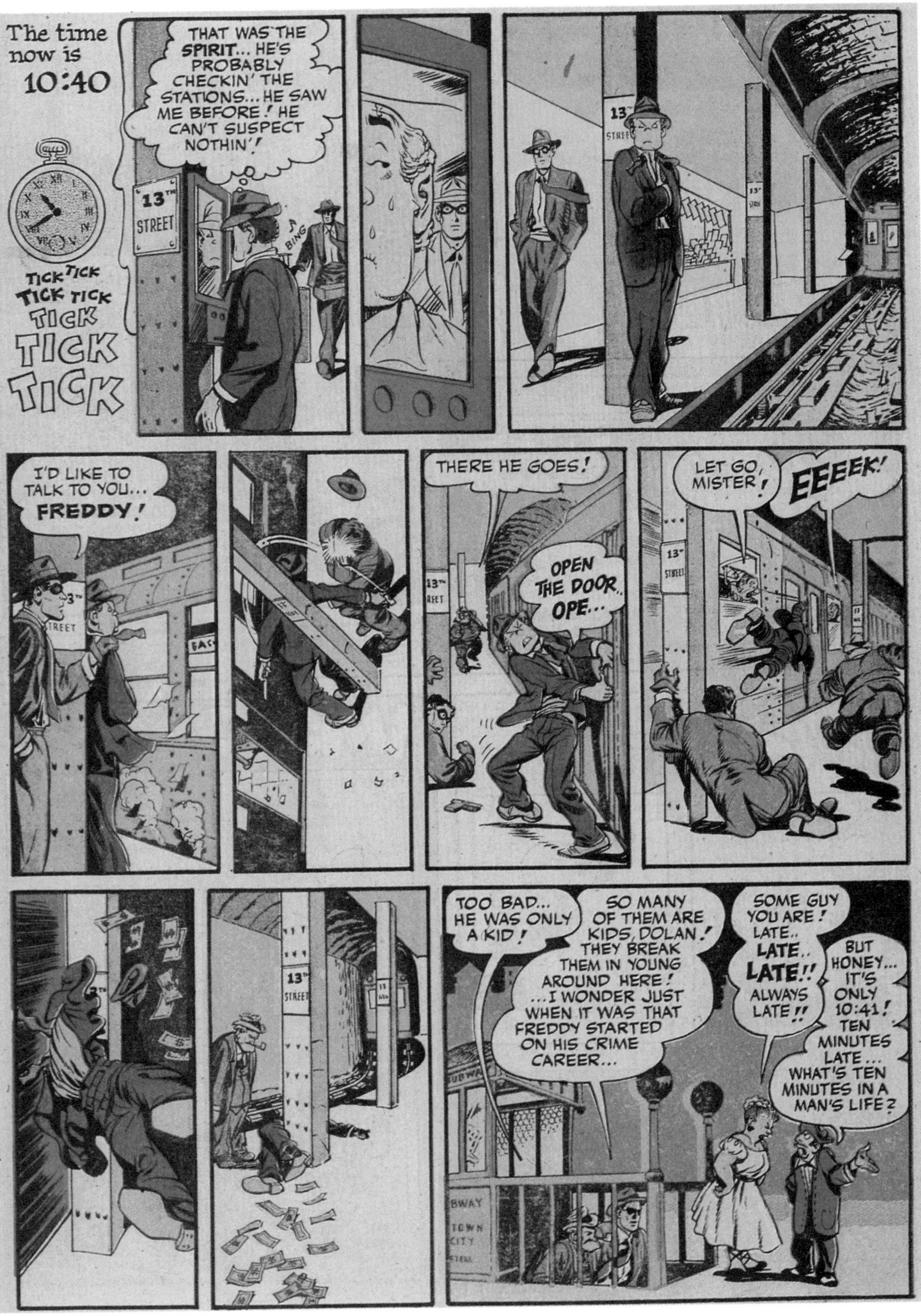
The time now is 10:40
TICK TICK TICK TICK TICK TICK TICK
THAT WAS THE SPIRIT... HE'S PROBABLY CHECKIN' THE STATIONS... HE SAW ME BEFORE! HE CAN'T SUSPECT NOTHIN'!
13TH STREET
BING
13TH STREET
I'D LIKE TO TALK TO YOU... FREDDY!
THERE HE GOES!
OPEN THE DOOR.. OPE...
LET GO, MISTER!
EEEEK!
13TH STREET
TOO BAD... HE WAS ONLY A KID!
SO MANY OF THEM ARE KIDS, DOLAN! THEY BREAK THEM IN YOUNG AROUND HERE! ...I WONDER JUST WHEN IT WAS THAT FREDDY STARTED ON HIS CRIME CAREER...
SOME GUY YOU ARE! LATE.. LATE.. LATE!! ALWAYS LATE!!
BUT HONEY... IT'S ONLY 10:41! TEN MINUTES LATE... WHAT'S TEN MINUTES IN A MAN'S LIFE?

About E.C.

The initials "E.C." on comic-book covers stood at first for "Educational Comics." When M. C. Gaines started E.C. in the mid-1940s, the company was indeed "educational," publishing comic-book versions of the Bible and American history. After Gaines died in a boating accident in 1947, his son William M. Gaines took over the company and shifted its emphasis toward more commercial fare—westerns, romance comics, and crime titles (E.C. came to stand for "Entertaining Comics"). In 1949, horror stories—told by the Vault Keeper and the Crypt Keeper—edged into E.C.'s crime comics, and in 1950, E.C. began publishing three unabashed horror titles. The success of these comic books spawned the flood of horror comics, from many publishers, in the early 1950s.

Also in 1950, E.C. began publishing two science-fiction comic books, *Weird Science* and *Weird Fantasy.* Earlier science-fiction comics were "space operas," along the lines of *Buck Rogers,* but the E.C. comic books tried to approximate, in comics form, the work of serious science-fiction writers. The science-fiction comic books did not sell well, but William Gaines kept them alive with the profits from the horror comics—a rare and probably unique instance of a publisher's supporting comic books because he cared about them.

Al Feldstein was the principal editor of the horror and science-fiction comic books. Unlike the editors of most comic books, Feldstein and the other E.C. editors wrote most of their own stories—and illustrated some of them, too. Like Will Eisner, they worked in the short-story form (E.C.'s stories were only six to eight pages long), but unlike Eisner, the E.C. editors had no need to incorporate continuing characters into their stories; except for the "hosts" of the horror comics, very few E.C. characters made more than one appearance.

Feldstein relied on literary models: he adhered to the idea that short stories had to have surprise endings, and he used captions to tell his stories, rather than to add meaning to the drawings that the captions accompanied. Harvey Kurtzman, the other major E.C. editor, did not lean on literary devices to the same extent. More important, he brought to his work as editor and writer a particularly valuable trait: in a field dominated by fantasies, he tried never to lose sight of reality.

Kurtzman, who was born in Manhattan in 1924, illustrated a number of science-fiction stories for E.C. before he began editing E.C.'s war comic books, *Two-Fisted Tales* and *Frontline Combat.* In the war comics, Kurtzman tried to depict the life of men in combat with a realism that was missing from other comic books. He engaged in orgies of research, spending countless hours in the New York Public Library. In one of the most famous examples of Kurtzman's desire for authenticity, he sent his assistant Jerry De Fuccio down in a submarine so that the onomatopoeic words he would use to represent the sounds made by a submerged submarine would be accurate.

Kurtzman relied heavily on such artists as Jack Davis and John Severin, but he illustrated some of his best war stories himself. His drawings were never slick, but his brushwork was flowing, direct, and energetic—qualities that were perfect for the subject matter—and the two war stories we have chosen for this book, *Air Burst* and *Corpse on the Imjin,* were illustrated as well as written by Kurtzman. *Air Burst,* published while the Korean war was still being fought, is notable for its sympathetic depiction of the Chinese enemy. *Corpse on the Imjin* gives war a psychological as well as a physical reality (in a caption, the American soldier's mind returns to childhood and "dunking" as he struggles in the water with the enemy soldier).

The war comics required so much work that they wore Kurtzman out, and in 1952, while recovering from a bout with jaundice, he decided he wanted to try something less demanding. This turned out to be *Mad*—which was, in its original incarnation as a comic book, a vigorous satirical assault on popular culture.

In *Mad,* Kurtzman spoofed movies, comic strips, and even "classic" popular fiction like *Frankenstein* and the Sherlock Holmes stories, but he may have felt a little uneasy about poking fun at artifacts that were more widely accepted as worthwhile than comic books were. In any case, Kurtzman was probably at his best when he was going after other comic books and "kiddie" TV shows like *Captain Video* and *Howdy Doody.* In *Superduperman,* Kurtzman ridicules the idea that within our unimpressive exteriors there lurk "supermen"—that one day those who scorn us will see our true worth and confess their error. (And along the way, he points out that an all-powerful hero's altruism cannot be taken for granted.) Similarly, Kurtzman bears down on *Howdy Doody,* where he finds a veneer of patronizing jollity that cannot camouflage a hard sell to a particularly vulnerable audience. On *Mad,* Kurtzman collaborated with several fine artists, two of whom, Wallace Wood and Bill Elder, are represented here. Wood and Elder themselves invented many of the bizarre details that enriched *Mad's* panels.

All of the E. C. artists were encouraged to work freely in their own styles (some publishers wanted their artists to squeeze themselves into an anonymous "house style"), but the editors always remained firmly in control. For example, when an artist named Bernard Krigstein was assigned by Al Feldstein to a story called *Master Race* in 1954, he was given six sheets of illustration board with the captions and the dialogue already lettered and in place; his job was to provide illustrations that matched this script. Instead, he expanded the story to eight pages (with the wary approval of Feldstein and William Gaines), by cutting up the lettering and pasting it on new boards. E.C.'s stories typically had six or seven panels per page; Krigstein added panels not just by making the story longer but by using more panels per page. Krigstein told John Benson and Bhob Stewart in an interview that where the script called for three panels, "I might have put in nine panels. Because it's what happens between these panels that's so fascinating." As Krigstein revised and expanded *Master Race,* he created one of the most interesting and admired of all comic-book stories.

Krigstein, who was born in Brooklyn in 1919, came late to E.C. (his work first appeared in issues with 1954 dates) after free-lancing for other comics publishers. He was greatly intrigued by the comics form, and particularly by the way stories are broken down into panels. More than most comic-book illustrators, he was aware of the effects possible by changing the shapes and arrangements of panels. In *Master Race,* Krigstein sometimes seems to be borrowing from film techniques, as many other cartoonists did, but he is up to something different. In the panels on the last page of *Master Race,* Krigstein has not imitated the flurry of images in a film with rapid cutting. He has instead dissected the action, giving his drawings a dreadful clarity that film could not match. His work has a cool objectivity that is unique in the work of the leading comic-book creators. Compare, for example, the death in the subway that comes on the last page of *Master Race* with the one that occurs on the last page of the 1949 *Spirit* story earlier in this book.

In 1954, a public outcry against comic books drove E.C.'s best sellers—the horror and crime comics—from the newsstands, and *Master Race* was published in the first issue of *Impact,* one of a half dozen "New Direction" titles that E.C. introduced late in 1954 and early in 1955 to take their place. The "New Direction" titles grasped desperately for a mature audience (one of the new titles was *Psychoanalysis*) and could not find it. The E.C. line—caught between declining sales and the new Comics Code—struggled for a year, until Gaines finally gave up and discontinued all of his comic books.

Mad survived. Gaines and Kurtzman had converted it into a twenty-five-cent, black-and-white magazine; as such, it was not subject to the Comics Code. Kurtzman and Gaines quarreled and Kurtzman left *Mad* after a few issues of the new magazine; he was replaced by Al Feldstein. *Mad* continues, as one of the great success stories in American publishing.

Kurtzman, after editing several new satire magazines that failed to catch on, did the *Little Annie Fanny* stories in *Playboy*. Bernard Krigstein worked for a time in commercial art, and more recently has been a teacher and a painter.

M.B.

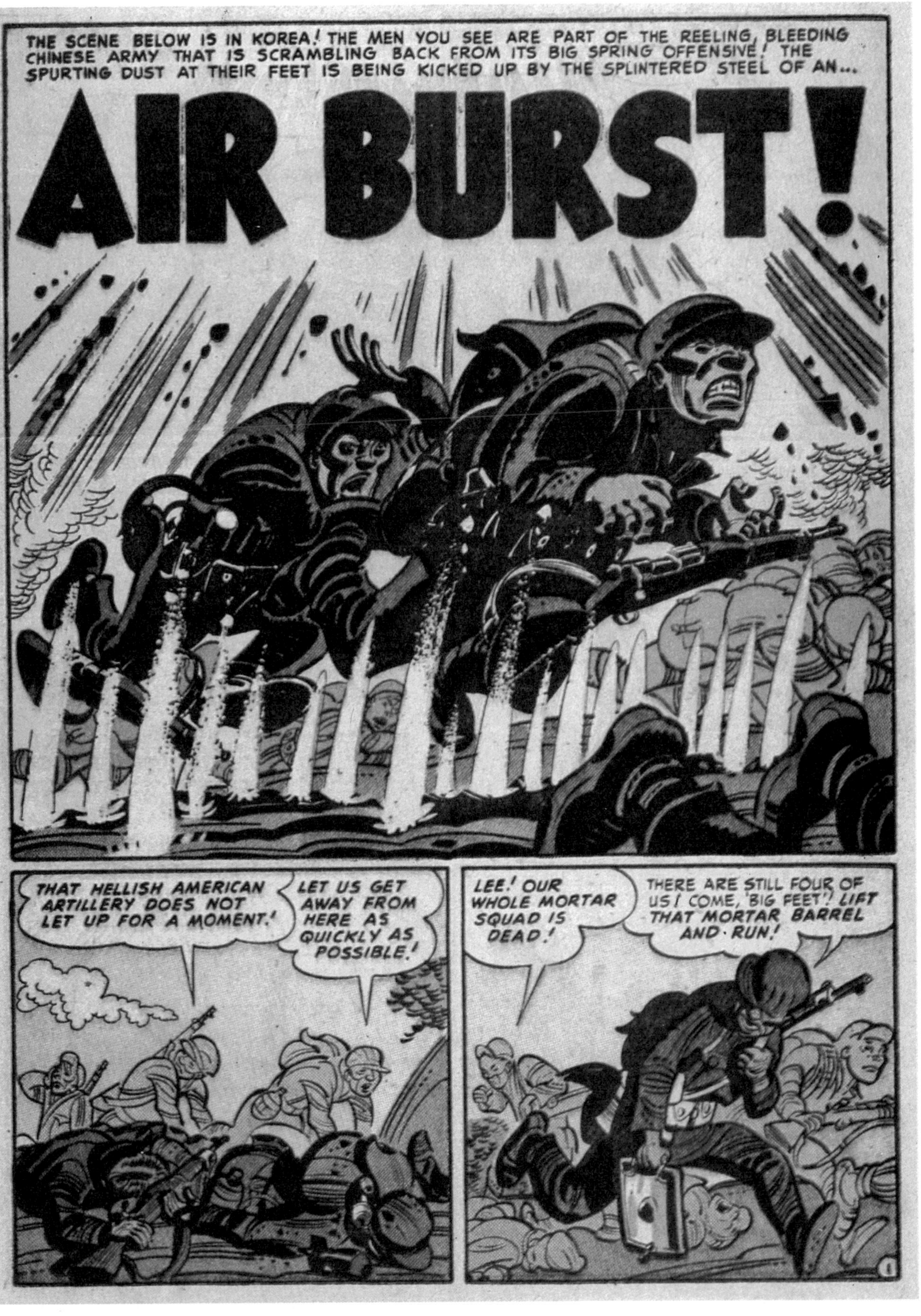

THE SCENE BELOW IS IN KOREA! THE MEN YOU SEE ARE PART OF THE REELING, BLEEDING CHINESE ARMY THAT IS SCRAMBLING BACK FROM ITS BIG SPRING OFFENSIVE! THE SPURTING DUST AT THEIR FEET IS BEING KICKED UP BY THE SPLINTERED STEEL OF AN...
AIR BURST!
THAT HELLISH AMERICAN ARTILLERY DOES NOT LET UP FOR A MOMENT!
LET US GET AWAY FROM HERE AS QUICKLY AS POSSIBLE!
LEE! OUR WHOLE MORTAR SQUAD IS DEAD!
THERE ARE STILL FOUR OF US! COME, 'BIG FEET'! LIFT THAT MORTAR BARREL AND RUN!

From *Frontline Combat* No. 4, Jan.-Feb. 1952.

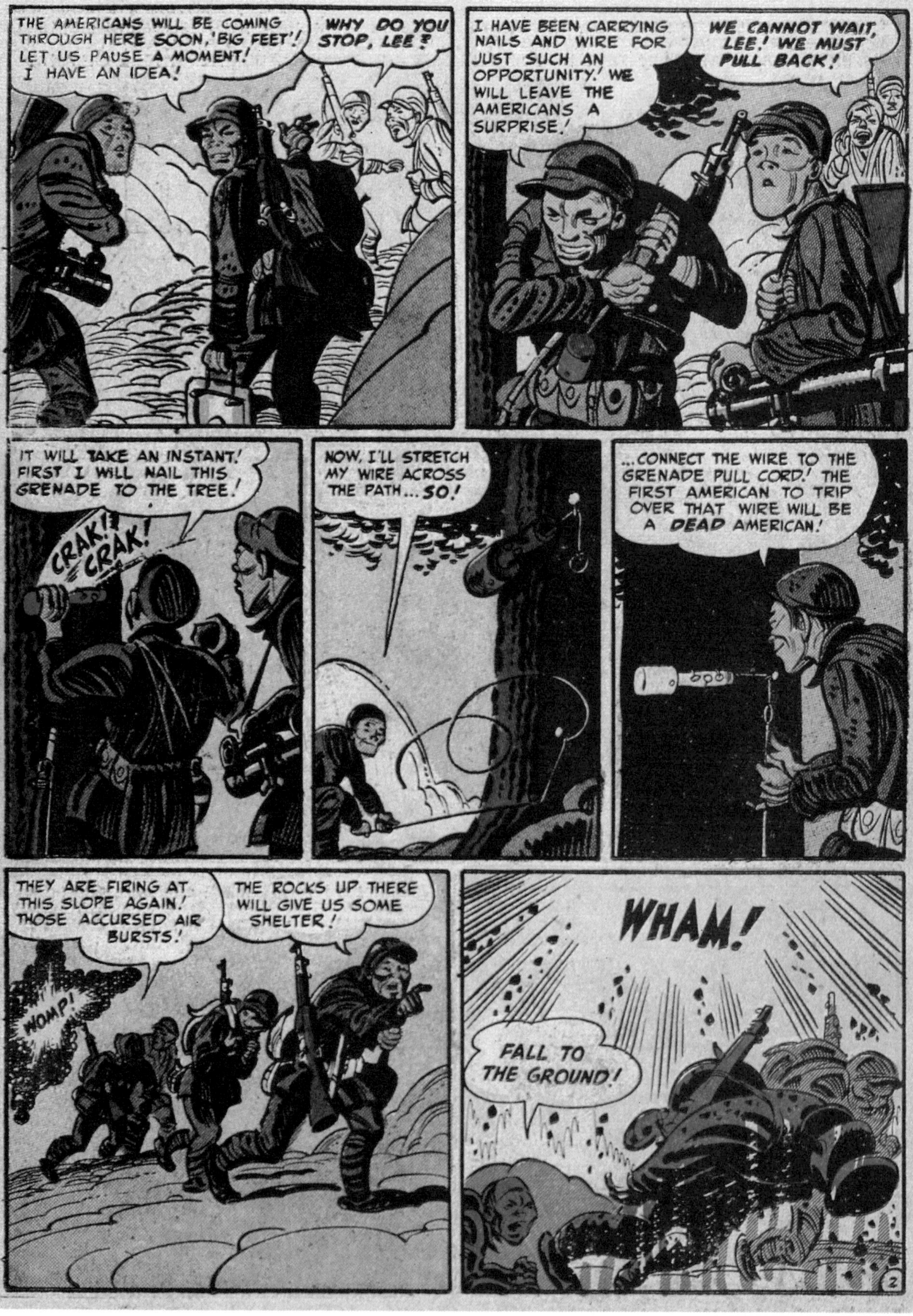
THE AMERICANS WILL BE COMING THROUGH HERE SOON, 'BIG FEET'! LET US PAUSE A MOMENT! I HAVE AN IDEA!
WHY DO YOU STOP, LEE?
I HAVE BEEN CARRYING NAILS AND WIRE FOR JUST SUCH AN OPPORTUNITY! WE WILL LEAVE THE AMERICANS A SURPRISE!
WE CANNOT WAIT, LEE! WE MUST PULL BACK!
IT WILL TAKE AN INSTANT! FIRST I WILL NAIL THIS GRENADE TO THE TREE!
CRAK! CRAK!
NOW, I'LL STRETCH MY WIRE ACROSS THE PATH... SO!
...CONNECT THE WIRE TO THE GRENADE PULL CORD! THE FIRST AMERICAN TO TRIP OVER THAT WIRE WILL BE A DEAD AMERICAN!
THEY ARE FIRING AT THIS SLOPE AGAIN! THOSE ACCURSED AIR BURSTS!
THE ROCKS UP THERE WILL GIVE US SOME SHELTER!
WOMP!
WHAM!
FALL TO THE GROUND!
2

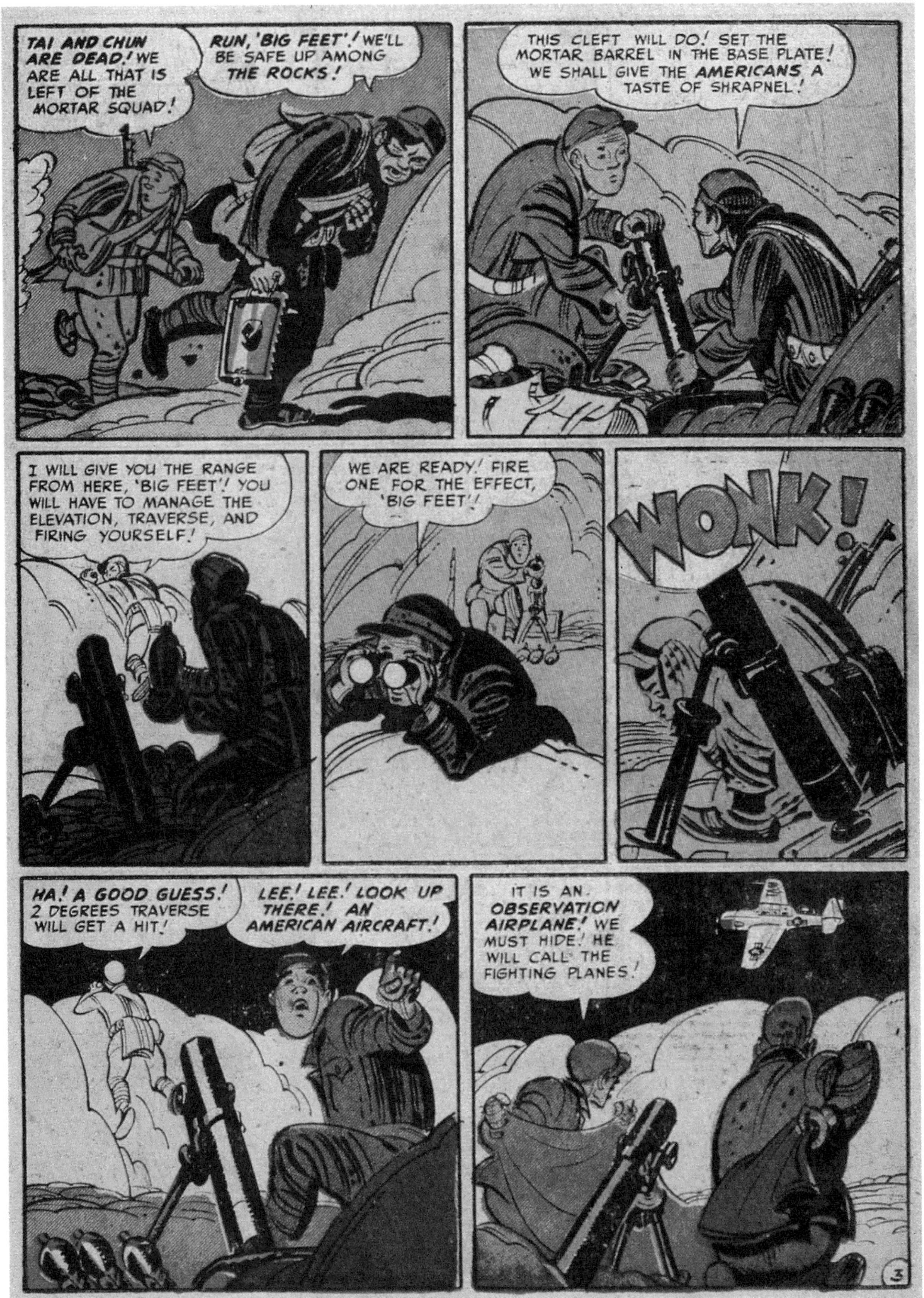
TAI AND CHUN ARE DEAD! WE ARE ALL THAT IS LEFT OF THE MORTAR SQUAD!
RUN, 'BIG FEET'! WE'LL BE SAFE UP AMONG THE ROCKS!
THIS CLEFT WILL DO! SET THE MORTAR BARREL IN THE BASE PLATE! WE SHALL GIVE THE AMERICANS A TASTE OF SHRAPNEL!
I WILL GIVE YOU THE RANGE FROM HERE, 'BIG FEET'! YOU WILL HAVE TO MANAGE THE ELEVATION, TRAVERSE, AND FIRING YOURSELF!
WE ARE READY! FIRE ONE FOR THE EFFECT, 'BIG FEET'!
WONK!
HA! A GOOD GUESS! 2 DEGREES TRAVERSE WILL GET A HIT!
LEE! LEE! LOOK UP THERE! AN AMERICAN AIRCRAFT!
IT IS AN OBSERVATION AIRPLANE! WE MUST HIDE! HE WILL CALL THE FIGHTING PLANES!
3

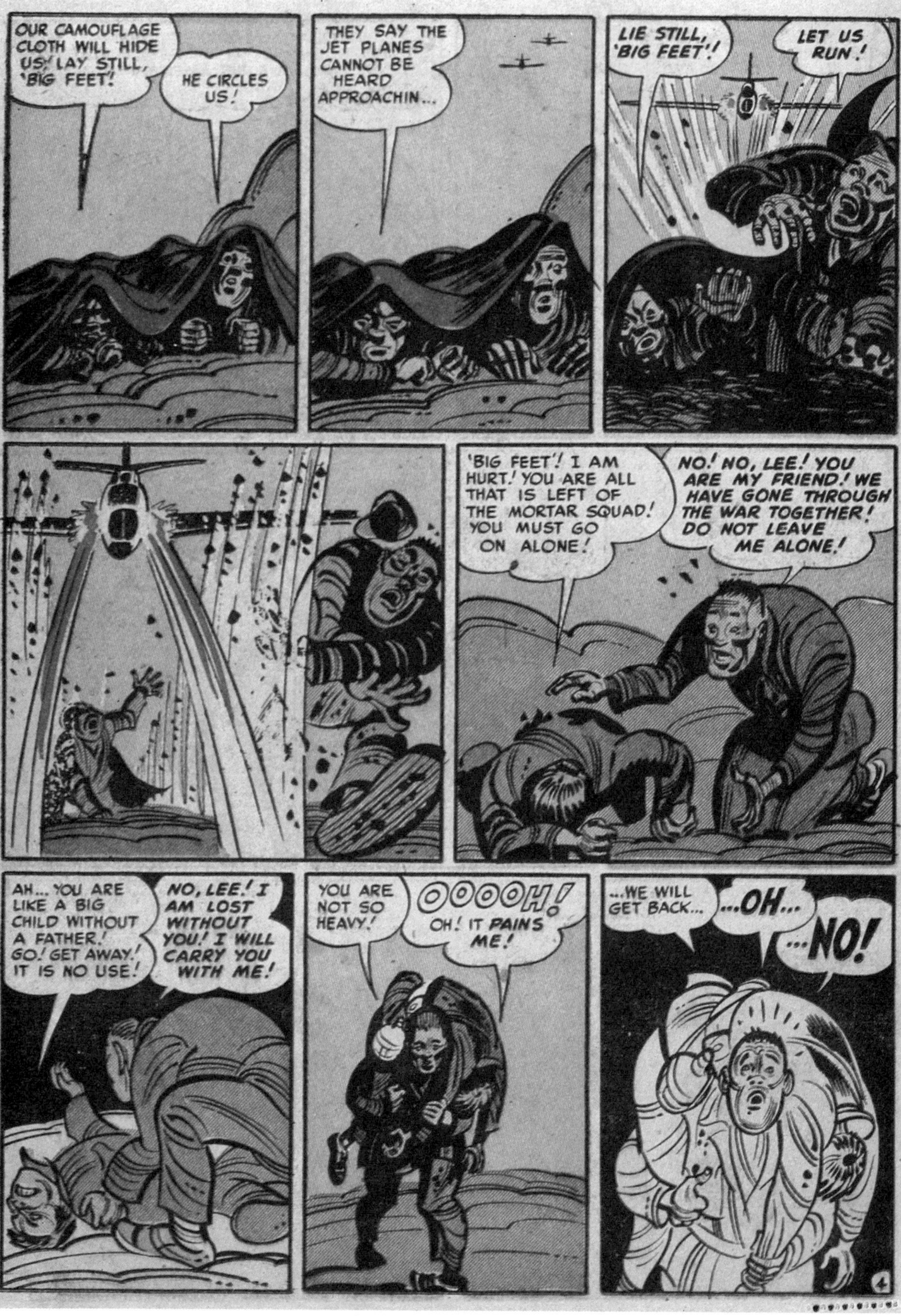

OUR CAMOUFLAGE CLOTH WILL HIDE US! LAY STILL, 'BIG FEET'!
HE CIRCLES US!
THEY SAY THE JET PLANES CANNOT BE HEARD APPROACHIN...
LIE STILL, 'BIG FEET'!
LET US RUN!
'BIG FEET'! I AM HURT! YOU ARE ALL THAT IS LEFT OF THE MORTAR SQUAD! YOU MUST GO ON ALONE!
NO! NO, LEE! YOU ARE MY FRIEND! WE HAVE GONE THROUGH THE WAR TOGETHER! DO NOT LEAVE ME ALONE!
AH... YOU ARE LIKE A BIG CHILD WITHOUT A FATHER! GO! GET AWAY! IT IS NO USE!
NO, LEE! I AM LOST WITHOUT YOU! I WILL CARRY YOU WITH ME!
YOU ARE NOT SO HEAVY!
OOOOH!
OH! IT PAINS ME!
...WE WILL GET BACK...
...OH...
...NO!
4

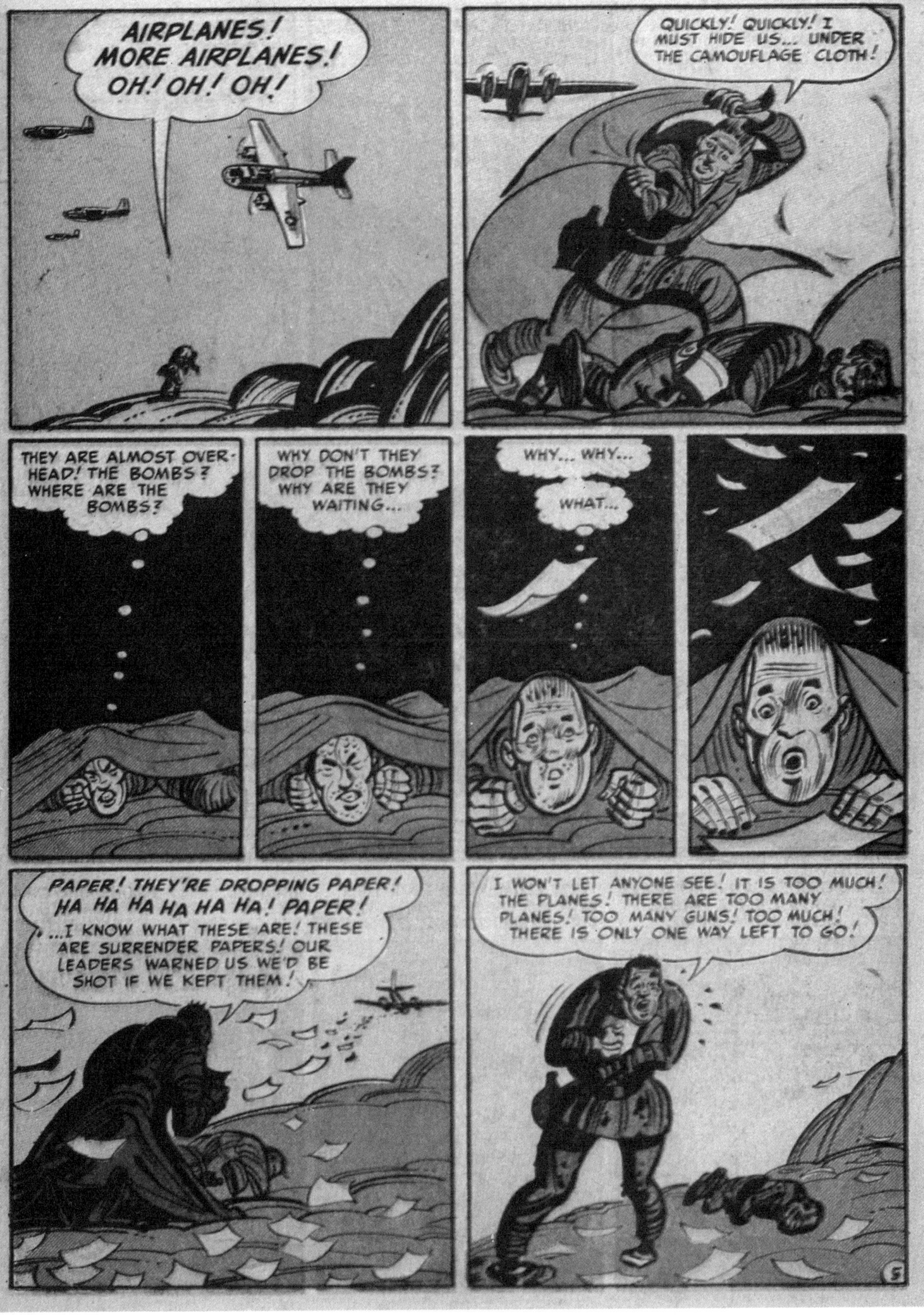
AIRPLANES! MORE AIRPLANES! OH! OH! OH!
QUICKLY! QUICKLY! I MUST HIDE US... UNDER THE CAMOUFLAGE CLOTH!
THEY ARE ALMOST OVER-HEAD! THE BOMBS? WHERE ARE THE BOMBS?
WHY DON'T THEY DROP THE BOMBS? WHY ARE THEY WAITING...
WHY... WHY...
WHAT...
PAPER! THEY'RE DROPPING PAPER! HA HA HA HA HA HA! PAPER! ...I KNOW WHAT THESE ARE! THESE ARE SURRENDER PAPERS! OUR LEADERS WARNED US WE'D BE SHOT IF WE KEPT THEM!
I WON'T LET ANYONE SEE! IT IS TOO MUCH! THE PLANES! THERE ARE TOO MANY PLANES! TOO MANY GUNS! TOO MUCH! THERE IS ONLY ONE WAY LEFT TO GO!
5

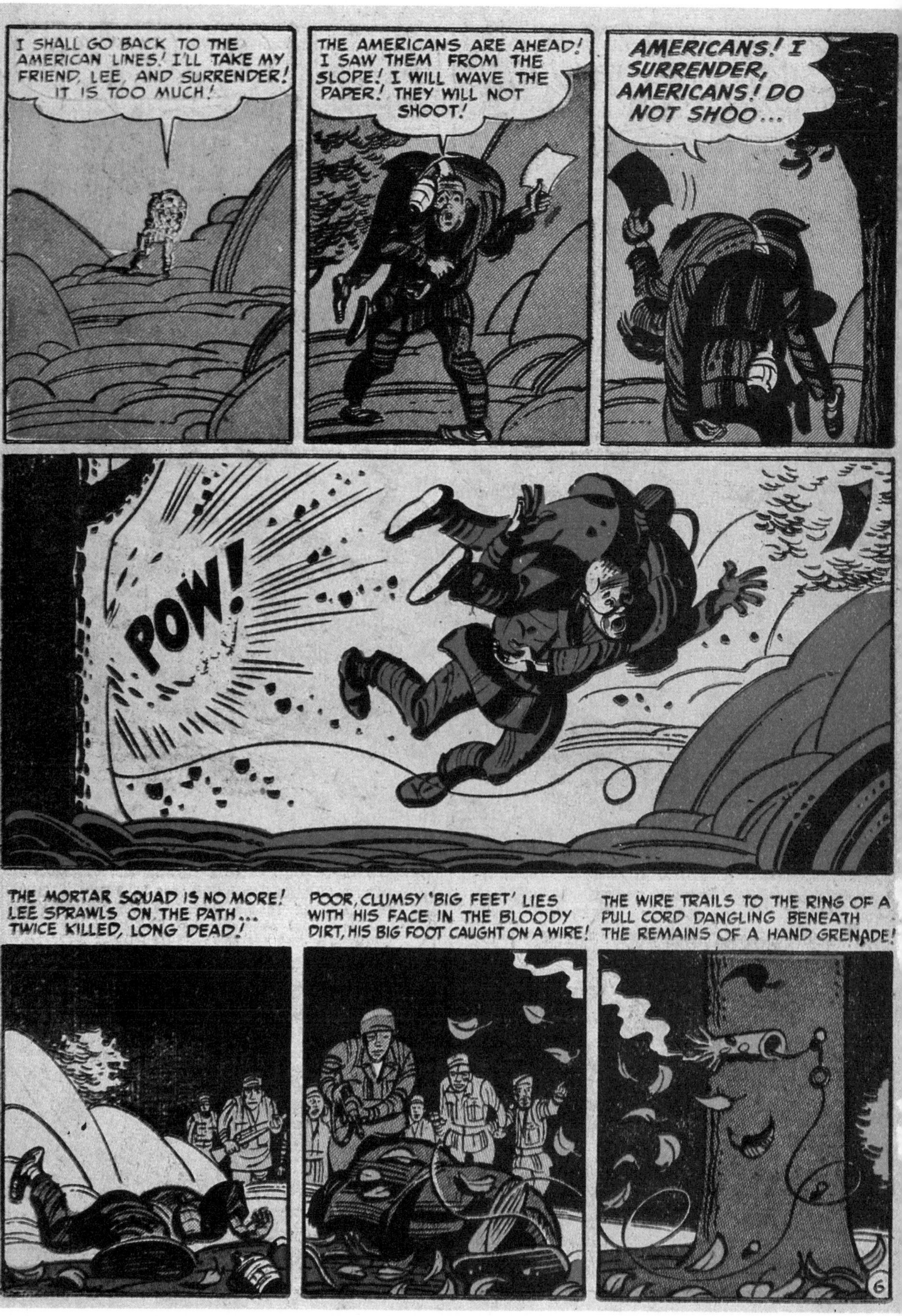

I SHALL GO BACK TO THE AMERICAN LINES! I'LL TAKE MY FRIEND, LEE, AND SURRENDER! IT IS TOO MUCH!
THE AMERICANS ARE AHEAD! I SAW THEM FROM THE SLOPE! I WILL WAVE THE PAPER! THEY WILL NOT SHOOT!
AMERICANS! I SURRENDER, AMERICANS! DO NOT SHOO...
POW!
THE MORTAR SQUAD IS NO MORE! LEE SPRAWLS ON THE PATH... TWICE KILLED, LONG DEAD!
POOR, CLUMSY 'BIG FEET' LIES WITH HIS FACE IN THE BLOODY DIRT, HIS BIG FOOT CAUGHT ON A WIRE!
THE WIRE TRAILS TO THE RING OF A PULL CORD DANGLING BENEATH THE REMAINS OF A HAND GRENADE!
6

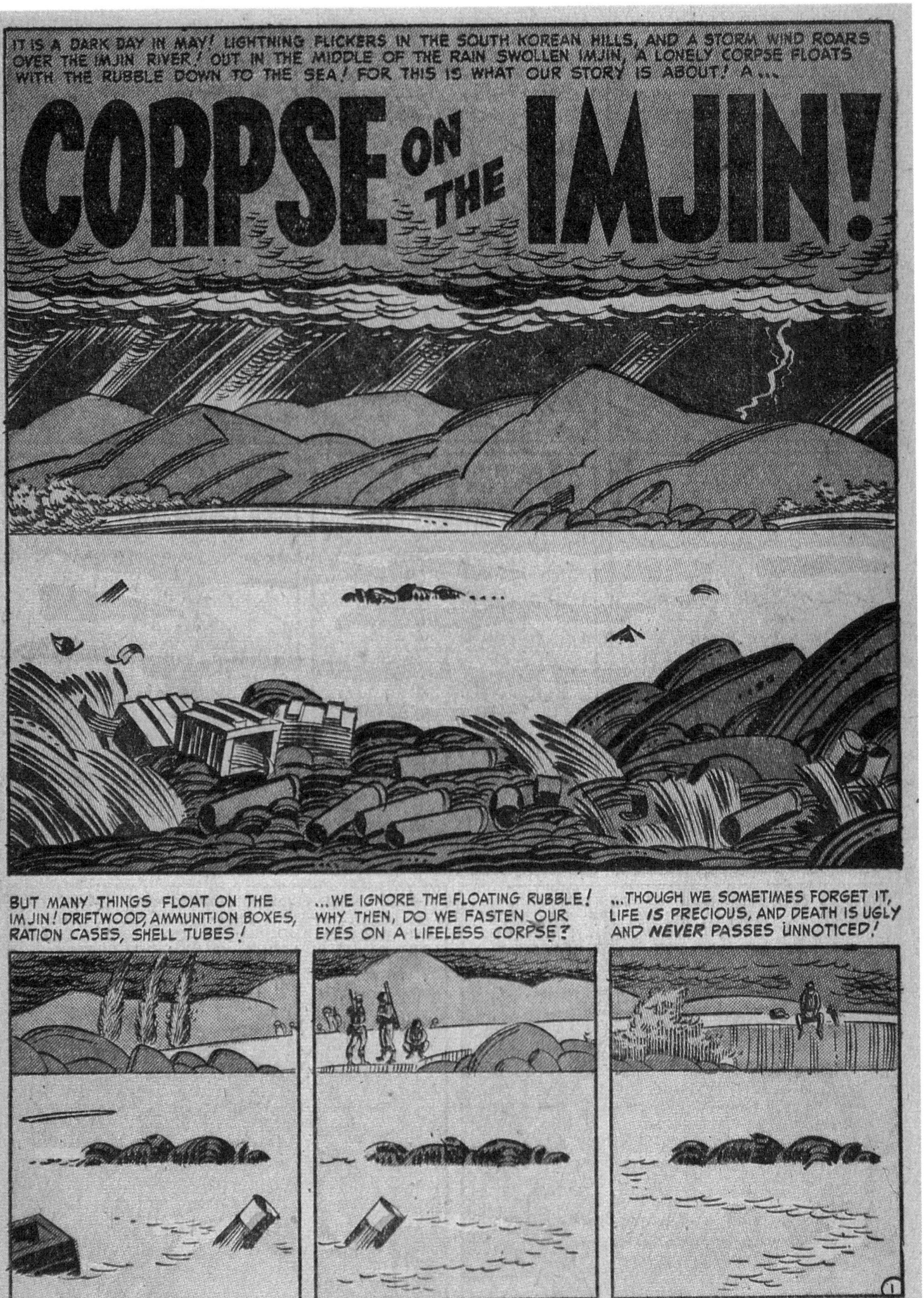
IT IS A DARK DAY IN MAY! LIGHTNING FLICKERS IN THE SOUTH KOREAN HILLS, AND A STORM WIND ROARS OVER THE IMJIN RIVER! OUT IN THE MIDDLE OF THE RAIN SWOLLEN IMJIN, A LONELY CORPSE FLOATS WITH THE RUBBLE DOWN TO THE SEA! FOR THIS IS WHAT OUR STORY IS ABOUT! A...
CORPSE ON THE IMJIN!
BUT MANY THINGS FLOAT ON THE IMJIN! DRIFTWOOD, AMMUNITION BOXES, RATION CASES, SHELL TUBES!
...WE IGNORE THE FLOATING RUBBLE! WHY THEN, DO WE FASTEN OUR EYES ON A LIFELESS CORPSE?
...THOUGH WE SOMETIMES FORGET IT, LIFE IS PRECIOUS, AND DEATH IS UGLY AND NEVER PASSES UNNOTICED!
1

From *Two-Fisted Tales* No. 25, Jan.-Feb. 1952.

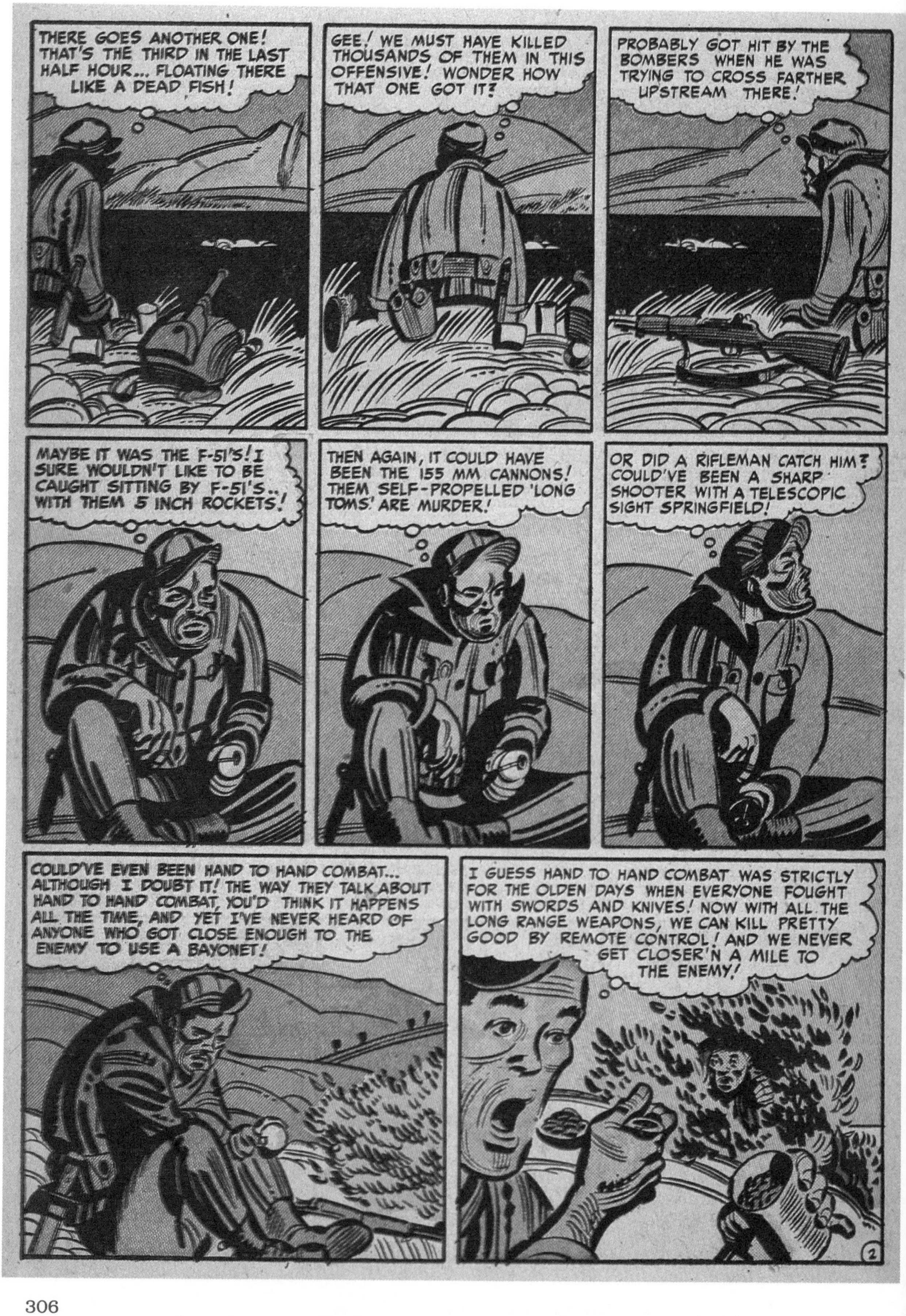
THERE GOES ANOTHER ONE! THAT'S THE THIRD IN THE LAST HALF HOUR... FLOATING THERE LIKE A DEAD FISH!
GEE! WE MUST HAVE KILLED THOUSANDS OF THEM IN THIS OFFENSIVE! WONDER HOW THAT ONE GOT IT?
PROBABLY GOT HIT BY THE BOMBERS WHEN HE WAS TRYING TO CROSS FARTHER UPSTREAM THERE!
MAYBE IT WAS THE F-51'S! I SURE WOULDN'T LIKE TO BE CAUGHT SITTING BY F-51'S.. WITH THEM 5 INCH ROCKETS!
THEN AGAIN, IT COULD HAVE BEEN THE 155 MM CANNONS! THEM SELF-PROPELLED 'LONG TOMS' ARE MURDER!
OR DID A RIFLEMAN CATCH HIM? COULD'VE BEEN A SHARP SHOOTER WITH A TELESCOPIC SIGHT SPRINGFIELD!
COULD'VE EVEN BEEN HAND TO HAND COMBAT... ALTHOUGH I DOUBT IT! THE WAY THEY TALK ABOUT HAND TO HAND COMBAT, YOU'D THINK IT HAPPENS ALL THE TIME, AND YET I'VE NEVER HEARD OF ANYONE WHO GOT CLOSE ENOUGH TO THE ENEMY TO USE A BAYONET!
I GUESS HAND TO HAND COMBAT WAS STRICTLY FOR THE OLDEN DAYS WHEN EVERYONE FOUGHT WITH SWORDS AND KNIVES! NOW WITH ALL THE LONG RANGE WEAPONS, WE CAN KILL PRETTY GOOD BY REMOTE CONTROL! AND WE NEVER GET CLOSER'N A MILE TO THE ENEMY!
2

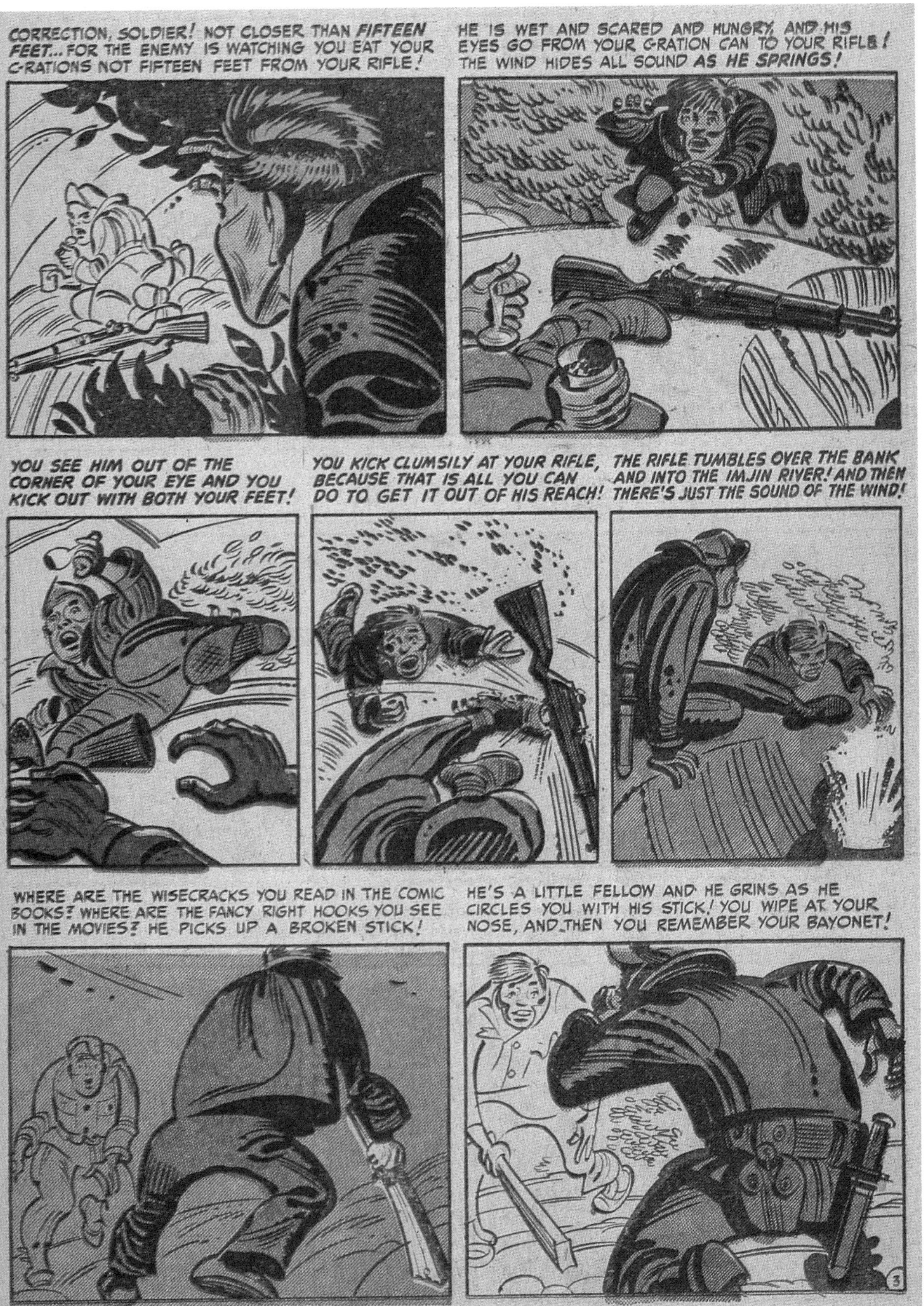
CORRECTION, SOLDIER! NOT CLOSER THAN FIFTEEN FEET... FOR THE ENEMY IS WATCHING YOU EAT YOUR C-RATIONS NOT FIFTEEN FEET FROM YOUR RIFLE!
HE IS WET AND SCARED AND HUNGRY, AND HIS EYES GO FROM YOUR C-RATION CAN TO YOUR RIFLE! THE WIND HIDES ALL SOUND AS HE SPRINGS!
YOU SEE HIM OUT OF THE CORNER OF YOUR EYE AND YOU KICK OUT WITH BOTH YOUR FEET!
YOU KICK CLUMSILY AT YOUR RIFLE, BECAUSE THAT IS ALL YOU CAN DO TO GET IT OUT OF HIS REACH!
THE RIFLE TUMBLES OVER THE BANK AND INTO THE IMJIN RIVER! AND THEN THERE'S JUST THE SOUND OF THE WIND!
WHERE ARE THE WISECRACKS YOU READ IN THE COMIC BOOKS? WHERE ARE THE FANCY RIGHT HOOKS YOU SEE IN THE MOVIES? HE PICKS UP A BROKEN STICK!
HE'S A LITTLE FELLOW AND HE GRINS AS HE CIRCLES YOU WITH HIS STICK! YOU WIPE AT YOUR NOSE, AND THEN YOU REMEMBER YOUR BAYONET!
3

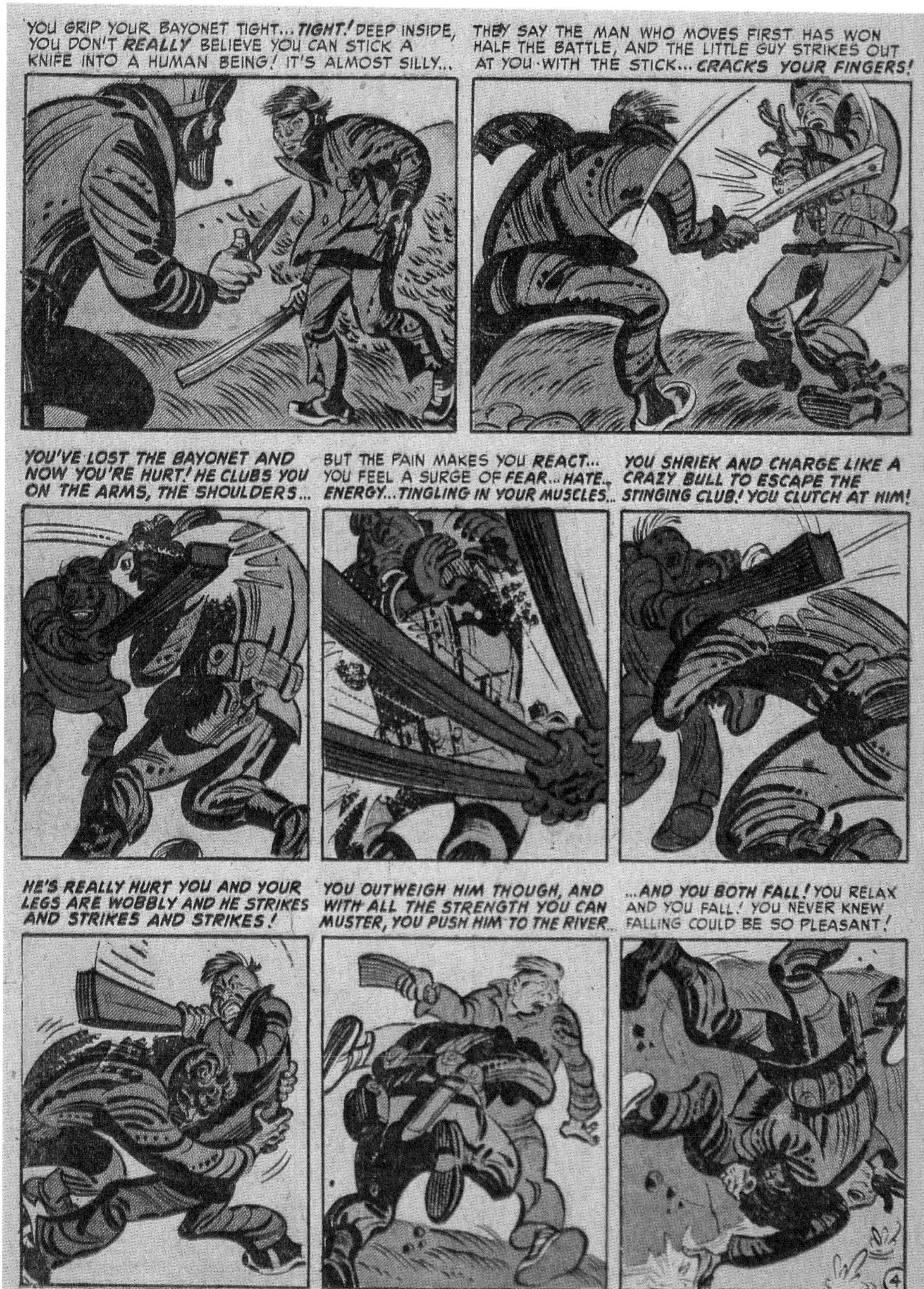

YOU GRIP YOUR BAYONET TIGHT... TIGHT! DEEP INSIDE, YOU DON'T REALLY BELIEVE YOU CAN STICK A KNIFE INTO A HUMAN BEING! IT'S ALMOST SILLY...
THEY SAY THE MAN WHO MOVES FIRST HAS WON HALF THE BATTLE, AND THE LITTLE GUY STRIKES OUT AT YOU WITH THE STICK... CRACKS YOUR FINGERS!
YOU'VE LOST THE BAYONET AND NOW YOU'RE HURT! HE CLUBS YOU ON THE ARMS, THE SHOULDERS...
BUT THE PAIN MAKES YOU REACT... YOU FEEL A SURGE OF FEAR... HATE.. ENERGY... TINGLING IN YOUR MUSCLES...
YOU SHRIEK AND CHARGE LIKE A CRAZY BULL TO ESCAPE THE STINGING CLUB! YOU CLUTCH AT HIM!
HE'S REALLY HURT YOU AND YOUR LEGS ARE WOBBLY AND HE STRIKES AND STRIKES AND STRIKES!
YOU OUTWEIGH HIM THOUGH, AND WITH ALL THE STRENGTH YOU CAN MUSTER, YOU PUSH HIM TO THE RIVER...
...AND YOU BOTH FALL! YOU RELAX AND YOU FALL! YOU NEVER KNEW FALLING COULD BE SO PLEASANT!
4

HE KICKS TO STAY UP, BUT YOU ARE HEAVIER AND YOU *PRESS HIM UNDER!*

IT REMINDS YOU OF SOMETHING...AND YOU *PRESS HIM UNDER!*

LIKE DUNKING, WHEN YOU WENT SWIMMING! YOU *PRESS HIM UNDER!*

YES...YES...LIKE DUNKING AT THE SWIMMING HOLE... YOU DUNK...*DUNK...DUNK...*

HIS HANDS HAVE STOPPED CLAWING AT THE AIR...HIS FEET HAVE STOPPED THRASHING...

...BLOOD AND BUBBLES ARE COMING TO THE SURFACE AND THE MAN YOU ARE HOLDING RELAXES!

IT SEEMS LIKE HOURS HAVE GONE BY! THE BUBBLES ARE BARELY TRICKLING UP AND ALL IS STILL!

SUDDENLY, YOUR MIND IS QUIET, AND YOUR RAGE COLLAPSES! THE WATER IS VERY COLD!

YOU'RE TIRED... YOUR BODY IS GASPING AND SHAKING WEAK... AND YOU'RE ASHAMED!

YOU STUMBLE AND SLOSH OUT OF THE RIVER AND RUN...RUN AWAY FROM THE BODY IN THE WATER!

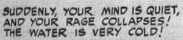

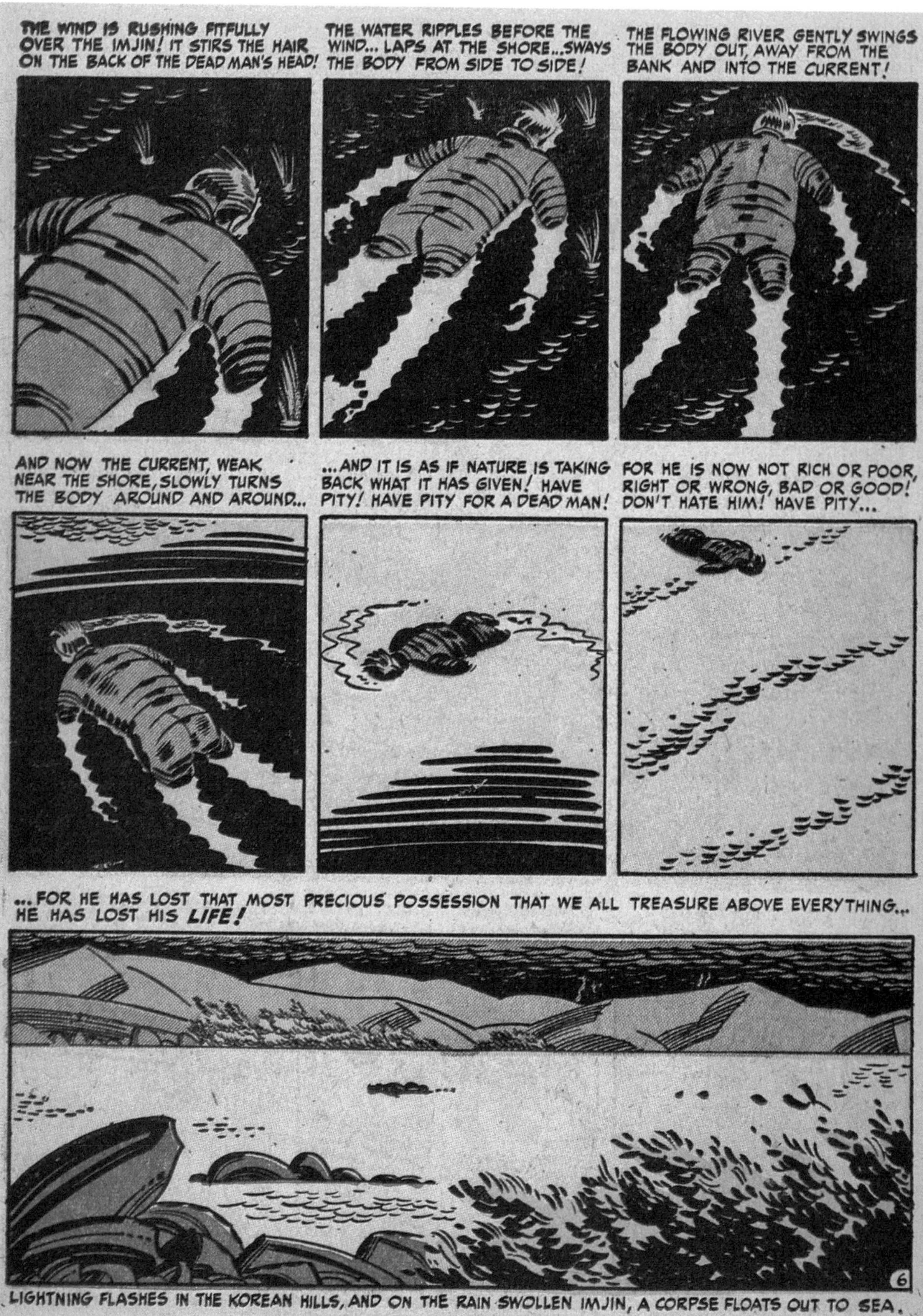
THE WIND IS RUSHING FITFULLY OVER THE IMJIN! IT STIRS THE HAIR ON THE BACK OF THE DEAD MAN'S HEAD!
THE WATER RIPPLES BEFORE THE WIND... LAPS AT THE SHORE...SWAYS THE BODY FROM SIDE TO SIDE!
THE FLOWING RIVER GENTLY SWINGS THE BODY OUT, AWAY FROM THE BANK AND INTO THE CURRENT!
AND NOW THE CURRENT, WEAK NEAR THE SHORE, SLOWLY TURNS THE BODY AROUND AND AROUND...
...AND IT IS AS IF NATURE IS TAKING BACK WHAT IT HAS GIVEN! HAVE PITY! HAVE PITY FOR A DEAD MAN!
FOR HE IS NOW NOT RICH OR POOR, RIGHT OR WRONG, BAD OR GOOD! DON'T HATE HIM! HAVE PITY...
...FOR HE HAS LOST THAT MOST PRECIOUS POSSESSION THAT WE ALL TREASURE ABOVE EVERYTHING... HE HAS LOST HIS LIFE!
6
LIGHTNING FLASHES IN THE KOREAN HILLS, AND ON THE RAIN SWOLLEN IMJIN, A CORPSE FLOATS OUT TO SEA.

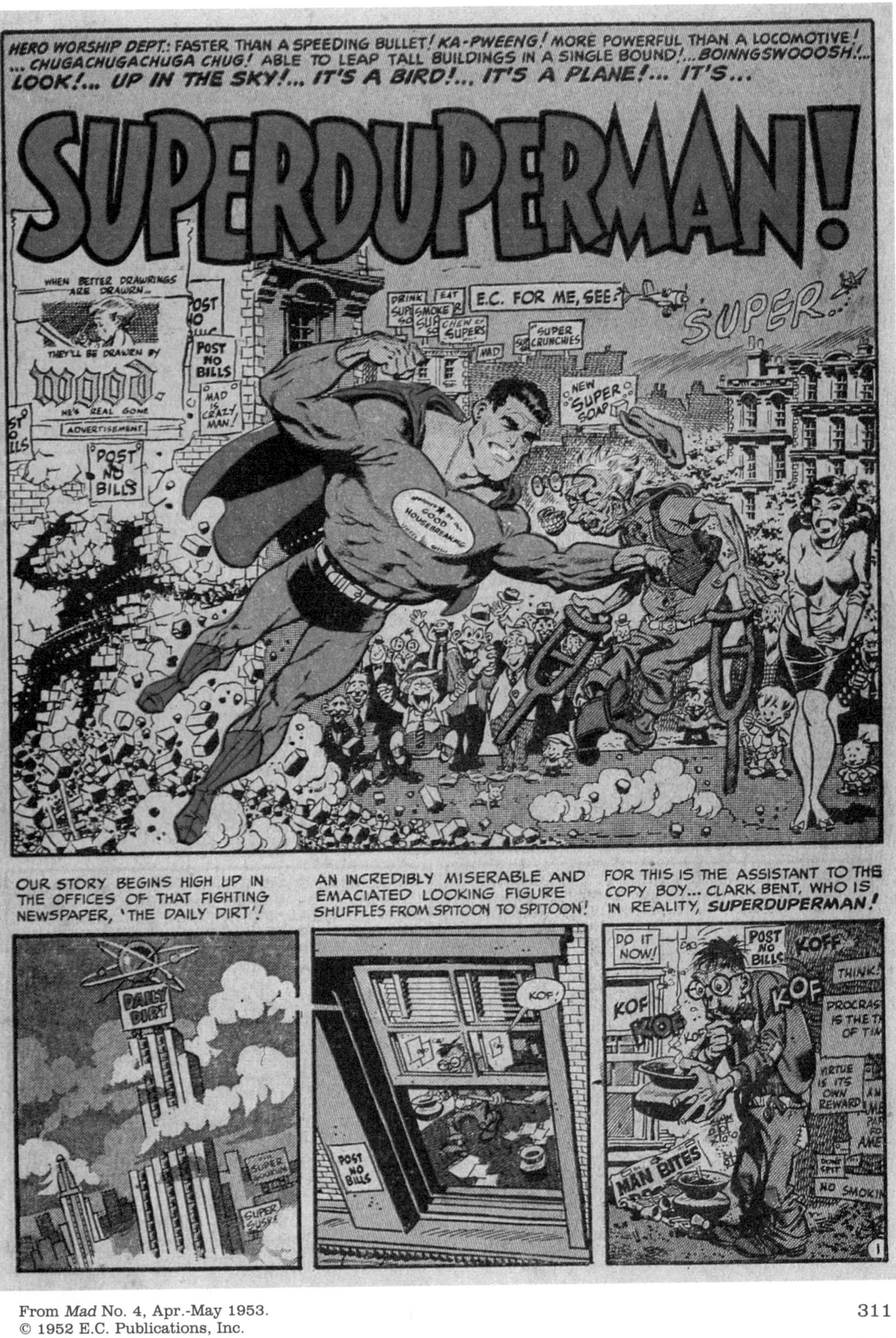
HERO WORSHIP DEPT.: FASTER THAN A SPEEDING BULLET! KA-PWEENG! MORE POWERFUL THAN A LOCOMOTIVE! ...CHUGACHUGACHUGA CHUG! ABLE TO LEAP TALL BUILDINGS IN A SINGLE BOUND!...BOINNGSWOOOSH!... LOOK!... UP IN THE SKY!... IT'S A BIRD!... IT'S A PLANE!... IT'S...
SUPERDUPERMAN!
WHEN BETTER DRAWRINGS ARE DRAWRN...
THEY'LL BE DRAWRN BY
WOOD
HE'S REAL GONE
ADVERTISEMENT
POST NO BILLS
MAD IS CRAZY MAN!
POST NO BILLS
E.C. FOR ME, SEE?
SUPER...
SUPER CRUNCHIES
CHEW SUPERS
NEW SUPER SOAP
GOOD HOUSEBREAKING
OUR STORY BEGINS HIGH UP IN THE OFFICES OF THAT FIGHTING NEWSPAPER, 'THE DAILY DIRT'!
AN INCREDIBLY MISERABLE AND EMACIATED LOOKING FIGURE SHUFFLES FROM SPITOON TO SPITOON!
FOR THIS IS THE ASSISTANT TO THE COPY BOY... CLARK BENT, WHO IS IN REALITY, SUPERDUPERMAN!
DAILY DIRT
KOF!
POST NO BILLS
DO IT NOW!
POST NO BILLS
KOFF
THINK!
KOF
KOF
KOF
VIRTUE IS ITS OWN REWARD
MAN BITES
NO SMOKIN
1

From *Mad* No. 4, Apr.-May 1953.

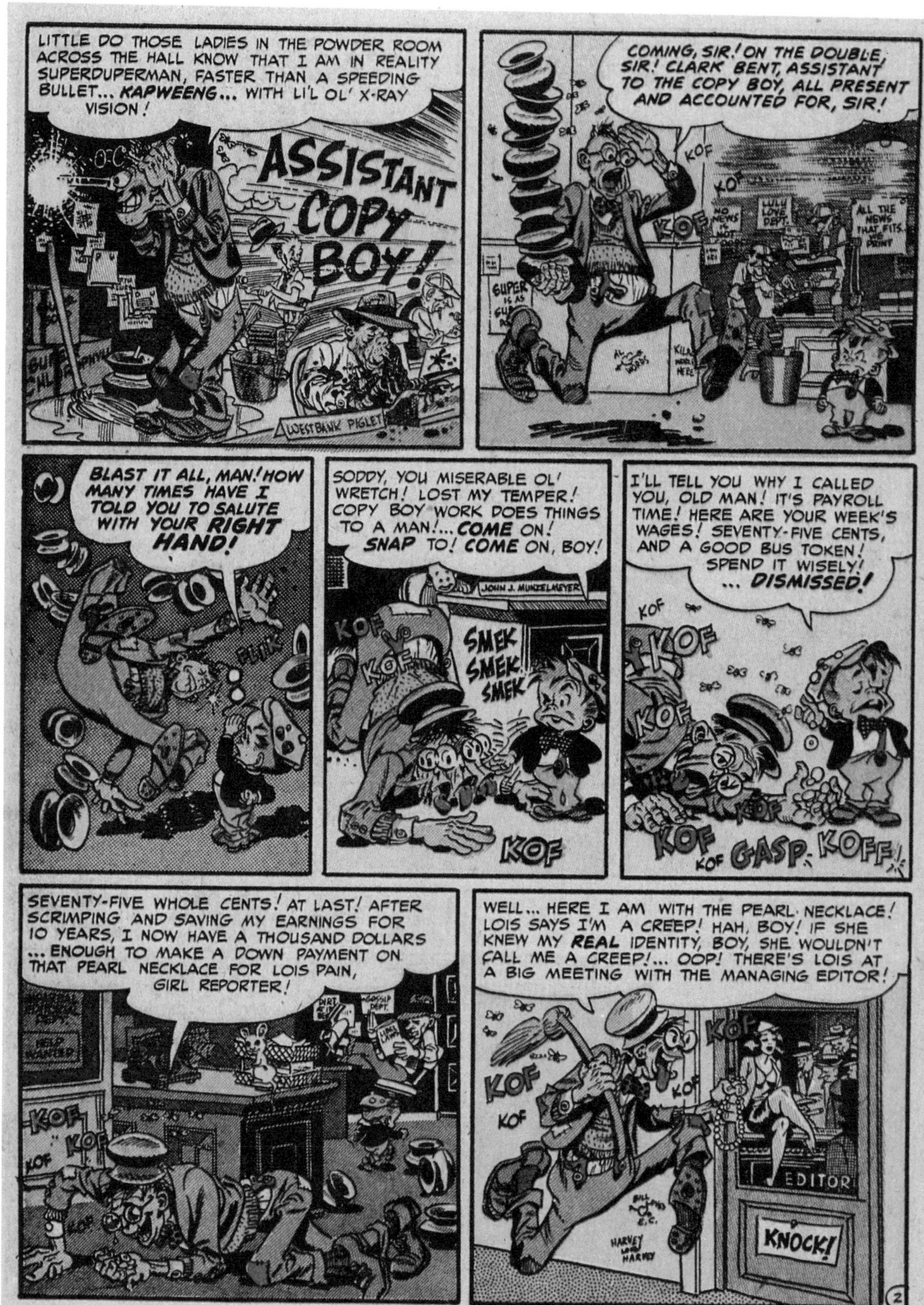

LITTLE DO THOSE LADIES IN THE POWDER ROOM ACROSS THE HALL KNOW THAT I AM IN REALITY SUPERDUPERMAN, FASTER THAN A SPEEDING BULLET... KAPWEENG... WITH LI'L OL' X-RAY VISION!
ASSISTANT COPY BOY!
WESTBANK PIGLET
COMING, SIR! ON THE DOUBLE, SIR! CLARK BENT, ASSISTANT TO THE COPY BOY, ALL PRESENT AND ACCOUNTED FOR, SIR!
KOF
KOF
KOF
LULU LOVE DEPT.
ALL THE NEWS THAT FITS WE PRINT
BLAST IT ALL, MAN! HOW MANY TIMES HAVE I TOLD YOU TO SALUTE WITH YOUR RIGHT HAND!
FLIK
SODDY, YOU MISERABLE OL' WRETCH! LOST MY TEMPER! COPY BOY WORK DOES THINGS TO A MAN!... COME ON! SNAP TO! COME ON, BOY!
JOHN J. MUNZELMEYER
KOF
KOF
SMEK
SMEK
SMEK
KOF
I'LL TELL YOU WHY I CALLED YOU, OLD MAN! IT'S PAYROLL TIME! HERE ARE YOUR WEEK'S WAGES! SEVENTY-FIVE CENTS, AND A GOOD BUS TOKEN! SPEND IT WISELY! ... DISMISSED!
KOF
KOF
KOF
KOF
KOF
KOF GASP KOFF
SEVENTY-FIVE WHOLE CENTS! AT LAST! AFTER SCRIMPING AND SAVING MY EARNINGS FOR 10 YEARS, I NOW HAVE A THOUSAND DOLLARS ... ENOUGH TO MAKE A DOWN PAYMENT ON THAT PEARL NECKLACE FOR LOIS PAIN, GIRL REPORTER!
HELP WANTED
GOSSIP DEPT.
KOF
KOF
KOF
KOF
WELL... HERE I AM WITH THE PEARL NECKLACE! LOIS SAYS I'M A CREEP! HAH, BOY! IF SHE KNEW MY REAL IDENTITY, BOY, SHE WOULDN'T CALL ME A CREEP!... OOP! THERE'S LOIS AT A BIG MEETING WITH THE MANAGING EDITOR!
KOF
KOF
KOF
KOF
EDITOR
KNOCK!
2

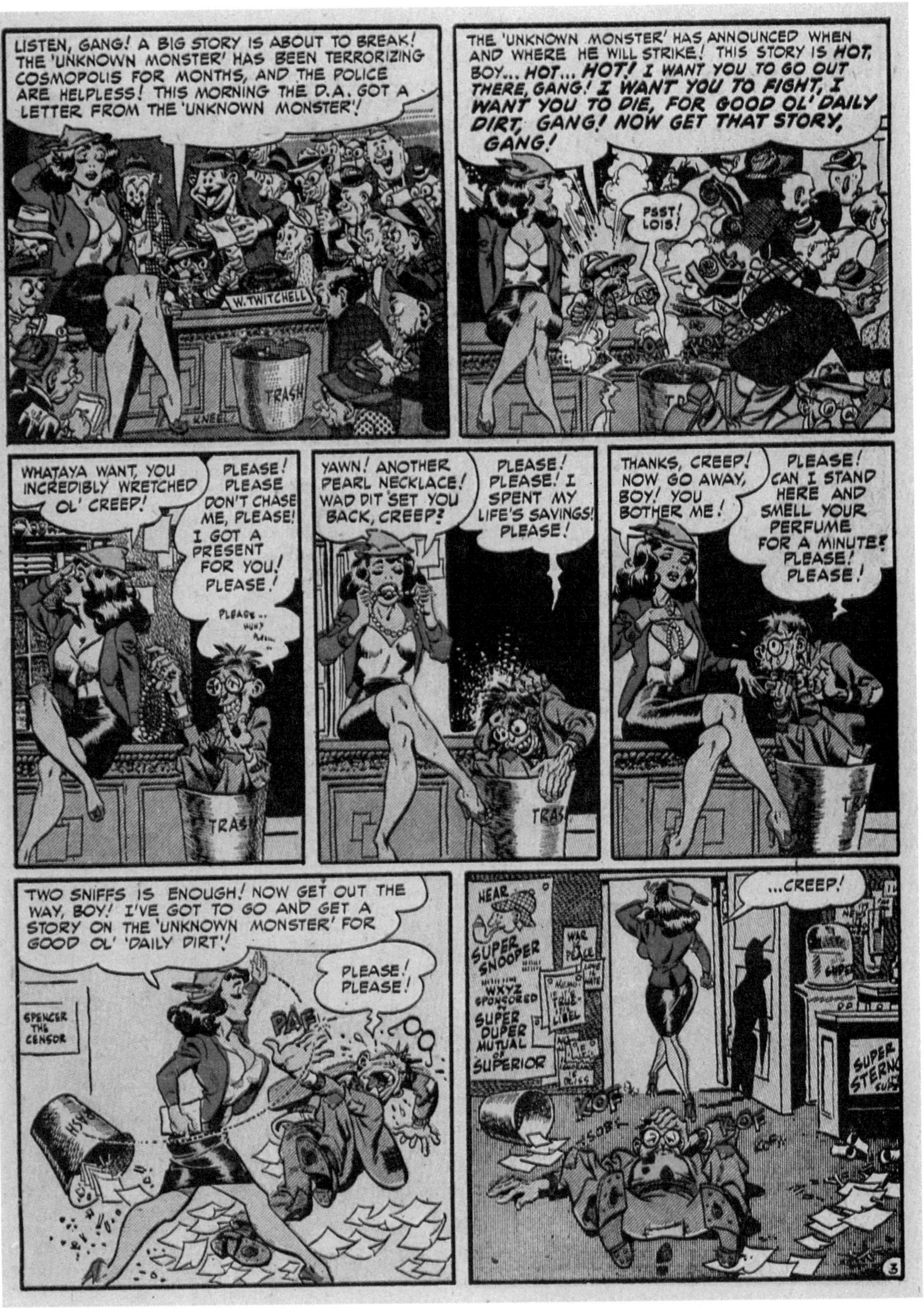
LISTEN, GANG! A BIG STORY IS ABOUT TO BREAK! THE 'UNKNOWN MONSTER' HAS BEEN TERRORIZING COSMOPOLIS FOR MONTHS, AND THE POLICE ARE HELPLESS! THIS MORNING THE D.A. GOT A LETTER FROM THE 'UNKNOWN MONSTER'!
W. TWITCHELL
TRASH
THE 'UNKNOWN MONSTER' HAS ANNOUNCED WHEN AND WHERE HE WILL STRIKE! THIS STORY IS HOT, BOY... HOT... HOT! I WANT YOU TO GO OUT THERE, GANG! I WANT YOU TO FIGHT, I WANT YOU TO DIE, FOR GOOD OL' DAILY DIRT, GANG! NOW GET THAT STORY, GANG!
PSST! LOIS!
WHATAYA WANT, YOU INCREDIBLY WRETCHED OL' CREEP!
PLEASE! PLEASE DON'T CHASE ME, PLEASE! I GOT A PRESENT FOR YOU! PLEASE!
TRASH
YAWN! ANOTHER PEARL NECKLACE! WAD DIT SET YOU BACK, CREEP?
PLEASE! PLEASE! I SPENT MY LIFE'S SAVINGS! PLEASE!
THANKS, CREEP! NOW GO AWAY, BOY! YOU BOTHER ME!
PLEASE! CAN I STAND HERE AND SMELL YOUR PERFUME FOR A MINUTE? PLEASE! PLEASE!
TWO SNIFFS IS ENOUGH! NOW GET OUT THE WAY, BOY! I'VE GOT TO GO AND GET A STORY ON THE 'UNKNOWN MONSTER' FOR GOOD OL' 'DAILY DIRT'!
PLEASE! PLEASE!
SPENCER THE CENSOR
PAF
...CREEP!
HEAR
SUPER SNOOPER
WXYZ
SPONSORED
SUPER DUPER MUTUAL OF SUPERIOR
WAR IS PEACE
LOVE IS HATE
TRUE IS LIBEL
SUPER STERNO
KOF
SOB
KOF
3

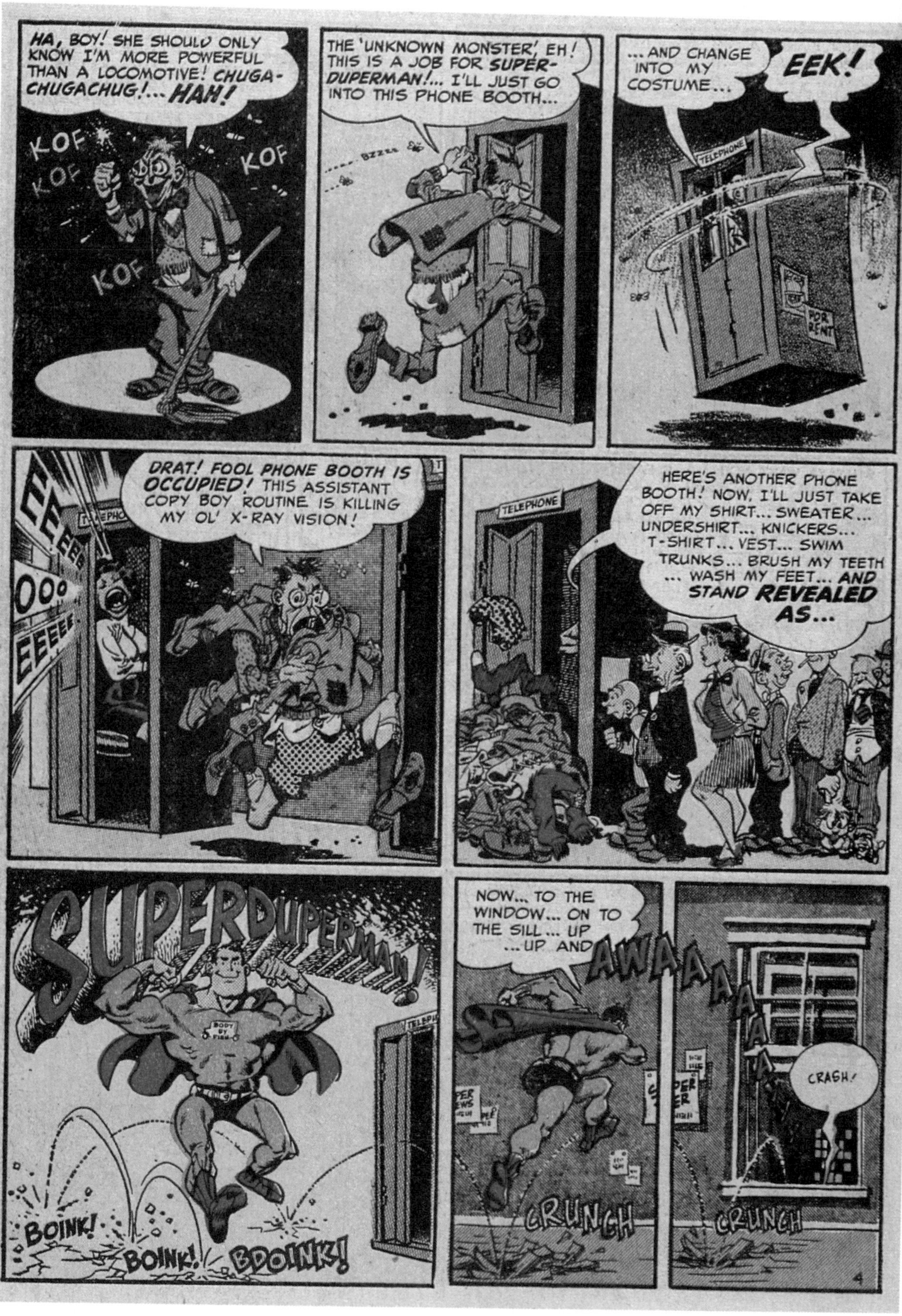
HA, BOY! SHE SHOULD ONLY KNOW I'M MORE POWERFUL THAN A LOCOMOTIVE! CHUGA-CHUGACHUG!... HAH!
KOF KOF KOF KOF
THE 'UNKNOWN MONSTER', EH! THIS IS A JOB FOR SUPER-DUPERMAN!... I'LL JUST GO INTO THIS PHONE BOOTH...
BZZZZ
... AND CHANGE INTO MY COSTUME...
EEK!
TELEPHONE
FOR RENT
DRAT! FOOL PHONE BOOTH IS OCCUPIED! THIS ASSISTANT COPY BOY ROUTINE IS KILLING MY OL' X-RAY VISION!
EEEEE OOO EEEEE
HERE'S ANOTHER PHONE BOOTH! NOW, I'LL JUST TAKE OFF MY SHIRT... SWEATER... UNDERSHIRT... KNICKERS... T-SHIRT... VEST... SWIM TRUNKS... BRUSH MY TEETH ... WASH MY FEET... AND STAND REVEALED AS...
TELEPHONE
SUPERDUPERMAN!
BODY BY FISH
BOINK! BOINK! BDOINK!
NOW... TO THE WINDOW... ON TO THE SILL... UP ...UP AND
AWAAAAAAAA
CRASH!
CRUNCH
CRUNCH
4

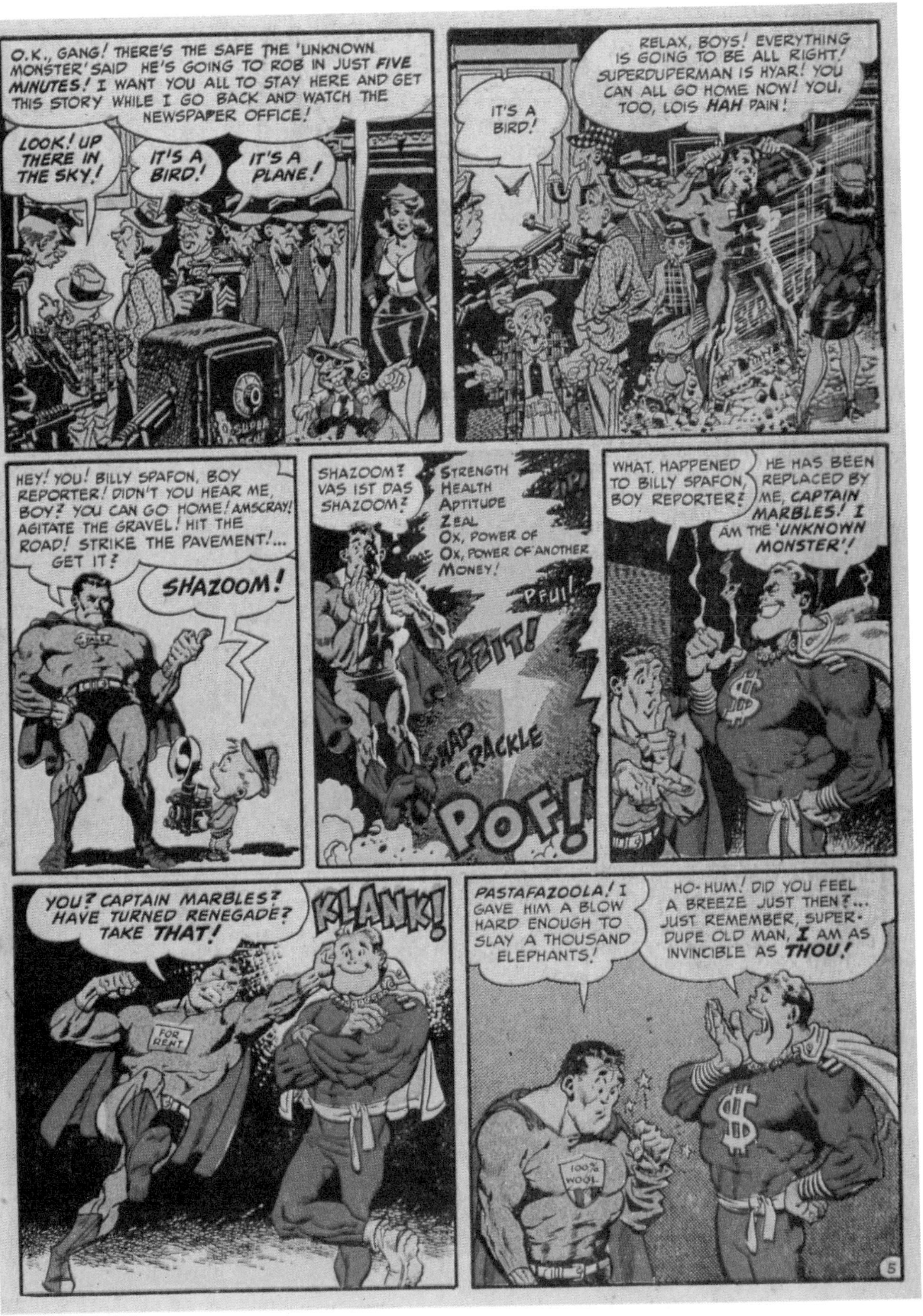
O.K., GANG! THERE'S THE SAFE THE 'UNKNOWN MONSTER' SAID HE'S GOING TO ROB IN JUST FIVE MINUTES! I WANT YOU ALL TO STAY HERE AND GET THIS STORY WHILE I GO BACK AND WATCH THE NEWSPAPER OFFICE!
LOOK! UP THERE IN THE SKY!
IT'S A BIRD!
IT'S A PLANE!
IT'S A BIRD!
RELAX, BOYS! EVERYTHING IS GOING TO BE ALL RIGHT! SUPERDUPERMAN IS HYAR! YOU CAN ALL GO HOME NOW! YOU, TOO, LOIS HAH PAIN!
HEY! YOU! BILLY SPAFON, BOY REPORTER! DIDN'T YOU HEAR ME, BOY? YOU CAN GO HOME! AMSCRAY! AGITATE THE GRAVEL! HIT THE ROAD! STRIKE THE PAVEMENT!... GET IT?
SHAZOOM!
SHAZOOM? VAS IST DAS SHAZOOM?
STRENGTH
HEALTH
APTITUDE
ZEAL
OX, POWER OF
OX, POWER OF ANOTHER
MONEY!
ZIP!
PFUI!
ZZIT!
SNAP CRACKLE
POF!
WHAT. HAPPENED TO BILLY SPAFON, BOY REPORTER?
HE HAS BEEN REPLACED BY ME, CAPTAIN MARBLES! I AM THE 'UNKNOWN MONSTER'!
YOU? CAPTAIN MARBLES? HAVE TURNED RENEGADE? TAKE THAT!
KLANK!
FOR RENT
PASTAFAZOOLA! I GAVE HIM A BLOW HARD ENOUGH TO SLAY A THOUSAND ELEPHANTS!
HO-HUM! DID YOU FEEL A BREEZE JUST THEN?... JUST REMEMBER, SUPER-DUPE OLD MAN, I AM AS INVINCIBLE AS THOU!
100% WOOL
5

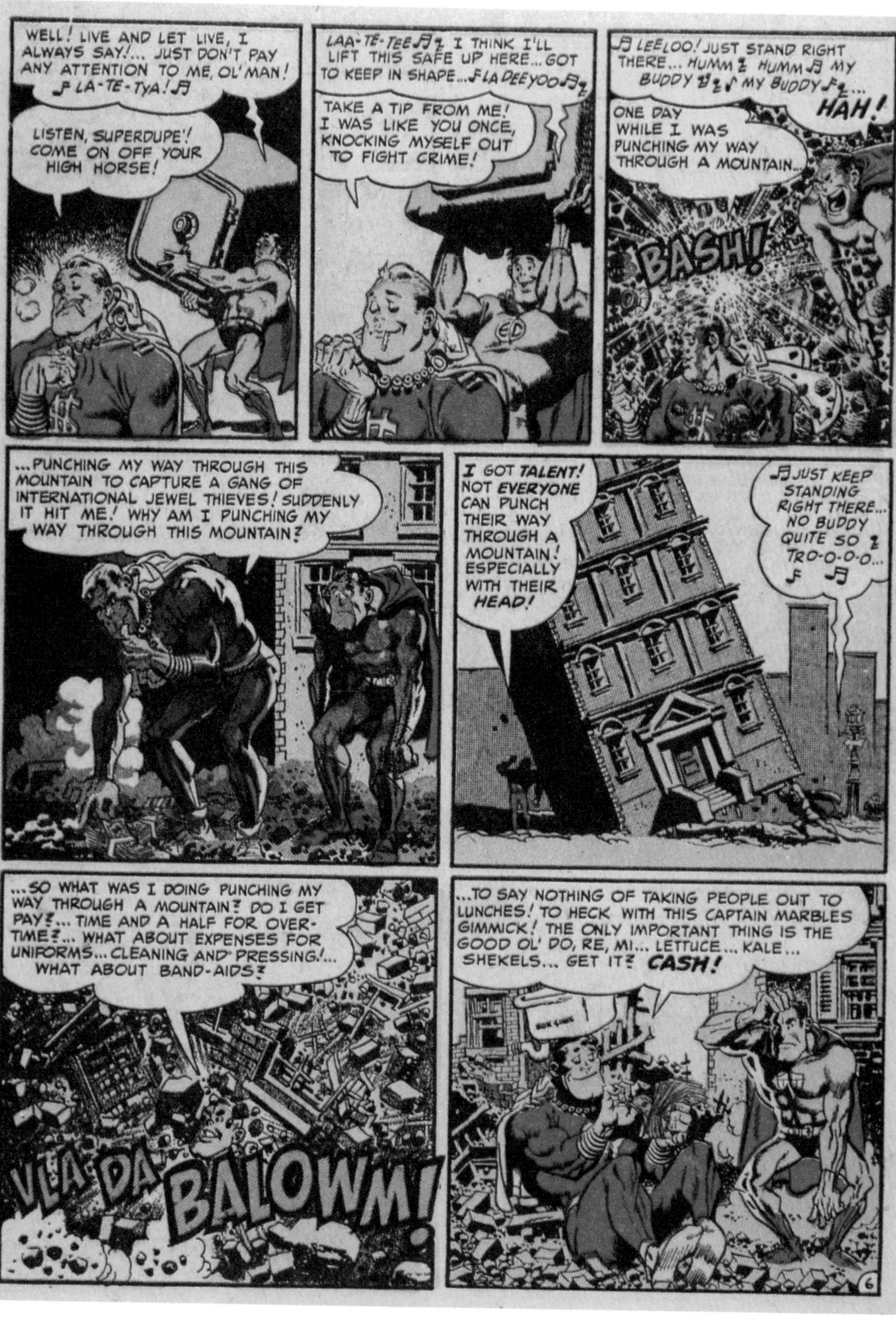
WELL! LIVE AND LET LIVE, I ALWAYS SAY!... JUST DON'T PAY ANY ATTENTION TO ME, OL' MAN! LA-TE-TYA!
LISTEN, SUPERDUPE! COME ON OFF YOUR HIGH HORSE!
LAA-TE-TEE I THINK I'LL LIFT THIS SAFE UP HERE... GOT TO KEEP IN SHAPE... LA DEEYOO
TAKE A TIP FROM ME! I WAS LIKE YOU ONCE, KNOCKING MYSELF OUT TO FIGHT CRIME!
LEELOO! JUST STAND RIGHT THERE... HUMM HUMM MY BUDDY MY BUDDY...
HAH!
ONE DAY WHILE I WAS PUNCHING MY WAY THROUGH A MOUNTAIN...
BASH!
...PUNCHING MY WAY THROUGH THIS MOUNTAIN TO CAPTURE A GANG OF INTERNATIONAL JEWEL THIEVES! SUDDENLY IT HIT ME! WHY AM I PUNCHING MY WAY THROUGH THIS MOUNTAIN?
I GOT TALENT! NOT EVERYONE CAN PUNCH THEIR WAY THROUGH A MOUNTAIN! ESPECIALLY WITH THEIR HEAD!
JUST KEEP STANDING RIGHT THERE... NO BUDDY QUITE SO TRO-O-O-O...
...SO WHAT WAS I DOING PUNCHING MY WAY THROUGH A MOUNTAIN? DO I GET PAY?... TIME AND A HALF FOR OVER-TIME?... WHAT ABOUT EXPENSES FOR UNIFORMS... CLEANING AND PRESSING!... WHAT ABOUT BAND-AIDS?
VLA DA BALOWM!
...TO SAY NOTHING OF TAKING PEOPLE OUT TO LUNCHES! TO HECK WITH THIS CAPTAIN MARBLES GIMMICK! THE ONLY IMPORTANT THING IS THE GOOD OL' DO, RE, MI... LETTUCE... KALE... SHEKELS... GET IT? CASH!
6

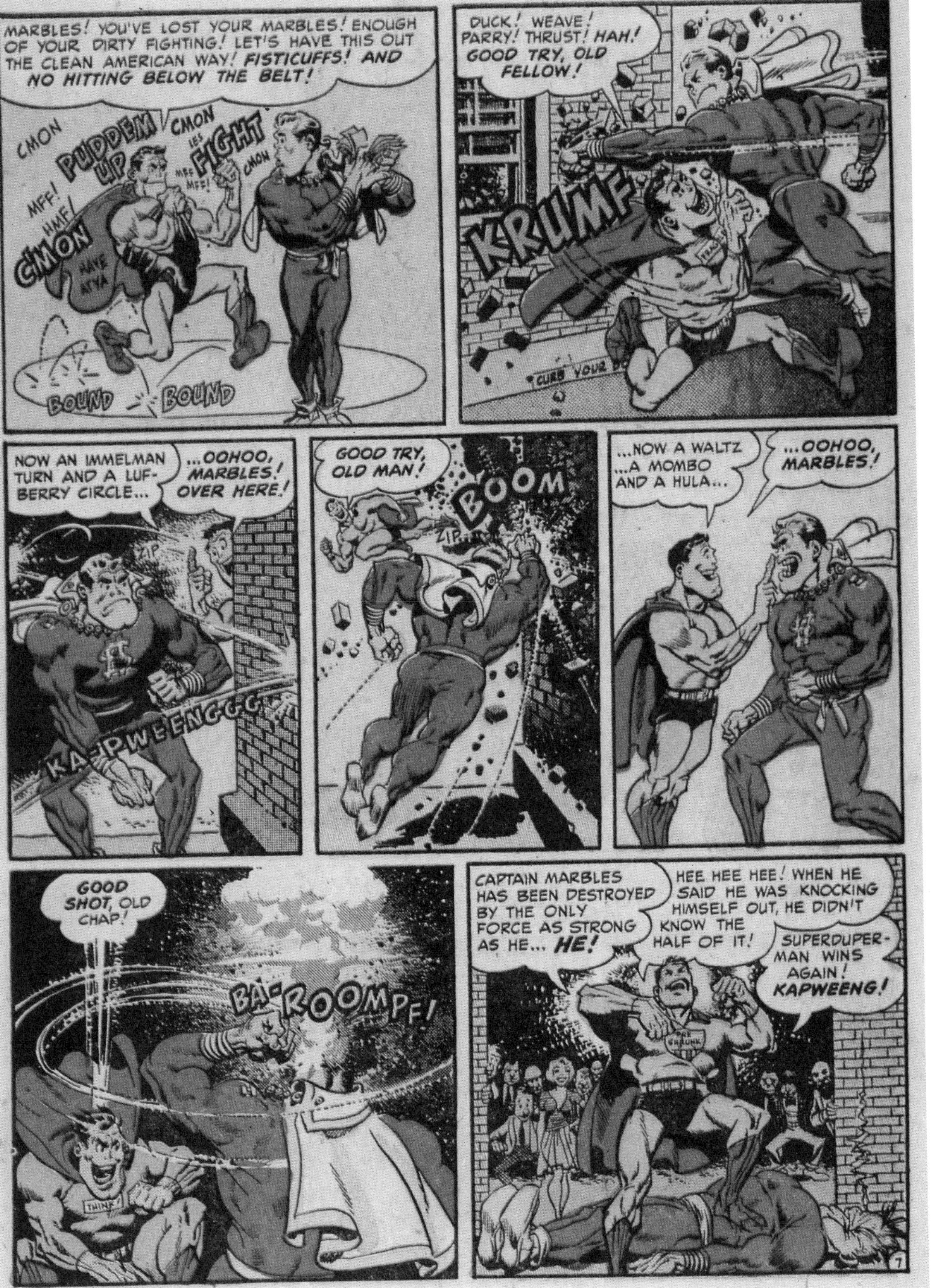
MARBLES! YOU'VE LOST YOUR MARBLES! ENOUGH OF YOUR DIRTY FIGHTING! LET'S HAVE THIS OUT THE CLEAN AMERICAN WAY! FISTICUFFS! AND NO HITTING BELOW THE BELT!
CMON
PUDDEM UP
CMON LES FIGHT
MFF!
HMF!
MFF MFF!
CMON
CMON
HAVE AT YA
BOUND
BOUND
DUCK! WEAVE! PARRY! THRUST! HAH! GOOD TRY, OLD FELLOW!
KRUMF
NOW AN IMMELMAN TURN AND A LUF-BERRY CIRCLE...
...OOHOO, MARBLES! OVER HERE!
ZIP
KA-PWEENGGG
GOOD TRY, OLD MAN!
BOOM
...NOW A WALTZ ...A MOMBO AND A HULA...
...OOHOO, MARBLES!
GOOD SHOT, OLD CHAP!
BA-ROOMPF!
THINK
CAPTAIN MARBLES HAS BEEN DESTROYED BY THE ONLY FORCE AS STRONG AS HE... HE!
HEE HEE HEE! WHEN HE SAID HE WAS KNOCKING HIMSELF OUT, HE DIDN'T KNOW THE HALF OF IT!
SUPERDUPER-MAN WINS AGAIN! KAPWEENG!
7

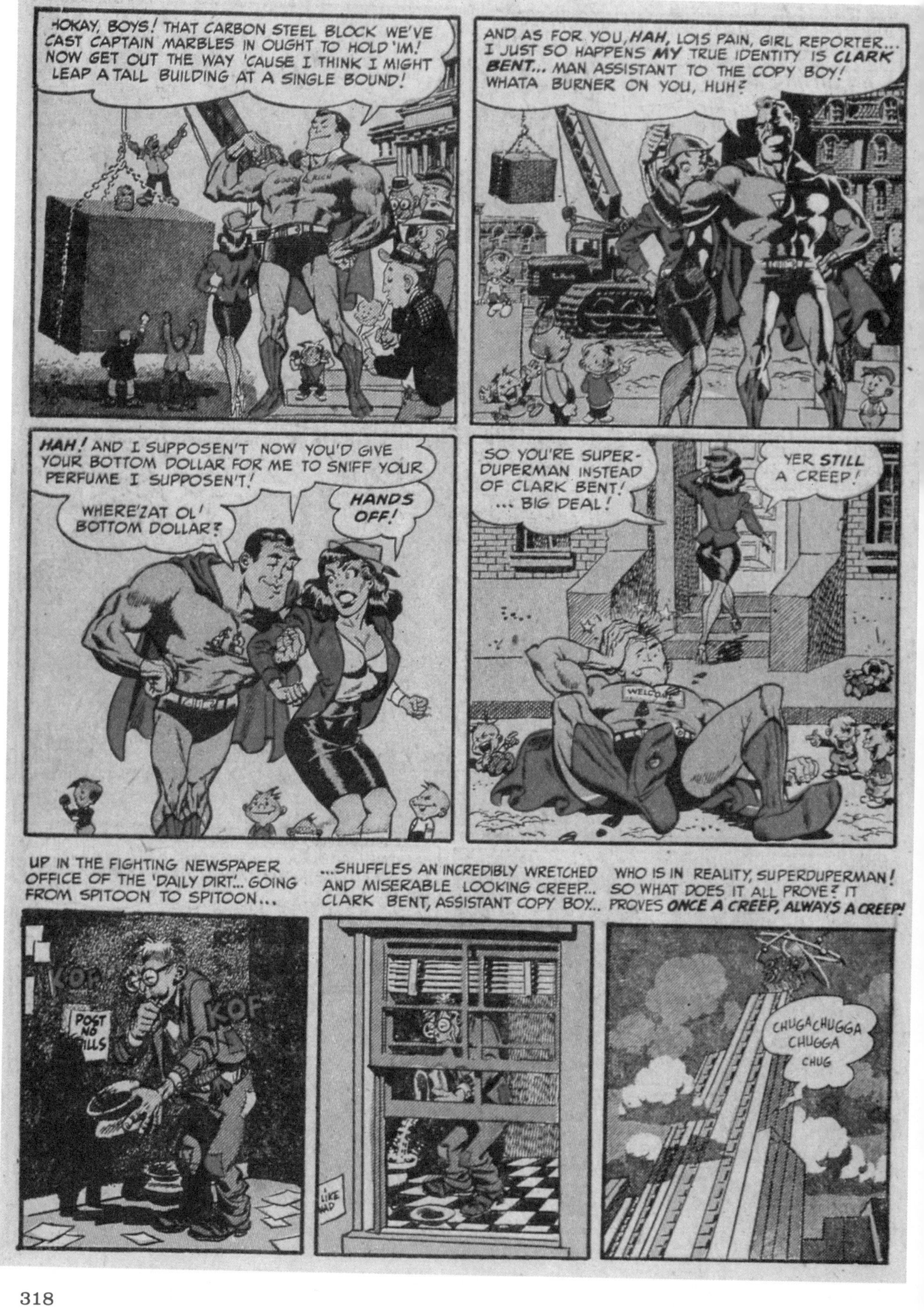
HOKAY, BOYS! THAT CARBON STEEL BLOCK WE'VE CAST CAPTAIN MARBLES IN OUGHT TO HOLD 'IM! NOW GET OUT THE WAY 'CAUSE I THINK I MIGHT LEAP A TALL BUILDING AT A SINGLE BOUND!
AND AS FOR YOU, HAH, LOIS PAIN, GIRL REPORTER... I JUST SO HAPPENS MY TRUE IDENTITY IS CLARK BENT... MAN ASSISTANT TO THE COPY BOY! WHATA BURNER ON YOU, HUH?
HAH! AND I SUPPOSEN'T NOW YOU'D GIVE YOUR BOTTOM DOLLAR FOR ME TO SNIFF YOUR PERFUME I SUPPOSEN'T!
WHERE'ZAT OL' BOTTOM DOLLAR?
HANDS OFF!
SO YOU'RE SUPER-DUPERMAN INSTEAD OF CLARK BENT! ... BIG DEAL!
YER STILL A CREEP!
UP IN THE FIGHTING NEWSPAPER OFFICE OF THE 'DAILY DIRT'... GOING FROM SPITOON TO SPITOON...
KOF
KOF
...SHUFFLES AN INCREDIBLY WRETCHED AND MISERABLE LOOKING CREEP... CLARK BENT, ASSISTANT COPY BOY...
WHO IS IN REALITY, SUPERDUPERMAN! SO WHAT DOES IT ALL PROVE? IT PROVES ONCE A CREEP, ALWAYS A CREEP!
CHUGA CHUGGA CHUGGA CHUG

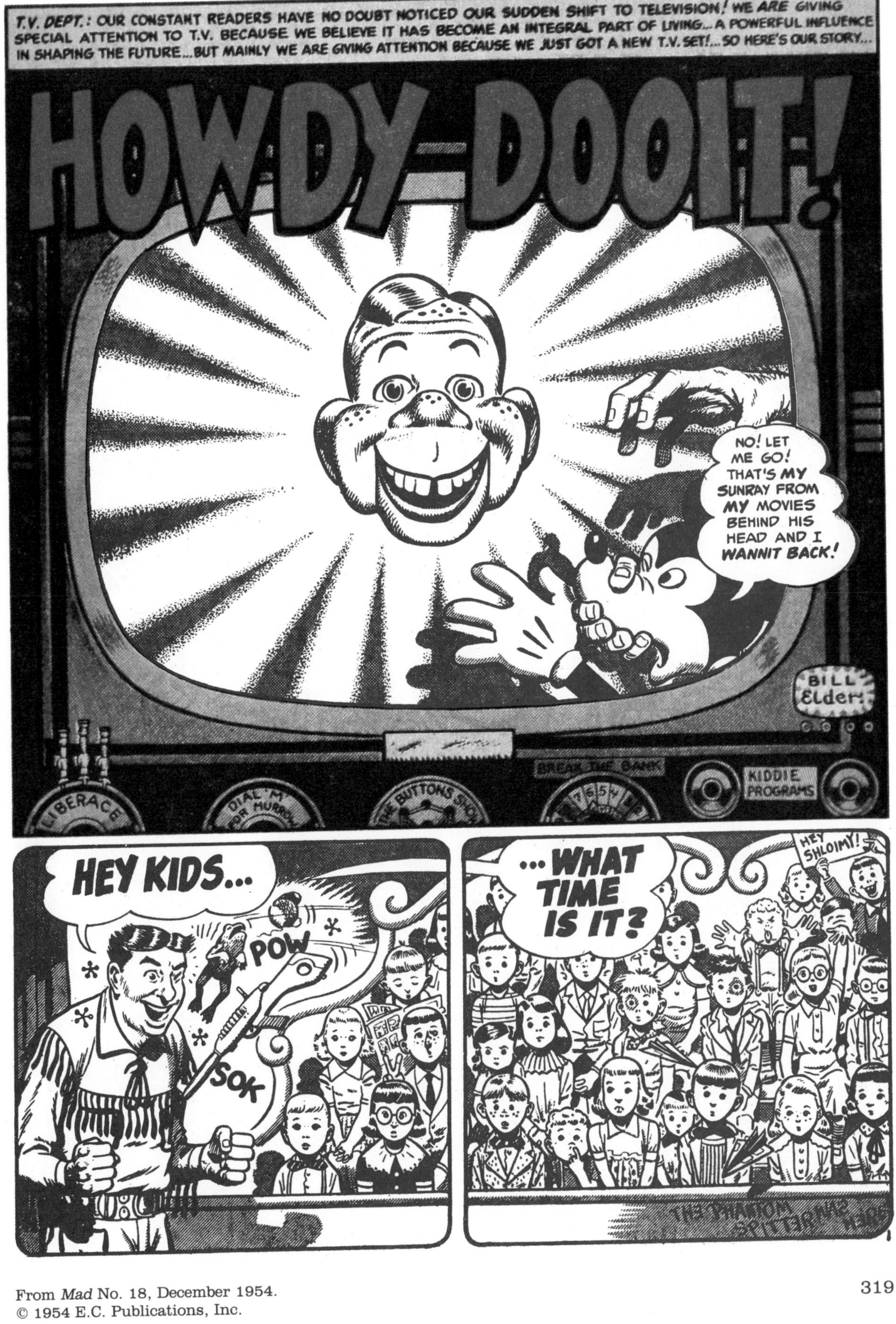
T.V. DEPT.: OUR CONSTANT READERS HAVE NO DOUBT NOTICED OUR SUDDEN SHIFT TO TELEVISION! WE ARE GIVING SPECIAL ATTENTION TO T.V. BECAUSE WE BELIEVE IT HAS BECOME AN INTEGRAL PART OF LIVING... A POWERFUL INFLUENCE IN SHAPING THE FUTURE...BUT MAINLY WE ARE GIVING ATTENTION BECAUSE WE JUST GOT A NEW T.V. SET!... SO HERE'S OUR STORY...
HOWDY-DOOIT!
NO! LET ME GO! THAT'S MY SUNRAY FROM MY MOVIES BEHIND HIS HEAD AND I WANNIT BACK!
BILL Elder
LIBERACE
BREAK THE BANK
KIDDIE PROGRAMS
HEY KIDS...
POW
SOK
...WHAT TIME IS IT?
HEY SHLOIMY!

From *Mad* No. 18, December 1954.

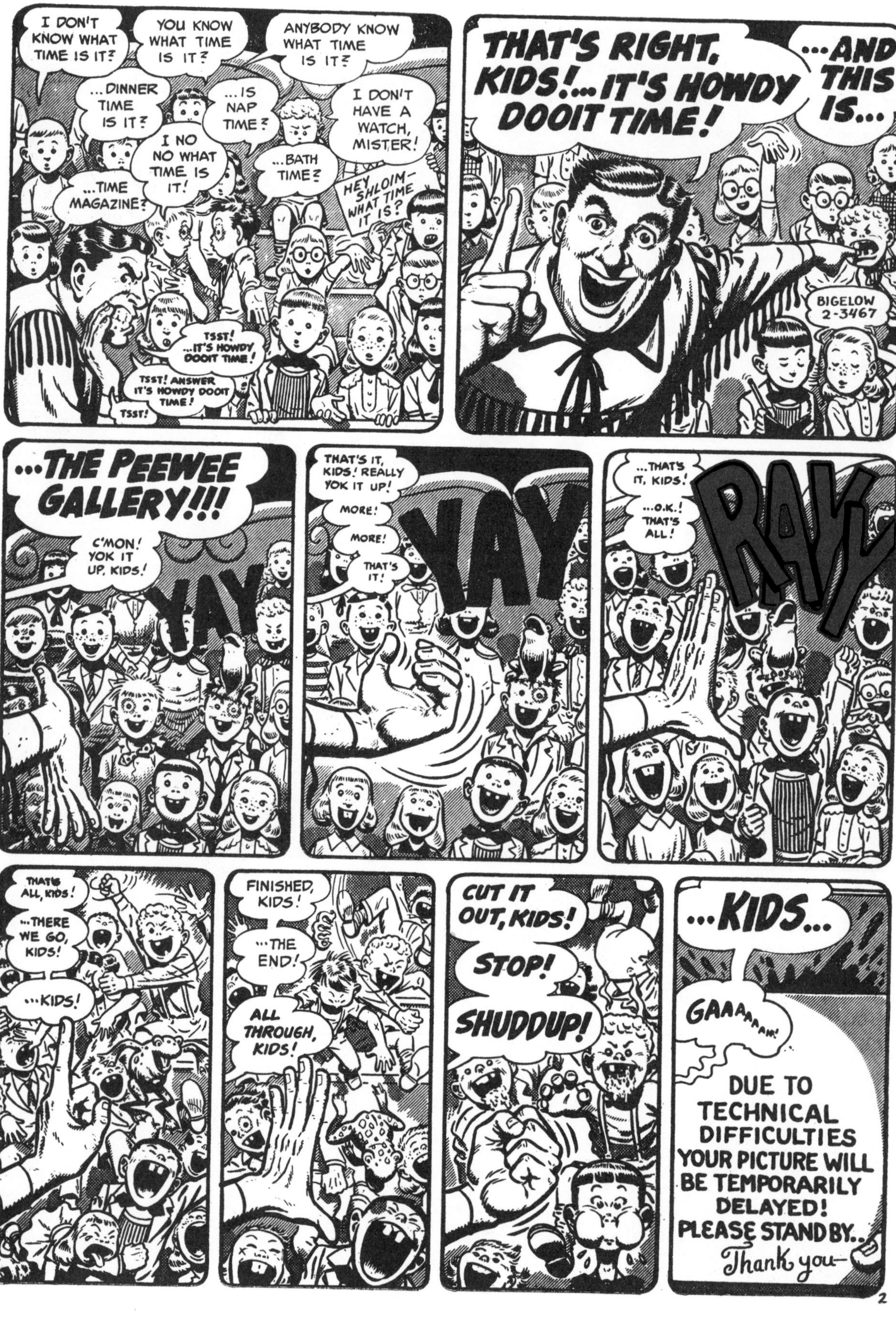
I DON'T KNOW WHAT TIME IS IT?
YOU KNOW WHAT TIME IS IT?
ANYBODY KNOW WHAT TIME IS IT?
...DINNER TIME IS IT?
...IS NAP TIME?
I DON'T HAVE A WATCH, MISTER!
I NO NO WHAT TIME IS IT!
...BATH TIME?
...TIME MAGAZINE?
HEY SHLOIM- WHAT TIME IT IS?
TSST! ...IT'S HOWDY DOOIT TIME!
TSST! ANSWER IT'S HOWDY DOOIT TIME!
TSST!
THAT'S RIGHT, KIDS!... IT'S HOWDY DOOIT TIME!
...AND THIS IS...
BIGELOW 2-3467
...THE PEEWEE GALLERY!!!
C'MON! YOK IT UP, KIDS!
YAY
THAT'S IT, KIDS! REALLY YOK IT UP!
MORE!
MORE!
THAT'S IT!
YAY
...THAT'S IT, KIDS!
...O.K.! THAT'S ALL!
RAY
THAT'S ALL, KIDS!
...THERE WE GO, KIDS!
...KIDS!
FINISHED, KIDS!
...THE END!
ALL THROUGH, KIDS!
CUT IT OUT, KIDS!
STOP!
SHUDDUP!
...KIDS...
GAAAAAAAK!
DUE TO TECHNICAL DIFFICULTIES YOUR PICTURE WILL BE TEMPORARILY DELAYED! PLEASE STAND BY...
Thank you-
2

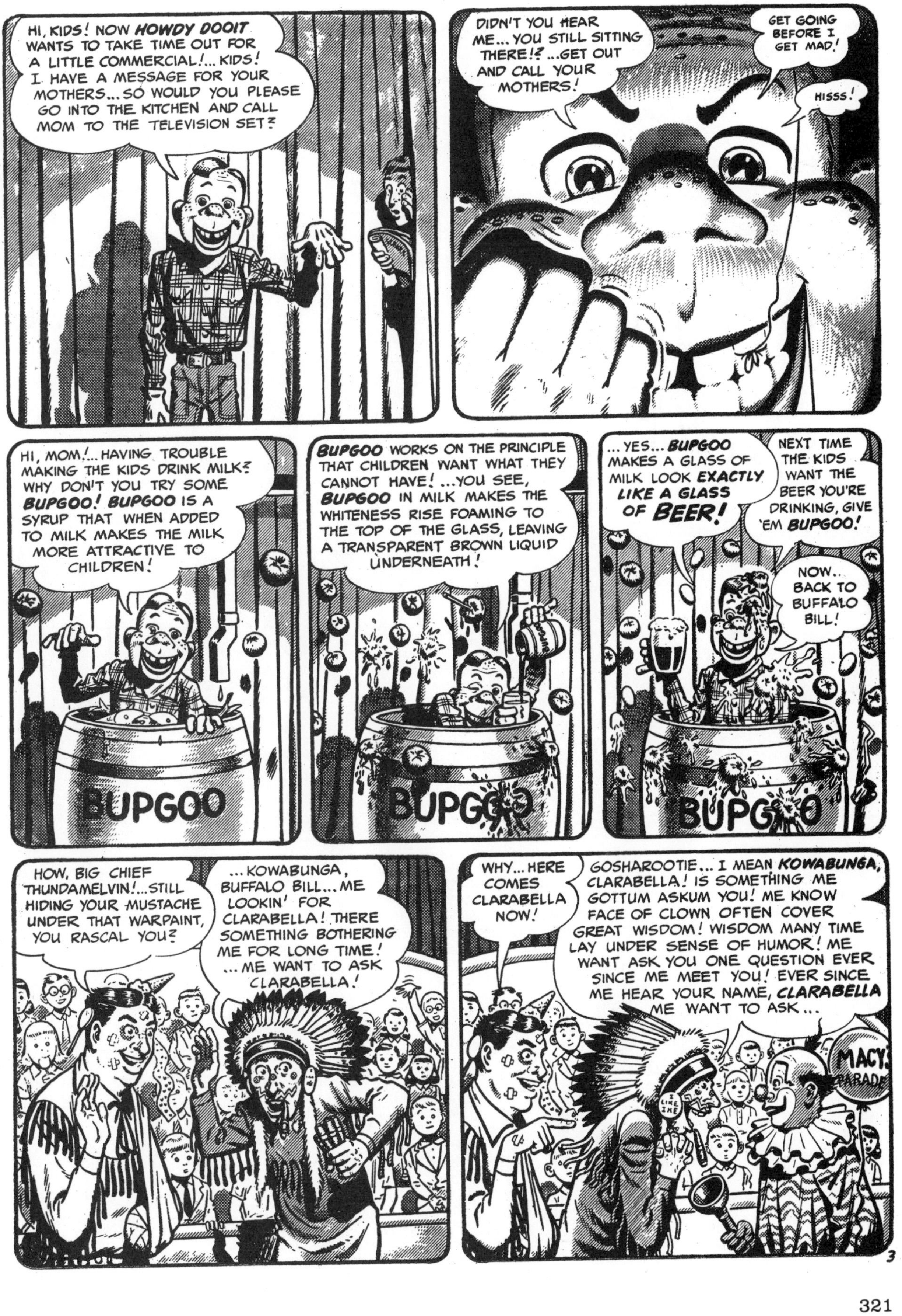
HI, KIDS! NOW HOWDY DOOIT WANTS TO TAKE TIME OUT FOR A LITTLE COMMERCIAL!... KIDS! I HAVE A MESSAGE FOR YOUR MOTHERS... SO WOULD YOU PLEASE GO INTO THE KITCHEN AND CALL MOM TO THE TELEVISION SET?
DIDN'T YOU HEAR ME... YOU STILL SITTING THERE!? ...GET OUT AND CALL YOUR MOTHERS!
GET GOING BEFORE I GET MAD!
HISSS!
HI, MOM!... HAVING TROUBLE MAKING THE KIDS DRINK MILK? WHY DON'T YOU TRY SOME BUPGOO! BUPGOO IS A SYRUP THAT WHEN ADDED TO MILK MAKES THE MILK MORE ATTRACTIVE TO CHILDREN!
BUPGOO
BUPGOO WORKS ON THE PRINCIPLE THAT CHILDREN WANT WHAT THEY CANNOT HAVE! ...YOU SEE, BUPGOO IN MILK MAKES THE WHITENESS RISE FOAMING TO THE TOP OF THE GLASS, LEAVING A TRANSPARENT BROWN LIQUID UNDERNEATH!
... YES... BUPGOO MAKES A GLASS OF MILK LOOK EXACTLY LIKE A GLASS OF BEER!
NEXT TIME THE KIDS WANT THE BEER YOU'RE DRINKING, GIVE 'EM BUPGOO!
NOW.. BACK TO BUFFALO BILL!
HOW, BIG CHIEF THUNDAMELVIN!... STILL HIDING YOUR MUSTACHE UNDER THAT WARPAINT, YOU RASCAL YOU?
... KOWABUNGA, BUFFALO BILL... ME LOOKIN' FOR CLARABELLA! THERE SOMETHING BOTHERING ME FOR LONG TIME! ... ME WANT TO ASK CLARABELLA!
WHY... HERE COMES CLARABELLA NOW!
GOSHAROOTIE... I MEAN KOWABUNGA, CLARABELLA! IS SOMETHING ME GOTTUM ASKUM YOU! ME KNOW FACE OF CLOWN OFTEN COVER GREAT WISDOM! WISDOM MANY TIME LAY UNDER SENSE OF HUMOR! ME WANT ASK YOU ONE QUESTION EVER SINCE ME MEET YOU! EVER SINCE ME HEAR YOUR NAME, CLARABELLA ME WANT TO ASK...
MACY'S PARADE
3

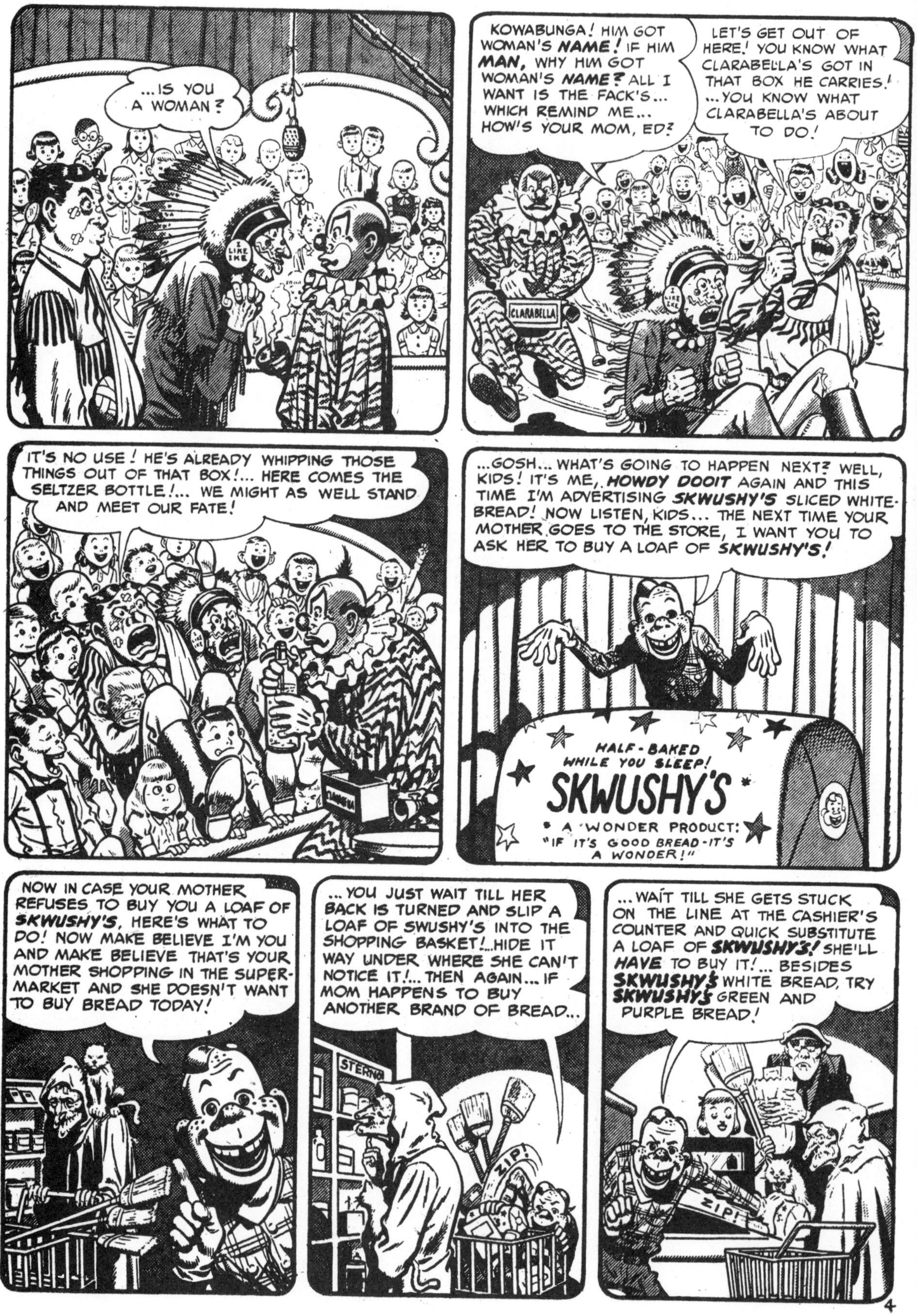
...IS YOU A WOMAN?
KOWABUNGA! HIM GOT WOMAN'S NAME! IF HIM MAN, WHY HIM GOT WOMAN'S NAME? ALL I WANT IS THE FACK'S... WHICH REMIND ME... HOW'S YOUR MOM, ED?
LET'S GET OUT OF HERE! YOU KNOW WHAT CLARABELLA'S GOT IN THAT BOX HE CARRIES! ...YOU KNOW WHAT CLARABELLA'S ABOUT TO DO!
CLARABELLA
IT'S NO USE! HE'S ALREADY WHIPPING THOSE THINGS OUT OF THAT BOX!... HERE COMES THE SELTZER BOTTLE!... WE MIGHT AS WELL STAND AND MEET OUR FATE!
...GOSH... WHAT'S GOING TO HAPPEN NEXT? WELL, KIDS! IT'S ME, HOWDY DOOIT AGAIN AND THIS TIME I'M ADVERTISING SKWUSHY'S SLICED WHITE-BREAD! NOW LISTEN, KIDS... THE NEXT TIME YOUR MOTHER GOES TO THE STORE, I WANT YOU TO ASK HER TO BUY A LOAF OF SKWUSHY'S!
HALF-BAKED WHILE YOU SLEEP!
SKWUSHY'S
A WONDER PRODUCT:
"IF IT'S GOOD BREAD-IT'S A WONDER!"
NOW IN CASE YOUR MOTHER REFUSES TO BUY YOU A LOAF OF SKWUSHY'S, HERE'S WHAT TO DO! NOW MAKE BELIEVE I'M YOU AND MAKE BELIEVE THAT'S YOUR MOTHER SHOPPING IN THE SUPER-MARKET AND SHE DOESN'T WANT TO BUY BREAD TODAY!
...YOU JUST WAIT TILL HER BACK IS TURNED AND SLIP A LOAF OF SWUSHY'S INTO THE SHOPPING BASKET!...HIDE IT WAY UNDER WHERE SHE CAN'T NOTICE IT!... THEN AGAIN... IF MOM HAPPENS TO BUY ANOTHER BRAND OF BREAD...
STERNO
ZIP!
...WAIT TILL SHE GETS STUCK ON THE LINE AT THE CASHIER'S COUNTER AND QUICK SUBSTITUTE A LOAF OF SKWUSHY'S! SHE'LL HAVE TO BUY IT!... BESIDES SKWUSHY'S WHITE BREAD, TRY SKWUSHY'S GREEN AND PURPLE BREAD!
ZIP!
4

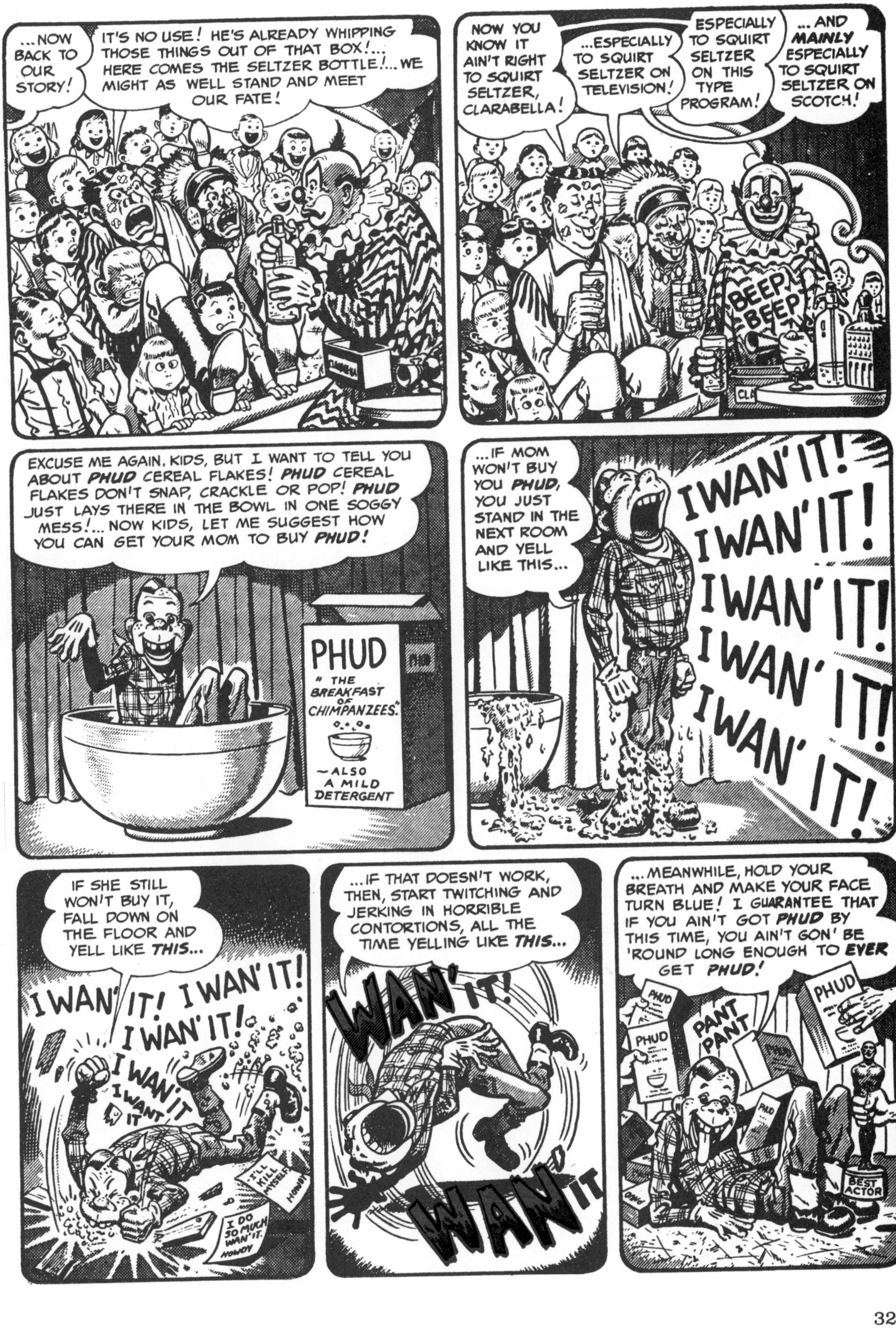

...NOW BACK TO OUR STORY!
IT'S NO USE! HE'S ALREADY WHIPPING THOSE THINGS OUT OF THAT BOX!... HERE COMES THE SELTZER BOTTLE!... WE MIGHT AS WELL STAND AND MEET OUR FATE!
NOW YOU KNOW IT AIN'T RIGHT TO SQUIRT SELTZER, CLARABELLA!
...ESPECIALLY TO SQUIRT SELTZER ON TELEVISION!
ESPECIALLY TO SQUIRT SELTZER ON THIS TYPE PROGRAM!
...AND MAINLY ESPECIALLY TO SQUIRT SELTZER ON SCOTCH!
BEEP BEEP
EXCUSE ME AGAIN, KIDS, BUT I WANT TO TELL YOU ABOUT PHUD CEREAL FLAKES! PHUD CEREAL FLAKES DON'T SNAP, CRACKLE OR POP! PHUD JUST LAYS THERE IN THE BOWL IN ONE SOGGY MESS!... NOW KIDS, LET ME SUGGEST HOW YOU CAN GET YOUR MOM TO BUY PHUD!
PHUD "THE BREAKFAST OF CHIMPANZEES." —ALSO A MILD DETERGENT
...IF MOM WON'T BUY YOU PHUD, YOU JUST STAND IN THE NEXT ROOM AND YELL LIKE THIS...
I WAN' IT! I WAN' IT! I WAN' IT! I WAN' IT! I WAN' IT!
IF SHE STILL WON'T BUY IT, FALL DOWN ON THE FLOOR AND YELL LIKE THIS...
I WAN' IT! I WAN' IT! I WAN' IT! I WAN' IT I WANT IT
I'LL KILL MYSELF
HOWDY
I DO SO MUCH WAN' IT. HOWDY
...IF THAT DOESN'T WORK, THEN, START TWITCHING AND JERKING IN HORRIBLE CONTORTIONS, ALL THE TIME YELLING LIKE THIS...
WAN' IT! WAN IT
...MEANWHILE, HOLD YOUR BREATH AND MAKE YOUR FACE TURN BLUE! I GUARANTEE THAT IF YOU AIN'T GOT PHUD BY THIS TIME, YOU AIN'T GON' BE 'ROUND LONG ENOUGH TO EVER GET PHUD!
PHUD
PHUD
PHUD
PANT PANT
BEST ACTOR
5

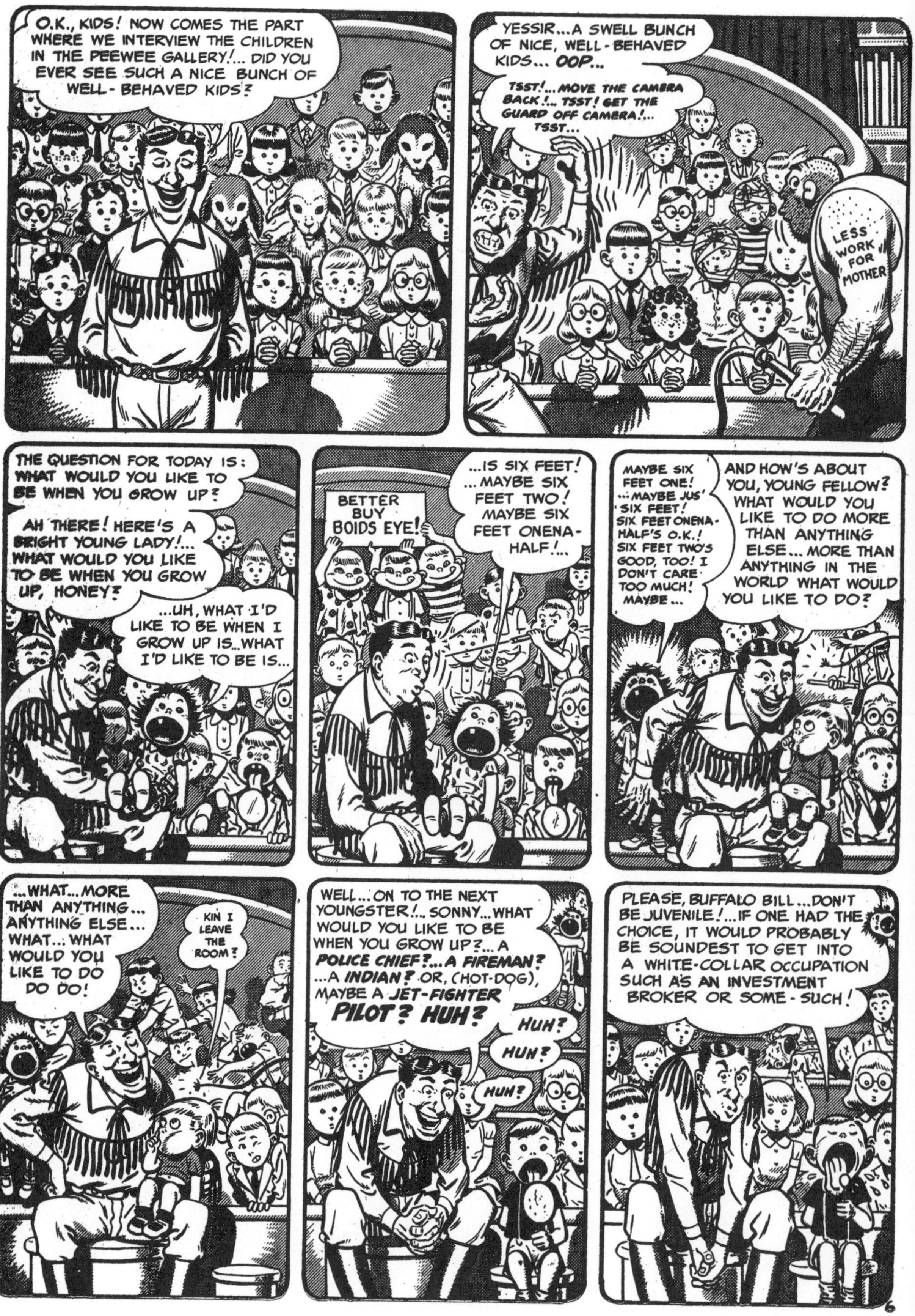
O.K., KIDS! NOW COMES THE PART WHERE WE INTERVIEW THE CHILDREN IN THE PEEWEE GALLERY!... DID YOU EVER SEE SUCH A NICE BUNCH OF WELL-BEHAVED KIDS?
YESSIR...A SWELL BUNCH OF NICE, WELL-BEHAVED KIDS... OOP...
TSST!... MOVE THE CAMERA BACK!.. TSST! GET THE GUARD OFF CAMERA!... TSST...
LESS WORK FOR MOTHER
THE QUESTION FOR TODAY IS: WHAT WOULD YOU LIKE TO BE WHEN YOU GROW UP?
AH THERE! HERE'S A BRIGHT YOUNG LADY!... WHAT WOULD YOU LIKE TO BE WHEN YOU GROW UP, HONEY?
...UH, WHAT I'D LIKE TO BE WHEN I GROW UP IS...WHAT I'D LIKE TO BE IS...
BETTER BUY BOIDS EYE!
...IS SIX FEET! ...MAYBE SIX FEET TWO! MAYBE SIX FEET ONENA-HALF!...
MAYBE SIX FEET ONE! ...MAYBE JUS' SIX FEET! SIX FEET ONENA-HALF'S O.K.! SIX FEET TWO'S GOOD, TOO! I DON'T CARE TOO MUCH! MAYBE...
AND HOW'S ABOUT YOU, YOUNG FELLOW? WHAT WOULD YOU LIKE TO DO MORE THAN ANYTHING ELSE... MORE THAN ANYTHING IN THE WORLD WHAT WOULD YOU LIKE TO DO?
...WHAT...MORE THAN ANYTHING... ANYTHING ELSE... WHAT... WHAT WOULD YOU LIKE TO DO DO DO!
KIN I LEAVE THE ROOM?
WELL... ON TO THE NEXT YOUNGSTER!... SONNY...WHAT WOULD YOU LIKE TO BE WHEN YOU GROW UP?... A POLICE CHIEF?... A FIREMAN? ...A INDIAN? OR, (HOT-DOG), MAYBE A JET-FIGHTER PILOT? HUH?
HUH?
HUH?
HUH?
PLEASE, BUFFALO BILL ...DON'T BE JUVENILE!...IF ONE HAD THE CHOICE, IT WOULD PROBABLY BE SOUNDEST TO GET INTO A WHITE-COLLAR OCCUPATION SUCH AS AN INVESTMENT BROKER OR SOME-SUCH!
6

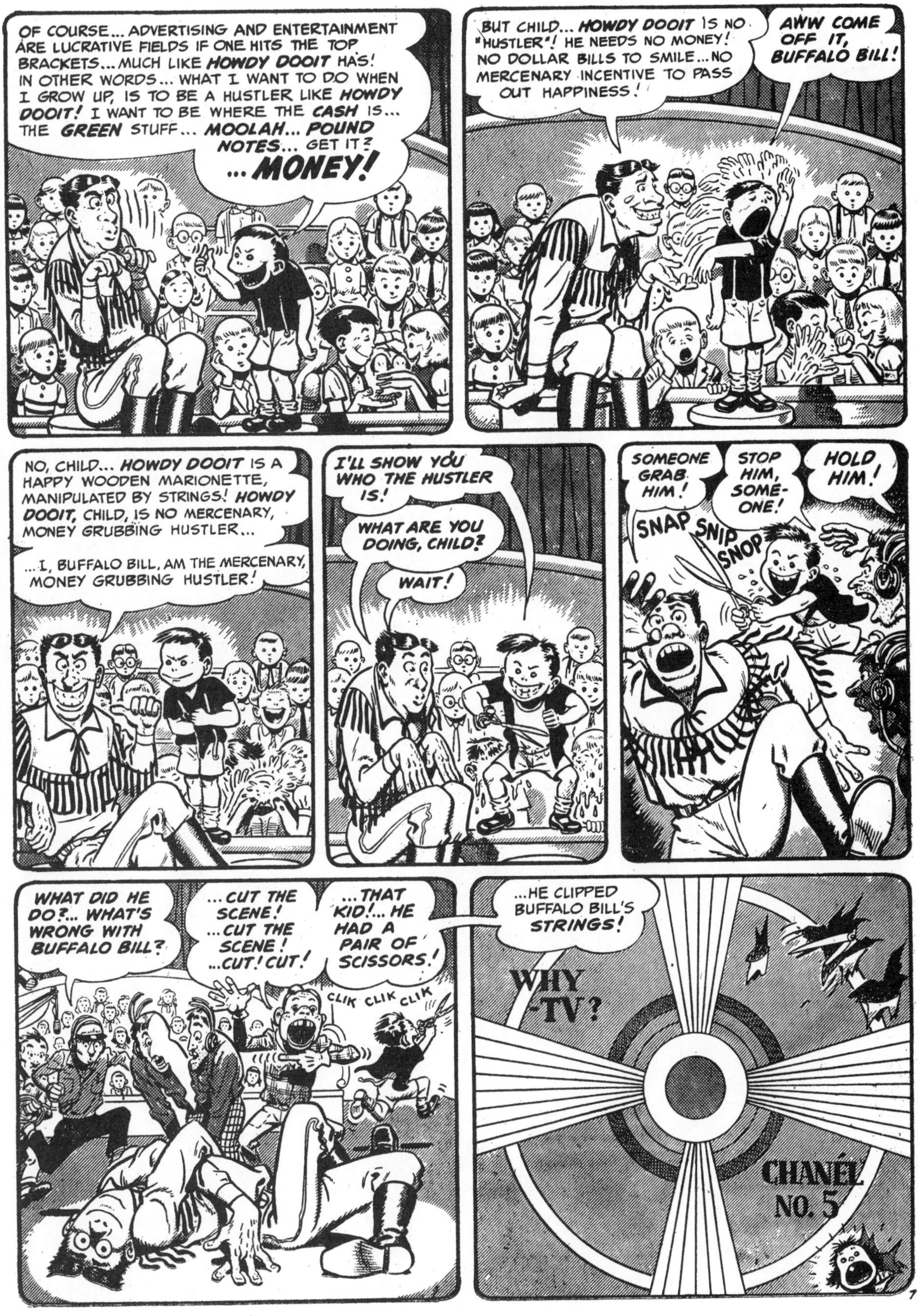
OF COURSE... ADVERTISING AND ENTERTAINMENT ARE LUCRATIVE FIELDS IF ONE HITS THE TOP BRACKETS... MUCH LIKE HOWDY DOOIT HAS! IN OTHER WORDS... WHAT I WANT TO DO WHEN I GROW UP, IS TO BE A HUSTLER LIKE HOWDY DOOIT! I WANT TO BE WHERE THE CASH IS... THE GREEN STUFF... MOOLAH... POUND NOTES... GET IT? ...MONEY!
BUT CHILD... HOWDY DOOIT IS NO "HUSTLER"! HE NEEDS NO MONEY! NO DOLLAR BILLS TO SMILE... NO MERCENARY INCENTIVE TO PASS OUT HAPPINESS!
AWW COME OFF IT, BUFFALO BILL!
NO, CHILD... HOWDY DOOIT IS A HAPPY WOODEN MARIONETTE, MANIPULATED BY STRINGS! HOWDY DOOIT, CHILD, IS NO MERCENARY, MONEY GRUBBING HUSTLER...
...I, BUFFALO BILL, AM THE MERCENARY, MONEY GRUBBING HUSTLER!
I'LL SHOW YOU WHO THE HUSTLER IS!
WHAT ARE YOU DOING, CHILD?
WAIT!
SOMEONE GRAB HIM!
STOP HIM, SOME-ONE!
HOLD HIM!
SNAP SNIP SNOP
WHAT DID HE DO?... WHAT'S WRONG WITH BUFFALO BILL?
...CUT THE SCENE! ...CUT THE SCENE! ...CUT! CUT!
...THAT KID!... HE HAD A PAIR OF SCISSORS!
CLIK CLIK CLIK
...HE CLIPPED BUFFALO BILL'S STRINGS!
WHY -TV?
CHANÉL NO. 5
7

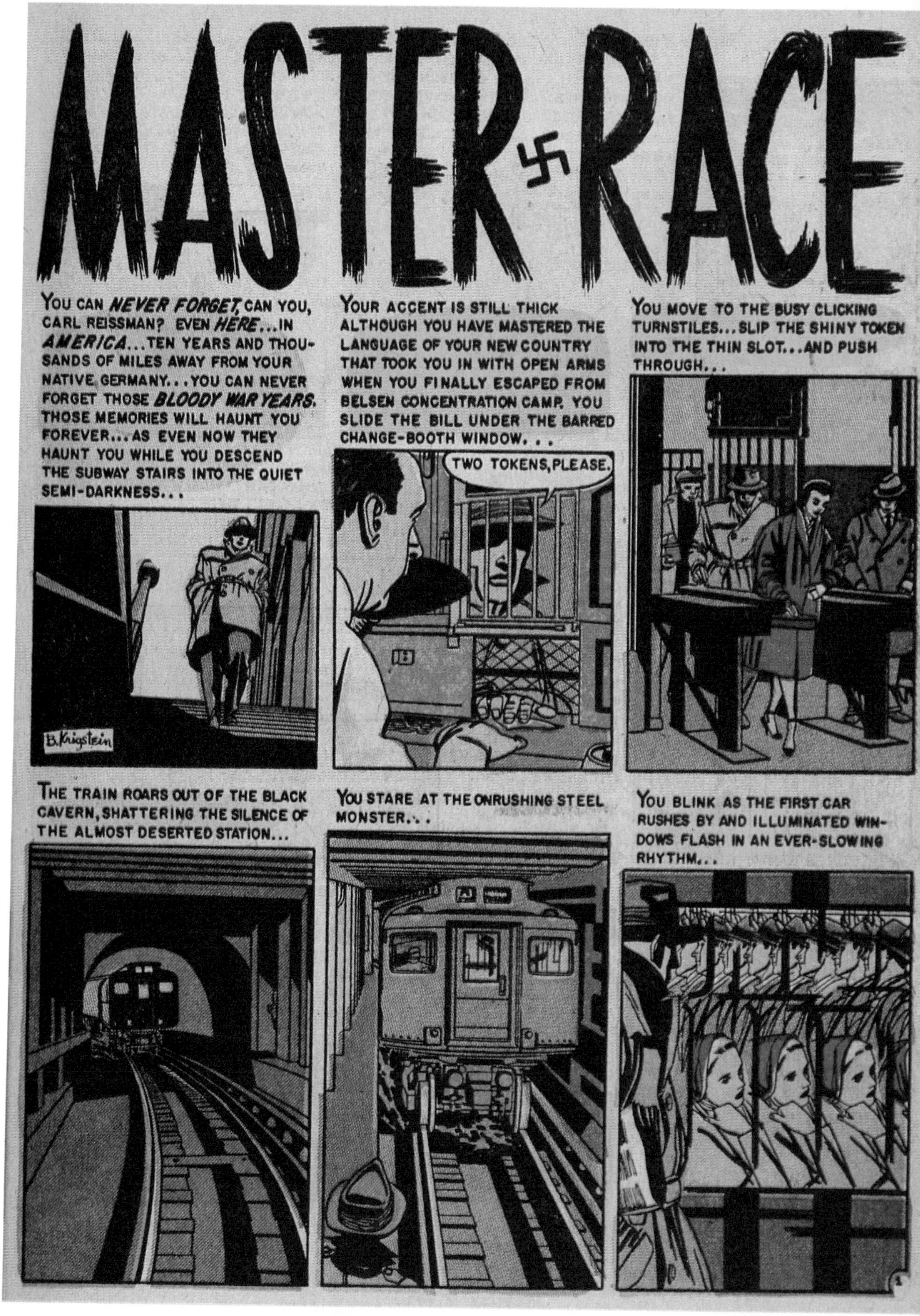
MASTER RACE
YOU CAN NEVER FORGET, CAN YOU, CARL REISSMAN? EVEN HERE...IN AMERICA...TEN YEARS AND THOUSANDS OF MILES AWAY FROM YOUR NATIVE GERMANY...YOU CAN NEVER FORGET THOSE BLOODY WAR YEARS. THOSE MEMORIES WILL HAUNT YOU FOREVER...AS EVEN NOW THEY HAUNT YOU WHILE YOU DESCEND THE SUBWAY STAIRS INTO THE QUIET SEMI-DARKNESS...
B. Krigstein
YOUR ACCENT IS STILL THICK ALTHOUGH YOU HAVE MASTERED THE LANGUAGE OF YOUR NEW COUNTRY THAT TOOK YOU IN WITH OPEN ARMS WHEN YOU FINALLY ESCAPED FROM BELSEN CONCENTRATION CAMP. YOU SLIDE THE BILL UNDER THE BARRED CHANGE-BOOTH WINDOW...
TWO TOKENS, PLEASE.
YOU MOVE TO THE BUSY CLICKING TURNSTILES...SLIP THE SHINY TOKEN INTO THE THIN SLOT...AND PUSH THROUGH...
THE TRAIN ROARS OUT OF THE BLACK CAVERN, SHATTERING THE SILENCE OF THE ALMOST DESERTED STATION...
YOU STARE AT THE ONRUSHING STEEL MONSTER...
YOU BLINK AS THE FIRST CAR RUSHES BY AND ILLUMINATED WINDOWS FLASH IN AN EVER-SLOWING RHYTHM...
1

From *Impact* No. 1, Mar.-Apr. 1955.

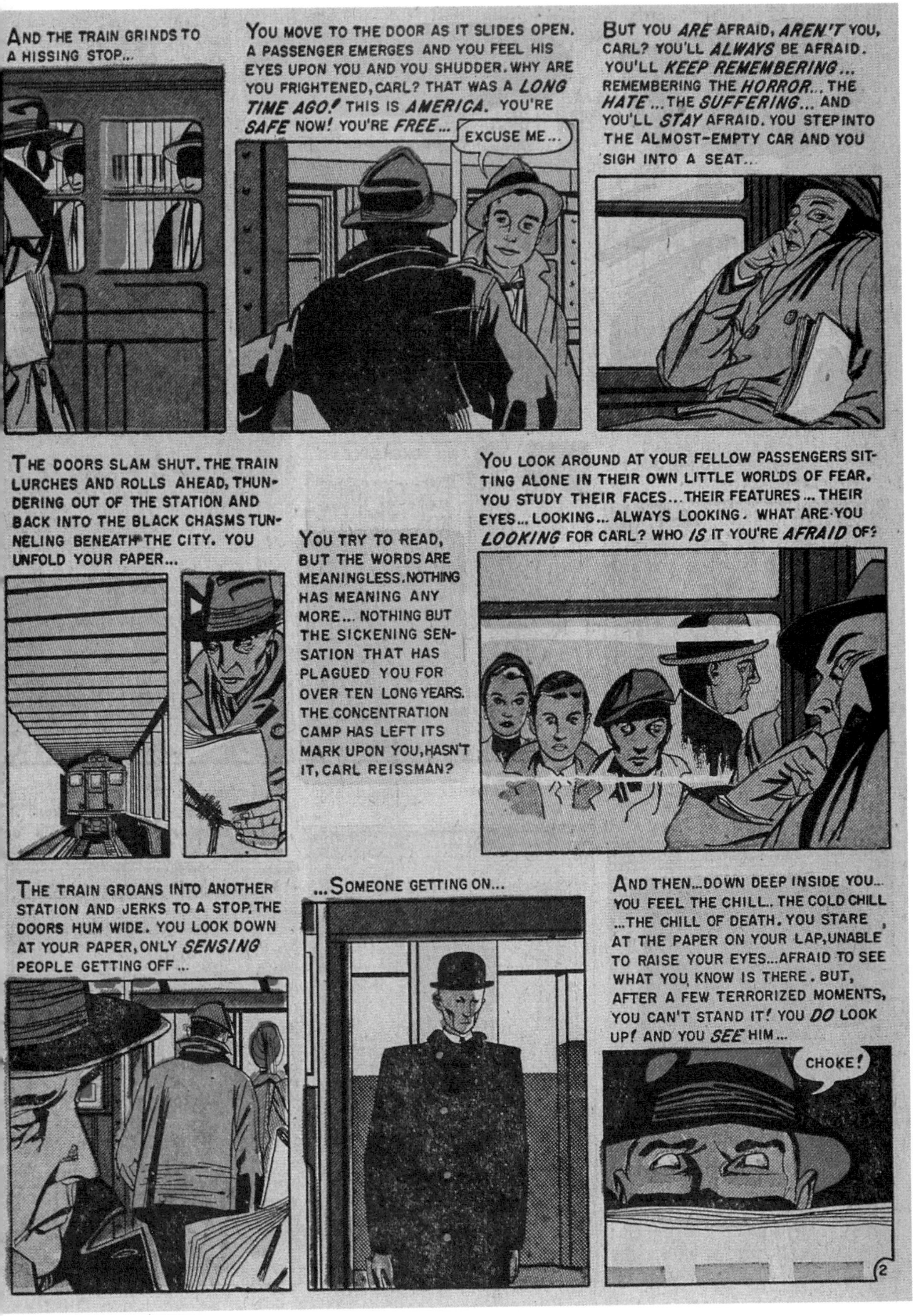
AND THE TRAIN GRINDS TO A HISSING STOP...
YOU MOVE TO THE DOOR AS IT SLIDES OPEN. A PASSENGER EMERGES AND YOU FEEL HIS EYES UPON YOU AND YOU SHUDDER. WHY ARE YOU FRIGHTENED, CARL? THAT WAS A LONG TIME AGO! THIS IS AMERICA. YOU'RE SAFE NOW! YOU'RE FREE...
EXCUSE ME...
BUT YOU ARE AFRAID, AREN'T YOU, CARL? YOU'LL ALWAYS BE AFRAID. YOU'LL KEEP REMEMBERING... REMEMBERING THE HORROR... THE HATE... THE SUFFERING... AND YOU'LL STAY AFRAID. YOU STEP INTO THE ALMOST-EMPTY CAR AND YOU SIGH INTO A SEAT...
THE DOORS SLAM SHUT. THE TRAIN LURCHES AND ROLLS AHEAD, THUNDERING OUT OF THE STATION AND BACK INTO THE BLACK CHASMS TUNNELING BENEATH THE CITY. YOU UNFOLD YOUR PAPER...
YOU TRY TO READ, BUT THE WORDS ARE MEANINGLESS. NOTHING HAS MEANING ANY MORE... NOTHING BUT THE SICKENING SENSATION THAT HAS PLAGUED YOU FOR OVER TEN LONG YEARS. THE CONCENTRATION CAMP HAS LEFT ITS MARK UPON YOU, HASN'T IT, CARL REISSMAN?
YOU LOOK AROUND AT YOUR FELLOW PASSENGERS SITTING ALONE IN THEIR OWN LITTLE WORLDS OF FEAR. YOU STUDY THEIR FACES... THEIR FEATURES... THEIR EYES... LOOKING... ALWAYS LOOKING. WHAT ARE YOU LOOKING FOR CARL? WHO IS IT YOU'RE AFRAID OF?
THE TRAIN GROANS INTO ANOTHER STATION AND JERKS TO A STOP. THE DOORS HUM WIDE. YOU LOOK DOWN AT YOUR PAPER, ONLY SENSING PEOPLE GETTING OFF...
...SOMEONE GETTING ON...
AND THEN... DOWN DEEP INSIDE YOU... YOU FEEL THE CHILL.. THE COLD CHILL ...THE CHILL OF DEATH. YOU STARE AT THE PAPER ON YOUR LAP, UNABLE TO RAISE YOUR EYES... AFRAID TO SEE WHAT YOU KNOW IS THERE. BUT, AFTER A FEW TERRORIZED MOMENTS, YOU CAN'T STAND IT! YOU DO LOOK UP! AND YOU SEE HIM...
CHOKE!
2

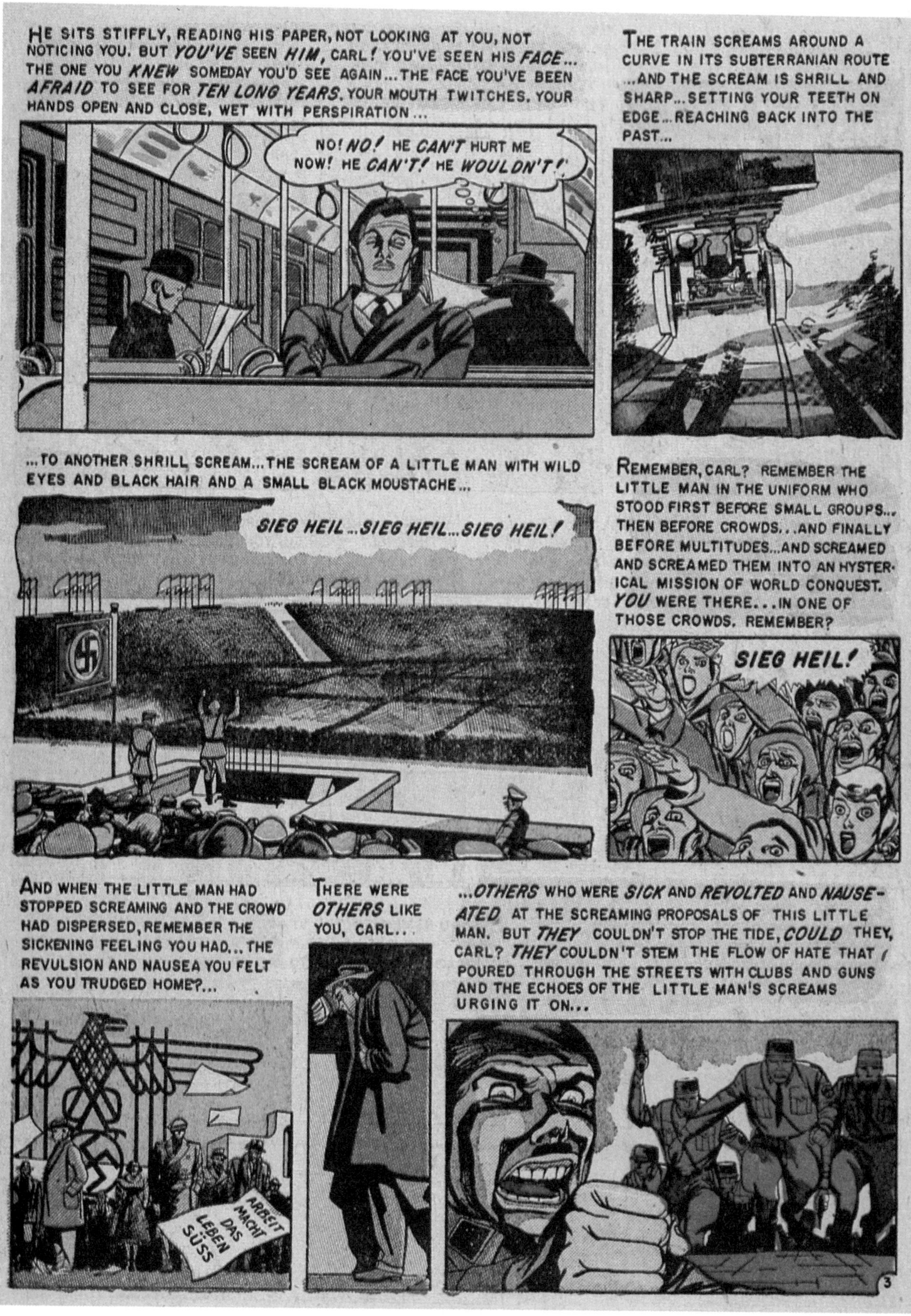
HE SITS STIFFLY, READING HIS PAPER, NOT LOOKING AT YOU, NOT NOTICING YOU. BUT YOU'VE SEEN HIM, CARL! YOU'VE SEEN HIS FACE... THE ONE YOU KNEW SOMEDAY YOU'D SEE AGAIN... THE FACE YOU'VE BEEN AFRAID TO SEE FOR TEN LONG YEARS. YOUR MOUTH TWITCHES. YOUR HANDS OPEN AND CLOSE, WET WITH PERSPIRATION...
NO! NO! HE CAN'T HURT ME NOW! HE CAN'T! HE WOULDN'T!
THE TRAIN SCREAMS AROUND A CURVE IN ITS SUBTERRANIAN ROUTE ...AND THE SCREAM IS SHRILL AND SHARP... SETTING YOUR TEETH ON EDGE... REACHING BACK INTO THE PAST...
...TO ANOTHER SHRILL SCREAM... THE SCREAM OF A LITTLE MAN WITH WILD EYES AND BLACK HAIR AND A SMALL BLACK MOUSTACHE...
SIEG HEIL...SIEG HEIL...SIEG HEIL!
REMEMBER, CARL? REMEMBER THE LITTLE MAN IN THE UNIFORM WHO STOOD FIRST BEFORE SMALL GROUPS... THEN BEFORE CROWDS... AND FINALLY BEFORE MULTITUDES... AND SCREAMED AND SCREAMED THEM INTO AN HYSTERICAL MISSION OF WORLD CONQUEST. YOU WERE THERE... IN ONE OF THOSE CROWDS. REMEMBER?
SIEG HEIL!
AND WHEN THE LITTLE MAN HAD STOPPED SCREAMING AND THE CROWD HAD DISPERSED, REMEMBER THE SICKENING FEELING YOU HAD... THE REVULSION AND NAUSEA YOU FELT AS YOU TRUDGED HOME?...
ARBEIT MACHT DAS LEBEN SÜSS
THERE WERE OTHERS LIKE YOU, CARL...
...OTHERS WHO WERE SICK AND REVOLTED AND NAUSEATED AT THE SCREAMING PROPOSALS OF THIS LITTLE MAN. BUT THEY COULDN'T STOP THE TIDE, COULD THEY, CARL? THEY COULDN'T STEM THE FLOW OF HATE THAT POURED THROUGH THE STREETS WITH CLUBS AND GUNS AND THE ECHOES OF THE LITTLE MAN'S SCREAMS URGING IT ON...
3

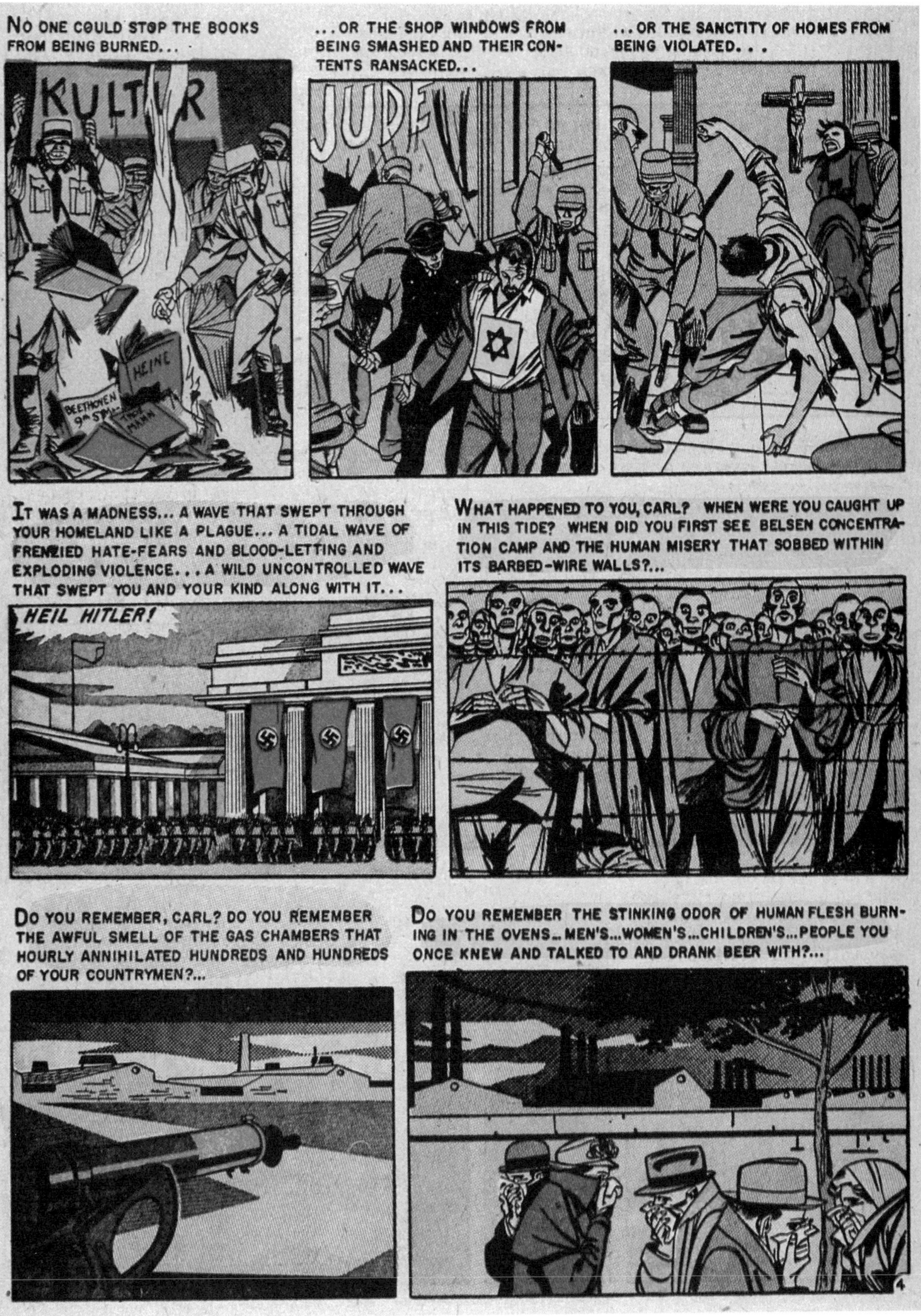
NO ONE COULD STOP THE BOOKS FROM BEING BURNED...
HEINE
BEETHOVEN 9th SYM...
...OR THE SHOP WINDOWS FROM BEING SMASHED AND THEIR CONTENTS RANSACKED...
JUDE
...OR THE SANCTITY OF HOMES FROM BEING VIOLATED...
IT WAS A MADNESS... A WAVE THAT SWEPT THROUGH YOUR HOMELAND LIKE A PLAGUE... A TIDAL WAVE OF FRENZIED HATE-FEARS AND BLOOD-LETTING AND EXPLODING VIOLENCE... A WILD UNCONTROLLED WAVE THAT SWEPT YOU AND YOUR KIND ALONG WITH IT...
HEIL HITLER!
WHAT HAPPENED TO YOU, CARL? WHEN WERE YOU CAUGHT UP IN THIS TIDE? WHEN DID YOU FIRST SEE BELSEN CONCENTRATION CAMP AND THE HUMAN MISERY THAT SOBBED WITHIN ITS BARBED-WIRE WALLS?...
DO YOU REMEMBER, CARL? DO YOU REMEMBER THE AWFUL SMELL OF THE GAS CHAMBERS THAT HOURLY ANNIHILATED HUNDREDS AND HUNDREDS OF YOUR COUNTRYMEN?...
DO YOU REMEMBER THE STINKING ODOR OF HUMAN FLESH BURNING IN THE OVENS... MEN'S...WOMEN'S...CHILDREN'S...PEOPLE YOU ONCE KNEW AND TALKED TO AND DRANK BEER WITH?...
4

DO YOU REMEMBER THE UNMERCIFUL TORTURES...THE SCREAMS IN THE NIGHT...THE PITIFUL WAILING OF THE DOOMED? DO YOU REMEMBER THE MAD EXPERIMENTS WITH HUMAN GUINEA PIGS...THE WANTON WASTE OF HUMAN LIFE?...

..THE BULBS THAT BURNED IN LAMPS ON DESKS IN THE CONCENTRATION CAMP OFFICES...GLOWING THROUGH THEIR HUMAN-SKIN-SHADES?...

LOOK, CARL! LOOK AT THE FACE OF THIS MAN SITTING ACROSS FROM YOU IN THIS NOW DESERTED SUBWAY CAR! LOOK... AND REMEMBER! REMEMBER THE GUARDS THAT GLEEFULLY CARRIED OUT THE SADISTIC ORDERS OF THE MASTER RACE...WHIPPING...KICKING... BEATING!... THE GUARDS THAT EAGERLY DRAGGED THE WOMEN AND CHILDREN TO THE WAITING, SMOKING OVENS!...

REMEMBER THE GUARDS THAT PUSHED AND SHOVED...HEAPING THE HELPLESS CAMP INMATES INTO THE FRESH DUG MASS GRAVES...

...LAUGHING WILDLY AS THEY BURIED THEIR VICTIMS ALIVE...SHOVELING THE DIRT DOWN UPON THEM, MUFFLING THEIR PATHETIC SCREAMS ...MUFFLING THEIR PATHETIC LIVES!...

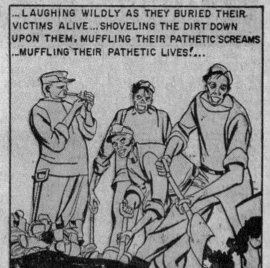

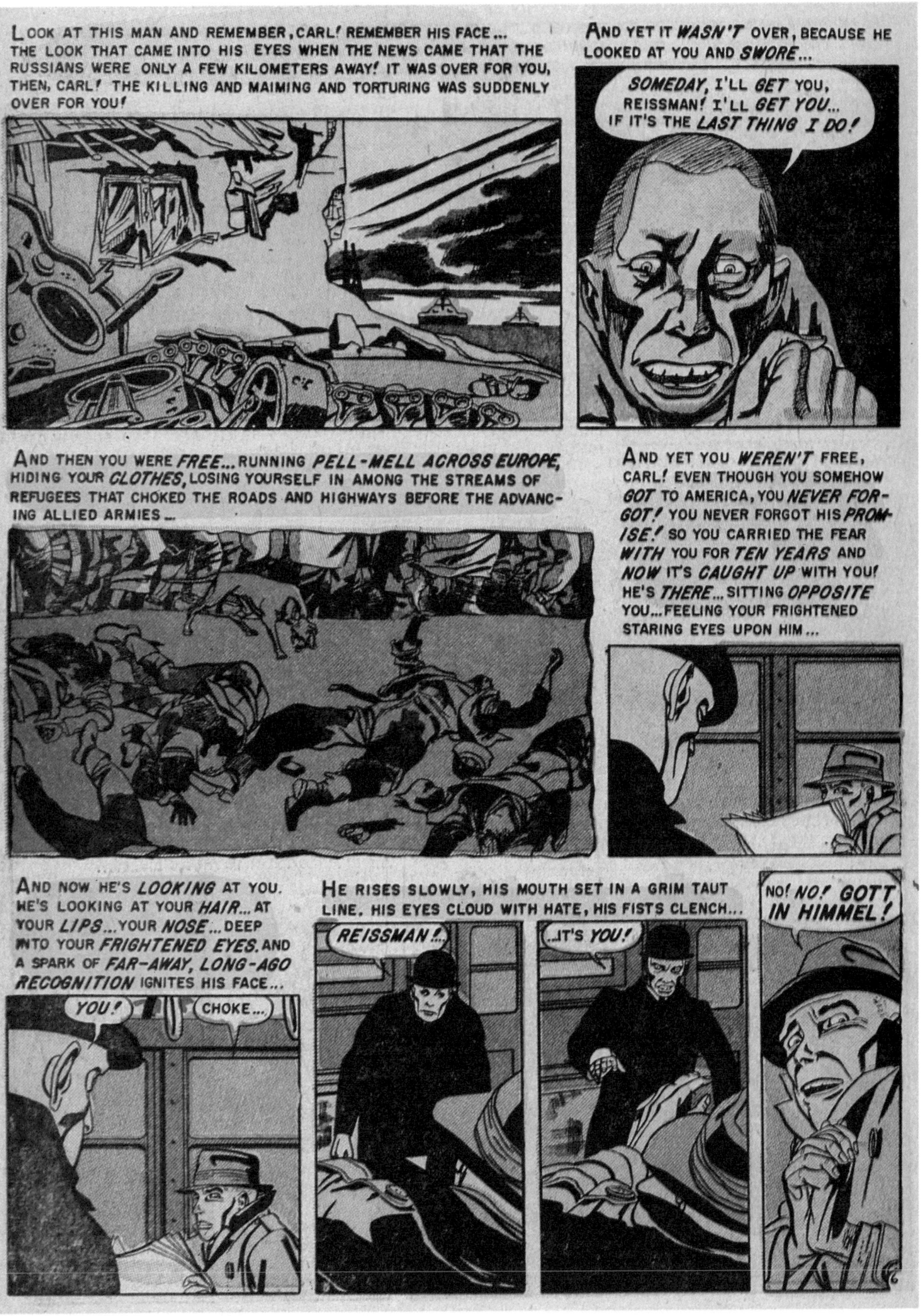

LOOK AT THIS MAN AND REMEMBER, CARL! REMEMBER HIS FACE... THE LOOK THAT CAME INTO HIS EYES WHEN THE NEWS CAME THAT THE RUSSIANS WERE ONLY A FEW KILOMETERS AWAY! IT WAS OVER FOR YOU, THEN, CARL! THE KILLING AND MAIMING AND TORTURING WAS SUDDENLY OVER FOR YOU!
AND YET IT WASN'T OVER, BECAUSE HE LOOKED AT YOU AND SWORE...
SOMEDAY, I'LL GET YOU, REISSMAN! I'LL GET YOU... IF IT'S THE LAST THING I DO!
AND THEN YOU WERE FREE... RUNNING PELL-MELL ACROSS EUROPE, HIDING YOUR CLOTHES, LOSING YOURSELF IN AMONG THE STREAMS OF REFUGEES THAT CHOKED THE ROADS AND HIGHWAYS BEFORE THE ADVANCING ALLIED ARMIES...
AND YET YOU WEREN'T FREE, CARL! EVEN THOUGH YOU SOMEHOW GOT TO AMERICA, YOU NEVER FORGOT! YOU NEVER FORGOT HIS PROMISE! SO YOU CARRIED THE FEAR WITH YOU FOR TEN YEARS AND NOW IT'S CAUGHT UP WITH YOU! HE'S THERE... SITTING OPPOSITE YOU... FEELING YOUR FRIGHTENED STARING EYES UPON HIM...
AND NOW HE'S LOOKING AT YOU. HE'S LOOKING AT YOUR HAIR... AT YOUR LIPS... YOUR NOSE... DEEP INTO YOUR FRIGHTENED EYES. AND A SPARK OF FAR-AWAY, LONG-AGO RECOGNITION IGNITES HIS FACE...
YOU!
CHOKE...
HE RISES SLOWLY, HIS MOUTH SET IN A GRIM TAUT LINE. HIS EYES CLOUD WITH HATE, HIS FISTS CLENCH...
REISSMAN!...
...IT'S YOU!
NO! NO! GOTT IN HIMMEL!

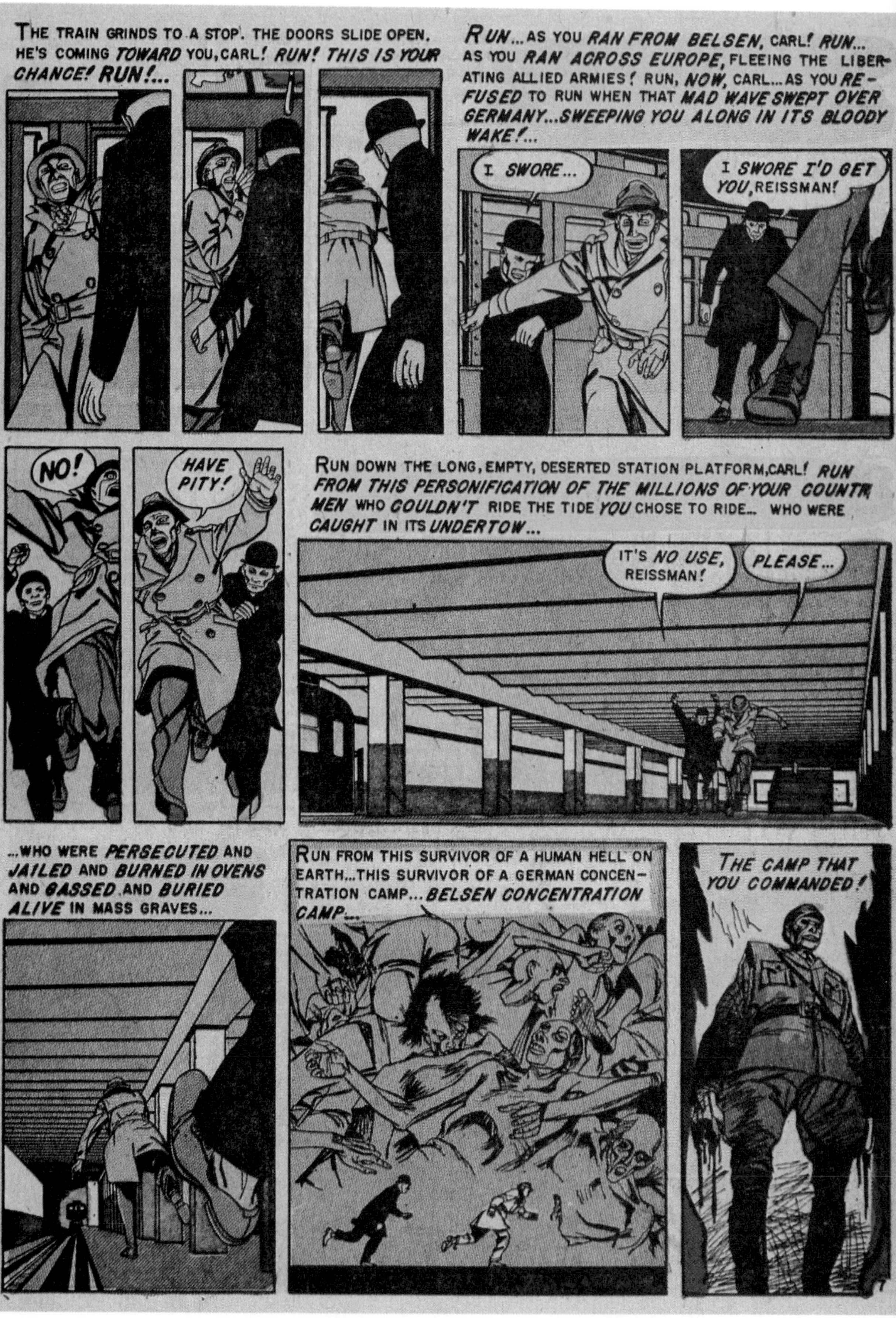

THE TRAIN GRINDS TO A STOP. THE DOORS SLIDE OPEN. HE'S COMING TOWARD YOU, CARL! RUN! THIS IS YOUR CHANCE! RUN!...
RUN... AS YOU RAN FROM BELSEN, CARL! RUN... AS YOU RAN ACROSS EUROPE, FLEEING THE LIBERATING ALLIED ARMIES! RUN, NOW, CARL... AS YOU REFUSED TO RUN WHEN THAT MAD WAVE SWEPT OVER GERMANY... SWEEPING YOU ALONG IN ITS BLOODY WAKE!...
I SWORE...
I SWORE I'D GET YOU, REISSMAN!
NO!
HAVE PITY!
RUN DOWN THE LONG, EMPTY, DESERTED STATION PLATFORM, CARL! RUN FROM THIS PERSONIFICATION OF THE MILLIONS OF YOUR COUNTRYMEN WHO COULDN'T RIDE THE TIDE YOU CHOSE TO RIDE... WHO WERE CAUGHT IN ITS UNDERTOW...
IT'S NO USE, REISSMAN!
PLEASE...
...WHO WERE PERSECUTED AND JAILED AND BURNED IN OVENS AND GASSED AND BURIED ALIVE IN MASS GRAVES...
RUN FROM THIS SURVIVOR OF A HUMAN HELL ON EARTH... THIS SURVIVOR OF A GERMAN CONCENTRATION CAMP... BELSEN CONCENTRATION CAMP...
THE CAMP THAT YOU COMMANDED!

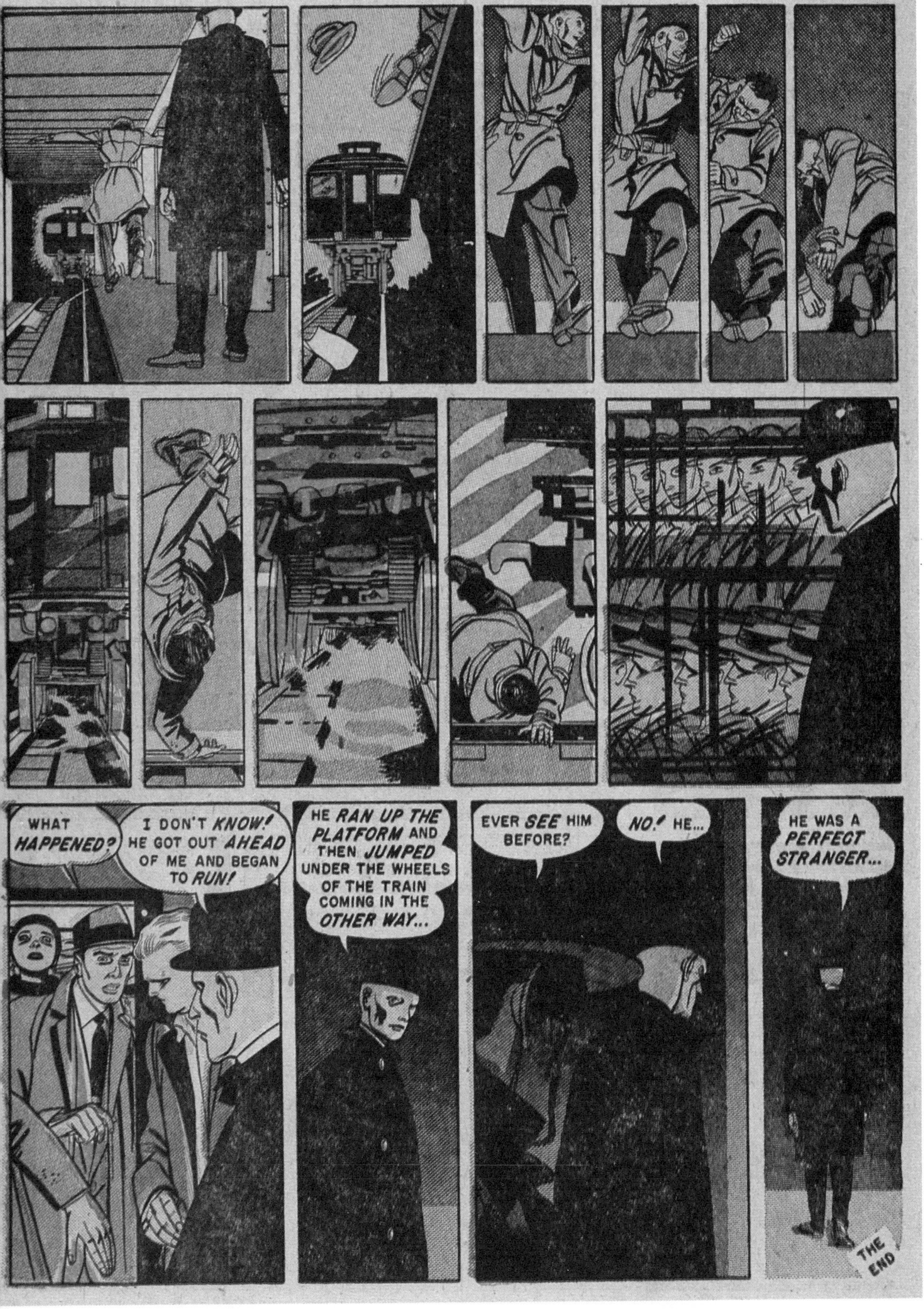

WHAT HAPPENED?
I DON'T KNOW! HE GOT OUT AHEAD OF ME AND BEGAN TO RUN!
HE RAN UP THE PLATFORM AND THEN JUMPED UNDER THE WHEELS OF THE TRAIN COMING IN THE OTHER WAY...
EVER SEE HIM BEFORE?
NO! HE...
HE WAS A PERFECT STRANGER...
THE END

A Selective, Annotated Bibliography

Most of the best research and writing about comic books has been published in comics "fanzines"—obscure magazines, with tiny circulations, that are devoted to discussions of comic books and related fields. We have cited a selection of those writings in this bibliography, along with some of the books and articles that have received more general distribution. Some "fanzines" can be found in large libraries, and in some cases back issues are available from the publishers or from University Microfilms. The addresses of the publishers are given when appropriate. And here are the addresses for the comics "fanzines" we will be listing several times below:

Fanfare (formerly *Graphic Story Magazine*)—Bill Spicer, 329 N. Avenue 66, Los Angeles, California 90042.

Funnyworld—University Microfilms International, 300 N. Zeeb Road, Ann Arbor, Michigan 48106.

Panels, Squa Tront—John Benson, 205 W. 80th Street, Apartment 2E, New York, New York 10024.

Please note: Inquiries about the price and availability of a publication should always be accompanied by a stamped, self-addressed envelope.

General

Bails, Jerry, and Hames Ware, eds. *The Who's Who of American Comic Books*, 4 vols., 1973–1976. (Jerry Bails, 21101 E. 11 Mile, Saint Clair Shores, Michigan 48081.) Biographical entries for more than 2,500 artists, writers, and editors.

Becker, Stephen. *Comic Art in America.* New York: Simon & Schuster, 1959. Chapter VII is about comic books.

Feiffer, Jules. *The Great Comic Book Heroes.* New York: Dial Press, 1965. Includes a dozen stories from super-hero comic books, in addition to Feiffer's nostalgic text.

Horn, Maurice, ed. *The World Encyclopedia of Comics.* New York: Chelsea House, 1976. This book remains the only comprehensive reference to the field (but reviewers have cited errors and omissions).

Lupoff, Dick, and Don Thompson, eds. *All in Color for a Dime.* New Rochelle, N. Y.: Arlington House, 1970. A collection of essays on comic books, some of which are listed individually below.

Overstreet, R. M. *The Comic Book Price Guide.* Tenth ed., 1980–1981. (Distributed by Harmony Books.) Some of the prices in this annual compilation may be taken with a grain of salt, but it contains reliable information about the publishing histories of many hundreds of titles.

Thompson, Don, and Dick Lupoff, eds. *The Comic-Book Book.* New Rochelle, N.Y.: Arlington House, 1974. A successor volume to *All in Color for a Dime,* and likewise composed of essays on comic books.

Waugh, Coulton. *The Comics.* New York: Macmillan, 1947. Chapter 20 is about comic books, and draws on interviews with M. C. Gaines and other pioneers.

On "Superman"

Kobler, John. "Up, Up and Awa-a-y! The Rise of Superman, Inc." *Saturday Evening Post,* June 21, 1941, p. 14.

White, Ted. "The Spawn of M. C. Gaines." In Lupoff and Thompson, eds., *All in Color for a Dime.*

On "Captain Marvel"

Lupoff, Dick. "The Big Red Cheese." In Lupoff and Thompson, eds., *All in Color for a Dime.*

On "Plastic Man" and Jack Cole

Thompson, Don. "The Rehabilitation of Eel O'Brian." In Thompson and Lupoff, eds., *The Comic-Book Book*.

On Basil Wolverton

Graphic Story Magazine No. 12, Fall 1970, and No. 14, Winter 1971–1972. Both issues are made up entirely of material by and about Wolverton.

On George Carlson

Ellison, Harlan. "Comic of the Absurd." In Lupoff and Thompson, eds., *All in Color for a Dime*.

On "Little Lulu" and John Stanley

Phelps, Don. "John Stanley." In the program book for the "Newcon" comics-fan convention, Boston, 1976.

Thompson, Maggie. "The Almost-Anonymous Mr. Stanley." *Funnyworld* 16 (Winter 1974–1975): 34.

On "Donald Duck" and Carl Barks

Barrier, Michael. "The Duck Man." In Thompson and Lupoff, eds., *The Comic-Book Book*.

Barrier, Michael. "Screenwriter for a Duck: Carl Barks at the Disney Studio." *Funnyworld* 21 (Fall 1979): 8.

Barrier, Michael. "Starting Out in the Comics: Carl Barks Becomes the Duck Man." *Funnyworld* 22 (1981): 12.

Boatner, E. B. "Carl Barks—From Duckburg to Calisota." In R. M. Overstreet, *The Comic Book Price Guide* 7 (1977–1978).

Summer, Edward. "Of Ducks and Men: Carl Barks Interviewed." *Panels* 2 (Spring 1981): 3.

On "Pogo" and Walt Kelly

Kelly, Walt. *Ten Ever-lovin' Blue-eyed Years with Pogo.* New York: Simon & Schuster, 1959.

The Okefenokee Star. (Swamp Yankee Studios, P.O. Box 2311, Bridgeport, Connecticut 06608.) Issued with the cooperation of Kelly's estate, this magazine has published a great deal of rare material by and about Walt Kelly.

Robinson, Murray. "Pogo's Papa." *Collier's,* March 8, 1952, p. 20.

On "The Spirit" and Will Eisner

Benson, John. "An Interview with Will Eisner." *Witzend* 6 (Spring 1969).

Eisner, Will (with John Benson). "Art & Commerce: An Oral Reminiscence." *Panels* 1 (Summer 1979): 5.

Feiffer, Jules (with John Benson). "Jules Feiffer Talks About the Spirit." *Panels* 1 (Summer 1979): 22.

Kyle, Richard. "Graphic Story Review." *Fantasy Illustrated (Graphic Story Magazine)* 6 (Summer/Fall 1966): 3.

Thompson, Maggie. "Blue Suit, Blue Mask, Blue Gloves—and No Socks." In Thompson and Lupoff, eds., *The Comic-Book Book*.

On E.C.

Benson, John. "Is War Hell? The Evolution of an Artist's Viewpoint." *Panels* 2 (Spring 1981): 18. On Harvey Kurtzman's war comic books.

Bray, Glenn. *The Illustrated Harvey Kurtzman Index.* 1976. (Glenn Bray, P.O. Box 4482, Sylmar, California 91342)

Durwood, Tom. "Harvey Kurtzman." *Crimmer's* (No. 3) (Spring 1976): 23. An interview.

Jacobs, Frank. *The Mad World of William M. Gaines.* Secaucus, N.J.: Lyle Stuart, Inc., 1972.

Spiegel, Ed. *"Fanfare* Interview: Editor of *Mad* Magazine, Al Feldstein." *Fanfare* 1 (Spring 1977): 16.

Squa Tront 6 (1975). An issue devoted to Bernard Krigstein. All issues of *Squa Tront* consist of material related to the E.C. comic books.

Thompson, Don. "The Spawn of the Son of M. C. Gaines." In Thompson and Lupoff, eds., *The Comic-Book Book.*

Reprints

Comic-book features have been reprinted in books with increasing frequency in recent years. Considering only the features represented in this book, *Superman, Batman,* and *Captain Marvel* (under the title of its 1970s revival, *Shazam!*) have been the subjects of collections published by Crown. Two collections of Carl Barks's *Donald Duck* and *Uncle Scrooge* have been published by Abbeville Press, but take warning that in these books substantial alterations were made in Barks's drawings and in his original dialogue. A collection of Barks's *Uncle Scrooge*—lovingly prepared and quite expensive—was scheduled for publication by Celestial Arts in 1982.

Will Eisner's *The Spirit* is being reprinted, in black and white, in a handsome bimonthly magazine, *The Spirit;* the magazine also publishes new work by Eisner. (Kitchen Sink Enterprises, Box 7, Princeton, Wisconsin 54968)

All E.C. comic books from 1950 to 1955 are being reprinted in slipcased sets; each set reprints, in several volumes, the complete run of an E.C. title in black and white, from the original artwork. To date, five sets— *Weird Science, Tales from the Crypt, Two-Fisted Tales, Weird Fantasy,* and *Shock SuspenStories*—have been published. (Russ Cochran, P.O. Box 469, West Plains, Missouri 65775)